A Military Atlas of the First World War

A map history of the War of 1914–18 on land, at sea and in the air

A Military Atlas

commentary by ALAN PALMER

Arthur Banks

of the

First World War

HEINEMANN EDUCATIONAL BOOKS

Heinemann Educational Books Ltd

LONDON EDINBURGH MELBOURNE AUCKLAND TORONTO
HONG KONG SINGAPORE KUALA LUMPUR
IBADAN NAIROBI JOHANNESBURG
LUSAKA NEW DELHI

ISBN 0435 32008 4

To the memories of my father, Arthur Thomas Banks,
who served his country throughout the Mesopotamian
Campaign and my uncle, Charles Banks, who fell
at Mons

Published by Heinemann Educational Books Ltd
48 Charles Street, London W1X 8AH
Printed and bound in Great Britain by
Morrison & Gibb Ltd, London and Edinburgh

PREFACE

It is now nearly a quarter of a century since I entered the specialised field of cartography and during that time I have been able to direct much of my effort into the fascinating, but technically complicated, area of military and historical map-production.

I soon discovered that the research material I needed was very widely scattered through many different libraries and military institutions and that much of my time would be spent in sifting through material and consulting veterans of past campaigns. At one time I longed to find some clear, reasonably-priced atlases of battles accompanied by succinct texts, tables, and diagrams. No such volumes seemed to exist, so far as I could discover. The idea of producing such an atlas myself took shape; from my researches and discussions with those who planned and took part in some of the actions I decided to compile my own cartographical record. This was the genesis of this present book.

In these times economy seems to dictate much that we do; therefore, my original plan to give detailed coverage to most of the important military campaigns has had to be modified. As a result, this book is necessarily briefer than the one I originally designed.

However, I hope that the book will be a convenient reference work which deals with those areas where a more detailed examination in cartographical terms has long been demanded.

Arthur Banks

ACKNOWLEDGEMENTS

During the research involved in the preparation of this atlas, I consulted some 1,300 historical reference works, examined and cross-checked 4,000 large- and small-scale maps (many of them of German or French origin), inspected several hundred technical manuals plus individual drawings, and attended numerous discussions with experts and veterans of the First World War.

Consequently, this must of necessity be a blanket appreciation of all those who were interested enough in my project to proffer advice and information in order to advance my work at various stages of the scheme.

In particular, I should like to thank General Sir James Marshall-Cornwall, Mr Michael Willis, and Mr Alan Palmer; all three went to enormous lengths to assist me and I am tremendously indebted to them.

In addition, the following persons deserve special mention and my gratitude: Dr R. Banks, Captain G. Bennett, Rear-Admiral P. Buckley, Captain L. Boswell, Captain E. Bush, Mrs J. Campbell, Miss R. Coombs, Major-General P. Essame, Miss S. Glover, Mr R. Holmes, Dr I. Nish, Mr V. Rigby, and Mr R. Welsh. Mr P. Richardson, Mr A. Hill, and Mr D. Heap of Heinemann Educational Books Limited extended endless encouragement and support to aid me in my task.

The librarians and staffs of the following organisations were generous in the facilities they placed at my disposal:

Imperial War Museum, Ministry of Defence, Royal Science Museum, Royal United Services Institute for Defence Studies, Royal Air Force Museum, H.M.S. *Vernon*, Hydrographic Department of the Admiralty, l'École Royale Militaire (Brussels), Turkish Naval Attaché's Office (London), United States Embassy (London), Belgian Embassy (London), and Surrey County Council Headquarters (Study and Information Department).

Finally, and above all, my wife deserves my deepest thanks: her devotion to my cause succoured me on so many occasions during the years of toil entailed in the research and preparation of this volume.

BIBLIOGRAPHICAL NOTE

Owing to the enormity of the research involved, it has proved impossible to itemise every reference work consulted, and the author feels that it would be unfair to specify particular accounts for recommended reading. However, he states that an essential first step for the serious student is to inspect the various military, naval, and aerial official histories of the belligerent powers. Usually these can be obtained from a central reference library or inspected at museums and institutions which specialise in military history and warfare.

CONTENTS

WAR ON THE EASTERN FRONT IN 1914

THE PERIPHERAL CAMPAIGNS

WEAPONS

THE WAR AT SEA

THE WAR IN THE AIR

THE PRE-WAR SITUATION

The coming of the Great War took the European peoples by surprise. In the spring of 1914 the nations of western and central Europe had been at peace with each other for forty-three years, a longer period free from conflict than ever before in their histories. Except in the south-eastern corner of the continent, where the Balkan peoples still sought complete independence from Turkish rule, frontiers had remained inviolate since the Franco-Prussian War. Two traditional battle cockpits, the Polish plains and the low-lying fields of Flanders, had escaped war not merely for forty years, but for a full century. Small wonder if the long European Peace lulled ordinary people into a false sense of security. Economists argued war was commercially so disruptive that no industrialised nation would resort to it; intellectuals maintained that international society was enlightened enough to scorn its folly.

Statesmen and generals remained less sanguine. There had, after all, been colonial campaigns throughout the armed peace. By 1914 the army of every European Great Power, except Germany and Austria-Hungary, had already been engaged in fighting since the turn of the century. If colonial disputes had not led to a general conflict it was because, as yet, they had never affected the vital interests of more than two Great Power rivals at the same time; but potentially they were dangerous, as the Agadir Crisis showed in 1911. Moreover no one could ignore the significance of the arms race. Naval and military expenditure by the Great Powers doubled in the last twenty years of the nineteenth century; it doubled again in the first decade of the twentieth. Where could the arms race finish, if not on the battlefield?

There was, too, uncertainty over the ability of the diplomats to safeguard peace much longer. By 1900 Europe was divided by rival alliances, with the Central Powers (Germany, Austria-Hungary, Italy) on one side and with France and Russia on the other. So long as potential opponents seemed equally strong, these alliances made for continuance of the peace rather than war. But by 1905 Russia, defeated in the Far East by Japan and weakened by the threat of revolution, had ceased to be militarily formidable. There was no genuine balance of strength between the Powers. Too many imponderables accumulated. What would the British do? The Liberal Government gave diplomatic support to its Entente partners, France and Russia, but evaded formal military obligations: in the last resort, only the 1839 pledge to uphold Belgium's neutrality counted in British reckoning. What, too, of Italy? Rivalry with Austria over territorial interests in the Adriatic made the Italians uncomfortable members of the Triple Alliance. Was Italy still a 'Central Power'? There was no doubt that the diplomatic system of 1900 had changed by 1914.

Yet mutual antagonism was growing in intensity rather than diminishing. The French still sought recovery of Alsace-Lorraine; the British were increasingly suspicious of Germany's naval shipbuilding programmes; Russian Pan-Slavism seemed to threaten the integrity of Austria-Hungary; and the Germans resented the web of encirclement which they believed others were weaving around them. Already these issues had provoked diplomatic crises, for which solutions were improvised by statesmen unready for war. But everyone in authority knew that once orders were given for mobilisation, the alliance system would work against any localisation of the conflict. Peace was fragile: the Sarajevo crime was to show it lay ultimately at the mercies of chance. The heir to the Austrian throne and his consort were assassinated in the Bosnian capital by a Serbian student on 28 June 1914. By the middle of August five European Great Powers and two of lesser standing were locked in battle from the Flanders Plain to the eastern foothills of the Carpathians.

1

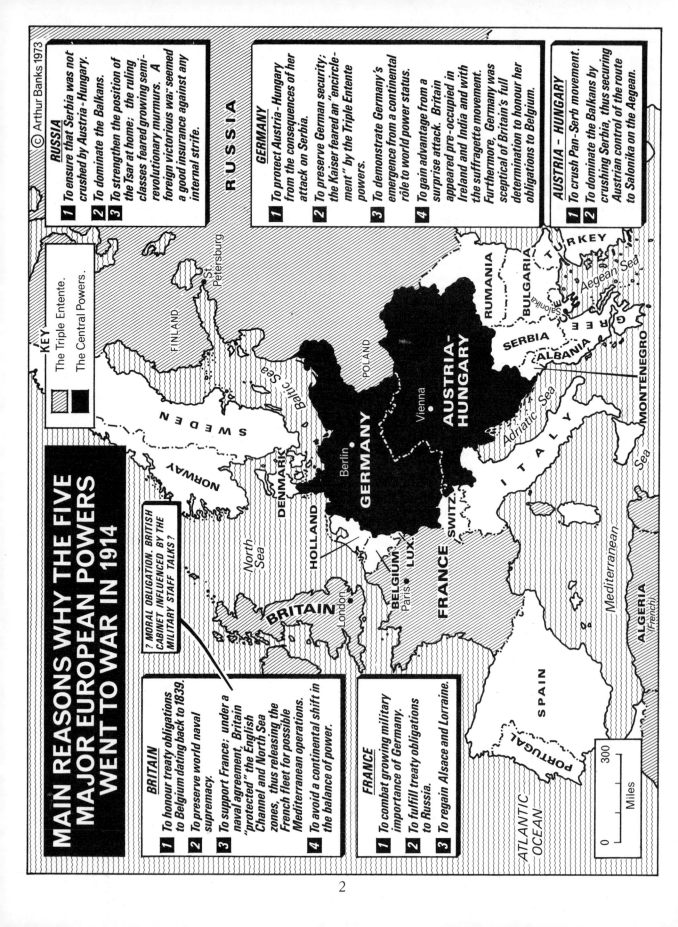

MAIN REASONS WHY THE FIVE MAJOR EUROPEAN POWERS WENT TO WAR IN 1914

© Arthur Banks 1973

KEY

The Triple Entente.

The Central Powers.

RUSSIA

1 *To ensure that Serbia was not crushed by Austria-Hungary.*

2 *To dominate the Balkans.*

3 *To strengthen the position of the Tsar at home: the ruling classes feared growing semi-revolutionary murmurs. A foreign victorious war seemed a good insurance against any internal strife.*

GERMANY

1 *To protect Austria-Hungary from the consequences of her attack on Serbia.*

2 *To preserve German security: the Kaiser feared an "encirclement" by the Triple Entente powers.*

3 *To demonstrate Germany's emergence from a continental rôle to world power status.*

4 *To gain advantage from a surprise attack. Britain appeared pre-occupied in Ireland and India and with the suffragette movement. Furthermore, Germany was sceptical of Britain's full determination to honour her obligations to Belgium.*

AUSTRIA – HUNGARY

1 *To crush Pan-Serb movement.*

2 *To dominate the Balkans by crushing Serbia, thus securing Austrian control of the route to Salonika on the Aegean.*

BRITAIN

1 *To honour treaty obligations to Belgium dating back to 1839.*

2 *To preserve world naval supremacy.*

3 *To support France: under a naval agreement, Britain "protected" the English Channel and North Sea zones, thus releasing the French fleet for possible Mediterranean operations.*

4 *To avoid a continental shift in the balance of power.*

? MORAL OBLIGATION. BRITISH CABINET INFLUENCED BY THE MILITARY STAFF TALKS?

FRANCE

1 *To combat growing military importance of Germany.*

2 *To fulfill treaty obligations to Russia.*

3 *To regain Alsace and Lorraine.*

RUSSIA

St Petersburg

FINLAND

SWEDEN

NORWAY

Baltic Sea

DENMARK

POLAND

GERMANY

Berlin

Vienna

AUSTRIA-HUNGARY

RUMANIA

BULGARIA

TURKEY

Aegean Sea

Salonika

SERBIA

ALBANIA

GREECE

MONTENEGRO

Adriatic Sea

ITALY

SWITZ.

North Sea

BRITAIN

London

HOLLAND

BELGIUM

LUX.

Paris

FRANCE

SPAIN

PORTUGAL

ALGERIA (French)

Mediterranean Sea

ATLANTIC OCEAN

0   300

Miles

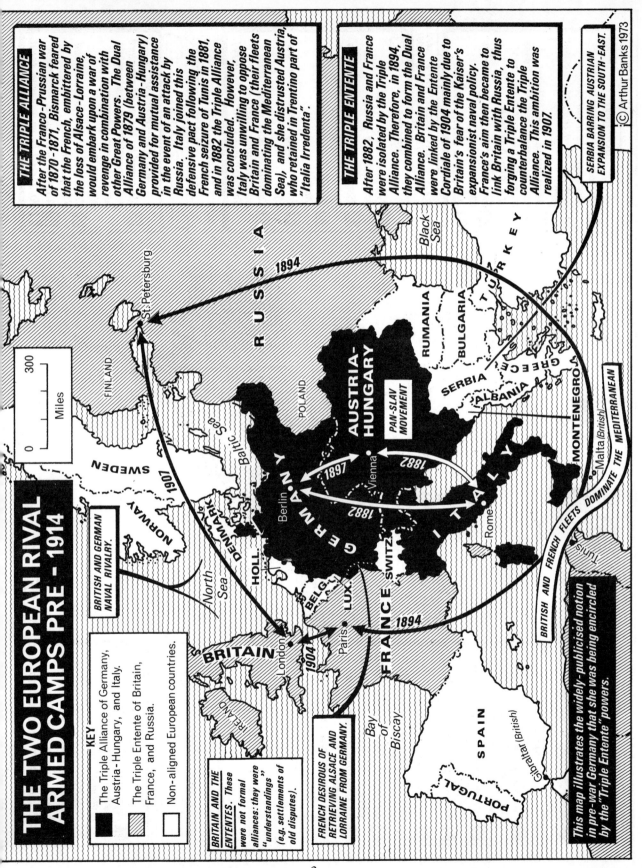

THE TWO EUROPEAN RIVAL ARMED CAMPS PRE - 1914

KEY

- ■ The Triple Alliance of Germany, Austria-Hungary, and Italy.
- ▨ The Triple Entente of Britain, France, and Russia.
- □ Non-aligned European countries.

BRITAIN AND THE ENTENTES. These were not formal alliances: they were "understandings" (e.g. settlements of old disputes).

FRENCH DESIROUS OF RETRIEVING ALSACE AND LORRAINE FROM GERMANY.

BRITISH AND GERMAN NAVAL RIVALRY.

THE TRIPLE ALLIANCE

After the Franco-Prussian war of 1870-1871, Bismarck feared that the French, embittered by the loss of Alsace-Lorraine, would embark upon a war of revenge in combination with other Great Powers. The Dual Alliance of 1879 (between Germany and Austria-Hungary) provided for mutual assistance in the event of an attack by Russia. Italy joined this defensive pact following the French seizure of Tunis in 1881, and in 1882 the Triple Alliance was concluded. However, Italy was unwilling to oppose Britain and France (their fleets dominating the Mediterranean Sea), and she distrusted Austria, who retained in Trentino part of "Italia Irredenta".

THE TRIPLE ENTENTE

After 1882, Russia and France were isolated by the Triple Alliance. Therefore, in 1894, they combined to form the Dual Alliance. Britain and France were linked by the Entente Cordiale of 1904 mainly due to Britain's fear of the Kaiser's expansionist naval policy. France's aim was then became to link Britain with Russia, thus forging a Triple Entente to counterbalance the Triple Alliance. This ambition was realized in 1907.

© Arthur Banks 1973

SERBIA BARRING AUSTRIAN EXPANSION TO THE SOUTH-EAST.

PAN-SLAV MOVEMENT

BRITISH AND FRENCH FLEETS DOMINATE THE MEDITERRANEAN

This map illustrates the widely-publicised notion in pre-war Germany that she was being encircled by the "Triple Entente" powers.

0 — 300 Miles

RUSSIA
FINLAND
SWEDEN
NORWAY
DENMARK
HOLL.
BELG.
LUX.
GERMANY
AUSTRIA-HUNGARY
POLAND
Baltic Sea
North Sea
BRITAIN
London
IRELAND
Paris
FRANCE
SWITZ.
ITALY
Berlin
Vienna
Rome
SPAIN
PORTUGAL
Bay of Biscay
Gibraltar (British)
Tunis
Malta (British)
MONTENEGRO
ALBANIA
GREECE
SERBIA
BULGARIA
RUMANIA
TURKEY
Black Sea
St. Petersburg

1894
1907
1904
1894
1897
1882
1882

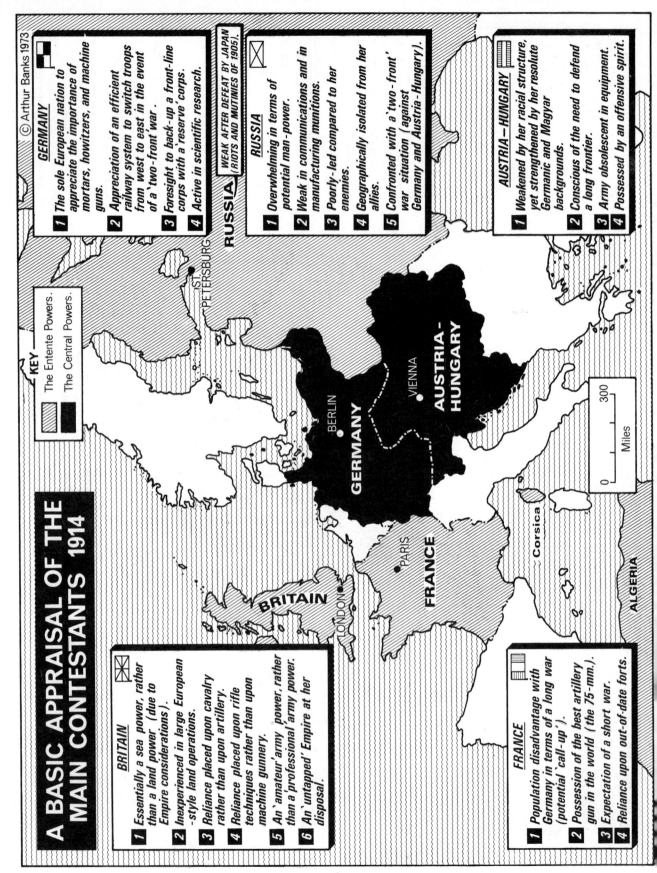

A BASIC APPRAISAL OF THE MAIN CONTESTANTS 1914

© Arthur Banks 1973

KEY

The Entente Powers.
The Central Powers.

GERMANY

1. The sole European nation to appreciate the importance of mortars, howitzers, and machine guns.
2. Appreciation of an efficient railway system to switch troops from west to east in the event of a 'two-front' war.
3. Foresight to back-up a front-line corps with a 'reserve' corps.
4. Active in scientific research.

RUSSIA WEAK AFTER DEFEAT BY JAPAN (RIOTS AND MUTINIES OF 1905).

1. Overwhelming in terms of potential man-power.
2. Weak in communications and in manufacturing munitions.
3. Poorly-led compared to her enemies.
4. Geographically isolated from her allies.
5. Confronted with a 'two-front' war situation (against Germany and Austria-Hungary).

AUSTRIA-HUNGARY

1. Weakened by her racial structure, yet strengthened by her resolute Germanic and Magyar backgrounds.
2. Conscious of the need to defend a long frontier.
3. Army obsolescent in equipment.
4. Possessed by an offensive spirit.

BRITAIN

1. Essentially a sea power, rather than a land power (due to Empire considerations).
2. Inexperienced in large European-style land operations.
3. Reliance placed upon cavalry rather than upon artillery.
4. Reliance placed upon rifle techniques rather than upon machine gunnery.
5. An 'amateur' army power, rather than a 'professional' army power.
6. An 'untapped' Empire at her disposal.

FRANCE

1. Population disadvantage with Germany in terms of a long war (potential 'call-up').
2. Possession of the best artillery gun in the world (the 75-mm.).
3. Expectation of a short war.
4. Reliance upon out-of-date forts.

ST. PETERSBURG

BERLIN

VIENNA

GERMANY

AUSTRIA-HUNGARY

FRANCE

PARIS

BRITAIN

LONDON

Corsica

ALGERIA

0   300
Miles

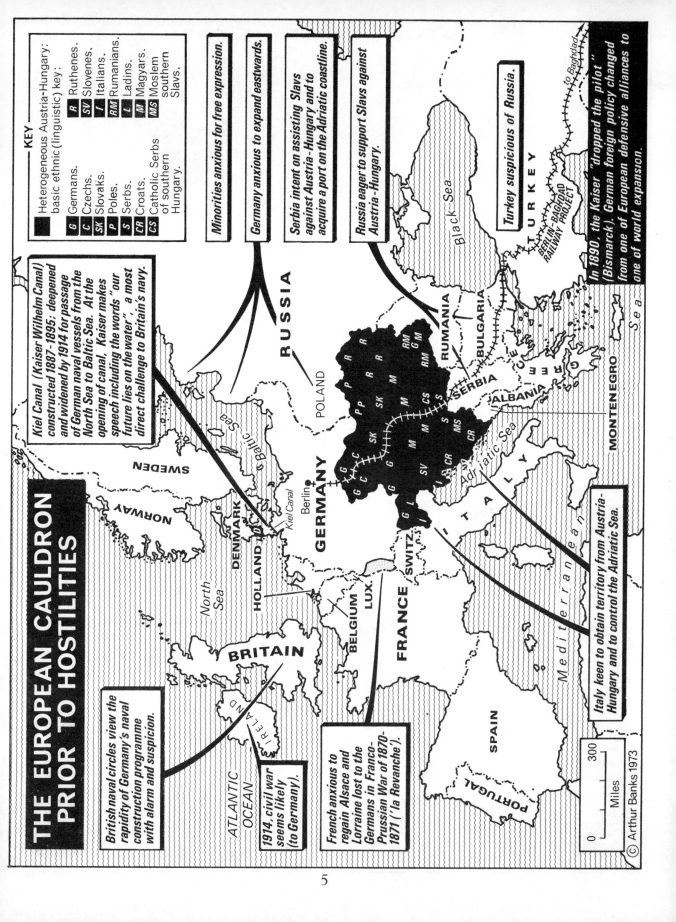

THE EUROPEAN CAULDRON PRIOR TO HOSTILITIES

KEY

Heterogeneous Austria-Hungary: basic ethnic (linguistic) key:

- **G** Germans.
- **C** Czechs.
- **SK** Slovaks.
- **P** Poles.
- **S** Serbs.
- **CR** Croats.
- **CS** Catholic Serbs of southern Hungary.
- **R** Ruthenes.
- **SV** Slovenes.
- **I** Italians.
- **RM** Rumanians.
- **L** Ladins.
- **M** Magyars.
- **MS** Moslem southern Slavs.

Kiel Canal (Kaiser Wilhelm Canal) constructed 1887-1895: deepened and widened by 1914 for passage of German naval vessels from the North Sea to Baltic Sea. At the opening of canal, Kaiser makes speech including the words "our future lies on the water", a most direct challenge to Britain's navy.

Minorities anxious for free expression.

Germany anxious to expand eastwards.

Serbia intent on assisting Slavs against Austria-Hungary and to acquire a port on the Adriatic coastline.

Russia eager to support Slavs against Austria-Hungary.

Turkey suspicious of Russia.

In 1890, the Kaiser "dropped the pilot" (Bismarck). German foreign policy changed from one of European defensive alliances to one of world expansion.

British naval circles view the rapidity of Germany's naval construction programme with alarm and suspicion.

1914, civil war seems likely (to Germany).

French anxious to regain Alsace and Lorraine lost to the Germans in Franco-Prussian War of 1870-1871 ('la Revanche').

Italy keen to obtain territory from Austria-Hungary and to control the Adriatic Sea.

BERLIN-BAGHDAD RAILWAY PROJECT

to Baghdad

0 — 300 Miles

© Arthur Banks 1973

5

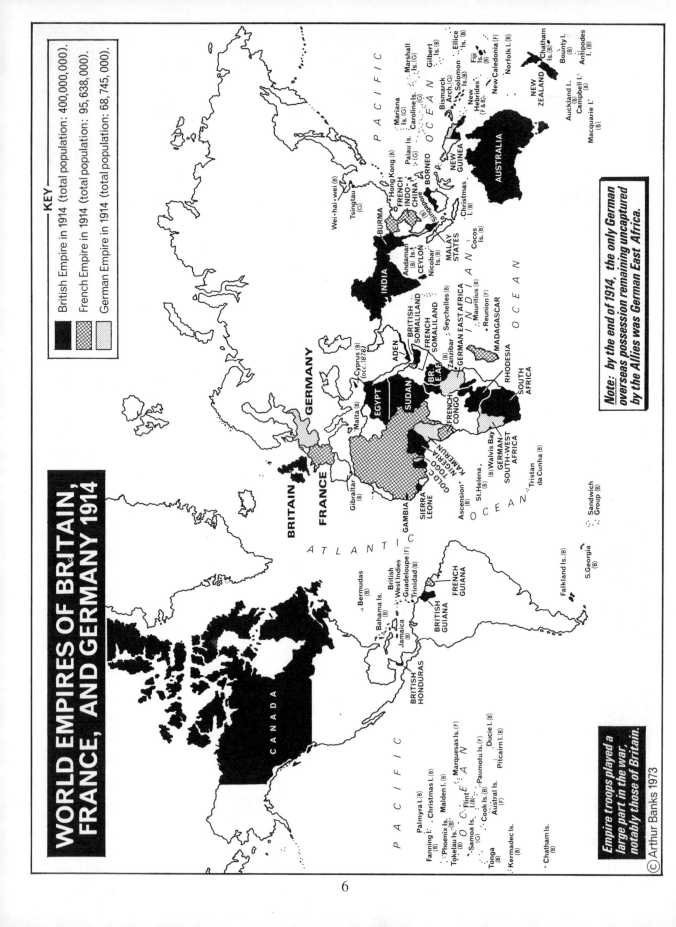

WORLD EMPIRES OF BRITAIN, FRANCE, AND GERMANY 1914

KEY

- British Empire in 1914 (total population: 400,000,000).
- French Empire in 1914 (total population: 95,638,000).
- German Empire in 1914 (total population: 68,745,000).

Note: by the end of 1914, the only German overseas possession remaining uncaptured by the Allies was German East Africa.

Empire troops played a large part in the war, notably those of Britain.

© Arthur Banks 1973

6

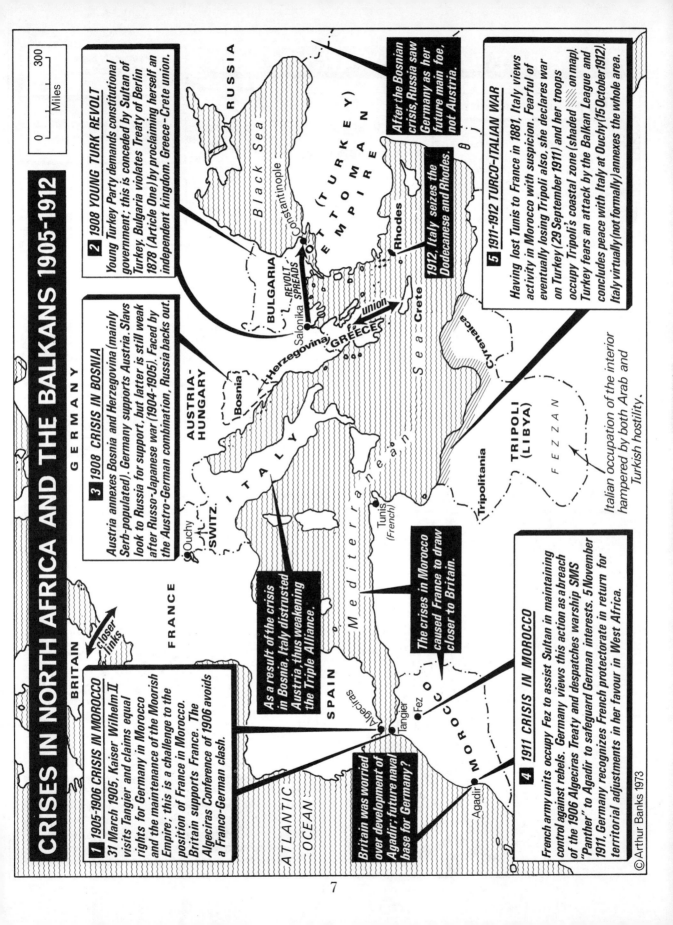

CRISES IN NORTH AFRICA AND THE BALKANS 1905-1912

1 1905-1906 CRISIS IN MOROCCO
31 March 1905, Kaiser Wilhelm II visits Tangier and claims equal rights for Germany in Morocco and the maintenance of the Moorish Empire; this is a challenge to the position of France in Morocco. Britain supports France. The Algeciras Conference of 1906 avoids a Franco-German clash.

2 1908 YOUNG TURK REVOLT
Young Turkey Party demands constitutional government; this is conceded by Sultan of Turkey. Bulgaria violates Treaty of Berlin 1878 (Article One) by proclaiming herself an independent kingdom. Greece-Crete union.

3 1908 CRISIS IN BOSNIA
Austria annexes Bosnia and Herzegovina (mainly Serb-populated). Germany supports Austria. Slavs look to Russia for support, but latter is still weak after Russo-Japanese war (1904-1905). Faced by the Austro-German combination, Russia backs out.

After the Bosnian crisis, Russia saw Germany as her future main foe, not Austria.

5 1911-1912 TURCO-ITALIAN WAR
Having lost Tunis to France in 1881, Italy views activity in Morocco with suspicion. Fearful of eventually losing Tripoli also, she declares war on Turkey (29 September 1911) and her troops occupy Tripoli's coastal zone (shaded ▨▨▨ on map). Turkey fears an attack by the Balkan League and concludes peace with Italy at Ouchy (15 October 1912). Italy virtually (not formally) annexes the whole area.

1912, Italy seizes the Dodecanese and Rhodes.

As a result of the crisis in Bosnia, Italy distrusted Austria, thus weakening the Triple Alliance.

The crises in Morocco caused France to draw closer to Britain.

4 1911 CRISIS IN MOROCCO
French army units occupy Fez to assist Sultan in maintaining control against rebels. Germany views this action as a breach of the 1906 Algeciras Treaty and despatches warship SMS "Panther" to Agadir to safeguard German interests. 5 November 1911, Germany recognizes French protectorate in return for territorial adjustments in her favour in West Africa.

Britain was worried over development of Agadir: future naval base for Germany?

Italian occupation of the interior hampered by both Arab and Turkish hostility.

closer links

RUSSIA

GERMANY

BRITAIN

FRANCE

SWITZ.

AUSTRIA-HUNGARY

ITALY

SPAIN

MOROCCO

Black Sea

Constantinople

OTTOMAN (TURKEY) EMPIRE

BULGARIA

Salonika

REVOLT SPREADS

Herzegovina

Bosnia

GREECE

Crete

union

Rhodes

Mediterranean Sea

Cyrenaica

TRIPOLI (LIBYA)

Tripolitania

FEZZAN

Tunis (French)

Ouchy

Algeciras

Tangier

Fez

Agadir

ATLANTIC OCEAN

0   300
Miles

© Arthur Banks 1973

7

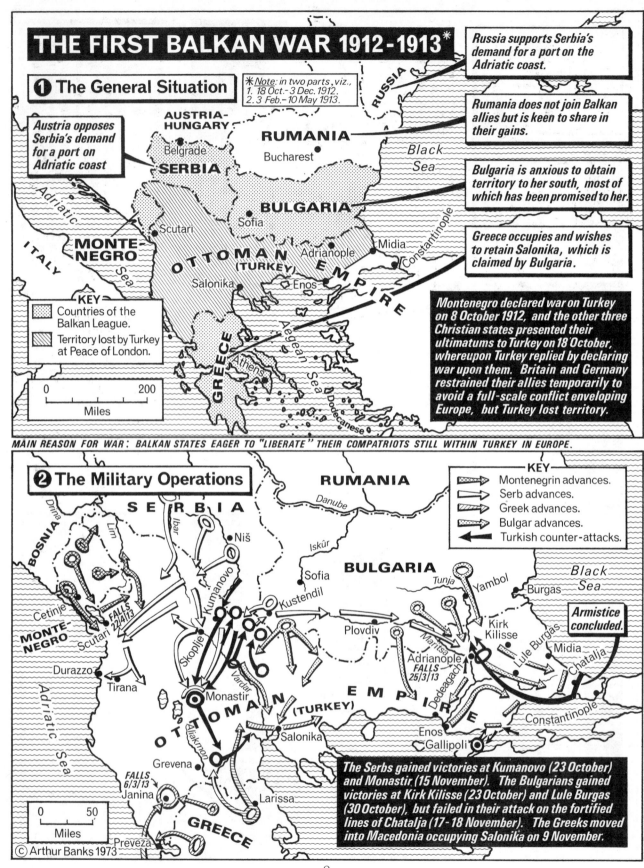

THE FIRST BALKAN WAR 1912-1913 *

① The General Situation

Note: in two parts, viz.,
1. 18 Oct.- 3 Dec. 1912.
2. 3 Feb.– 10 May 1913.

Russia supports Serbia's demand for a port on the Adriatic coast.

Austria opposes Serbia's demand for a port on Adriatic coast

Rumania does not join Balkan allies but is keen to share in their gains.

Bulgaria is anxious to obtain territory to her south, most of which has been promised to her.

Greece occupies and wishes to retain Salonika, which is claimed by Bulgaria.

AUSTRIA-HUNGARY

RUMANIA

Belgrade

SERBIA

Bucharest

Black Sea

BULGARIA

Adriatic

Sofia

Scutari

ITALY

MONTE-NEGRO

Midia

Adrianople

Constantinople

OTTOMAN (TURKEY) EMPIRE

Salonika

Enos

Montenegro declared war on Turkey on 8 October 1912, and the other three Christian states presented their ultimatums to Turkey on 18 October, whereupon Turkey replied by declaring war upon them. Britain and Germany restrained their allies temporarily to avoid a full-scale conflict enveloping Europe, but Turkey lost territory.

KEY
- Countries of the Balkan League.
- Territory lost by Turkey at Peace of London.

Aegean Sea

GREECE

Athens

Dodecanese

0   200

Miles

MAIN REASON FOR WAR: BALKAN STATES EAGER TO "LIBERATE" THEIR COMPATRIOTS STILL WITHIN TURKEY IN EUROPE.

② The Military Operations

RUMANIA

KEY
- ⬡⬡⬢➤ Montenegrin advances.
- ➤ Serb advances.
- ⬡⬢➤ Greek advances.
- ⬢⬢⬢➤ Bulgar advances.
- ◀ Turkish counter-attacks.

SERBIA

Danube

Drina

BOSNIA

Lim

Ibar

Niš

Iskûr

BULGARIA

Sofia

Tunja

Yambol

Black Sea

Burgas

Cetinje

Kumanovo

Kustendil

Armistice concluded.

MONTE-NEGRO

FALLS 22/4/13

Scutari

Skopje

Plovdiv

Kirk Kilisse

Lule Burgas

Midia

Durazzo

Vardar

Marica

Adrianople FALLS 25/3/13

Dedeagach

Chatalja

Tirana

Monastir

OTTOMAN

(TURKEY)

EMPIRE

Constantinople

Aliakmon

Salonika

Grevena

Enos

Gallipoli

FALLS 6/3/13

Janina

Larissa

The Serbs gained victories at Kumanovo (23 October) and Monastir (15 November). The Bulgarians gained victories at Kirk Kilisse (23 October) and Lule Burgas (30 October), but failed in their attack on the fortified lines of Chatalja (17-18 November). The Greeks moved into Macedonia occupying Salonika on 9 November.

0   50

Miles

GREECE

Preveza

© Arthur Banks 1973

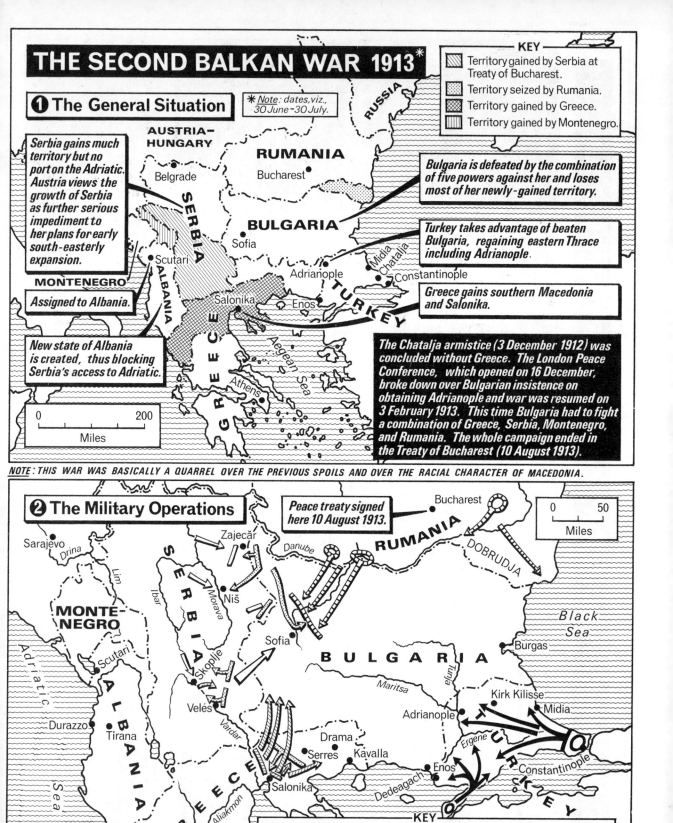

THE SECOND BALKAN WAR 1913*

❶ The General Situation

Note: dates, viz., 30 June - 30 July.

Serbia gains much territory but no port on the Adriatic. Austria views the growth of Serbia as further serious impediment to her plans for early south-easterly expansion.

MONTENEGRO
Assigned to Albania.

New state of Albania is created, thus blocking Serbia's access to Adriatic.

AUSTRIA–HUNGARY

RUSSIA

RUMANIA
Bucharest •

Belgrade •

SERBIA

Sofia •

BULGARIA

ALBANIA

Scutari •

Adrianople •

Midia
Chatalja
Constantinople •

TURKEY

Salonika •

Enos •

GREECE

Athens •

Aegean Sea

Bulgaria is defeated by the combination of five powers against her and loses most of her newly-gained territory.

Turkey takes advantage of beaten Bulgaria, regaining eastern Thrace including Adrianople.

Greece gains southern Macedonia and Salonika.

KEY
▨ Territory gained by Serbia at Treaty of Bucharest.
░ Territory seized by Rumania.
▩ Territory gained by Greece.
▥ Territory gained by Montenegro.

The Chatalja armistice (3 December 1912) was concluded without Greece. The London Peace Conference, which opened on 16 December, broke down over Bulgarian insistence on obtaining Adrianople and war was resumed on 3 February 1913. This time Bulgaria had to fight a combination of Greece, Serbia, Montenegro, and Rumania. The whole campaign ended in the Treaty of Bucharest (10 August 1913).

0 _____ 200
Miles

NOTE: THIS WAR WAS BASICALLY A QUARREL OVER THE PREVIOUS SPOILS AND OVER THE RACIAL CHARACTER OF MACEDONIA.

❷ The Military Operations

Peace treaty signed here 10 August 1913.

0 ___ 50
Miles

Sarajevo •

MONTE-NEGRO

Drina
Lim
Ibar

SERBIA

Zajecar •

Danube

Bucharest •

RUMANIA

DOBRUDJA

Morava

Niš •

Black Sea

Scutari •

Skoplje •

Sofia •

BULGARIA

Burgas •

Adriatic Sea

Veles •

Vardar

Maritsa

Tunja

Kirk Kilisse •
Midia •

ALBANIA

Durazzo •
Tirana •

Drama •
Serres •

Kavalla •

Adrianople •

Ergene

TURKEY

Salonika •

Enos •

Dedeagach •

Constantinople •

GREECE

Aliakmon

Janina •

CORFU

Larissa •

© Arthur Banks 1973

KEY
⬅ Bulgarian advances and movements.
⬜➡ Serbian counter-attacks.
▨➡ Greek counter-attacks.
▦➡ Rumanian counter-attacks.
➡ Turkish counter-attacks.

9

THE 'SPARK'–ASSASSINATION OF FRANZ FERDINAND 28 JUNE 1914

The assassination of Archduke Franz Ferdinand (heir to the throne of Austria–Hungary) and his wife at Sarajevo, capital of Bosnia, was the spark igniting a chain reaction sequence that led to the outbreak of war in 1914. A group of conspirators associated with two Balkan Slav societies (the 'Black Hand' and the 'Young Bosnia') were involved in the plot, which was put into operation on St Vitus Day (a Serbian festival).
The first attempt failed, but the Archduke, who was on an official visit to Sarajevo, went on to the Town Hall as arranged. The return route was altered but the driver of the Archduke's car misunderstood the change of plan (due to poor briefing) and followed the leading car into Franz Josef Street. Princip, one of the conspirators, saw the car reversing into Appel Quay, ran into the road and shot the Archduke and Duchess.

CLARIFICATION NOTE : 'BLACK HAND' WAS A SECRET SERBIAN SOCIETY, WHEREAS 'YOUNG BOSNIA' WAS A MOVEMENT, PARTLY CULTURAL.

THE TRAGIC FAMILY HISTORY OF FRANZ JOSEF (EMPEROR OF AUSTRIA)

1867. His brother, Emperor of Mexico, was executed.
1889. His son, Crown Prince Rudolf, died mysteriously.
1898. His wife, Empress Elizabeth, was assassinated.

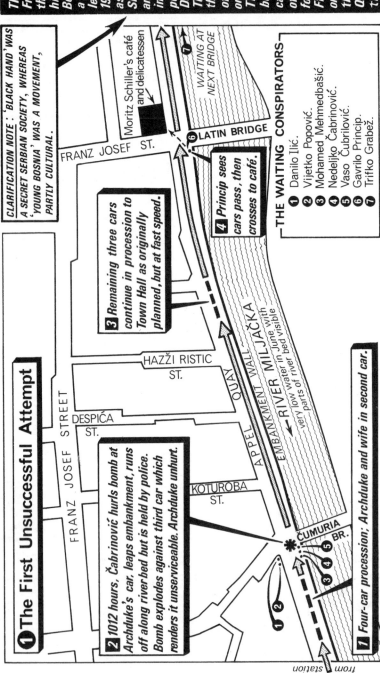

❶ The First Unsuccessful Attempt

2 1012 hours, Čabrinović hurls bomb at Archduke's car, leaps along river bed but is held by police. Bomb explodes against third car which renders it unserviceable. Archduke unhurt.

3 Remaining three cars continue in procession to Town Hall as originally planned, but at fast speed.

4 Princip sees cars pass, then crosses to café.

1 Four-car procession; Archduke and wife in second car.

Moritz Schiller's café and delicatessen

LATIN BRIDGE

FRANZ JOSEF ST.

FRANZ JOSEF STREET

DESPIĆA ST.

HAZZI RISTIC ST.

KOTUROBA ST.

CUMURIA BR.

APPEL QUAY

EMBANKMENT WALL

RIVER MILJAČKA very low water in June with parts of river bed visible

WAITING AT NEXT BRIDGE

from station

THE WAITING CONSPIRATORS
❶ Danilo Ilić.
❷ Vijetko Popović.
❸ Mohamed Mehmedbašić.
❹ Nedeljko Čabrinović.
❺ Vaso Čubrilović.
❻ Gavrilo Princip.
❼ Trifko Grabež.

❷ The Second Successful Attempt

Princip (positioned at Schiller's store) fires two shots from Browning automatic at five yards range (1045 hours). Archduke and wife mortally wounded.

LATIN BR.

FRANZ JOSEF STREET

MILJAČKA

RIVER

APPEL QUAY

visit to museum

KEY
– – – Return route from Town Hall as originally planned (before Čabrinović's bomb action).
••••• Revised return route (after bomb action).
S Moritz Schiller's delicatessen/café shop.
G Position of car during Princip's action.

© Arthur Banks 1973

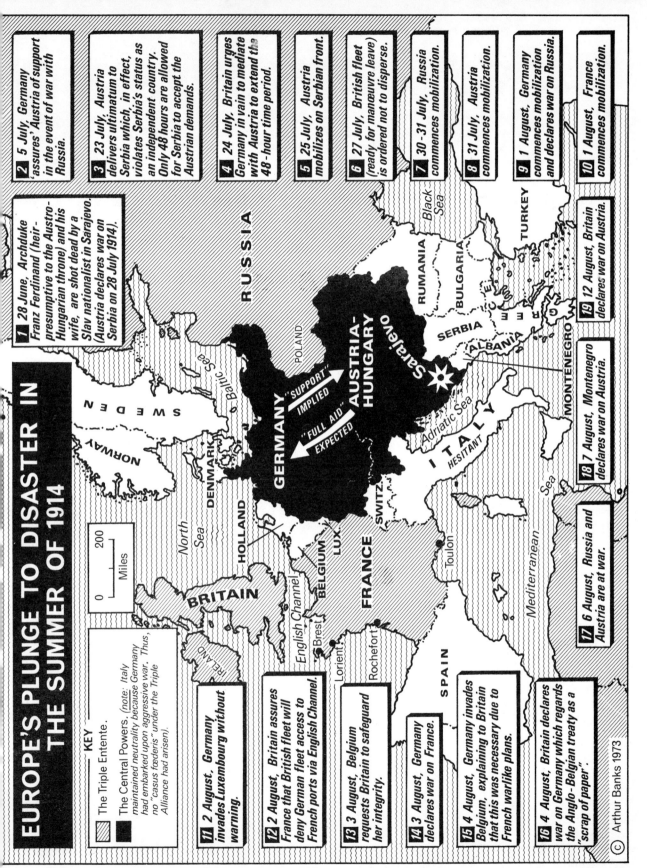

EUROPE'S PLUNGE TO DISASTER IN THE SUMMER OF 1914

KEY

The Triple Entente.

The Central Powers. *(note: Italy maintained neutrality because Germany had embarked upon aggressive war. Thus, no "casus foederis" under the Triple Alliance had arisen).*

0   200
Miles

1 28 June, Archduke Franz Ferdinand (heir-presumptive to the Austro-Hungarian throne) and his wife, are shot dead by a Slav nationalist in Sarajevo. (Austria declares war on Serbia on 28 July 1914).

2 5 July, Germany 'assures' Austria of support in the event of war with Russia.

3 23 July, Austria delivers ultimatum to Serbia which, in effect, violates Serbia's status as an independent country. Only 48 hours are allowed for Serbia to accept the Austrian demands.

4 24 July, Britain urges Germany in vain to mediate with Austria to extend the 48-hour time period.

5 25 July, Austria mobilizes on Serbian front.

6 27 July, British fleet (ready for manoeuvre leave) is ordered not to disperse.

7 30-31 July, Russia commences mobilization.

8 31 July, Austria commences mobilization.

9 1 August, Germany commences mobilization and declares war on Russia.

10 1 August, France commences mobilization.

11 2 August, Germany invades Luxembourg without warning.

12 2 August, Britain assures France that British fleet will deny German fleet access to French ports via English Channel.

13 3 August, Belgium requests Britain to safeguard her integrity.

14 3 August, Germany declares war on France.

15 4 August, Germany invades Belgium, explaining to Britain that this was necessary due to French warlike plans.

16 4 August, Britain declares war on Germany which regards the Anglo-Belgian treaty as a "scrap of paper".

17 6 August, Russia and Austria are at war.

18 7 August, Montenegro declares war on Austria.

19 12 August, Britain declares war on Austria.

© Arthur Banks 1973

11

WAR ON THE WESTERN FRONT IN 1914

There had never been so great a concentration of military forces as in August 1914. A little over a century before, Napoleon (who, with Voltaire, believed fortune favoured 'the big battalions') staggered his contemporaries by gathering a Grand Army of 500,000 men to invade Russia. Yet, within a fortnight of the outbreak of war in 1914, the Germans had three times that number in France and Belgium alone. At the same time there were over a million Frenchmen on the Western Front, with three million reservists on call; both the Russians and the Austrians had more than a million and a quarter field troops along their frontiers; and by the end of the year a million volunteers in Britain had come forward for Kitchener's 'New Army'. Napoleon's Marshals counted their big battalions in hundreds of thousands; the commanders of 1914 thought in millions.

These huge numbers determined the character of the war. Military theorists in both France and Germany had long believed victory would come to the nation able rapidly to mobilise its mass of manpower and deploy its forces effectively in the field. It was assumed that the key to success lay in an offensive spirit and that the outcome of the war would be decided by a single campaign on each Front. Kitchener warned the British Cabinet the war would last for at least three years, but his colleagues doubted his powers of judgment. In Berlin that August the Kaiser told departing troops, 'You will be home before the leaves have fallen from the trees'; and few public figures in London, Paris or St Petersburg (soon to be renamed Petrograd) believed the fighting would continue for more than six months. The great tragedy for Europe is that when rapid victory eluded the combatants, the armies—still massive in numbers—became deadlocked in trench warfare, the big battalions checked by the unexpected defensive power of machine guns and exposed to the fury of weapons which the authorities had underrated. It was this transformation of the battlefield which wasted so many lives. Casualties were heavy during the 'war of movement': they were heavier still during the long agony of the 'war of attrition'. At a conservative estimate over the world as a whole—with land fighting in three continents and with warships engaged on every

ocean—one sailor, soldier or airman was killed for every ten seconds the war lasted; and it continued in the end for fifty-one months.

Yet, at the outset, it seemed as if the fighting would indeed 'all be over by Christmas'. The Schlieffen Plan, finally adopted by the German General Staff at the end of 1905, proposed a holding operation against the Russians (who, it was assumed, would be slow to mobilise) in the East while the bulk of the German Army struck against France with an enveloping movement through Flanders and Picardy which would invest Paris from the west and south and thus force the French armies eastwards on to their own defences from Nancy to Belfort. British intervention, though regarded as probable once Belgium was invaded, was discounted as negligible. France defeated, the Germans planned to use the network of railways to move their forces eastwards and destroy the Russian menace. This plan, which was modified by Moltke (Chief of the German General Staff since 1906) in the three years immediately preceding the war, came within an ace of success. The French grand design—Plan XVII—to some extent played into German hands, for it committed two armies to an attack on Lorraine, away from the principal threat to the heart of France. Even when amended after the German invasion of Luxembourg, Plan XVII still ignored the strength of the enemy's thrust into western Belgium. So successful were the Germans that on 30 August the readers of *The Times* in England were startled to learn that 'the investment of Paris cannot be banished from the field of possibility'. What the public was not told was that the French, exhausting themselves by courageous counter-attacks in the spirit of Napoleonic battle panoramas, had already suffered nearly a third of a million casualties (dead, missing, wounded). One out of every ten officers in the whole French army (not merely the regiments in the field) was killed or incapacitated before the end of August 1914.

Moltke's variation on the Schlieffen Plan failed for three principal reasons. He lost touch with his army commanders, who showed excessive independence of manoeuvre; he was so worried by reports of the

Russian advance into East Prussia that he weakened his right wing by detaching troops to the East (compare pages 19, 88 and 89); and he failed to see that three weeks of forced marches in intensive heat and blazing sunshine had reduced the efficiency of the invading armies. When General von Kluck began to move his tired troops south-eastwards, exposing the right flank of the German First Army to the Paris garrison (page 54), the fate of the whole war was in the balance. The French commander-in-chief, Joffre, supported by the Military Governor of Paris, General Gallieni, ordered the French Sixth, Fifth and Ninth Armies (Generals Maunoury, Franchet d'Espèrey and Foch) together with the British Expeditionary Force (Field-Marshal Sir John French) to counter-attack across the lower Marne and its tributaries on 5–6 September. There followed the series of inter-related engagements, the legendary 'miracle of the Marne', fought along a front of more than 125 miles. Momentarily the nerve of the German High Command seemed to crack; Paris and France were saved; the German knock-out blow— which had stunned France in 1870 and which was to stun France again in 1940—was thrust aside.

If the Allies had not themselves been so weary and cautious that September, they might well have turned the German retreat from the Marne into a sensational defeat. As it was, the Germans found they could stabilise their line north of Rheims and along the river Aisne. Moltke retired from active service and was replaced as Chief of the German General Staff by General von Falkenhayn, who at once determined to consolidate the German hold on Belgium, through which the invaders had passed like a scythe in the first weeks of war. When Brussels was occupied on 20 August five divisions of the Belgian Army (80,000 men) fell back on Antwerp, the great fortress-port on the Schelde. So long as the Belgians held Antwerp (from which they made a number of sorties to relieve pressure on the French and British on the Marne and the Aisne) there was a possibility of using the city as a point from which to attack the German right flank. This threat the Germans were determined to eradicate. The First Lord of the Admiralty, Churchill, sought to stiffen resistance in Antwerp by a personal visit and by sending from England a naval division, which was hastily trained and inadequately armed. In the event, the Belgians placed excessive reliance on outdated forts and redoubts which could not withstand the pounding of German artillery. Antwerp duly surrendered to General von Beseler on

9 October, but the main Belgian army withdrew by way of Ghent and Bruges to the line of a canalised small river, the Yser. There, inspired by their courageous King Albert, the Belgians resisted a German advance towards Dunkirk, eventually opening the sluices of Nieuport and bringing the North Sea in flood to the aid of the defenders.

While Beseler was besieging Antwerp, both the Germans and the Allies were engaged in a complicated movement from the Aisne to cover the Channel ports. At times during this 'race for the sea' it seemed as if both sides were risking envelopment by the other during their outflanking operations. Briefly there was hope that the British would capture Lille and open up a route towards Brussels, but they failed to penetrate the town in strength. All six divisions of the B.E.F. were moved northwards from the Aisne to Flanders. By the end of the second week in October they had established a salient around Ypres, Armentières and Neuve Chapelle. It was here that they faced Falkenhayn's principal attempt to break through the Allied positions and take Calais and Boulogne.

The first battle of Ypres (October–November 1914) virtually destroyed the old peacetime British regular army and began to take heavy toll of the new territorial infantry battalions as well. 50,000 British soldiers fell at Ypres that autumn, one division losing two-thirds of its infantry in three weeks of combat. Hardest hit were the original 'old contemptibles', the men who had gone forward to Mons in August (page 47) and retreated for a gruelling fortnight before turning back south of the Marne and forcing the Germans northwards to the Belgian frontier. By the end of November over half of the men who had crossed to France three months previously were casualties, one in ten of them dead. The Germans lost twice as many soldiers as the British at Ypres, yet they never broke through. They penetrated the British line at Gheluvelt on the Menin Road (31 October) but were ejected in a surprise counter attack by the 2nd Battalion of the Worcestershire Regiment, subsequently supported by French units. The city of Ypres was never captured by the Germans, even though fighting raged continuously around the ruined mediaeval cloth town for four years. Ypres and its salient acquired a symbolic significance for the British which was out of all proportion to its strategic value. There were two later battles within the Ypres Salient: in the spring of 1915 (pages 138–143) and from June to November 1917 (pages 172–173); and a final penetration of the German positions in September 1918 (page 196).

Winter set in before the First Battle of Ypres was over. There was no longer any danger of an outright German victory, but equally there was little prospect of an Allied breakthrough. First Ypres marked the end of open warfare: henceforth the opposing armies on the Western Front were paralysed by barbed wire, by entrenchments, by minefields, and by machine-gun emplacements. In another sense, too, First Ypres marked a change of character in the war. The first month of fighting had shown divisions and suspicion between the Allied commanders, especially between the British and the French. The close proximity of British, French and Belgian lines around Ypres helped to weld together the Allied command, although it was difficult to forget old prejudices. The mud-filled disease-ridden trenches bred a sense of communal adversity. At the same time First Ypres showed the extent of Allied resources, for in the line were not only the first battalions of Kitchener's 'new army', but Zouave regiments from French Algeria and Indians from Lahore. Before the fighting died away at the salient in 1918, they were to be joined by units from Canada, Senegal and finally the United States. The cemeteries around Ypres, and the great monument to those 'with no known grave', bear silent testimony to the world-wide character of this most wasteful of wars.

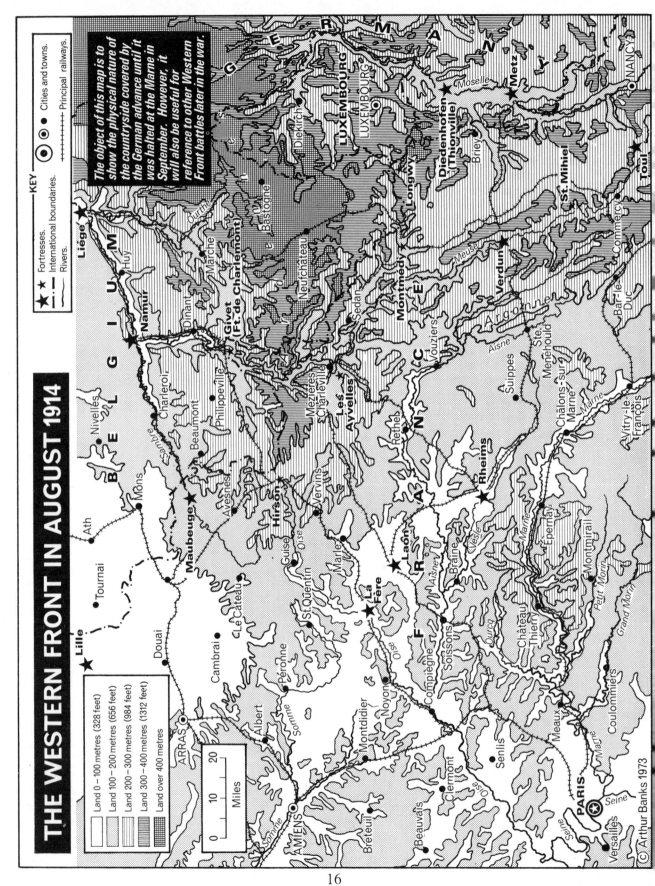

THE WESTERN FRONT IN AUGUST 1914

KEY

Fortresses.
Cities and towns.
International boundaries.
Principal railways.
Rivers.

The object of this map is to show the physical nature of the countryside covered by the German advance until it was halted at the Marne in September. However, it will also be useful for reference to other Western Front battles later in the war.

Land 0 – 100 metres (328 feet)
Land 100 – 200 metres (656 feet)
Land 200 – 300 metres (984 feet)
Land 300 – 400 metres (1312 feet)
Land over 400 metres

Miles
0   10   20

16

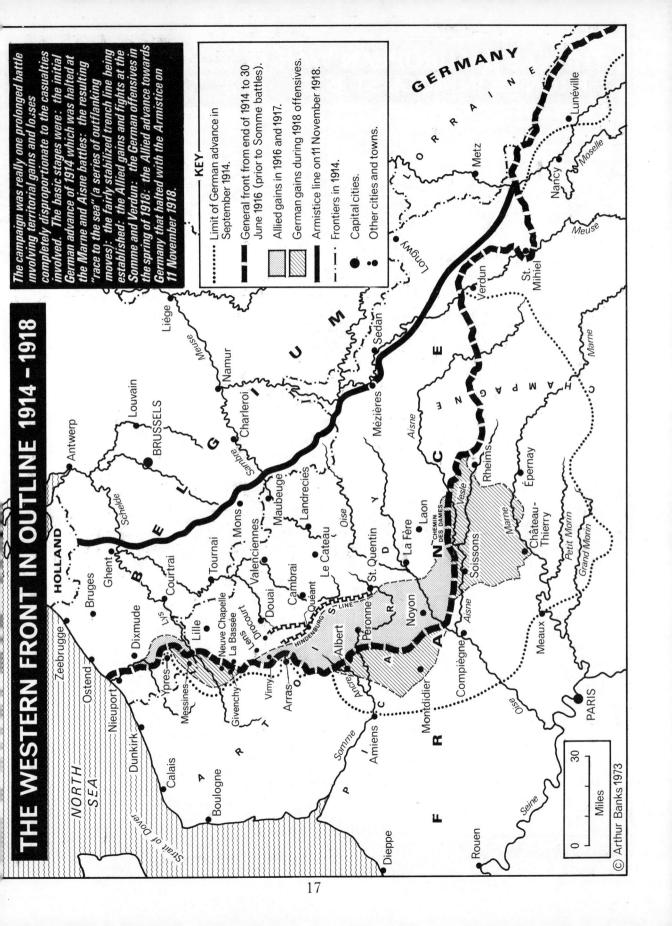

THE WESTERN FRONT IN OUTLINE 1914 – 1918

The campaign was really one prolonged battle involving territorial gains and losses completely disproportionate to the casualties involved. The basic stages were: the initial German advance of 1914 which was halted at the Marne and Aisne battles: the resulting "race to the sea" (a series of outflanking moves): the fairly stabilized trench line being established: the Allied gains and fights at the Somme and Verdun: the German offensives in the spring of 1918: the Allied advance towards Germany that halted with the Armistice on 11 November 1918.

KEY

······ Limit of German advance in September 1914.

❙❙❙ General front from end of 1914 to 30 June 1916 (prior to Somme battles).

▦ Allied gains in 1916 and 1917.

▨ German gains during 1918 offensives.

▬ Armistice line on 11 November 1918.

–··– Frontiers in 1914.

● Capital cities.

• Other cities and towns.

NORTH SEA

Strait of Dover

HOLLAND

GERMANY

BELGIUM

FRANCE

LORRAINE

CHAMPAGNE

HINDENBURG LINE

CHEMIN DES DAMES

Zeebrugge
Ostend
Nieuport
Dunkirk
Calais
Boulogne
Dieppe
Rouen
Dixmude
Bruges
Ghent
Ypres
Messines
Courtrai
Tournai
Lille
Neuve Chapelle
La Bassée
Givenchy
Vimy
Arras
Lens
Drocourt
Douai
Valenciennes
Mons
Maubeuge
Cambrai
Quéant
Landrecies
Le Cateau
St. Quentin
Péronne
Albert
Amiens
Montdidier
Noyon
Compiègne
Meaux
PARIS
La Fère
Laon
Soissons
Château-Thierry
Épernay
Rheims
Mézières
Sedan
Charleroi
Namur
Louvain
Antwerp
BRUSSELS
Liége
Verdun
St. Mihiel
Longwy
Metz
Nancy
Lunéville

Schelde
Lys
Somme
Ancre
Oise
Sambre
Meuse
Aisne
Vesle
Marne
Petit Morin
Grand Morin
Seine
Moselle
Meuse

30
Miles
0

© Arthur Banks 1973

17

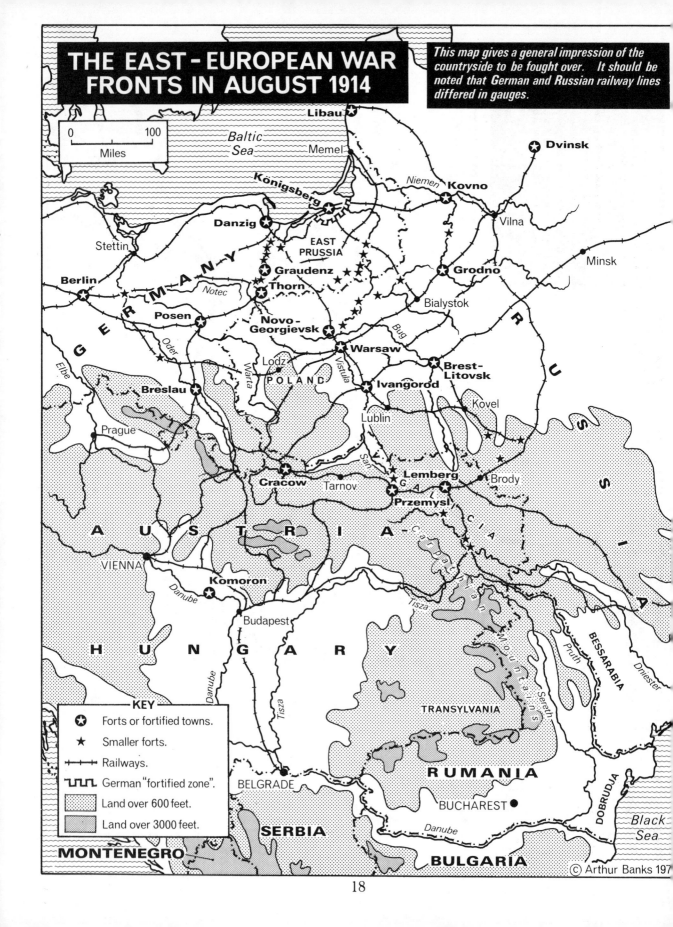

THE EAST - EUROPEAN WAR FRONTS IN AUGUST 1914

This map gives a general impression of the countryside to be fought over. It should be noted that German and Russian railway lines differed in gauges.

0   100
Miles

Libau
Baltic Sea
Memel
Dvinsk
Königsberg
Niemen
Kovno
Vilna
Minsk
Danzig
EAST PRUSSIA
Stettin
Graudenz
Grodno
Berlin
Notec
Thorn
Bialystok
Posen
Novo-Georgievsk
Bug
Oder
Warsaw
Brest-Litovsk
Lodz
Warta
Vistula
Kovel
Breslau
POLAND
Ivangorod
Prague
Lublin
San
Cracow
Tarnov
Lemberg
Brody
Przemysl
Komoron
VIENNA
Danube
AUSTRIA-
Budapest
Tisza
HUNGARY
Danube
BESSARABIA
Pruth
Dniester
TRANSYLVANIA
Sereth
RUMANIA
DOBRUDJA
Black Sea
BELGRADE
BUCHAREST
SERBIA
BULGARIA
MONTENEGRO

GERMANY
RUSSIA
GALICIA
Carpathian Mountains
Elbe

KEY
- ✪ Forts or fortified towns.
- ★ Smaller forts.
- ┼┼┼ Railways.
- ⊓⊔⊓⊔ German "fortified zone".
- Land over 600 feet.
- Land over 3000 feet.

© Arthur Banks 197

18

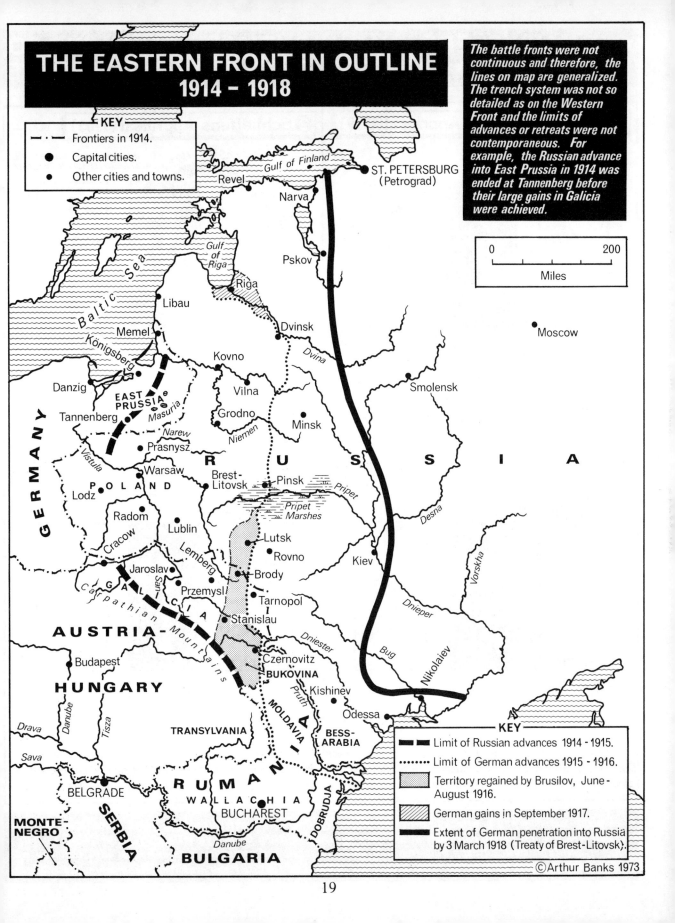

THE EASTERN FRONT IN OUTLINE
1914 – 1918

The battle fronts were not continuous and therefore, the lines on map are generalized. The trench system was not so detailed as on the Western Front and the limits of advances or retreats were not contemporaneous. For example, the Russian advance into East Prussia in 1914 was ended at Tannenberg before their large gains in Galicia were achieved.

KEY
–·–· Frontiers in 1914.
● Capital cities.
• Other cities and towns.

0   200
Miles

KEY
▬▬ Limit of Russian advances 1914 - 1915.
····· Limit of German advances 1915 - 1916.
▦ Territory regained by Brusilov, June - August 1916.
▨ German gains in September 1917.
▬▬ Extent of German penetration into Russia by 3 March 1918 (Treaty of Brest-Litovsk).

ⓒArthur Banks 1973

Baltic Sea
Gulf of Finland
Gulf of Riga
Revel
Narva
ST. PETERSBURG (Petrograd)
Pskov
Riga
Libau
Memel
Königsberg
Danzig
Dvinsk
Dvina
Moscow
Kovno
EAST PRUSSIA
Masuria
Tannenberg
Vilna
Grodno
Narew
Niemen
Minsk
Smolensk
GERMANY
Vistula
Prasnysz
R U S S I A
Warsaw
P O L A N D
Lodz
Brest-Litovsk
Pinsk
Pripet
Pripet Marshes
Radom
Lublin
Desna
Cracow
Lutsk
Jaroslav
Lemberg
Rovno
Kiev
Przemysl
Brody
San
G A L I C I A
Tarnopol
Vorskha
Stanislau
AUSTRIA-HUNGARY
Carpathian Mountains
Dniester
Czernovitz
BUKOVINA
Dnieper
Bug
Budapest
Kishinev
Nikolaiev
HUNGARY
MOLDAVIA
Pruth
BESS-ARABIA
Drava
Danube
Tisza
TRANSYLVANIA
Odessa
Sava
R U M A N I A
BELGRADE
WALLACHIA
BUCHAREST
MONTE-NEGRO
SERBIA
DOBRUDJA
Danube
BULGARIA

19

GERMANY'S PRE-WAR NIGHTMARE OF HAVING TO FIGHT A LAND CAMPAIGN ON TWO FRONTS AT ONCE

❶ The Elder Moltke's Appraisal (1879)

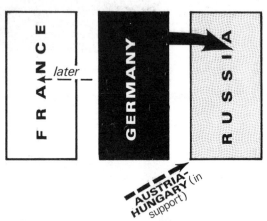

RUSSIA *must be dealt with FIRST.* Count von Waldersee (Moltke's successor) agreed with this provided that the offensive against Russia be conducted in summer weather.

❷ Schlieffen's Appraisal (1905)

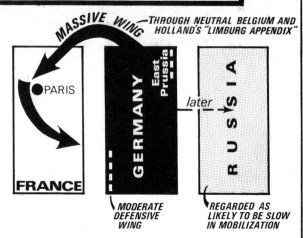

THROUGH NEUTRAL BELGIUM AND HOLLAND'S "LIMBURG APPENDIX"

MASSIVE WING

PARIS
East Prussia

MODERATE DEFENSIVE WING

REGARDED AS LIKELY TO BE SLOW IN MOBILIZATION

FRANCE *must be dealt with FIRST in a rapid campaign while Russia is kept at bay by means of a holding or delaying operation in East Prussia. Austria in support.*

❸ Schlieffen's Revised Appraisal (1912)

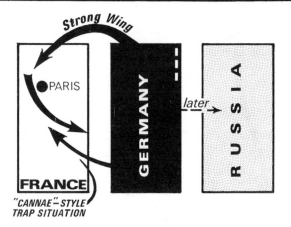

Strong Wing

PARIS

later

"CANNAE"-STYLE TRAP SITUATION

Apparently Schlieffen studied Hannibal's victory at Cannae (216 B.C.) in detail and, as a consequence, revised his own plan. But the German right wing was to be kept strong.

❹ The Younger Moltke's Appraisal (1914)

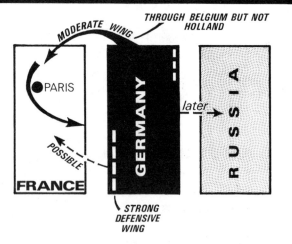

THROUGH BELGIUM BUT NOT HOLLAND

MODERATE WING

PARIS

later

POSSIBLE

STRONG DEFENSIVE WING

Moltke (nephew of Bismarck's general) strengthened his defensive wing at the expense of his right wing: he omitted ersatz "back up" formations at rear of right wing armies.

In all plans, Germany had to attack first to obviate her fighting an all-out war on two fronts simultaneously: the two potential enemies had to be fought in sequence to avoid splitting Germany's main effort. Everything hinged upon her ability to switch troops from front to front with speed and precision. Even in August 1914, Germany was not powerful enough to launch two major offensives at the same time. Her fear was that SHE might be attacked first!

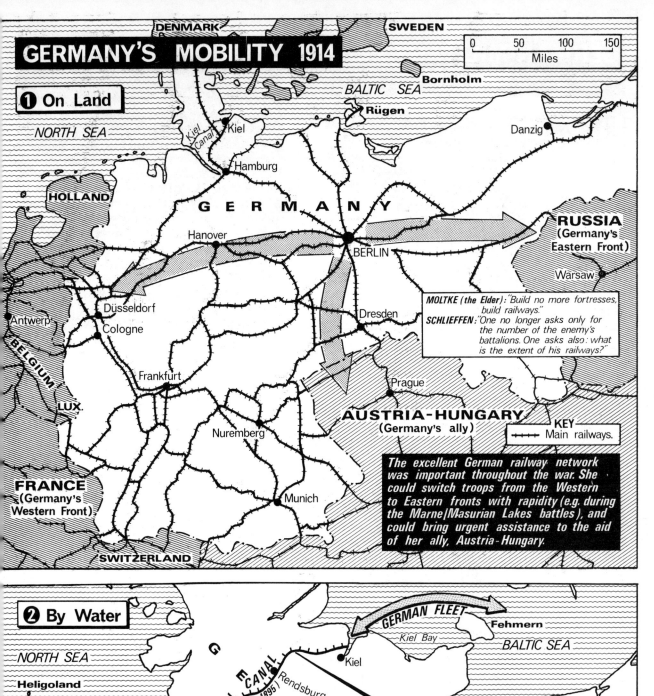

GERMANY'S MOBILITY 1914

❶ On Land

DENMARK · SWEDEN

BALTIC SEA

Bornholm

Rügen

NORTH SEA

Kiel · Kiel Canal

Danzig

Hamburg

HOLLAND

G E R M A N Y

Hanover

BERLIN

RUSSIA
(Germany's Eastern Front)

Warsaw

Düsseldorf

Antwerp

Cologne

Dresden

BELGIUM

LUX.

Frankfurt

Prague

> MOLTKE (the Elder): "Build no more fortresses, build railways."
> SCHLIEFFEN: "One no longer asks only for the number of the enemy's battalions. One asks also: what is the extent of his railways?"

AUSTRIA - HUNGARY
(Germany's ally)

KEY
╫═══ Main railways.

Nuremberg

FRANCE
(Germany's Western Front)

Munich

> The excellent German railway network was important throughout the war. She could switch troops from the Western to Eastern fronts with rapidity (e.g. during the Marne/Masurian Lakes battles), and could bring urgent assistance to the aid of her ally, Austria - Hungary.

SWITZERLAND

0   50   100   150
Miles

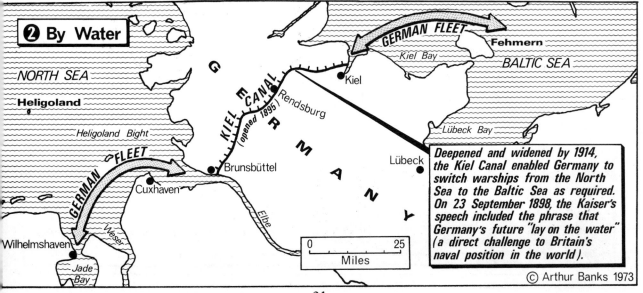

❷ By Water

NORTH SEA

GERMAN FLEET

Fehmern

Kiel Bay

BALTIC SEA

G
E
R
M
A
N
Y

KIEL CANAL (opened 1895)

Rendsburg

Kiel

Heligoland

Heligoland Bight

Lübeck Bay

Brunsbüttel

Lübeck

GERMAN FLEET

Cuxhaven

Elbe

Weser

> Deepened and widened by 1914, the Kiel Canal enabled Germany to switch warships from the North Sea to the Baltic Sea as required. On 23 September 1898, the Kaiser's speech included the phrase that Germany's future "lay on the water" (a direct challenge to Britain's naval position in the world).

Wilhelmshaven

Jade Bay

0   25
Miles

© Arthur Banks 1973

21

GERMAN MILITARY PLANS 1905-1914

In the years before 1914, German military planners were haunted by fear of an all-out war on two fronts simultaneously (that is, against Russia and France). In 1905, Field-Marshal Graf Alfred Schlieffen prepared a plan based on an assumption that Russia (calculated to be slower in mobilization than France) could be held temporarily at bay, while the bulk of German military power be directed at securing a rapid victory over France. Thus, Schlieffen's plan dealt almost exclusively with the Western Front. Moltke, Schlieffen's successor as Chief of the German General Staff, modified the scheme on several occasions before the war, and an amended version was put into operation in August 1914. Despite initial successes, the plan failed to produce the expected quick victory, and the Western Front became a scene of almost rigid trench warfare until 1918.

❶ A War on Two Fronts

GERMANY (efficient rail network linking both fronts)

HOLLAND · Belgium · Lux. · Paris · FRANCE · Switz. · Poland · RUSSIA · Austria-Hungary (Allied with Germany)

0 — 200 Miles

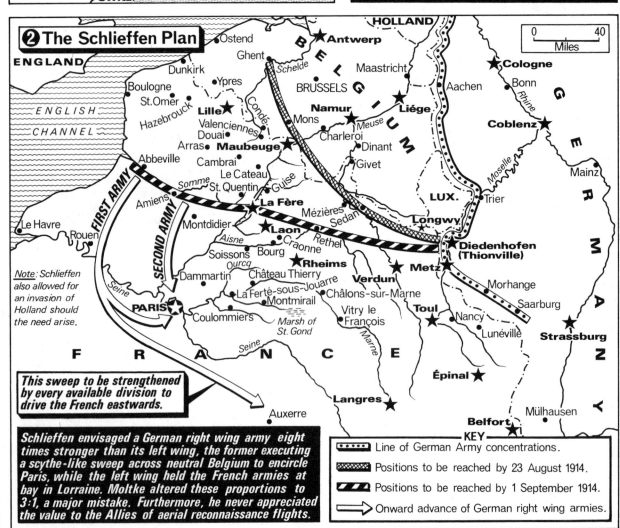

❷ The Schlieffen Plan

0 — 40 Miles

Note: Schlieffen also allowed for an invasion of Holland should the need arise.

This sweep to be strengthened by every available division to drive the French eastwards.

Schlieffen envisaged a German right wing army eight times stronger than its left wing, the former executing a scythe-like sweep across neutral Belgium to encircle Paris, while the left wing held the French armies at bay in Lorraine. Moltke altered these proportions to 3:1, a major mistake. Furthermore, he never appreciated the value to the Allies of aerial reconnaissance flights.

KEY

- •••••• Line of German Army concentrations.
- ▨▨▨▨ Positions to be reached by 23 August 1914.
- ▧▧▧▧ Positions to be reached by 1 September 1914.
- ⟹ Onward advance of German right wing armies.

ACTUAL GERMAN ADVANCE
17 AUGUST - 5 SEPTEMBER 1914

0   50

Miles

NORTH
SEA

HOLLAND

Essen

Ostend

Nieuport

Antwerp   BELGIAN
ARMY

Düsseldorf

Schelde

Dunkirk

FIRST ARMY

Maastricht

Cologne

Ypres

BRUSSELS   Louvain

Aachen

O.H.L.
(MOLTKE)

Schelde

Lys

BELGIUM

Liége

Rhine

Lille

SECOND ARMY

Namur

Coblenz

Mons

Charleroi

ARMY

Scarpe

Valenciennes

Maubeuge

THIRD

Dinant

Arras

FIRST ARMY

Cambrai

Le
Cateau

Somme

St.
Quentin

Guise

Meuse

ARDENNES

LUX.

Amiens

SECOND ARMY

La Fère
(obsolete)

Laon

THIRD ARMY

Sedan

ARMY

Longwy

GERMANY

O.H.L. MOVES 29 AUG.

Moselle

LUXEMBOURG

Trier

Compiègne

Aisne

FOURTH

Diedenhofen
(Thionville)

Saarbrücken

Oise

FIRST ARMY

Rheims

FIFTH ARMY

Metz

Moselle

SIXTH
ARMY

Marne

Châlons-sur-
Marne

Argonne Forest

THIRD ARMY

Verdun

Meaux

St.Mihiel

PARIS

B.E.F.

NINTH
ARMY
(new)

FOURTH
ARMY

Toul

SECOND ARMY

SIXTH ARMY

Strassburg

Melun

FIFTH
ARMY

Provins

FRANCE

Seine

Meuse

Moselle

FIRST ARMY

SEVENTH ARMY

VOSGES

Épinal

Rhine

Ill

Langres

Mülhausen

Saône

Belfort

Montbeliard

Basle

— KEY —

Position of German Armies on 17 August 1914.

The German advance, 18 August - 5 September 1914.

German positions on 5 September 1914.

French

British

Belgian

Allied positions on 5 September 1914.

★ Military fortresses or fortified towns.

Dijon

Besançon

Doubs

SWITZ.

*This map shows von Kluck's
First Army altering its advance
to a south-easterly direction.*

Arthur Banks 1973

23

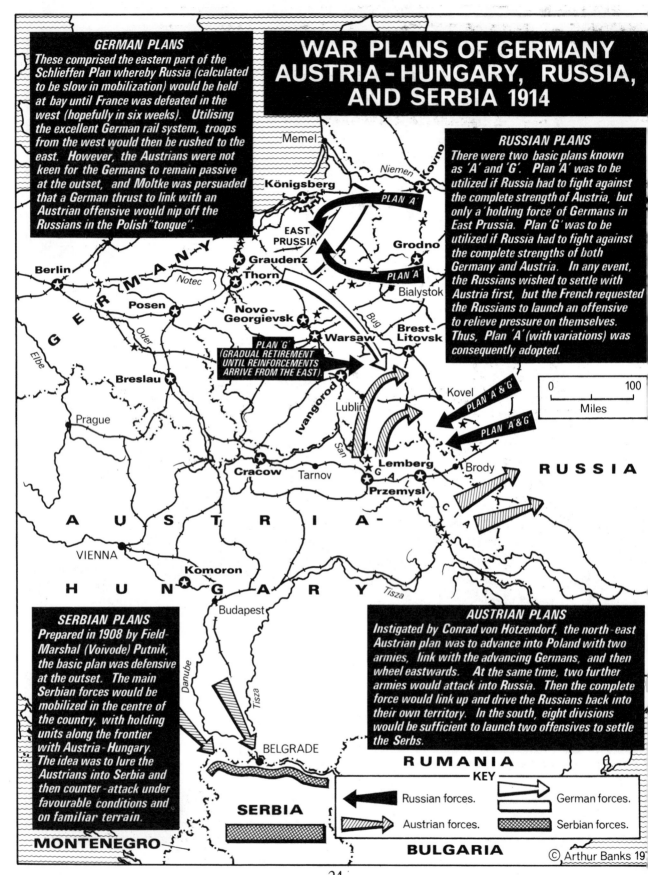

WAR PLANS OF GERMANY AUSTRIA - HUNGARY, RUSSIA, AND SERBIA 1914

GERMAN PLANS

These comprised the eastern part of the Schlieffen Plan whereby Russia (calculated to be slow in mobilization) would be held at bay until France was defeated in the west (hopefully in six weeks). Utilising the excellent German rail system, troops from the west would then be rushed to the east. However, the Austrians were not keen for the Germans to remain passive at the outset, and Moltke was persuaded that a German thrust to link with an Austrian offensive would nip off the Russians in the Polish "tongue".

RUSSIAN PLANS

There were two basic plans known as 'A' and 'G'. Plan 'A' was to be utilized if Russia had to fight against the complete strength of Austria, but only a 'holding force' of Germans in East Prussia. Plan 'G' was to be utilized if Russia had to fight against the complete strengths of both Germany and Austria. In any event, the Russians wished to settle with Austria first, but the French requested the Russians to launch an offensive to relieve pressure on themselves. Thus, Plan 'A' (with variations) was consequently adopted.

AUSTRIAN PLANS

Instigated by Conrad von Hötzendorf, the north-east Austrian plan was to advance into Poland with two armies, link with the advancing Germans, and then wheel eastwards. At the same time, two further armies would attack into Russia. Then the complete force would link up and drive the Russians back into their own territory. In the south, eight divisions would be sufficient to launch two offensives to settle the Serbs.

SERBIAN PLANS

Prepared in 1908 by Field-Marshal (Voivode) Putnik, the basic plan was defensive at the outset. The main Serbian forces would be mobilized in the centre of the country, with holding units along the frontier with Austria-Hungary. The idea was to lure the Austrians into Serbia and then counter-attack under favourable conditions and on familiar terrain.

Memel
Niemen
Königsberg
EAST PRUSSIA
PLAN 'A'
Kovno
Grodno
PLAN 'A'
Bialystok
Berlin
Notec
Graudenz
Thorn
Posen
Novo-Georgievsk
Warsaw
Bug
Brest-Litovsk
GERMANY
Oder
Elbe
Breslau
PLAN 'G'
(GRADUAL RETIREMENT UNTIL REINFORCEMENTS ARRIVE FROM THE EAST).
Ivangorod
Kovel
PLAN 'A & G'
PLAN 'A & G'
Prague
Lublin
San
0   100
Miles
Cracow
Tarnov
Lemberg
Brody
RUSSIA
Przemysl
AUSTRIA-
VIENNA
Komoron
HUNGARY
Budapest
Tisza
Danube
Tisza
BELGRADE
RUMANIA
SERBIA
MONTENEGRO
BULGARIA

KEY

Russian forces.
German forces.
Austrian forces.
Serbian forces.

24

© Arthur Banks 19

FRENCH PRE-WAR MILITARY PLANS 1914

© Arthur Banks 1973

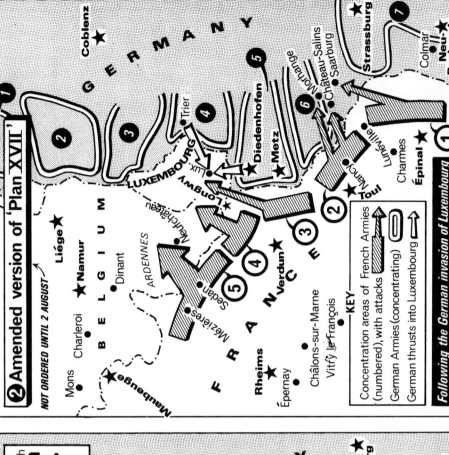

① Joffre's 'Plan XVII'

OFFICIALLY APPROVED BY WAR MINISTER ON 20 MAY 1913. ISSUED TO THE PROSPECTIVE ARMY COMMANDERS ON 15 MAY 1914.

KEY
- Concentration areas of French Armies (numbered)
- Proposed thrusts
- Military fortresses

GROUPE D'ALSACE

PART OF FIRST ARMY

(IN RESERVE)

This plan was prepared on an assumption that a Franco-German war, fought across common frontiers, would avoid violating nearby neutral territory (Belgium's status of neutrality had been "guaranteed" by France and Prussia [Germany] in 1839 & 1871). The plan involved a rapid mobilization of 3,000,000 troops and 4,000 troop-trains.

② Amended version of 'Plan XVII'

NOT ORDERED UNTIL 2 AUGUST

FORMED ON 11 AUGUST

ARMÉE D'ALSACE

KEY
- Concentration areas of French Armies (numbered), with attacks
- German Armies (concentrating)
- German thrusts into Luxembourg

Following the German invasion of Luxembourg on 2 August 1914, a variation of the original plan was ordered. The French right wing was to remain as hitherto, but the Fourth Army was to move up between the Third and Fifth Armies to facilitate a strong left wing thrust.

The basic weakness of both plans lay in the fact that Germany could strike first, a position which the French felt morally unable to assume in 1914.

25

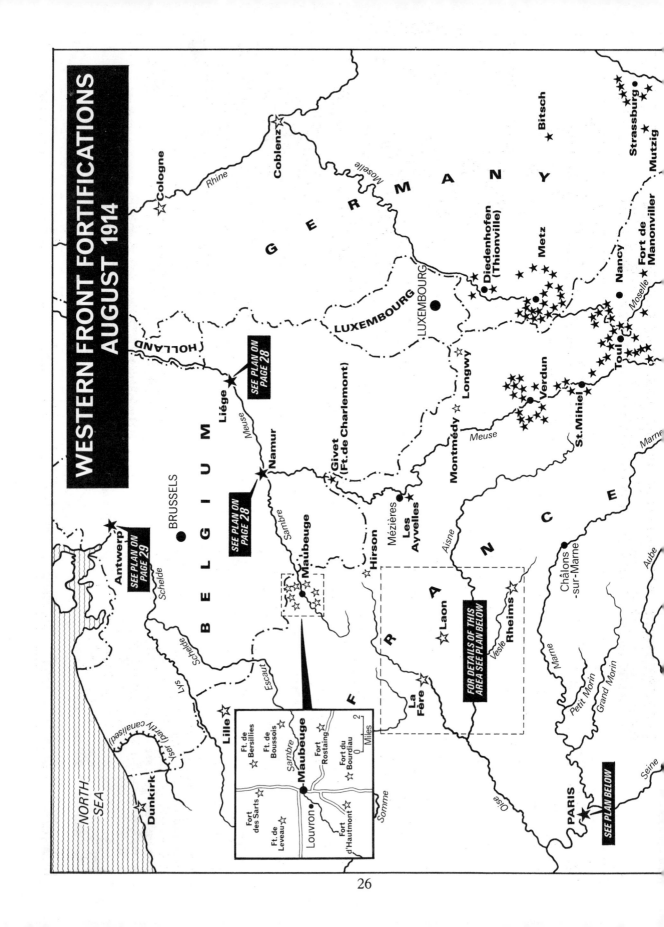

WESTERN FRONT FORTIFICATIONS AUGUST 1914

GERMANY

Cologne

Rhine

Coblenz

Moselle

Bitsch

Strassburg

Mutzig

Diedenhofen (Thionville)

Metz

Fort de Manonviller

Nancy

HOLLAND

LUXEMBOURG

LUXEMBOURG

Moselle

Liége

SEE PLAN ON PAGE 28

Meuse

Longwy

Toul

Verdun

Namur

SEE PLAN ON PAGE 28

BELGIUM

BRUSSELS

Givet (Ft.de Charlemont)

Montmédy

St.Mihiel

Meuse

Marne

Antwerp

SEE PLAN ON PAGE 29

Schelde

Sambre

Maubeuge

Hirson

Mézières

Les Ayvelles

FRANCE

Aisne

Châlons -sur-Marne

Aube

Lille

Escaut

Laon

Vesle

Rheims

FOR DETAILS OF THIS AREA SEE PLAN BELOW

Marne

Grand Morin

Lys

Yser (partly canalised)

La Fère

Petit Morin

Dunkirk

NORTH SEA

Fort de Bersillies

Fort de Boussois

Fort Rostaing

Fort du Bourdiau

Lille

Sambre

Maubeuge

Miles

0 2

Fort des Sarts

Ft.de Leveau

Louvron

Fort d'Hautmont

Somme

Oise

PARIS

SEE PLAN BELOW

Seine

26

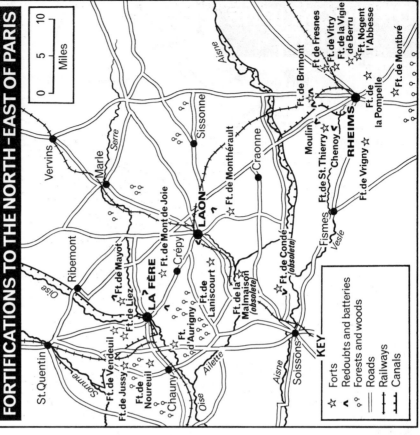

FORTIFICATIONS TO THE NORTH-EAST OF PARIS

Miles
0 5 10

Ft. de Fresnes
Ft. de Vitry ☆
Ft. de la Vigie de Berru ☆
Ft. Nogent l'Abbesse ☆
Ft. de Montbré ☆
Ft. de Brimont
RHEIMS
Ft. de la Pompelle ☆
Moulin
Ft. de St. Thierry ☆
Chenoy ☆
Ft. de Vigny ☆
Aisne
Sissonne
Craonne
Fismes
Vesle
Vervins
Serre
Marle
Ft. de Monthérault
Ft. de Condé (obsolete)
Soissons
LAON
Ft. de Mont de Joie
Crépy
Ribemont
Oise
Ft. de Mayot
Ft. de Liez
LA FÈRE
Ft. de Laniscourt
Ft. d'Aurigny
Ft. de la Malmaison (obsolete)
St. Quentin
Ft. de Vendeuil
Ft. de Jussy
Ft. de Noureuil
Chauny
Somme
Allette
Aisne
Oise

KEY
☆ Forts
⌃ Redoubts and batteries
ᵒᵖ Forests and woods
═══ Roads
╂╂╂ Railways
─────── Canals

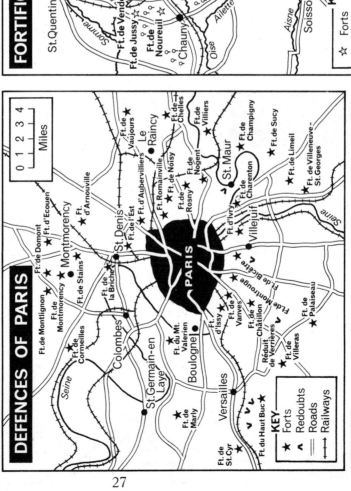

DEFENCES OF PARIS

Miles
0 1 2 3 4

Ft. de Domont
Ft. d'Ecouen
Ft. de Vaujours
Le Raincy
Ft. de Chelles
Ft. de Villiers
Ft. de Montmorency
Montmorency
Ft. de Stains
Ft. d'Arnouville
Ft. de Romainville
Ft. de Noisy
Ft. de Nogent
Ft. de Champigny
St. Maur
Ft. de Sucy
Colombes
Ft. de Cormeilles
Ft. de la Briche
St. Denis
Ft. de l'Est
Ft. d'Aubervilliers
Ft. de Rosny
PARIS
Ft. d'Ivry
Ft. de Charenton
Ft. de Limeil
Ft. de Villeneuve-St. Georges
St. Germain-en Laye
Ft. du Mt. Valérien
Boulogne
Versailles
Ft. d'Issy
Ft. de Vanves
Ft. de Montrouge
Ft. de Bicêtre
Villejuif
Réduit de Verrières
Ft. de Châtillon
Ft. de Palaiseau
Ft. de Marly
Ft. de Villeras
Ft. de St. Cyr
Ft. du Haut Buc
Seine

KEY
★ Forts
⌃ Redoubts
═══ Roads
╂╂╂ Railways

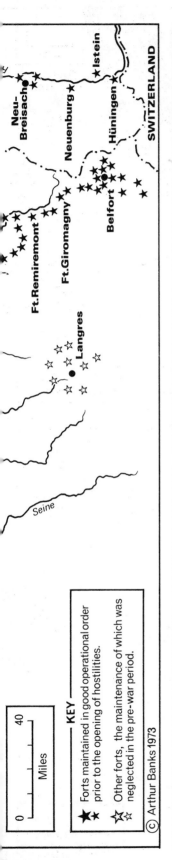

Neu-Breisach ★
Neuenburg ★
★ Istein
Hüningen ★
SWITZERLAND
Ft. Remiremont ★
Ft. Giromagny ★
Belfort ★
Langres ☆

KEY
Miles
0 40

★ Forts maintained in good operational order prior to the opening of hostilities.

☆ Other forts, the maintenance of which was neglected in the pre-war period.

© Arthur Banks 1973

Seine

This map depicts the system of fortifications that adorned the Western Front area prior to the commencement of hostilities. Many of the northern French fortresses were virtually obsolete or in a state of disrepair and the three Belgian fortresses had been designed in the 1880's and 1890's, long before the advent of "Dicke Bertha" and "Schlanke Emma".

27

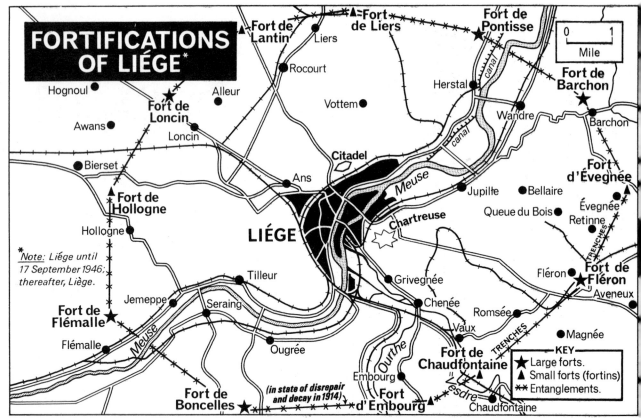

FORTIFICATIONS OF LIÉGE*

Fort de Lantin
Fort de Liers
Fort de Pontisse
Liers
Rocourt
Herstal
Fort de Barchon
canal
Hognoul
Alleur
Vottem
Wandre
Barchon
Fort de Loncin
Awans
Loncin
canal
Jupille
Bellaire
Fort d'Évegnée
Bierset
Ans
Citadel
Meuse
Queue du Bois
Évegnée
Retinne
Fort de Hollogne
Chartreuse
Fort de Fléron
Hollogne
LIÉGE
Fléron
Aveneux
*Note: Liége until 17 September 1946; thereafter, Liège.
Grivegnée
Romsée
Magnée
Tilleur
Chenée
Fort de Flémalle
Jemeppe
Seraing
Vaux
TRENCHES
Flémalle
Ougrée
Ourthe
Fort de Chaudfontaine

KEY
★ Large forts.
▲ Small forts (fortins).
⚹⚹ Entanglements.

Embourg
Fort d'Embourg
Vesdre
Chaudfontaine
Fort de Boncelles
(in state of disrepair and decay in 1914)

The main forts were pentagonal in shape, whereas the smaller 'fortins' were triangular. All consisted of works beneath ground level, with the guns being housed in steel cupolas which could be raised and lowered again at will. The designer was Henri Brialmont.

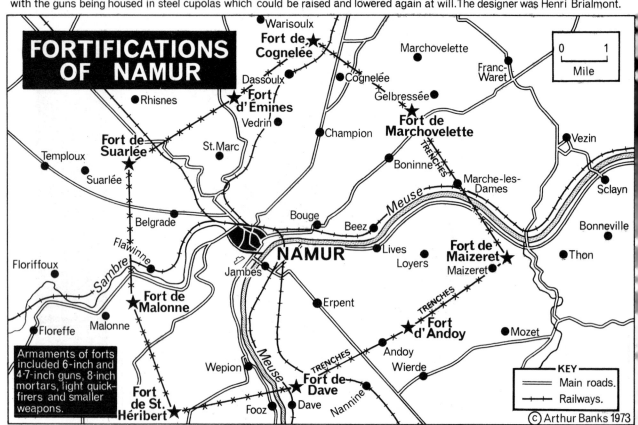

FORTIFICATIONS OF NAMUR

Warisoulx
Fort de Cognelée
Marchovelette
Franc-Waret
Dassoulx
Cognelée
Rhisnes
Gelbressée
Fort d'Émines
Vedrin
Champion
Fort de Marchovelette
Vezin
Fort de Suarlée
St. Marc
Boninne
Temploux
Marche-les-Dames
Sclayn
Suarlée
TRENCHES
Belgrade
Bouge
Meuse
Bonneville
Flawinne
Beez
Fort de Maizeret
Thon
Floriffoux
NAMUR
Lives
Loyers
Maizeret
Sambre
Jambes
Fort de Malonne
Erpent
Fort d'Andoy
Mozet
Floreffe
Malonne
Andoy
Wierde
Meuse
Wepion
Fort de St. Héribert
Fort de Dave
Fooz
Dave
Nannine

Armaments of forts included 6-inch and 4·7-inch guns, 8-inch mortars, light quick-firers and smaller weapons.

KEY
═══ Main roads.
—+— Railways.

© Arthur Banks 1973

28

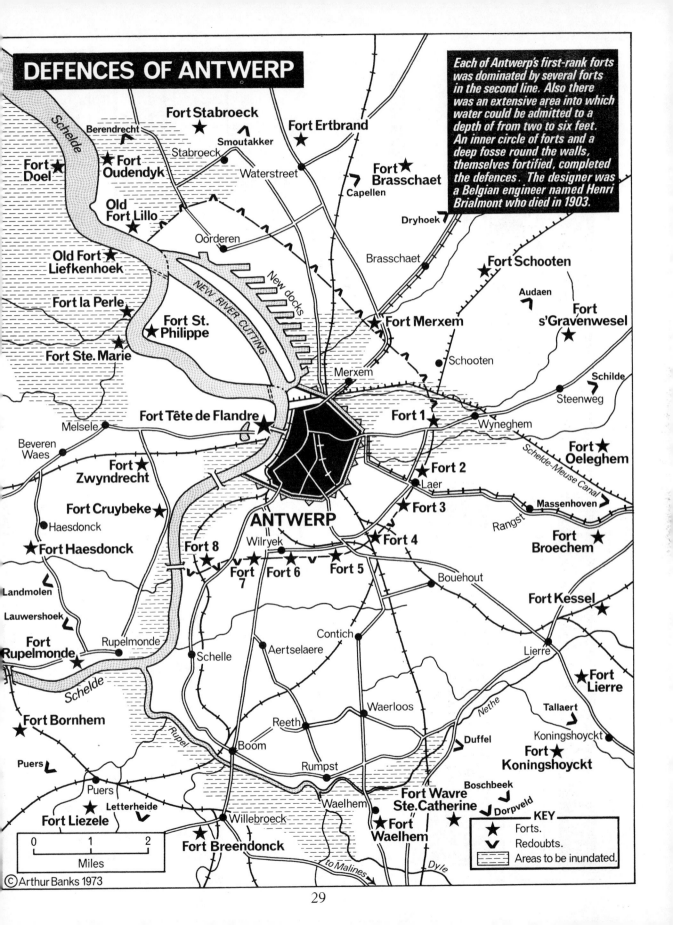

DEFENCES OF ANTWERP

Each of Antwerp's first-rank forts was dominated by several forts in the second line. Also there was an extensive area into which water could be admitted to a depth of from two to six feet. An inner circle of forts and a deep fosse round the walls, themselves fortified, completed the defences. The designer was a Belgian engineer named Henri Brialmont who died in 1903.

Schelde

Fort Stabroeck ★
Berendrecht
Smoutakker
Fort Ertbrand ★
Stabroeck
Waterstreet
Fort ★ Doel
★ Fort Oudendyk
Old Fort Lillo
Fort ★ Brasschaet
Capellen
Dryhoek
Oorderen
Brasschaet
Old Fort ★ Liefkenhoek
Fort Schooten ★
Audaen
Fort la Perle ★
NEW RIVER CUTTING
New docks
Fort ★ s'Gravenwesel
Fort St. ★ Philippe
Fort ★ Ste. Marie
Schooten
Schilde
Merxem
★ Fort Merxem
Steenweg
Fort Tête de Flandre ★
Fort 1 ★
Wyneghem
Melsele
Schelde-Meuse Canal
Fort ★ Oeleghem
Beveren Waes
Fort ★ Zwyndrecht
★ Fort 2
Laer
Massenhoven
ANTWERP
★ Fort 3
Rangst
Fort ★ Broechem
Fort Cruybeke ★
Wilryek
★ Fort 4
Haesdonck
★ Fort Haesdonck
Fort 8
★ Fort 5
Bouehout
Fort Kessel ★
Landmolen
Fort 7
Fort 6
Lauwershoek
Contich
Lierre
Fort ★ Rupelmonde
Rupelmonde
Schelle
Aertselaere
Fort ★ Lierre
Fort Bornhem ★
Reeth
Waerloos
Nethe
Tallaert
Puers
Boom
Koningshoyckt
Puers
Rupel
Rumpst
Duffel
Fort ★ Koningshoyckt
Letterheide
Waelhem
Boschbeek
Fort Liezele ★
Willebroeck
Fort Wavre Ste.Catherine
Dorpveld
Fort Breendonck ★
★ Fort Waelhem
to Malines
Dyle

KEY
★ Forts.
⌐ Redoubts.
▦ Areas to be inundated.

0   1   2
Miles

© Arthur Banks 1973

29

ARMY CONCENTRATIONS ON THE WESTERN FRONT AUGUST 1914

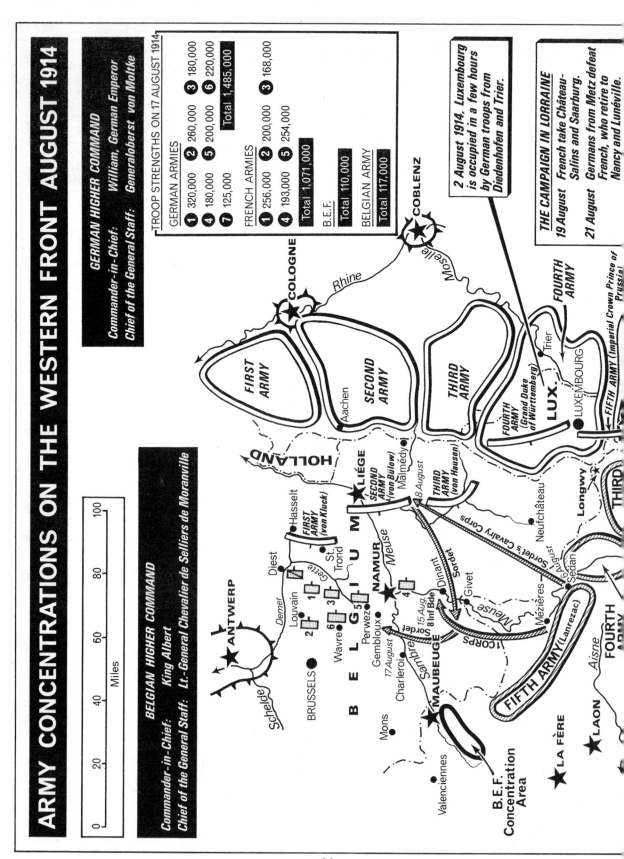

GERMAN HIGHER COMMAND

Commander-in-Chief: *William, German Emperor*
Chief of the General Staff: *Generaloberst von Moltke*

TROOP STRENGTHS ON 17 AUGUST 1914

GERMAN ARMIES

1 320,000	**2** 260,000	**3** 180,000
4 180,000	**5** 200,000	**6** 220,000
7 125,000		Total 1,485,000

FRENCH ARMIES

1 256,000	**2** 200,000	**3** 168,000
4 193,000	**5** 254,000	
		Total 1,071,000

B.E.F.
Total 110,000

BELGIAN ARMY
Total 117,000

2 August 1914. Luxembourg is occupied in a few hours by German troops from Diedenhofen and Trier.

THE CAMPAIGN IN LORRAINE

19 August *French take Château-Salins and Saarburg.*
21 August *Germans from Metz defeat French, who retire to Nancy and Lunéville.*

BELGIAN HIGHER COMMAND

Commander-in-Chief: *King Albert*
Chief of the General Staff: *Lt.-General Chevalier de Selliers de Moranville*

0 20 40 60 80 100
Miles

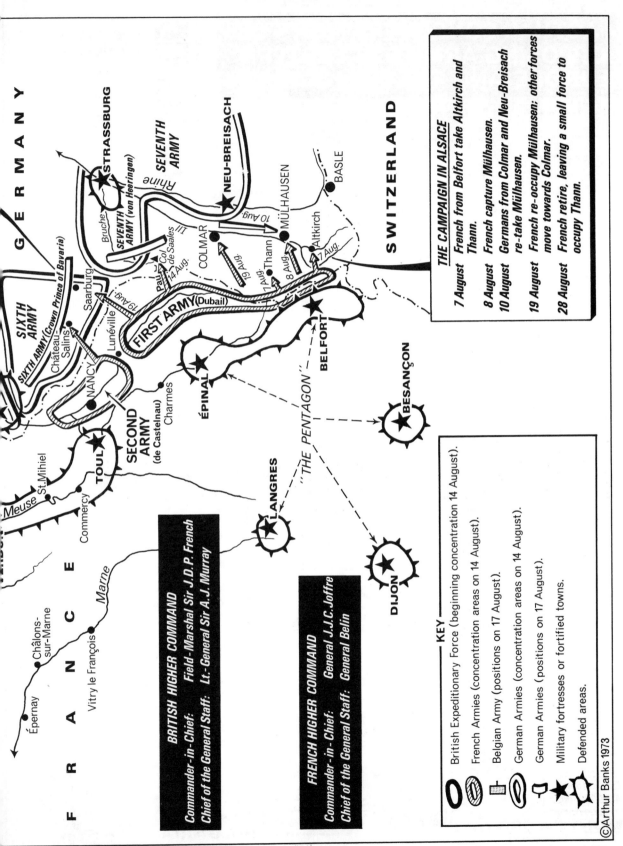

GERMANY

FRANCE

SWITZERLAND

SIXTH ARMY (Crown Prince of Bavaria)

SIXTH ARMY

Saarburg

SEVENTH ARMY (von Heeringen)

SEVENTH ARMY

STRASSBURG

Bruche

Rhine

NEU-BREISACH

Col de Saales

Paul Col

14 Aug.

COLMAR

19 Aug.

III

MÜLHAUSEN

10 Aug.

BASLE

Château-Salins

Lunéville

19 Aug.

Thann

7 Aug.

8 Aug.

7 Aug.

Altkirch

NANCY

SECOND ARMY (de Castelnau)

FIRST ARMY (Dubail)

Charmes

ÉPINAL

"THE PENTAGON"

BELFORT

BESANÇON

TOUL

St.Mihiel

LANGRES

Meuse

Commercy

DIJON

Marne

Châlons-sur-Marne

Épernay

Vitry le François

THE CAMPAIGN IN ALSACE

7 August	French from Belfort take Altkirch and Thann.
8 August	French capture Mülhausen.
10 August	Germans from Colmar and Neu-Breisach re-take Mülhausen.
19 August	French re-occupy Mülhausen; other forces move towards Colmar.
28 August	French retire, leaving a small force to occupy Thann.

BRITISH HIGHER COMMAND
Commander-in-Chief: Field-Marshal Sir J.D.P. French
Chief of the General Staff: Lt.-General Sir A.J. Murray

FRENCH HIGHER COMMAND
Commander-in-Chief: General J.J.C. Joffre
Chief of the General Staff: General Belin

KEY

⬭ British Expeditionary Force (beginning concentration 14 August).

⬯ French Armies (concentration areas on 14 August).

🏴 Belgian Army (positions on 17 August).

⬭ German Armies (concentration areas on 14 August).

⬗ German Armies (positions on 17 August).

★ Military fortresses or fortified towns.

✦ Defended areas.

©Arthur Banks 1973

31

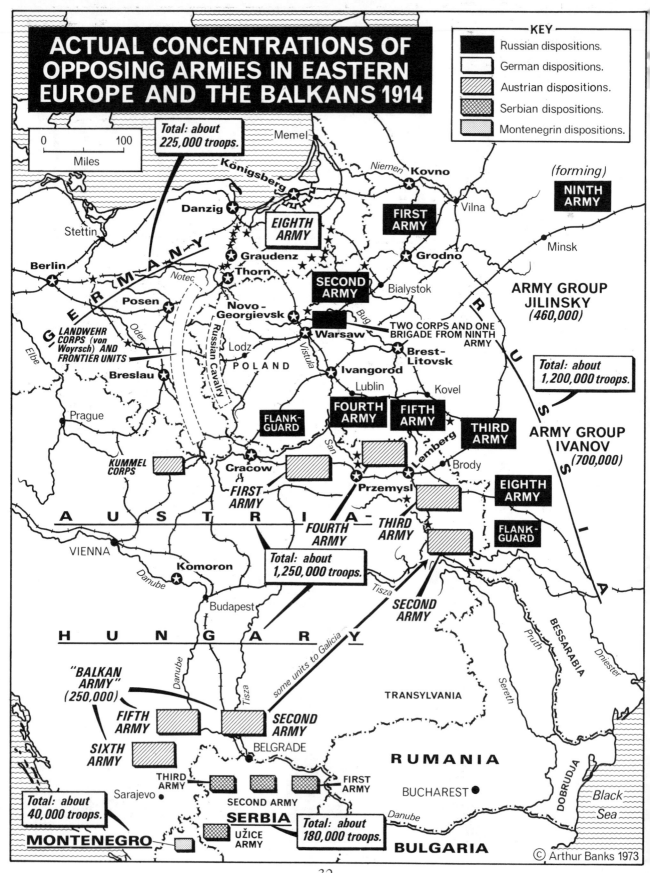

ACTUAL CONCENTRATIONS OF OPPOSING ARMIES IN EASTERN EUROPE AND THE BALKANS 1914

KEY
- Russian dispositions.
- German dispositions.
- Austrian dispositions.
- Serbian dispositions.
- Montenegrin dispositions.

0   100
Miles

Total: about 225,000 troops.

Memel

(forming)
NINTH ARMY

Königsberg

Niemen Kovno

Danzig

Vilna

FIRST ARMY

Minsk

Stettin

EIGHTH ARMY

G E R M A N Y

Graudenz

Grodno

Berlin

Thorn

SECOND ARMY

Bialystok

ARMY GROUP JILINSKY (460,000)

Notec

Posen

Novo-Georgievsk

Bug

Oder

Warsaw

TWO CORPS AND ONE BRIGADE FROM NINTH ARMY

LANDWEHR CORPS (von Woyrsch) AND FRONTIER UNITS

Russian Cavalry

Lodz

Brest-Litovsk

P O L A N D

Vistula

Elbe

Breslau

Ivangorod

Lublin

Kovel

Total: about 1,200,000 troops.

Prague

FLANK-GUARD

FOURTH ARMY

FIFTH ARMY

San

THIRD ARMY

ARMY GROUP IVANOV (700,000)

R U S S I A

KUMMEL CORPS

Cracow

Lemberg

Brody

EIGHTH ARMY

Przemysl

FIRST ARMY

A U S T R I A

FOURTH ARMY

THIRD ARMY

FLANK-GUARD

VIENNA

Danube

Komoron

Total: about 1,250,000 troops.

Tisza

SECOND ARMY

BESSARABIA

Pruth

Budapest

Dniester

H U N G A R Y

some units to Galicia

Sereth

TRANSYLVANIA

Danube

Tisza

"BALKAN ARMY" (250,000)

FIFTH ARMY

SECOND ARMY

Belgrade

RUMANIA

DOBRUDJA

SIXTH ARMY

THIRD ARMY

FIRST ARMY

BUCHAREST

Black Sea

Sarajevo

SECOND ARMY

SERBIA

Total: about 40,000 troops.

UŽICE ARMY

Danube

Total: about 180,000 troops.

MONTENEGRO

BULGARIA

© Arthur Banks 1973

THREE IMPORTANT GUNS IN 1914

French 75-mm. field gun (Model 1897)

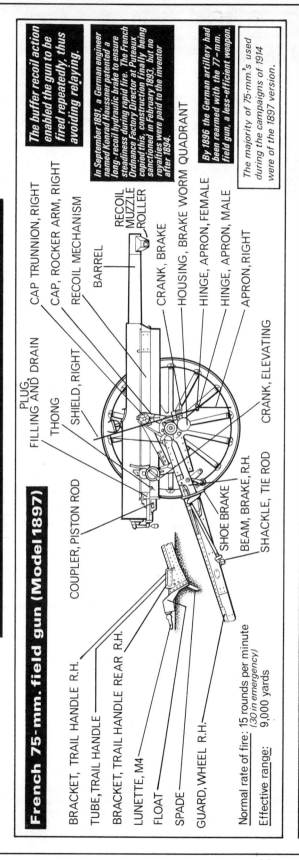

The buffer recoil action enabled the gun to be fired repeatedly, thus avoiding relaying.

In September 1891, a German engineer named Konrad Haussner patented a long-recoil hydraulic brake to ensure steadiness during rapid fire. The French Ordnance Factory Director at Puteaux copied this, construction finally being sanctioned in February 1893, but no royalties were paid to the inventor after 1894.

By 1896 the German artillery had been rearmed with the 77-mm. field gun, a less-efficient weapon.

The majority of 75-mm.'s used during the campaigns of 1914 were of the 1897 version.

CAP TRUNNION, RIGHT
CAP, ROCKER ARM, RIGHT
RECOIL MECHANISM
BARREL
RECOIL MUZZLE ROLLER
CRANK, BRAKE
HOUSING, BRAKE WORM QUADRANT
HINGE, APRON, FEMALE
HINGE, APRON, MALE
APRON, RIGHT
CRANK, ELEVATING

PLUG, FILLING AND DRAIN
THONG
SHIELD, RIGHT

SHOE BRAKE
BEAM, BRAKE, R.H.
SHACKLE, TIE ROD

BRACKET, TRAIL HANDLE R.H.
TUBE, TRAIL HANDLE
BRACKET, TRAIL HANDLE REAR R.H.
COUPLER, PISTON ROD
LUNETTE, M4
FLOAT
SPADE
GUARD, WHEEL R.H.

Normal rate of fire: 15 rounds per minute
(30 in emergency)
Effective range: 9,000 yards

Austrian 30·5-cm. howitzer (Model 1911)

Normal rate of fire: 1 round every 6 minutes
Effective range: 13,000 yards

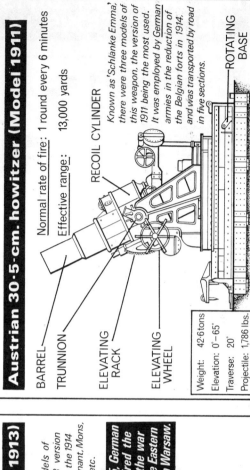

Known as 'Schlanke Emma,' there were three models of this weapon, the version of 1911 being the most used. It was employed by German armies in the reduction of the Belgian forts in 1914, and was transported by road in five sections.

RECOIL CYLINDER
ROTATING BASE

BARREL
TRUNNION
ELEVATING RACK
ELEVATING WHEEL

Weight: 42·6 tons
Elevation: 0°–65°
Traverse: 20°
Projectile: 1,786 lbs.

German 15-cm. field howitzer (Model 1913)

There were four models of this weapon. The 1913 version was employed during the 1914 battles at Charleroi, Dinant, Mons, the Marne, the Aisne, etc.

On 3 January 1915, German 15-cm. howitzers fired the first gas shells of the war near Bolimow on the Eastern Front, 40 miles from Warsaw.

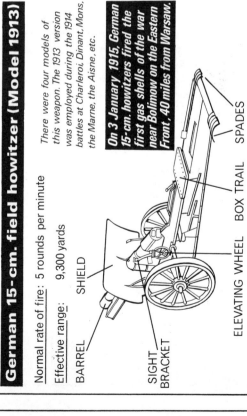

SPADES
BOX TRAIL
ELEVATING WHEEL
SIGHT BRACKET
SHIELD
BARREL

Normal rate of fire: 5 rounds per minute
Effective range: 9,300 yards

RIVAL INFANTRY DIVISIONAL ORGANIZATIONS IN 1914

The infantry division was the standard component of corps and armies. These diagrams give approximate comparisons between the main contending forces.

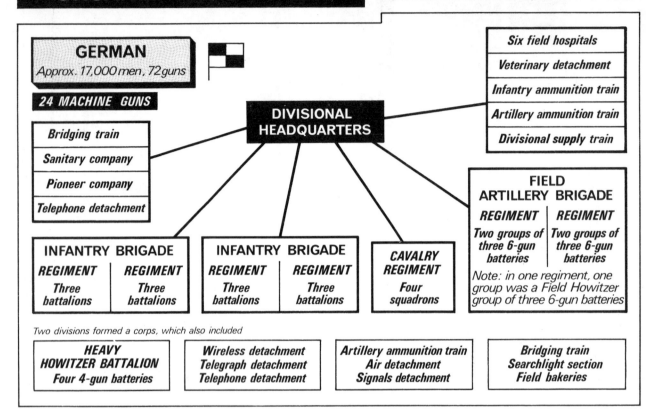

GERMAN
Approx. 17,000 men, 72 guns

24 MACHINE GUNS

| Bridging train |
| Sanitary company |
| Pioneer company |
| Telephone detachment |

DIVISIONAL HEADQUARTERS

| Six field hospitals |
| Veterinary detachment |
| Infantry ammunition train |
| Artillery ammunition train |
| Divisional supply train |

FIELD ARTILLERY BRIGADE

REGIMENT	REGIMENT
Two groups of three 6-gun batteries	Two groups of three 6-gun batteries

Note: in one regiment, one group was a Field Howitzer group of three 6-gun batteries

INFANTRY BRIGADE

REGIMENT	REGIMENT
Three battalions	Three battalions

INFANTRY BRIGADE

REGIMENT	REGIMENT
Three battalions	Three battalions

CAVALRY REGIMENT
Four squadrons

Two divisions formed a corps, which also included

| HEAVY HOWITZER BATTALION Four 4-gun batteries | Wireless detachment Telegraph detachment Telephone detachment | Artillery ammunition train Air detachment Signals detachment | Bridging train Searchlight section Field bakeries |

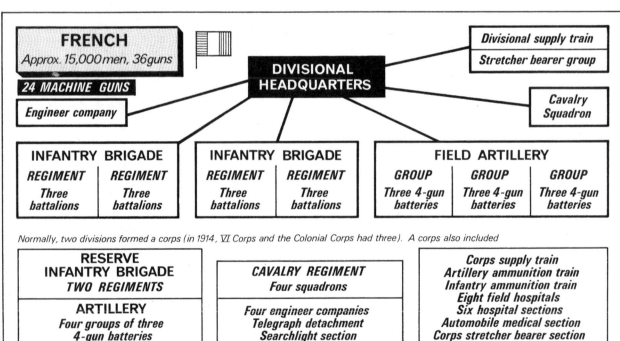

FRENCH
Approx. 15,000 men, 36 guns

24 MACHINE GUNS

| Engineer company |

DIVISIONAL HEADQUARTERS

| Divisional supply train |
| Stretcher bearer group |

Cavalry Squadron

INFANTRY BRIGADE

REGIMENT	REGIMENT
Three battalions	Three battalions

INFANTRY BRIGADE

REGIMENT	REGIMENT
Three battalions	Three battalions

FIELD ARTILLERY

GROUP	GROUP	GROUP
Three 4-gun batteries	Three 4-gun batteries	Three 4-gun batteries

Normally, two divisions formed a corps (in 1914, VI Corps and the Colonial Corps had three). A corps also included

| RESERVE INFANTRY BRIGADE TWO REGIMENTS ARTILLERY Four groups of three 4-gun batteries | CAVALRY REGIMENT Four squadrons Four engineer companies Telegraph detachment Searchlight section | Corps supply train Artillery ammunition train Infantry ammunition train Eight field hospitals Six hospital sections Automobile medical section Corps stretcher bearer section |

© Arthur Banks 1973

34

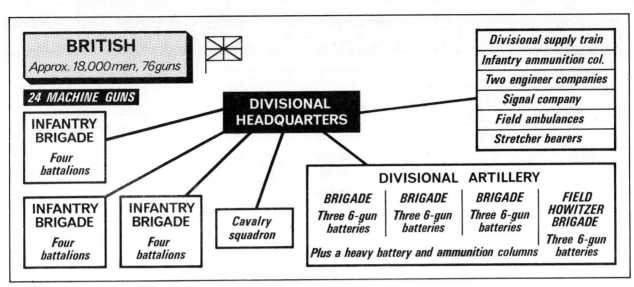

BRITISH
Approx. 18,000 men, 76 guns

24 MACHINE GUNS

DIVISIONAL HEADQUARTERS

- Divisional supply train
- Infantry ammunition col.
- Two engineer companies
- Signal company
- Field ambulances
- Stretcher bearers

INFANTRY BRIGADE
Four battalions

INFANTRY BRIGADE
Four battalions

INFANTRY BRIGADE
Four battalions

Cavalry squadron

DIVISIONAL ARTILLERY

BRIGADE	**BRIGADE**	**BRIGADE**	**FIELD HOWITZER BRIGADE**
Three 6-gun batteries	*Three 6-gun batteries*	*Three 6-gun batteries*	*Three 6-gun batteries*

Plus a heavy battery and ammunition columns

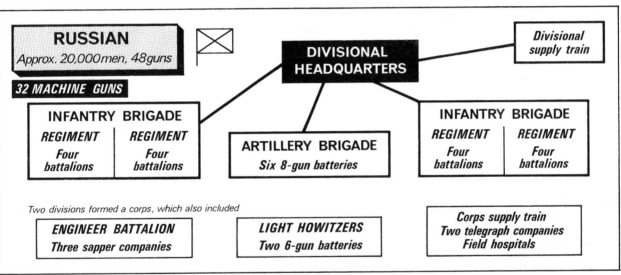

RUSSIAN
Approx. 20,000 men, 48 guns

32 MACHINE GUNS

DIVISIONAL HEADQUARTERS

- Divisional supply train

INFANTRY BRIGADE

REGIMENT	**REGIMENT**
Four battalions	*Four battalions*

ARTILLERY BRIGADE
Six 8-gun batteries

INFANTRY BRIGADE

REGIMENT	**REGIMENT**
Four battalions	*Four battalions*

Two divisions formed a corps, which also included

ENGINEER BATTALION
Three sapper companies

LIGHT HOWITZERS
Two 6-gun batteries

Corps supply train
Two telegraph companies
Field hospitals

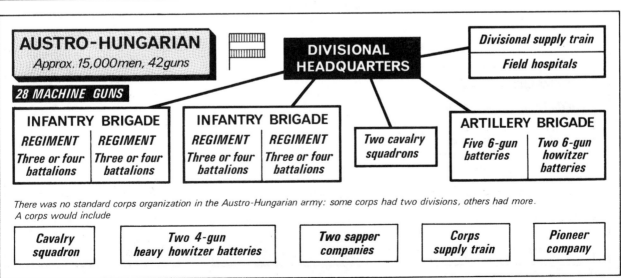

AUSTRO-HUNGARIAN
Approx. 15,000 men, 42 guns

28 MACHINE GUNS

DIVISIONAL HEADQUARTERS

- Divisional supply train
- Field hospitals

INFANTRY BRIGADE

REGIMENT	**REGIMENT**
Three or four battalions	*Three or four battalions*

INFANTRY BRIGADE

REGIMENT	**REGIMENT**
Three or four battalions	*Three or four battalions*

Two cavalry squadrons

ARTILLERY BRIGADE

Five 6-gun batteries	*Two 6-gun howitzer batteries*

There was no standard corps organization in the Austro-Hungarian army: some corps had two divisions, others had more. A corps would include

Cavalry squadron

Two 4-gun heavy howitzer batteries

Two sapper companies

Corps supply train

Pioneer company

RIVAL CAVALRY DIVISIONAL ORGANIZATIONS IN 1914

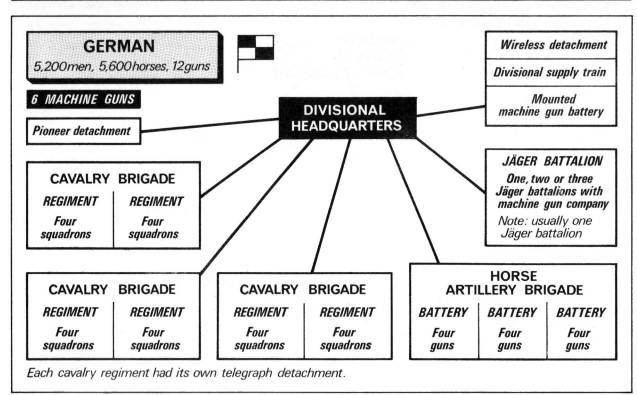

GERMAN
5,200 men, 5,600 horses, 12 guns

6 MACHINE GUNS

Pioneer detachment

DIVISIONAL HEADQUARTERS

Wireless detachment

Divisional supply train

Mounted machine gun battery

JÄGER BATTALION
One, two or three Jäger battalions with machine gun company

Note: usually one Jäger battalion

CAVALRY BRIGADE
REGIMENT	REGIMENT
Four squadrons	Four squadrons

CAVALRY BRIGADE
REGIMENT	REGIMENT
Four squadrons	Four squadrons

CAVALRY BRIGADE
REGIMENT	REGIMENT
Four squadrons	Four squadrons

HORSE ARTILLERY BRIGADE
BATTERY	BATTERY	BATTERY
Four guns	Four guns	Four guns

Each cavalry regiment had its own telegraph detachment.

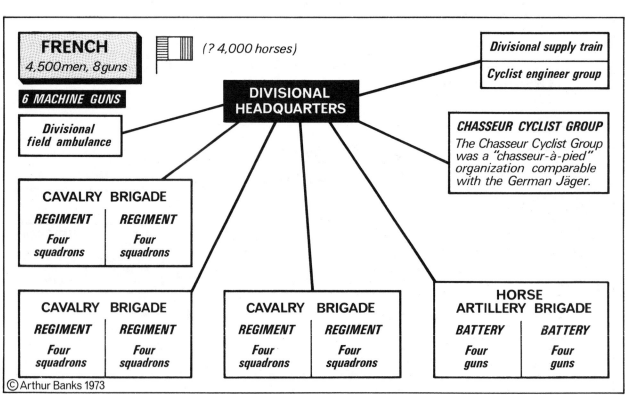

FRENCH
4,500 men, 8 guns

(? 4,000 horses)

6 MACHINE GUNS

Divisional field ambulance

DIVISIONAL HEADQUARTERS

Divisional supply train

Cyclist engineer group

CHASSEUR CYCLIST GROUP
The Chasseur Cyclist Group was a "chasseur-à-pied" organization comparable with the German Jäger.

CAVALRY BRIGADE
REGIMENT	REGIMENT
Four squadrons	Four squadrons

CAVALRY BRIGADE
REGIMENT	REGIMENT
Four squadrons	Four squadrons

CAVALRY BRIGADE
REGIMENT	REGIMENT
Four squadrons	Four squadrons

HORSE ARTILLERY BRIGADE
BATTERY	BATTERY
Four guns	Four guns

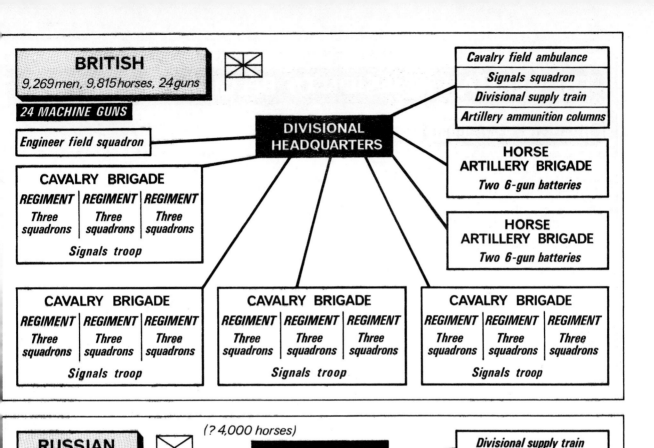

BRITISH
9,269 men, 9,815 horses, 24 guns

24 MACHINE GUNS

Engineer field squadron

DIVISIONAL HEADQUARTERS

Cavalry field ambulance
Signals squadron
Divisional supply train
Artillery ammunition columns

HORSE ARTILLERY BRIGADE
Two 6-gun batteries

HORSE ARTILLERY BRIGADE
Two 6-gun batteries

CAVALRY BRIGADE		
REGIMENT	REGIMENT	REGIMENT
Three squadrons	Three squadrons	Three squadrons
Signals troop		

CAVALRY BRIGADE		
REGIMENT	REGIMENT	REGIMENT
Three squadrons	Three squadrons	Three squadrons
Signals troop		

CAVALRY BRIGADE		
REGIMENT	REGIMENT	REGIMENT
Three squadrons	Three squadrons	Three squadrons
Signals troop		

CAVALRY BRIGADE		
REGIMENT	REGIMENT	REGIMENT
Three squadrons	Three squadrons	Three squadrons
Signals troop		

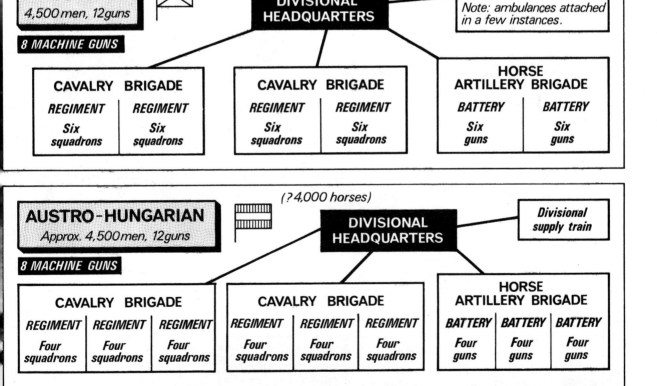

RUSSIAN
4,500 men, 12 guns

8 MACHINE GUNS

(? 4,000 horses)

DIVISIONAL HEADQUARTERS

Divisional supply train
Note: ambulances attached in a few instances.

CAVALRY BRIGADE	
REGIMENT	REGIMENT
Six squadrons	Six squadrons

CAVALRY BRIGADE	
REGIMENT	REGIMENT
Six squadrons	Six squadrons

HORSE ARTILLERY BRIGADE	
BATTERY	BATTERY
Six guns	Six guns

AUSTRO-HUNGARIAN
Approx. 4,500 men, 12 guns

8 MACHINE GUNS

(? 4,000 horses)

DIVISIONAL HEADQUARTERS

Divisional supply train

CAVALRY BRIGADE		
REGIMENT	REGIMENT	REGIMENT
Four squadrons	Four squadrons	Four squadrons

CAVALRY BRIGADE		
REGIMENT	REGIMENT	REGIMENT
Four squadrons	Four squadrons	Four squadrons

HORSE ARTILLERY BRIGADE		
BATTERY	BATTERY	BATTERY
Four guns	Four guns	Four guns

THE GERMAN INVASION OF BELGIUM AUGUST 1914

Situation 17-24 August

NORTH SEA

H O L L A N D

OSTEND

BRUGES

Nieuport

DUNKIRK

Dixmude

Yser

GHENT

Schelde

Schelde

Dendre

Bergues

81 Territorial Division

Roulers

Lys

B E L G

Ypres

Courtrai

Oudenarde

Grammont

II

FIRST AR

Cassel

Hazebrouck

Warneton

Renaix

II

II

II

Enghien

IV

II

Armentières

Lys

II Cav. Corps

24 Aug.

II Cav. Corps

Schelde

24 Aug.

Ath

Dendre

24 Aug.

IV

II

II

IX

LILLE

Cysoing

82 Territorial Division

TOURNAI

Antoing

Leuze

Peruwelz

II

IV

III

II

IX

Cana

GROUP D'AMADE (Reserve)

Béthune

II Cav. Corps (von der Marwitz)

24 Aug.

II

Condé

IX

MONS

Binc

Lens

23 August

88 Terr. Div.

24 Aug.

St. Amand

19 Inf. Bde.

II

B. E. F.

I

I C
Co

Douai

Scarpe

Marchiennes

84 Terr. D.

Cav. Div.

5 Cav. Bde.

ARRAS

HQ, GROUP D'AMADE

Schelde

Valenciennes

Bavai

MAUBEUGE

53 & 69 R.Ds.

53 R.D.

F R A N C E

Le Quesnoy

Solesmes

XVIII

KEY TO ALLIED DISPOSITIONS

- French Fifth Army, 21 August position.
- French Fifth Army, 22 August positions.
- French Fifth Army, 24 August positions.
- British Expeditionary Force, 22/23 August.

Note: Corps are shown by Roman numerals

Cambrai

Sambre

Helpe

Avesnes

Landrecies

Royal Flying Corps HQ was at Maubeuge aerodrome. It consisted of 63 aeroplanes and 860 personnel.

Le Cateau

GHQ, B.E.F.

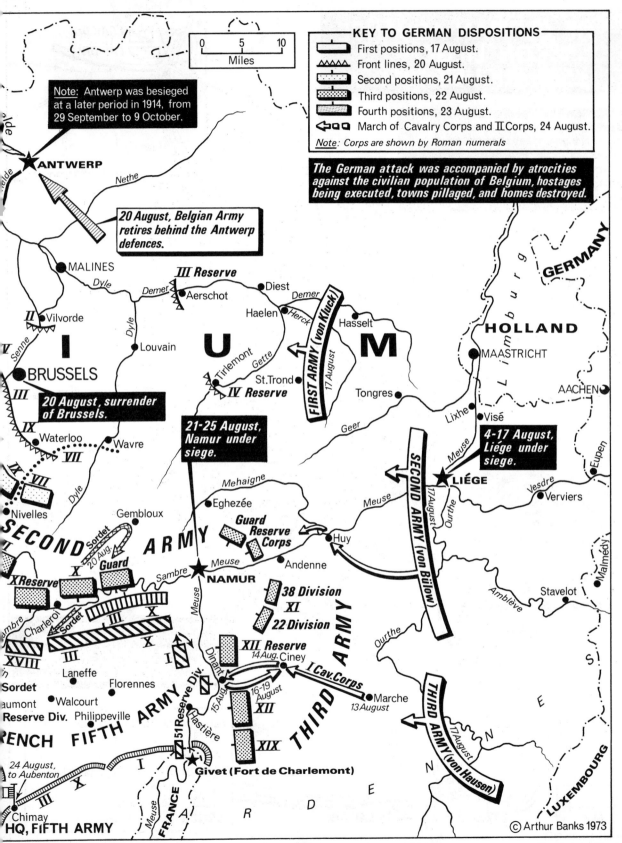

KEY TO GERMAN DISPOSITIONS

First positions, 17 August.
Front lines, 20 August.
Second positions, 21 August.
Third positions, 22 August.
Fourth positions, 23 August.
March of Cavalry Corps and II Corps, 24 August.

Note: Corps are shown by Roman numerals

The German attack was accompanied by atrocities against the civilian population of Belgium, hostages being executed, towns pillaged, and homes destroyed.

0   5   10
Miles

<u>Note:</u> Antwerp was besieged at a later period in 1914, from 29 September to 9 October.

★ ANTWERP

Nethe

20 August, Belgian Army retires behind the Antwerp defences.

● MALINES

Dyle

III Reserve
Aerschot

● Diest

Demer

Herck

● Hasselt

FIRST ARMY (von Kluck)
17 August

HOLLAND

Limburg

GERMANY

● MAASTRICHT

● Haelen

II ● Vilvorde

V

Senne

I

BRUSSELS

● Louvain

Dyle

Tirlemont

Gette

IV Reserve

St.Trond

● Tongres

Geer

● Lixhe

● Visé

AACHEN ●

20 August, surrender of Brussels.

III

IX

● Waterloo   ● Wavre

VII

IX   VII

Nivelles

Dyle

21-25 August, Namur under siege.

Mehaigne

● Eghezée

Guard Reserve Corps

● Huy

● Andenne

SECOND ARMY (von Bülow)
17 August

★ LIÉGE

Vesdre

● Verviers

4-17 August, Liége under siege.

Eupen

Gembloux

SECOND   ARMY

Sordet
20 Aug.

X   **Guard**

X Reserve

Sambre   Charleroi

Sordet   III   X

III   X

XVIII

III

● Laneffe

● Florennes

Meuse

★ NAMUR

38 Division

XI

22 Division

XII Reserve
14 Aug. Ciney

15 Aug.

16-19 August

I Cav. Corps

● Marche
13 August

THIRD   ARMY

Ourthe

● Stavelot

Amblève

THIRD ARMY (von Hausen)
17 August

Malmédy

Sordet

aumont

Reserve Div.   ● Philippeville

● Walcourt

51 Reserve Div.

Hastière

XII

XIX

Givet (Fort de Charlemont)

ENCH   **FIFTH   ARMY**

I

Meuse

FRANCE

A   R   D   E   N   N   E   S

24 August, to Aubenton

X   III

● Chimay

HQ, FIFTH ARMY

LUXEMBOURG

© Arthur Banks 1973

39

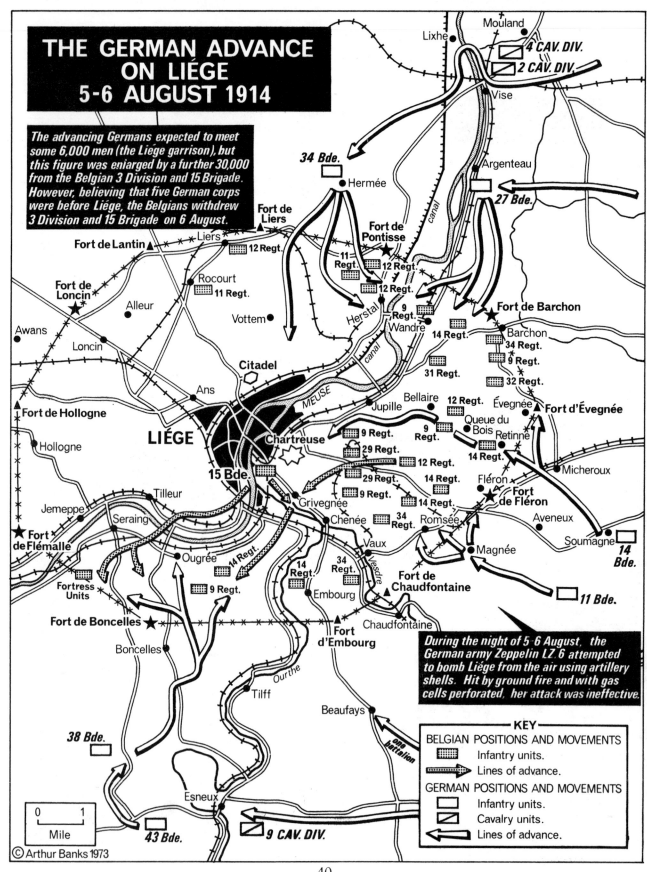

THE GERMAN ADVANCE ON LIÉGE 5-6 AUGUST 1914

The advancing Germans expected to meet some 6,000 men (the Liége garrison), but this figure was enlarged by a further 30,000 from the Belgian 3 Division and 15 Brigade. However, believing that five German corps were before Liége, the Belgians withdrew 3 Division and 15 Brigade on 6 August.

During the night of 5-6 August, the German army Zeppelin LZ.6 attempted to bomb Liége from the air using artillery shells. Hit by ground fire and with gas cells perforated, her attack was ineffective.

Mouland
4 CAV. DIV.
2 CAV. DIV.
Lixhe
Vise
Argenteau
34 Bde.
Hermée
27 Bde.
Fort de Liers
Fort de Pontisse
Liers
12 Regt.
11 Regt.
12 Regt.
Fort de Lantin
Rocourt
12 Regt.
Fort de Loncin
11 Regt.
9 Regt.
Fort de Barchon
Alleur
Herstal
Wandre
14 Regt.
Barchon
34 Regt.
9 Regt.
Awans
Vottem
32 Regt.
Loncin
canal
31 Regt.
Citadel
MEUSE
Bellaire
12 Regt.
Évegnée
Fort d'Évegnée
Ans
Jupille
9 Regt.
Queue du Bois
Retinne
Fort de Hollogne
Chartreuse
9 Regt.
29 Regt.
14 Regt.
LIÉGE
12 Regt.
Micheroux
Hollogne
29 Regt.
14 Regt.
Fléron
15 Bde.
9 Regt.
14 Regt.
Fort de Fléron
Tilleur
Grivegnée
34 Regt.
Romsée
Avenenx
Jemeppe
Chenée
Seraing
Vaux
Magnée
Soumagne
Fort de Flémalle
14 Regt.
Vesdre
14 Bde.
Ougrée
14 Regt.
34 Regt.
Fort de Chaudfontaine
11 Bde.
Fortress Units
9 Regt.
Embourg
Fort de Boncelles
Chaudfontaine
Boncelles
Fort d'Embourg
Ourthe
Tilff
Beaufays
one battalion
38 Bde.

0   1
Mile

Esneux
43 Bde.
9 CAV. DIV.

KEY
BELGIAN POSITIONS AND MOVEMENTS
Infantry units.
Lines of advance.
GERMAN POSITIONS AND MOVEMENTS
Infantry units.
Cavalry units.
Lines of advance.

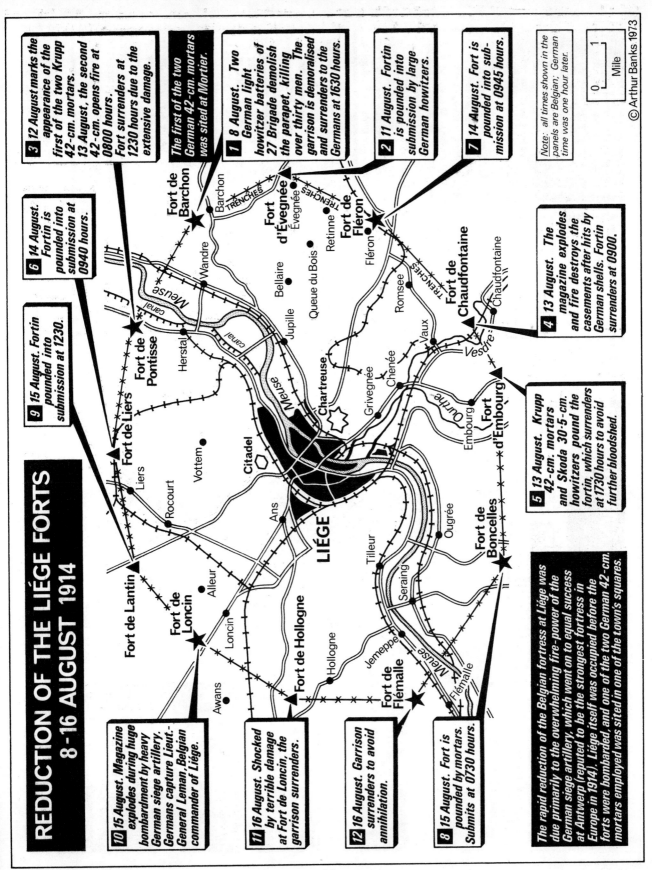

REDUCTION OF THE LIÉGE FORTS 8-16 AUGUST 1914

3 12 August marks the appearance of the first of the two Krupp 42-cm. mortars. 13 August, the second 42-cm. opens fire at 0800 hours. Fort surrenders at 1230 hours due to the extensive damage.

The first of the two German 42-cm. mortars was sited at Mortier.

1 8 August. Two German light howitzer batteries of 27 Brigade demolish the parapet, killing over thirty men. The garrison is demoralised and surrenders to the Germans at 1630 hours.

2 11 August. Fortin is pounded into submission by large German howitzers.

7 14 August. Fort is sub-mission at 0945 hours.

6 14 August. Fortin is pounded into submission at 0940 hours.

9 15 August. Fortin pounded into submission at 1230.

Note: all times shown in the panels are Belgian; German time was one hour later.

0   1
Mile

© Arthur Banks 1973

4 13 August. The magazine explodes and fire destroys the casements after hits by German shells. Fortin surrenders at 0900.

5 13 August. Krupp 42-cm. mortars and Skoda 30·5-cm. howitzers pound the fortin, which surrenders at 1730 hours to avoid further bloodshed.

10 15 August. Magazine explodes during huge bombardment by heavy German siege artillery. Germans capture Lieut.-General Leman, Belgian commander of Liége.

11 16 August. Shocked by terrible damage at Fort de Loncin, the garrison surrenders.

12 16 August. Garrison surrenders to avoid annihilation.

8 15 August. Fort is pounded by mortars. Submits at 0730 hours.

The rapid reduction of the Belgian fortress at Liége was due primarily to the overwhelming fire-power of the German siege artillery, which went on to equal success at Antwerp (reputed to be the strongest fortress in Europe in 1914). Liége itself was occupied before the forts were bombarded, and one of the two German 42-cm. mortars employed was sited in one of the town's squares.

Fort de Barchon
Barchon
TRENCHES
Fort d'Évegnée
Évegnée
Retinne
Fort de Fléron
Fléron
TRENCHES
Fort de Chaudfontaine
Chaudfontaine
Vesdre
Fort d'Embourg
Embourg
Ourthe
Vaux
Chenée
Romsee
Grivegnée
Queue du Bois
Bellaire
Jupille
Meuse
Canal
Wandre
Fort de Pontisse
Herstal
Chartreuse
Citadel
LIÉGE
Vottem
Liers
Fort de Liers
Rocourt
Ans
Tilleur
Seraing
Ougrée
Fort de Boncelles
Fort de Lantin
Alleur
Loncin
Fort de Loncin
Awans
Fort de Hollogne
Hollogne
Jemeppe
Flémalle
Fort de Flémalle
Meuse

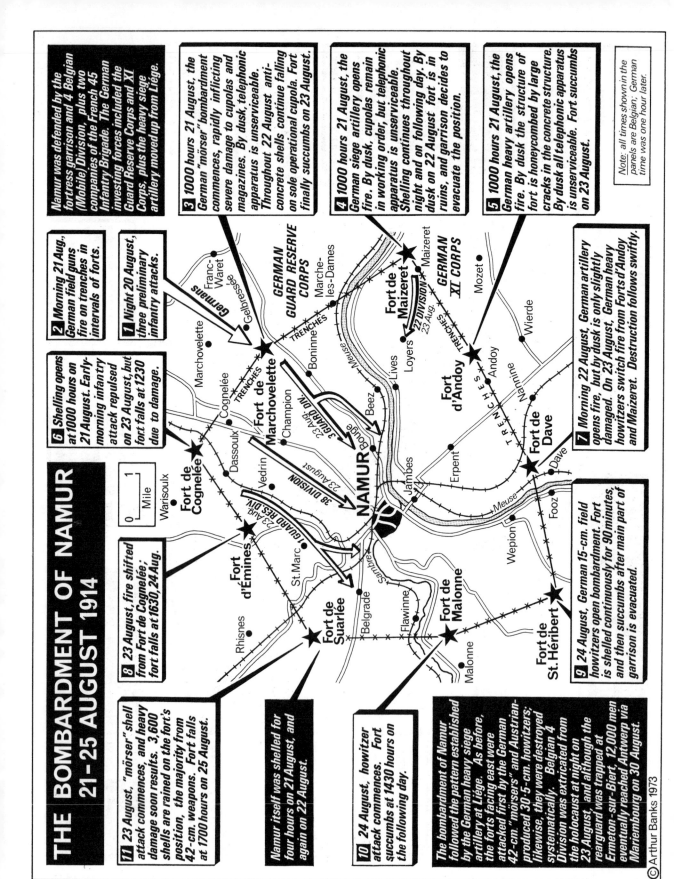

THE BOMBARDMENT OF NAMUR 21–25 AUGUST 1914

Namur was defended by the fortress garrison and 4 Belgian (Mobile) Division, plus two companies of the French 45 Infantry Brigade. The German investing forces included the Guard Reserve Corps and XI Corps, plus the heavy siege artillery moved up from Liége.

1 Night 20 August, three preliminary infantry attacks.

2 Morning 21 Aug., German field guns fire on trenches in intervals of forts.

3 1000 hours 21 August, the German "mörser" bombardment commences, rapidly inflicting severe damage to cupolas and magazines. By dusk, telephonic apparatus is unserviceable. Throughout 22 August anti-concrete shells continue falling on sole operational cupola. Fort finally succumbs on 23 August.

4 1000 hours 21 August, the German siege artillery opens fire. By dusk, cupolas remain in working order, but telephonic apparatus is unserviceable. Shelling continues throughout night and on following day. By dusk on 22 August fort is in ruins, and garrison decides to evacuate the position.

5 1000 hours 21 August, the German heavy artillery opens fire. By dusk the structure of fort is honeycombed by large cracks in the concrete structure. By dusk all telephonic apparatus is unserviceable. Fort succumbs on 23 August.

Note: all times shown in the panels are Belgian; German time was one hour later.

6 Shelling opens at 1000 hours on 21 August. Early-morning infantry attack repulsed on 23 August, but fort falls at 1230 due to damage.

7 Morning 22 August, German artillery opens fire, but by dusk is only slightly damaged. On 23 August, German heavy howitzers switch fire from Forts d'Andoy and Maizeret. Destruction follows swiftly.

8 23 August, fire shifted from Fort de Cognelée; fort falls at 1630, 24 Aug.

9 24 August, German 15-cm. field howitzers open bombardment. Fort is shelled continuously for 90 minutes, and then succumbs after main part of garrison is evacuated.

10 24 August, howitzer attack commences. Fort succumbs at 1430 hours on the following day.

11 23 August, "mörser" shell attack commences, and heavy damage soon results. 3,600 shells are rained on the fort's position, the majority from 42-cm. weapons. Fort falls at 1700 hours on 25 August.

Namur itself was shelled for four hours on 21 August, and again on 22 August.

The bombardment of Namur followed the pattern established by the German heavy siege artillery at Liége. As before, the forts facing east were attacked first by the German 42-cm. "mörsers" and Austrian-produced 30·5-cm. howitzers; likewise, they were destroyed systematically. Belgian 4 Division was extricated from the holocaust at night on 23 August, and although the rearguard was trapped at Ermeton-sur-Biert, 12,000 men eventually reached Antwerp via Mariembourg on 30 August.

© Arthur Banks 1973

Map labels: Franc-Waret, Gelbressée, Germans, GERMAN GUARD RESERVE CORPS, Marche-les-Dames, TRENCHES, Boninnes, Lives, Loyers, Fort de Maizeret, Maizeret, GERMAN XI CORPS, Mozet, Wierde, Fort d'Andoy, Andoy, Nannine, Marchovelette, Cognelée, Fort de Marchovelette, Champion, Beez, Meuse, NAMUR, Jambes, Erpent, Fort de Dave, Dave, Dassoulx, Vedrin, Fort de Cognelée, Warisoulx, St. Marc, Fort d'Emines, Belgrade, Flawinne, Sambre, Fort de Malonne, Malonne, Wepion, Fooz, Fort de St. Héribert, Rhisnes, Fort de Suarlée, 3 GUARD DIV., 38 DIVISION, GUARD RES. DIV.

Scale: 0 1 Mile

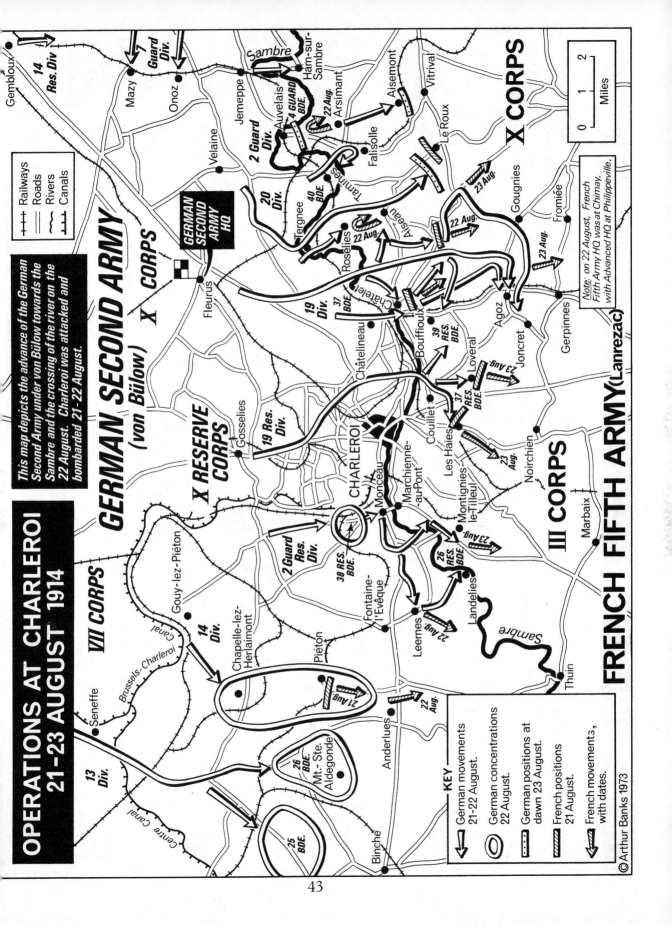

OPERATIONS AT CHARLEROI 21–23 AUGUST 1914

This map depicts the advance of the German Second Army under von Bülow towards the Sambre and the crossing of the river on the 22 August. Charleroi was attacked and bombarded 21–22 August.

GERMAN SECOND ARMY
(von Bülow)

FRENCH FIFTH ARMY (Lanrezac)

Note: on 22 August, French Fifth Army HQ was at Chimay, with Advanced HQ at Philippeville.

GERMAN SECOND ARMY HQ

X CORPS

X RESERVE CORPS

VII CORPS

X CORPS

X CORPS

III CORPS

KEY
- German movements 21–22 August.
- German concentrations 22 August.
- German positions at dawn 23 August.
- French positions 21 August.
- French movements, with dates.

Railways
Roads
Rivers
Canals

Miles
0 1 2

© Arthur Banks 1973

Place names and units

14 Res. Div.
7 Guard Div.
Gembloux
Mazy
Onoz
Jemeppe
Velaine
2 Guard Div.
Auvelais
4 Guard BDE.
22 Aug.
Arsimant
Ham-sur-Sambre
Sambre
Aisemont
Vitrival
Le Roux
Falisolle
Tamines
20 Div.
40 BDE.
Tergnée
23 Aug.
Gougnies
Fromiée
Gerpinnes
22 Aug.
Aiseau
Roselies
22 Aug.
19 Div.
37 BDE.
Fleurus
Châtelet
Bouffioulx
39 RES. BDE.
Agoz
23 Aug.
Joncret
Châtelineau
Gosselies
19 Res. Div.
Loveral
37 RES. BDE.
23 Aug.
Couillet
Noirchien
CHARLEROI
Monceau
Marchienne-au-Pont
Les Haies
Montignies-le-Tilleul
23 Aug.
Marbaix
2 Guard Res. Div.
38 RES. BDE.
Fontaine-l'Évêque
26 RES. BDE.
Landelies
22 Aug.
Thuin
Sambre
Gouy-lez-Piéton
Chapelle-lez-Herlaimont
Piéton
Leernes
14 Div.
Brussels-Charleroi Canal
21 Aug.
Anderlues
22 Aug.
13 Div.
Seneffe
26 BDE.
Mt.-Ste.-Aldegonde
Binche
25 BDE.
Centre Canal

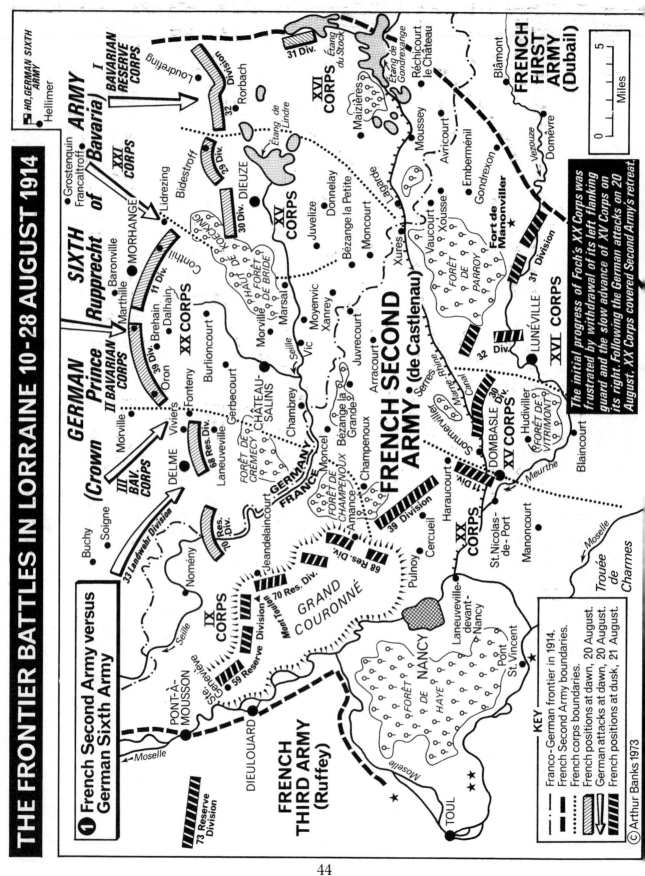

THE FRONTIER BATTLES IN LORRAINE 10-28 AUGUST 1914

1 French Second Army versus German Sixth Army

■ HQ, GERMAN SIXTH ARMY

Hellimer

GERMAN SIXTH ARMY (Crown Prince Rupprecht of Bavaria)

I BAVARIAN RESERVE CORPS

XXI CORPS

II BAVARIAN CORPS

III BAV. CORPS

XX CORPS

FRENCH FIRST ARMY (Dubail)

XVI CORPS

XV CORPS

FRENCH SECOND ARMY (de Castlenau)

Grostenquin
Francaltroff
Rorbach
31 Div.
Étang du Stock
Étang de Gondrexange
Réchicourt le Château
Blâmont
Loudrefing
Division
32
Rorbach
XVI CORPS
Maizières
Moussey
Avricourt
Embermenil
Gondrexon
Domèvre
Vezouze
Bidestroff
29 Div.
Étang de Lindre
Lagarde
Xousse
Vaucourt
Fort de Manonviller
Lidrezing
30 Div. DIEUZE
Juvelize
Donnelay
Bézange la Petite
Moncourt
Xures
FORÊT DE PARROY
31 Division
MORHANGE
Baronville
Marthille
KOECKING
Marsal
Moyenvic
Xanrey
Arracourt
LUNÉVILLE
32 Div.
Conthil
11 Div.
HAUT DE KOECKING
FORÊT DE BRIDE
Morville
Seille
Vic
Juvrecourt
Serres
Marne-Rhine Canal
Hudiviller
FORÊT DE VITRIMONT
Brehain
39 Div.
Dalhain
Burlioncourt
Chambrey
Bézange la Grande
Champenoux
Sommerviller
DOMBASLE 30 Div. XV CORPS
Blaincourt
Oron
Fonteny
CHÂTEAU-SALINS
Gerbecourt
Moncel
Blaincourt
DELME
68 Res. Div.
Laneuveville
FORÊT DE CRÉMECY
FORÊT DE CHAMPENOUX
Amance
39 Division
11 Div.
Meurthe
Morville
Vivier
GERMANY
FRANCE
Harancourt
St. Nicolas-de-Port
Manoncourt
Buchy
Soigne
70 Res. Div.
33 Landwehr Division
Jeandelaincourt
68 Res. Div.
70 Res. Div.
Pulnoy
Cercueil
XX CORPS
Moselle
Troués de Charmes
Nomény
Mont Toulon
GRAND COURONNÉ
Laneuveville-devant-Nancy
Pont St. Vincent
Moselle
IX CORPS
Ste. Geneviève
59 Reserve Division
FORÊT DE HAYE
NANCY
Seille
PONT-À-MOUSSON
DIEULOUARD
FRENCH THIRD ARMY (Ruffey)
Moselle
TOUL

73 Reserve Division

The initial progress of Foch's XX Corps was frustrated by withdrawal of its left flanking guard and the slow advance of XV Corps on its right. Following the German attacks on 20 August, XX Corps covered Second Army's retreat.

KEY

—·— Franco-German frontier in 1914.
━━ French Second Army boundaries.
······· French corps boundaries.
▨▨ French positions at dawn, 20 August.
⟹ German attacks at dawn, 20 August.
▧▧ French positions at dusk, 21 August.

0 5 Miles

© Arthur Banks 1973

44

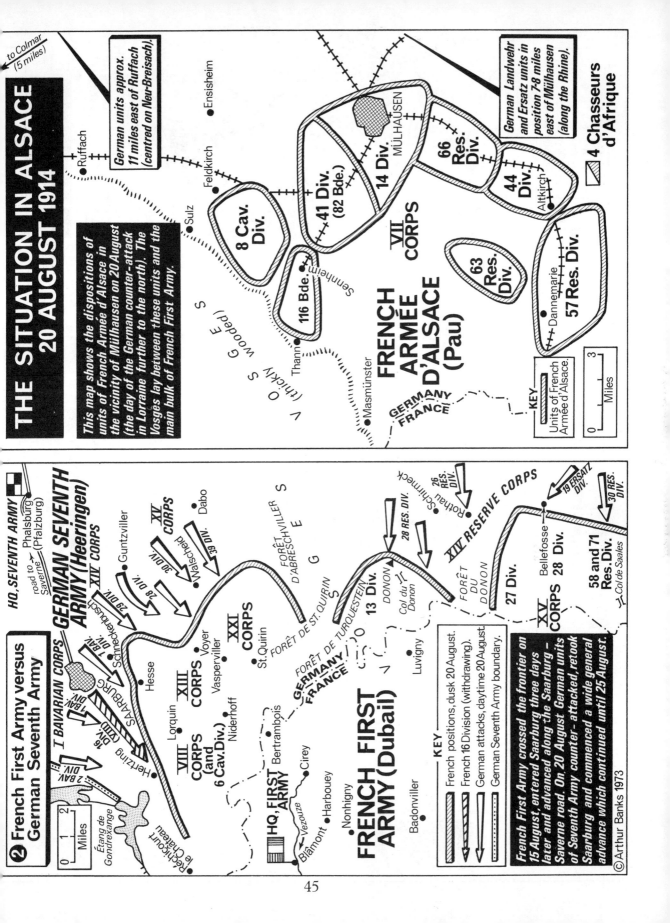

THE SITUATION IN ALSACE 20 AUGUST 1914

This map shows the dispositions of units of French Armée d'Alsace in the vicinity of Mülhausen on 20 August (the day of the German counter-attack in Lorraine further to the north). The Vosges lay between these units and the main bulk of French First Army.

to Colmar (5 miles)

German units approx. 11 miles east of Ruffach (centred on Neu-Breisach).

• Ruffach

• Ensisheim

• Feldkirch

MÜLHAUSEN

German Landwehr and Ersatz units in position 7-8 miles east of Mülhausen (along the Rhine).

41 Div. (82 Bde.)

14 Div.

66 Res. Div.

44 Div.

• Sulz

8 Cav. Div.

VII CORPS

4 Chasseurs d'Afrique

• Altkirch

116 Bde.

63 Res. Div.

57 Res. Div.

Sennheim

FRENCH ARMÉE D'ALSACE (Pau)

• Dannemarie

• Thann

V O S G E S (thickly wooded)

• Masmünster

GERMANY
FRANCE

KEY
Units of French Armée d'Alsace.

0   3
Miles

---

❷ French First Army versus German Seventh Army

HQ, SEVENTH ARMY

Phalsburg (Pfalzburg)

road to Saverne →

GERMAN SEVENTH ARMY (Heeringen)

XIV CORPS

• Guntzviller

• Dabo

XV CORPS

39 DIV.

Wascheid

F O R Ê T D'ABRESCHVILLER

30 DIV.

Schenbusch

29 DIV.

28 DIV.

Schneckei

I BAVARIAN CORPS

1 BAV. DIV.

SAARBURG

1 BAV. DIV.

Hertzing

• Hesse

Niderhoff

XIII CORPS

• Voyer

Vasperviller

XXI CORPS

• Lorquin

• St. Quirin

FORÊT DE ST. QUIRIN

26 RES. DIV.

•Schirmeck

Rothau•

XIV RESERVE CORPS

28 RES. DIV.

13 Div.

DONON

Col du Donon

F O R Ê T   D U   D O N O N

27 Div.

19 ERSATZ DIV.

• Bellefosse

30 RES. DIV.

XV CORPS

28 Div.

16 DIV.

2 BAV. DIV.

Réchicourt le Château

Étang de Gondrexange

VIII CORPS (and 6 Cav.Div.)

Bertrambois

FORÊT DE TURQUESTEIN

Luvigny •

GERMANY
FRANCE

• Blâmont

• Cirey

• Harbouey

• Nonhigny

• Vezouze

Col de Saales

58 and 71 Res. Div.

HQ, FIRST ARMY

FRENCH FIRST ARMY (Dubail)

• Badonviller

KEY
French positions, dusk 20 August.
French 16 Division (withdrawing).
German attacks, daytime 20 August.
German Seventh Army boundary.

French First Army crossed the frontier on 15 August, entered Saarburg three days later and advanced along the Saarburg – Saverne road. On 20 August German units of Seventh Army counter-attacked, retook Saarburg and commenced a wide general advance which continued until 25 August.

0 1 2
Miles

© Arthur Banks 1973

45

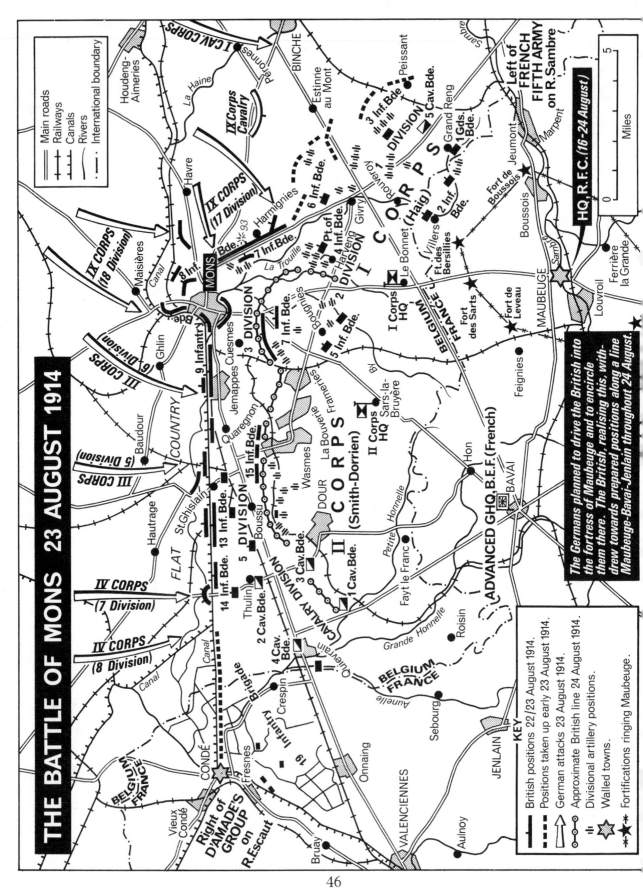

THE BATTLE OF MONS 23 AUGUST 1914

KEY

Main roads	
Railways	
Canals	
Rivers	
International boundary	

British positions 22/23 August 1914.
Positions taken up early 23 August 1914.
German attacks 23 August 1914.
Approximate British line 24 August 1914.
Divisional artillery positions.
Walled towns.
Fortifications ringing Maubeuge.

The Germans planned to drive the British into the fortress of Maubeuge and to encircle them there. The British, realising this, withdrew towards prepared positions along a line Maubeuge-Bavai-Jenlain throughout 24 August.

HQ, R.F.C. (16-24 August)

Miles

Left of FRENCH FIFTH ARMY on R.Sambre

I CAV.CORPS

IX Corps Cavalry

IX CORPS (17 Division)

IX CORPS (18 Division)

III CORPS (6 Division)

III CORPS (5 Division)

IV CORPS (7 Division)

IV CORPS (8 Division)

Right of D'AMADE'S GROUP on R.Escaut

I CORPS (Haig)

II CORPS (Smith-Dorrien)

ADVANCED GHQ, B.E.F. (French)

CAVALRY DIVISION

FLAT COUNTRY

3 Inf. Bde.
5 Cav. Bde.
6 Inf. Bde.
1 Gds. Bde.
2 Inf. Bde.
7 Inf. Bde.
8 Inf. Bde.
4 Inf. Bde.
9 Infantry Bde.
3 DIVISION
5 Inf. Bde.
2 DIVISION
7 Inf. Bde.
15 Inf. Bde.
13 Inf. Bde.
14 Inf. Bde.
1 Cav. Bde.
2 Cav. Bde.
3 Cav. Bde.
4 Cav. Bde.
5 DIVISION
I Corps HQ
II Corps HQ
Infantry Brigade

MONS
BINCHE
Péronnes
Houdeng-Aimeries
Havre
Maisières
Ghlin
Jemappes
Cuesmes
Quaregnon
Baudour
Hautrage
St.Ghislain
Thulin
Boussu
Wasmes
Dour
La Bouverie
Frameries
Sars-la-Bruyère
Estinne au Mont
Harmignies
Harveng
Givry
Bougnies
Nouvelles
Pt. of
La Trouille
Grand Reng
Peissant
Villers
Ft.des Bersillies
Le Bonnet
Fort de Boussois
Boussois
Fort des Sarts
Fort de Leveau
MAUBEUGE
Feignies
Hon
BAVAI
Honnelle
Petite Honnelle
Fayt le Franc
Grande Honnelle
Roisin
Quiévrain
Crespin
Fresnes
Vieux Condé
CONDÉ
VALENCIENNES
Onnaing
Sebourg
Aulnoy
Bruay
JENLAIN
Louvroil
Ferrière la Grande
Marpent
Jeumont

BELGIUM FRANCE

La Haine
Canal
Samb(re)
Sambre
Annelle

19

93

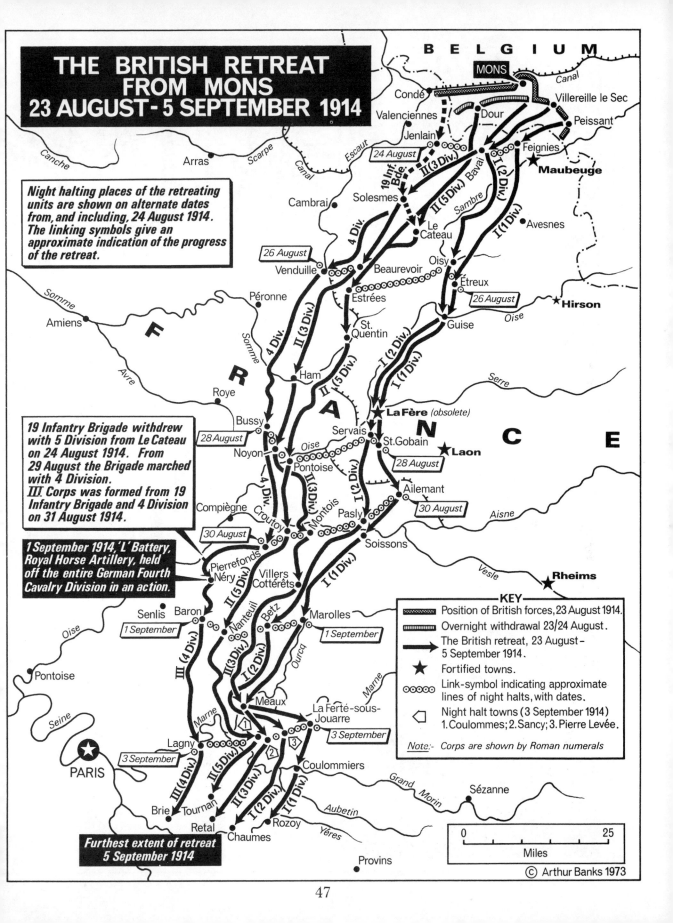

THE BRITISH RETREAT FROM MONS 23 AUGUST - 5 SEPTEMBER 1914

Night halting places of the retreating units are shown on alternate dates from, and including, 24 August 1914. The linking symbols give an approximate indication of the progress of the retreat.

19 Infantry Brigade withdrew with 5 Division from Le Cateau on 24 August 1914. From 29 August the Brigade marched with 4 Division. III Corps was formed from 19 Infantry Brigade and 4 Division on 31 August 1914.

1 September 1914, 'L' Battery, Royal Horse Artillery, held off the entire German Fourth Cavalry Division in an action.

Furthest extent of retreat 5 September 1914

BELGIUM
MONS
Canal
Condé
Villereille le Sec
Valenciennes
Dour
Peissant
Jenlain
II (3 Div.)
Feignies
24 August
19 Inf. Bde.
I (2 Div.)
Maubeuge
Arras
Scarpe
Canal
Escaut
Bavai
Sambre
Avesnes
Cambrai
Solesmes
II (5 Div.)
4 Div.
Le Cateau
I (1 Div.)
26 August
Venduille
Beaurevoir
Oisy
Péronne
Estrées
Étreux
Hirson
Somme
Venduille
St. Quentin
26 August
Guise
Amiens
F
Somme
4 Div.
II (3 Div.)
Ham
II (5 Div.)
Oise
Serre
Avre
R
Roye
A
La Fère (obsolete)
Bussy
Servais
N
C
E
28 August
Oise
St.Gobain
Noyon
I (2 Div.)
Laon
Pontoise
I (1 Div.)
Ailemant
28 August
Compiègne
4 Div.
II (3 Div.)
Montois
Pasly
30 August
Croutoy
30 August
Soissons
Aisne
Pierrefonds
II (5 Div.)
Néry
Villers Cotterêts
I (1 Div.)
Vesle
Rheims
Senlis
Baron
III (4 Div.)
Nanteuil
Betz
Marolles
1 September
Oise
1 September
II (3 Div.)
I (2 Div.)
Ourcq
1 September
Pontoise
Marne
Meaux
La Ferté-sous-Jouarre
Seine
Marne
①
③
3 September
PARIS
Lagny
II (5 Div.)
②
3 September
Coulommiers
Grand Morin
Sézanne
3 September
III (4 Div.)
II (3 Div.)
I (2 Div.)
I (1 Div.)
Brie Tournan
Aubetin
Retal
Rozoy
Chaumes
Yères
Provins

KEY
Position of British forces, 23 August 1914.
Overnight withdrawal 23/24 August.
The British retreat, 23 August – 5 September 1914.
★ Fortified towns.
ooooo Link-symbol indicating approximate lines of night halts, with dates.
◁ Night halt towns (3 September 1914) 1. Coulommes; 2. Sancy; 3. Pierre Levée.
Note:- Corps are shown by Roman numerals

0 ———— 25
Miles

© Arthur Banks 1973

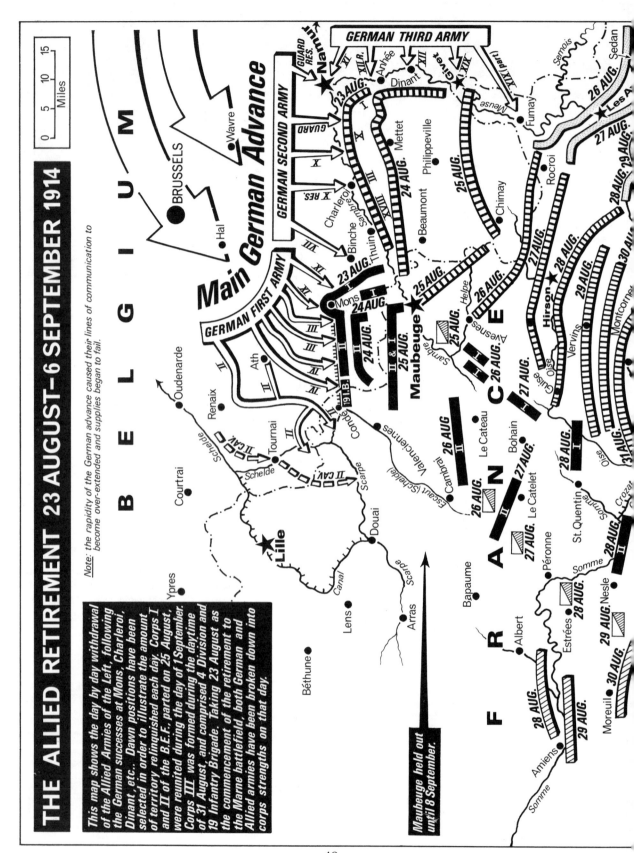

THE ALLIED RETIREMENT 23 AUGUST–6 SEPTEMBER 1914

This map shows the day by day withdrawal of the Allied Armies of the Left, following the German successes at Mons, Charleroi, Dinant, etc.. Dawn positions have been selected in order to illustrate the amount of territory relinquished each day. Corps I and II of the B.E.F. parted on 25 August, were reunited during the day of 1 September. Corps III was formed during the daytime of 31 August, and comprised 4 Division and 19 Infantry Brigade. Taking 23 August as the commencement of the retirement to the Marne battlefield, both German and Allied armies have been broken down into corps strengths on that day.

Note: the rapidity of the German advance caused their lines of communication to become over-extended and supplies began to fail.

Maubeuge held out until 8 September.

GERMAN THIRD ARMY

GERMAN SECOND ARMY

GERMAN FIRST ARMY

Main German Advance

BELGIUM

FRANCE

BRUSSELS

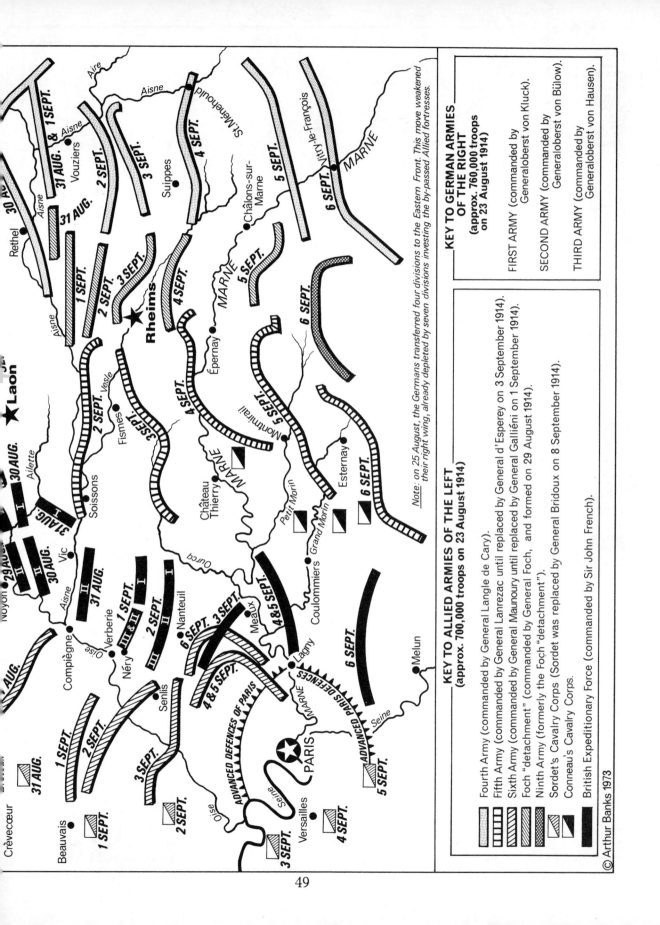

KEY TO ALLIED ARMIES OF THE LEFT
(approx. 700,000 troops on 23 August 1914)

Fourth Army (commanded by General Langle de Cary).

Fifth Army (commanded by General Lanrezac until replaced by General d'Esperey on 3 September 1914).

Sixth Army (commanded by General Maunoury until replaced by General Galliéni on 1 September 1914).

Foch "detachment" (commanded by General Foch, and formed on 29 August 1914).

Ninth Army (formerly the Foch "detachment").

Sordet's Cavalry Corps (Sordet was replaced by General Bridoux on 8 September 1914).

Conneau's Cavalry Corps.

British Expeditionary Force (commanded by Sir John French).

KEY TO GERMAN ARMIES OF THE RIGHT
(approx. 760,000 troops on 23 August 1914)

FIRST ARMY (commanded by Generaloberst von Kluck).

SECOND ARMY (commanded by Generaloberst von Bülow).

THIRD ARMY (commanded by Generaloberst von Hausen).

Note: on 25 August, the Germans transferred four divisions to the Eastern Front. This move weakened their right wing, already depleted by seven divisions investing the by-passed Allied fortresses.

© Arthur Banks 1973

49

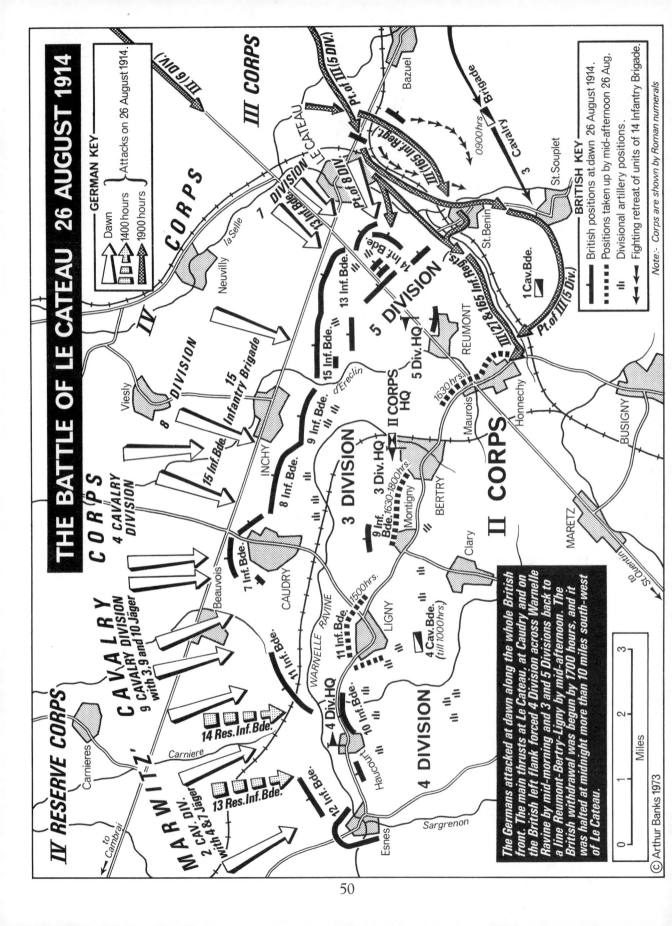

THE BATTLE OF LE CATEAU 26 AUGUST 1914

GERMAN KEY

Dawn
1400 hours
1900 hours

Attacks on 26 August 1914.

BRITISH KEY

British positions at dawn 26 August 1914.
Positions taken up by mid-afternoon 26 Aug.
Divisional artillery positions.
Fighting retreat of units of 14 Infantry Brigade.

Note:- Corps are shown by Roman numerals

III CORPS

III CORPS

IV CORPS

('6 DIV.') III

DIVISION

LE CATEAU

Pt. of III (5 DIV.)

Bazuel

Pt. of 8 DIV.

III (165 Inf. Regt.)

0900 hrs.

Cavalry

3

St. Souplet

13 Inf. Bde.

1

7

la Selle

Neuvilly

13 Inf. Bde.

14 Inf. Bde.

St. Benin

III (27 & 165 Inf. Regts.)

5 DIVISION

1 Cav. Bde.

Pt. of III (5 Div.)

Viesly

8 DIVISION

15

Infantry Brigade

15 Inf. Bde.

15 Inf. Bde.

d'Ereclin

REUMONT

5 Div. HQ

1630 hrs.

Maurois

Honnechy

BUSIGNY

8 DIVISION

15 Inf. Bde.

8 Inf. Bde.

9 Inf. Bde.

II CORPS HQ

3 DIVISION

3 Div. HQ

1630-1800 hrs.

II CORPS

MARETZ

to St. Quentin

INCHY

CAVALRY CORPS

9 CAVALRY DIVISION
with 3, 9 and 10 Jäger

4 CAVALRY DIVISION

7 Inf. Bde.

CAUDRY

WARNELLE RAVINE

11 Inf. Bde.

1500 hrs.

9 Inf. Bde.

Montigny

BERTRY

Clary

LIGNY

MARETZ

Beauvois

11 Inf. Bde.

11 Inf. Bde.

4 Cav. Bde.
(till 1000 hrs.)

4 DIVISION

M A R W I T Z

2 CAV. DIV.
with 4 & 7 Jäger

Carnieres

Carniere

14 Res. Inf. Bde.

13 Res. Inf. Bde.

4 Div. HQ

10 Inf. Bde.

1000 hrs.

Haucourt

Esnes

12 Inf. Bde.

Sargrenon

IV RESERVE CORPS

to Cambrai

The Germans attacked at dawn along the whole British front. The main thrusts were at Le Cateau, at Caudry and on the British left flank forced 4 Division across Warnelle Ravine by mid-morning and 3 and 5 Divisions back to a line Reumont–Bertry–Ligny by mid-afternoon. The British withdrawal was begun by 1700 hours, and it was halted at midnight more than 10 miles south-west of Le Cateau.

© Arthur Banks 1973

0   1   2   3
Miles

50

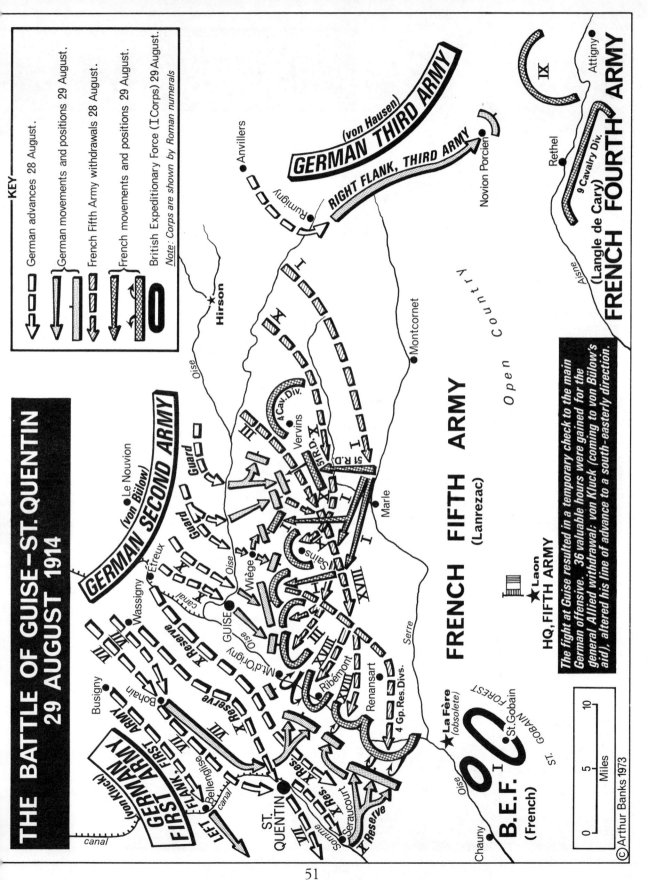

THE BATTLE OF GUISE–ST.QUENTIN 29 AUGUST 1914

KEY

⬜⬜▷ German advances 28 August.

German movements and positions 29 August.

French Fifth Army withdrawals 28 August.

French movements and positions 29 August.

British Expeditionary Force (I Corps) 29 August.

Note: Corps are shown by Roman numerals

GERMAN SECOND ARMY
(von Bülow)

GERMAN THIRD ARMY
(von Hausen)

RIGHT FLANK, THIRD ARMY

FRENCH FOURTH ARMY
(Langle de Cary)

GERMAN FIRST ARMY
(von Kluck)

FRENCH FIFTH ARMY
(Lanrezac)

HQ, FIFTH ARMY

B.E.F.
(French)

The fight at Guise resulted in a temporary check to the main German offensive. 36 valuable hours were gained for the general Allied withdrawal: von Kluck (coming to von Bülow's aid), altered his line of advance to a south-easterly direction.

0   5   10
Miles

© Arthur Banks 1973

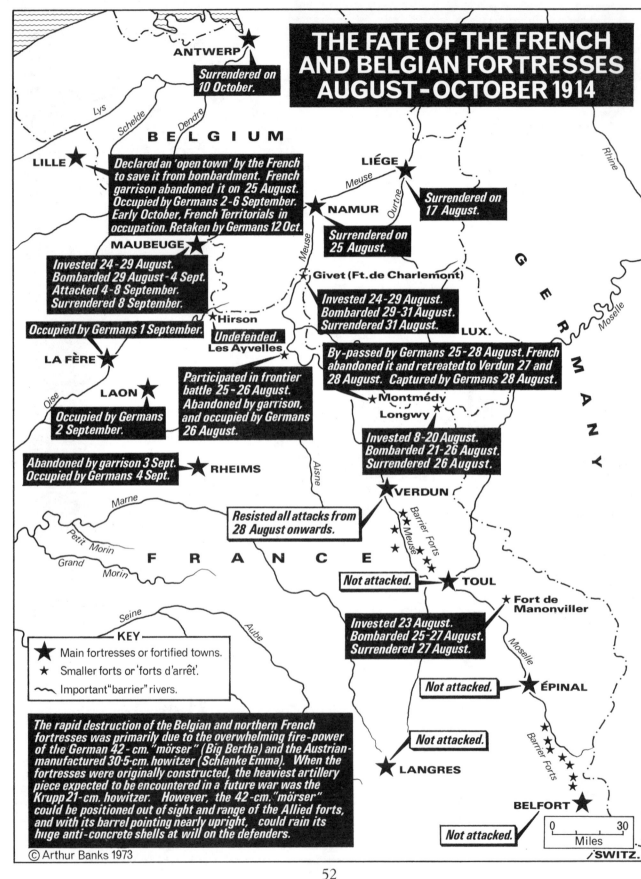

THE FATE OF THE FRENCH AND BELGIAN FORTRESSES AUGUST–OCTOBER 1914

ANTWERP
Surrendered on 10 October.

BELGIUM

LILLE
Declared an 'open town' by the French to save it from bombardment. French garrison abandoned it on 25 August. Occupied by Germans 2–6 September. Early October, French Territorials in occupation. Retaken by Germans 12 Oct.

LIÉGE
Surrendered on 17 August.

NAMUR
Surrendered on 25 August.

MAUBEUGE
Invested 24–29 August. Bombarded 29 August–4 Sept. Attacked 4–8 September. Surrendered 8 September.

Givet (Ft. de Charlemont)
Invested 24–29 August. Bombarded 29–31 August. Surrendered 31 August.

Occupied by Germans 1 September.

Hirson
Les Ayvelles Undefended.

LA FÈRE

LUX.

By-passed by Germans 25–28 August. French abandoned it and retreated to Verdun 27 and 28 August. Captured by Germans 28 August.

Participated in frontier battle 25–26 August. Abandoned by garrison, and occupied by Germans 26 August.

Montmédy
Longwy
Invested 8–20 August. Bombarded 21–26 August. Surrendered 26 August.

LAON
Occupied by Germans 2 September.

Abandoned by garrison 3 Sept. Occupied by Germans 4 Sept.
RHEIMS

Resisted all attacks from 28 August onwards.

VERDUN

Barrier Forts

FRANCE

Not attacked.
TOUL

Fort de Manonviller
Invested 23 August. Bombarded 25–27 August. Surrendered 27 August.

Not attacked.
ÉPINAL

Not attacked.

KEY
★ Main fortresses or fortified towns.
⋆ Smaller forts or 'forts d'arrêt'.
〜 Important "barrier" rivers.

LANGRES

Barrier Forts

The rapid destruction of the Belgian and northern French fortresses was primarily due to the overwhelming fire-power of the German 42-cm. "mörser" (Big Bertha) and the Austrian-manufactured 30·5-cm. howitzer (Schlanke Emma). When the fortresses were originally constructed, the heaviest artillery piece expected to be encountered in a future war was the Krupp 21-cm. howitzer. However, the 42-cm. "mörser" could be positioned out of sight and range of the Allied forts, and with its barrel pointing nearly upright, could rain its huge anti-concrete shells at will on the defenders.

BELFORT

Not attacked.

0 — 30
Miles

SWITZ.

© Arthur Banks 1973

52

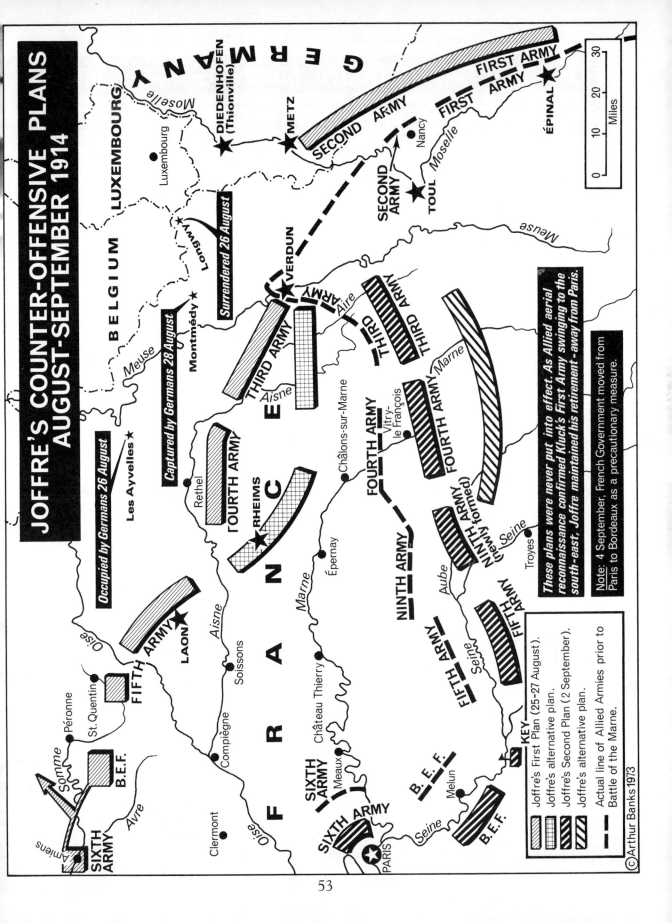

JOFFRE'S COUNTER-OFFENSIVE PLANS AUGUST–SEPTEMBER 1914

GERMANY

BELGIUM

LUXEMBOURG

FRANCE

Occupied by Germans 26 August

Captured by Germans 28 August

Surrendered 26 August

These plans were never put into effect. As Allied aerial reconnaissance confirmed Kluck's First Army swinging to the south-east, Joffre maintained his retirement - away from Paris.

Note: 4 September, French Government moved from Paris to Bordeaux as a precautionary measure.

KEY
- Joffre's First Plan (25-27 August).
- Joffre's alternative plan.
- Joffre's Second Plan (2 September).
- Joffre's alternative plan.
- Actual line of Allied Armies prior to Battle of the Marne.

FIRST ARMY
SECOND ARMY
FIRST ARMY
SECOND ARMY
THIRD ARMY
FOURTH ARMY
NINTH ARMY (Newly formed)
FIFTH ARMY
SIXTH ARMY
B.E.F.

DIEDENHOFEN (Thionville)
METZ
Nancy
TOUL
ÉPINAL
Luxembourg
Longwy
VERDUN
Montmédy
Les Ayvelles
Rethel
RHEIMS
Épernay
Châlons-sur-Marne
Vitry-le François
Troyes
LAON
Soissons
Compiègne
Clermont
St. Quentin
Péronne
Amiens
Château Thierry
Meaux
Melun
PARIS

Moselle
Moselle
Meuse
Meuse
Aisne
Aire
Aisne
Marne
Marne
Marne
Aube
Seine
Seine
Seine
Oise
Oise
Somme
Avre

Miles
0 10 20 30

© Arthur Banks 1973

53

THE FIRST BATTLE OF THE MARNE 5-10 SEPTEMBER 191[4]

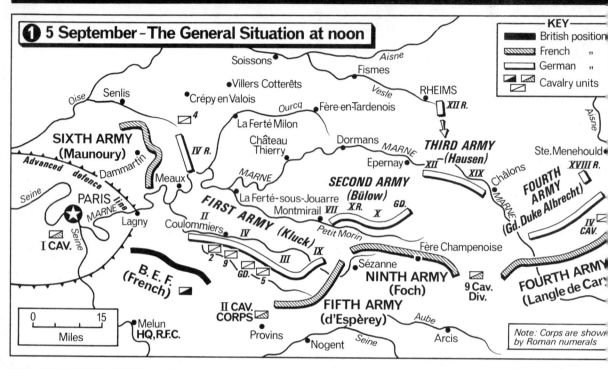

① 5 September – The General Situation at noon

KEY
- British position[s]
- French "
- German "
- Cavalry units

Aisne

Soissons

Fismes

Vesle

RHEIMS

XII R.

Senlis

Villers Cotterêts

Crépy en Valois

Oise

Ourcq

Fère-en-Tardenois

La Ferté Milon

THIRD ARMY
(Hausen)
XII

Ste. Menehould

4

IV R.

Château Thierry

Dormans

MARNE

Epernay

XIX

Châlons

XVIII R.

Aisne

SIXTH ARMY
(Maunoury)

Dammartin

Advanced defence line

Meaux

MARNE

FOURTH ARMY
(Gd. Duke Albrecht)

Seine

PARIS

MARNE

Lagny

La Ferté-sous-Jouarre

FIRST ARMY (Kluck)

Montmirail *VII*

SECOND ARMY
(Bülow)
X R. *X* *GD.*

IV CAV.

Coulommiers

II

IV

Petit Morin

Fère Champenoise

I CAV.

2 *9*

GD.

III

IX

5

Sézanne

NINTH ARMY
(Foch)

9 Cav. Div.

FOURTH ARM[Y]
(Langle de Car[y])

B. E. F.
(French)

II CAV. CORPS

FIFTH ARMY
(d'Espèrey)

Provins

Aube

Arcis

0   15
Miles

Melun
HQ, R.F.C.

Nogent

Seine

Note: Corps are show[n] by Roman numerals

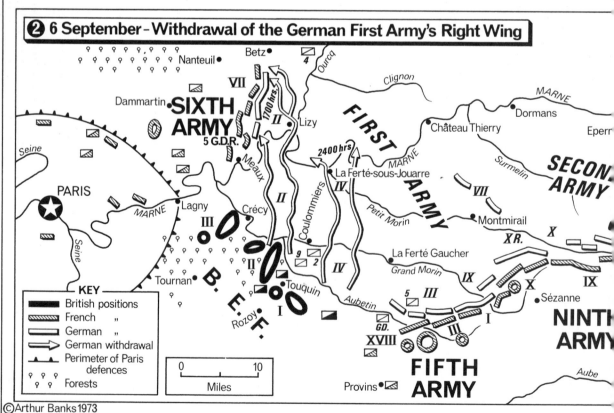

② 6 September – Withdrawal of the German First Army's Right Wing

Betz

4

Nanteuil

Ourcq

Clignon

MARNE

Dormans

VII

FIRST

Château Thierry

Eper[nay]

Dammartin

SIXTH ARMY

1700 hrs.

II

Lizy

ARMY

Surmelin

SECON[D] ARMY

5 G.D.R.

Meaux

2400 hrs

La Ferté-sous-Jouarre

VII

Seine

PARIS

II

IV

MARNE

X R.

Lagny

Crécy

Coulommiers

Petit Morin

Montmirail

X

III

II

9 *2*

IV

La Ferté Gaucher

IX

X

IX

Tournan

B.

Touquin

I

La Ferté Gaucher

Grand Morin

Aubetin

5 *III*

Sézanne

Rozoy

E. F.

NIN[TH]

GD.

I

ARM[Y]

XVIII

KEY
- ▬ British positions
- ▨ French "
- ▭ German "
- ⇨ German withdrawal
- ▲▲ Perimeter of Paris defences
- ♀♀♀ Forests

0   10
Miles

Provins

FIFTH ARMY

Aube

© Arthur Banks 1973

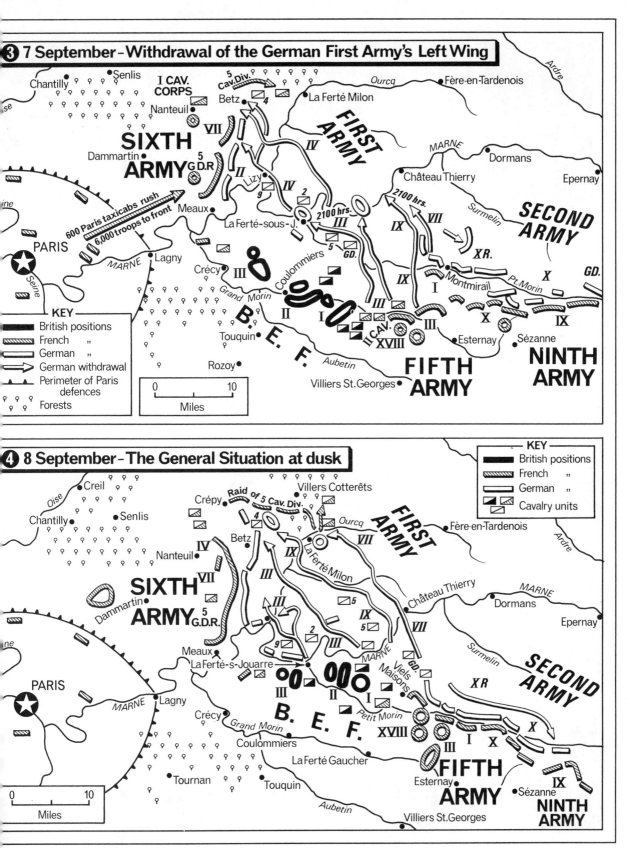

❸ 7 September – Withdrawal of the German First Army's Left Wing

Ardre

Chantilly • Senlis

I CAV. CORPS

5 Cav.Div.

Ourcq

Fère-en-Tardenois

Betz

La Ferté Milon

Nanteuil

VII

FIRST ARMY

MARNE

Dormans

SIXTH ARMY

IV

Château Thierry

Epernay

Dammartin

G.D.R. 5

II

Lizy

IV

2

2100 hrs.

Surmelin

SECOND ARMY

600 Paris taxicabs rush 6,000 troops to front

Meaux

La Ferté-sous-J.

III

2100 hrs.

IX

VII

XR.

PARIS

Seine

MARNE

Lagny

Crécy

III

Grand Morin

Coulommiers

5

GD.

IX

I

Montmirail

Pt.Morin

X

GD.

Touquin

II

I

III

X

IX

KEY

▬ British positions
▨ French   "
▭ German   "
⇨ German withdrawal
▲ Perimeter of Paris defences
♀ ♀ Forests

B. E. F.

II CAV.

XVIII

Esternay

Sézanne

Rozoy •

Aubetin

FIFTH ARMY

NINTH ARMY

Villiers St.Georges

0   10
Miles

---

❹ 8 September – The General Situation at dusk

KEY

▬ British positions
▨ French   "
▭ German   "
▨ Cavalry units

Oise • Creil

Crépy

Raid of 5 Cav. Div.

Villers Cotterêts

Chantilly • Senlis

Betz

Ourcq

La Ferté Milon

FIRST ARMY

Fère-en-Tardenois

Nanteuil

IV

III

IX

VII

SIXTH ARMY

VII

III

III

IX

5

Château Thierry

MARNE

Dormans

Dammartin

G.D.R. 5

III

2

9

IX

5

VII

Epernay

Meaux

La Ferté-s-Jouarre

III

MARNE

Viels Maisons

gd.

Surmelin

SECOND ARMY

PARIS

MARNE

Lagny

III

II

I

Crécy

Grand Morin

Petit Morin

XR

X

Coulommiers

B. E. F.

XVIII

I

IX

X

La Ferté Gaucher

III

Tournan • Touquin

Aubetin

Esternay

FIFTH ARMY

IX

Sézanne

NINTH ARMY

Villiers St.Georges

0   10
Miles

THE FIRST BATTLE OF THE MARNE – continued

5 9 September – The British Attack across the Marne

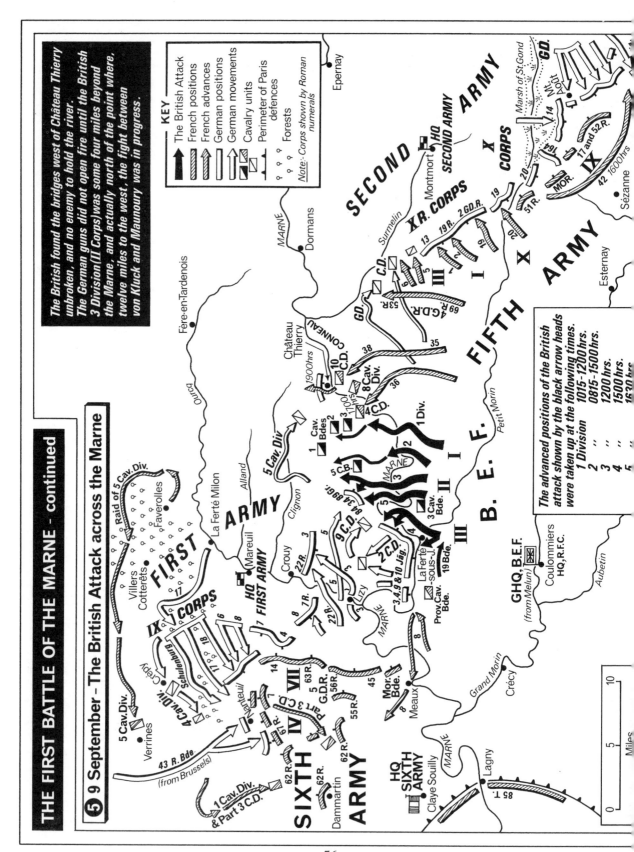

The British found the bridges west of Château Thierry unbroken, and no enemy to hold the river. The German guns did not open fire until the British 3 Division (II Corps) was some four miles beyond the Marne, and actually north of the point where, twelve miles to the west, the fight between von Kluck and Maunoury was in progress.

KEY

⬆	The British Attack
	French positions
	French advances
	German positions
	German movements
	Cavalry units
	Perimeter of Paris defences
♀ ♀ ♀	Forests

Note:- Corps shown by Roman numerals

The advanced positions of the British attack shown by the black arrow heads were taken up at the following times.

1 Division			1015-1200 hrs.
2	,,		0815-1500 hrs.
3	,,		1200 hrs.
4	,,		1500 hrs.
5			1630 hrs.

56

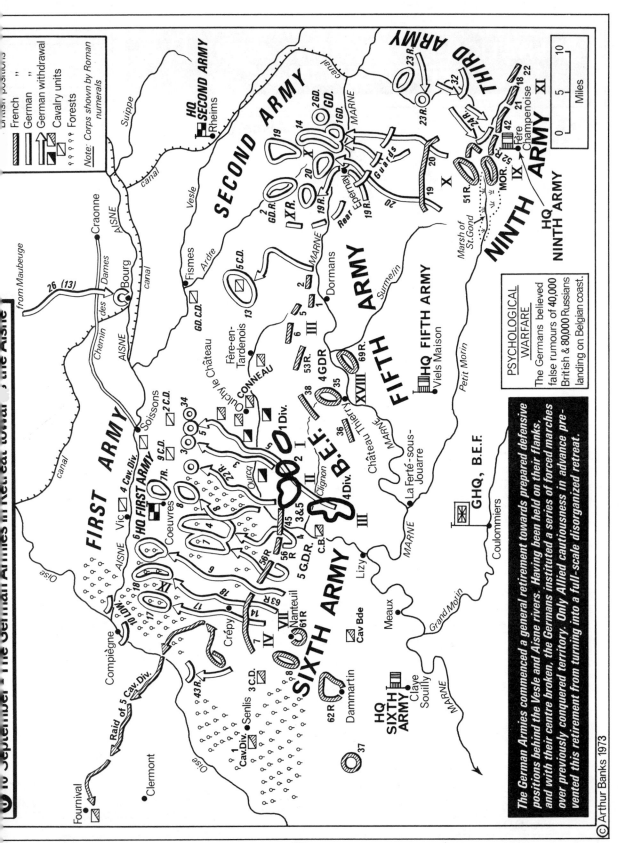

Note: Corps shown by Roman numerals

British positions
French "
German "
German withdrawal
Cavalry units
Forests

PSYCHOLOGICAL
WARFARE
The Germans believed
false rumours of 40,000
British & 80,000 Russians
landing on Belgian coast.

The German Armies commenced a general retirement towards prepared defensive
positions behind the Vesle and Aisne rivers. Having been held on their flanks,
and with their centre broken, the Germans instituted a series of forced marches
over previously conquered territory. Only Allied cautiousness in advance prevented this retirement from turning into a full-scale disorganized retreat.

© Arthur Banks 1973

Miles
0   5   10

57

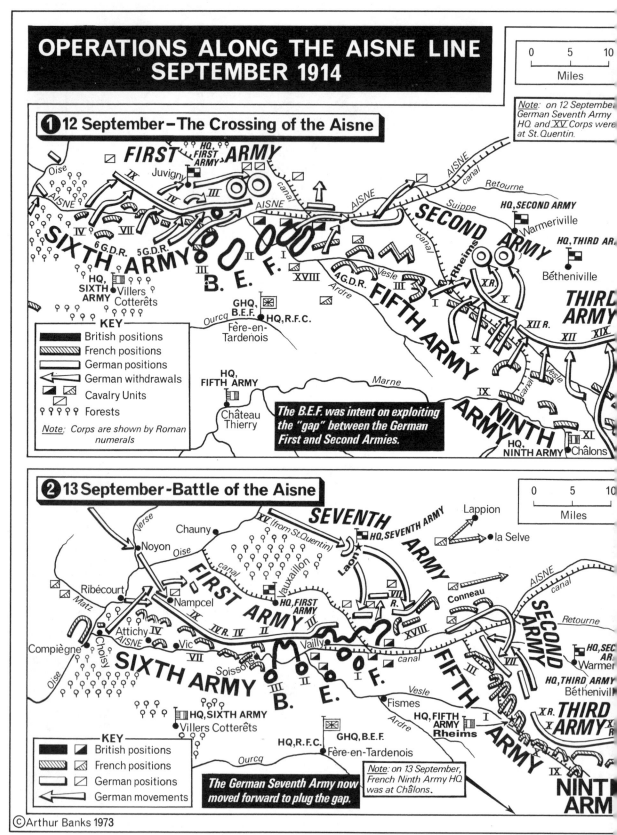

OPERATIONS ALONG THE AISNE LINE SEPTEMBER 1914

0 5 10
Miles

Note: on 12 September, German Seventh Army HQ and XV Corps were at St.Quentin.

❶ 12 September – The Crossing of the Aisne

HQ, FIRST ARMY
FIRST ARMY
Juvigny
Oise
AISNE
IX
IV
III
canal
AISNE
AISNE
canal
Retourne
HQ, SECOND ARMY
Warmeriville
SECOND ARMY
Suippe
HQ, THIRD AR.
Bétheniville
6 G.D.R. 5 G.D.R.
SIXTH ARMY
II
B.E.F.
I
XVIII
4 G.D.R.
Vesle
Ardre
Rheims
X.R.
X
THIRD ARMY
HQ, SIXTH ARMY
Villers Cotterêts
III
FIFTH ARMY
XII R.
XII XIX
X
Ourcq
GHQ, B.E.F.
HQ, R.F.C.
Fère-en-Tardenois
Vesle
IX
HQ, FIFTH ARMY
Marne
canal
NINTH ARMY
XI
Châlons

KEY
▅	British positions
▨	French positions
▢	German positions
⬅	German withdrawals
◪ ⊠	Cavalry Units
♀♀♀♀♀	Forests

Note: Corps are shown by Roman numerals

Château Thierry

HQ, NINTH ARMY

The B.E.F. was intent on exploiting the "gap" between the German First and Second Armies.

❷ 13 September – Battle of the Aisne

0 5 10
Miles

Verse
Chauny
SEVENTH ARMY
Lappion
Noyon
Oise
XV (from St.Quentin)
HQ, SEVENTH ARMY
la Selve
Ribécourt
canal
Vauxaillon
Laon
VII
R.
Conneau
AISNE
canal
Matz
Nampcel
HQ, FIRST ARMY
XVIII
SECOND ARMY
Retourne
Compiègne
Choisy
Attichy
IV
AISNE
Vic
IV.R. IV
II
III
Vailly
canal
HQ, SEC AR.
Warmer
Oise
VII
Soissons
I
B. E. F.
III
HQ, THIRD ARMY
Bétheniville
FIRST ARMY
FIFTH ARMY
SIXTH ARMY
Vesle
X.R.
THIRD ARMY
HQ, SIXTH ARMY
Villers Cotterêts
Fismes
Ardre
HQ, FIFTH ARMY
Rheims
HQ, R.F.C.
GHQ, B.E.F.
Fère-en-Tardenois
Ourcq
IX
NINTH ARMY

KEY
▅	◪	British positions
▨	⊠	French positions
▢	◪	German positions
⬅		German movements

Note: on 13 September, French Ninth Army HQ was at Châlons.

The German Seventh Army now moved forward to plug the gap.

© Arthur Banks 1973

58

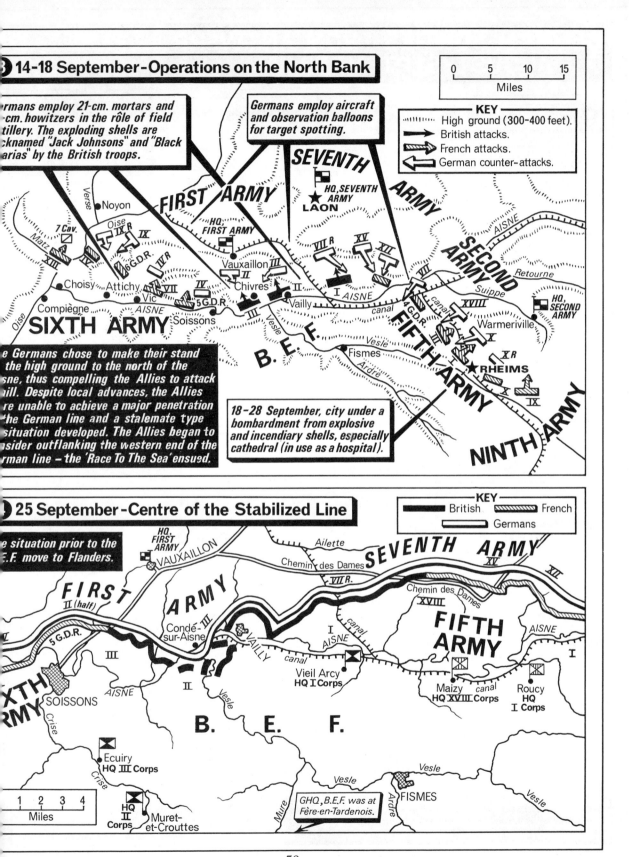

14-18 September - Operations on the North Bank

rmans employ 21-cm. mortars and
-cm. howitzers in the rôle of field
tillery. The exploding shells are
cknamed "Jack Johnsons" and "Black
arias" by the British troops.

Germans employ aircraft
and observation balloons
for target spotting.

KEY
- .... High ground (300-400 feet).
- → British attacks.
- ⇏ French attacks.
- ⇐ German counter-attacks.

0   5   10   15
Miles

SEVENTH

FIRST ARMY

ARMY

HQ, SEVENTH
ARMY
LAON

Verse ● Noyon

7 Cav.

Oise

HQ,
FIRST ARMY

AISNE

Matz

XIII

IX R
IX

6 G.D.R.

IV R

VII R   XV   XII

SECOND

ARMY

Retourne

Vauxaillon

Choisy ● Attichy

VII

IV

Chivres

I AISNE

4 G.D.R.

XVIII

Suippe

HQ,
SECOND
ARMY

● Vic

5 G.D.R.

Vailly

canal

canal

● Warmeriville

Compiègne
Oise

AISNE

III

Soissons

II

Vesle

FIFTH ARMY

III

X

X R

Choisy

SIXTH ARMY

B. E. F.

Vesle

● Fismes

Ardre

★ RHEIMS

IX

e Germans chose to make their stand
the high ground to the north of the
sne, thus compelling the Allies to attack
ill. Despite local advances, the Allies
re unable to achieve a major penetration
the German line and a stalemate type
situation developed. The Allies began to
nsider outflanking the western end of the
rman line – the 'Race To The Sea'ensued.

18-28 September, city under a
bombardment from explosive
and incendiary shells, especially
cathedral (in use as a hospital).

NINTH ARMY

25 September - Centre of the Stabilized Line

KEY
- ▬▬▬ British
- ▨▨▨ French
- ▭ Germans

e situation prior to the
.E.F. move to Flanders.

HQ,
FIRST
ARMY
VAUXAILLON

Ailette

Chemin des Dames

SEVENTH ARMY

XV

FIRST

ARMY

VII R.

XII

II (half)

Chemin des Dames

5 G.D.R.

Condé-
sur-Aisne

III

VAILLY

XVIII

I
AISNE

canal

FIFTH
ARMY

AISNE

I

III

II

Vieil Arcy
HQ I Corps

Maizy
HQ XVIII Corps

canal

Roucy
HQ
I Corps

IXTH
RMY

SOISSONS

AISNE

Crise

B.   E.   F.

Vesle

Ecuiry
HQ III Corps

Crise

Vesle

Vesle

1 2 3 4
Miles

HQ
II
Corps

Muret-
et-Crouttes

Mure

Ardre

● FISMES

Vesle

GHQ, B.E.F. was at
Fère-en-Tardenois.

BELGIAN SORTIES FROM ANTWERP AUGUST-SEPTEMBER 1914

The main object of the sorties was to divert part of German strength from their main lines of advance into France. There was also the minor hope that some sort of breakthrough in the German rear might be won.

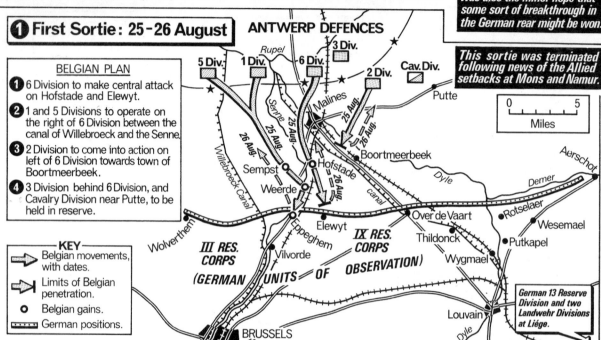

① First Sortie: 25-26 August

This sortie was terminated following news of the Allied setbacks at Mons and Namur.

ANTWERP DEFENCES

BELGIAN PLAN

❶ 6 Division to make central attack on Hofstade and Elewyt.

❷ 1 and 5 Divisions to operate on the right of 6 Division between the canal of Willebroeck and the Senne.

❸ 2 Division to come into action on left of 6 Division towards town of Boortmeerbeek.

❹ 3 Division behind 6 Division, and Cavalry Division near Putte, to be held in reserve.

― KEY ―

⇨ Belgian movements, with dates.

⇥ Limits of Belgian penetration.

○ Belgian gains.

▭▭▭ German positions.

German 13 Reserve Division and two Landwehr Divisions at Liége.

III RES. CORPS (GERMAN UNITS OF OBSERVATION)

0 ―――― 5 Miles

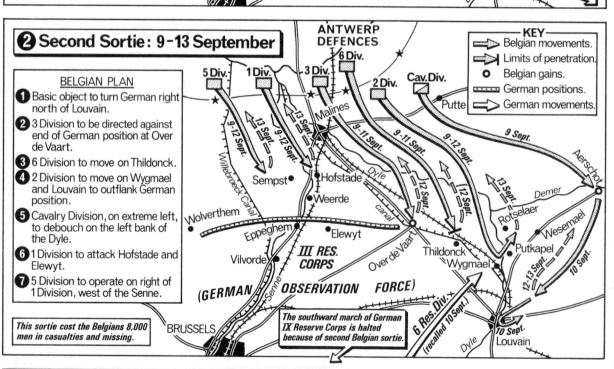

② Second Sortie: 9-13 September

ANTWERP DEFENCES

― KEY ―

⇨ Belgian movements.

⇥ Limits of penetration.

○ Belgian gains.

▭▭▭ German positions.

⇨ German movements.

BELGIAN PLAN

❶ Basic object to turn German right north of Louvain.

❷ 3 Division to be directed against end of German position at Over de Vaart.

❸ 6 Division to move on Thildonck.

❹ 2 Division to move on Wygmael and Louvain to outflank German position.

❺ Cavalry Division, on extreme left, to debouch on the left bank of the Dyle.

❻ 1 Division to attack Hofstade and Elewyt.

❼ 5 Division to operate on right of 1 Division, west of the Senne.

This sortie cost the Belgians 8,000 men in casualties and missing.

III RES. CORPS (GERMAN OBSERVATION FORCE)

The southward march of German IX Reserve Corps is halted because of second Belgian sortie.

On 22 September, 700 Belgian cyclist volunteers arranged in seven detachments, left Antwerp to destroy railway lines of communication in enemy-occupied region outside the fortress. Main lines were severed in Limbourg, Brabant and Hainaut provinces, disrupting German transport. Most cyclists returned to Antwerp, but some were captured.

A third sortie, requested by Joffre on 24 September, never materialised as the Germans launched <u>their</u> offensive on Antwerp shortly after Joffre's request.

BOMBARDMENT OF THE ANTWERP FORTS
28 SEPTEMBER – 9 OCTOBER 1914

Note: all times shown in panels are Belgian; German time was one hour later.

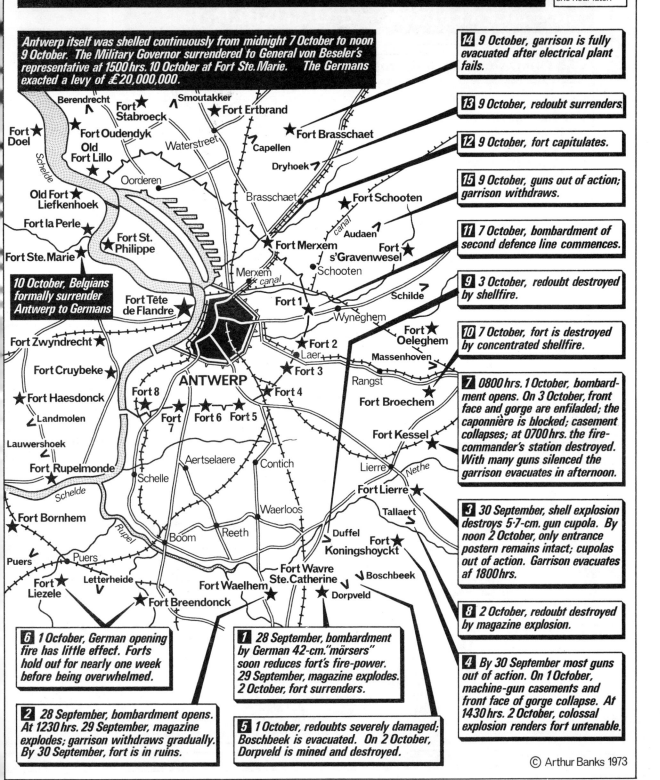

Antwerp itself was shelled continuously from midnight 7 October to noon 9 October. The Military Governor surrendered to General von Beseler's representative at 1500 hrs. 10 October at Fort Ste. Marie. The Germans exacted a levy of £20,000,000.

10 October, Belgians formally surrender Antwerp to Germans

14 9 October, garrison is fully evacuated after electrical plant fails.

13 9 October, redoubt surrenders.

12 9 October, fort capitulates.

15 9 October, guns out of action; garrison withdraws.

11 7 October, bombardment of second defence line commences.

9 3 October, redoubt destroyed by shellfire.

10 7 October, fort is destroyed by concentrated shellfire.

7 0800 hrs. 1 October, bombardment opens. On 3 October, front face and gorge are enfiladed; the caponnière is blocked; casement collapses; at 0700 hrs. the fire-commander's station destroyed. With many guns silenced the garrison evacuates in afternoon.

3 30 September, shell explosion destroys 5·7-cm. gun cupola. By noon 2 October, only entrance postern remains intact; cupolas out of action. Garrison evacuates at 1800 hrs.

8 2 October, redoubt destroyed by magazine explosion.

4 By 30 September most guns out of action. On 1 October, machine-gun casements and front face of gorge collapse. At 1430 hrs. 2 October, colossal explosion renders fort untenable.

6 1 October, German opening fire has little effect. Forts hold out for nearly one week before being overwhelmed.

1 28 September, bombardment by German 42-cm."mörsers" soon reduces fort's fire-power. 29 September, magazine explodes. 2 October, fort surrenders.

2 28 September, bombardment opens. At 1230 hrs. 29 September, magazine explodes; garrison withdraws gradually. By 30 September, fort is in ruins.

5 1 October, redoubts severely damaged; Boschbeek is evacuated. On 2 October, Dorpveld is mined and destroyed.

© Arthur Banks 1973

61

THE GERMAN VICTORY AT ANTWERP
26 SEPTEMBER – 9 OCTOBER 1914

0 ___ 5
Miles

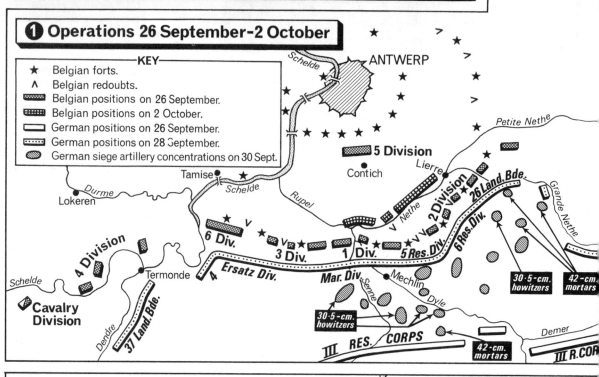

① Operations 26 September–2 October

KEY
★ Belgian forts.
∧ Belgian redoubts.
▨ Belgian positions on 26 September.
▨ Belgian positions on 2 October.
▭ German positions on 26 September.
▭ German positions on 28 September.
◢ German siege artillery concentrations on 30 Sept.

ANTWERP

Schelde

Petite Nethe

5 Division
Contich
Lierre
26 Land. Bde.

Grande Nethe

Tamise
Schelde
Rupel
Nethe
2 Division
6 Res. Div.

Durme
Lokeren

6 Div.
3 Div.
1 Div.
5 Res. Div.
30·5-cm. howitzers
42-cm. mortars

4 Division
Termonde
4 Ersatz Div.
Mar. Div.
Mechlin
Senne
Dyle

Schelde
Cavalry Division
Dendre
37 Land. Bde.
30·5-cm. howitzers
III RES. CORPS
42-cm. mortars
Demer
III R. COR

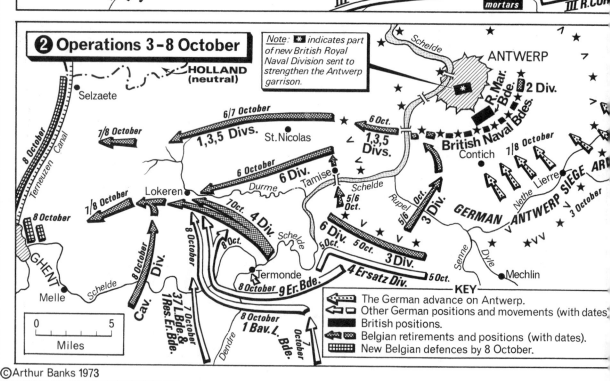

② Operations 3–8 October

Note: ✱ indicates part of new British Royal Naval Division sent to strengthen the Antwerp garrison.

ANTWERP
Schelde
R. Mar. Bde.
2 Div.

HOLLAND (neutral)
Selzaete

6/7 October
7/8 October
1,3,5 Divs.
St. Nicolas
6 Oct.
1,3,5 Divs.

British Naval Bdes.
Contich
7/8 October
Lierre
Nethe

Terneuzen Canal
8 October
8 October

6 October
6 Div.

7/8 October
Lokeren
Durme
Tamise
Schelde
5/6 Oct.
Rupel
Oct.
3 Div.
GERMAN
ANTWERP SIEGE AR
3 October

7 Oct.
4 Div.
Schelde
6 Div.
5 Oct.
3 Div.
Senne
Dyle
Mechlin

8 Oct.
8 October
GHENT
Melle
Schelde
Cav. Div.
Termonde
9 Er. Bde.
4 Ersatz Div.
5 Oct.

0 ___ 5
Miles

7 October
37 L.Bde. & 1Res.Er.Bde.
8 October
1 Bav. L. Bde.
7 October
Dendre

KEY
◀▭ The German advance on Antwerp.
◀▭ Other German positions and movements (with dates)
▬ British positions.
◀▨ Belgian retirements and positions (with dates).
▥▥▥ New Belgian defences by 8 October.

© Arthur Banks 1973

62

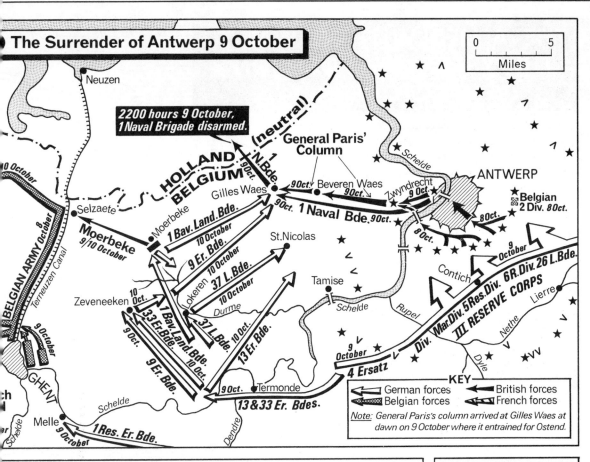

The Surrender of Antwerp 9 October

0 | 5
Miles

Neuzen

2200 hours 9 October, 1 Naval Brigade disarmed.

General Paris' Column

HOLLAND (neutral)
BELGIUM

Scheldt

ANTWERP

1 N.Bde.
90ct.
Beveren Waes
90ct.
Zwyndrecht
9 Oct

Gilles Waes
90ct. 1 Naval Bde. 90ct.
8 Oct

Moerbeke
Selzaete
1 Bav. Land. Bde.
10 October

Belgian 2 Div. 80ct.
80ct.

BELGIAN ARMY 8 October

Terneuzen Canal

Moerbeke
9/10 October

9 Er. Bde.
10 October

St. Nicolas

9 October

Contich
6R.Div. 26 L.Bde.

37 L.Bde.
10 October

Mar.Div. 5Res.Div.

Lierre

9 October

Zeveneeken
10 Oct.
7 Bav.Land.Bde.
33 Er.Bde.
90ct.
37 L.Bde. 10 Oct.
Durme
Tamise
Scheldt
Rupel
III RESERVE CORPS
Nethe
Dyle

13 Er. Bde.

4 Ersatz
9 October

GHENT
9 Er. Bde.
90ct.

9 October

Melle
1 Res. Er. Bde.
90ct. Termonde
13 & 33 Er. Bdes.

Scheldt
Dendre

KEY
⟵ German forces   ⟵ British forces
⟵ Belgian forces   ⟵ French forces

Note: General Paris's column arrived at Gilles Waes at dawn on 9 October where it entrained for Ostend.

German 42-cm. (16·5-inch) L/16 Mortar "Gamma"

...July 1906, in accordance with the ...man General Staff directive, the ...llerie - Prüfungs - Kommission ...ested Krupp to design a mortar of ...t 40 cm. which could be transported ...ailway. Two equipments were ...ed initially, and another three in ... making five available on outbreak ...ar in 1914.

Elevation:	43°- 66°
Traverse:	45°
Weight with platform:	75 tons
Muzzle velocity:	1,312 ft-secs.
Maximum range: (anti-concrete shell)	15,500 yards

...l rate of fire: 1 round every 6 minutes

280 men served a 2-gun battery

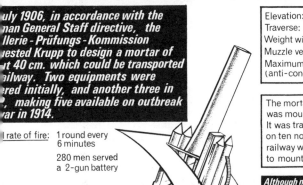

The mortar had a recoiling barrel and was mounted on an iron platform. It was transported in separate loads on ten normal-gauge 25/30-ton railway wagons, and took ten hours to mount.

Although named a 'Mörser' by the German forces, the 42 was technically a howitzer as it was capable of being elevated and pivoted on trunnions, whereas mortars have rear trunnions on fixed beds.

The first naval battery to be armed with the original two mortars was formed and trained in the summer of 1912.

...weapon was known as "Big Bertha" or "Fat Bertha".

German 42-cm. H.E. Shell

Weight (shell complete): 2,052 lb.
Bursting charge: 234 lb.

A
B
1540mm.
C
25mm.

Thickness of walls: at A, 295mm.
at B, 52mm.
at C, 46mm.
Thickness of base: 95 mm.
Width of driving band: 50 mm.
Construction material: Steel

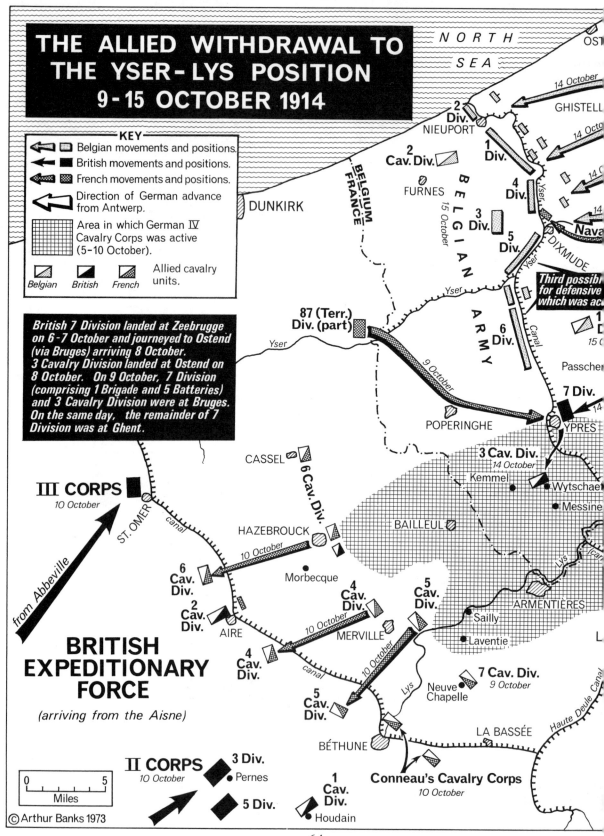

THE ALLIED WITHDRAWAL TO THE YSER-LYS POSITION 9-15 OCTOBER 1914

KEY
- ← ⬜ Belgian movements and positions.
- ← ⬛ British movements and positions.
- ← ▨ French movements and positions.
- ← Direction of German advance from Antwerp.
- ▦ Area in which German IV Cavalry Corps was active (5-10 October).
- Allied cavalry units. Belgian / British / French

British 7 Division landed at Zeebrugge on 6-7 October and journeyed to Ostend (via Bruges) arriving 8 October. 3 Cavalry Division landed at Ostend on 8 October. On 9 October, 7 Division (comprising 1 Brigade and 5 Batteries) and 3 Cavalry Division were at Bruges. On the same day, the remainder of 7 Division was at Ghent.

NORTH SEA

OST

GHISTELL

14 October

2 Div. NIEUPORT

2 Cav. Div.

1 Div.

4 Div.

FURNES

3 Div.

5 Div.

Yser

BELGIAN ARMY

DIXMUDE

Nava

15 October

Third possib for defensive which was ac

87 (Terr.) Div. (part)

Yser

Yser

6 Div.

Canal

Passchen

9 October

POPERINGHE

7 Div.

YPRES

CASSEL

6 Cav. Div.

3 Cav. Div.
14 October

Kemmel

Wytschae

Messine

III CORPS
10 October

ST. OMER

canal

HAZEBROUCK
10 October

BAILLEUL

Lys

from Abbeville

Morbecque

6 Cav. Div.

2 Cav. Div.

AIRE

4 Cav. Div.

4 Cav. Div.

10 October

MERVILLE

5 Cav. Div.

Sailly

Laventie

ARMENTIÈRES

BRITISH EXPEDITIONARY FORCE

(arriving from the Aisne)

5 Cav. Div.

canal

10 October

Lys

Neuve Chapelle

7 Cav. Div.
9 October

Haute Deule Canal

BÉTHUNE

LA BASSÉE

II CORPS
10 October

3 Div.
• Pernes

1 Cav. Div.

Conneau's Cavalry Corps
10 October

0 ___ 5
Miles

© Arthur Banks 1973

5 Div.
• Houdain

64

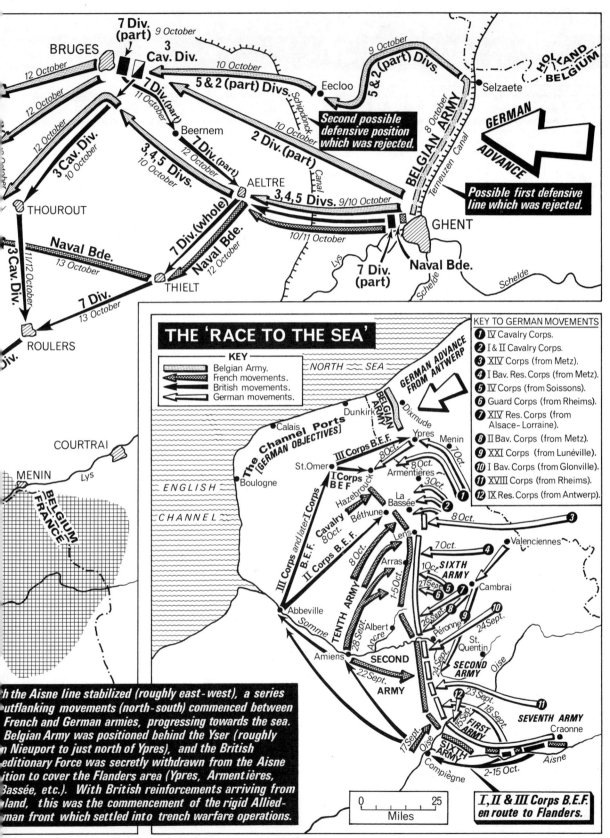

DEFENCE OF THE CHANNEL PORTS AUTUMN 1914

With Antwerp and also Ostend behind them, the German aim was to sever the sea link with England.

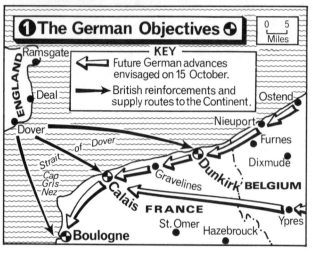

❶ The German Objectives ✚

KEY
← Future German advances envisaged on 15 October.
→ British reinforcements and supply routes to the Continent.

0 — 5
Miles

Ramsgate
ENGLAND
Deal
Dover
Strait of Dover
Cap Gris Nez
Boulogne
Calais
Gravelines
Dunkirk
St. Omer
Hazebrouck
FRANCE
Nieuport
Furnes
Dixmude
Ostend
BELGIUM
Ypres

❷ The Belgian Bulwark

0 — 1 — 2
Miles

Lombartzyde
Westende
2 DIV.
Nieuport
Slype
St. Georges
Mannekensvere
2 DIV.
Schoore
1 DIV.
1 DIV.
Schoorbakke
Ghistelles
2 CAV. DIV.
(in reserve)
canal
2 DIVISION
1 DIVISION
Tervaete
4 DIVISION
4 DIV.
Keyem
4 DIV.
Beerst
GERMAN RESERVE CORPS (von Beseler)
Couckelaere
BELGIAN ARMY (King Albert)
Lampernisse
3 DIVISION (in reserve)
Rear-Admiral Ronarc'h
Zarren
Clercken
Woumen
Dixmude
5 DIVISION
"Fort of Knocke"
Driegrachten
5 DIV.
Merckem
Forest of Houthulst
canal
6 DIVISION
Bixschoote
1 CAVALRY DIVISION
Steenstraat
Langemarck
Boesinghe
to Ypres

This map shows the situation on 15 October 1914.

KEY
▨ Belgian Army.
▧ French Marine Fusiliers.
← German advances.

❸ The Allied Line from the Sea

0 — 5
Miles

NORTH SEA
Ostend
Middelkerke
Ghistelles
Slype
Mannekensvere
Schoore
Keyem
Nieuport
Sand Dunes
canal
BELGIAN ARMY
III RESERVE CORPS
Beerst
Furnes
Dixmude
Zarren
Clercken
Lampernisse
canal
Lo
Woumen
Merckem
Yser (canalised)
Forest of Houthulst
Bixschoote
Poelcapelle
87 & 89 Territorial Divs.
Elverdinghe
Langemarck
Passchendaele
Poperinghe
Boesinghe
Ypres
7 DIV.
Zonnebeke
Hooge
Gheluvelt
Vlamertinghe
Dickebusch
Wytschaete
Kemmel
CAV. CORPS
Douve
Messines
XIX CORPS
Gheluwe
Comines
Lys
Bailleul
Ploegsteert Wood
BELGIUM
FRANCE
Nieppe
Steenwerck
III CORPS
Neuf Berquin
DE MITRY
CONNEAU
Lys
Lys
VII CORPS
Layes Brook
Armentières
IV CAV. CORPS
Ennetières
Fournes
II CAV. CORPS
Aubers
Deule
XIII CORPS
LILLE
II CORPS
Béthune
La Bassée
canal
1 CAV. CORPS
Lawe
canal

Withdrawal of German cavalry due to relief by XIX Corps and VII Corps.

KEY
▤ Belgian Army.
▬ B.E.F.
▨ French units.
┄ German positions.
← German movements.

This map illustrates the Allied barrier to the German thrusts towards the Channel ports and the basic situation 15 October.

© Arthur Banks 1973

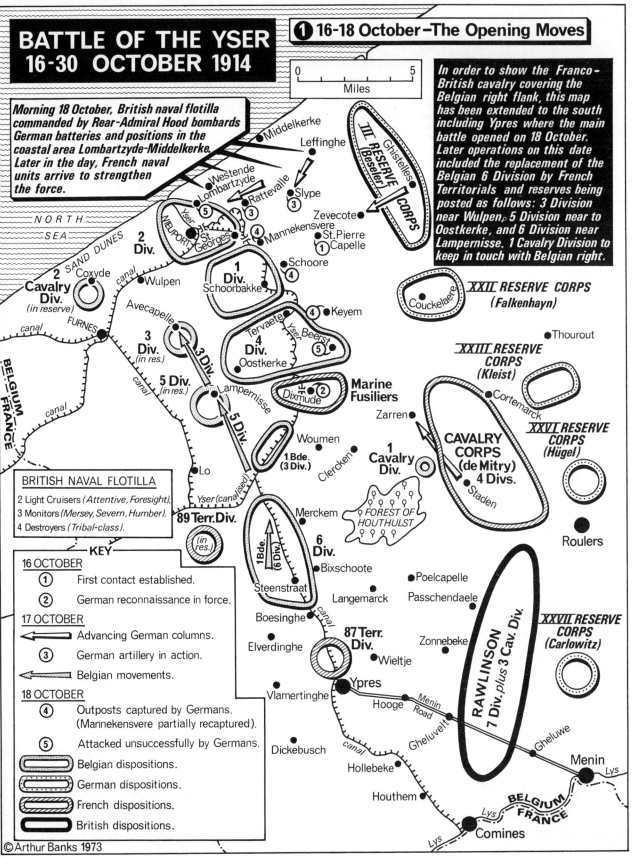

BATTLE OF THE YSER 16-30 OCTOBER 1914

① 16-18 October – The Opening Moves

0 — Miles — 5

In order to show the Franco-British cavalry covering the Belgian right flank, this map has been extended to the south including Ypres where the main battle opened on 18 October. Later operations on this date included the replacement of the Belgian 6 Division by French Territorials and reserves being posted as follows: 3 Division near Wulpen, 5 Division near to Oostkerke, and 6 Division near Lampernisse. 1 Cavalry Division to keep in touch with Belgian right.

Morning 18 October, British naval flotilla commanded by Rear-Admiral Hood bombards German batteries and positions in the coastal area Lombartzyde-Middelkerke. Later in the day, French naval units arrive to strengthen the force.

NORTH SEA

SAND DUNES

III RESERVE CORPS (Beseler) Ghistelles

Middelkerke
Leffinghe
Westende
Lombartzyde
Rattevalle
Slype ③
Zevecote
Mannekensvere
St.Pierre Capelle ①
NIEUPORT
St. Georges ④
⑤
⑤

2 Div.
2 Cavalry Div. *(in reserve)*
Coxyde
Wulpen
canal
Avecapelle
FURNES
canal
canal
canal

1 Div. ①
Schoorbakke
Schoore ④
Keyem ④
Tervaete **4 Div.** ⑤ Beerst
Oostkerke
Yser

3 Div. *(in res.)*
5 Div. *(in res.)*
Lampernisse
Dixmude ② **Marine Fusiliers**

Couckelaere
XXII RESERVE CORPS *(Falkenhayn)*

Thourout

XXIII RESERVE CORPS *(Kleist)*
Cortemarck

Zarren
CAVALRY CORPS (de Mitry) 4 Divs.
Staden

XXVI RESERVE CORPS *(Hügel)*

Roulers

Lo
Woumen
1 Bde. (3 Div.)
Clercken
1 Cavalry Div.
FOREST OF HOUTHULST

Yser (canalised)

BRITISH NAVAL FLOTILLA
2 Light Cruisers *(Attentive, Foresight).*
3 Monitors *(Mersey, Severn, Humber).*
4 Destroyers *(Tribal-class).*

89 Terr. Div. *(in res.)*

Merckem
6 Div.
Bixschoote
1 Bde. (6 Div.)
Steenstraat
Poelcapelle
Passchendaele

XXVII RESERVE CORPS *(Carlowitz)*

BELGIUM FRANCE

canal

Langemarck
Boesinghe
Elverdinghe
87 Terr. Div.
Zonnebeke
Wieltje
Ypres
Vlamertinghe
Hooge
Menin Road
Gheluvelt
Gheluwe

RAWLINSON 7 Div. plus 3 Cav. Div.

Menin
Lys

Dickebusch
Hollebeke
Houthem
Comines
Lys
Lys

BELGIUM FRANCE

KEY

16 OCTOBER
① First contact established.
② German reconnaissance in force.

17 OCTOBER
⟵ Advancing German columns.
③ German artillery in action.
⟵ Belgian movements.

18 OCTOBER
④ Outposts captured by Germans. (Mannekensvere partially recaptured).
⑤ Attacked unsuccessfully by Germans.
▭ Belgian dispositions.
▭ German dispositions.
▭ French dispositions.
▭ British dispositions.

© Arthur Banks 1973

67

BATTLE OF THE YSER – continued

② Operations 19-20 October

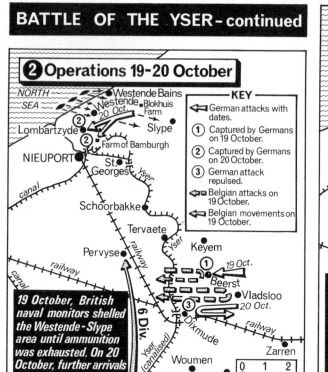

KEY

⬅ German attacks with dates.
① Captured by Germans on 19 October.
② Captured by Germans on 20 October.
③ German attack repulsed.
⬅◻ Belgian attacks on 19 October.
⬅ Belgian movements on 19 October.

19 October, British naval monitors shelled the Westende-Slype area until ammunition was exhausted. On 20 October, further arrivals strengthened flotilla.

```
0    1    2
     Miles
```

③ 21 October – Completion of the German Concentration

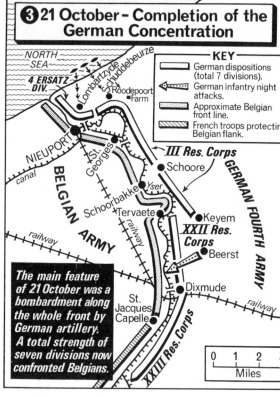

KEY

◻ German dispositions (total 7 divisions).
⬅ German infantry night attacks.
▦ Approximate Belgian front line.
▨ French troops protecting Belgian flank.

The main feature of 21 October was a bombardment along the whole front by German artillery. A total strength of seven divisions now confronted Belgians.

```
0    1    2
     Miles
```

④ Naval Operations: Evening 21 October – Morning 31 October

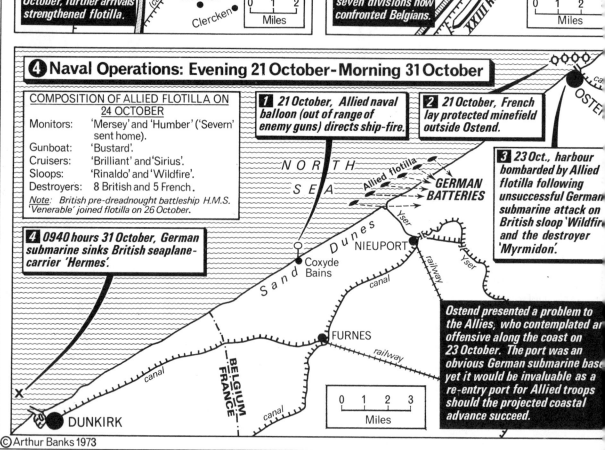

COMPOSITION OF ALLIED FLOTILLA ON 24 OCTOBER

Monitors: 'Mersey' and 'Humber' ('Severn' sent home).
Gunboat: 'Bustard'.
Cruisers: 'Brilliant' and 'Sirius'.
Sloops: 'Rinaldo' and 'Wildfire'.
Destroyers: 8 British and 5 French.

Note: British pre-dreadnought battleship H.M.S. 'Venerable' joined flotilla on 26 October.

4 *0940 hours 31 October, German submarine sinks British seaplane-carrier 'Hermes'.*

1 *21 October, Allied naval balloon (out of range of enemy guns) directs ship-fire.*

2 *21 October, French lay protected minefield outside Ostend.*

3 *23 Oct., harbour bombarded by Allied flotilla following unsuccessful German submarine attack on British sloop 'Wildfire' and the destroyer 'Myrmidon'.*

Ostend presented a problem to the Allies, who contemplated an offensive along the coast on 23 October. The port was an obvious German submarine base, yet it would be invaluable as a re-entry port for Allied troops should the projected coastal advance succeed.

```
0    1    2    3
       Miles
```

At the outbreak of war, three "river" monitors were being built for the Brazilian Government by Vickers at Barrow. As the Royal Navy was in need of shallow-draft craft for coastal use, the British Government purchased all three on 8 August 1914.

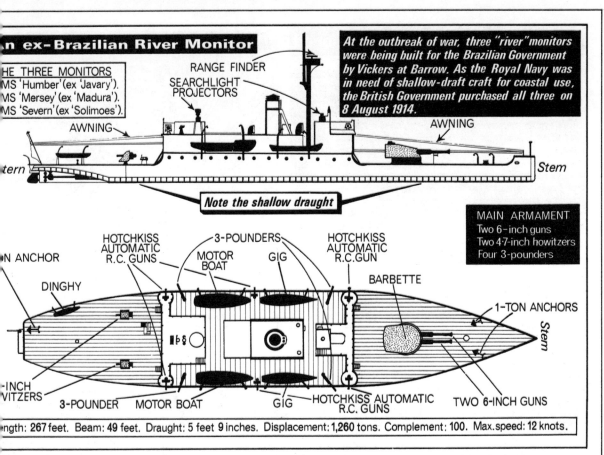

HE THREE MONITORS
MS 'Humber' (ex 'Javary').
MS 'Mersey' (ex 'Madura').
MS 'Severn' (ex 'Solimoes').

RANGE FINDER
SEARCHLIGHT PROJECTORS
AWNING
AWNING
tern
Stem

Note the shallow draught

MAIN ARMAMENT
Two 6-inch guns
Two 4.7-inch howitzers
Four 3-pounders

N ANCHOR
DINGHY
HOTCHKISS AUTOMATIC R.C. GUNS
3-POUNDERS
MOTOR BOAT
GIG
HOTCHKISS AUTOMATIC R.C. GUN
BARBETTE
1-TON ANCHORS
Stem
-INCH WITZERS
3-POUNDER
MOTOR BOAT
GIG
HOTCHKISS AUTOMATIC R.C. GUNS
TWO 6-INCH GUNS

ngth: 267 feet. Beam: 49 feet. Draught: 5 feet 9 inches. Displacement: 1,260 tons. Complement: 100. Max. speed: 12 knots.

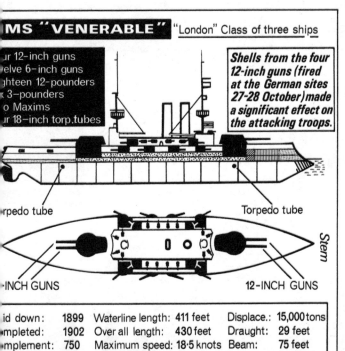

MS "VENERABLE" "London" Class of three ships

Shells from the four 12-inch guns (fired at the German sites 27-28 October) made a significant effect on the attacking troops.

ur 12-inch guns
elve 6-inch guns
ghteen 12-pounders
x 3-pounders
o Maxims
ur 18-inch torp. tubes

rpedo tube
Torpedo tube
Stem
-INCH GUNS
12-INCH GUNS

id down:	1899	Waterline length:	411 feet	Displace.:	15,000 tons
mpleted:	1902	Over all length:	430 feet	Draught:	29 feet
emplement:	750	Maximum speed:	18·5 knots	Beam:	75 feet

5 Military Operations 22-23 October

4 22 October, Belgian attacks.

3 22 October, German attack repulsed by 4 Line Regiment.

Heavy fire from German artillery.

5 23 October, arrival of French 42 Division.

2 22 October, Belgian counter-attack fails to dislodge German units.

1 Night 21/22 October, Germans establish footing on west bank of Yser. They deploy infantry and guns.

Yser
Lombartzyde
Farm of Bamburgh canal
NIEUPORT
St Georges
One Bde.
canal
Schoorbakke
(French 42 Div.)
Yser
Tervaete

0   1
Mile

BATTLE OF THE YSER-continued

By 24 October, Belgian resistance was deteriorating due to exhaustion of troops, lack of ammunition, and only a few reinforcements arriving (French 42 Division). However, as the whole area was intersected by canals and ditches, a possibility existed of flooding the countryside to a depth sufficient to render the attacking Germans unoperational. Stated briefly, this entailed damming 22 culverts under the Nieuport – Dixmude railway embankment to contain the rising waters in the east, followed by opening the Nieuport sluices to admit the sea. This manœuvre was accomplished successfully and by 30 October the drive by the Germans along the coast was virtually at an end.

NIEUPORT'S SLUICES AND CHANNELS

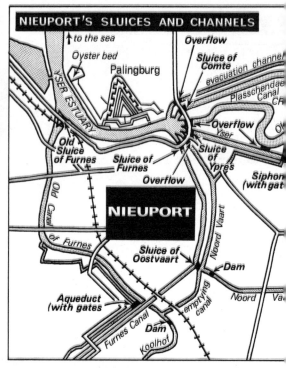

to the sea
Oyster bed
Palingburg
Overflow
Sluice of Comte
evacuation channel
Plasschendael Canal
YSER ESTUARY
Old Sluice of Furnes
Sluice of Furnes
Overflow Yser
Sluice of Ypres
Overflow
Siphon (with gat
NIEUPORT
Noord Vaart
Sluice of Oostvaart
Dam
Old Canal of Furnes
Aqueduct (with gates
emptying canal
Furnes Canal
Dam
Koolhof
Noord Va

THE OLD SLUICE OF FURNES

On 26 October, efforts to manipulate doors failed due to inadequate housing.

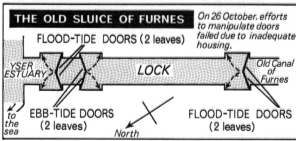

FLOOD-TIDE DOORS (2 leaves)
YSER ESTUARY
LOCK
Old Canal of Furnes
to the sea
EBB-TIDE DOORS (2 leaves)
North
FLOOD-TIDE DOORS (2 leaves)

❻ The Irrigated Countryside

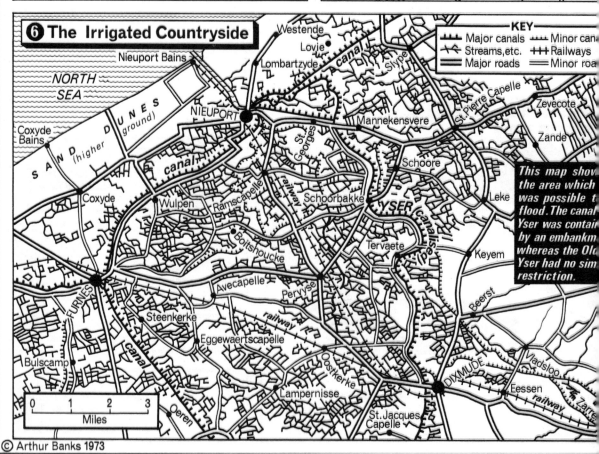

KEY
Major canals Minor cana
Streams, etc. Railways
Major roads Minor roa

Westende
Lovie
Lombartzyde
NORTH SEA
Nieuport Bains
canal
Slype
St. Pierre Capelle
Zevecote
Zande
Coxyde Bains
SAND DUNES (higher ground)
NIEUPORT
Mannekensvere
Schoore
Leke
Coxyde
canal
St Georges
railway
Schoorbakke
YSER (canalise
This map sho
the area which
was possible t
flood. The cana
Yser was contain
by an embankm
whereas the Old
Yser had no sim
restriction.
Wulpen
Ramscapelle
Boitshoucke
Tervaete
Keyem
FURNES
Avecapelle
Pervyse
railway
Beerst
Steenkerke
Eggewaertscapelle
Bulscamp
canal
Oostkerke
DIXMUDE
Vladsloo
Eessen
railway
Lampernisse
Oeren
St. Jacques Capelle

0   1   2   3
Miles

© Arthur Banks 1973

70

Military Operations 24-30 October

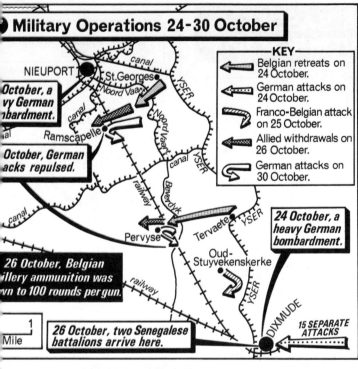

KEY

⬅ Belgian retreats on 24 October.

⬅ German attacks on 24 October.

↝ Franco-Belgian attack on 25 October.

⬅ Allied withdrawals on 26 October.

↝ German attacks on 30 October.

NIEUPORT

St.Georges

canal

Noord Vaart

YSER

October, a
vy German
mbardment.

canal

Ramscapelle

Noord Vaart

canal

YSER

October, German
acks repulsed.

railway

Beverdijk

Pervyse

Tervaete

YSER

24 October, a heavy German bombardment.

Oud-Stuyvekenskerke

YSER

26 October, Belgian
illery ammunition was
wn to 100 rounds per gun.

railway

DIXMUDE

15 SEPARATE ATTACKS ⬅

1 Mile

26 October, two Senegalese battalions arrive here.

BELGIAN ENGINEERING OPERATIONS AT NIEUPORT

The operational procedures were extremely complex, depending for success upon tides from the North Sea being propitious, force and direction of winds being correct, plus the actual manipulation of sluice gates being feasible. At the old sluice of Furnes, the two sets of flood-tide doors needed to be held open permanently with the one set of ebb-tide doors freed from their racks so that they opened and closed according to the water pressure from rising and receding tides. At other sluices, doors and gates required to be operated manually for each manœuvre; that is, opened at high tides and closed before low tides. *(The full moon of 29 October assisted operations by causing a very high tide).*

21 October. 1100 hours. Old Yser's overflow is opened; water rapidly inundates creek; Noord Vaart-Old Yser siphon closed to avoid flooding 2 Division's established position.

25 October. Foch contemplates flooding area east of Dunkirk, but delays plan temporarily.

26 October. Attempt fails at old sluice of Furnes.

28 October. Second try succeeds; waters rise.

29 October. 1930 hours, gates of N.Vaart opened.

30 October. Manœuvre repeated; floods spread.

The Inundated Countryside

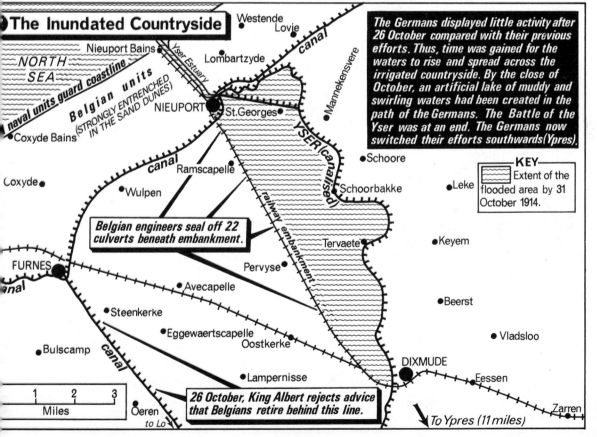

Westende
Lovie

Yser Estuary

canal

Nieuport Bains

Lombartzyde

NORTH SEA

naval units guard coastline

Belgian units
(STRONGLY ENTRENCHED IN THE SAND DUNES)

Mannekensvere

NIEUPORT

St.Georges

Coxyde Bains

canal

Ramscapelle

Schoore

Coxyde

Wulpen

Schoorbakke

YSER (canalised)

railway embankment

Belgian engineers seal off 22 culverts beneath embankment.

Tervaete

FURNES

canal

Avecapelle

Pervyse

Steenkerke

Eggewaertscapelle
Oostkerke

Bulscamp

canal

Lampernisse

26 October, King Albert rejects advice that Belgians retire behind this line.

Oeren
to Lo

Leke

Keyem

Beerst

Vladsloo

DIXMUDE

Eessen

Zarren

↓ To Ypres (11 miles)

1 2 3
Miles

The Germans displayed little activity after 26 October compared with their previous efforts. Thus, time was gained for the waters to rise and spread across the irrigated countryside. By the close of October, an artificial lake of muddy and swirling waters had been created in the path of the Germans. The Battle of the Yser was at an end. The Germans now switched their efforts southwards (Ypres).

KEY

▦ Extent of the flooded area by 31 October 1914.

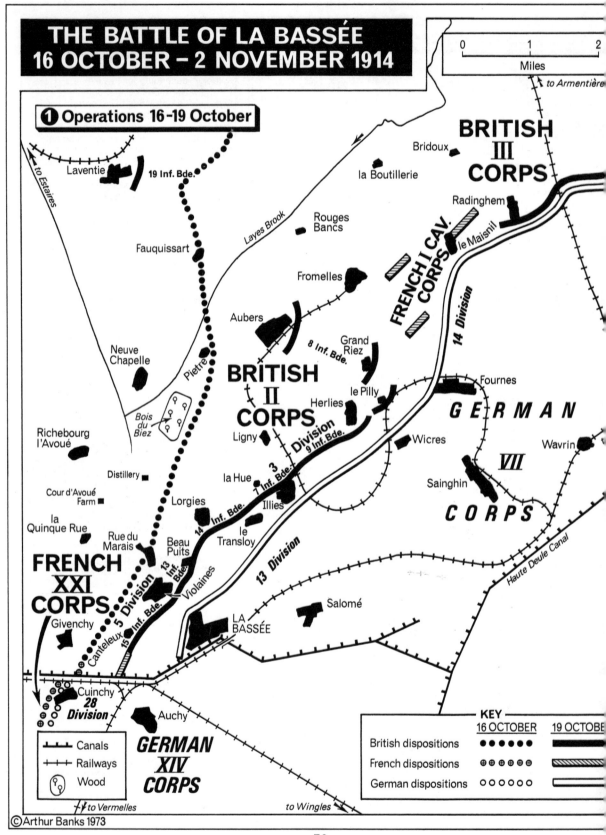

THE BATTLE OF LA BASSÉE
16 OCTOBER – 2 NOVEMBER 1914

0   1   2
Miles

① Operations 16-19 October

to Armentières

BRITISH III CORPS

Bridoux

la Boutillerie

Radinghem

le Maisnil

Laventie

19 Inf. Bde.

Layes Brook

Rouges Bancs

FRENCH I CAV. CORPS

Fauquissart

Fromelles

14 Division

to Estaires

Aubers

Grand Riez

8 Inf. Bde.

Neuve Chapelle

Fournes

Pietre

BRITISH II CORPS

Herlies

le Pilly

GERMAN

Bois du Biez

Richebourg l'Avoué

Ligny

Wicres

Wavrin

Distillery

Division

9 Inf. Bde.

VII

Cour d'Avoué Farm

la Hue

3 Inf. Bde.

Illies

Sainghin

CORPS

la Quinque Rue

Lorgies

7 Inf. Bde.

Rue du Marais

Beau Puits

14 Inf. Bde.

le Transloy

13 Division

Haute Deule Canal

FRENCH XXI CORPS

13 Inf. Bde.

Violaines

Givenchy

Canteleux

5 Division

15 Inf. Bde.

Salomé

LA BASSÉE

Cuinchy

28 Division

Auchy

GERMAN XIV CORPS

KEY

	16 OCTOBER	19 OCTOBER
British dispositions	● ● ● ● ●	▬▬▬
French dispositions	⊕ ⊕ ⊕ ⊕ ⊕	▨▨▨
German dispositions	○ ○ ○ ○ ○	▭▭▭

Canals

Railways

Wood

to Vermelles

to Wingles

© Arthur Banks 1973

72

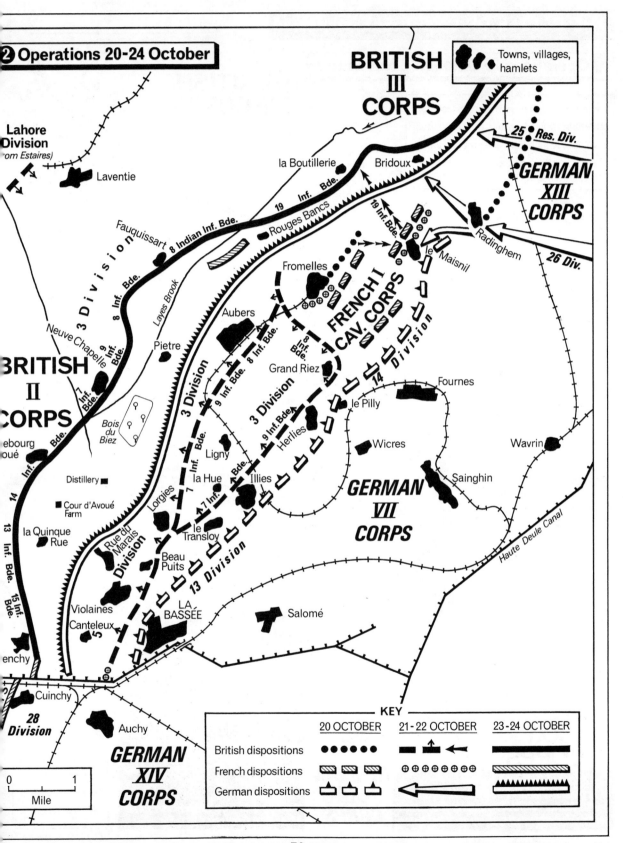

② Operations 20-24 October

Towns, villages, hamlets

BRITISH III CORPS

Lahore Division *(from Estaires)*

Laventie

la Boutillerie

Bridoux

25 Res. Div.

GERMAN XIII CORPS

Radinghem

26 Div.

3 Division

Fauquissart

8 Indian Inf. Bde.

19 Inf. Bde.

Rouges Bancs

19 Inf. Bde.

le Maisnil

8 Inf. Bde.

Layes Brook

Fromelles

FRENCH I CAV. CORPS

Neuve Chapelle

9 Inf. Bde.

Pietre

Aubers

8 Inf. Bde.

9 Inf. Bde.

Grand Riez

14 Division

Fournes

BRITISH II CORPS

7 Inf. Bde.

3 Division

3 Division

le Pilly

Bois du Biez

9 Inf. Bde.

Herlies

Wicres

Wavrin

ebourg oué

Ligny

9 Inf. Bde.

Illies

Sainghin

Distillery

la Hue

7 Inf. Bde.

7 Inf. Bde.

GERMAN VII CORPS

Cour d'Avoué Farm

Lorgies

le Transloy

la Quinque Rue

15 Inf. Bde.

Rue du Marais

5 Division

Beau Puits

13 Division

Haute Deule Canal

Salomé

Violaines

Canteleux

LA BASSÉE

enchy

Cuinchy

Auchy

28 Division

GERMAN XIV CORPS

	0		1	
	Mile			

KEY

	20 OCTOBER	21-22 OCTOBER	23-24 OCTOBER
British dispositions	●●●●●●	▬ ↑ ←	▬▬▬
French dispositions	⬛⬛⬛	⊕⊕⊕⊕⊕⊕	▨▨▨
German dispositions	⌂⌂⌂	⬅	▲▲▲▲

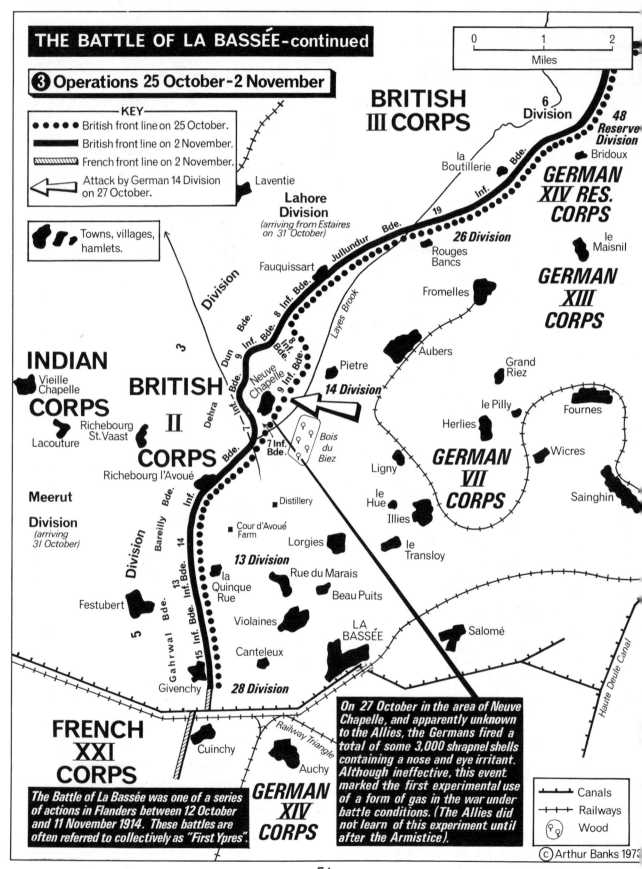

THE BATTLE OF LA BASSÉE-continued

③ Operations 25 October–2 November

KEY

• • • • British front line on 25 October.

▬▬▬ British front line on 2 November.

▨▨▨ French front line on 2 November.

⬅ Attack by German 14 Division on 27 October.

◆◆ Towns, villages, hamlets.

0   1   2
Miles

BRITISH III CORPS

6 Division

48 Reserve Division

Bridoux

la Boutillerie

GERMAN XIV RES. CORPS

Inf. Bde.

19 Inf.

26 Division

Rouges Bancs

le Maisnil

GERMAN XIII CORPS

Laventie

Lahore Division *(arriving from Estaires on 31 October)*

Jullundur Bde.

Fromelles

Fauquissart

Layes Brook

Aubers

8 Inf. Bde.

Pietre

Grand Riez

Division

3

Dun Bde.

9 Inf. Bde.

le Pilly

Fournes

INDIAN CORPS

Vieille Chapelle

BRITISH II CORPS

Neuve Chapelle

9 Inf. Bde.

14 Division

Herlies

Wicres

Richebourg St. Vaast

Dehra

Inf. Bde.

7

Bde.

7 Inf. Bde.

Bois du Biez

Ligny

GERMAN VII CORPS

Sainghin

Lacouture

Meerut Division *(arriving 31 October)*

Richebourg l'Avoué

Inf.

Bareilly Bde.

14

Distillery

le Hue

Illies

Division

Cour d'Avoué Farm

Lorgies

le Transloy

13 Inf. Bde.

13 Division

la Quinque Rue

Rue du Marais

Beau Puits

Festubert

Gahrwal Bde.

Inf. Bde.

15 Inf. Bde.

Violaines

LA BASSÉE

Salomé

5

Canteleux

Givenchy

28 Division

Haute Deule Canal

FRENCH XXI CORPS

Railway Triangle

Cuinchy

Auchy

GERMAN XIV CORPS

The Battle of La Bassée was one of a series of actions in Flanders between 12 October and 11 November 1914. These battles are often referred to collectively as "First Ypres".

On 27 October in the area of Neuve Chapelle, and apparently unknown to the Allies, the Germans fired a total of some 3,000 shrapnel shells containing a nose and eye irritant. Although ineffective, this event marked the first experimental use of a form of gas in the war under battle conditions. (The Allies did not learn of this experiment until after the Armistice).

┼┼ Canals

┼┼┼ Railways

♀♀ Wood

© Arthur Banks 1973

74

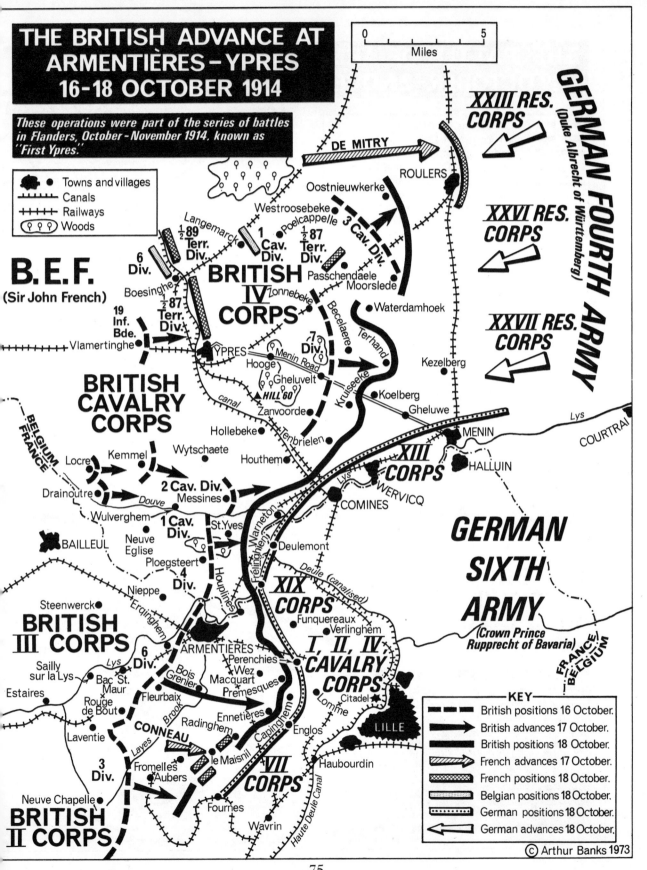

THE BRITISH ADVANCE AT ARMENTIÈRES – YPRES 16-18 OCTOBER 1914

These operations were part of the series of battles in Flanders, October – November 1914, known as "First Ypres."

0 ___ 5
Miles

Key
- Towns and villages
- Canals
- Railways
- Woods

B.E.F.
(Sir John French)

GERMAN FOURTH ARMY (Duke Albrecht of Württemberg)

XXIII RES. CORPS

XXVI RES. CORPS

XXVII RES. CORPS

DE MITRY

ROULERS

Oostnieuwkerke

Westroosebeke

Poelcappelle

3 Cav. Div.

Langemarck

½ 89 Terr. Div.

1 Cav. Div.

½ 87 Terr. Div.

6 Div.

Passchendaele

Moorslede

BRITISH IV CORPS

Boesinghe

½ 87 Terr. Div.

Zonnebeke

Becelaere

Waterdamhoek

Terhand

19 Inf. Bde.

Vlamertinghe

YPRES

Menin Road

7 Div.

Hooge

Gheluvelt

Kruiseeke

Kezelberg

HILL 60

Zanvoorde

Koelberg

Gheluwe

BRITISH CAVALRY CORPS

canal

Hollebeke

Tenbrielen

MENIN

Lys

COURTRAI

BELGIUM FRANCE

Locre

Kemmel

Wytschaete

Houthem

XIII CORPS

HALLUIN

Drainoutre

2 Cav. Div.

Messines

Douve

WERVICQ

Lys

COMINES

GERMAN SIXTH ARMY
(Crown Prince Rupprecht of Bavaria)

Wulverghem

1 Cav. Div.

St. Yves

Warneton

Deulemont

BAILLEUL

Neuve Eglise

Ploegsteert

4 Div.

Houplines

Frelinghien

Deule (canalised)

Nieppe

XIX CORPS

Funquereaux

Verlinghem

Steenwerck

BRITISH III CORPS

Erquinghem

6 Div.

Lys

ARMENTIÈRES

Perenchies

Wez

Macquart

Premesques

T, II, IV, CAVALRY CORPS

Sailly sur la Lys

Bois Grenier

Fleurbaix

Brook

Radinghem

Ennetières

Capinghem

Englos

Lomme

Citadel

FRANCE BELGIUM

Bac St. Maur

Estaires

Rouge de Bout

CONNEAU

Laventie

Layes

le Maisnil

Fromelles

Aubers

3 Div.

VII CORPS

Fournes

Haubourdin

LILLE

Neuve Chapelle

BRITISH II CORPS

Wavrin

Haute Deule Canal

KEY
- — — British positions 16 October.
- ——▶ British advances 17 October.
- ━━━ British positions 18 October.
- ▨▶ French advances 17 October.
- ▦ French positions 18 October.
- ▒ Belgian positions 18 October.
- ▪▪▪ German positions 18 October.
- ◀━━ German advances 18 October.

© Arthur Banks 1973

75

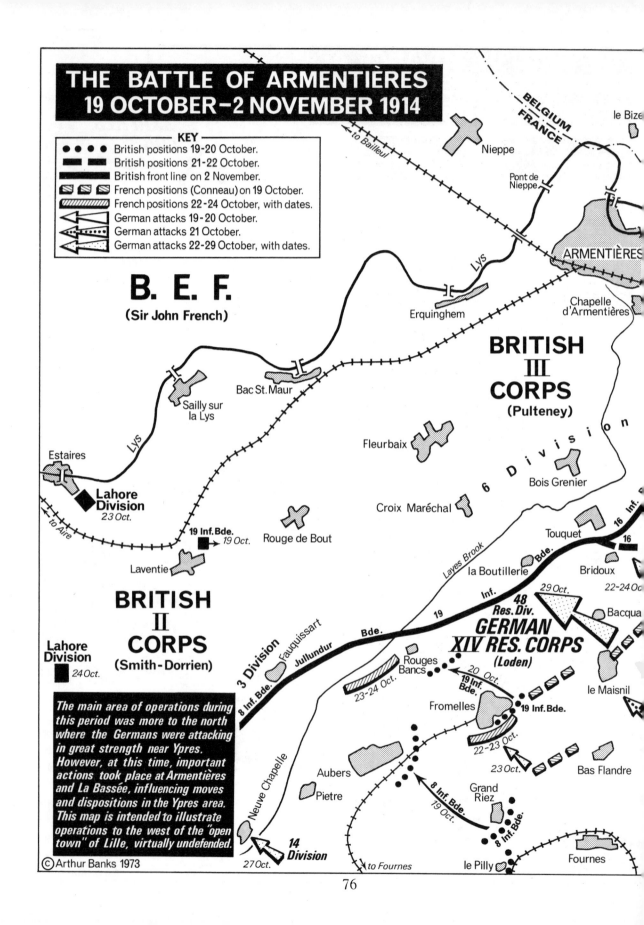

THE BATTLE OF ARMENTIÈRES
19 OCTOBER–2 NOVEMBER 1914

KEY
- •••• British positions 19-20 October.
- British positions 21-22 October.
- British front line on 2 November.
- French positions (Conneau) on 19 October.
- French positions 22-24 October, with dates.
- German attacks 19-20 October.
- German attacks 21 October.
- German attacks 22-29 October, with dates.

B. E. F.
(Sir John French)

BELGIUM
FRANCE

to Bailleul

le Bize

Nieppe

Pont de Nieppe

ARMENTIÈRES

Lys

Chapelle d'Armentières

Erquinghem

BRITISH III CORPS
(Pulteney)

Bac St.Maur

Sailly sur la Lys

Fleurbaix

6 Division

Bois Grenier

Estaires

Lys

Lahore Division
23 Oct.

to Aire

Croix Maréchal

Touquet

16 Inf. Bde.

16

19 Inf. Bde.
19 Oct.

Rouge de Bout

Laventie

la Boutillerie

Bridoux

22-24 Oc

Lahore Division
24 Oct.

BRITISH II CORPS
(Smith-Dorrien)

3 Division

8 Inf. Bde.

Fauquissart

Jullundur

Bde.

Inf.

19

48 Res. Div.

29 Oct.

GERMAN XIV RES. CORPS
(Loden)

Bacqua

le Maisnil

Rouges Bancs

20 Oct.

19 Inf. Bde.

19 Inf. Bde.

Fromelles

23-24 Oct.

22-23 Oct.

23 Oct.

Bas Flandre

The main area of operations during this period was more to the north where the Germans were attacking in great strength near Ypres. However, at this time, important actions took place at Armentières and La Bassée, influencing moves and dispositions in the Ypres area. This map is intended to illustrate operations to the west of the "open town" of Lille, virtually undefended.

Neuve Chapelle

Aubers

Pietre

8 Inf. Bde.
19 Oct.

Grand Riez

8 Inf. Bde.

14 Division
27 Oct.

to Fournes

le Pilly

Fournes

© Arthur Banks 1973

76

Comines/Menin

40 Division

Frélinghien

GERMAN XIX CORPS (Laffert)

Lys

le Ruage

Houplines
4 Division

Fort de Bondues

Deule (canalised)

to Comines

0   1   2
Miles

These operations formed part of the series of battles fought in Flanders in 1914 known as "First Ypres."

Fort Carnot

Funquereau

Epinette

Verlinghem

24 Division

Inf. Bde. taken over by 4 Div. 23-24 Oct.

Rue du Bois

17 Inf. Bde.

20 Oct.
17 Inf. Bde.

Perenchies

Wez Macquart

SENARMONT BATTERY

Premesques

22-24 Oct.

18 Inf. Bde.

Paradis
20 Oct.

18 Inf. Bde.

Mont de Premesques

Lomme

Capinghem

22-24 Oct.
le Touquet

le Quesne

Ennetières

25 Reserve Division

22-24 Oct.

la Vallée

18 Inf. Bde.

Citadel

Fort d'Englos

Englos

GERMAN XIII CORPS (Fabeck)

Inf. Bde.

ghem

18 Inf. Bde.

26 Division

16 Inf. Bde.

Escobecques

LILLE
Occupied by Germans on 12 October

Division

Erquinghem le Sec

Loos

Beaucamps

GERMAN SIXTH ARMY

Haubourdin

(Crown Prince Rupprecht of Bavaria)

GERMAN VII CORPS (Claer)

Haute Deule Canal

to La Bassée

🏘 Towns, villages, hamlets   ⚏ Bridges   ┿┿┿ Railways   ┷┷┷ Canals

77

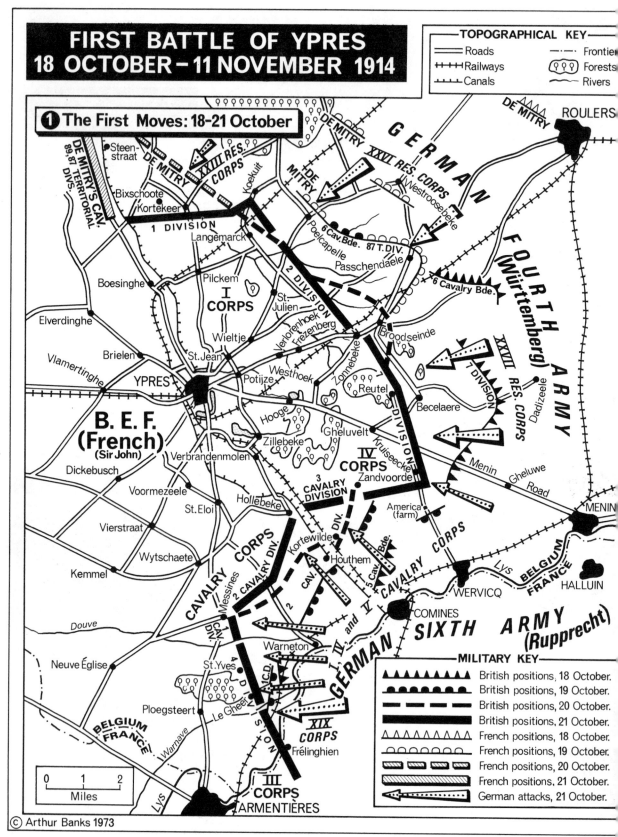

FIRST BATTLE OF YPRES
18 OCTOBER – 11 NOVEMBER 1914

TOPOGRAPHICAL KEY
Roads
Railways
Canals
Frontier
Forests
Rivers

❶ The First Moves: 18-21 October

DE MITRY'S CAV. 89,87 TERRITORIAL DIVS.

Steenstraat

DE MITRY

XXIII RES. CORPS

Koekuit

DE MITRY

ROULERS

G E R M A N

XXVI RES. CORPS

Westroosebeke

Bixschoote

Kortekeer

1 DIVISION

Langemarck

6 Cav. Bde.

Poelcapelle

87 T. DIV.

Passchendaele

F O U R T H

Boesinghe

Pilckem

I CORPS

St. Julien

2 DIVISION

6 Cavalry Bde.

Elverdinghe

Wieltje

Verlorenhoek

Frezenberg

Broodseinde

A R M Y

(Württemberg)

Brielen

St. Jean

Westhoek

Zonnebeke

XXVII RES. CORPS

Vlamertinghe

Potijze

Reutel

7 DIVISION

Dadizeele

YPRES

Hooge

Gheluvelt

Becelaere

B. E. F.
(French)
(Sir John)

Zillebeke

IV CORPS

Kruiseecke

Verbrandenmolen

3 CAVALRY DIVISION

Zandvoorde

Menin

Gheluwe

Road

MENIN

Dickebusch

Voormezeele

Hollebeke

America (farm)

St. Eloi

Kortewilde

DIV.

CAVALRY CORPS

Vierstraat

CAVALRY CORPS

CAV.

Houthem

5 Cav. Bde.

Lys

BELGIUM FRANCE

HALLUIN

Wytschaete

2 CAVALRY DIV.

2

WERVICQ

Kemmel

Messines

CAV. DIV.

IV and V

COMINES

Douve

SIXTH

A R M Y

Warneton

GERMAN

(Rupprecht)

Neuve Église

St. Yves

4 DIV.

CD

MILITARY KEY

BELGIUM FRANCE

Ploegsteert

Le Gheer

Warnave

XIX CORPS

Frélinghien

British positions, 18 October.
British positions, 19 October.
British positions, 20 October.
British positions, 21 October.
French positions, 18 October.
French positions, 19 October.
French positions, 20 October.
French positions, 21 October.
German attacks, 21 October.

0   1   2
Miles

LYS

III CORPS

ARMENTIÈRES

© Arthur Banks 1973

78

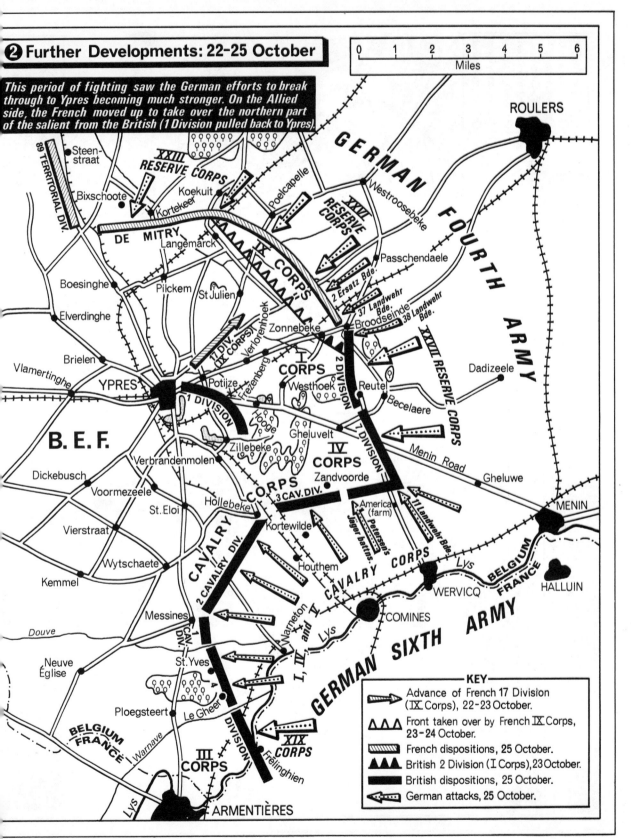

② Further Developments: 22-25 October

This period of fighting saw the German efforts to break through to Ypres becoming much stronger. On the Allied side, the French moved up to take over the northern part of the salient from the British (1 Division pulled back to Ypres).

0 1 2 3 4 5 6
Miles

ROULERS

GERMAN FOURTH ARMY

Steen-straat

89 TERRITORIAL DIV.

XXIII RESERVE CORPS

Koekuit

Poelcapelle

Westroosebeke

Bixschoote

Kortekeer

DE MITRY

Langemarck

IX CORPS

XXVI RESERVE CORPS

Passchendaele

Boesinghe

Pilckem

St Julien

2 Ersatz Bde.

37 Landwehr Bde.

Broodseinde

38 Landwehr Bde.

Elverdinghe

Zonnebeke

Brielen

17 DIV. IX CORPS

Verlorenhoek

I CORPS

2 DIVISION

Dadizeele

Vlamertinghe

Frezenberg

XXVII RESERVE CORPS

Reutel

Becelaere

YPRES

Potijze

1 DIVISION

Westhoek

Hooge

7 DIVISION

B. E. F.

Zillebeke

Gheluvelt

IV CORPS

Menin Road

Dickebusch

Verbrandenmolen

Zandvoorde

Gheluwe

Voormezeele

3 CAV. DIV.

American (farm)

11 Landwehr Bde.

MENIN

St. Eloi

Hollebeke

CORPS

Petersen's Jäger batts.

Vierstraat

Kortewilde

CAVALRY CORPS

Lys

Wytschaete

CAVALRY DIV.

Houthem

WERVICQ

BELGIUM FRANCE

HALLUIN

Kemmel

2 CAVALRY DIV.

Narneton and I Lys

COMINES

Messines

I, IV, and V

GERMAN SIXTH ARMY

Douve

1 CAV. DIV.

Neuve Église

St. Yves

Ploegsteert

Le Gheer

KEY

BELGIUM FRANCE

Warnave

III CORPS

4 DIVISION

XIX CORPS

Frélinghien

Lys

ARMENTIÈRES

Advance of French 17 Division (IX Corps), 22-23 October.	
Front taken over by French IX Corps, 23-24 October.	
French dispositions, 25 October.	
British 2 Division (I Corps), 23 October.	
British dispositions, 25 October.	
German attacks, 25 October.	

79

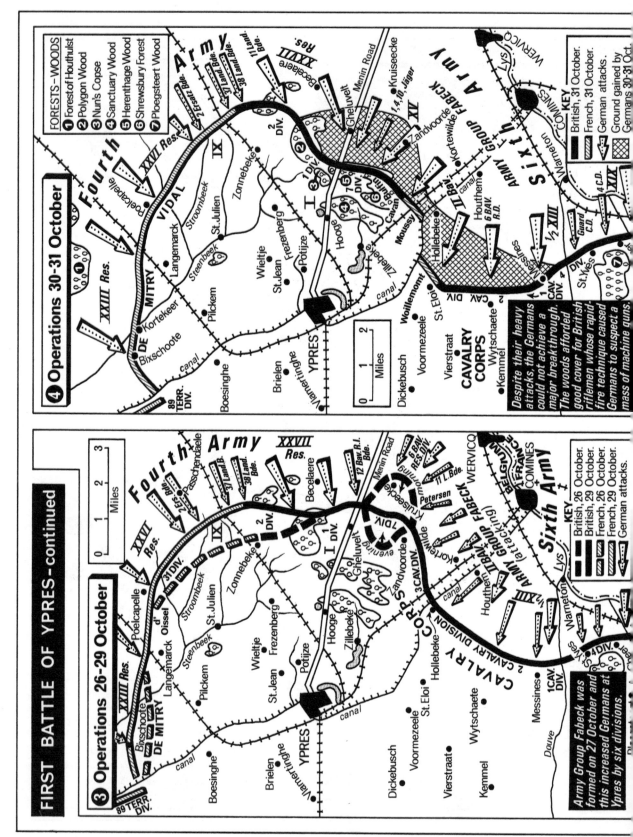

FIRST BATTLE OF YPRES – continued

④ Operations 30-31 October

FORESTS – WOODS
1. Forest of Houthulst
2. Polygon Wood
3. Nun's Copse
4. Sanctuary Wood
5. Herenthage Wood
6. Shrewsbury Forest
7. Ploegsteert Wood

KEY
British, 31 October.
French, 31 October.
German attacks.
Ground gained by
Germans 30-31 Oct.

Despite their heavy attacks, the Germans could not achieve a major breakthrough. The woods afforded good cover for British riflemen whose rapid-fire technique caused Germans to suspect a mass of machine guns.

Fourth Army
Fifth Res.
XXVII Res.
2 Ersatz Bde.
37 Land. Bde.
38 Land. Bde.
11 Land. Bde.
XXVI Res.
Becelaere
Menin Road
Kruiseecke
1,4,10. Jäger
XV
Gheluvelt
Zandvoorde
Kortewilde
XXIII Res.
VIDAL
DE MITRY
Poelcapelle
Langemarck
Steenbeek
Stroombeek
Zonnebeek
St. Julien
Kortekeer
DE
Bixschoote
canal
Pilckem
Wieltje
St. Jean
Frezenberg
Potijze
Hooge
Zillebeke
canal
IX
I DIV.
2 DIV.
7 DIV.
Cavan
II Bav.
6 BAV. R.D.
Houthem
ARMY GROUP FABECK
Hollebeke
Messines
Moussy
Woillemont
St. Eloi
Sixth Army
WERVICQ
COMINES
Lys
Warneton
St. Yves
Guard C.D.
4 C.D.
XIX
1 CAV. DIV.
Div.
2 CAV. DIV.
CAVALRY CORPS
Dickebusch
Voormezeele
Vierstraat
Wytschaete
Kemmel
YPRES
Boesinghe
Brielen
Vlamertinghe
89 TERR. DIV.

Miles: 0 1 2

③ Operations 26-29 October

KEY
British, 26 October.
British, 29 October.
French, 26 October.
French, 29 October.
German attacks.

Army Group Fabeck was formed on 27 October and this increased Germans at Ypres by six divisions.

Fourth Army
XXVII Res.
2 Ers. Bde.
37 Land. Bde.
38 Land. Bde.
12 Bav. R.I. Bde.
6 BAV. RES. DIV.
11 Bde.
Petersen
FABECK
WERVICQ
COMINES
BELGIUM
FRANCE
Sixth Army
XXIII Res.
Passchendaele
Becelaere
Menin Road
Kruiseecke
XXVI Res.
DE MITRY
d' Oissel
Poelcapelle
Langemarck
31 DIV.
Stroombeek
Steenbeek
Zonnebeke
St. Julien
Bisschoote
IX
2 DIV.
1 DIV.
Gheluvelt
7 DIV.
Kortewilde
Zandvoorde
II Bav. Group (King)
III ARMY attacking (evening)
3 CAV. DIV.
CAVALRY CORPS
2 CAVALRY DIVISION
Houthem
Hollebeke
canal
XIII
1/2 XIII
Warneton
St. Yves
1 CAV. DIV.
4 DIV.
Messines
Lys
Douve
Pilckem
Wieltje
St. Jean
Frezenberg
Potijze
Hooge
Zillebeke
canal
YPRES
Dickebusch
Voormezeele
Vierstraat
St. Eloi
Wytschaete
Kemmel
Boesinghe
Brielen
Vlamertinghe
89 TERR. DIV.

Miles: 0 1 2 3

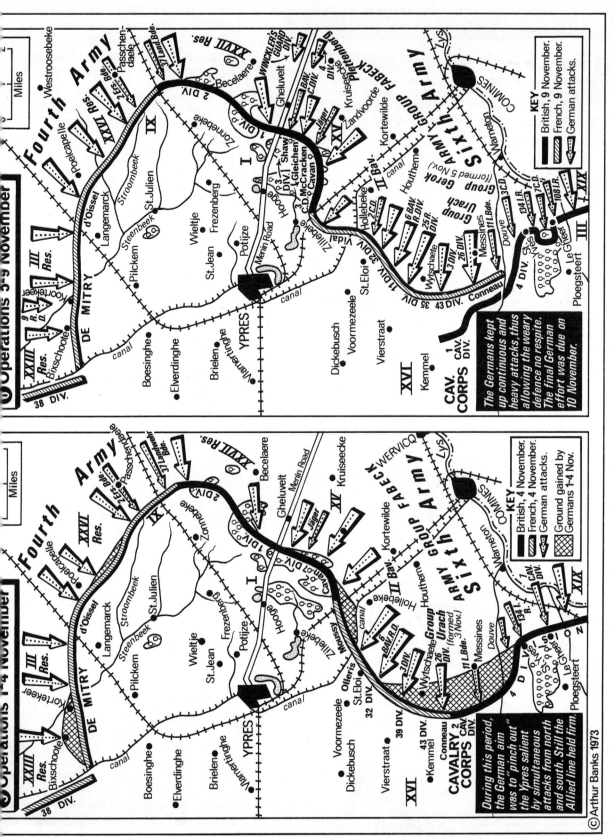

Operations 5-9 November (top map)

Fourth Army

Miles

37 Land.Bde.
Westroosebeke
Passchen-daele
2EF.Bde.
XXVII Res.
Becelaere
Poelcapelle
XXII Res.
d'Oissel
Langemarck
St.Julien
Stroombeek
Zonnebeke
2 DIV.
Gheluvelt
WINCKLER'S GUARD DIV.
BAV. C.D.
DIV.
Kruiseecke
Plettenberg
III Res.
Steenbeek
Pilckem
Frezenberg
Wieltje
St.Jean
Potijze
Hooge
DIV. Shaw
Gleichen
C.D. McCracken
Cavan
Jäger
XV
Zandvoorde
Kortewilde
FABECK
Kortekeer
9 R.D.
R.D.
Bixschoote
XXIII Res.
Boesinghe
Elverdinghe
Brielen
Vlamertinghe
canal
YPRES
canal
DE MITRY
I
Zillebeke
St.Eloi
Voormezeele
Dickebusch
Vierstraat
Kemmel
XVI
CAV. CORPS
1 CAV. DIV.
II Bav.
Hollebeke
2 C.D.
Vidal
6 Bav. R.DIV.
25 R. DIV.
Wytschaete
30 DIV.
Messines
26 DIV.
43 DIV.
Conneau
Houthem
Warneton
COMINES
Group Gerok (formed 5 Nov.)
Group Urach
Lys
11 L.Bde.
134 I.R.
7 C.D.
108 I.R.
Le Gheer
Ploegsteert
Douve
III
XIX
4 DIV.
Sixth Army
GROUP FABECK
38 DIV.

KEY
British, 9 November.
French, 9 November.
German attacks.

The Germans kept up continuous and heavy attacks, thus allowing the weary defence no respite. The final German effort was due on 10 November.

Operations 1-4 November (bottom map)

Fourth Army

Miles

37 Land.Bde.
Langemarck Bde.
Passchendaele
2EF.Bde.
XXVII Res.
Becelaere
Poelcapelle
XXII Res.
d'Oissel
Langemarck
St.Julien
Stroombeek
Zonnebeke
2 DIV.
Gheluvelt
Menin Road
Kruiseecke
III Res.
Steenbeek
Pilckem
Frezenberg
Wieltje
St.Jean
Potijze
Hooge
1 DIV.
Cavan
Jäger
XV
Kortewilde
FABECK
Kortekeer
XXIII Res.
Bixschoote
Boesinghe
Elverdinghe
Brielen
Vlamertinghe
canal
YPRES
canal
DE MITRY
32 DIV.
I
Zillebeke
Ollezis
St.Eloi
Voormezeele
Dickebusch
Vierstraat
39 DIV.
43 DIV.
Kemmel
XVI
CAVALRY CORPS
2 CAV. DIV.
Conneau
II Bav.
Hollebeke
6 Bav. R.D.
Group Urach (formed 3 Nov.)
Wytschaete
30 DIV.
26 DIV.
11 L.Bde.
Messines
Houthem
Warneton
COMINES
Sixth Army
GROUP FABECK
WERVICQ
Lys
134 I.R.
7 CAV. DIV.
Le Gheer
Ploegsteert
Douve
4 DIV.
III
XIX
38 DIV.

KEY
British, 4 November.
French, 4 November.
German attacks.
Ground gained by Germans 1-4 Nov.

During this period, the German aim was to "pinch out" the Ypres salient by simultaneous attacks from north and south. Still the Allied line held firm.

© Arthur Banks 1973

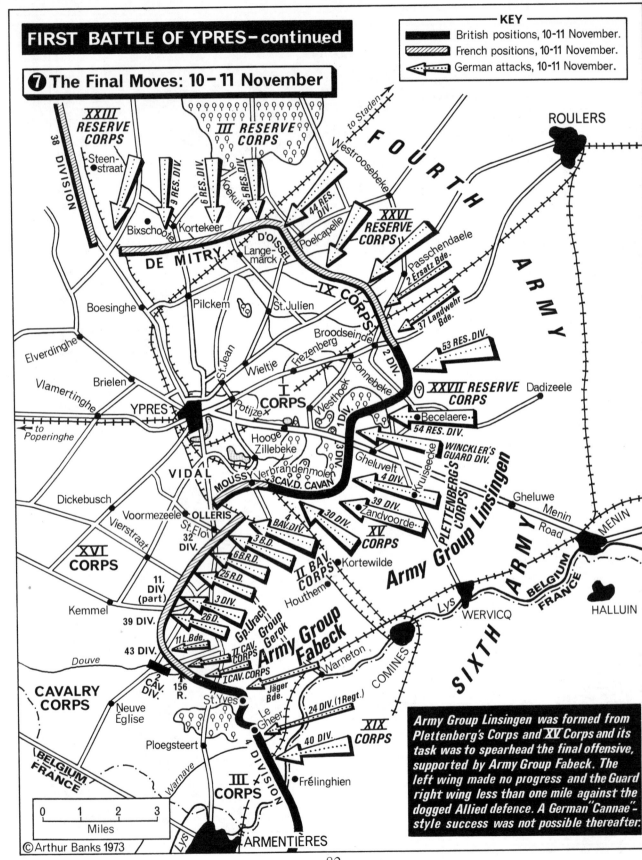

FIRST BATTLE OF YPRES – continued

7 The Final Moves: 10–11 November

ROULERS

XXIII RESERVE CORPS

38 DIVISION

Steen-straat

III RESERVE CORPS

9 RES. DIV.

6 RES. DIV.

5 RES. DIV.

Koekuit

44 RES. DIV.

Bixschoote   Kortekeer

D'OISSEL

XXVI RESERVE CORPS

to Staden

Westroosebeke

FOURTH ARMY

DE MITRY

Langemarck

Poelcapelle

Passchendaele

2 Ersatz Bde.

Boesinghe

Pilckem

St.Julien

IX CORPS

Broodseinde

37 Landwehr Bde.

Elverdinghe

St.Jean

Wieltje

Frezenberg

Zonnebeke

2 DIV.

53 RES. DIV.

Vlamertinghe

Brielen

to Poperinghe

YPRES

Potize

I CORPS

Westhoek

1 DIV.

XXVII RESERVE CORPS

Dadizeele

Becelaere

54 RES. DIV.

Hooge
Zillebeke

3 DIV.

Gheluvelt

Kruiseecke

WINCKLER'S GUARD DIV.

VIDAL

Dickebusch

Verbrandenmolen

MOUSSY 3 CAV.D. CAVAN.

4 DIV.

39 DIV.

Zandvoorde

PLETTENBERG'S CORPS

Gheluwe

Menin Road

MENIN

Voormezeele   OLLERIS

Vierstraat

St.Eloi

32 DIV.

4 BAV.DIV.

3 B.D.

30 DIV.

XV CORPS

Army Group Linsingen

XVI CORPS

11. DIV. (part)

6 B.R.D.

25 R.D.

II BAV. CORPS

Kortewilde

Army Group Fabeck

Lys

BELGIUM
FRANCE

WERVICQ

HALLUIN

Kemmel

39 DIV.

3 DIV.

26 D.

Houthem

Douve

43 DIV.

11 L.Bde.

Gp. Urach

Group Gerok

II CAV. CORPS

I CAV. CORPS

Warneton

COMINES

SIXTH ARMY

CAVALRY CORPS

2 CAV. DIV.

156 R.

St.Yves

Jäger Bde.

24 DIV.(1 Regt.)

Neuve Église

Le Gheer

40 DIV.

XIX CORPS

Ploegsteert

4 DIVISION

BELGIUM
FRANCE

Warnave

Frélinghien

III CORPS

Lys

ARMENTIÈRES

© Arthur Banks 1973

0 1 2 3
Miles

> Army Group Linsingen was formed from Plettenberg's Corps and XV Corps and its task was to spearhead the final offensive, supported by Army Group Fabeck. The left wing made no progress and the Guard right wing less than one mile against the dogged Allied defence. A German "Cannae"-style success was not possible thereafter.

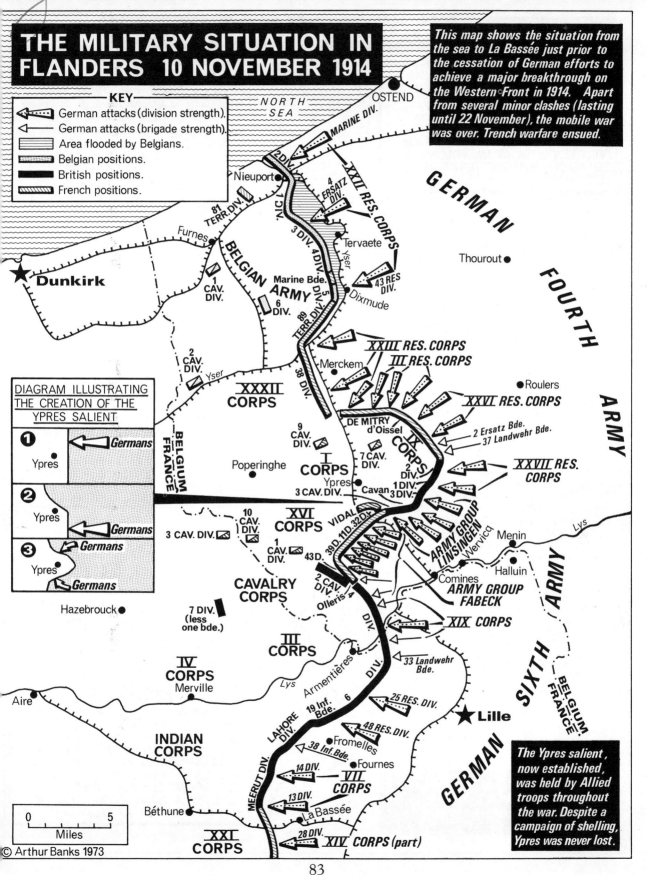

THE MILITARY SITUATION IN FLANDERS 10 NOVEMBER 1914

KEY
- German attacks (division strength).
- German attacks (brigade strength).
- Area flooded by Belgians.
- Belgian positions.
- British positions.
- French positions.

This map shows the situation from the sea to La Bassée just prior to the cessation of German efforts to achieve a major breakthrough on the Western Front in 1914. Apart from several minor clashes (lasting until 22 November), the mobile war was over. Trench warfare ensued.

NORTH SEA

OSTEND

MARINE DIV.

GERMAN

FOURTH ARMY

2 DIV.

Nieuport

4 ERSATZ DIV.

XXII RES. CORPS

81 TERR. DIV.

Furnes

3 DIV. 4 DIV.

Tervaete

Yser

Thourout

BELGIAN ARMY

Marine Bde.

Dixmude

43 RES. DIV.

Dunkirk

1 CAV. DIV.

6 DIV.

5

89 TERR. DIV.

Merckem

XXIII RES. CORPS

III RES. CORPS

Roulers

2 CAV. DIV.

Yser

38 DIV.

XXXII CORPS

DE MITRY d'Oissel

XXVI RES. CORPS

IX CORPS

2 Ersatz Bde.
37 Landwehr Bde.

DIAGRAM ILLUSTRATING THE CREATION OF THE YPRES SALIENT

1 Ypres — Germans

BELGIUM FRANCE

9 CAV. DIV.

I CORPS

Poperinghe

7 CAV. DIV.

Ypres

3 CAV. DIV.

Cavan

2 DIV.
1 DIV.
3 DIV.

XXVII RES. CORPS

2 Ypres — Germans

3 Ypres — Germans

10 CAV. DIV.

XVI CORPS

VIDAL

39 D. 11 D. 32 D.

Menin

Lys

1 CAV. DIV.

43 D.

ARMY GROUP LINSINGEN

Wervicq

Halluin

Hazebrouck

CAVALRY CORPS

2 CAV. DIV.

Olleris

Comines

ARMY GROUP FABECK

7 DIV. (less one bde.)

4 DIV.

XIX CORPS

III CORPS

Armentières

33 Landwehr Bde.

IV CORPS
Merville

Lys

DIV.

LAHORE DIV.

19 Inf. Bde.

6

25 RES. DIV.

Lille

GERMAN SIXTH ARMY

BELGIUM FRANCE

Aire

INDIAN CORPS

48 RES. DIV.

Fromelles

MEERUT DIV.

38 Inf. Bde.

Fournes

14 DIV.

VII CORPS

Béthune

13 DIV.

La Bassée

28 DIV.

XIV CORPS (part)

The Ypres salient, now established, was held by Allied troops throughout the war. Despite a campaign of shelling, Ypres was never lost.

XXI CORPS

0 _____ 5
Miles

© Arthur Banks 1973

83

SMALL DETONATORS: BIG EXPLOSIONS!

0 · 200
Miles

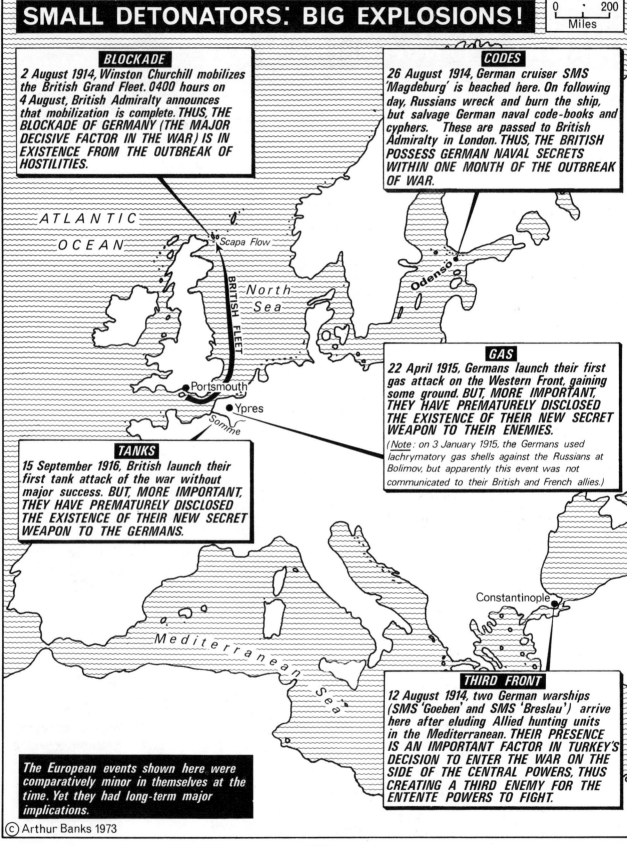

BLOCKADE
2 August 1914, Winston Churchill mobilizes the British Grand Fleet. 0400 hours on 4 August, British Admiralty announces that mobilization is complete. THUS, THE BLOCKADE OF GERMANY (THE MAJOR DECISIVE FACTOR IN THE WAR) IS IN EXISTENCE FROM THE OUTBREAK OF HOSTILITIES.

CODES
26 August 1914, German cruiser SMS 'Magdeburg' is beached here. On following day, Russians wreck and burn the ship, but salvage German naval code-books and cyphers. These are passed to British Admiralty in London. THUS, THE BRITISH POSSESS GERMAN NAVAL SECRETS WITHIN ONE MONTH OF THE OUTBREAK OF WAR.

GAS
22 April 1915, Germans launch their first gas attack on the Western Front, gaining some ground. BUT, MORE IMPORTANT, THEY HAVE PREMATURELY DISCLOSED THE EXISTENCE OF THEIR NEW SECRET WEAPON TO THEIR ENEMIES.
(Note: on 3 January 1915, the Germans used lachrymatory gas shells against the Russians at Bolimov, but apparently this event was not communicated to their British and French allies.)

TANKS
15 September 1916, British launch their first tank attack of the war without major success. BUT, MORE IMPORTANT, THEY HAVE PREMATURELY DISCLOSED THE EXISTENCE OF THEIR NEW SECRET WEAPON TO THE GERMANS.

THIRD FRONT
12 August 1914, two German warships (SMS 'Goeben' and SMS 'Breslau') arrive here after eluding Allied hunting units in the Mediterranean. THEIR PRESENCE IS AN IMPORTANT FACTOR IN TURKEY'S DECISION TO ENTER THE WAR ON THE SIDE OF THE CENTRAL POWERS, THUS CREATING A THIRD ENEMY FOR THE ENTENTE POWERS TO FIGHT.

The European events shown here, were comparatively minor in themselves at the time. Yet they had long-term major implications.

ATLANTIC OCEAN

North Sea

BRITISH FLEET

Scapa Flow

Odenso

Portsmouth

Ypres

Somme

Mediterranean Sea

Constantinople

© Arthur Banks 1973

84

THE WAR ON THE EASTERN FRONT

There were four other theatres of war in Europe during the autumn of 1914. Eight hundred miles to the east of the Belgian cockpit, Russian and German armies clashed in the marchlands of East Prussia while to their south other forces manoeuvred for position in the great plains of the Vistulan Basin. The principal Austrian army was concentrated at the outbreak of war in Galicia, with the well-forested range of the Carpathians in its rear, an admirable position for withstanding any Russian onslaught (compare pages 24 and 32). Farther south still, nearly four hundred miles across the Austro-Hungarian empire, another quarter of a million soldiers from Franz Josef's multinational empire were assigned the duty of 'punishing' Serbia. The commander of this Balkan Army was the former Governor of Bosnia, General Potiorek, who had been sitting in front of Archduke Franz Ferdinand on that fateful day in Sarajevo. But Potiorek, like all other Austro-Hungarian commanders, was subordinate to General Conrad von Hötzendorf, the Austrian Chief of Staff, who established his first headquarters in the reputedly impregnable Galician fortress town of Przemysl.

Although Conrad had hoped to cut off the Russians in Poland by joint Austro-German operations uniting the commands in East Prussia and Galicia, there was in fact little co-ordination between the various eastern European armies. The first shots in the whole war were fired by two monitors of the Austro-Hungarian Danube flotilla, which bombarded Belgrade on 29 July, five days before the opening of hostilities in western Europe. But thereafter all was peaceful until the middle of the second week in August when Conrad sent his First and Fourth armies northward into Russian Poland, while the first units of the Russian 1st Army invaded East Prussia, and Potiorek's troops crossed the river Sava and seized the Serbian town of Sabac.

The most dramatic of these undertakings was the Russian incursion towards the historic Prussian coronation city, Königsberg, some ninety miles from the frontier. The Schlieffen Plan had anticipated a German holding operation against Russia for some six or seven weeks, before the full weight of German arms was shifted to the West. On paper, there was no reason for German alarm, even though the invaders had a numerical superiority of more than four to one. But on 20 August three German army corps clashed with Rennenkampf's Russian First Army at Gumbinnen and did not distinguish themselves (pages 88–89). The German commander, Prittwitz, was worried by news that the Russian Second Army, under Samsonov, was threatening his southern flank, and sent alarming messages to Moltke's headquarters in the West. The situation was saved by one of Prittwitz's staff officers, Lieutenant-Colonel Max von Hoffmann, who knew there was a deep personal vendetta between Samsonov and Rennenkampf. Hoffmann proposed that the Germans should concentrate against Samsonov, leaving the route towards Königsberg apparently open for Rennenkampf (who would not resist this bait simply to aid the rival he so detested). Thus began the deployment for the battle of Tannenberg, three days of agony for the Russians, in which the Second Army was destroyed and its commander shot himself in despair.

Tannenberg, like the Marne, became a legendary victory. The discovery of a Russian staff officer's body on the battlefield, with detailed military directives in his pocket, helped the Germans considerably; and so did the incredible folly of the three Russian head-quarters in sending unciphered operations orders by wireless, with the Germans able to note down every word (see page 98). The ease of their victory made the Germans despise their Russian opponents and they therefore suffered heavy casualties in rash frontal assaults on Rennenkampf's army, which was caught at the Masurian Lakes in the first week of September. But the Masurian Lakes completed the triumph of Tannenberg: the Russians, after nibbling at the edge of East Prussia for twenty-eight days, were thrown back across the frontier, broken and demoralised. No Russian army penetrated German territory again until 1945.

The twin victories enabled the German people to find a heroic father-figure to idolise for the remainder of the War and beyond. Paul von Hindenburg was six weeks short of his sixty-seventh birthday when, on 22 August, he was summoned from obscure retirement to replace Prittwitz on the Eastern Front. Hindenburg had been decorated for bravery both in the 1866 war with Austria and the 1870 war with France and he had witnessed the proclamation of the German Empire at Versailles in 1871. No one could describe him as a strategic genius. His greatest asset was his rocklike imperturbability. The brain behind his triumphs belonged to his deputy, Ludendorff, who had already distinguished himself in reducing the Liége forts (page 41); and, at least on the Eastern Front, Ludendorff owed much to Hoffmann, who understood the Russian military mind. But, in Germany, sentiment and propaganda combined to turn Hindenburg into a colossus of victory.

Austria-Hungary discovered no such idol. Conrad's decision to send the First and Fourth armies northwards from Galicia was based upon a false assumption. He thought that the Russian commander-in-chief, Grand Duke Nicholas, had ordered the commander of the South-Western Army Group, General Ivanov, to concentrate around Lublin. In reality the Russians were farther south-east, threatening Lemberg (Lvov) where Ivanov had, in his turn, wrongly assumed the main Austrian forces to be. There was, in consequence, a curious week of shadow-boxing before Conrad turned to meet the challenge to his flank from Ivanov (see pages 100–101). Conrad made the mistake of opening up a gap in the north which was filled by the Russian Fifth Army. Fearing he might be encircled, Conrad ordered a general retreat on 11 September, and found it impossible to stabilise the Front until the Russians had penetrated over a hundred miles, reaching the Carpathian passes into Hungary. The Austrians thus sustained a humiliating defeat, with the Russians capturing two provincial capitals, Lemberg (the fourth largest city in Austria-Hungary) and Czernowitz, as well as beseiging Przemsyl. The Slav contingents in the Austro-Hungarian Army (particularly the Czechs) had little heart for a war against 'Mother Russia', but large-scale desertions did not begin until the spring of 1915, and it is clear that the disaster reflects as much on Conrad and his staff as on the quality of the troops they commanded. Eventually the Austrians were saved by an offensive mounted by Hindenburg in central Poland and threatening Warsaw. An abortive Russian counter-offensive in Poland at the end of October threatened Silesia but brought down a massive German response from the north, when Mackensen's Ninth Army fell on the Russians at Lodz and as winter set in, destroyed all prospects of avenging Tannenberg. Though the Russians had triumphed in Galicia, the first four months of fighting against the Germans had proved disastrous and left the Russian artillery desperately short of shells.

Yet the strangest development of the war was in Serbia. For Putnik, the Serbian commander-in-chief, had successfully repelled Potiorek's first incursion across the river Sava, and nipped another offensive (across the river Drina) in the bud. At the end of November Potiorek tried again and captured Belgrade on 2 December, sweeping the Serbs back into the mountain heart of the Kingdom. Yet, though short of men and munitions, the Serbs made a surprise counter-attack and within eleven days had recovered their capital. 'On the whole territory of the Serbian Government there remains not one free enemy soldier', ran a proud communiqué on 15 December. Austria's humiliation was complete. Small wonder the German High Command began privately to wonder if they were allied to a living Empire or a corpse.

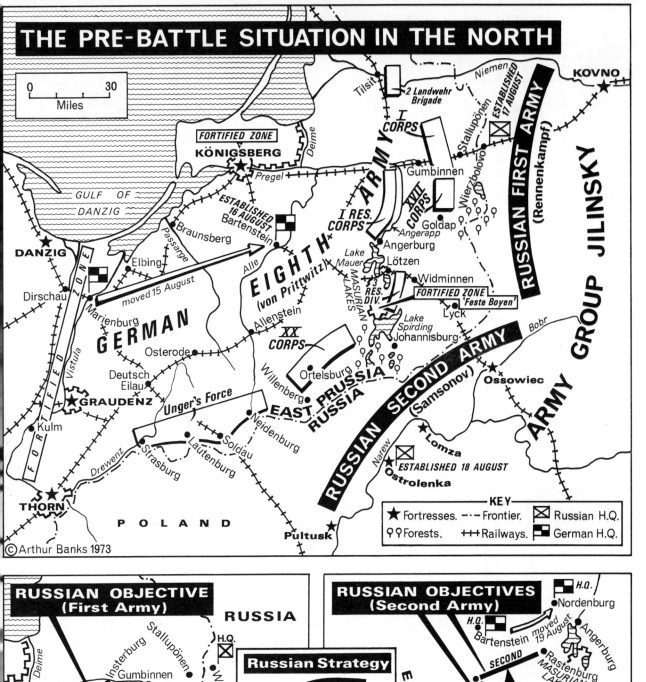

THE PRE-BATTLE SITUATION IN THE NORTH

0 ——— 30
Miles

KOVNO

Niemen

Tilsit

2 Landwehr Brigade

I CORPS

ESTABLISHED 17 AUGUST

Stallupönen

RUSSIAN FIRST ARMY
(Rennenkampf)

FORTIFIED ZONE
KÖNIGSBERG

Deime

Pregel

GULF OF DANZIG

ESTABLISHED 16 AUGUST
Bartenstein

EIGHTH

I RES. CORPS

XVII CORPS

Gumbinnen

Wierzbolovo

Goldap

Angerapp

Angerburg

Lötzen

Widminnen

Braunsberg

Passarge

DANZIG

Elbing

Alle

ARMY

(von Prittwitz)

Lake Mauer

3 RES. DIV.

FORTIFIED ZONE
'Feste Boyen'

Lyck

ARMY GROUP JILINSKY

Dirschau

moved 15 August

Marienburg

GERMAN

Allenstein

XX CORPS

Lake Spirding

Johannisburg

Bobr

Osterode

Deutsch Eilau

GRAUDENZ

Vistula

Unger's Force

Willenberg

Ortelsburg

EAST
PRUSSIA

RUSSIA

RUSSIAN SECOND ARMY
(Samsonov)

Ossowiec

Kulm

Strasburg

Lautenburg

Soldau

Neidenburg

Drewenz

Narew

Lomza

ESTABLISHED 18 AUGUST

Ostrolenka

THORN

P O L A N D

Pultusk

© Arthur Banks 1973

KEY
★ Fortresses.   ·–·– Frontier.   ⊠ Russian H.Q.
ꝯꝯ Forests.   +++ Railways.   ▪ German H.Q.

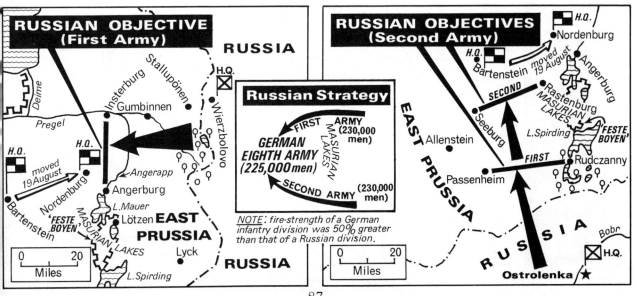

RUSSIAN OBJECTIVE
(First Army)

RUSSIA

Deime

Pregel

Insterburg

Stallupönen

Gumbinnen

H.Q.

Wierzbolovo

H.Q.

H.Q.

moved 19 August

Nordenburg

Bartenstein

Angerapp

Angerburg

'FESTE BOYEN'

L.Mauer

Lötzen

EAST PRUSSIA

Lyck

RUSSIA

L. Spirding

0 ——— 20
Miles

Russian Strategy

FIRST ARMY
(230,000 men)

GERMAN EIGHTH ARMY
(225,000 men)

MASURIAN LAKES

SECOND ARMY
(230,000 men)

<u>NOTE</u>: fire-strength of a German infantry division was 50% greater than that of a Russian division.

RUSSIAN OBJECTIVES
(Second Army)

H.Q.

Nordenburg

H.Q.

Bartenstein

moved 19 August

Angerburg

SECOND

Seeburg

Rastenburg

MASURIAN LAKES

L.Spirding

'FESTE BOYEN'

Allenstein

FIRST

Rudczanny

Passenheim

EAST PRUSSIA

RUSSIA

Bobr

0 ——— 20
Miles

Ostrolenka ★ ⊠H.Q.

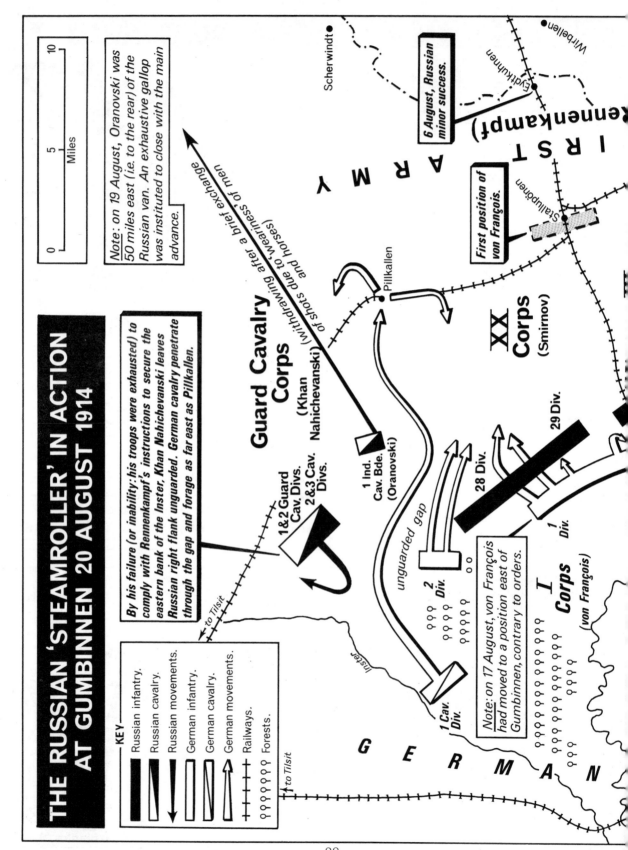

THE RUSSIAN 'STEAMROLLER' IN ACTION AT GUMBINNEN 20 AUGUST 1914

KEY

- ▬ Russian infantry.
- ◣ Russian cavalry.
- ↓ Russian movements.
- ▭ German infantry.
- ◻ German cavalry.
- ⇧ German movements.
- ┼┼┼ Railways.
- ♀♀♀♀♀ Forests.

Note: on 19 August, Oranovski was 50 miles east (i.e. to the rear) of the Russian van. An exhaustive gallop was instituted to close with the main advance.

By his failure (or inability: his troops were exhausted) to comply with Rennenkampf's instructions to secure the eastern bank of the Inster, Khan Nahichevanski leaves Russian right flank unguarded. German cavalry penetrate through the gap and forage as far east as Pillkallen.

Note: on 17 August, von François had moved to a position east of Gumbinnen, contrary to orders.

Guard Cavalry Corps

(Khan Nahichevanski) (withdrawing due to weariness) of shots and horses)

Guard Cavalry after a brief exchange

1 & 2 Guard Cav. Divs.
2 & 3 Cav. Divs.

1 Ind. Cav. Bde. (Oranovski)

1 Cav. Div.

2 Div.

unguarded gap

I Corps
(von François)

1 Div.

28 Div.

29 Div.

XX Corps
(Smirnov)

Pillkallen

First position of von François.

Stallupönen

FIRST **A**RMY **(Rennenkampf)**

6 August, Russian minor success.

Eydtkuhnen

Scherwindt

Wirballen

Inster

to Tilsit

to Tilsit

G E R M A N

0   5   10
Miles

88

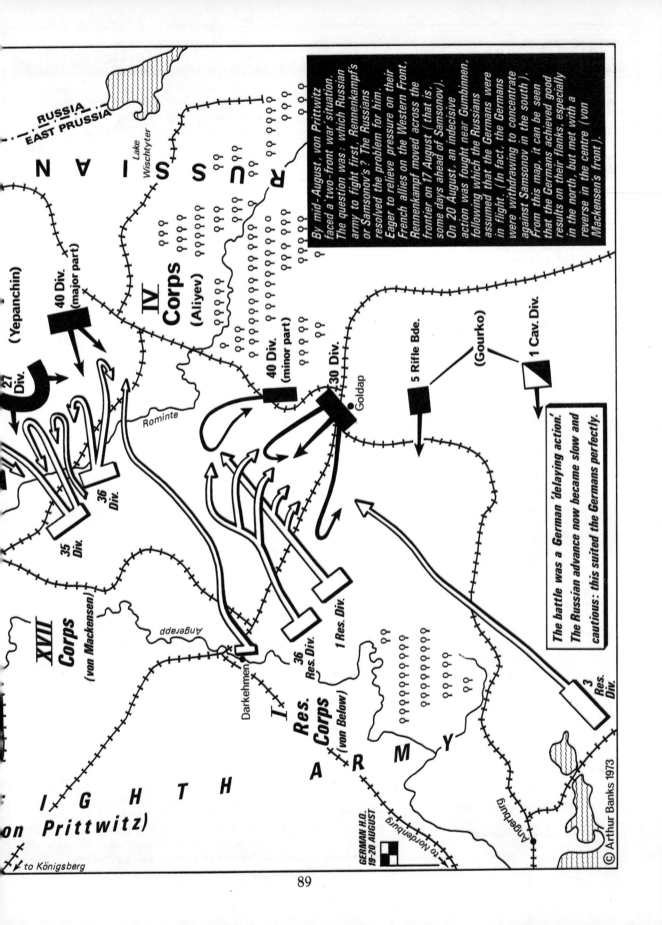

By mid-August, von Prittwitz faced a 'two-front war' situation. The question was: which Russian army to fight first, Rennenkampf's or Samsonov's? The Russians resolved the problem for him. Eager to relieve pressure on their French allies on the Western Front, Rennenkampf moved across the frontier on 17 August (that is, some days ahead of Samsonov). On 20 August, an indecisive action was fought near Gumbinnen, following which the Germans assumed that the Russians were in flight. (In fact, the Germans were withdrawing to concentrate against Samsonov in the south). From this map, it can be seen that the Germans achieved good results on their flanks, especially in the north, but met with a reverse in the centre (von Mackensen's front).

The battle was a German 'delaying action'. The Russian advance now became slow and cautious: this suited the Germans perfectly.

RUSSIA
EAST PRUSSIA

N   A   S   S   I   A   N   R

Lake Wischtyter

(Yepanchin)

27 Div.

40 Div. (major part)

IV Corps (Aliyev)

40 Div. (minor part)

30 Div.

Goldap

5 Rifle Bde.

(Gourko)

1 Cav. Div.

Rominte

36 Div.

35 Div.

XVII Corps (von Mackensen)

Angerapp

1 Res. Div.

36 Res. Div.

Darkehmen

I Res. Corps (von Below)

3 Res. Div.

E   I   G   H   T   H   A   R   M   Y

on Prittwitz)

to Königsberg

© Arthur Banks 1973

GERMAN H.Q. 19-20 AUGUST

to Nordenburg

Angerburg

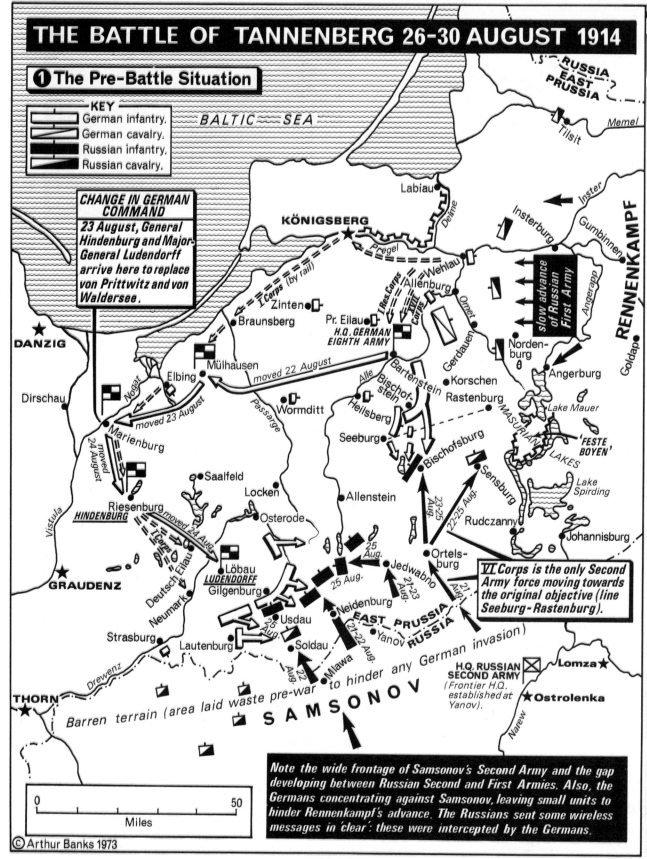

THE BATTLE OF TANNENBERG 26-30 AUGUST 1914

① The Pre-Battle Situation

KEY
- German infantry.
- German cavalry.
- Russian infantry.
- Russian cavalry.

RUSSIA EAST PRUSSIA

BALTIC SEA

CHANGE IN GERMAN COMMAND
23 August, General Hindenburg and Major-General Ludendorff arrive here to replace von Prittwitz and von Waldersee.

Memel

Tilsit

Labiau

Inster

Insterburg

Gumbinnen

KÖNIGSBERG

Wehlau

Allenburg

slow advance of Russian First Army

RENNENKAMPF

Pregel

Deine

I Corps (by rail)

Zinten

I Res. Corps

XVII Corps

Angerapp

Braunsberg

Pr. Eilau

H.Q. GERMAN EIGHTH ARMY

Ornet

Gerdauen

Nordenburg

Angerburg

Goldap

DANZIG

Elbing

Mülhausen

moved 22 August

Nogat

Bartenstein

Korschen

Rastenburg

Lake Mauer

'FESTE BOYEN'

MASURIAN LAKES

Dirschau

moved 23 August

Passarge

Wormditt

Alle

Bischof-stein

Heilsberg

Seeburg

Bischofsburg

Marienburg

moved 24 August

Saalfeld

Locken

Allenstein

Sensburg

Lake Spirding

Rudczanny

Vistula

HINDENBURG

Osterode

moved 24 Aug.

I Corps

25 Aug.

22-25 Aug.

23-25 Aug.

Ortels-burg

Johannisburg

GRAUDENZ

Deutsch Eilau

Löbau

LUDENDORFF

Gilgenburg

25 Aug.

25 Aug.

Jedwabno

21-23 Aug.

21 Aug.

VI Corps is the only Second Army force moving towards the original objective (line Seeburg-Rastenburg).

Neumark

Usdau

Neidenburg

EAST PRUSSIA

Yanov

RUSSIA

25 Aug.

21-22 Aug.

Strasburg

Lautenburg

Soldau

Mlawa

22 Aug.

to hinder any German invasion)

H.Q. RUSSIAN SECOND ARMY
(*Frontier H.Q. established at Yanov*).

Lomza

Drewenz

THORN

Barren terrain (area laid waste pre-war

S A M S O N O V

Narew

Ostrolenka

Note the wide frontage of Samsonov's Second Army and the gap developing between Russian Second and First Armies. Also, the Germans concentrating against Samsonov, leaving small units to hinder Rennenkampf's advance. The Russians sent some wireless messages in 'clear': these were intercepted by the Germans.

0   50
Miles

© Arthur Banks 1973

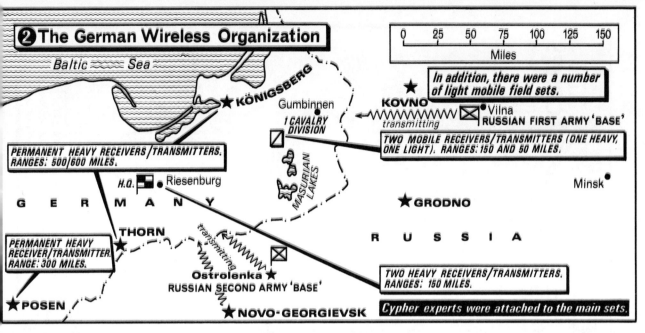

② The German Wireless Organization

Baltic ～ Sea

★ KÖNIGSBERG

Gumbinnen

1 CAVALRY DIVISION

★ KOVNO

In addition, there were a number of light mobile field sets.

•Vilna
RUSSIAN FIRST ARMY 'BASE'

transmitting

TWO MOBILE RECEIVERS/TRANSMITTERS (ONE HEAVY, ONE LIGHT). RANGES: 150 AND 50 MILES.

0 25 50 75 100 125 150
Miles

PERMANENT HEAVY RECEIVERS/TRANSMITTERS. RANGES: 500/600 MILES.

H.Q. • Riesenburg

MASURIAN LAKES

Minsk •

G E R M A N Y

★ GRODNO

R U S S I A

THORN ★

transmitting

PERMANENT HEAVY RECEIVER/TRANSMITTER. RANGE: 300 MILES.

Ostrolenka ★
RUSSIAN SECOND ARMY 'BASE'

TWO HEAVY RECEIVERS/TRANSMITTERS. RANGES: 150 MILES.

★ POSEN

★ NOVO-GEORGIEVSK

Cypher experts were attached to the main sets.

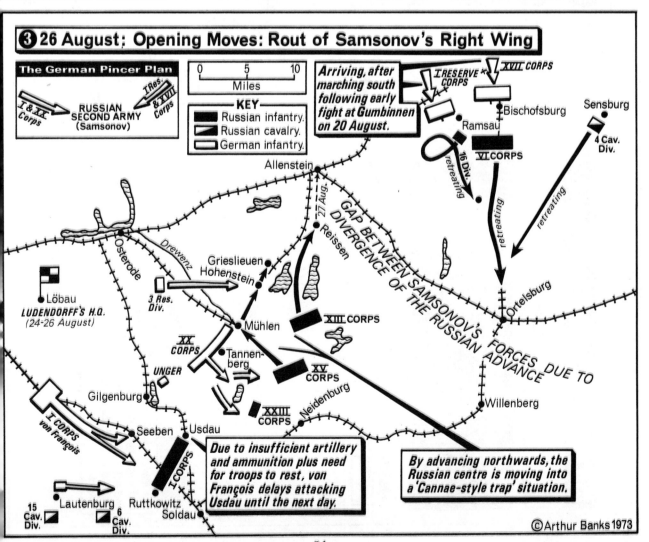

③ 26 August: Opening Moves: Rout of Samsonov's Right Wing

The German Pincer Plan

I & XX Corps
I Res. & XVII Corps
RUSSIAN SECOND ARMY (Samsonov)

0 5 10
Miles

— KEY —
Russian infantry.
Russian cavalry.
German infantry.

Arriving, after marching south following early fight at Gumbinnen on 20 August.

I RESERVE CORPS

XVII CORPS

Bischofsburg

Sensburg

Ramsau

16 Div. retreating

VI CORPS

4 Cav. Div.

Allenstein

27 Aug.

GAP BETWEEN DIVERGENCE OF THE RUSSIAN

Reissen

retreating

retreating

Osterode

Drewenz

Grieslieuen
Hohenstein

Löbau
LUDENDORFF'S H.Q. (24-26 August)

3 Res. Div.

Mühlen

XIII CORPS

Ortelsburg

FORCES DUE TO

XX CORPS

Tannenberg

UNGER

XV CORPS

Gilgenburg

Neidenburg

XXIII CORPS

Willenberg

Seeben

Usdau

I CORPS von François

I CORPS

Due to insufficient artillery and ammunition plus need for troops to rest, von François delays attacking Usdau until the next day.

By advancing northwards, the Russian centre is moving into a 'Cannae-style trap' situation.

15 Cav. Div.

Lautenburg

6 Cav. Div.

Ruttkowitz

Soldau

RUSSIAN ADVANCE

© Arthur Banks 1973

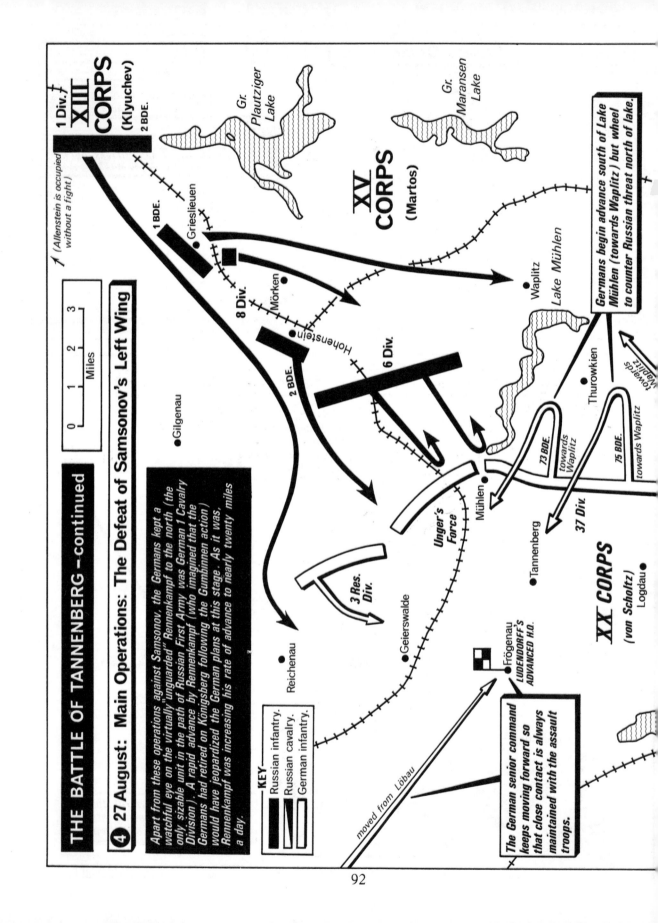

THE BATTLE OF TANNENBERG – continued

④ 27 August: Main Operations: The Defeat of Samsonov's Left Wing

Apart from these operations against Samsonov, the Germans kept a watchful eye on the virtually "unguarded" Rennenkampf to the north (the only sizable unit in the path of Russian First Army was German 1 Cavalry Division). A rapid advance by Rennenkampf (who imagined that the Germans had retired on Königsberg following the Gumbinnen action) would have jeopardized the German plans at this stage. As it was, Rennenkampf was increasing his rate of advance to nearly twenty miles a day.

KEY
- Russian infantry.
- Russian cavalry.
- German infantry.

Miles
0 1 2 3

↗ (Allenstein is occupied without a fight)

XIII CORPS (Klyuchev)
1 Div.
2 BDE.

Gr. Plautziger Lake

XV CORPS (Martos)

Gr. Maransen Lake

1 BDE.
●Grieslieuen

8 Div.
●Mörken

Hohenstein

2 BDE.

6 Div.

●Waplitz
Lake Mühlen

●Gilgenau

Reichenau●

3 Res. Div.
●Geierswalde

Unger's Force

●Mühlen

Thurowkien

73 BDE.
towards Waplitz

75 BDE.
towards Waplitz
towards Waplitz

37 Div.

●Tannenberg

XX CORPS (von Scholtz)
Logdau●

Frögenau
LUDENDORFF'S ADVANCED H.Q.

moved from Löbau

Germans begin advance south of Lake Mühlen (towards Waplitz) but wheel to counter Russian threat north of lake.

The German senior command keeps moving forward so that close contact is always maintained with the assault troops.

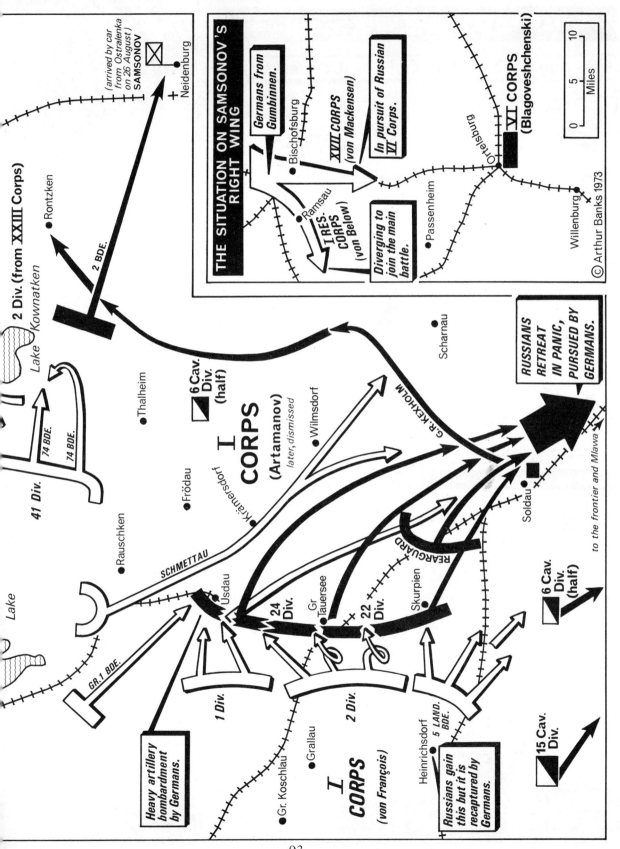

THE SITUATION ON SAMSONOV'S RIGHT WING

Germans from Gumbinnen.

XVII CORPS (von Mackensen)
In pursuit of Russian VI Corps.

I RES. CORPS (von Below)
Diverging to join the main battle.

VI CORPS (Blagoveshchenski)

Bischofsburg

Ramsau

Ortelsburg

Passenheim

Willenburg

© Arthur Banks 1973

0   5   10
Miles

2 Div. (from XXIII Corps)

(arrived by car from Ostralenka on 26 August) SAMSONOV

Neidenburg

Rontzken

2 BDE.

Lake Kownatken

Thalheim

6 Cav. Div. (half)

I CORPS (Artamanov) later, dismissed

Wilmsdorf

Frödau

Krämersdorf

Rauschken

41 Div.

74 BDE.

74 BDE.

Lake

SCHMETTAU

GR. 1 BDE.

Usdau

1 Div.

Gr. Koschlau

Grallau

I CORPS (von François)

24 Div.

Gr Tauersee

2 Div.

22 Div.

Skurpien

Heinrichsdorf

5 LAND. BDE.

REARGUARD

G.R. KEXHOLM

Scharnau

Soldau

RUSSIANS RETREAT IN PANIC, PURSUED BY GERMANS.

to the frontier and Mlawa

6 Cav. Div. (half)

15 Cav. Div.

Heavy artillery bombardment by Germans.

Russians gain this but it is recaptured by Germans.

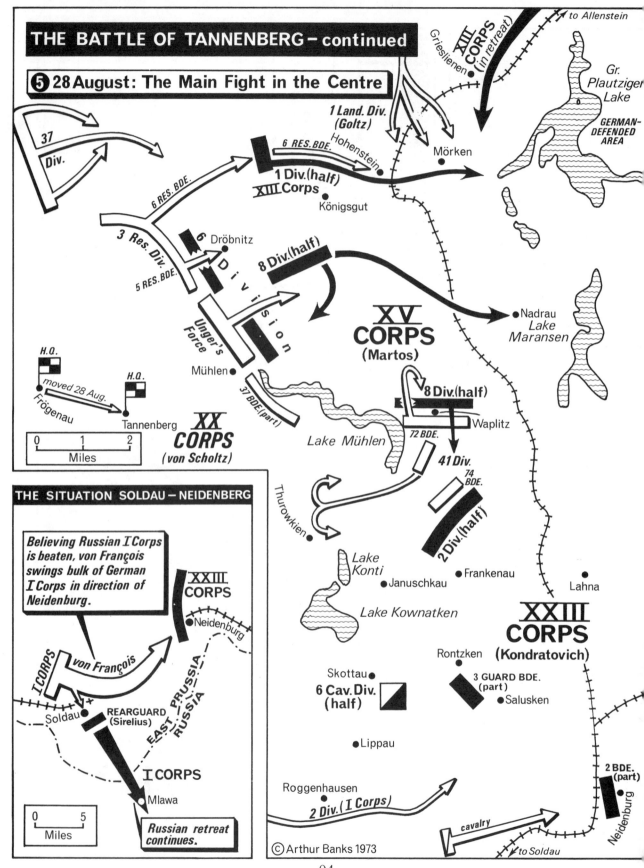

THE BATTLE OF TANNENBERG – continued

⑤ 28 August: The Main Fight in the Centre

37 Div.

XIII CORPS (in retreat)

to Allenstein

Grieslienen

Gr. Plautziger Lake

GERMAN-DEFENDED AREA

1 Land. Div. (Goltz)

6 RES. BDE.

Hohenstein

Mörken

6 RES. BDE.

1 Div.(half)

XIII Corps

Königsgut

3 Res. Div.

6 Dröbnitz

5 RES. BDE.

8 Div.(half)

Nadrau

Lake Maransen

Division

Unger's Force

XV CORPS (Martos)

H.Q.

moved 28 Aug.

H.Q.

Frögenau

Tannenberg

Mühlen

37 BDE. (part)

8 Div.(half)

Waplitz

72 BDE.

Lake Mühlen

41 Div.

74 BDE.

| 0 | 1 | 2 |

Miles

XX CORPS (von Scholtz)

2 Div.(half)

Thurowkien

Lake Konti

Januschkau

Frankenau

Lahna

Lake Kownatken

XXIII CORPS (Kondratovich)

THE SITUATION SOLDAU – NEIDENBERG

Believing Russian I Corps is beaten, von François swings bulk of German I Corps in direction of Neidenburg.

XXIII CORPS

Neidenburg

I CORPS

von François

EAST PRUSSIA

RUSSIA

Soldau

REARGUARD (Sirelius)

I CORPS

Mlawa

| 0 | | 5 |

Miles

Russian retreat continues.

Rontzken

Skottau

6 Cav. Div. (half)

3 GUARD BDE. (part)

Salusken

Lippau

2 BDE. (part)

Neidenburg

Roggenhausen

2 Div. (I Corps)

cavalry

to Soldau

© Arthur Banks 1973

94

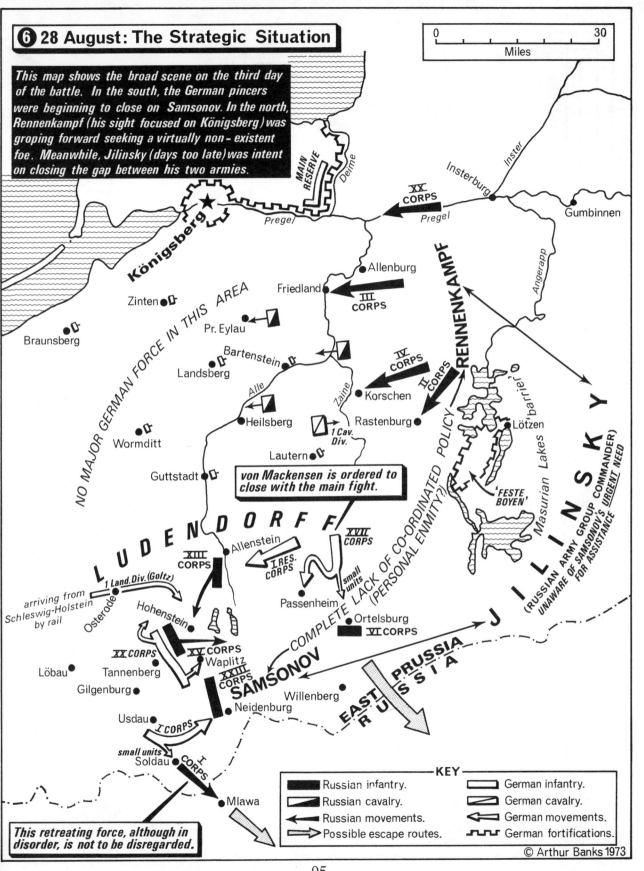

6 28 August: The Strategic Situation

This map shows the broad scene on the third day of the battle. In the south, the German pincers were beginning to close on Samsonov. In the north, Rennenkampf (his sight focused on Königsberg) was groping forward seeking a virtually non-existent foe. Meanwhile, Jilinsky (days too late) was intent on closing the gap between his two armies.

0   30
Miles

MAIN RESERVE

Deime

Insterburg

Inster

XX CORPS

Pregel

Pregel

Gumbinnen

Königsberg

Zinten

Braunsberg

Pr. Eylau

Allenburg

Friedland

III CORPS

RENNENKAMPF

Angerapp

NO MAJOR GERMAN FORCE IN THIS AREA

Bartenstein

Landsberg

Alle

Heilsberg

Zaine

IV CORPS

II CORPS

Korschen

Rastenburg

Lötzen

Masurian Lakes

'lake barrier'

Wormditt

1 Cav. Div.

Lautern

von Mackensen is ordered to close with the main fight.

Guttstadt

'FESTE BOYEN'

J I L I N S K Y

(RUSSIAN ARMY GROUP COMMANDER) UNAWARE OF SAMSONOV'S *URGENT NEED* FOR ASSISTANCE

L U D E N D O R F F

Allenstein

XVII CORPS

COMPLETE LACK OF CO-ORDINATED POLICY (PERSONAL ENMITY?)

XIII CORPS

I RES. CORPS

small units

Passenheim

arriving from Schleswig-Holstein by rail

1 Land.Div.(Goltz)

Osterode

Hohenstein

Ortelsburg

VI CORPS

Löbau

XX CORPS

Tannenberg

XV CORPS

Waplitz

XXIII CORPS

SAMSONOV

Willenberg

EAST PRUSSIA RUSSIA

J I L I N S K Y

Gilgenburg

Usdau

I CORPS

Neidenburg

small units

Soldau

I CORPS

Mlawa

This retreating force, although in disorder, is not to be disregarded.

KEY

◼ Russian infantry.		▢ German infantry.	
◪ Russian cavalry.		▨ German cavalry.	
◀— Russian movements.		⟵ German movements.	
⟹ Possible escape routes.		ᔕᔕᔕ German fortifications.	

© Arthur Banks 1973

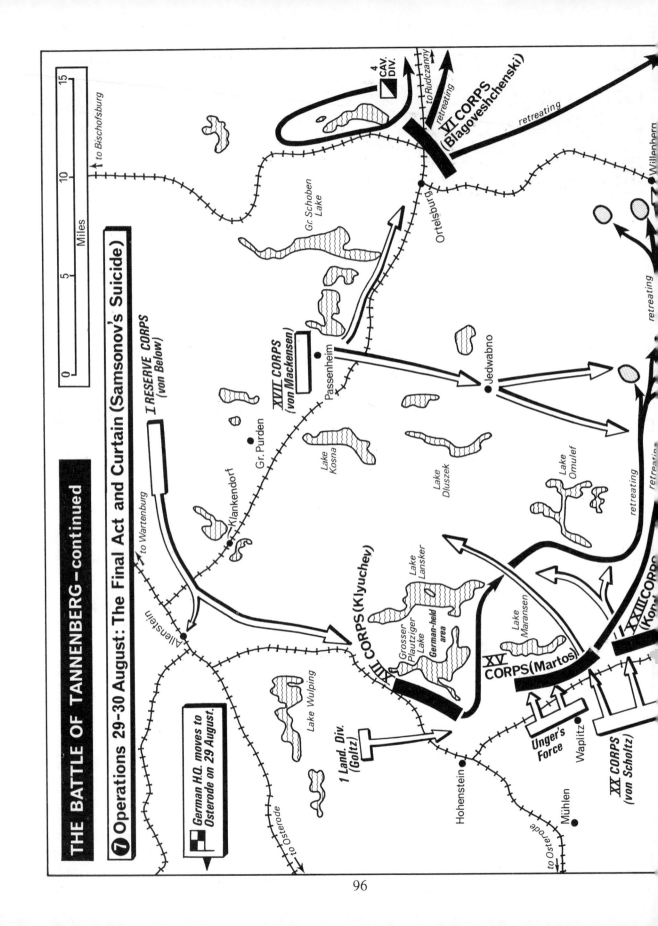

THE BATTLE OF TANNENBERG–continued

⑦ Operations 29-30 August: The Final Act and Curtain (Samsonov's Suicide)

German H.Q. moves to Osterode on 29 August.

Miles
0   5   10   15

to Bischofsburg

4 CAV. DIV.

to Rudczanny

retreating

VI CORPS (Blagoveshchenski)

retreating

Willenberg

Ortelsburg

Gr. Schoben Lake

I RESERVE CORPS (von Below)

XVII CORPS (von Mackensen)

Passenheim

Jedwabno

Gr. Purden

Klankendort

Lake Kosna

Lake Dluszek

Lake Omulef

retreating

to Wartenburg

Lake Lansker

Grosser Plautziger Lake

German-held area

Lake Maransen

XIII CORPS (Klyuchev)

XV CORPS (Martos)

XXIII CORPS (Kon...

Allenstein

to Osterode

Lake Wulping

1 Land. Div. (Goltz)

Unger's Force

Waplitz

XX CORPS (von Scholtz)

Hohenstein

Mühlen

to Osterode

to Osterode

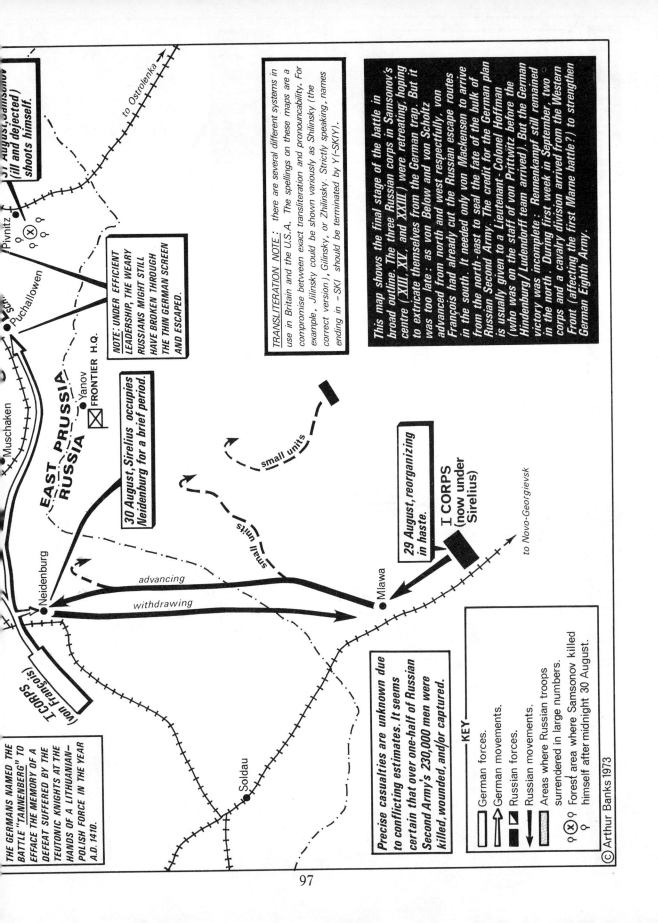

31 August, Samsonov (ill and dejected) shoots himself.

to Ostrolenka

Pivnitz

Puchallowen

NOTE: UNDER EFFICIENT LEADERSHIP, THE WEARY RUSSIANS MIGHT STILL HAVE BROKEN THROUGH THE THIN GERMAN SCREEN AND ESCAPED.

TRANSLITERATION NOTE: there are several different systems in use in Britain and the U.S.A. The spellings on these maps are a compromise between exact transliteration and pronounceability. For example, Jilinsky could be shown variously as Shilinsky (the correct version), Gilinsky, or Zhilinsky. Strictly speaking, names ending in –SKI should be terminated by Y(–SKIY).

This map shows the final stage of the battle in broad outline. The three Russian corps in Samsonov's centre (XIII, XV, and XXIII) were retreating, hoping to extricate themselves from the German trap. But it was too late: as von Below and von Scholtz advanced from north and west respectively, von François had already cut the Russian escape routes in the south. It needed only von Mackensen to arrive from the north-east to seal the fate of the bulk of Russian Second Army. The credit for the German plan is usually given to a Lieutenant-Colonel Hoffman (who was on the staff of von Prittwitz before the Hindenburg/Ludendorff team arrived.) But the German victory was incomplete: Rennenkampf still remained in the north. During first week in September, two corps and a cavalry division arrived from the Western Front (affecting the first Marne battle?) to strengthen German Eighth Army.

EAST PRUSSIA
RUSSIA

Muschaken

Yanov FRONTIER H.Q.

30 August, Sirelius occupies Neidenburg for a brief period.

small units

I CORPS (now under Sirelius)

29 August, reorganizing in haste.

to Novo-Georgievsk

Neidenburg

Mlawa

advancing

withdrawing

small units

I CORPS (von François)

THE GERMANS NAMED THE BATTLE "TANNENBERG" TO EFFACE THE MEMORY OF A DEFEAT SUFFERED BY THE TEUTONIC KNIGHTS AT THE HANDS OF A LITHUANIAN-POLISH FORCE IN THE YEAR A.D. 1410.

Precise casualties are unknown due to conflicting estimates. It seems certain that over one-half of Russian Second Army's 230,000 men were killed, wounded, and/or captured.

Soldau

— KEY —
- German forces.
- German movements.
- Russian forces.
- Russian movements.
- Areas where Russian troops surrendered in large numbers.
- Forest area where Samsonov killed himself after midnight 30 August.

© Arthur Banks 1973

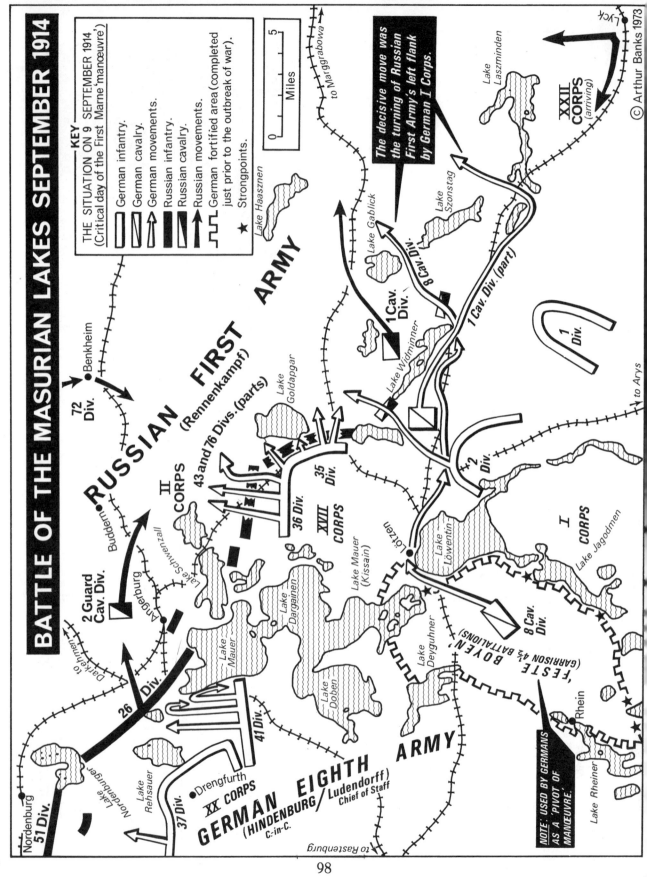

BATTLE OF THE MASURIAN LAKES SEPTEMBER 1914

© Arthur Banks 1973

KEY

THE SITUATION ON 9 SEPTEMBER 1914
(Critical day of the First Marne 'manoeuvre')

- German infantry.
- German cavalry.
- German movements.
- Russian infantry.
- Russian cavalry.
- Russian movements.
- German fortified area (completed just prior to the outbreak of war).
- ★ Strongpoints.

Miles 0 5

RUSSIAN FIRST ARMY (Rennenkampf)

The decisive move was the turning of Russian First Army's left flank by German I Corps.

XXII CORPS (arriving)

to Marggrabowa

LYCK

Lake Laszminden

Lake Haasznen

Lake Szonstag

Lake Gablick

8 Cav. Div.

1 Cav. Div.

1 Cav. Div. (part)

to Arys

1 Div.

Lake Widminner

Lake Goldapgar

2 Div.

72 Div.

Benkheim

Buddern

II CORPS

43 and 76 Divs. (parts)

36 Div.

35 Div.

XVII CORPS

Lake Mauer (Kissain)

Löttzen

Lake Löwentin

I CORPS

Lake Jagodmen

8 Cav. Div.

'FESTE BOYEN' (GARRISON 4½ BATTALIONS)

Lake Deyguhner

Lake Dargainen

Lake Doben

Rhein

Lake Rheiner

2 Guard Cav. Div.

Angerburg

Lake Schwenzall

26 Div.

Lake Mauer

41 Div.

Drengfurth

37 Div.

XX CORPS

GERMAN EIGHTH ARMY

(HINDENBURG/Ludendorff) C-in-C.
Chief of Staff

to Rastenburg

to Dehmen

Nordenburg

51 Div.

Lake Rehsauer

Lake Nordenburg

NOTE: USED BY GERMANS AS A 'PIVOT OF MANOEUVRE'.

SERBIA IN TRAVAIL AND TRIUMPH 1914

*Punitive expedition: so-called by the Austrians *after* it had failed.

① Serbia's Strategic Position

Anti-Serbia: hence pro-Central Powers.

Berlin
GERMANY
Poland
Berlin-Baghdad railway project
Vienna
AUSTRIA-HUNGARY
RUSSIA
AREA OF OPERATIONS IN 1914
ITALY
RUMANIA
SERBIA
BULGARIA
Constantinople
GREECE
TURKEY

Railway link runs through Serbia.

0   100   200
Miles

② Austria's "Strafexpedition"*

12-24 AUGUST
AUSTRIAN SECOND ARMY

ONLY PART SECOND ARMY ENGAGED. (some units diverted to Galicia)

Sava
Shabatz
BELGRADE
Danube
AUSTRIAN FIFTH ARMY
XIII CORPS
VIII CORPS
Jadar
SERBIAN MAIN FORCE
Serbian units guarding Belgrade
Kolubara
Drina
Valjevo (Putnik's H.Q.)
AUSTRIAN SIXTH ARMY
Uzhitse
SERBIAN UZHITSE (UZICE) GROUP

STRENGTHS	
Austrians:	190,000
Serbians:	180,000
CASUALTIES	
Austrians:	38,000
Serbians:	18,000

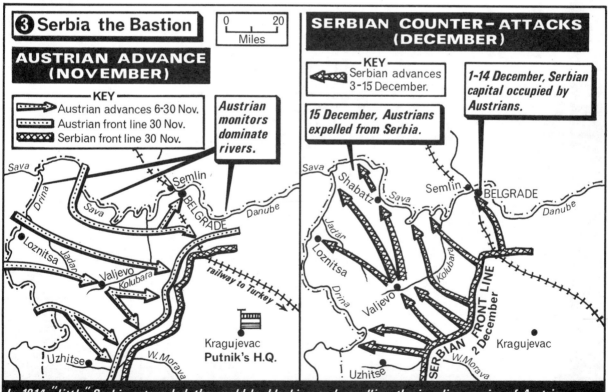

③ Serbia the Bastion

0   20
Miles

AUSTRIAN ADVANCE (NOVEMBER)

KEY
→ Austrian advances 6-30 Nov.
···· Austrian front line 30 Nov.
XXXX Serbian front line 30 Nov.

Austrian monitors dominate rivers.

Sava
Drina
Sava
Semlin
BELGRADE
Danube
Loznitsa
Jadar
Valjevo
Kolubara
railway to Turkey
Uzhitse
W. Morava
Kragujevac
Putnik's H.Q.

SERBIAN COUNTER-ATTACKS (DECEMBER)

KEY
⇚ Serbian advances 3-15 December.

15 December, Austrians expelled from Serbia.

1-14 December, Serbian capital occupied by Austrians.

Sava
Shabatz
Sava
Semlin
BELGRADE
Danube
Jadar
Loznitsa
Kolubara
Drina
Valjevo
SERBIAN FRONT LINE 2 December
Kragujevac
Uzhitse
W. Morava

In 1914, "little" Serbia astounded the world by blocking and repelling the invading armies of Austria-Hungary. German reaction was derisive: "Allies? We are shackled to a corpse." It is important to note that part only of Austrian Second Army was engaged in August, and these units were gradually withdrawn to fight on the Galician front. However, a Serbian Army equalled little more than an Austrian corps.

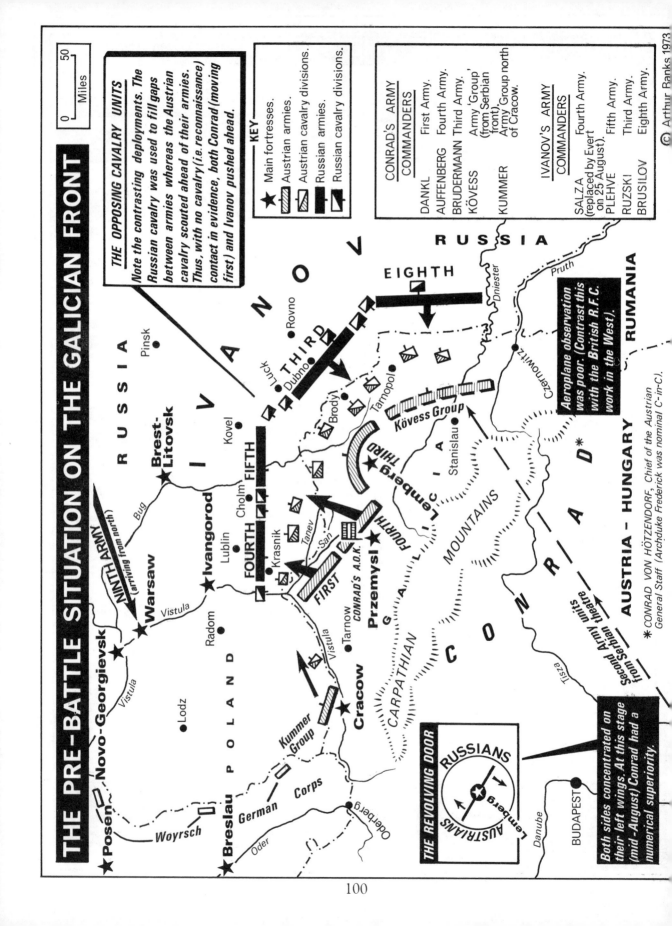

THE PRE-BATTLE SITUATION ON THE GALICIAN FRONT

© Arthur Banks 1973

THE OPPOSING CAVALRY UNITS

Note the contrasting deployments. The Russian cavalry was used to fill gaps between armies whereas the Austrian cavalry scouted ahead of their armies. Thus, with no cavalry (i.e. reconnaissance) contact in evidence, both Conrad (moving first) and Ivanov pushed ahead.

KEY

★ Main fortresses.

▨ Austrian armies.

▧ Austrian cavalry divisions.

▬ Russian armies.

▭ Russian cavalry divisions.

CONRAD'S ARMY COMMANDERS

DANKL — First Army.
AUFFENBERG — Fourth Army.
BRUDERMANN — Third Army.
KÖVESS — Army 'Group (from Serbian front).
KUMMER — Army Group north of Cracow.

IVANOV'S ARMY COMMANDERS

SALZA (replaced by Evert on 25 August). — Fourth Army.
PLEHVE — Fifth Army.
RUZSKI — Third Army.
BRUSILOV — Eighth Army.

Aeroplane observation was poor. (Contrast this with the British R.F.C. work in the West).

RUSSIA

EIGHTH

RUSSIA

Pinsk

Rovno

Brest-Litovsk

Kovel

Luck

Dubno

THIRD

Dniester

Pruth

Czernowitz

RUMANIA

Brody

Tarnopol

Kövess Group

Stanislau

MOUNTAINS

GALICIA

CARPATHIAN

AUSTRIA – HUNGARY

* CONRAD VON HÖTZENDORF, Chief of the Austrian General Staff (Archduke Frederick was nominal C-in-C).

NINTH ARMY (arriving from north)

Warsaw

Ivangorod

Vistula

Radom

Bug

Lublin

Cholm

FIFTH

FOURTH

Krasnik

Tanev

San

Lemberg

Tarnow

Tarnow

Przemysl

FIRST

CONRAD'S A.O.K.

FOURTH

THIRD

Second Army units from Serbian theatre

Tisza

BUDAPEST

Danube

Posen – Novo-Georgievsk

Breslau

POLAND

Lodz

Oderberg

Oder

Kummer Group

German Corps

Woyrsch

Cracow

THE REVOLVING DOOR

RUSSIANS

Lemberg

AUSTRIANS

Both sides concentrated on their left wings. At this stage (mid-August) Conrad had a numerical superiority.

THE NORTHERN CLASH

② 26-30 AUGUST
RUSSIAN FIFTH ARMY

Bug

XXI CORPS

XIX CORPS

V CORPS

THREE DIVISIONS FROM THIRD ARMY, PLUS CAVALRY.

Komarov

XXV CORPS

XVII CORPS

VI CORPS

IX CORPS

II CORPS

Sokokiya

AUSTRIAN FOURTH ARMY (Auffenberg)

Por.

Wieprz

FIRST ARMY'S RIGHT WING

① 23-25 AUGUST
RUSSIAN FOURTH ARMY

FIFTH ARMY'S RIGHT WING

Wieprz

Por.

Bistritza

GRENADIER CORPS

XVI CORPS

XIV CORPS

Krasnik

V CORPS

I CORPS

13 Cav. Div.

Vistula

AUSTRIAN FIRST ARMY

FOURTH ARMY'S LEFT WING

Austrian First Army clashed with Russian Fourth Army which withdrew. Russian Fifth Army on Fourth Army's left, wheeled right thus exposing its left flank to the Austrian Fourth Army. Strengthened on his right by divisions under Archduke Josef Ferdinand, Auffenberg sensed an opportunity to envelop the Russians.

④ 2 SEPTEMBER
RUSSIAN FIFTH ARMY (Plehve)

AUSTRIAN FOURTH ARMY

RUSSIAN THIRD ARMY

③ 31 AUGUST-1 SEPT.
RUSSIAN FIFTH ARMY

Bug

RUSSIAN ATTACK DEVELOPING ?

Archduke J. Ferdinand

Huczwa

XVII CORPS

VI CORPS

II CORPS

I CORPS

Komarov

AUSTRIAN FOURTH ARMY

Por.

RUSSIAN ATTACK DEVELOPING ?

Austrian right and left flanks (believing enemy units to be moving towards their rears) fell back and the Russians escaped being encircled. Auffenberg reversed his main force and marched south to aid the now-threatened Austrian Third Army (see next page). The advancing Russian Third Army swung north-west to aid Plehve.

© Arthur Banks 1973

THE CONFLICTING PLANS

CONRAD'S ASSUMPTION

0 — 50 Miles

RUSSIA

MAIN RUSSIAN FORCE (STILL CONCENTRATING)

Lutsk

WEAK RUSSIAN FORCE

Dniester

RUMANIA

Cholm

Bug

Lublin

KÖVESS 'GROUP'

Czernowitz

Lemberg

THIRD ARMY

Przemysl

FOURTH ARMY

San

FIRST ARMY

Ivangorod

Vistula

Cracow

KUMMER GROUP

POLAND

AUSTRIA-HUNGARY

Austrian 'holding' units

POWERFUL AUSTRIAN ADVANCE TO CRUSH MAIN (AND UNREADY) OPPOSITION

Both assumptions were incorrect and exactly opposite to the facts, possibly due to inadequate intelligence and poor cavalry reconnaissance. Each side wished to fight the other's main force.

IVANOV'S ASSUMPTION

0 — 50 Miles

RUSSIA

MAIN RUSSIAN ADVANCE

EIGHTH ARMY

Lutsk

THIRD ARMY

Dniester

RUMANIA

Russian units (ready to intercept assumed Austrian retreat).

Bug

FIFTH ARMY

Cholm

Lemberg

Czernowitz

FOURTH ARMY

San

Przemysl

MAIN AUSTRIAN FORCE

Lublin

Ivangorod

Vistula

Cracow

WEAK AUSTRIAN FORCE

POLAND

AUSTRIA-HUNGARY

101

LEMBERG-PRZEMYSL OPERATIONS

The Austro-Hungarian armies were multi-racial: the graph below gives a broad guide to their heterogenous make-up.

① The Russian Advance on Lemberg

26-31 AUGUST

RUSSIAN THIRD ARMY (Ruzski)

AUSTRIAN THIRD ARMY (Brudermann)

Cavalry

XXI

XI

IX

X

Lemberg

Dniester

Brzezany

Złota Lipa

KÖVESS "GROUP" part SECOND ARMY (rest confronting Serbia)

VII

XII

VIII

XXIV

G. Lipa

Halicz

RUSSIAN EIGHTH ARMY (Brusilov)

Dniester

KEY
- Russian attacks (corps shown).
- x — Russian army boundary.
- Austrian line 26 August.
- Austrian retreat (in disorder).

0 10 20 30
Miles

(Senior officers largely of German race)

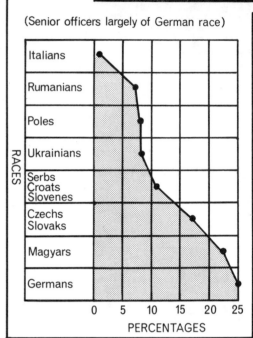

RACES						
Italians						
Rumanians						
Poles						
Ukrainians						
Serbs Croats Slovenes						
Czechs Slovaks						
Magyars						
Germans						

0   5   10   15   20   25
PERCENTAGES

② The Overall Scene in Outline

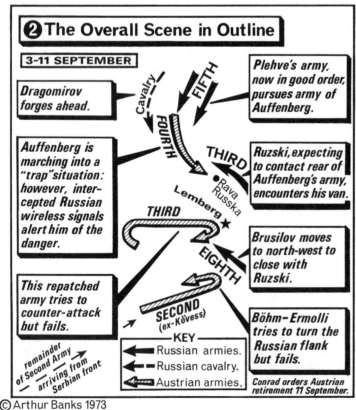

3-11 SEPTEMBER

Dragomirov forges ahead.

Cavalry

FIFTH

FOURTH

THIRD

Lemberg

Rava Russka

THIRD

EIGHTH

SECOND (ex-Kövess)

Auffenberg is marching into a "trap" situation: however, intercepted Russian wireless signals alert him of the danger.

This repatched army tries to counter-attack but fails.

Plehve's army, now in good order, pursues army of Auffenberg.

Ruzski, expecting to contact rear of Auffenberg's army, encounters his van.

Brusilov moves to north-west to close with Ruzski.

Böhm-Ermolli tries to turn the Russian flank but fails.

Conrad orders Austrian retirement 11 September.

remainder of Second Army arriving from Serbian front

KEY
- Russian armies.
- Russian cavalry.
- Austrian armies.

③ The Austrian Retreat

11 SEPT.-3 OCT.

0   20
Miles

Vistula

Ivangorod

Lublin

Fresh army arriving.

NINTH

FOURTH

FIFTH

FIRST

FIRST

FOURTH

Cracow

Vistula Tarnow

Dunajetz

Gorlice

San

Przemysl

THIRD

SECOND

THIRD

Rava Russka

Lemberg

EIGHTH

Dniester

Invested by Russians 24 Sept.- 9 Oct.

KEY
- Russian armies (attacking).
- Austrian line 11 September.
- Austrian armies (retreating).
- Austrian line (3 October).
- ✂ Fierce clash.

© Arthur Banks 1973

102

THE DISCORDANT VIEWS OF CONRAD & MOLTKE

Four double-gauge railway lines running west to east across Germany form the basis of her military mobility. (Two corps west → east Sept.).

BELGIUM
WESTERN FRONT
FRANCE

GERMANY
● Berlin

"NEGLECTED" RAILWAY

Vienna ●
AUSTRIA-HUNGARY

R U S S I A

E. PRUSSIA
EASTERN FRONT
POLAND

MOLTKE

This commander's attention is fixed upon the Western Front: he desires a quick victory over France so that he can switch Germany's military might against Russia. He is irritated by Conrad's exhortations for aid, regarding them as a distraction from the main task in hand.

14 September 1914, von Falkenhayn replaces Moltke (who has bungled application of amended Schlieffen Plan). The new Chief of the German General Staff recognizes Conrad's plight but is adamant that any German aid to Austria must come from East Prussia, not the Western Front.

Moltke's irritation with Conrad turns to disdain when Austria fails to defeat "little" Serbia in August and the Serbs raid Hungary (Sept.).

SERBIA

CONRAD

This commander expects German aid from the outset (it was implied rather than promised): he feels betrayed and snubbed. (Austria's main foe is Russia, not France).

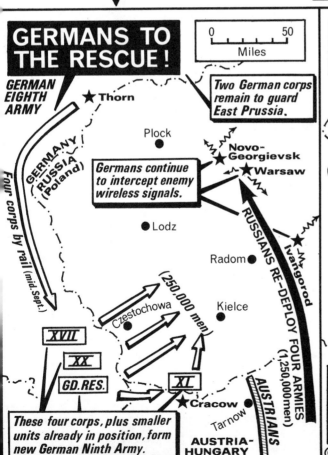

GERMANS TO THE RESCUE!

0 — 50 Miles

GERMAN EIGHTH ARMY

★ Thorn

● Plock

Four corps by rail (mid. Sept.)

GERMANY (RUSSIA (Poland))

Germans continue to intercept enemy wireless signals.

★ Novo-Georgievsk
★ Warsaw

● Lodz

RUSSIANS RE-DEPLOY FOUR ARMIES (1,250,000 men)

★ Ivangorod

● Radom

(250,000 men)

Czestochowa

Kielce

Two German corps remain to guard East Prussia.

XVII
XX
GD.RES.
XI

★ Cracow
Tarnow
AUSTRIANS
AUSTRIA-HUNGARY

These four corps, plus smaller units already in position, form new German Ninth Army.

CENTRAL POWERS ON THE MOVE

0 — 20 Miles

Vistula
Plock ●
② Novo-Georgievsk
★ Warsaw ⑤
④
★ Ivangorod

G E R M A N Y

● Lodz

P O L A N D

GERMANS
GERMANS

Radom ● Hindenburg

⑨

San

● Czestochowa

AUSTRIANS

Vistula

AUSTRIA-HUNGARY

★ Cracow

KEY

GER. AUS.

Central Powers' line 28 September (start of advance).

Central Powers' line 17 October (limit of advance).

Central Powers' drives.

● Russian armies.

© Arthur Banks 1973

103

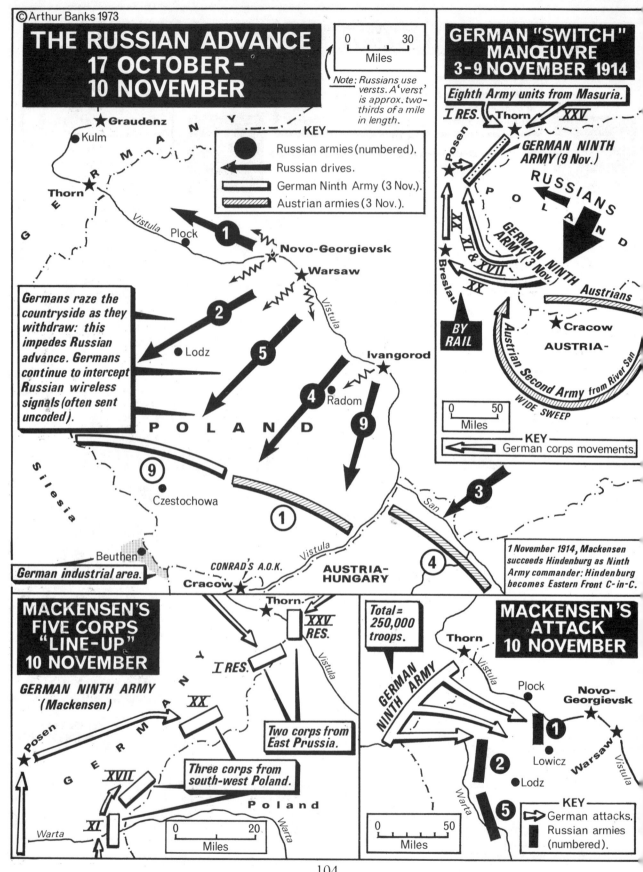

© Arthur Banks 1973

THE RUSSIAN ADVANCE 17 OCTOBER – 10 NOVEMBER

0   30
Miles

Note: Russians use versts. A 'verst' is approx. two-thirds of a mile in length.

KEY
●   Russian armies (numbered).
←   Russian drives.
▭   German Ninth Army (3 Nov.).
▨   Austrian armies (3 Nov.).

Graudenz
Kulm
Thorn
Plock
Novo-Georgievsk
Warsaw
Vistula

GERMANY

Germans raze the countryside as they withdraw: this impedes Russian advance. Germans continue to intercept Russian wireless signals (often sent uncoded).

Lodz
Ivangorod
Radom

P O L A N D

Silesia

Czestochowa

Beuthen

German industrial area.

CONRAD'S A.O.K.

Cracow

AUSTRIA-HUNGARY

San

Vistula

GERMAN "SWITCH" MANŒUVRE 3–9 NOVEMBER 1914

Eighth Army units from Masuria.

I RES.   Thorn   XXV

Posen

GERMAN NINTH ARMY (9 Nov.)

R U S S I A N S

GERMAN NINTH ARMY (3 Nov.)

Breslau

XX XI & XVII
XX

Austrians

BY RAIL

Cracow

AUSTRIA-

Austrian Second Army from River San

WIDE SWEEP

P O L A N D

0   50
Miles

KEY
←   German corps movements.

1 November 1914, Mackensen succeeds Hindenburg as Ninth Army commander: Hindenburg becomes Eastern Front C-in-C.

MACKENSEN'S FIVE CORPS "LINE-UP" 10 NOVEMBER

GERMAN NINTH ARMY (Mackensen)

Posen

Thorn

XXV RES.

I RES.

XX

XVII

XI

Warta

GERMANY

P O L A N D

Warta

Two corps from East Prussia.

Three corps from south-west Poland.

0   20
Miles

MACKENSEN'S ATTACK 10 NOVEMBER

Total = 250,000 troops.

Thorn

Vistula

Plock

Novo-Georgievsk

GERMAN NINTH ARMY

Lowicz

Warsaw

Vistula

Lodz

Warta

0   50
Miles

KEY
⇒   German attacks.
▮   Russian armies (numbered).

104

THE BATTLE OF LODZ 18-25 NOVEMBER 1914

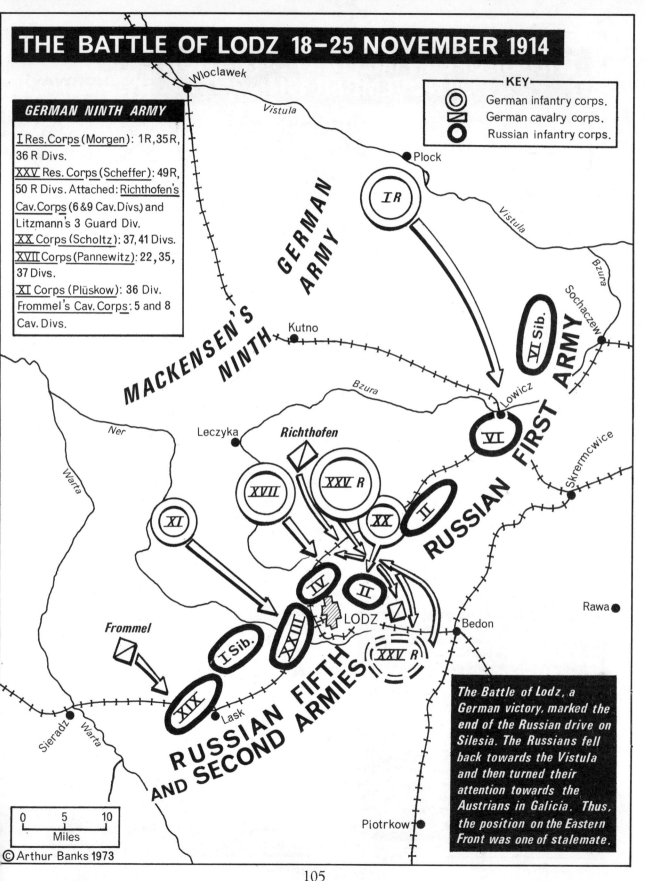

KEY
- German infantry corps.
- German cavalry corps.
- Russian infantry corps.

GERMAN NINTH ARMY

<u>I</u> Res. Corps (<u>Morgen</u>): 1R, 35R, 36 R Divs.

<u>XXV</u> Res. Corps (<u>Scheffer</u>): 49R, 50 R Divs. Attached: <u>Richthofen's Cav. Corps</u> (6 & 9 Cav. Divs.) and <u>Litzmann's 3 Guard Div.</u>

<u>XX</u> Corps (<u>Scholtz</u>): 37, 41 Divs.

<u>XVII</u> Corps (<u>Pannewitz</u>): 22, 35, 37 Divs.

<u>XI</u> Corps (<u>Plüskow</u>): 36 Div.

<u>Frommel's Cav. Corps</u>: 5 and 8 Cav. Divs.

GERMAN ARMY

MACKENSEN'S NINTH

RUSSIAN FIRST ARMY

RUSSIAN FIFTH AND SECOND ARMIES

Richthofen

Frommel

LODZ

The Battle of Lodz, a German victory, marked the end of the Russian drive on Silesia. The Russians fell back towards the Vistula and then turned their attention towards the Austrians in Galicia. Thus, the position on the Eastern Front was one of stalemate.

0 5 10
Miles

© Arthur Banks 1973

Place names: Wloclawek, Vistula, Plock, Bzura, Sochaczew, Kutno, VI Sib., Lowicz, Ner, Leczyka, VI, Skrerncwice, Warta, XVII, XXV R, XX, II, XI, IV, II, Rawa, XIII, Bedon, I Sib., XXV R, XIX, Lask, Sieradz, Warta, Piotrkow

105

THE EUROPEAN MILITARY SITUATION
30 NOVEMBER 1914

0 — 200
Miles

NORWAY
CHRISTIANIA

SWEDE

Skagerrak

Kattegat

DENMARK

COPEN

NORTH
SEA

Kiel
Canal

HELIGOLAND

Kiel

Hamburg

IRELAND

Dublin

Elbe

Bremen

GERMA

BERL

Manchester

THE
HAGUE   Amsterdam

Dresden

BRITAIN

LONDON

Antwerp

Rhine

Glasgow

Edinburgh

Southampton

BRUSSELS
BELGIUM   Liège

Frankfurt

Pr

LUX.

ATLANTIC

English   Channel

Rouen

2 August, occupied
by Germans.

OCEAN

Brest

Aisne

PARIS   Marne

Munich

Dan

Seine

Belfort

Bay of
Biscay

Loire

BERNE

Innsbruc

SWITZ.

FRANCE

Rhône

Milan   Venice

Tr

Bordeaux

Turin

Po

Genoa

A

Marseilles

Florence

I
T
A
L

ROM

Towards the end of November 1914 the initial
energetic thrusts of the Central Powers had
exhausted themselves. After four months
of activity (the Central Powers meeting with
determined resistance on both the Eastern
and Western Fronts), the war had reached
a position of stalemate. This map depicts
the "de facto" situation that existed at this
stage of operations. As opposed to large-
scale movements, the campaign settled
into a localised trench-warfare situation,
each side testing the other, rather than
initiating a definite major advance.
Consequently the mobile war switched to
other areas (e.g. the war at sea, in the air,
the Dardanelles, Mesopotamia, etc.) in the
hope of achieving "side-show" breakthroughs
that would affect the main battle fronts.

SPAIN

Barcelona

CORSICA

BALEARIC ISLANDS

SARDINIA

TYRRHEN

SEA

Pale

MEDITERRANEAN

Bizerta

Oran

ALGIERS

Bone   TUNIS

© Arthur Banks 1973

106

KEY

The Entente Powers and associates on 30 November 1914.

The Central Powers on 30 November 1914. *Note: Britain declared war on Turkey on 5 November 1914.*

Neutral states on 30 November 1914.

The Western and Eastern fronts on 30 November 1914.

Gulf of Bothnia

FINLAND

PETROGRAD

Gulf of Finland

STOCKHOLM

Reval

Moscow

BALTIC SEA

Riga

Libau

Smolensk

Kovno

Gumbinnen

Vilna

Königsberg

Minsk

R U S S I A

Danzig

Grodno

Tannenberg

Vistula

Brest-Litovsk

Posen

Lodz

Warsaw

Kiev

Oder

POLAND

Dnieper

Lemberg

Dniester

Odessa

Pruth

Pressburg

Tisza

VIENNA

Budapest

AUSTRIA - HUNGARY

Drava

29 November, vacated by Serbs.

RUMANIA

BUCHAREST

B L A C K   S E A

Sava

Frontier operations.

BELGRADE

Danube

BULGARIA

SERBIA

SOFIA

CONSTANTINOPLE

Angora

MONTE-NEGRO

ALBANIA

Salonika

Brindisi

GREECE

Dardanelles

OTTOMAN EMPIRE [TURKEY]

AEGEAN SEA

IONIAN SEA

ATHENS

Smyrna

Messina

RHODES

5 November, annexed by Britain.

CYPRUS

SICILY

SEA

CRETE

107

THE SITUATION AT THE END OF THE YEAR 1914

By the end of the year 1914 there was deadlock on every battlefront in Europe. From the Swiss frontier northwards fortified lines ran by way of the Vosges, the hills of the Meuse, the Argonne and the Chemin des Dames to the Aisne and up to Armentières and the Ypres Salient, reaching down to the inundated fields around Dixmude and so to the sand dunes of the North Sea. A tenth of metropolitan France, including the main French coalfields, and almost the whole of Belgium were behind the German trenches, and remained so throughout the war. The line of the Western Front did not move as much as ten miles in either direction for the following two and a half years. In the East, stalemate had come only through the onset of winter and there were no continuous systems of entrenchment to rule out a war movement. Yet there seemed little prospect of a decisive victory, and both sides had by now abandoned all hope of a short war.

Both the British and the German public were surprised by what was happening in the war at sea. After more than a decade of naval rivalry it was assumed there would be a naval battle between the great capital ships at an early date. But the Kaiser personally vetoed an engagement which might have destroyed his battle fleet until after the enemy fleet had been weakened by other means. The Germans accordingly made extensive use of their submarines (see page 246) and of minefields, although there was a sharp clash between cruisers and destroyers in Heligoland Bight at the end of August (see pages 242–245) and twice the German battle-cruisers took advantage of the long winter nights to cross the North Sea and bombard the East coast of England (see page 255). It was accepted in Britain that the days of isolation were over, a point emphasised on Christmas Eve when the first aerial bombs were dropped on English soil, at Dover.

The main clashes of sea power were, however, on the oceans. Vice-Admiral von Spee's squadron caused havoc in the Pacific and won a naval victory off Coronel before being defeated at the Falkland Islands early in December (pages 238, 240–241). The German cruiser *Emden* effectively disrupted trade in the East Indies (page 239), but by the end of the year, the British had reasserted their naval supremacy, clearing the seas of surface raiders and virtually destroying Germany's overseas commerce. Japanese, Australian and New Zealand forces mopped up Germany's island possessions in the Pacific, and British and Japanese troops occupied Kiaochow (the small German protectorate on the coast of China) in November. General von Lettow-Vorbeck retained firm control of German East Africa (pages 216–218) and the South Africans were in some difficulty in German South-West Africa but Togoland had surrendered and there was minimal resistance in the interior of the Cameroons.

The attention of the British outside Europe was from now on primarily concentrated on the Ottoman Empire. Turkey, long under the influence of Germany militarily, entered the War early in November, hoping to gain territory from Russia in the Caucasus and to recover, with German backing, her influence in the Balkans. The handing over by Germany to Turkey of the battle-cruiser *Goeben* and the cruiser *Breslau* (page 237) finally decided Turkey's course of action. Militarily Turkey was a distraction both to Britain and Russia, but her entry into the war suggested a possible alternative strategy—of toppling Germany, not on the main battlefronts, but by destroying her supports and entering Central Europe by the back door. It seemed the only way to make the war once more fluid. From such ideas developed the Dardanelles and Gallipoli campaigns, and belatedly the expedition to Salonika.

THE GALLIPOLI CAMPAIGN

The attempt to force the Dardanelles and gain control of Constantinople and the Straits was the first strategically imaginative project of the war. Its origins lie in a proposal made by Churchill to the War Council of 25 November 1914. He argued that 'the ideal method of defending Egypt' and the Suez Canal from an invading Turkish army 'was by an attack on the Gallipoli Peninsula' which, if successful, would enable the Allies to 'dictate terms at Constantinople'. Subsequently the possibilities of using British naval power to open up a new front against the enemy appealed to other members of the War Council, including Lloyd George, Admiral Sir John Fisher and the Secretary of the Council, Colonel Hankey. There was much debate over the best place for a landing, Lloyd George urging the occupation of Salonika and the transportation by rail of an army to aid Serbia against Austria-Hungary, and this plan was favoured by two leading French Generals, Gallieni and Franchet d'Espèrey. The Dardanelles project had, however, three major advantages: it appeared to be primarily a naval operation; it would rally Turkey's traditional enemies among the Balkan nations to the Allied side; and it would open up a short warm-water route for supplies to Russia. It was this third consideration which was decisive: for at the end of December gloomy reports were received from Petrograd, indicating an acute shortage of munitions and appealing for British help in relieving Turkish pressure on the Russian armies in the Caucasus. The War Council agreed on a naval expedition 'with Constantinople as its objective' on 15 January 1915.

The Gallipoli enterprise falls into four distinctive phases (which may be studied in pages 110–129, supplemented for naval and submaritime operations by pages 252–254). Naval bombardments on 19 and 26 February were followed by nearly three weeks of abortive minesweeping before the principal attempt by capital ships to force the passage of the Dardanelles on 18 March. Preparations were then made for using British, Australian and New Zealand troops for a series of landings on the Gallipoli peninsula while a French army corps temporarily occupied Kum Kale on the mainland and made a feint assault on Besika Bay. These landings were carried out on 25 April in an atmosphere of almost crusading ardour, but without proper landing craft and with no real training in amphibious operations. The Anzacs established themselves in a cove of steep cliffs and backed by a gorge covered in scrub, where it was difficult to penetrate more than half a mile inland. The British made more headway at Cape Helles, but suffered appalling casualties. Further landings in early August came near to success, but by the end of the summer the troops on the peninsula were as effectively pinned down in a network of trenches as the armies in France and Flanders; four thousand men died in seeking to secure four hundred yards on a mile front. Kitchener went out to investigate in November and accepted the inevitability of evacuation. The final phase, the withdrawal from Anzac and Suvla in December and from Helles a fortnight later, was the most successful aspect of the campaign.

The expedition failed because of confused leadership, insufficient co-ordination, inadequate planning, and sheer lack of troops and firepower; perhaps, too, it failed because the landings were made at the tip of the peninsula rather than at its neck, where there would have been greater freedom of manouvere. Failure at the Dardanelles cost Churchill his predominant position in the War Council; it deprived the Allies of a grand Balkan alliance against Berlin; above all, it completed the isolation of Russia. Gallipoli, with its high hopes twice nearly realised, was a tragic disappointment which discredited imaginative strategic thought in London for many years ahead.

TURKISH DEFENCES AT THE DARDANELLES 1915

This map depicts the Turkish defences guarding the Dardanelles prior to the Allied naval attacks during February and March 1915. Following a Russian request to the Western Allies at the end of 1914 for a "second front" to be created against Turkey to ease pressure on the Russian forces in the Caucasus, British naval authorities devised a three-point plan to force the Dardanelles passage. First, a naval bombardment of the entrance forts; secondly, a minefield-clearing operation; thirdly, a naval force to sail right through the Dardanelles to the Sea of Marmara, and thence on to the Turkish capital of Constantinople.

Vice-Admiral Carden, commander of the British squadron in the Aegean, considered that he would require the following units to successfully force the Dardanelles passage: 12 battleships, 3 battlecruisers, 3 light cruisers, 16 destroyers, 6 submarines, 4 seaplanes, 12 minesweepers, and a plentiful supply of ammunition.

KEY TO MINEFIELDS

1. 26 February 1915.
3. 5 November 1914 - 19 February 1915.
4. 5 November 1914 - 15 February 1915.
7. 5 November 1914 - 15 February 1915.
8. 5 November 1914 - 19 February 1915.
11. 8 March 1915 (laid by 'Nousret').

Note: The correct name for Achi Baba was Alchi Tepe: this was due to a spelling error on British maps, but Achi Baba became the accepted name.

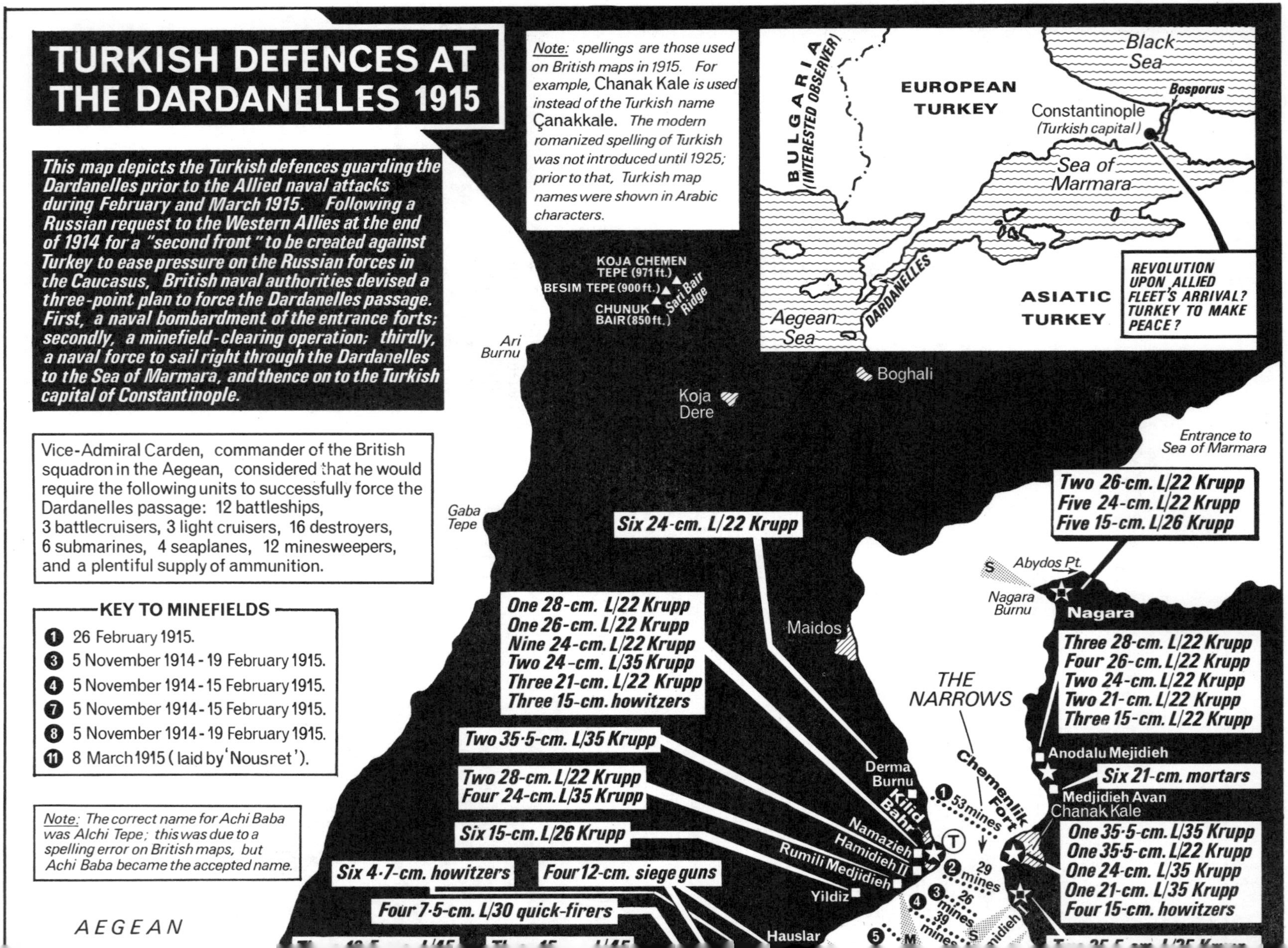

Note: spellings are those used on British maps in 1915. For example, Chanak Kale is used instead of the Turkish name Çanakkale. The modern romanized spelling of Turkish was not introduced until 1925; prior to that, Turkish map names were shown in Arabic characters.

REVOLUTION UPON ALLIED FLEET'S ARRIVAL? TURKEY TO MAKE PEACE?

Inset map labels

Black Sea — Bosporus — Constantinople (Turkish capital) — Sea of Marmara — EUROPEAN TURKEY — ASIATIC TURKEY — BULGARIA (INTERESTED OBSERVER) — DARDANELLES — Aegean Sea

Map labels

Entrance to Sea of Marmara — Nagara — Abydos Pt. — Nagara Burnu — Anodolu Mejidieh — Medjidieh Avan — Chanak Kale — THE NARROWS — Chemenlik Fort — Kilid Bahr — Derma Burnu — Namazieh — Hamidieh — Rumili Medjidieh — Yildiz — Hauslar — Maidos — Boghali — Koja Dere — Ari Burnu — Gaba Tepe — KOJA CHEMEN TEPE (971ft.) — BESIM TEPE (900ft.) — CHUNUK BAIR (850ft.) — AEGEAN

Gun emplacement boxes

- Two 26-cm. L/22 Krupp / Five 24-cm. L/22 Krupp / Five 15-cm. L/26 Krupp
- Three 28-cm. L/22 Krupp / Four 26-cm. L/22 Krupp / Two 24-cm. L/22 Krupp / Two 21-cm. L/22 Krupp / Three 15-cm. L/22 Krupp
- Six 21-cm. mortars
- One 35.5-cm. L/35 Krupp / One 35.5-cm. L/22 Krupp / One 24-cm. L/35 Krupp / One 21-cm. L/22 Krupp / Four 15-cm. howitzers
- Six 24-cm. L/22 Krupp
- One 28-cm. L/22 Krupp / One 26-cm. L/22 Krupp / Nine 24-cm. L/22 Krupp / Two 24-cm. L/35 Krupp / Three 21-cm. L/22 Krupp / Three 15-cm. howitzers
- Two 35.5-cm. L/35 Krupp
- Two 28-cm. L/22 Krupp / Four 24-cm. L/35 Krupp
- Six 15-cm. L/26 Krupp
- Six 4.7-cm. howitzers
- Four 12-cm. siege guns
- Four 7.5-cm. L/30 quick-firers

Minefield markers

53 mines — 29 mines — 26 mines — 39 mines

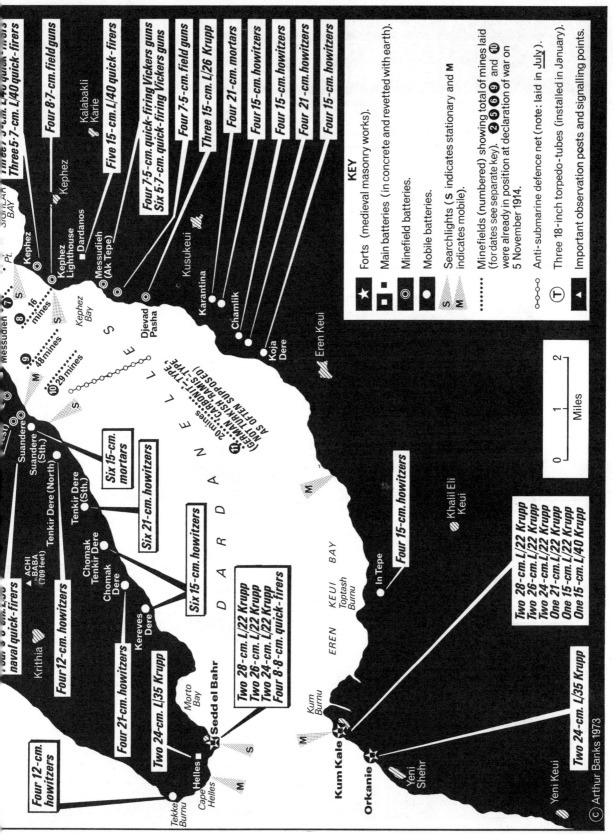

✳ *Note: on 3 November 1914, four Allied warships had bombarded Sedd el Bahr and Kum Kale using 12-inch guns.*

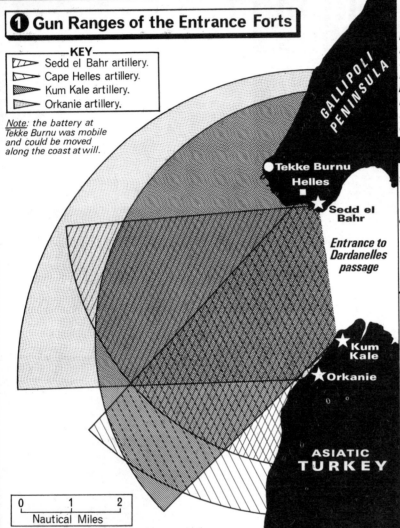

❶ Gun Ranges of the Entrance Forts

—KEY—
- Sedd el Bahr artillery.
- Cape Helles artillery.
- Kum Kale artillery.
- Orkanie artillery.

Note: the battery at Tekke Burnu was mobile and could be moved along the coast at will.

GALLIPOLI PENINSULA

● Tekke Burnu
■ Helles
★ Sedd el Bahr

Entrance to Dardanelles passage

★ Kum Kale
★ Orkanie

ASIATIC TURKEY

```
0        1        2
|_____|_____|
   Nautical Miles
```

GUN RANGES OF TURK[...] ENTRANCE WORKS

Allied estimated maxim[...] ranges of the main guns [...]
L/35 . . . . 12,000 y[...]
L/22 . . . . 10,000 y[...]
(effective ranges rather [...])

NOTES ON GUN CALIBRES

L/35	24-cm. Krupp	9·4–
L/22	28-cm. Krupp	11–
L/22	26-cm. Krupp	10·2–
L/22	24-cm. Krupp	9·4–
L/22	21-cm. Krupp	8·2–
L/22	15-cm. Krupp	5·9–
L/40	15-cm.	5·9–
	12-cm. howitzer	4·7–
	8·8-cm. quick-firer	3·4–

MAIN ALLIED NAVAL ORGANISAT[...]

FIRST DIVISION (British)
'Inflexible' *(flagship)*; 'Agamemnon', and 'Que[...] Elizabeth' *(both en route from Malta)*

SECOND DIVISION (British)
'Vengeance' *(flagship)*; 'Albion', 'Cornwallis', 'Irresistible', 'Triumph'.

THIRD DIVISION (French)
'Suffren' *(flagship)*; 'Bouvet', 'Charlemagne[...] 'Gaulois'.

THE ALLIED PLAN

1. **Long-range bombardment.** (This sta[...] commenced at 0951 hours).
2. **Medium-range bombardment.** (This s[...] commenced at 1400 hours).
3. **Short-range bombardment.** (This sta[...] never materialised).

Note: Main armament of warships to be emp[...] for Stage 1, secondary armament for Stage 2, [...] main armament again for Stage 3 (to complet[...] obliterate the forts and defence remnants, i[...]

TARGETS OF SHIPS (STAGE ON[...])

'Inflexible'	→ Sedd el [...]
'Triumph'	→ Helles
'Cornwallis'	→ Orkanie
'Suffren'	→ Kum Ka[...]

('Bouvet' spotting; 'Gaulois' patrolling off Besik[...])

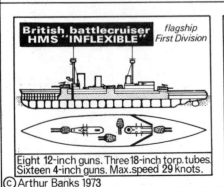

British battlecruiser HMS "INFLEXIBLE" *flagship First Division*

Eight 12-inch guns. Three 18-inch torp. tubes. Sixteen 4-inch guns. Max. speed 29 knots.

© Arthur Banks 1973

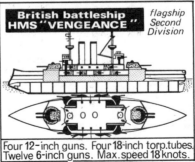

British battleship HMS "VENGEANCE" *flagship Second Division*

Four 12-inch guns. Four 18-inch torp. tubes. Twelve 6-inch guns. Max. speed 18 knots.

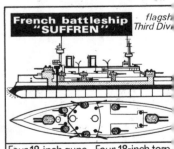

French battleship "SUFFREN" *flagsh[...] Third Div[...]*

Four 12-inch guns. Four 18-inch torp[...] Ten 6·4-inch guns. Max. speed 16 kn[...]

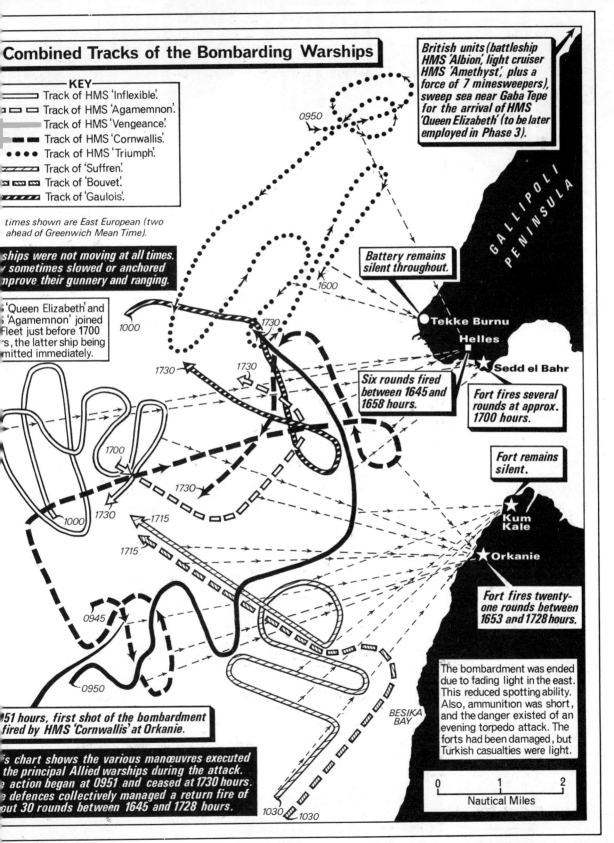

Combined Tracks of the Bombarding Warships

KEY

- ▭ Track of HMS 'Inflexible'.
- ▭▭▭ Track of HMS 'Agamemnon'.
- Track of HMS 'Vengeance'.
- ▬▬▬ Track of HMS 'Cornwallis'.
- ●●●● Track of HMS 'Triumph'.
- ▱▱▱ Track of 'Suffren'.
- ▨▨▨ Track of 'Bouvet'.
- ▨▨▨ Track of 'Gaulois'.

times shown are East European (two ahead of Greenwich Mean Time).

ships were not moving at all times. sometimes slowed or anchored mprove their gunnery and ranging.

'Queen Elizabeth' and 'Agamemnon' joined Fleet just before 1700 rs, the latter ship being mitted immediately.

British units (battleship HMS 'Albion', light cruiser HMS 'Amethyst', plus a force of 7 minesweepers), sweep sea near Gaba Tepe for the arrival of HMS 'Queen Elizabeth' (to be later employed in Phase 3).

Battery remains silent throughout.

Six rounds fired between 1645 and 1658 hours.

Fort fires several rounds at approx. 1700 hours.

Fort remains silent.

Fort fires twenty-one rounds between 1653 and 1728 hours.

The bombardment was ended due to fading light in the east. This reduced spotting ability. Also, ammunition was short, and the danger existed of an evening torpedo attack. The forts had been damaged, but Turkish casualties were light.

51 hours, first shot of the bombardment fired by HMS 'Cornwallis' at Orkanie.

s chart shows the various manœuvres executed the principal Allied warships during the attack. e action began at 0951 and ceased at 1730 hours. e defences collectively managed a return fire of ut 30 rounds between 1645 and 1728 hours.

GALLIPOLI PENINSULA

Tekke Burnu
Helles
Sedd el Bahr
Kum Kale
Orkanie
BESIKA BAY

0 1 2
Nautical Miles

0950
1600
1000
1730
1730
1730
1700
1730
1715
1715
0945
1000
1730
0950
1030 1030

113

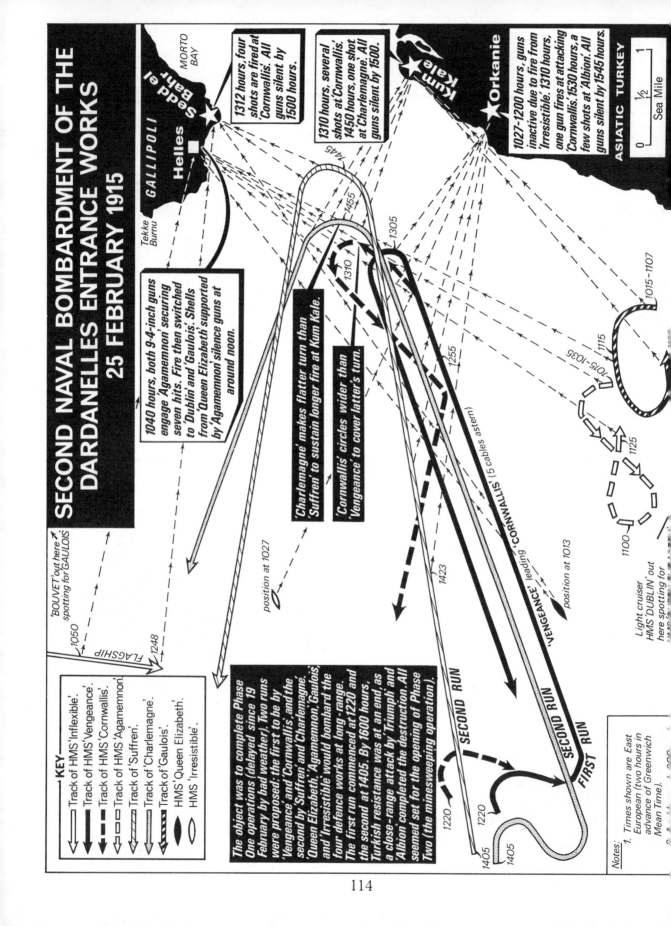

SECOND NAVAL BOMBARDMENT OF THE DARDANELLES ENTRANCE WORKS 25 FEBRUARY 1915

1312 hours, four shots are fired at 'Cornwallis'. All guns silent by 1500 hours.

1310 hours, several shots at 'Cornwallis', 1450 hours, one shot at Charlemagne. All guns silent by 1500.

1027-1200 hours, guns inactive due to fire from 'Irresistible'. 1310 hours, one gun fires at attacking 'Cornwallis'. 1530 hours, a few shots at 'Albion'. All guns silent by 1545 hours.

MORTO BAY

Sedd el Bahr

GALLIPOLI

Helles

Tekke Burnu

Kum Kale

Orkanie

ASIATIC TURKEY

0   ½   1
Sea Mile

1040 hours, both 9.4-inch guns engage 'Agamemnon', securing seven hits. Fire then switched to 'Dublin' and 'Gaulois'. Shells from 'Queen Elizabeth' silence guns at around noon.

'BOUVET' out here spotting for GAULOIS

1050

1248

FLAGSHIP

'Charlemagne' makes flatter turn than 'Suffren' to sustain longer fire at Kum Kale.

'Cornwallis' circles wider than 'Vengeance' to cover latter's turn.

position at 1027

1445

1455

1305

1310

1255

'VENGEANCE' leading 'CORNWALLIS' (5 cables astern)

position at 1013

1423

1015-1107

1115

1015-1038

1125

1100

Light cruiser HMS 'DUBLIN' out here spotting for

SECOND RUN

FIRST RUN

SECOND RUN

1220

1220

1405

1405

The object was to complete Phase One operations (delayed since 19 February by bad weather). Two runs were proposed: the first to be by 'Vengeance' and 'Cornwallis', and the second by 'Suffren' and Charlemagne'. 'Queen Elizabeth', 'Agamemnon' 'Gaulois', and 'Irresistible' would bombard the four defence works at long-range. The first run commenced at 1220 and the second at 1405. By 1600 hours, Turkish resistance was at an end, as a close-range attack by 'Triumph' and 'Albion' completed the destruction. All seemed set for the opening of Phase Two (the minesweeping operation).

KEY
— Track of HMS 'Inflexible'.
— Track of HMS 'Vengeance'.
— Track of HMS 'Cornwallis'.
— Track of HMS 'Agamemnon'.
— Track of 'Suffren'.
— Track of 'Charlemagne'.
— Track of 'Gaulois'.
— HMS 'Queen Elizabeth'.
— HMS 'Irresistible'.

Notes:
1. Times shown are East European (two hours in advance of Greenwich Mean Time).

114

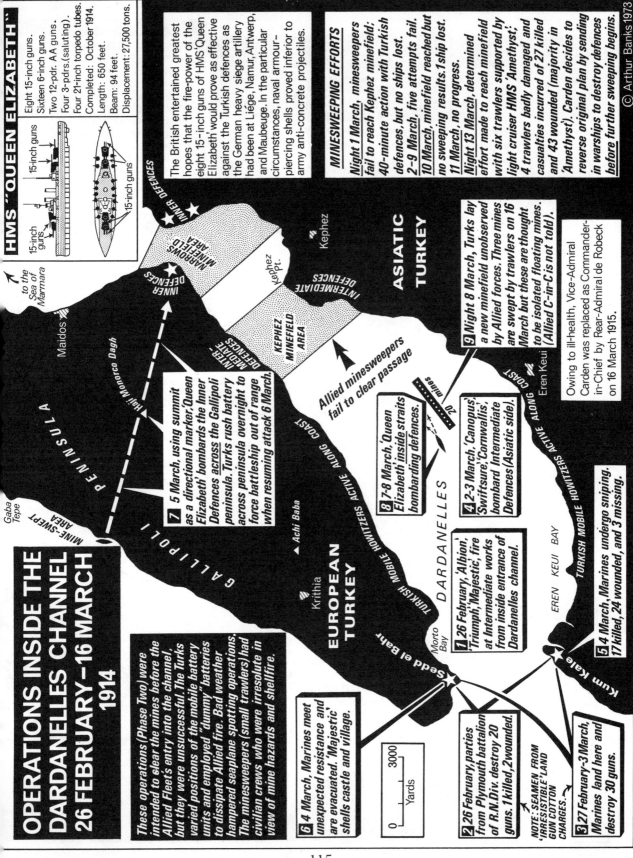

OPERATIONS INSIDE THE DARDANELLES CHANNEL 26 FEBRUARY–16 MARCH 1914

HMS "QUEEN ELIZABETH"

Eight 15-inch guns.
Sixteen 6-inch guns.
Two 12-pdr. AA guns.
Four 3-pdrs.(saluting).
Four 21-inch torpedo tubes.
Completed: October 1914.
Length: 650 feet.
Beam: 94 feet.
Displacement: 27,500 tons.

15-inch guns
15-inch guns
15-inch guns
15-inch guns

The British entertained greatest hopes that the fire-power of the eight 15-inch guns of HMS'Queen Elizabeth' would prove as effective against the Turkish defences as the German heavy siege artillery had been at Liège, Namur, Antwerp, and Maubeuge. In the particular circumstances, naval armour–piercing shells proved inferior to army anti-concrete projectiles.

MINESWEEPING EFFORTS

Night 1 March, minesweepers fail to reach Kephez minefield: 40-minute action with Turkish defences, but no ships lost.
2–9 March, five attempts fail.
10 March, minefield reached but no sweeping results. 1 ship lost.
11 March, no progress.
Night 13 March, determined effort made to reach minefield with six trawlers supported by light cruiser HMS 'Amethyst'. 4 trawlers badly damaged and casualties incurred of 27 killed and 43 wounded (majority in 'Amethyst'). Carden decides to reverse original plan by sending in warships to destroy defences *before further sweeping begins.*

© Arthur Banks 1973

to the Sea of Marmara

Maidos

GALLIPOLI PENINSULA

Hali Monoroco Dagh

INNER DEFENCES
INNER DEFENCES
MARROWS MINEFIELD AREA
INTERMEDIATE DEFENCES
KEPHEZ MINEFIELD AREA
INTERMEDIATE DEFENCES

Kephez
Kephez Pt.

ASIATIC TURKEY

Allied minesweepers fail to clear passage

Gaba Tepe
MINE-SWEPT AREA

Achi Baba
Krithia

EUROPEAN TURKEY

DARDANELLES

TURKISH MOBILE HOWITZERS ACTIVE ALONG COAST

TURKISH MOBILE HOWITZERS ACTIVE ALONG COAST

Sedd el Bahr
Morto Bay

EREN KEUI BAY

Kum Kale
Eren Keui

mines
20

These operations (Phase Two) were intended to clear the mines before the Allied Fleet's entry into the channel, but they were unsuccessful. The Turks varied positions of the mobile batteries units and employed "dummy" batteries to dissipate Allied fire. Bad weather hampered seaplane spotting operations. The minesweepers (small trawlers) had civilian crews who were irresolute in view of mine hazards and shellfire.

7 5 March, using summit as a directional marker, 'Queen Elizabeth' bombards the Inner Defences across the Gallipoli peninsula. Turks rush battery across peninsula overnight to force battleship out of range when resuming attack 6 March.

8 7-8 March, 'Queen Elizabeth' inside straits bombarding defences.

9 Night 8 March, Turks lay a new minefield unobserved by Allied forces. Three mines are swept by trawlers on 16 March but these are thought to be isolated floating mines. (Allied C–in–C is not told).

Owing to ill-health, Vice-Admiral Carden was replaced as Commander-in-Chief by Rear-Admiral de Robeck on 16 March 1915.

4 2-3 March, 'Canopus', 'Swiftsure', 'Cornwallis', bombard Intermediate Defences (Asiatic side).

1 26 February, 'Albion', 'Triumph','Majestic', fire at Intermediate works from inside entrance of Dardanelles channel.

5 4 March, Marines undergo sniping. 17 killed, 24 wounded, and 3 missing.

6 4 March, Marines meet unexpected resistance and are evacuated. 'Majestic' shells castle and village.

2 26 February, parties from Plymouth battalion of R.N.Div. destroy 20 guns. 1 killed, 2 wounded.

3 27 February–3 March, Marines land here and destroy 30 guns.

NOTE: SEAMEN FROM 'IRRESISTIBLE' LAND GUN COTTON CHARGES.

0   3000
Yards

THE ALLIED FAILURE TO FORCE THE DARDANELLES PASSAGE 18 MARCH 1915

1030 hours, preceded by destroyers, the Allied fleet of 17 battleships and 1 battlecruiser entered the straits and advanced to allotted positions. Line 'A' opened fire at 1130 and Line 'B' was advanced at 1206. By 1345, the defences were inactive; consequently the minesweepers were ordered up supported by Second Division (to relieve Line 'B'). Moving out, 'Bouvet' was mined at 1355, then capsized and sank in two minutes. 1610 'Irresistible' was mined; 1614 'Inflexible' suffered a similar fate. At 1715 'Gaulois' was badly holed and had to beached. 1805 'Ocean' was mined and abandoned. Thus one-third of the capital ships were either sunk or incapacitated and the naval attempt to force the Dardanelles was called off. Prematurely? By 16 April, a British destroyer—minesweeping "fast" force was in existence ("Beagle"-class ships). This fact is not generally appreciated.

The attack of 18 March was intended to bre the stalemate situation of Phase Two in wh the minesweeper crews were reluctant to pursue their operations until the capital sh had silenced the Turkish main batteries. Tl Allied plan allowed for the trawlers to begi sweeping operations two hours after star of the long-range bombardment, whereup they were to clear a channel 900 yards bro past Kephez Point into Sari Sighlar Bay. *(It should be noted that the Allied naval comma was unaware of the full extent of the Turkish m fields despite detailed Intelligence reports whic had not been passed on).*

Prior to the attack, the Allies worried over the alleged existence of torpedo-tubes on both sides of the channel. In fact, there were only three tubes in position, all at Kilid Bahr. Each tube was equipped with two torpedoes, but only one tube could fire right across the width of the Narrows, the others less than halfway across.

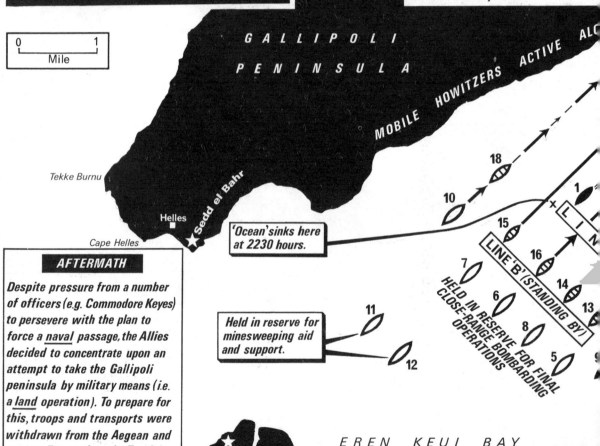

0 —— 1 Mile

SARI TEPE

KRITHIA

GALLIPOLI PENINSULA

MOBILE HOWITZERS ACTIVE ALC

Tekke Burnu

Helles

Sedd el Bahr

Cape Helles

'Ocean' sinks here at 2230 hours.

18

10

1

15

16

LINE 'B' (STANDING BY)

14

13

7

HELD IN RESERVE FOR FINAL CLOSE-RANGE BOMBARDING OPERATIONS

6

8

5

11

Held in reserve for minesweeping aid and support.

12

AFTERMATH

Despite pressure from a number of officers (e.g. Commodore Keyes) to persevere with the plan to force a naval passage, the Allies decided to concentrate upon an attempt to take the Gallipoli peninsula by military means (i.e. a land operation). To prepare for this, troops and transports were withdrawn from the Aegean and sent to Egypt: thus, the Turkish defenders gained a valuable respite.

Kum Kale

EREN KEUI BAY

Toptash Burnu

MOB

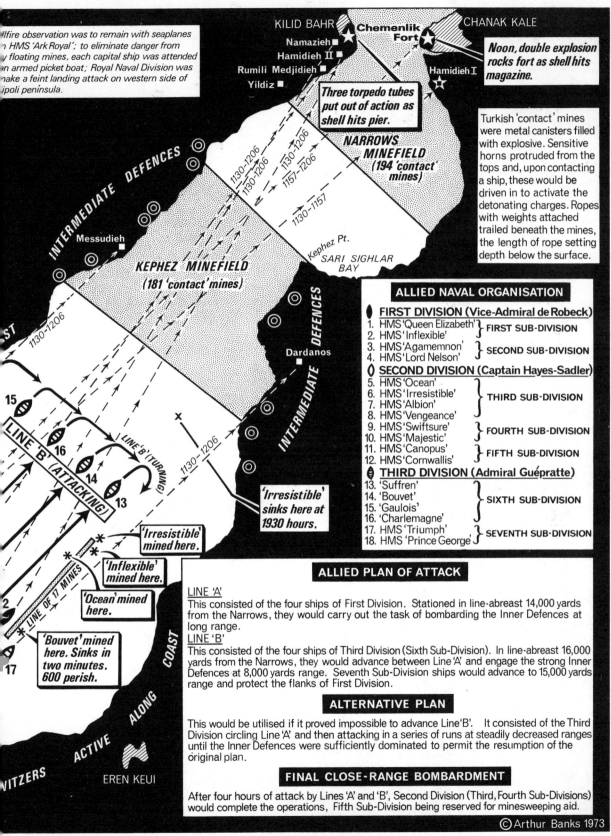

Illfire observation was to remain with seaplanes in HMS 'Ark Royal'; to eliminate danger from floating mines, each capital ship was attended an armed picket boat; Royal Naval Division was make a feint landing attack on western side of ipoli peninsula.

KILID BAHR   CHANAK KALE

Chemenlik Fort

Namazieh
Hamidieh II
Rumili Medjidieh
Yildiz

Hamidieh I

Noon, double explosion rocks fort as shell hits magazine.

Three torpedo tubes put out of action as shell hits pier.

NARROWS MINEFIELD (194 'contact' mines)

1130-1206
1130-1206
1130-1206
1157-1206
1130-1157

Turkish 'contact' mines were metal canisters filled with explosive. Sensitive horns protruded from the tops and, upon contacting a ship, these would be driven in to activate the detonating charges. Ropes with weights attached trailed beneath the mines, the length of rope setting depth below the surface.

Kephez Pt.

SARI SIGHLAR BAY

INTERMEDIATE DEFENCES

Messudieh

KEPHEZ MINEFIELD (181 'contact' mines)

1130-1206

INTERMEDIATE DEFENCES

Dardanos

15

LINE 'B' (TURNING)

LINE 'B' (ATTACKING)

16

14

13

1130-1206

'Irresistible' sinks here at 1930 hours.

'Irresistible' mined here.

'Inflexible' mined here.

LINE OF 17 MINES

2

'Ocean' mined here.

'Bouvet' mined here. Sinks in two minutes. 600 perish.

17

COAST

ACTIVE ALONG

WITZERS   EREN KEUI

ALLIED NAVAL ORGANISATION

FIRST DIVISION (Vice-Admiral de Robeck)
1. HMS 'Queen Elizabeth' } **FIRST SUB-DIVISION**
2. HMS 'Inflexible'
3. HMS 'Agamemnon' } **SECOND SUB-DIVISION**
4. HMS 'Lord Nelson'
SECOND DIVISION (Captain Hayes-Sadler)
5. HMS 'Ocean'
6. HMS 'Irresistible' } **THIRD SUB-DIVISION**
7. HMS 'Albion'
8. HMS 'Vengeance'
9. HMS 'Swiftsure' } **FOURTH SUB-DIVISION**
10. HMS 'Majestic'
11. HMS 'Canopus' } **FIFTH SUB-DIVISION**
12. HMS 'Cornwallis'
THIRD DIVISION (Admiral Guépratte)
13. 'Suffren'
14. 'Bouvet' } **SIXTH SUB-DIVISION**
15. 'Gaulois'
16. 'Charlemagne'
17. HMS 'Triumph' } **SEVENTH SUB-DIVISION**
18. HMS 'Prince George'

ALLIED PLAN OF ATTACK

LINE 'A'
This consisted of the four ships of First Division. Stationed in line-abreast 14,000 yards from the Narrows, they would carry out the task of bombarding the Inner Defences at long range.
LINE 'B'
This consisted of the four ships of Third Division (Sixth Sub-Division). In line-abreast 16,000 yards from the Narrows, they would advance between Line 'A' and engage the strong Inner Defences at 8,000 yards range. Seventh Sub-Division ships would advance to 15,000 yards range and protect the flanks of First Division.

ALTERNATIVE PLAN

This would be utilised if it proved impossible to advance Line 'B'. It consisted of the Third Division circling Line 'A' and then attacking in a series of runs at steadily decreased ranges until the Inner Defences were sufficiently dominated to permit the resumption of the original plan.

FINAL CLOSE-RANGE BOMBARDMENT

After four hours of attack by Lines 'A' and 'B', Second Division (Third, Fourth Sub-Divisions) would complete the operations, Fifth Sub-Division being reserved for minesweeping aid.

© Arthur Banks 1973

117

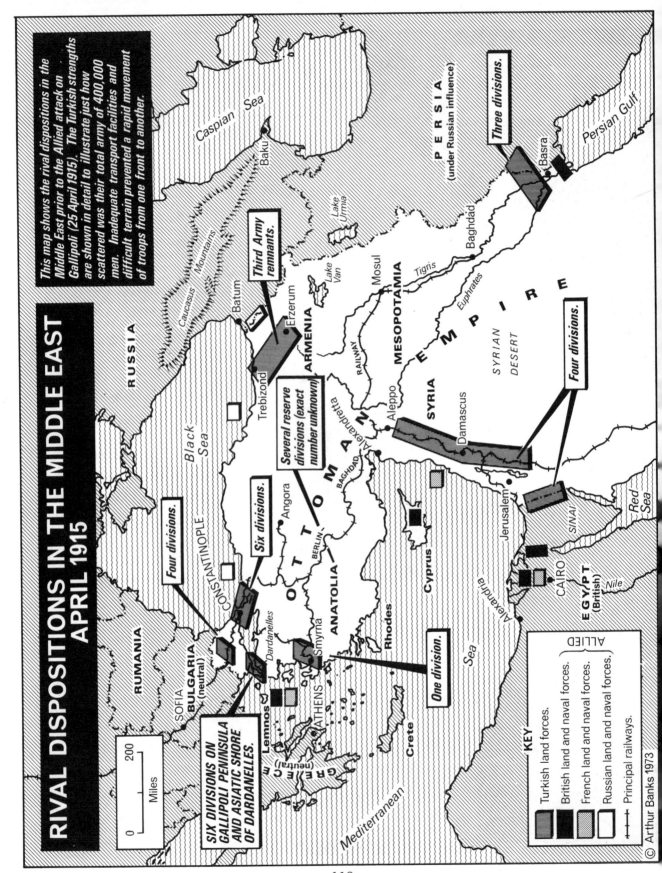

RIVAL DISPOSITIONS IN THE MIDDLE EAST
APRIL 1915

This map shows the rival dispositions in the Middle East prior to the Allied attack on Gallipoli (25 April 1915). The Turkish strengths are shown in detail to illustrate just how scattered was their total army of 400,000 men. Inadequate transport facilities and difficult terrain prevented a rapid movement of troops from one front to another.

Caspian Sea

PERSIA
(under Russian influence)

Three divisions.

Basra

Persian Gulf

Baghdad

Lake Urmia

Mosul

MESOPOTAMIA

Tigris

Euphrates

Third Army remnants.

Erzerum

ARMENIA

Lake Van

E M P I R E

Batum

Caucasus Mountains

RUSSIA

Trebizond

Several reserve divisions (exact number unknown).

Four divisions.

SYRIAN DESERT

Aleppo

SYRIA

Damascus

Black Sea

RAILWAY

Alexandretta

Angora

Six divisions.

O T T O M A N

BAGHDAD-

BERLIN-

Jerusalem

SINAI

Red Sea

CONSTANTINOPLE

Four divisions.

RUMANIA

SOFIA

BULGARIA
(neutral)

Dardanelles

Smyrna

ANATOLIA

Rhodes

Cyprus

CAIRO

EGYPT
(British)

Nile

Alexandria

One division.

SIX DIVISIONS ON GALLIPOLI PENINSULA AND ASIATIC SHORE OF DARDANELLES.

Lemnos

ATHENS

GREECE
(neutral)

Crete

Mediterranean

Aegean Sea

KEY

	ALLIED
Turkish land forces.	
British land and naval forces.	
French land and naval forces.	
Russian land and naval forces.	
Principal railways.	

0   200   Miles

© Arthur Banks 1973

118

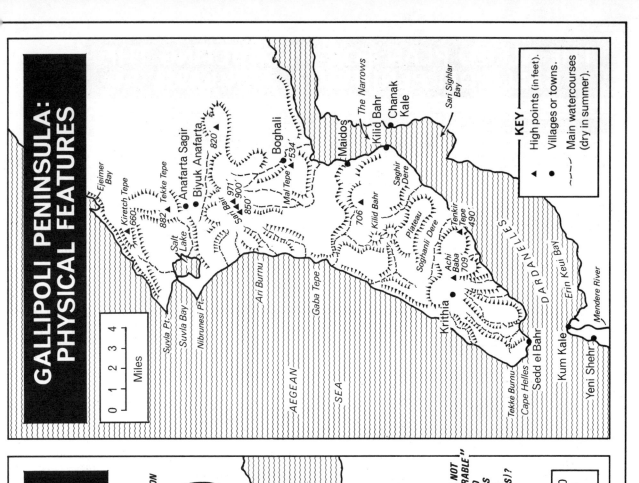

GALLIPOLI PENINSULA: PHYSICAL FEATURES

KEY

▲ High points (in feet).

● Villages or towns.

〜 Main watercourses (dry in summer).

Miles: 0 1 2 3 4

Ejeimer Bay, Kiretch Tepe 660', Salt Lake, Suvla Pt., Suvla Bay, Nibrunesi Pt., Anafarta Sagir, Biyuk Anafarta, 882', Tekke Tepe, 820', Boghali, Mal Tepe, 534', 971', 900', 850', Sari Bair, Ari Burnu, Gaba Tepe, Kilid Bahr, 706', Plateau, Soghanli Dere, Saghir Dere, Achi Baba 709', Tenkir Tepe 490', Krithia, AEGEAN SEA, Maidos, The Narrows, Kilid Bahr, Chanak Kale, Sari Sighlar Bay, DARDANELLES, Erin Keui Bay, Mendere River, Tekke Burnu, Cape Helles, Sedd el Bahr, Kum Kale, Yeni Shehr

---

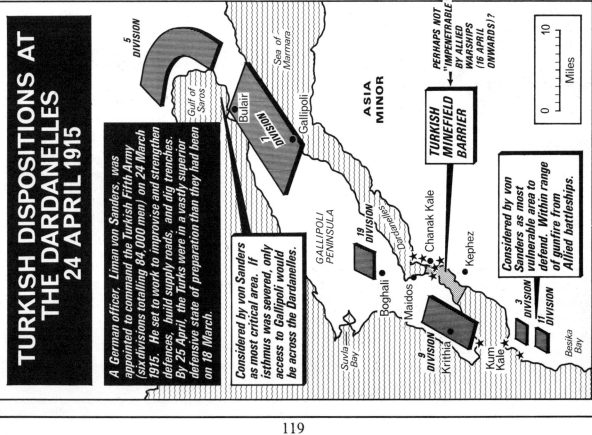

TURKISH DISPOSITIONS AT THE DARDANELLES 24 APRIL 1915

A German officer, Liman von Sanders, was appointed to command the Turkish Fifth Army (six divisions totalling 84,000 men) on 24 March 1915. He set to work to improvise and strengthen defences, build supply roads, and dig trenches. By 25 April, the Turks were in a vastly superior defensive state of preparation than they had been on 18 March.

Considered by von Sanders as most critical area. If isthmus was severed, only access to Gallipoli would be across the Dardanelles.

PERHAPS NOT "IMPENETRABLE" BY ALLIED WARSHIPS (16 APRIL ONWARDS)!?

TURKISH MINEFIELD BARRIER

Considered by von Sanders as most vulnerable area to defend. Within range of gunfire from Allied battleships.

5 DIVISION, Gulf of Saros, Bulair, 7 DIVISION, Sea of Marmara, Gallipoli, ASIA MINOR, Chanak Kale, Kephez, 19 DIVISION, GALLIPOLI PENINSULA, Boghali, Maidos, Dardanelles, Suvla Bay, 9 DIVISION, Krithia, Kum Kale, 3 DIVISION, 11 DIVISION, Besika Bay

Miles: 0 10

© Arthur Banks 1973

THE ALLIED PLAN FOR ASSAULTING THE GALLIPOLI PENINSULA APRIL 1915

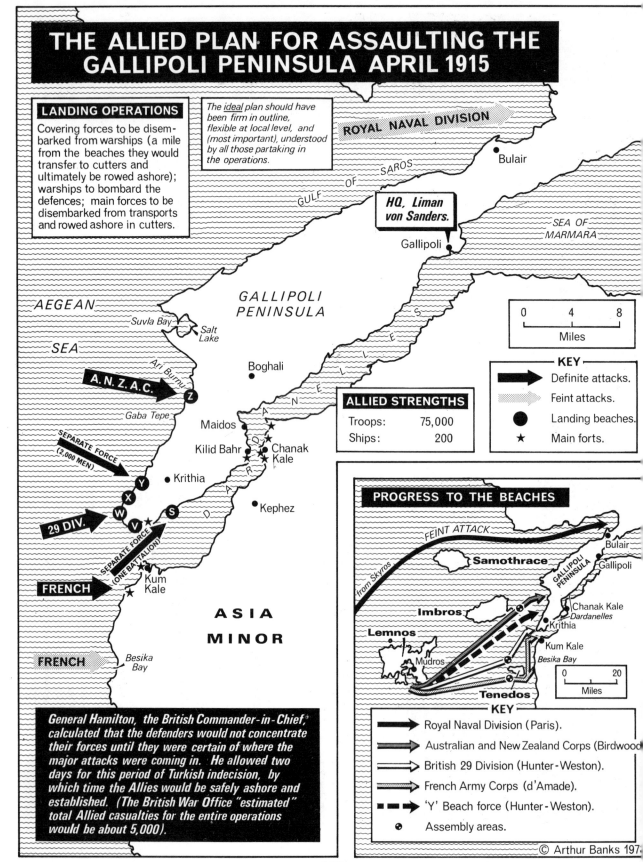

LANDING OPERATIONS

Covering forces to be disembarked from warships (a mile from the beaches they would transfer to cutters and ultimately be rowed ashore); warships to bombard the defences; main forces to be disembarked from transports and rowed ashore in cutters.

The ideal plan should have been firm in outline, flexible at local level, and (most important), understood by all those partaking in the operations.

ROYAL NAVAL DIVISION

Bulair

GULF OF SAROS

HQ, Liman von Sanders.

Gallipoli

SEA OF MARMARA

GALLIPOLI PENINSULA

AEGEAN

SEA

Suvla Bay

Salt Lake

Ari Burnu

A.N.Z.A.C.

Z

Gaba Tepe

Boghali

SEPARATE FORCE (2,000 MEN)

Maidos

Kilid Bahr

Chanak Kale

Y

Krithia

X

W

29 DIV.

V

S

SEPARATE FORCE (ONE BATTALION)

Kephez

FRENCH

Kum Kale

FRENCH

Besika Bay

ASIA

MINOR

ALLIED STRENGTHS

Troops:	75,000
Ships:	200

KEY

→ Definite attacks.

⇒ Feint attacks.

● Landing beaches.

★ Main forts.

0   4   8
Miles

PROGRESS TO THE BEACHES

FEINT ATTACK

from Skyros

Samothrace

GALLIPOLI PENINSULA

Bulair

Gallipoli

Imbros

Chanak Kale

Dardanelles

Lemnos

Krithia

Mudros

Kum Kale

Besika Bay

Tenedos

0   20
Miles

KEY

→ Royal Naval Division (Paris).

⇒ Australian and New Zealand Corps (Birdwood)

⇒ British 29 Division (Hunter-Weston).

⇒ French Army Corps (d'Amade).

▰▰▰► 'Y' Beach force (Hunter-Weston).

⊕ Assembly areas.

General Hamilton, the British Commander-in-Chief, calculated that the defenders would not concentrate their forces until they were certain of where the major attacks were coming in. He allowed two days for this period of Turkish indecision, by which time the Allies would be safely ashore and established. (The British War Office "estimated" total Allied casualties for the entire operations would be about 5,000).

THE ALLIED LANDINGS ON THE GALLIPOLI PENINSULA 25 APRIL 1915

0   1   2   3

Miles

THE A.N.Z.A.C. LANDINGS THE LANDINGS WERE MADE AT AN INCORRECT AND DISADVANTAGEOUS POINT. REASONS SUGGESTED FOR THE ERROR INCLUDE AN UNFORESEEN NORTHERLY CURRENT, LAST-MINUTE PLAN VARIATIONS, THE MOVEMENT OF A MARKER BUOY BY TURKS, AND SOME MISINTERPRETED SIGNALS.

Ari Burnu

AEGEAN SEA

Gaba Tepe

1 HMS 'London'.   Intended landing area.
2 HMS 'Prince of Wales'.   Actual landing position.
3 HMS 'Queen'.   'Tows' to shore.

TURKEY IN EUROPE

HQ, Turkish 19 Division (in reserve under Mustapha Kemal Pasha).

Boghali

Sari Bair Ridge

LANDING FORCE

Ari Burnu

Koja Dere

MAIN FORCE

Mal Tepe

to Sea of Marmara

Gaba Tepe

Maidos

GALLIPOLI PENINSULA

Australian submarine AE 2 sinks Turkish gunboat.

AEGEAN SEA

Kum Tepe

TURKISH 9 DIV. (Sami)

Kilid Bahr

Chanak Kale

NARROWS MINEFIELD

0600 hours, 2,000 troops land from 'Athemyst' and 'Sapphire' without opposition.

Sari Tepe

MAIN FORCE

Achi Baba

Krithia

KEPHEZ MINEFIELD

0630 hours, three battalions land from 'Implacable' without a casualty.

Y

TURKEY IN ASIA

Gully Beach

X

Dardanelles

0750 hours, three companies get ashore covered by guns of 'Cornwallis'.

W

S

0600 hours, Turks inflict 533 casualties on British, but troops get ashore.

V

Sedd el Bahr

0625 hours, 'River Clyde' attempts to land 1,500 men. Turks open fusillade on boat-causeway to shore. British suffer 1,200 casualties.

To achieve success, the Allies required: a unified command; knowledge of the opposing defences and unit strengths; accurate maps of the terrain; the element of surprise. <u>They possessed none of these essentials.</u>

INITIAL REACTIONS BY THE DEFENDERS
Liman von Sanders, the German commander, was at Bulair viewing the feint attack by the Royal Naval Division. (This was the landing area most feared by him). He ordered all available troops at Gallipoli town to race to the "threatened" isthmus. Meanwhile, reports of the extent of the various attacks around the peninsula alarmed him greatly. A report of an enemy submarine within the Dardanelles caused him to dismiss any idea of ferrying troop reinforcements across the Dardanelles from the Asiatic shore.

KEY

—— Allied objectives by dusk 25 April.

--- Positions actually gained by dusk 25 April.

Turkish infantry units (companies or platoons).

Turkish artillery batteries.

● Landing beaches.

© Arthur Banks 1973

121

THE ALLIED ADVANCE ON THE HELLES FRONT 28 APRIL – 4 JUNE

to Anzac, Suvla, & Sari Bair

0   ½   1
Mile

KEY
- British front line, dusk 4 June.
- French front line, dusk 4 June.
- British front line, 9 May.
- French front line, 9 May.
- British front line, 6 May.
- French front line, 6 May.
- British front line, dusk 28 April.
- French front line, dusk 28 April.

ALLIED BATTLE CASUALTIES
British & Dominion:	40,000
French:	20,000

Allied casualties from disease were twice the figures shown above: "the sufferings of the troops were terrible...."
CLEMENT ATTLEE to AUTHOR on 22 April 1965 in London.

4 June, fierce resistance by Turks at Third Battle of Krithia.

KRITHIA

to Achi Baba

Gully Ravine

TRENCHES

TRENCHES

TRENCHES

road

TRENCHES

TRENCHES

TRENCHES

TRENCHES

TRENCHES

Kereves dry Dere

dry

GULLY BEACH

BRITISH ADVANCE

INADEQUATE ARTILLERY AND AMMUNITION (naval guns inaccurate against small trench targets)

FRENCH ADVANCE

AEGEAN SEA

'X' BEACH

dry

dry

dry

Kirte Dere

Kanli Dere

dry

BAKERY BEACH

▲ Hill 114

dry

Morto Bay

Cape Tekke

'W' BEACH

▲ Hill 138

▲ Hill 141

'S' BEACH

Eski Hissarlik

SEDD EL BAHR

THE KRITHIA BATTLES 1915
1 28 April.
2 6-8 May.
3 4 June.

Cape Helles   'V' BEACH

DARDANELLES

After 4 June, Allied progress was slight, and the French were eager for fresh landings to be made in size on the Asiatic shore near Kum Kale. In an attempt to break the trench deadlock to the south of Krithia, the British planned new attacks to the north, at Suvla Bay and upon Sari Bair.

© Arthur Banks 1973

122

FRESH BRITISH LANDINGS 1915

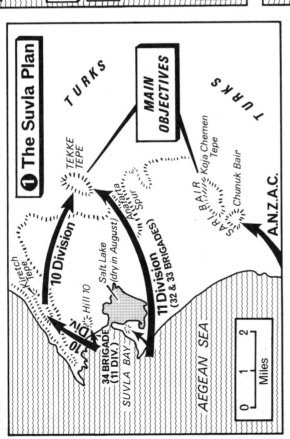

❶ The Suvla Plan

TURKS

TURKS

MAIN OBJECTIVES

A.N.Z.A.C.

TEKKE TEPE

Koja Chemen Tepe

Anafarta Spur

B A I R

Chunuk Bair

Kiretch Tepe

Hill 10

Salt Lake (Dry in August)

10 DIV.

34 BRIGADE (11 DIV.)

SUVLA BAY

AEGEAN SEA

10 Division

11 Division (32 & 33 BRIGADES)

0 1 2 Miles

❷ The Landings of 11 Division Night 6/7 August

THE INCORRECT LANDFALL OF 34 BRIGADE WAS SIMILAR TO THE ERROR MADE ON 25 APRIL AT ARI BURNU.

Turkish outposts.

Turkish outposts

TURKS (not in strength)

Chocolate Hill

KARAKOL RIDGE
Kiretch Tepe

Ghazi Baba

Beach

Spit

Cut

SUVLA BAY

DRY SALT LAKE

Hill 10

Lala Baba

Nibrunesi Beach

Suvla Pt.

Nibrunesi Pt.

32 BRIGADE

33 BRIGADE

Intended landing area of 34 Brigade.

Actual landing area of 34 Brigade.

0 1 Mile

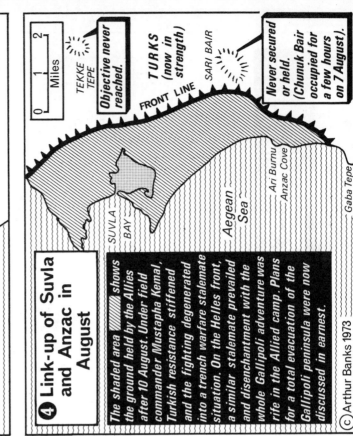

❸ The Landings of 10 Division Morning 7 August

THIS MAP SHOWS MORE LANDINGS DEVIATING FROM THE ORIGINAL PLAN. THUS, THE INVADERS WERE SCATTERED AND DISORGANIZED FROM OUTSET.

British destroyer fires shell into lake to test if surface is firm for possible infantry advance. (It is not).

Landing area of five battalions.

Intended landing area of whole 10 Division.

Landing area of 30 and 31 Brigades.

KARAKOL RIDGE

Kiretch Tepe

Ghazi Baba

Beach

Cut

DRY SALT LAKE

Hill 10

Lala Baba

SUVLA BAY

Suvla Pt.

Nibrunesi Beach

Nibrunesi Pt.

NOTE:
AT THIS PERIOD, THE TOTAL TURKISH STRENGTH AT SUVLA WAS ONLY 1,500.

0 ½ Mile

❹ Link-up of Suvla and Anzac in August

Objective never reached.

TEKKE TEPE

T U R K S (now in strength)

FRONT LINE

SARI BAIR

Never secured or held. (Chunuk Bair occupied for a few hours on 7 August).

SUVLA BAY

Aegean Sea

Ari Burnu

Anzac Cove

Gaba Tepe

0 1 2 Miles

The shaded area shows the ground held by the Allies after 10 August. Under field commander Mustapha Kemal, Turkish resistance stiffened and the fighting degenerated into a trench warfare stalemate situation. On the Helles front, a similar stalemate prevailed and disenchantment with the whole Gallipoli adventure was rife in the Allied camp. Plans for a total evacuation of the Gallipoli peninsula were now discussed in earnest.

© Arthur Banks 1973

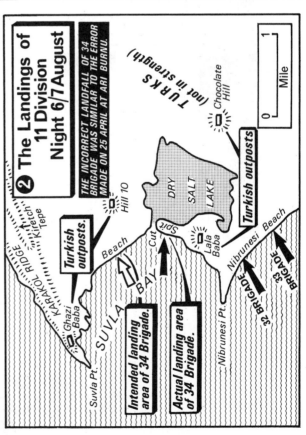

123

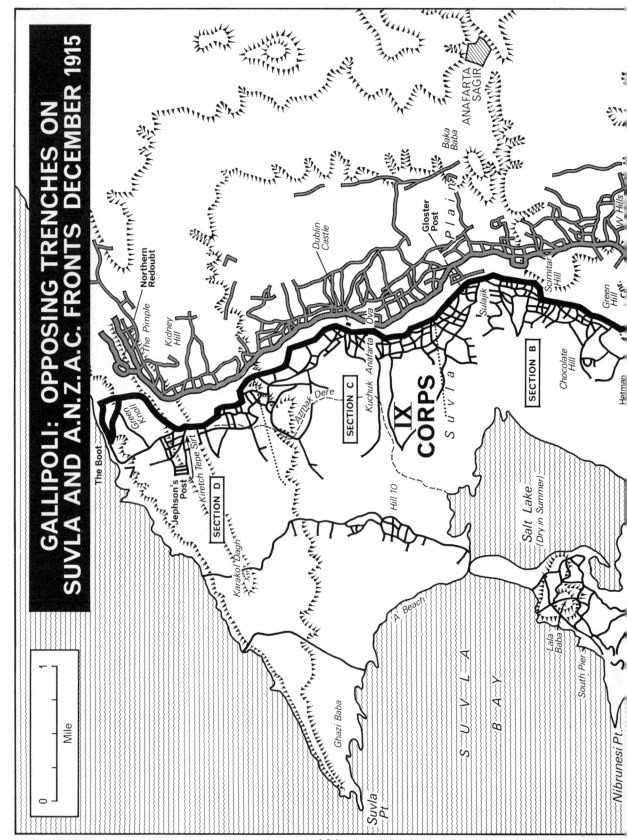

GALLIPOLI: OPPOSING TRENCHES ON SUVLA AND A.N.Z.A.C. FRONTS DECEMBER 1915

0 Mile 1

The Boot

Green Knoll

Jephson's Post

Kiretch Tepe Sirt

SECTION D

Karakol Dagh

Ghazi Baba

Suvla Pt.

The Pimple

Kidney Hill

Northern Redoubt

Azmak Dere

SECTION C

Kuchuk Anafarta Ova

Dublin Castle

Hill 10

'A' Beach

S — U — V — L — A

B — A — Y

SUVLA BAY

Salt Lake
(Dry in Summer)

Lala Baba

South Pier

Nibrunesi Pt.

IX CORPS

Suvla Plain

Gloster Post

Sulajik

SECTION B

Chocolate Hill

Hetman

Scimitar Hill

Green Hill

W Hills

Baka Baba

ANAFARTA SAGIR

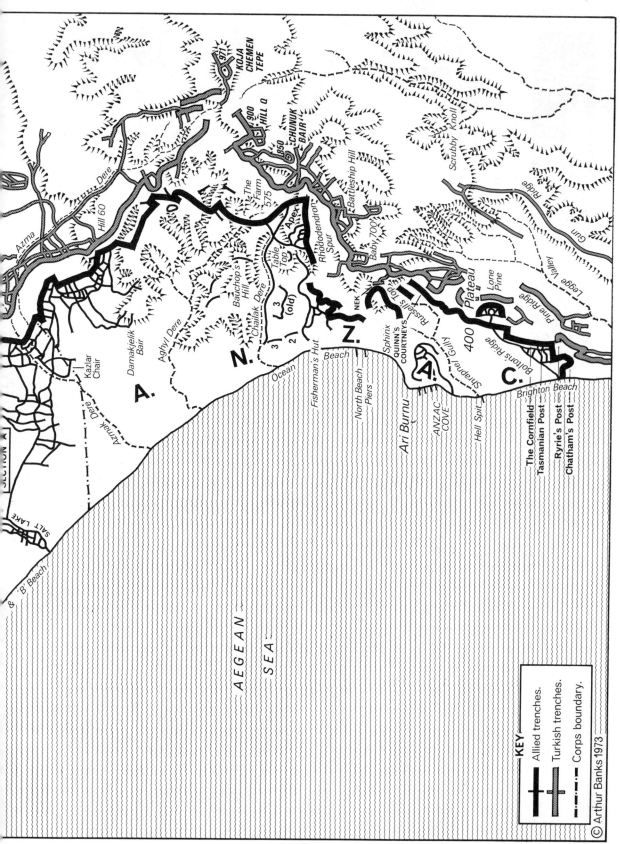

971

KOJA
CHEMEN
TEPE

900
HILL Q

CHUNUK
BAIR

850

The
Farm
575

Battleship Hill

Scrubby Knoll

Hill 60

Azma

Dere

Rhododendron
Spur

Apex

Table
Top

Baby 700

Gun Ridge

Legge Valley

Bauchop's
Hill

Aghyl Dere

Chailak Dere

NEK

Russell's Top

Plateau

Lone
Pine

Pine Ridge

Damakjelik Bair

3
2
(old)

Sphinx

QUINN'S
COURTNEYS

400

Bolton's Ridge

Kazlar
Chair

A.

N.

Z.

A.

C.

Ocean

Fisherman's Hut
Beach

North Beach
Piers

Ari Burnu

Shrapnel Gully

Hell Spit

Brighton Beach

Aztack Dere

ANZAC
COVE

SECTION A

The Cornfield
Tasmanian Post
Ryrie's Post
Chatham's Post

A E G E A N

S E A

SALT LAKE

& 'B' Beach

KEY
Allied trenches.
Turkish trenches.
Corps boundary.

© Arthur Banks 1973

125

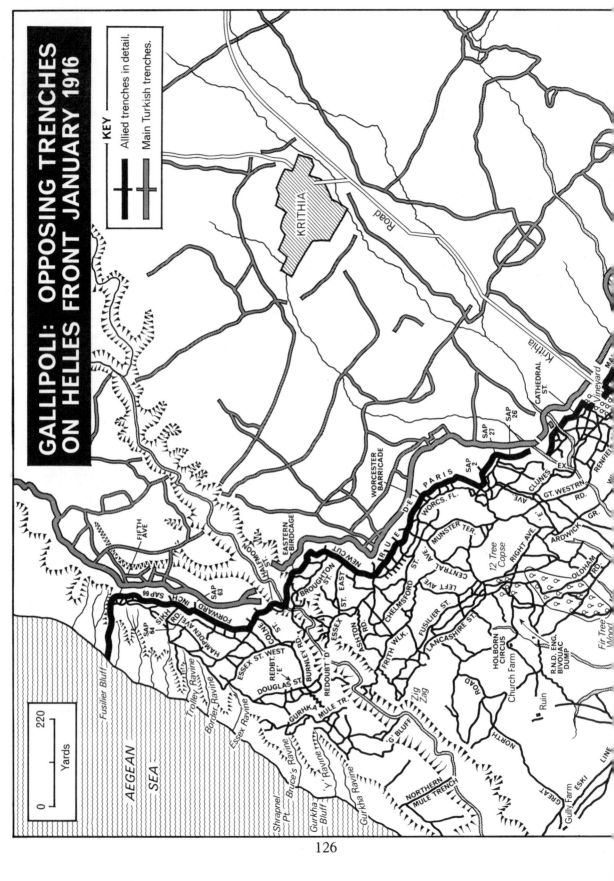

GALLIPOLI: OPPOSING TRENCHES ON HELLES FRONT JANUARY 1916

KEY
━━━━ Allied trenches in detail.
▦▦▦▦ Main Turkish trenches.

KRITHIA

Krithia Road

AEGEAN SEA

0   220
Yards

Fusilier Bluff

Shrapnel Pt.—Bruce's Ravine

Gurkha Bluff

Trolley Ravine

Border Ravine

Essex Ravine

'Y' Ravine

Gurkha Ravine

NORTHERN MULE TRENCH

FIFTH AVE

HALFMOON ST.

EASTERN BIRDCAGE

WORCESTER BARRICADE

SAP 66

SIKH RD.

SAP 64

SAP 63

HAMPDEN AVE

FORWARD INCH

COL. ST.

BROUGHTON ST.

NEW CUT

ESSEX ST.

ESSEX ST. WEST

REDBT. 'D'

REDOUBT 'E'

BURNLEY RD.

DOUGLAS ST.

GURHKA

MULE TR.

ASHTON RD.

CHELMSFORD ST.

FRITH WLK.

FUSILIER ST.

LANCASHIRE ST.

'G' BLUFF

Zig Zag

RUE DE PARIS

WORCS. FL.

ST. AVE.

CENTRAL AVE.

LEFT AVE.

MUNSTER TER.

12 Tree Copse

RIGHT AVE.

'E'

GT. WESTRN RD.

CLUNES AVE.

ARDWICK GR.

OLDHAM RD.

HOLBORN CIRCUS

Church Farm

Ruin

NORTH ROAD

R.N.D. ENG. BIVOUAC DUMP

Fir Tree Wood

Gully Farm

ESKI LINE

GREAT

SAP 27

SAP 26

SAP 2

CATHEDRAL ST.

Vineyard

EX

RENFIELD

WE

MA

Krithia

126

© Arthur Banks 1973

127

THE EVACUATIONS OF THE SUVLA AND A.N.Z.A.C. POSITIONS

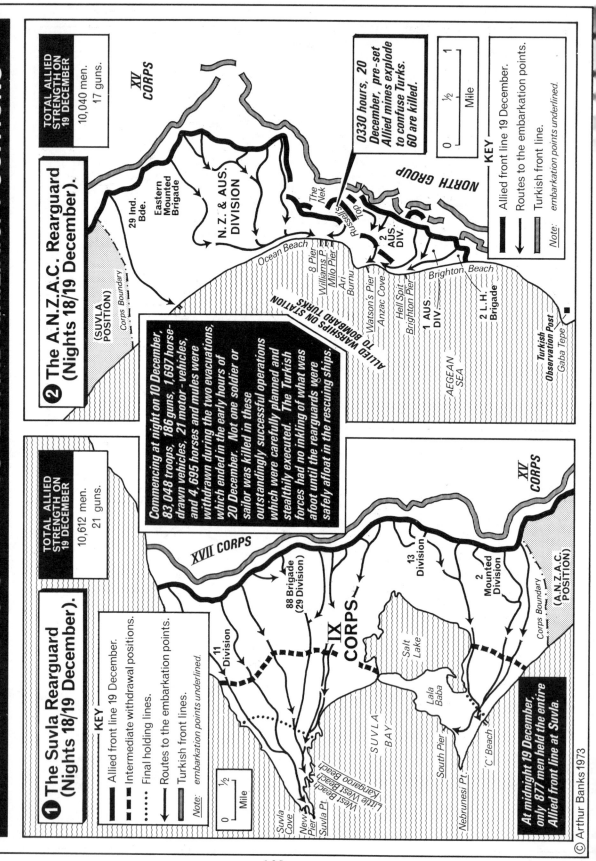

TOTAL ALLIED STRENGTH ON 19 December
10,040 men.
17 guns.

XV CORPS

❷ The A.N.Z.A.C. Rearguard (Nights 18/19 December).

0330 hours, 20 December, pre-set Allied mines explode to confuse Turks. 60 are killed.

NORTH GROUP

KEY
▬▬▬ Allied front line 19 December.
→ Routes to the embarkation points.
▨▨▨ Turkish front line.
Note: embarkation points underlined.

29 Ind. Bde.

Eastern Mounted Brigade

N.Z. & AUS. DIVISION

(SUVLA POSITION)

Corps Boundary

The Nek

Russell's Top

2 AUS. DIV.

Ocean Beach

8 Pier
Williams P.
Milo Pier
Ari Burnu
Watson's Pier
Anzac Cove
Hell Spit
Brighton Pier

Brighton Beach

1 AUS. DIV.

2 L.H. Brigade

AEGEAN SEA

Turkish Observation Post

Gaba Tepe

ALLIED WARSHIPS ON STATION TO BOMBARD TURKS

Commencing at night on 10 December, 83,048 troops, 186 guns, 1,697 horse-drawn vehicles, 21 motor-vehicles, and 4,695 horses and mules were withdrawn during the two evacuations, which ended in the early hours of 20 December. Not one soldier or sailor was killed in these outstandingly successful operations which were carefully planned and stealthily executed. The Turkish forces had no inkling of what was afoot until the rearguards were safely afloat in the rescuing ships.

TOTAL ALLIED STRENGTH ON 19 December
10,612 men.
21 guns.

❶ The Suvla Rearguard (Nights 18/19 December).

XVII CORPS

88 Brigade (29 Division)

IX CORPS

13 Division

2 Mounted Division

Corps Boundary

(A.N.Z.A.C. POSITION)

XV CORPS

11 Division

Salt Lake

Lala Baba

SUVLA BAY

South Pier

C Beach

Nebrunesi Pt.

Suvla Cove
New Pier
Suvla Pt.
West Beach
Little West Beach
Kangaroo Beach

KEY
▬▬▬ Allied front line 19 December.
▬ ▬ ▬ Intermediate withdrawal positions.
· · · · Final holding lines.
→ Routes to the embarkation points.
▨▨▨ Turkish front lines.
Note: embarkation points underlined.

0   ½   Mile

0   ½   1   Mile

At midnight 19 December, only 877 men held the entire Allied front line at Suvla.

© Arthur Banks 1973

128

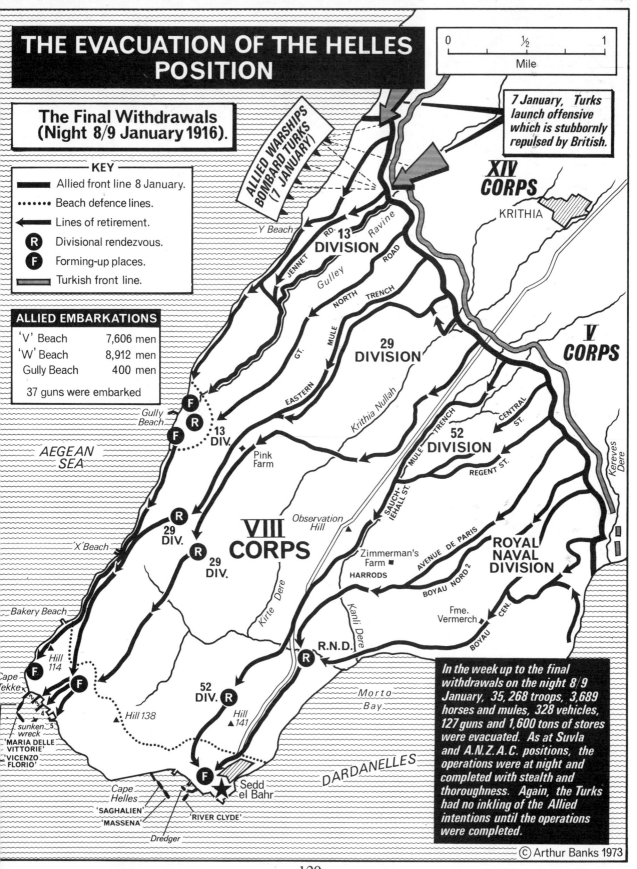

THE EVACUATION OF THE HELLES POSITION

The Final Withdrawals (Night 8/9 January 1916).

KEY
- ──── Allied front line 8 January.
- •••• Beach defence lines.
- ◀━━ Lines of retirement.
- Ⓡ Divisional rendezvous.
- Ⓕ Forming-up places.
- ▨▨▨ Turkish front line.

ALLIED EMBARKATIONS

'V' Beach	7,606 men
'W' Beach	8,912 men
Gully Beach	400 men

37 guns were embarked

ALLIED WARSHIPS BOMBARD TURKS (7 JANUARY)

7 January, Turks launch offensive which is stubbornly repulsed by British.

XIV CORPS

KRITHIA

V CORPS

Y Beach

RD. 13 DIVISION Ravine

ROAD

JENNET

Gulley

NORTH TRENCH

GT.

MULE

29 DIVISION

EASTERN

Krithia Nullah

MULE TRENCH

52 DIVISION

CENTRAL ST.

REGENT ST.

Kereves Dere

AEGEAN SEA

Gully Beach

Ⓕ Ⓡ Ⓕ 13 DIV.

Pink Farm

Observation Hill

VIII CORPS

SAUCH-IEHALL ST.

Zimmerman's Farm

HARRODS

AVENUE DE PARIS

BOYAU NORD 2

ROYAL NAVAL DIVISION

Ⓡ 29 DIV.

'X'Beach

Ⓡ 29 DIV.

Fme. Vermerch

CEN.

BOYAU

Bakery Beach

Kirte Dere

Kanli Dere

R.N.D.

Ⓡ

Morto Bay

Ⓕ Hill 114

Cape Tekke

Ⓕ

Hill 138

52 DIV. Ⓡ

Hill 141

sunken wreck

'MARIA DELLE VITTORIE'

'VICENZO FLORIO'

Ⓕ

Cape Helles

'SAGHALIEN'

'MASSENA'

Dredger

'RIVER CLYDE'

★ Sedd el Bahr

DARDANELLES

In the week up to the final withdrawals on the night 8/9 January, 35,268 troops, 3,689 horses and mules, 328 vehicles, 127 guns and 1,600 tons of stores were evacuated. As at Suvla and A.N.Z.A.C. positions, the operations were at night and completed with stealth and thoroughness. Again, the Turks had no inkling of the Allied intentions until the operations were completed.

THE WAR IN 1915

The Dardanelles and Gallipoli dominated the minds of the political leaders in Whitehall during the opening months of 1915. But Sir John French and his generals across the Channel bitterly opposed any plans which might divert troops from the Western Front, and Joffre agreed with them. French and his principal subordinate, Haig, wished to attack the Germans in Belgium as soon as the weather was favourable. Joffre had hopes of a two-pronged thrust later in the spring in Artois and Champagne, intended to break through the German lines and sweep across Belgium west of the Ardennes. Reality fell short of expectation that year on every sector of the Western Front: the British gained the town of Neuve Chapelle at the cost of heavy casualties in March (pages 136–137); the German offensive in the West during April sought to eliminate the Ypres Salient, but, despite the use of poison gas, their success was limited to a few villages; and later frontal assaults by the British and the French in Artois, at Loos, and in Champagne, though shaking the vertebrae of the German defensive system, failed to crack the spinal cord. The newspapers continued to carry long casualty lists which, together with the frustrations of Gallipoli, emphasised the terrible burden of the War on families far from the battlefronts. The first Zeppelin raids (pages 286–290) brought a new terror to English homes.

The news from other fronts was no more encouraging. At first it seemed that the Russians would make some progress on the southern sector of the Eastern Front, for they at last captured the fortress of Przemysl on 22 March. But Falkenhayn, unlike Moltke in the previous year, was prepared to co-ordinate strategy with Conrad. In May a massive Austro-German offensive began in Galicia, breaking through four lines of Russian defences at Gorlice and forcing a general withdrawal from the Carpathians. The Russians were driven out of Przemysl, out of Galicia, and out of Poland as well. When the campaign ended, half a million Russians were in prisoner-of-war cages. Nor was this the limit of Falkenhayn's success. In October Mackensen, the victor of Gorlice, set up his headquarters in southern Hungary and took command of a joint Austro–Germano–Bulgarian army which overran Serbia (page 160) and gave Germany control of a continuous railway route from Berlin to Constantinople and the Middle East. The Allied response to Bulgaria's alliance with Germany was, at last, to establish a base at Salonika, but no effective aid could be given to Serbia.

Bulgaria's entry into the German camp was preceded by Italy's adhesion to the Allied cause in May 1915. But, though it was hoped in London and Paris that Italy would pose a new threat to Austria-Hungary, this Front, too, was soon paralysed by defensive trench warfare (page 200–201). Briefly it seemed possible that the German U-Boat campaign, and especially the sinking of the Cunard liner *Lusitania* with the loss of 128 American lives on 6 May, would bring the United States into the War, but the Germans gave informal assurances that passenger ships would not be sunk without warning, and America maintained her neutrality.

By the end of the year the war seemed as rapacious of lives and material as ever, and there was no prospect of peace. Among the Allies, and especially in Britain, indignation mounted at the lack of munitions. On both sides governments began to take unprecedented measures to organise their economy for a long war. The task was to prove too great for Tsarist Russia.

GERMAN CARTOGRAPHIC PROPAGANDA 1915

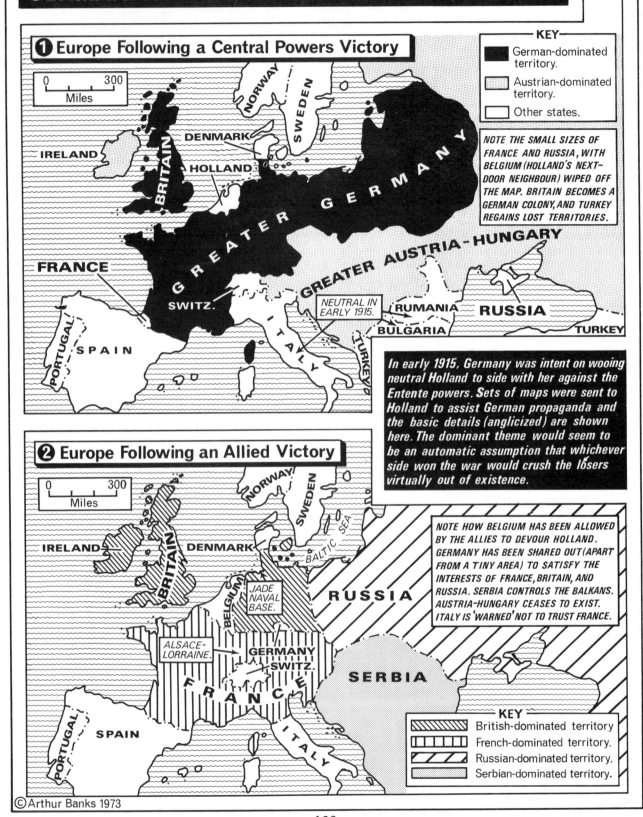

❶ Europe Following a Central Powers Victory

0   300
Miles

NORWAY

SWEDEN

DENMARK

IRELAND

BRITAIN

HOLLAND

GREATER GERMANY

FRANCE

SWITZ.

ITALY

TURKEY

PORTUGAL

SPAIN

GREATER AUSTRIA-HUNGARY

NEUTRAL IN EARLY 1915.

RUMANIA

BULGARIA

RUSSIA

TURKEY

KEY
- ■ German-dominated territory.
- ▨ Austrian-dominated territory.
- □ Other states.

NOTE THE SMALL SIZES OF FRANCE AND RUSSIA, WITH BELGIUM (HOLLAND'S NEXT-DOOR NEIGHBOUR) WIPED OFF THE MAP. BRITAIN BECOMES A GERMAN COLONY, AND TURKEY REGAINS LOST TERRITORIES.

In early 1915, Germany was intent on wooing neutral Holland to side with her against the Entente powers. Sets of maps were sent to Holland to assist German propaganda and the basic details (anglicized) are shown here. The dominant theme would seem to be an automatic assumption that whichever side won the war would crush the losers virtually out of existence.

❷ Europe Following an Allied Victory

0   300
Miles

NORWAY

SWEDEN

BALTIC SEA

IRELAND

BRITAIN

DENMARK

BELGIUM

JADE NAVAL BASE.

RUSSIA

ALSACE-LORRAINE.

GERMANY

SWITZ.

FRANCE

SERBIA

PORTUGAL

SPAIN

ITALY

NOTE HOW BELGIUM HAS BEEN ALLOWED BY THE ALLIES TO DEVOUR HOLLAND. GERMANY HAS BEEN SHARED OUT (APART FROM A TINY AREA) TO SATISFY THE INTERESTS OF FRANCE, BRITAIN, AND RUSSIA. SERBIA CONTROLS THE BALKANS. AUSTRIA-HUNGARY CEASES TO EXIST. ITALY IS 'WARNED' NOT TO TRUST FRANCE.

KEY
- ▨ British-dominated territory
- ▥ French-dominated territory.
- ▧ Russian-dominated territory.
- ▤ Serbian-dominated territory.

© Arthur Banks 1973

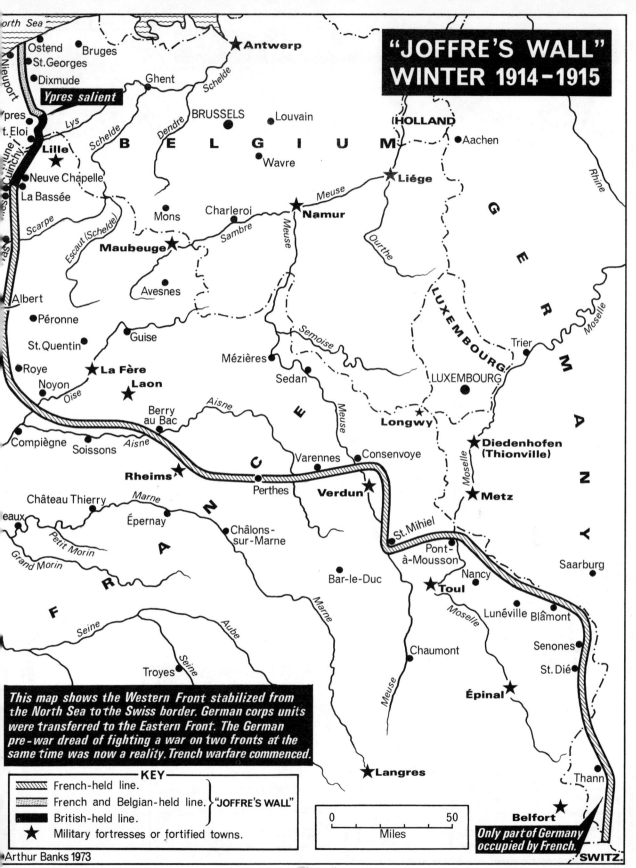

"JOFFRE'S WALL"
WINTER 1914-1915

North Sea

Ostend
Bruges
St.Georges
Dixmude

Nieuport

Ypres salient

pres
t.Eloi

Ghent

Schelde

Dendre

BRUSSELS

Louvain

HOLLAND

Aachen

Lille

Cuinchy

Neuve Chapelle
La Bassée

B E L G I U M

Wavre

Liége

Namur

Meuse

Scarpe

Mons
Charleroi

Sambre

Meuse

Ourthe

G

Maubeuge

Escaut (Schelde)

Avesnes

Meuse

Rhine

Albert
Péronne

Guise

Semoise

LUXEMBOURG

Moselle

St.Quentin

Roye
Noyon

La Fère

Mézières

Trier

E

Laon

Oise

Aisne

Berry
au Bac

Sedan

Meuse

LUXEMBOURG

Compiègne
Soissons

Aisne

C

Varennes

Consenvoye

Longwy

Diedenhofen
(Thionville)

Rheims

Perthes

Verdun

Metz

Château Thierry

Marne

N

Châlons-
sur-Marne

St.Mihiel

Pont-
à-Mousson

Saarburg

eaux

Épernay

Petit Morin

Grand Morin

Seine

F

R

A

Bar-le-Duc

Marne

Nancy

Toul

Lunéville Blâmont

Moselle

Senones

Aube

Chaumont

St.Dié

Seine

Troyes

Meuse

Épinal

This map shows the Western Front stabilized from
the North Sea to the Swiss border. German corps units
were transferred to the Eastern Front. The German
pre-war dread of fighting a war on two fronts at the
same time was now a reality. Trench warfare commenced.

Langres

Thann

KEY

French-held line.
French and Belgian-held line. "JOFFRE'S WALL"
British-held line.
Military fortresses or fortified towns.

0   50
Miles

Belfort

Only part of Germany
occupied by French.

Arthur Banks 1973

SWITZ.

133

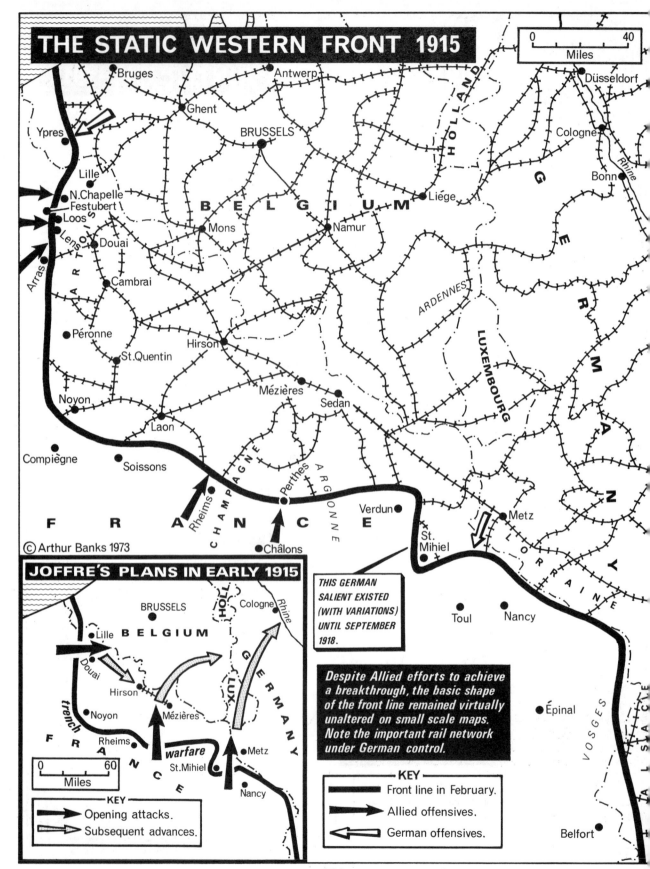

THE STATIC WESTERN FRONT 1915

0 — 40
Miles

Bruges
Antwerp
Düsseldorf
Ghent
Ypres
Cologne
Rhine
Lille
BELGIUM
Liége
Bonn
N.Chapelle
Festubert
Loos
Mons
Namur
GERMANY
Douai
Lens
ARTOIS
Arras
Cambrai
ARDENNES
Péronne
Hirson
LUXEMBOURG
St.Quentin
Mézières
Noyon
Sedan
Laon
Compiègne
Soissons
Rheims
Perthes
CHAMPAGNE
ARGONNE
FRANCE
Verdun
Metz
Châlons
St. Mihiel
LORRAINE

© Arthur Banks 1973

THIS GERMAN
SALIENT EXISTED
(WITH VARIATIONS)
UNTIL SEPTEMBER
1918.

Toul
Nancy

*Despite Allied efforts to achieve
a breakthrough, the basic shape
of the front line remained virtually
unaltered on small scale maps.
Note the important rail network
under German control.*

Épinal

VOSGES
ALSACE

Belfort

JOFFRE'S PLANS IN EARLY 1915

BRUSSELS
Cologne
Rhine
HOLLAND
Lille
BELGIUM
Douai
GERMANY
Hirson
LUX.
trench
Noyon
Mézières
Rheims
FRANCE
warfare
St.Mihiel
Metz
Nancy

0 — 60
Miles

— KEY —
Opening attacks.
Subsequent advances.

— KEY —
Front line in February.
Allied offensives.
German offensives.

THE MOBILE EASTERN FRONT 1915

0   50   100
Miles

Riga

Libau
Fell on 8 May.

Not captured by Germans.

Memel

BALTIC SEA

Dvinsk

Dvina

Stormed by Germans 17-18 August.

Kovno

Germany's aim was to make the Eastern Front safe and passive so that she could switch her main assault to the Western Front (she did not hope to completely defeat Russia). Rather than instituting an "enveloping" operation, she decided to attempt a "breakthrough" attack between Gorlice and Tarnow. This commenced on 2 May 1915, in concert with the Austrians. This front contrasts sharply with the Western Front during 1915.

Königsberg

Danzig

EAST PRUSSIA

MASURIAN LAKES

Niemen

Graudenz

Vistula

Grodno

Narew

RUSSIA

Thorn

Vistula

Capitulated on 20 August.

Fell on 2 September.

Entered by Germans on 5 August.

Novo-Georgievsk

Warsaw

Bug

Brest-Litovsk

North of this position, the front line remained as shown (with minor variations) until the end of 1917.

POLAND

Vistula

Ivangorod

Surrendered on 26 August.

Pripet

South of this position, the front line remained as shown (with minor variations) until June 1916.

Fell on 5 August.

San

Evacuated by Russians on 22 June.

Vistula

Tarnow

Cracow

GALICIA

Lemberg

2 MAY 1915

Przemysl

GERMAN ELEVENTH ARMY

Gorlice

Fell on 3 June.

CARPATHIAN MOUNTAINS

Dniester

Pruth

Tisza

---KEY---

Opening assault by German and Austrian armies.

Advances by German and Austrian armies.

Front line, 2 May.

Front line, 1 June.

Front line, 16 July.

Front line, 15 August.

Front line, 1 September.

Front line, winter 1915.

THE BATTLE OF NEUVE CHAPELLE 10-12 MARCH 1915

① 10 March–The Opening Attack

0730 hours 10 March, a British artillery bombardment commenced along the whole front. At 0805 hours the range was lengthened some 300 yards to include Neuve Chapelle, and the infantry commenced their advance which continued until dusk. The Germans began rapid consolidation of their new position, strengthening strongpoints and wiring.

The British employed some 300 guns which was thought to be a huge concentration at the time.

0 500 Yards

AUBERS
1 Batt. 15 INF. REGT.
Les Mottes Farm
Moulin du Pietre
13 DIV.
Bas Pommereau
Haut Pommereau
2 Companies
GERMAN VII CORPS
Pietre
La Russie
2 Companies
2 Companies 11 JÄGER
Halpegarbe
14 DIV.
Brook
Bois du Biez
16 INF. REGT.
Smith Dorrien Trench
Lalyes
Neuve Chapelle
1 Battalion
GERMAN FRONT LINE
BRITISH FRONT LINE
Quadrilateral
Moated Grange
Orchard
2 Companies 11 JÄGER
Neuburquisseart
BRITISH IV CORPS
7 DIV.
22 Inf Bde.
23 Inf Bde.
25 Inf Bde.
8 DIV.
Pont Logy
Port Arthur
MEERUT DIV.
INDIAN CORPS
Garhwal Bde.
2 Battalions

BRITISH KEY
1	2 Middlesex	6	2/Devon	11	2/3rd Gurkhas
2	2/Scottish Rifles	7	1/Royal Irish Rifles	12	2/Leics.
3	2/Lincs.	8	Rifle Brigade	13	3/London
4	2/Royal Berks.	9	13/London	14	1/39th.Garhwal Rifles
5	2/West Yorks.	10	2/39th.Garhwal Rifles		

☆ German strongpoints

② 11 March–New German Line Established

0645 hours 11 March, the offensive was resumed, but was largely ineffectual due to difficulties in concentrating a further artillery bombardment on to the new German positions. Mist impaired visibility.

Note: the Quadrilateral was a large self- contained work, strongly defended with machine-guns.

0 500 Yards

AUBERS
13 Division
DUSK ADVANCE
Les Mottes Farm
Bas Pommereau
Haut Pommereau
GERMAN VII CORPS
Pietre
Halpegarbe
Moulin du Pietre
DUSK ADVANCE
La Russie
14 Division
DUSK ADVANCE
Lligny le Petit
DUSK ADVANCE
Quadrilateral
BROOK
Bois du Biez
LALYES
Smith- Dorrien Trench
Moated Grange
Orchard
7 Division
BRITISH IV CORPS
8 Division
NEUVE CHAPELLE
Pont Logy
INDIAN CORPS
Meerut Division
Port Arthur

KEY
▬▬▬	New German line.
⇨	German reinforcements.
▬ ▬	British front line.

136

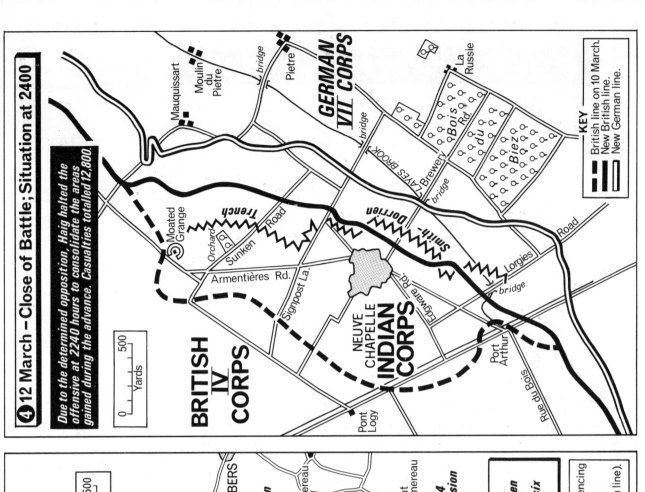

④ 12 March – Close of Battle; Situation at 2400

Due to the determined opposition, Haig halted the offensive at 2240 hours to consolidate the areas gained during the advance. Casualties totalled 12,800.

GERMAN VII CORPS

Mauquissart
Moulin du Pietre
bridge
Pietre
La Russie
bridge
LAYES BROOK
Brewery
bridge
Bois du Biez

Moated Grange
Orchard
Sunken Road
Trench
Smith-Dorrien
Armentières Rd.
Signpost La.
Edgware Rd.
Lorgies
bridge
Road

NEUVE CHAPELLE
INDIAN CORPS

BRITISH IV CORPS

Port Arthur
Pont Logy
Rue du Bois

500
Yards
0

KEY
British line on 10 March.
New British line.
New German line.

---

③ 12 March – German Counter-Attacks

The German infantry counter-attacks were preceded by an artillery bombardment (at 0430 hours) along the length of the front held by the British IV and Indian Corps. This mostly affected rear areas, the front-line trenches remaining intact.

500
Yards
0

AUBERS
Les Mottes Farm
Moulin du Pietre
13 Division
Bas Pommereau
Haut Pommereau
14 Division
Pietre

GERMAN VII CORPS

La Russie
Bois du Biez

Quadrilateral
RIGHT ATTACK
RIGHT-CENTRE ATTACK
LEFT-CENTRE ATTACK
LAYES BROOK
LEFT ATTACK

7 Division
Moated Grange
Orchard
8 Division
NEUVE CHAPELLE
INDIAN CORPS
Meerut Division

BRITISH IV CORPS

Pont Logy
Port Arthur

GERMAN FORCES
16,000 men employed in ten assault battalions, four support battalions, and six reserve battalions.

KEY
German counter-attacks (commencing 0500 hours).
British front line.
Smith-Dorrien Trench (old trench line).

© Arthur Banks 1973

137

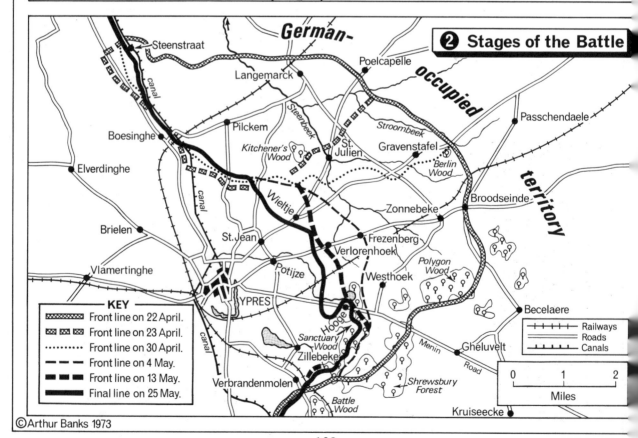

"SECOND YPRES" APRIL-MAY 1915

① The Battle Area

Note on farm names: most farms were not named on military maps in use at this stage of the war in the vicinity of Ypres, and were simply referred to by the grid square in which they were situated. This caused some confusion, and the fighting powers began to bestow their own versions of names to various farms. On these maps, British-used names have been employed. Using 'Mouse Trap Farm' (British version) as an example, it was known as 'Chateau du Nord' to the French and Belgians, 'Wieltje Chateau' to the Germans, and 'Shell Trap Farm' to the Canadians.

Note on ridges: these have been emphasised solely for clarity. In reality, they are low gradual spurs with gradients rarely exceeding 1 in 20. Highest points about 250 feet.

FARMS
1. South Zwaanhof
2. Fusilier
3. Turco
4. Welch
5. Canadian
6. Oblong
7. Vanheule
8. Mouse Trap
9. Hampshire
10. Foch
11. Belle Alliance
12. Boetleer's
13. Bellewaarde
14. Château
15. White Château

● Villages
■ Farms
🌳 Woods

With the exception of Langemarck (population 7,500) and Boesinghe (population 2,500), the villages around Ypres were small, and their populations were less than 1,000.

0   1
Mile

Steenstraat, Poelcapelle, Langemarck, Lekkerboterbeek, Stroombeek Ridge, Passchendaele, Stroombeek, Boesinghe, Pilckem, Pilckem Ridge, Gravenstafel, St. Julien, Gravenstafel Ridge, Mouse Ridge, Haanebeek, Zonnebeke Ridge, Brielen, Hill Top Ridge, Wieltje, Zonnebeke, Broodseinde, St. Jean Ridge, Frezenberg, St. Jean, Verlorenhoek, RIDGE, Potijze, YPRES, Zillebeke, Westhoek, Bellewaarde Ridge, Hooge, Becelaere, Zillebeke Lake, YPRES, Gheluvelt, Verbrandenmolen, Hill 60, Kruiseecke

② Stages of the Battle

German-occupied territory

Steenstraat, Poelcapelle, Langemarck, Passchendaele, Pilckem, Boesinghe, Kitchener's Wood, St. Julien, Stroombeek, Gravenstafel, Berlin Wood, Broodseinde, Elverdinghe, Wieltje, Zonnebeke, Brielen, St. Jean, Frezenberg, Verlorenhoek, Polygon Wood, Vlamertinghe, Potijze, Westhoek, YPRES, Becelaere, Sanctuary Wood, Hooge, Menin Road, Gheluvelt, Zillebeke, Verbrandenmolen, Shrewsbury Forest, Battle Wood, Kruiseecke

KEY
- ▨▨▨ Front line on 22 April.
- ▨ ▨ ▨ Front line on 23 April.
- ·········· Front line on 30 April.
- – – – Front line on 4 May.
- ▬ ▬ ▬ Front line on 13 May.
- ▬▬▬ Final line on 25 May.

┼┼┼┼ Railways
═══ Roads
⊥⊥⊥ Canals

0   1   2
Miles

© Arthur Banks 1973

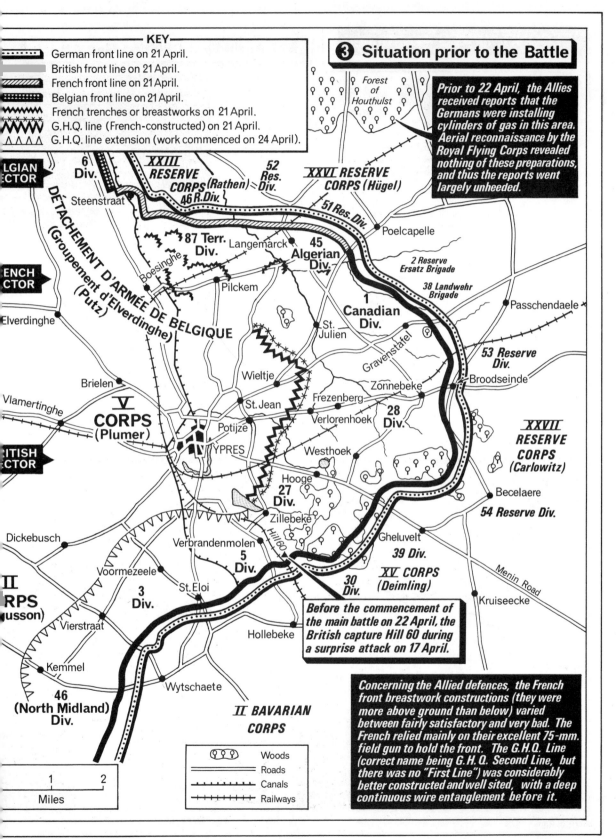

KEY
- German front line on 21 April.
- British front line on 21 April.
- French front line on 21 April.
- Belgian front line on 21 April.
- French trenches or breastworks on 21 April.
- G.H.Q. line (French-constructed) on 21 April.
- G.H.Q. line extension (work commenced on 24 April).

③ Situation prior to the Battle

Prior to 22 April, the Allies received reports that the Germans were installing cylinders of gas in this area. Aerial reconnaissance by the Royal Flying Corps revealed nothing of these preparations, and thus the reports went largely unheeded.

Forest of Houthulst

BELGIAN SECTOR

6 Div.

XXIII RESERVE CORPS (Rathen)

46 R.Div.

52 Res. Div.

XXVI RESERVE CORPS (Hügel)

51 Res. Div.

Steenstraat

DÉTACHEMENT D'ARMÉE DE BELGIQUE (Groupement d'Elverdinghe) (Putz)

FRENCH SECTOR

87 Terr. Div.

Langemarck

Boesinghe

Pilckem

45 Algerian Div.

Poelcapelle

2 Reserve Ersatz Brigade

38 Landwehr Brigade

Elverdinghe

St. Julien

1 Canadian Div.

Passchendaele

Gravenstafel

53 Reserve Div.

Brielen

V CORPS (Plumer)

Wieltje

Frezenberg

Zonnebeke

Broodseinde

Vlamertinghe

St. Jean

Verlorenhoek

28 Div.

XXVII RESERVE CORPS (Carlowitz)

BRITISH SECTOR

Potijze

YPRES

Westhoek

Becelaere

Hooge

27 Div.

54 Reserve Div.

Dickebusch

Zillebeke

Hill 60

Gheluvelt

39 Div.

Verbrandenmolen

5 Div.

30 Div.

XV CORPS (Deimling)

Menin Road

Voormezeele

St. Eloi

Kruiseecke

II CORPS (Fergusson)

3 Div.

Hollebeke

Before the commencement of the main battle on 22 April, the British capture Hill 60 during a surprise attack on 17 April.

Vierstraat

Kemmel

Wytschaete

46 (North Midland) Div.

II BAVARIAN CORPS

Concerning the Allied defences, the French front breastwork constructions (they were more above ground than below) varied between fairly satisfactory and very bad. The French relied mainly on their excellent 75-mm. field gun to hold the front. The G.H.Q. Line (correct name being G.H.Q. Second Line, but there was no "First Line") was considerably better constructed and well sited, with a deep continuous wire entanglement before it.

| Miles | 1 | 2 |

- Woods
- Roads
- Canals
- Railways

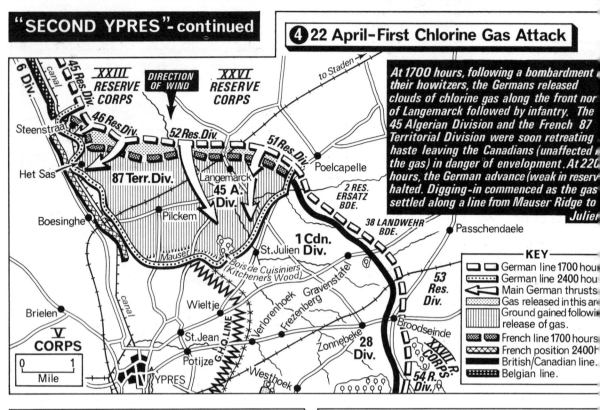
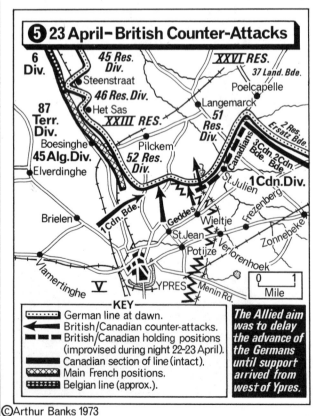
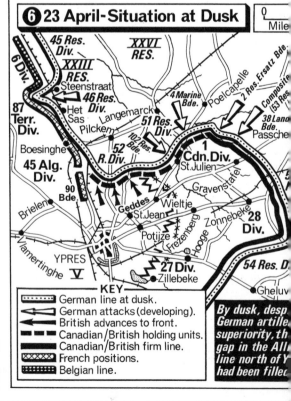

"SECOND YPRES" - continued

❹ 22 April–First Chlorine Gas Attack

At 1700 hours, following a bombardment their howitzers, the Germans released clouds of chlorine gas along the front nor of Langemarck followed by infantry. The 45 Algerian Division and the French 87 Territorial Division were soon retreating haste leaving the Canadians (unaffected the gas) in danger of envelopment. At 220 hours, the German advance (weak in reserv halted. Digging-in commenced as the gas settled along a line from Mauser Ridge to Julier

KEY
- German line 1700 hou
- German line 2400 hou
- Main German thrusts
- Gas released in this ar
- Ground gained followi release of gas.
- French line 1700 hours
- French position 2400h
- British/Canadian line.
- Belgian line.

Map labels: to Staden, 6 Div., canal, XXIII RESERVE CORPS, 45 Res. Div., DIRECTION OF WIND, XXVI RESERVE CORPS, 46 Res. Div., Steenstraat, 52 Res. Div., 51 Res. Div., Poelcapelle, Het Sas, 87 Terr. Div., Langemarck, 45 A. Div., 2 RES. ERSATZ BDE., Boesinghe, Pilckem, Mauser, Bois de Cuisiniers (Kitchener's Wood), St. Julien, 1 Cdn. Div., 38 LANDWEHR BDE., Passchendaele, Brielen, Wieltje, G.H.Q. LINE, Verlorenhoek, Gravenstafel, Frezenberg, 53 Res. Div., Broodseinde, V CORPS, St. Jean, Potijze, Zonnebeke, 28 Div., XXIII R. CORPS, YPRES, Westhoek, 54 R. Div.

0 | 1 Mile

❺ 23 April–British Counter-Attacks

Map labels: 6 Div., 45 Res. Div., XXVI RES., 37 Land. Bde., Steenstraat, 46 Res. Div., Poelcapelle, 87 Terr. Div., Het Sas, XXIII RES., Langemarck, 51 Res. Div., 2 Res. Ersatz Bde., Boesinghe, Pilckem, 52 Res. Div., Canadians, 3 Cdn. 2 Cdn. Bde. Bde., Elverdinghe, St. Julien, 1 Cdn. Div., Geddes, Wieltje, Frezenberg, Brielen, 1 Cdn. Bde., St. Jean, Verlorenhoek, Zonnebeke, Potijze, Vlamertinghe, V, YPRES, Menin Rd.

0 | 1 Mile

KEY
- German line at dawn.
- British/Canadian counter-attacks.
- British/Canadian holding positions (improvised during night 22-23 April).
- Canadian section of line (intact).
- Main French positions.
- Belgian line (approx.).

The Allied aim was to delay the advance of the Germans until support arrived from west of Ypres.

❻ 23 April–Situation at Dusk

0 Mile

Map labels: 45 Res. Div., XXVI RES., 6 Div., XXIII RES., Steenstraat, 46 Res. Div., Langemarck, 4 Marine Bde., Poelcapelle, 2 Res. Ersatz Composite 53 Res., 87 Terr. Div., Het Sas, Pilckem, 51 Res. Div., 38 Land Bde., Passche, Boesinghe, 52 R. Div., 10 Res. Bde., 1 Cdn. Div., St. Julien, 45 Alg. Div., Gravenstafel, 90 Bde., Geddes, Wieltje, Brielen, St. Jean, Frezenberg, Zonnebeke, 28 Div., Potijze, Hooge, Vlamertinghe, V, YPRES, 27 Div., Zillebeke, 54 Res. D., Gheluv

KEY
- German line at dusk.
- German attacks (developing).
- British advances to front.
- Canadian/British holding units.
- Canadian/British firm line.
- French positions.
- Belgian line.

By dusk, desp German artille superiority, th gap in the Alli line north of Y had been fille

140

7 24 April – Battle of St. Julien

0130 hours, Germans occupy Lizerne. Belgians stem further progress.

Fierce house-to-house fighting.

French Attack 1330 hrs.

46 Res. Div. · XXIII RES. · 102 Res. Bde. · XXVI RES. · 51 R. Div. · 4 Marine Bde. · 2 Res. Ersatz Bde. · Composite Bde. (53 Res. Bde.) · 37 Land. Bde. · 38 Land. Bde. · 52 R. Div. · 53 Res. Div. · XXVII R. · 54 Res. Div.

Lizerne · Passchendaele · St. Julien · Zonnebeke · St. Jean · Frezenberg · Potijze · Hooge · Westhoek · Zillebeke · Gheluvelt · YPRES · V CORPS

KEY
- German line at dawn.
- Main German thrusts.
- Ground gained by Germans. Gas released at **G** (0400 hours).

Allied units have been omitted for clarity. German artillery batteries dominated area.

8 25 April – Situation at Dusk

Throughout the day, the German artillery shelled Allied units and positions in the salient.

Taken and held by Germans.

XXIII RES. · XXVI RES. · 51 R. Div. · 52 R. Div. · 53 Res. Div. · XXVII RES. · 54 R. Div.

Steenstraat · Poelcapelle · Langemarck · Pilckem · Boesinghe · St. Julien · Brielen · St. Jean · Wieltje · Frezenberg · Potijze · Westhoek · Zonnebeke · Hooge · Zillebeke · Gheluvelt · YPRES

Noon, Lahore Division (Indian) concentrates at Ouderdom, five miles south-west of Ypres.

During the evening, the bulk of the Canadian Division was pulled back into reserve. Its casualties since 22 April: 1,700 dead and 2,500 wounded.

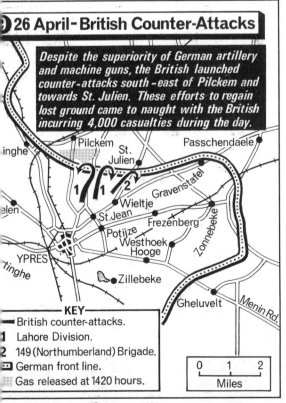

9 26 April – British Counter-Attacks

Despite the superiority of German artillery and machine guns, the British launched counter-attacks south-east of Pilckem and towards St. Julien. These efforts to regain lost ground came to naught with the British incurring 4,000 casualties during the day.

Pilckem · St. Julien · Passchendaele · Wieltje · Gravenstafel · St. Jean · Frezenberg · Potijze · Westhoek · Hooge · Zonnebeke · Zillebeke · Gheluvelt · Menin Rd. · YPRES

KEY
- British counter-attacks.
- **1** Lahore Division.
- **2** 149 (Northumberland) Brigade.
- German front line.
- Gas released at 1420 hours.

0 1 2 Miles

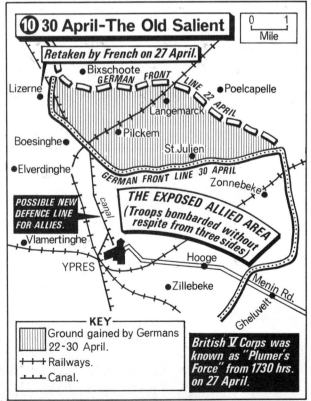

10 30 April – The Old Salient

Retaken by French on 27 April.

GERMAN FRONT LINE 22 APRIL

GERMAN FRONT LINE 30 APRIL

THE EXPOSED ALLIED AREA (Troops bombarded without respite from three sides)

POSSIBLE NEW DEFENCE LINE FOR ALLIES.

Bixschoote · Lizerne · Poelcapelle · Langemarck · Boesinghe · Pilckem · St. Julien · Elverdinghe · Zonnebeke · Vlamertinghe · Hooge · YPRES · Zillebeke · Menin Rd. · Gheluvelt · canal

KEY
- Ground gained by Germans 22–30 April.
- Railways.
- Canal.

British V Corps was known as "Plumer's Force" from 1730 hrs. on 27 April.

0 1 Mile

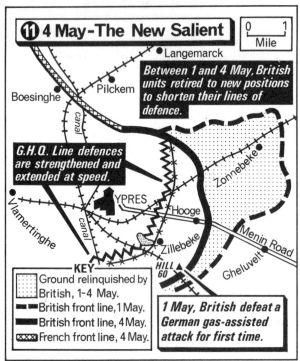

⑪ 4 May–The New Salient

0 1 Mile

Between 1 and 4 May, British units retired to new positions to shorten their lines of defence.

Langemarck

Boesinghe · Pilckem

G.H.Q. Line defences are strengthened and extended at speed.

Zonnebeke

YPRES

Hooge

Vlamertinghe · canal · Zillebeke · Menin Road · Gheluvelt

HILL 60

KEY
Ground relinquished by British, 1–4 May.
British front line, 1 May.
British front line, 4 May.
French front line, 4 May.

1 May, British defeat a German gas-assisted attack for first time.

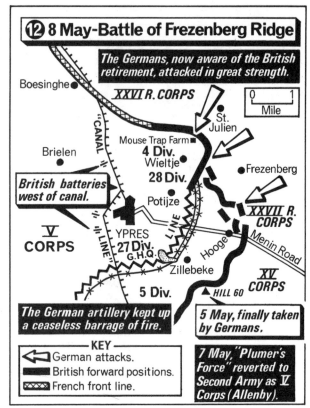

⑫ 8 May–Battle of Frezenberg Ridge

The Germans, now aware of the British retirement, attacked in great strength.

Boesinghe · XXVI R. CORPS · St. Julien

Mouse Trap Farm · 4 Div. · Wieltje · 28 Div. · Frezenberg

Brielen

British batteries west of canal.

Potijze · XXVII R. CORPS

"CANAL" "LINE"

V CORPS · YPRES · 27 Div. · G.H.Q. · Hooge · Menin Road · Zillebeke · XV CORPS

5 Div. · HILL 60

0 1 Mile

The German artillery kept up a ceaseless barrage of fire.

5 May, finally taken by Germans.

KEY
German attacks.
British forward positions.
French front line.

7 May, "Plumer's Force" reverted to Second Army as V Corps (Allenby).

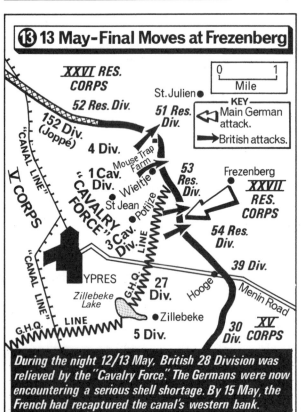

⑬ 13 May–Final Moves at Frezenberg

XXVI RES. CORPS · 52 Res. Div. · St. Julien · 51 Res. Div.

152 Div. (Joppé) · 4 Div. · Mouse Trap Farm

"CANAL LINE"

V CORPS · "1 Cav. Div." · "CAVALRY FORCE" · Wieltje · St Jean · Potijze · "3 Cav. Div." · 53 Res. Div. · Frezenberg · XXVII RES. CORPS

54 Res. Div.

YPRES · Zillebeke Lake · 27 Div. · Hooge · Menin Road · 39 Div.

"CANAL LINE" · G.H.Q. LINE · Zillebeke · 5 Div. · 30 Div. · XV CORPS

0 1 Mile

KEY
Main German attack.
British attacks.

During the night 12/13 May, British 28 Division was relieved by the "Cavalry Force". The Germans were now encountering a serious shell shortage. By 15 May, the French had recaptured the canal's western bank.

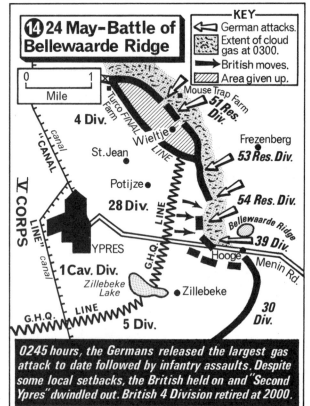

⑭ 24 May–Battle of Bellewaarde Ridge

KEY
German attacks.
Extent of cloud gas at 0300.
British moves.
Area given up.

0 1 Mile

4 Div. · "Turco FINAL Farm" · Mouse Trap Farm · 51 Res. Div.

Wieltje

St. Jean · Frezenberg · 53 Res. Div.

"CANAL LINE" · canal

V CORPS · Potijze · 28 Div. · 54 Res. Div. · Bellewaarde Ridge · 39 Div.

YPRES · 1 Cav. Div. · Zillebeke Lake · G.H.Q. LINE · Hooge · Menin Rd. · Zillebeke

G.H.Q. LINE · 5 Div. · 30 Div.

0245 hours, the Germans released the largest gas attack to date followed by infantry assaults. Despite some local setbacks, the British held on and "Second Ypres" dwindled out. British 4 Division retired at 2000.

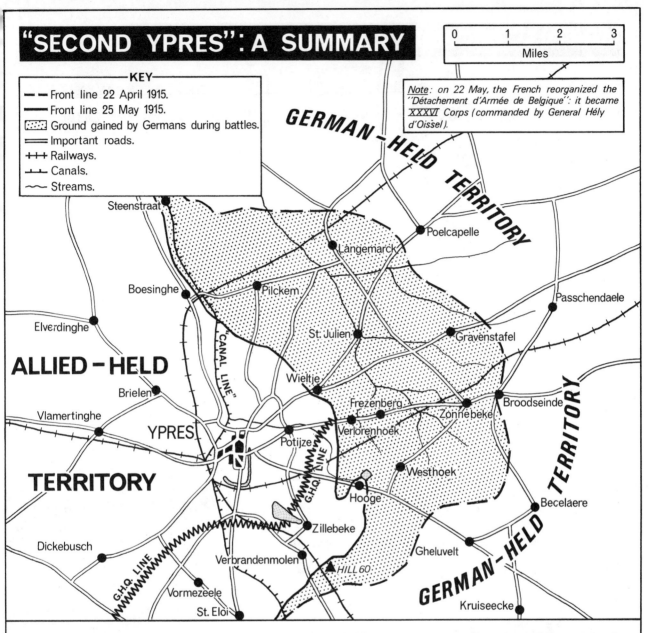

"SECOND YPRES": A SUMMARY

KEY

- – – Front line 22 April 1915.
- ––– Front line 25 May 1915.
- :::: Ground gained by Germans during battles.
- ══ Important roads.
- +++ Railways.
- ⊥⊥ Canals.
- ～～ Streams.

Miles
0   1   2   3

Note: on 22 May, the French reorganized the ''Détachement d'Armée de Belgique'': it became XXXVI Corps (commanded by General Hély d'Oissel).

GERMAN–HELD TERRITORY

Steenstraat
Poelcapelle
Langemarck
Boesinghe
Pilckem
Passchendaele
Elverdinghe
St. Julien
Gravenstafel
ALLIED–HELD
CANAL LINE
Wieltje
Brielen
Frezenberg
Zonnebeke
Broodseinde
Vlamertinghe
Verlorenhoek
YPRES
Potijze
Westhoek
TERRITORY
G.H.Q. LINE
Hooge
Becelaere
Zillebeke
GERMAN–HELD TERRITORY
Dickebusch
G.H.Q. LINE
Verbrandenmolen
Gheluvelt
▲ HILL 60
Vormezeele
Kruiseecke
St. Eloi

BRITISH CASUALTIES (59,275)	
1 Cavalry Division :	1,203
2 Cavalry Division :	244
3 Cavalry Division :	1,618
4 Division :	10,859
5 Division :	7,994
27 Division:	7,263
28 Division :	15,533
50 Division :	5,204
1 Canadian Division :	5,469
Lahore Division :	3,888

© Arthur Banks 1973

GERMAN CASUALTIES (34,933)	
XXIII Reserve Corps :	10,592
XXVI Reserve Corps :	12,845
XXVII Reserve Corps :	8,652
XV Corps :	2,844

FRENCH CASUALTIES (10,000)
ESTIMATE   *Precise figs. unknown*

BELGIAN CASUALTIES (1,530)

BY THE CLOSE OF "SECOND YPRES" THE GERMANS HAD GAINED SOME GROUND BUT THE SALIENT STILL REMAINED, ALBEIT REDUCED IN SIZE. MORE IMPORTANT FOR THE FUTURE, THEY HAD DISCLOSED THEIR SECRET WEAPON (GAS) PREMATURELY, AS THEY WERE NOT SUFFICIENTLY EQUIPPED TO EXPLOIT THEIR INITIAL SUCCESS OF 22 APRIL. ON THE BRITISH SIDE, THE BATTLES WERE MARKED BY INDECISION AMONG THE HIGHER RANKS AS TO THE CORRECT DEFENSIVE ACTION TO EMPLOY, AND GENERAL SMITH-DORRIEN (2 ARMY COMMANDER) WAS DISMISSED ON 6 MAY AS A RESULT OF DISSENSION BETWEEN HIMSELF AND THE COMMANDER-IN-CHIEF, FIELD-MARSHAL SIR JOHN FRENCH.

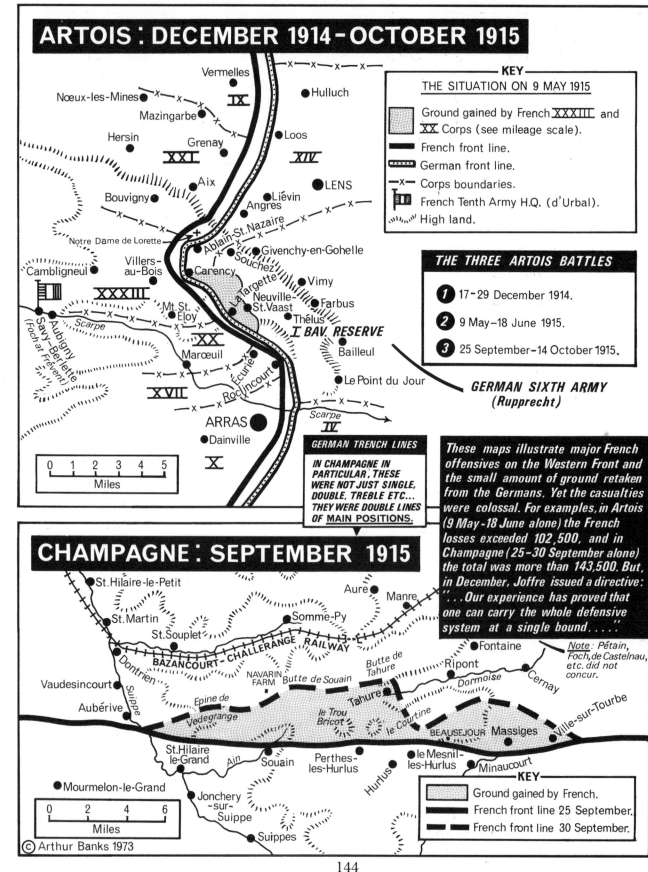

ARTOIS : DECEMBER 1914 – OCTOBER 1915

Vermelles

Nœux-les-Mines

Mazingarbe

IX

Hulluch

Hersin

Grenay

Loos

XXI

Aix

XIV

LENS

Bouvigny

Liévin

Angres

Ablain-St.Nazaire

Notre Dame de Lorette

Givenchy-en-Gohelle

Villers-au-Bois

Souchez

Carency

Camblingeul

Largette

Vimy

Neuville-St.Vaast

Farbus

XXXIII

Mt.St. Eloy

Thélus

I BAV. RESERVE

Aubigny
Savy–Berlette
(Foch at Frévent)

Scarpe

XX

Bailleul

Marœuil

Ecurie

Le Point du Jour

XVII

Roclincourt

Scarpe

ARRAS

IV

Dainville

X

KEY

THE SITUATION ON 9 MAY 1915

Ground gained by French XXXIII and XX Corps (see mileage scale).

——— French front line.

▬▬▬ German front line.

-x- Corps boundaries.

🏰 French Tenth Army H.Q. (d'Urbal).

⌒⌒ High land.

THE THREE ARTOIS BATTLES

❶ 17–29 December 1914.

❷ 9 May–18 June 1915.

❸ 25 September–14 October 1915.

GERMAN SIXTH ARMY (Rupprecht)

0 1 2 3 4 5
Miles

GERMAN TRENCH LINES

IN CHAMPAGNE IN PARTICULAR, THESE WERE NOT JUST SINGLE, DOUBLE, TREBLE ETC... THEY WERE DOUBLE LINES OF MAIN POSITIONS.

These maps illustrate major French offensives on the Western Front and the small amount of ground retaken from the Germans. Yet the casualties were colossal. For examples, in Artois (9 May–18 June alone) the French losses exceeded 102,500, and in Champagne (25–30 September alone) the total was more than 143,500. But, in December, Joffre issued a directive: "...Our experience has proved that one can carry the whole defensive system at a single bound....."

Note: Pétain, Foch, de Castelnau, etc. did not concur.

CHAMPAGNE : SEPTEMBER 1915

St.Hilaire-le-Petit

Aure

Manre

St.Martin

St.Souplet

Somme-Py

Fontaine

BAZANCOURT-CHALLERANGE RAILWAY

Butte de Tahure

Ripont

Cernay

NAVARIN FARM

Butte de Souain

Dormoise

Vaudesincourt

Suippe

Epine de Védegrange

Tahure

Aubérive

le Trou Bricot

le Courtine

Ville-sur-Tourbe

BEAUSEJOUR

Massiges

St.Hilaire le-Grand

Ain

Souain

Perthes-les-Hurlus

le Mesnil-les-Hurlus

Minaucourt

Mourmelon-le-Grand

Hurlus

KEY

Ground gained by French.

▬▬ French front line 25 September.

▬ ▬ French front line 30 September.

Jonchery-sur-Suippe

0 2 4 6
Miles

Suippes

© Arthur Banks 1973

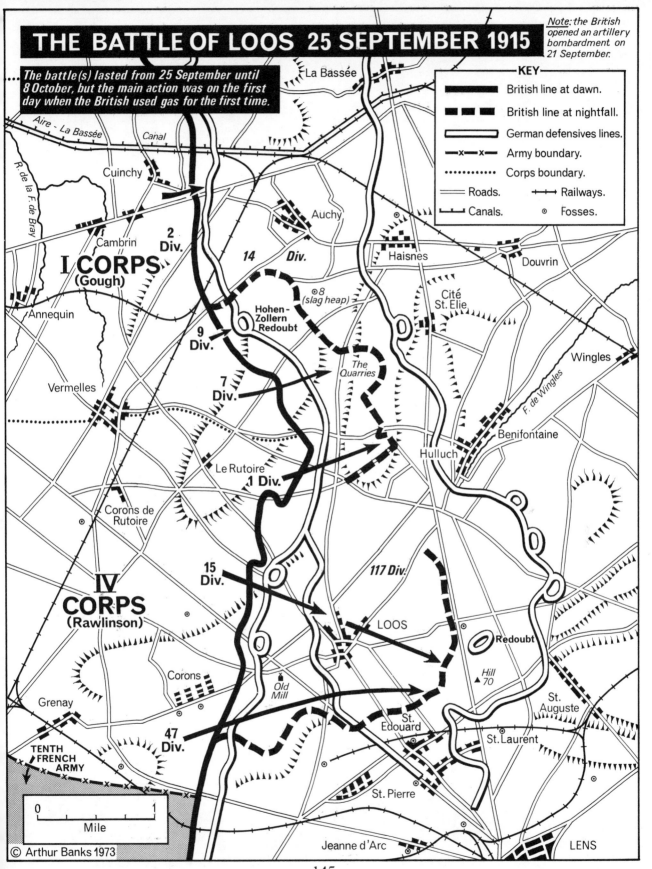

THE BATTLE OF LOOS 25 SEPTEMBER 1915

Note: the British opened an artillery bombardment on 21 September.

The battle(s) lasted from 25 September until 8 October, but the main action was on the first day when the British used gas for the first time.

KEY

▬▬▬▬	British line at dawn.
▬ ▬ ▬	British line at nightfall.
▭▭▭	German defensives lines.
x—x—x	Army boundary.
••••••	Corps boundary.
——	Roads.
+++	Railways.
⊥⊥⊥	Canals.
⊙	Fosses.

La Bassée

Aire - La Bassée
Canal

Cuinchy

Auchy

Haisnes

Douvrin

Cambrin

2 Div.

14 Div.

I CORPS (Gough)

R. de la F. de Bray

Annequin

⊙8 (slag heap)

Cité St. Elie

Wingles

Hohen-Zollern Redoubt

9 Div.

Vermelles

7 Div.

The Quarries

F. de Wingles

Benifontaine

Le Rutoire

Hulluch

1 Div.

Corons de Rutoire

IV CORPS (Rawlinson)

15 Div.

117 Div.

LOOS

Redoubt

Corons

Hill 70

St. Auguste

Old Mill

Grenay

47 Div.

St. Edouard

St. Laurent

St. Pierre

TENTH FRENCH ARMY

0   1
Mile

© Arthur Banks 1973

Jeanne d'Arc

LENS

145

THE WAR IN 1916

The costly failures of 1915 had led to changes in command before the end of the year. In the autumn, against the advice of his ministers, Tsar Nicholas II assumed command on the Eastern Front, sending Grand Duke Nicholas to hold the Caucasus against the Turks (page 163). The heavy casualties at Loos discredited Sir John French who, in December, was replaced as British commander-in-chief by Sir Douglas Haig. At the same time Kitchener, though remaining War Minister, surrendered responsibility for operations to a new Chief of the Imperial General Staff, Sir William Robertson, an ex-footman who had enlisted as a private thirty-nine years before. Only in France did Joffre's supremacy pass unchallenged.

Haig and Robertson were a formidable partnership. They insisted that, after the frustrations of Gallipoli, the Western Front was to have priority over all other Fronts. This decision was endorsed by the Cabinet on 28 December 1915; it was welcomed by Joffre. His own plans for 1916 looked for wearing-down operations by his allies preparatory to a major offensive by the French later in the spring. But the initiative on the Western Front was seized by the Germans. Falkenhayn won the Kaiser's consent for a different concept of military operations: he proposed massive attack on a narrow sector where reasons of national sentiment would 'compel the French General Staff to throw in every man they have'. The sector he recommended for this attempt 'to bleed France white' (Falkenhayn's own expression) was Verdun, the historic city on the Meuse whose fall in 1792 precipitated the panic September massacres in revolutionary Paris.

The battle of Verdun, which began with a concentrated artillery barrage on 21 February 1916 and continued for 300 days, overshadowed—and to some extent predetermined—all other military events of the year. Verdun, like Ypres, never fell to the Germans; it consumed Joffre's reserves; it left the French Army permanently shell-shocked; but it also brought disillusionment to the Germans, who sustained a third of a million casualties in occupying a crater filled wasteland one-sixth the size of the Isle of Wight. Never again was morale steady, either in France or Germany.

Ultimately the defenders of Verdun were relieved by actions elsewhere. By midsummer Haig, supported by Foch's Sixth Army, was ready to attack on the Somme. 20,000 British soldiers perished on the first day of the battle, more than were killed in action during the five years of Wellington's Peninsular Campaign. Yet, despite the terrible losses, Haig continued to pound the German lines on the Somme, employing in September, for the first time, tanks to cross trenches and destroy machine gun nests. The Somme was a traumatic as Verdun.

Success in 1916 came on the south-west sector of the Eastern Front where General Brusilov convinced the Tsar that it was possible to break through the Austrian defences and, if assisted by an enveloping movement farther north, to knock Austria-Hungary out of the war. Brusilov forced the Austrians to fall back sixty or seventy miles in confusion: the Germans rushed divisions from the Western Front to plug the gap, the Austrians relaxed pressure on Italy, and even a Turkish Corps was hurried to Galicia. The northern attack never materialised, but Brusilov gained a remarkable triumph, sufficient to tempt Rumania into the war as an ally, although the Rumanians were speedily defeated (page 162). The victory over Rumania was won by Mackensen and Falkenhayn, who had been replaced as Chief of the German General Staff by Hindenburg when the Kaiser despaired of his Verdun policy at the end of August.

At sea, 1916 was the year of Jutland (pages 256–261), of intensified measures by the British to blockade Germany, and of a fifty per cent increase over the 1915 figures for the tonnage of Allied shipping sunk by U-boats. The outlook for 1917 was ominous.

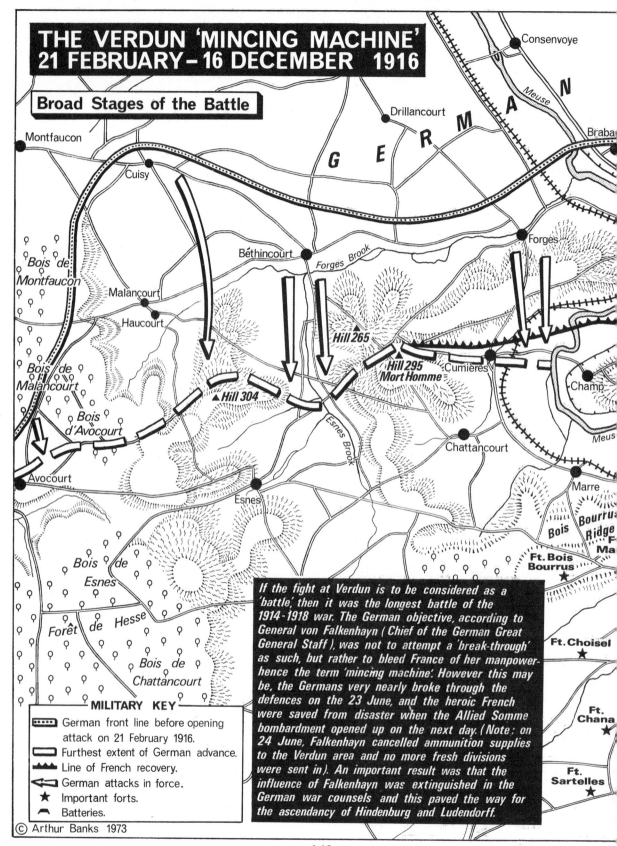

THE VERDUN 'MINCING MACHINE' 21 FEBRUARY – 16 DECEMBER 1916

Broad Stages of the Battle

Consenvoye

Drillancourt

GERMAN

Montfaucon

Braba

Cuisy

Meuse

Bois de Montfaucon

Béthincourt

Forges Brook

Forges

Malancourt

Hill 265

Haucourt

Hill 295 Mort Homme

Cumières

Bois de Malancourt

Champ

Bois d'Avocourt

Hill 304

Meus

Avocourt

Chattancourt

Esnes

Marre

Bois Bourru Ridge

Bois de Esnes

Ft. Bois Bourrus ★

Forêt de Hesse

Ft. Choisel ★

Bois de Chattancourt

If the fight at Verdun is to be considered as a 'battle', then it was the longest battle of the 1914-1918 war. The German objective, according to General von Falkenhayn (Chief of the German Great General Staff), was not to attempt a 'break-through' as such, but rather to bleed France of her manpower - hence the term 'mincing machine'. However this may be, the Germans very nearly broke through the defences on the 23 June, and the heroic French were saved from disaster when the Allied Somme bombardment opened up on the next day. (Note: on 24 June, Falkenhayn cancelled ammunition supplies to the Verdun area and no more fresh divisions were sent in). An important result was that the influence of Falkenhayn was extinguished in the German war counsels and this paved the way for the ascendancy of Hindenburg and Ludendorff.

Ft. Chana ★

MILITARY KEY

- German front line before opening attack on 21 February 1916.
- Furthest extent of German advance.
- Line of French recovery.
- German attacks in force.
- ★ Important forts.
- Batteries.

Ft. Sartelles ★

© Arthur Banks 1973

148

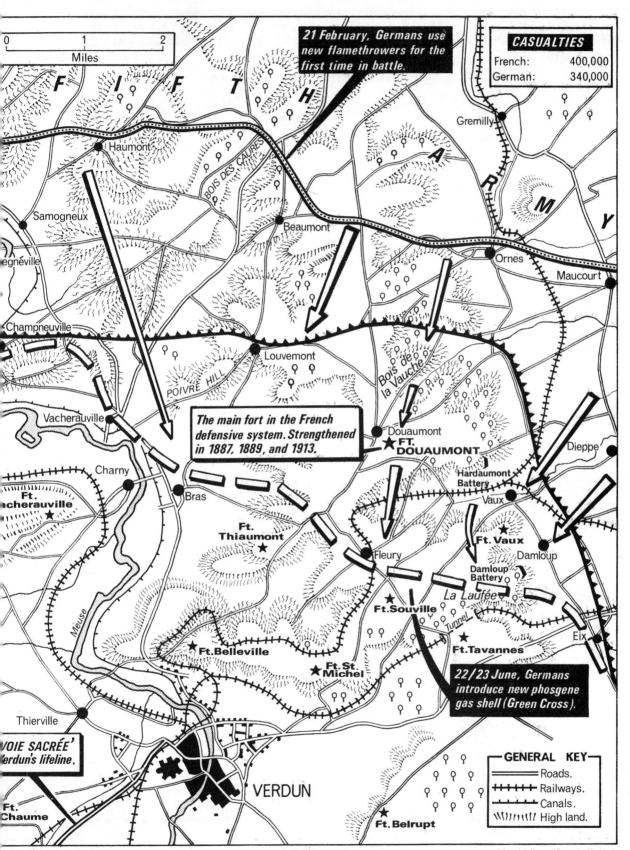

21 February, Germans use new flamethrowers for the first time in battle.

CASUALTIES	
French:	400,000
German:	340,000

F I F T H   A R M Y

Gremilly

Haumont

BOIS DES CAURES

Samogneux

Beaumont

Ornes

Maucourt

egnéville

Champneuville

Louvemont

Bois de la Vauche

POIVRE HILL

Dieppe

Vacherauville

The main fort in the French defensive system. Strengthened in 1887, 1889, and 1913.

Douaumont

★ FT. DOUAUMONT

Charny

Hardaumont Battery

Ft. acherauville ★

Bras

Vaux

Ft. Thiaumont ★

Fleury

★ Ft. Vaux

Damloup

Meuse

Damloup Battery

La Laufée

★ Ft.Souville

Eix

Ft.Belleville ★

Tunnel

★ Ft.Tavannes

★ Ft.St. Michel

22/23 June, Germans introduce new phosgene gas shell (Green Cross).

Thierville

VOIE SACRÉE' erdun's lifeline.

VERDUN

Ft. Chaume

★ Ft. Belrupt

— GENERAL KEY —
Roads.
Railways.
Canals.
High land.

149

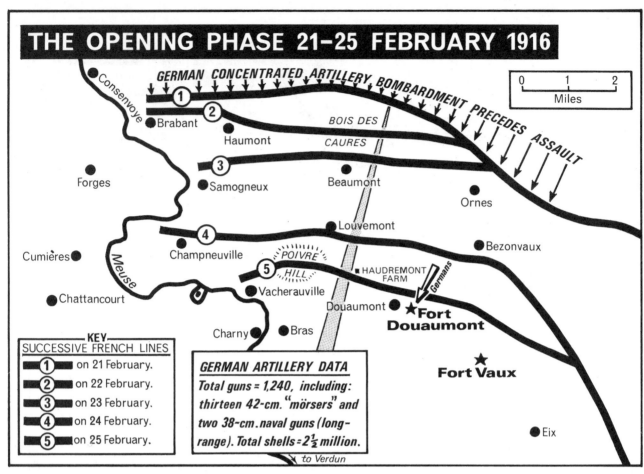

THE OPENING PHASE 21–25 FEBRUARY 1916

GERMAN CONCENTRATED ARTILLERY BOMBARDMENT PRECEDES ASSAULT

0 1 2
Miles

Consenvoye

① Brabant

② Haumont

BOIS DES CAURES

③ Samogneux

Forges

Beaumont

Ornes

Meuse

④ Champneuville

Louvemont

Bezonvaux

Cumières

POIVRE HILL

⑤

HAUDREMONT FARM

Vacherauville

Germans

Chattancourt

Douaumont

★ Fort Douaumont

Charny

Bras

★ Fort Vaux

Eix

KEY
SUCCESSIVE FRENCH LINES
① on 21 February.
② on 22 February.
③ on 23 February.
④ on 24 February.
⑤ on 25 February.

GERMAN ARTILLERY DATA
Total guns = 1,240, including: thirteen 42-cm. "mörsers" and two 38-cm. naval guns (long-range). Total shells = 2½ million.

↓ to Verdun

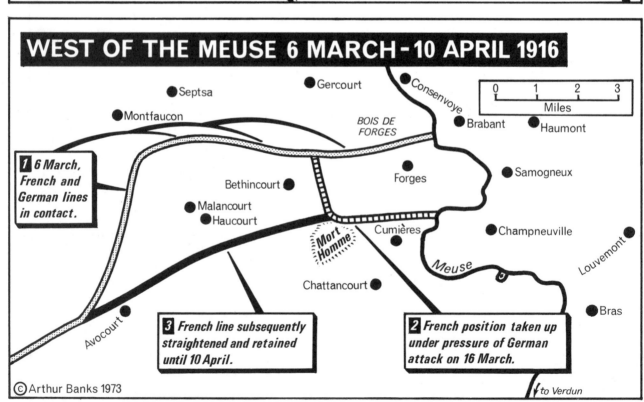

WEST OF THE MEUSE 6 MARCH – 10 APRIL 1916

Septsa

Gercourt

Consenvoye

0 1 2 3
Miles

Montfaucon

BOIS DE FORGES

Brabant

Haumont

1 *6 March, French and German lines in contact.*

Bethincourt

Forges

Samogneux

Malancourt
Haucourt

Cumières

Champneuville

Mort Homme

Meuse

Louvemont

Chattancourt

Bras

Avocourt

3 *French line subsequently straightened and retained until 10 April.*

2 *French position taken up under pressure of German attack on 16 March.*

© Arthur Banks 1973

↓ to Verdun

150

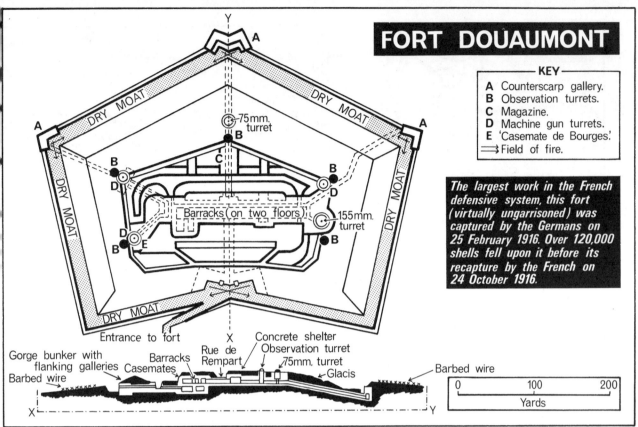

FORT DOUAUMONT

KEY
A Counterscarp gallery.
B Observation turrets.
C Magazine.
D Machine gun turrets.
E 'Casemate de Bourges'.
⟹ Field of fire.

The largest work in the French defensive system, this fort (virtually ungarrisoned) was captured by the Germans on 25 February 1916. Over 120,000 shells fell upon it before its recapture by the French on 24 October 1916.

75mm. turret

DRY MOAT

Barracks (on two floors)

155mm. turret

Entrance to fort

Rue de Rempart

Concrete shelter
Observation turret
75mm. turret
Glacis

Gorge bunker with flanking galleries
Barracks
Casemates
Barbed wire
Barbed wire

0   100   200
Yards

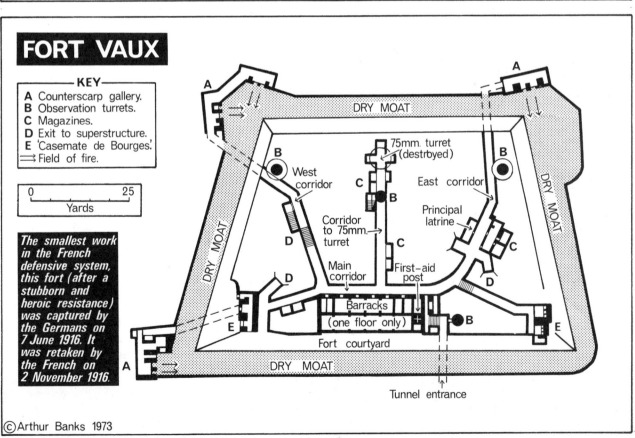

FORT VAUX

KEY
A Counterscarp gallery.
B Observation turrets.
C Magazines.
D Exit to superstructure.
E 'Casemate de Bourges'.
⟹ Field of fire.

0   25
Yards

The smallest work in the French defensive system, this fort (after a stubborn and heroic resistance) was captured by the Germans on 7 June 1916. It was retaken by the French on 2 November 1916.

DRY MOAT

75mm. turret (destroyed)

West corridor

East corridor

Corridor to 75mm. turret

Principal latrine

Main corridor

First-aid post

Barracks (one floor only)

Fort courtyard

DRY MOAT

Tunnel entrance

© Arthur Banks 1973

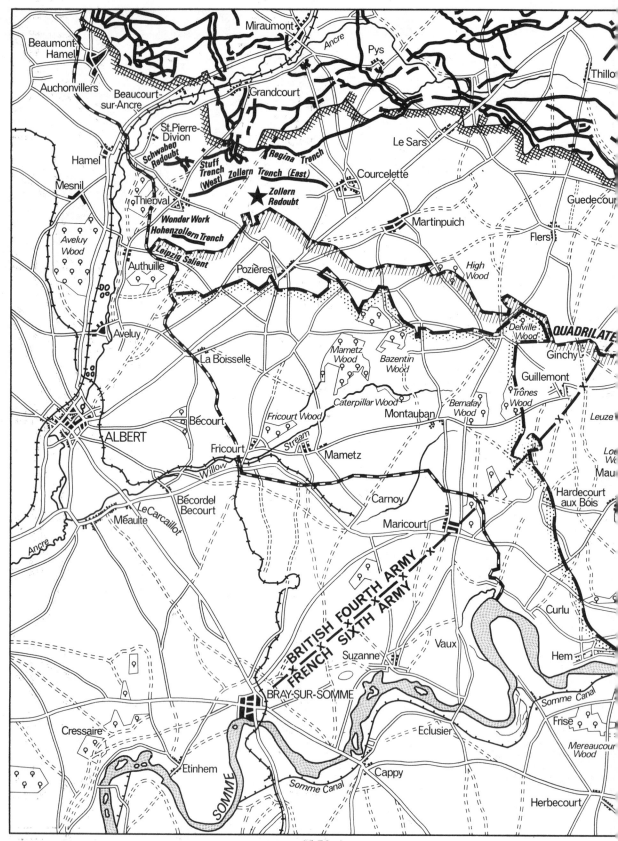

Beaumont-Hamel
Auchonvillers
Beaucourt-sur-Ancre
Miraumont
Ancre
Pys
Thillo
Grandcourt
St.Pierre-Divion
Le Sars
Hamel
Schwaben Redoubt
Regina Trench
Mesnil
Stuff Trench (West)
Zollern Trench (East)
Courcelette
Guedecour
Thiepval
Zollern Redoubt
Wonder Work
Martinpuich
Hohenzollern Trench
Flers
Aveluy Wood
Leipzig Salient
Pozières
High Wood
Authuille
Deſville Wood
QUADRILATE
Aveluy
La Boisselle
Mametz Wood
Bazentin Wood
Ginchy
Guillemont
Trônes Wood
Leuze
Caterpillar Wood
Bécourt
Fricourt Wood
Montauban
Bernafay Wood
Loe Wo
ALBERT
Fricourt
Stream
Mametz
Hardecourt aux Bóis
Mau
Willow
Bécordel Becourt
Carnoy
LeCarcaillot
Méaulte
Maricourt
Ancre
Curlu
BRITISH FOURTH ARMY
FRENCH SIXTH ARMY
Vaux
Hem
Suzanne
Cressaire
BRAY-SUR-SOMME
Somme Canal
Frise
Eclusier
Mereaucour Wood
Etinhem
Cappy
SOMME
Somme Canal
Herbecourt

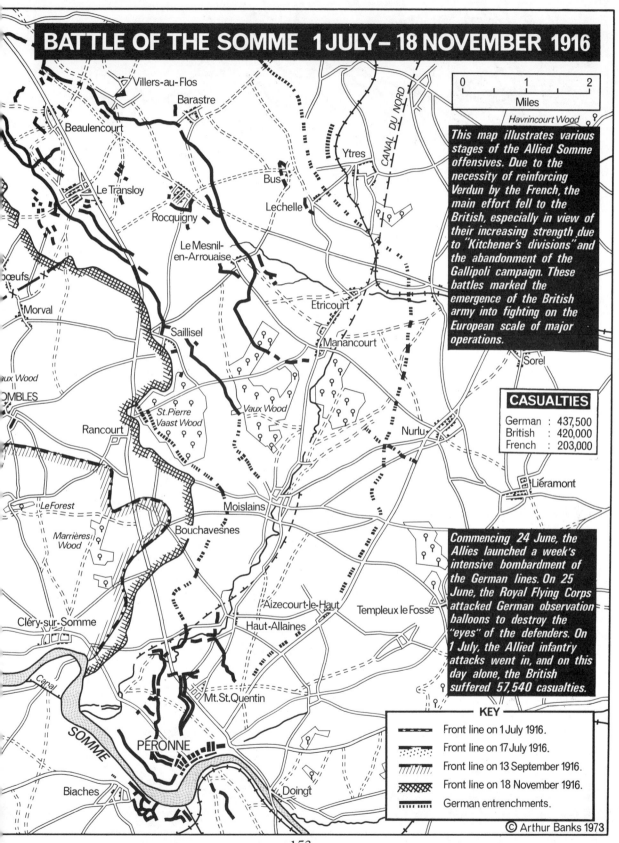

BATTLE OF THE SOMME 1 JULY – 18 NOVEMBER 1916

Villers-au-Flos
Barastre
Beaulencourt
Le Transloy
Bus
Lechelle
Rocquigny
Le Mesnil-
en-Arrouaise
Bœufs
Morval
Saillisel
Etricourt
Vaux Wood
Manancourt
aux Wood
OMBLES
St. Pierre
Vaast Wood
Vaux Wood
Sorel
Rancourt
Nurlu
Liéramont
Le Forest
Moislains
Marrières
Wood
Bouchavesnes
Aizecourt-le-Haut
Templeux le Fossé
Clèry-sur-Somme
Haut-Allaines
Canal
Mt. St. Quentin
SOMME
PÉRONNE
Biaches
Doingt

Ytres
CANAL DU NORD
Havrincourt Wood

This map illustrates various stages of the Allied Somme offensives. Due to the necessity of reinforcing Verdun by the French, the main effort fell to the British, especially in view of their increasing strength due to "Kitchener's divisions" and the abandonment of the Gallipoli campaign. These battles marked the emergence of the British army into fighting on the European scale of major operations.

CASUALTIES

German : 437,500
British : 420,000
French : 203,000

Commencing 24 June, the Allies launched a week's intensive bombardment of the German lines. On 25 June, the Royal Flying Corps attacked German observation balloons to destroy the "eyes" of the defenders. On 1 July, the Allied infantry attacks went in, and on this day alone, the British suffered 57,540 casualties.

KEY

- Front line on 1 July 1916.
- Front line on 17 July 1916.
- Front line on 13 September 1916.
- Front line on 18 November 1916.
- German entrenchments.

© Arthur Banks 1973

0   1   2
Miles

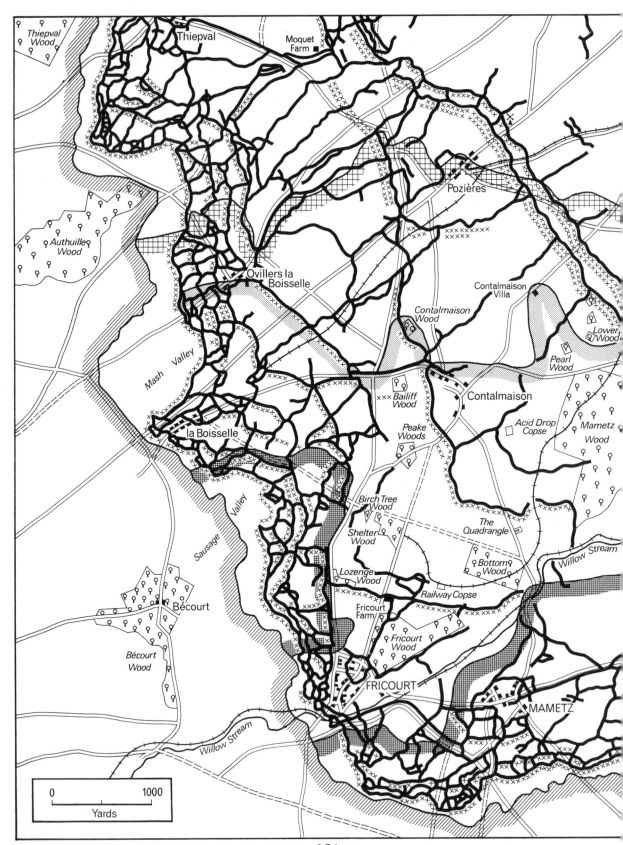

Thiepval Wood

Thiepval

Moquet Farm

Pozières

Authuille Wood

Ovillers la Boisselle

Contalmaison Villa

Contalmaison Wood

Lower Wood

Pearl Wood

Mash Valley

Bailiff Wood

Contalmaison

Acid Drop Copse

Mametz Wood

Peake Woods

la Boisselle

Birch Tree Wood

The Quadrangle

Sausage Valley

Shelter Wood

Willow Stream

Lozenge Wood

Bottom Wood

Bécourt

Railway Copse

Fricourt Farm

Bécourt Wood

Fricourt Wood

FRICOURT

MAMETZ

Willow Stream

0   1000
Yards

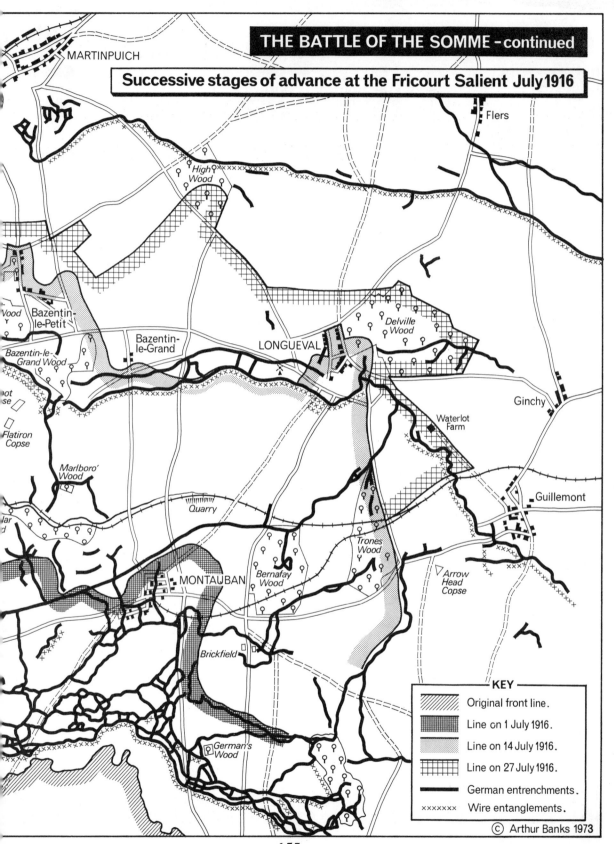

THE BATTLE OF THE SOMME - continued

Successive stages of advance at the Fricourt Salient July 1916

MARTINPUICH

Flers

High Wood

Bazentin-le-Petit

Bazentin-le-Grand

LONGUEVAL

Delville Wood

Bazentin-le-Grand Wood

Ginchy

Flatiron Copse

Waterlot Farm

Marlboro' Wood

Quarry

Guillemont

Trones Wood

Bernafay Wood

Arrow Head Copse

MONTAUBAN

Brickfield

German's Wood

KEY

⧄	Original front line.
▨	Line on 1 July 1916.
░	Line on 14 July 1916.
▦	Line on 27 July 1916.
▬	German entrenchments.
xxxxxxx	Wire entanglements.

© Arthur Banks 1973

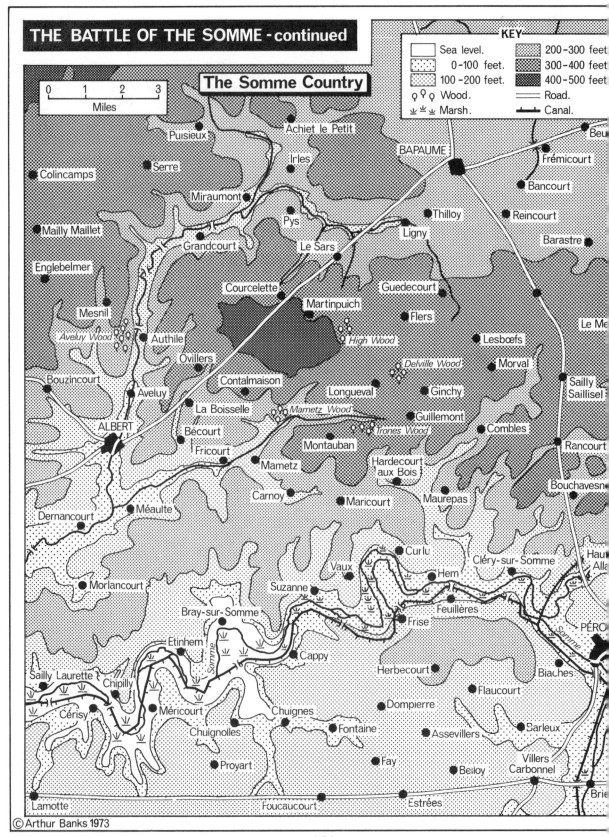

THE BATTLE OF THE SOMME - continued

The Somme Country

0 1 2 3
Miles

Puisieux
Achiet le Petit
Beu
BAPAUME
Frémicourt
Irles
Colincamps
Serre
Bancourt
Miraumont
Pys
Thilloy
Reincourt
Mailly Maillet
Ligny
Grandcourt
Le Sars
Barastre
Englebelmer
Courcelette
Guedecourt
Martinpuich
Flers
Le Me
Mesnil
High Wood
Aveluy Wood
Authile
Lesbœufs
Ovillers
Delville Wood
Morval
Bouzincourt
Contalmaison
Longueval
Ginchy
Sailly
Saillisel
Aveluy
Mametz Wood
La Boisselle
Guillemont
Combles
Bécourt
Trones Wood
Rancourt
ALBERT
Montauban
Fricourt
Bouchavesn
Mametz
Hardecourt
aux Bois
Carnoy
Maricourt
Maurepas
Dernancourt
Méaulte
Curlu
Cléry-sur-Somme
Hau
Alla
Vaux
Morlancourt
Hem
Suzanne
Feuillères
PÉRO
Bray-sur-Somme
Frise
Somme
Etinhem
Cappy
Herbecourt
Biaches
Sailly Laurette
Chipilly
Flaucourt
Chuignes
Dompierre
Cérisy
Méricourt
Barleux
Chuignolles
Fontaine
Assevillers
Villers
Carbonnel
Proyart
Fay
Belloy
Bri
Lamotte
Foucaucourt
Estrées

© Arthur Banks 1973

156

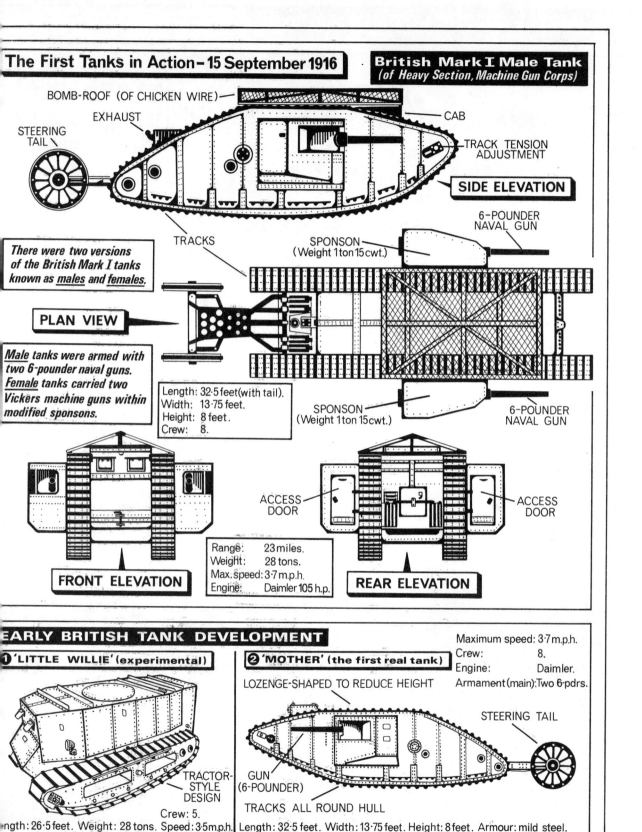

The First Tanks in Action – 15 September 1916

British Mark I Male Tank
(of Heavy Section, Machine Gun Corps)

BOMB-ROOF (OF CHICKEN WIRE)

EXHAUST

STEERING TAIL

CAB

TRACK TENSION ADJUSTMENT

SIDE ELEVATION

TRACKS

6-POUNDER NAVAL GUN

SPONSON (Weight 1 ton 15 cwt.)

There were two versions of the British Mark I tanks known as males and females.

PLAN VIEW

Male tanks were armed with two 6-pounder naval guns. Female tanks carried two Vickers machine guns within modified sponsons.

Length: 32·5 feet (with tail).
Width: 13·75 feet.
Height: 8 feet.
Crew: 8.

SPONSON (Weight 1 ton 15 cwt.)

6-POUNDER NAVAL GUN

ACCESS DOOR

ACCESS DOOR

Range: 23 miles.
Weight: 28 tons.
Max. speed: 3·7 m.p.h.
Engine: Daimler 105 h.p.

FRONT ELEVATION

REAR ELEVATION

EARLY BRITISH TANK DEVELOPMENT

Maximum speed: 3·7 m.p.h.
Crew: 8.
Engine: Daimler.
Armament (main): Two 6-pdrs.

❶ 'LITTLE WILLIE' (experimental)

TRACTOR-STYLE DESIGN

Crew: 5.

ngth: 26·5 feet. Weight: 28 tons. Speed: 3·5 m.p.h.

❷ 'MOTHER' (the first real tank)

LOZENGE-SHAPED TO REDUCE HEIGHT

STEERING TAIL

GUN (6-POUNDER)

TRACKS ALL ROUND HULL

Length: 32·5 feet. Width: 13·75 feet. Height: 8 feet. Armour: mild steel.

THE BATTLE OF THE SOMME – conclusion

A Basic Summary

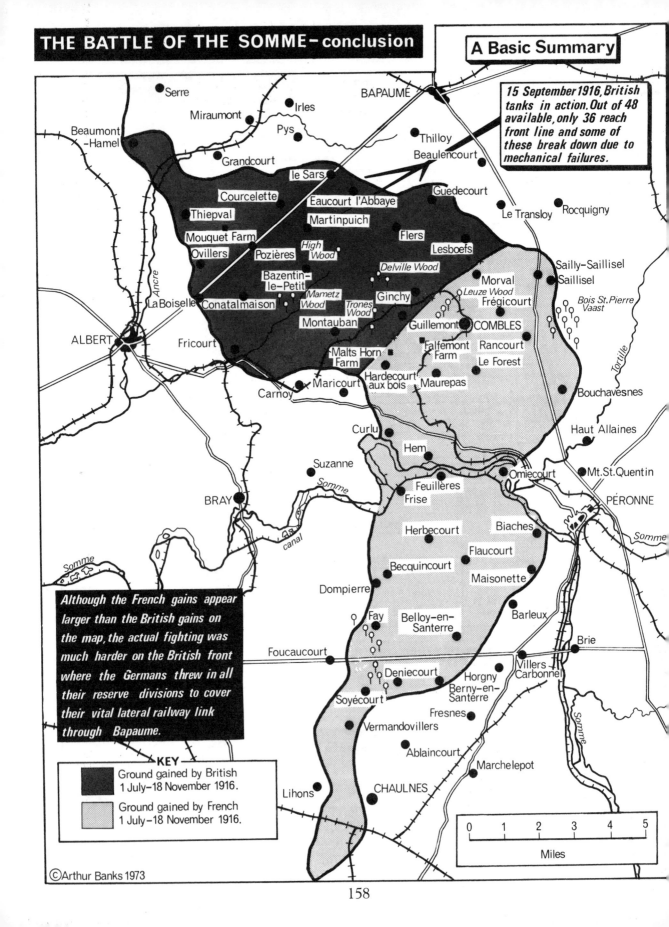

15 September 1916, British tanks in action. Out of 48 available, only 36 reach front line and some of these break down due to mechanical failures.

Serre
Miraumont
Irles
Pys
BAPAUME
Thilloy
Beaumont-Hamel
Grandcourt
Beaulencourt
le Sars
Guedecourt
Le Transloy
Rocquigny
Courcelette
Eaucourt l'Abbaye
Thiepval
Martinpuich
Mouquet Farm
Flers
Ovillers
Pozières
High Wood
Lesboefs
Sailly-Saillisel
Saillisel
Delville Wood
Bazentin-le-Petit
Morval
Leuze Wood
Bois St.Pierre Vaast
Mametz Wood
Ginchy
Frégicourt
La Boiselle
Conatalmaison
Trones Wood
Guillemont
COMBLES
ALBERT
Montauban
Falfemont Farm
Rancourt
Fricourt
Malts Horn Farm
Le Forest
Bouchavesnes
Hardecourt aux bois
Maurepas
Maricourt
Carnoy
Haut Allaines
Curlu
Hem
Mt.St.Quentin
Suzanne
Omiecourt
Somme
Feuillères
Frise
PÉRONNE
BRAY
Herbecourt
Biaches
Somme
Flaucourt
canal
Becquincourt
Maisonette
Somme
Dompierre
Barleux
Fay
Belloy-en-Santerre
Brie
Foucaucourt
Deniecourt
Horgny
Villers Carbonnel
Berny-en-Santerre
Soyécourt
Fresnes
Vermandovillers
Somme
Ablaincourt
Marchelepot
Lihons
CHAULNES

Although the French gains appear larger than the British gains on the map, the actual fighting was much harder on the British front where the Germans threw in all their reserve divisions to cover their vital lateral railway link through Bapaume.

KEY

Ground gained by British 1 July–18 November 1916.

Ground gained by French 1 July–18 November 1916.

0 1 2 3 4 5

Miles

©Arthur Banks 1973

THE FRENCH RECOVERY AT VERDUN OCTOBER – DECEMBER 1916

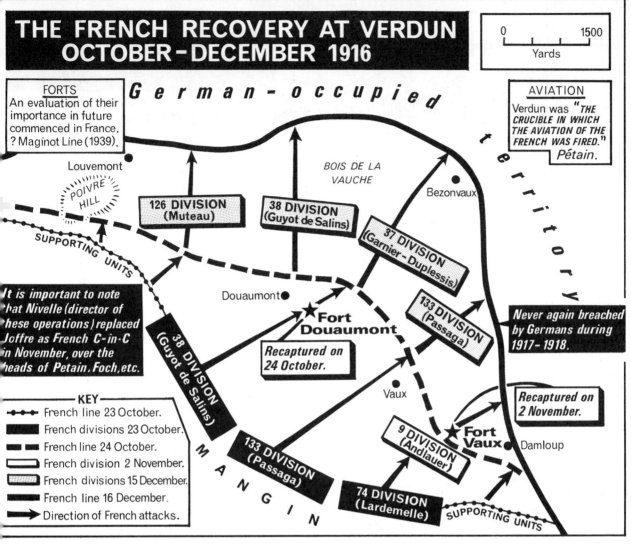

G e r m a n - o c c u p i e d   t e r r i t o r y

FORTS
An evaluation of their importance in future commenced in France. ? Maginot Line (1939).

AVIATION
Verdun was *"THE CRUCIBLE IN WHICH THE AVIATION OF THE FRENCH WAS FIRED."* Pétain.

Louvemont

BOIS DE LA VAUCHE

POIVRE HILL

Bezonvaux

126 DIVISION (Muteau)

38 DIVISION (Guyot de Salins)

37 DIVISION (Garnier-Duplessis)

SUPPORTING UNITS

It is important to note that Nivelle (director of these operations) replaced Joffre as French C-in-C in November, over the heads of Petain, Foch, etc.

Douaumont

★ **Fort Douaumont**

Recaptured on 24 October.

38 DIVISION (Guyot de Salins)

133 DIVISION (Passaga)

Never again breached by Germans during 1917-1918.

Vaux

Recaptured on 2 November.

9 DIVISION (Andlauer)

★ **Fort Vaux**

Damloup

KEY
- •–•–• French line 23 October.
- ▬ French divisions 23 October.
- ▬ ▬ French line 24 October.
- ▭ French division 2 November.
- ▨ French divisions 15 December.
- ═══ French line 16 December.
- → Direction of French attacks.

M A N G I N

133 DIVISION (Passaga)

74 DIVISION (Lardemelle)

SUPPORTING UNITS

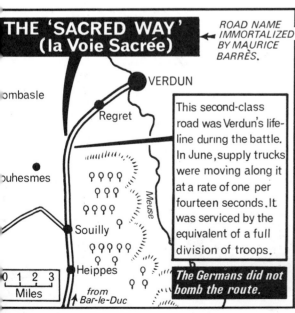

THE 'SACRED WAY' (la Voie Sacrée)

ROAD NAME IMMORTALIZED BY MAURICE BARRÈS.

ombasle

VERDUN

Regret

This second-class road was Verdun's lifeline during the battle. In June, supply trucks were moving along it at a rate of one per fourteen seconds. It was serviced by the equivalent of a full division of troops.

ouhesmes

Meuse

Souilly

Heippes

0 1 2 3
Miles

from Bar-le-Duc

The Germans did not bomb the route.

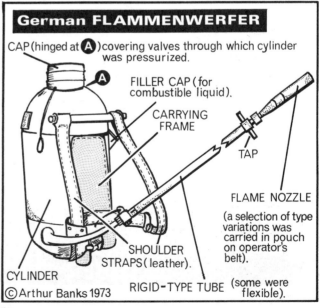

German FLAMMENWERFER

CAP (hinged at **A**) covering valves through which cylinder was pressurized.

FILLER CAP (for combustible liquid).

CARRYING FRAME

TAP

FLAME NOZZLE
(a selection of type variations was carried in pouch on operator's belt).

SHOULDER STRAPS (leather).

CYLINDER

RIGID-TYPE TUBE (some were flexible).

© Arthur Banks 1973

159

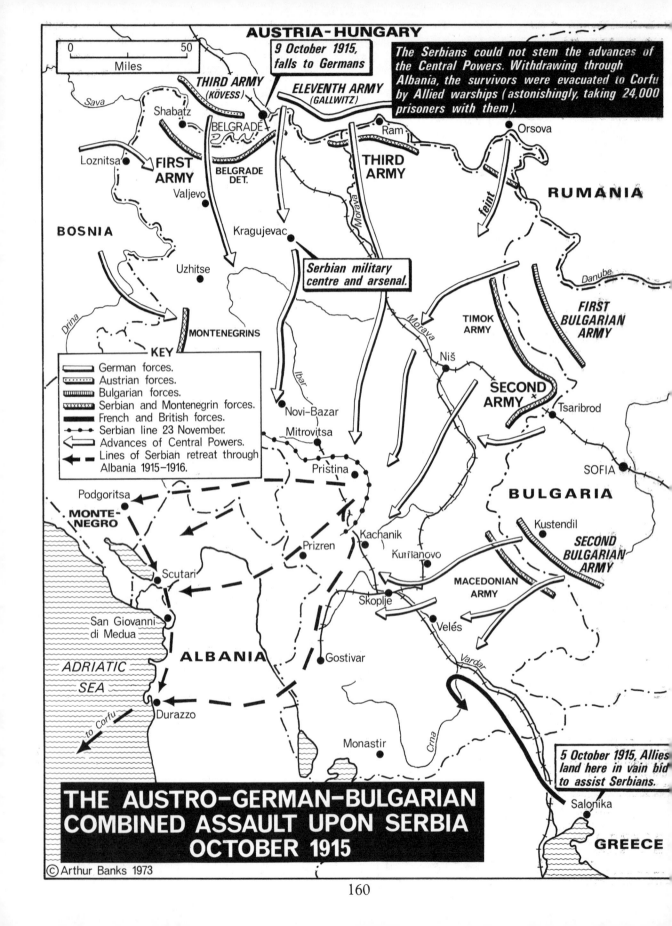

AUSTRIA-HUNGARY

9 October 1915, falls to Germans

The Serbians could not stem the advances of the Central Powers. Withdrawing through Albania, the survivors were evacuated to Corfu by Allied warships (astonishingly, taking 24,000 prisoners with them).

0 — 50
Miles

Sava

THIRD ARMY *(KÖVESS)*

ELEVENTH ARMY *(GALLWITZ)*

Shabatz

BELGRADE

Ram

Orsova

Loznitsa

FIRST ARMY

BELGRADE DET.

THIRD ARMY

feint

RUMANIA

Valjevo

BOSNIA

Kragujevac

Morava

Serbian military centre and arsenal.

Uzhitse

Danube

FIRST BULGARIAN ARMY

Drina

MONTENEGRINS

TIMOK ARMY

Morava

Niš

KEY

▭ German forces.
▭ Austrian forces.
▭ Bulgarian forces.
▭ Serbian and Montenegrin forces.
▬ French and British forces.
•—• Serbian line 23 November.
⇦ Advances of Central Powers.
◄▬ Lines of Serbian retreat through Albania 1915–1916.

Ibar

Novi-Bazar

Mitrovitsa

SECOND ARMY

Tsaribrod

Pristina

SOFIA

BULGARIA

Podgoritsa

MONTE-NEGRO

Kachanik

Prizren

Kurrianovo

Kustendil

SECOND BULGARIAN ARMY

Scutari

Skoplje

MACEDONIAN ARMY

San Giovanni di Medua

Velés

ALBANIA

Gostivar

Vardar

ADRIATIC SEA

to Corfu

Durazzo

Monastir

Crna

5 October 1915, Allies land here in vain bid to assist Serbians.

THE AUSTRO-GERMAN-BULGARIAN COMBINED ASSAULT UPON SERBIA OCTOBER 1915

Salonika

GREECE

© Arthur Banks 1973

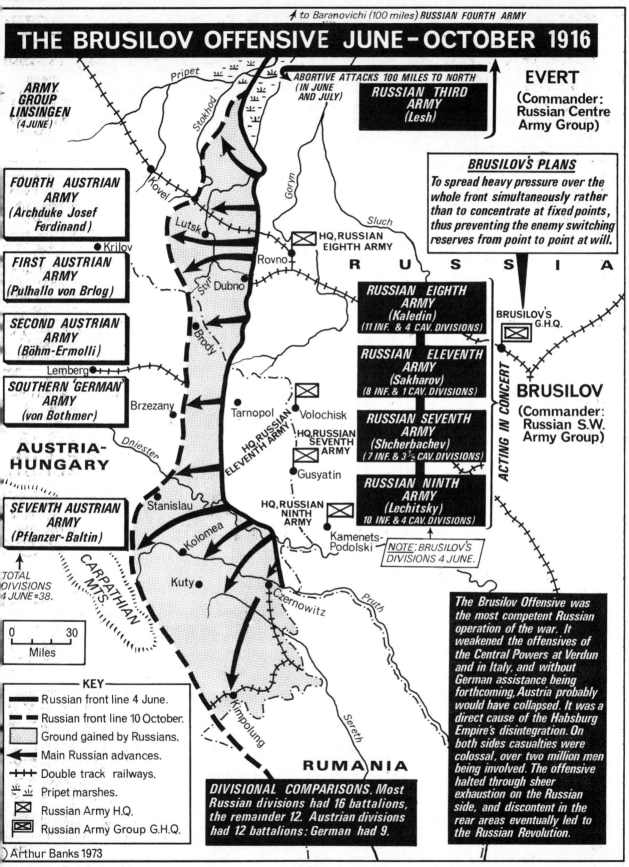

THE BRUSILOV OFFENSIVE JUNE–OCTOBER 1916

↑ to Baranovichi (100 miles) RUSSIAN FOURTH ARMY

ARMY GROUP LINSINGEN (4 JUNE)

ABORTIVE ATTACKS 100 MILES TO NORTH (IN JUNE AND JULY)

RUSSIAN THIRD ARMY (Lesh)

EVERT (Commander: Russian Centre Army Group)

FOURTH AUSTRIAN ARMY (Archduke Josef Ferdinand)

FIRST AUSTRIAN ARMY (Pulhallo von Brlog)

SECOND AUSTRIAN ARMY (Böhm-Ermolli)

SOUTHERN 'GERMAN' ARMY (von Bothmer)

AUSTRIA-HUNGARY

SEVENTH AUSTRIAN ARMY (Pflanzer-Baltin)

TOTAL DIVISIONS 4 JUNE = 38.

Pripet

Stokhod

Kovel

Lutsk

Krilov

Styr

Dubno

Brody

Lemberg

Brzezany

Dniester

Stanislau

Kolomea

CARPATHIAN MTS.

Kuty

Kimpolung

Goryn

Sluch

HQ, RUSSIAN EIGHTH ARMY

Rovno

Tarnopol

HQ RUSSIAN ELEVENTH ARMY

Volochisk

HQ RUSSIAN SEVENTH ARMY

Gusyatin

HQ, RUSSIAN NINTH ARMY

Kamenets-Podolski

Czernowitz

Pruth

Sereth

RUSSIA

BRUSILOV'S PLANS
To spread heavy pressure over the whole front simultaneously rather than to concentrate at fixed points, thus preventing the enemy switching reserves from point to point at will.

RUSSIAN EIGHTH ARMY (Kaledin) (11 INF. & 4 CAV. DIVISIONS)

RUSSIAN ELEVENTH ARMY (Sakharov) (8 INF. & 1 CAV. DIVISIONS)

RUSSIAN SEVENTH ARMY (Shcherbachev) (7 INF. & 3½ CAV. DIVISIONS)

RUSSIAN NINTH ARMY (Lechitsky) (10 INF. & 4 CAV. DIVISIONS)

NOTE: BRUSILOV'S DIVISIONS 4 JUNE.

BRUSILOV'S G.H.Q.

ACTING IN CONCERT

BRUSILOV (Commander: Russian S.W. Army Group)

The Brusilov Offensive was the most competent Russian operation of the war. It weakened the offensives of the Central Powers at Verdun and in Italy, and without German assistance being forthcoming, Austria probably would have collapsed. It was a direct cause of the Habsburg Empire's disintegration. On both sides casualties were colossal, over two million men being involved. The offensive halted through sheer exhaustion on the Russian side, and discontent in the rear areas eventually led to the Russian Revolution.

RUMANIA

KEY
— Russian front line 4 June.
-- Russian front line 10 October.
▓ Ground gained by Russians.
← Main Russian advances.
+++ Double track railways.
⚒ Pripet marshes.
⊠ Russian Army H.Q.
⊠ Russian Army Group G.H.Q.

DIVISIONAL COMPARISONS. Most Russian divisions had 16 battalions, the remainder 12. Austrian divisions had 12 battalions: German had 9.

© Arthur Banks 1973

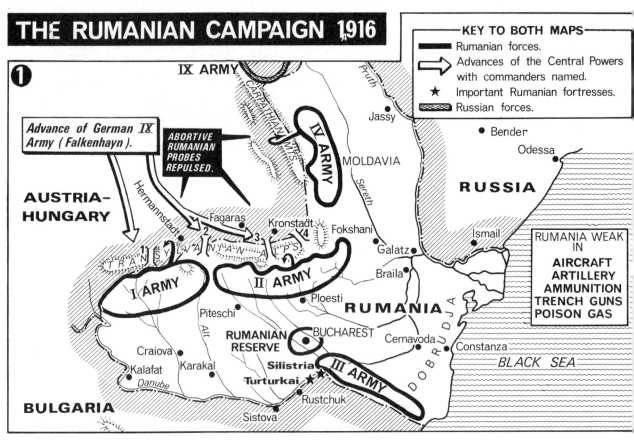

THE RUMANIAN CAMPAIGN 1916

KEY TO BOTH MAPS
- ▬▬ Rumanian forces.
- ⇨ Advances of the Central Powers with commanders named.
- ★ Important Rumanian fortresses.
- ▨ Russian forces.

①

IX ARMY

IV ARMY

MOLDAVIA

Jassy

Bender

Odessa

Advance of German IX. Army (Falkenhayn).

ABORTIVE RUMANIAN PROBES REPULSED.

AUSTRIA-HUNGARY

Hermannstadt

Fagaras

Kronstadt

Fokshani

Galatz

Braila

Ismail

RUSSIA

RUMANIA WEAK IN AIRCRAFT ARTILLERY AMMUNITION TRENCH GUNS POISON GAS

TRANSYLVANIAN ALPS

I ARMY

II ARMY

Piteschi

Ploesti

RUMANIA

Cernavoda

Constanza

BLACK SEA

RUMANIAN RESERVE

BUCHAREST

DOBRUDJA

Craiova

Karakal

Silistria

Turturkai

III ARMY

Kalafat

Danube

Rustchuk

BULGARIA

Sistova

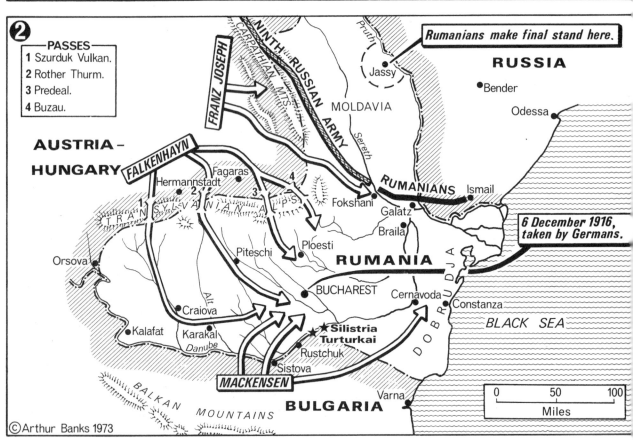

②

PASSES
1 Szurduk Vulkan.
2 Rother Thurm.
3 Predeal.
4 Buzau.

FRANZ JOSEPH

NINTH RUSSIAN ARMY

Rumanians make final stand here.

Jassy

RUSSIA

Bender

Odessa

MOLDAVIA

Sereth

Pruth

AUSTRIA-HUNGARY

FALKENHAYN

Hermannstadt

Fagaras

TRANSYLVANIAN ALPS

Fokshani

RUMANIANS

Ismail

6 December 1916, taken by Germans.

Galatz

Braila

Orsova

Piteschi

Ploesti

RUMANIA

Alt

Craiova

BUCHAREST

Cernavoda

Constanza

BLACK SEA

DOBRUDJA

Kalafat

Karakal

★Silistria
Turturkai

Danube

Rustchuk

Sistova

MACKENSEN

BALKAN MOUNTAINS

Varna

BULGARIA

0   50   100
Miles

©Arthur Banks 1973

162

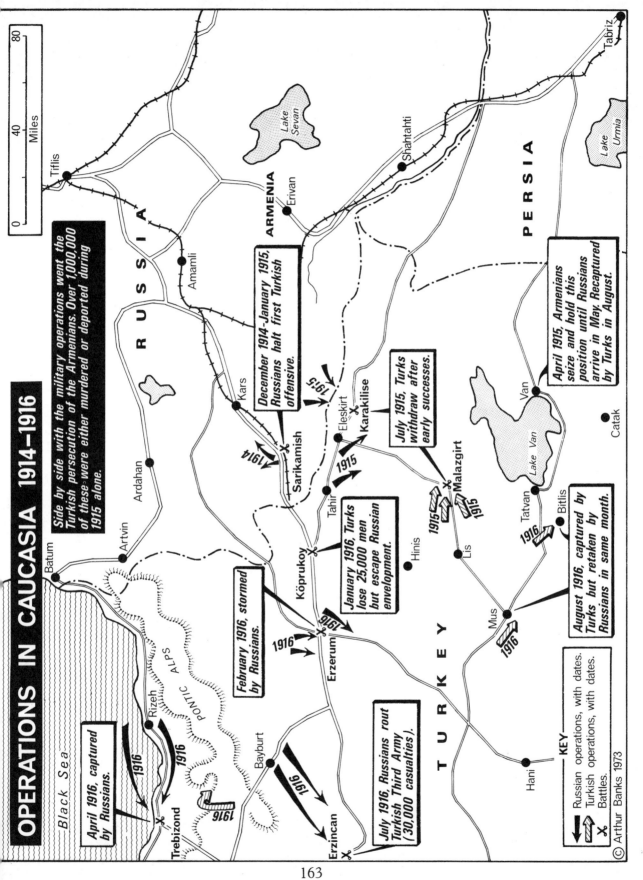

OPERATIONS IN CAUCASIA 1914–1916

Side by side with the military operations went the Turkish persecution of the Armenians. Over 1,000,000 of these were either murdered or deported during 1915 alone.

Black Sea

80 40 0
Miles

Tiflis

Lake Sevan

Tabriz

Lake Urmia

Shahtahti

Erivan

ARMENIA

RUSSIA

PERSIA

Amamli

Kars

Ardahan

Artvin

Batum

Rizeh

Trebizond

PONTIC ALPS

Bayburt

Erzincan

Erzerum

Köprukoy

Tahir

Sarikamish

Eleskirt
Karakilise

Malazgirt

Van

Lake Van

Catak

Tatvan

Bitlis

Lis

Mus

Hinis

Hani

April 1916, captured by Russians.

December 1914–January 1915, Russians halt first Turkish offensive.

July 1915, Turks withdraw after early successes.

April 1915, Armenians seize and hold this position until Russians arrive in May. Recaptured by Turks in August.

January 1916, Turks lose 25,000 men but escape Russian envelopment.

February 1916, stormed by Russians.

August 1916, captured by Turks but retaken by Russians in same month.

July 1916, Russians rout Turkish Third Army (30,000 casualties).

1914 1915 1916

KEY

→ Russian operations, with dates.
⇨ Turkish operations, with dates.
✕ Battles.

© Arthur Banks 1973

THE WAR IN 1917

The wasteful slaughter of 1916 was followed by a year of astonishing political change and upheaval. When, on 1 February 1917, the Germans announced a resumption of unrestricted U-Boat warfare, they knew that they ran the risk of bringing America into the conflict, but they calculated that they could eliminate Russia and France on land and starve the British into surrender before the effects of American belligerency were felt in Europe. In the event, the United States was finally brought to declare war on Germany in April 1917 as much by evidence of German intrigues in Mexico (the Zimmermann telegram) as by the submarine (see page 214). The fall of the Tsarist autocracy and the establishment of a democratic Provisional Government in Russia (page 177) made it easier for Congress to accept the idea of war; but British and French hopes that the Provisional Government would purge corruption and make Russia again an efficient military partner proved ill-founded. The so-called Kerensky Offensive of July 1917 soon petered out (page 176); the Russian people were apathetic and anxious only for 'peace and bread'. When in the first week of November Lenin's Bolsheviks seized power in Petrograd, Russia virtually withdrew from the war, opened negotiations with Germany and her allies, and concluded a separate peace (the Treaty of Brest-Litovsk, March 1918) by which Russia surrendered Poland, the Ukraine, the Baltic provinces, Finland and much of the Caucasus (see page 178).

Bolshevik propaganda contributed to unrest elsewhere in the Allied camp, notably among the French and Russians in Macedonia (page 204) and among mutinous French units on the Western Front (page 168). Although there was disaffection among the Austro-Hungarian forces, their morale was strengthened by the combined Austro-German victory over the Italians at Caporetto (page 202), in which the rout was only halted by the arrival of British and French reinforcements. The principal successes of the Allies during 1917 were in Asia. The Tigris port of Kut (where the first British expedition of Mesopotamia had been forced to surrender to the Turks in the spring of 1916) was retaken in February and Baghdad captured a fortnight later. The most dramatic victory was won by Allenby in Palestine, enabling the British to enter Jerusalem at the beginning of December. (For Mesopotamia see pages 206–210 and for Palestine see pages 211–213.)

On the Western Front Nivelle had succeeded Joffre in the second week of December 1916. The new commander-in-chief planned an offensive towards Laon, and persisted in his project even when the Germans withdrew to stronger defensive positions. The offensive was a disaster; Nivelle was replaced by Pétain, who with great skill gradually restored the confidence of the French soldiery. But there was little the French Army could do for the remainder of the year. Haig hoped to defeat the Germans in Flanders, a policy which appealed to the British naval chiefs, since it would have eliminated the U-boat bases on the Belgian coast. Heavy bombardments and rain made the ground impassable, and the 'third battle of Ypres' came to a disastrous halt in the mud of Passchendaele. Earlier in the year the Canadians gained a striking success at Vimy Ridge, north-east of Arras, and the British Second Army (which included an Australian and New Zealand Corps) won a comprehensive local victory at Messines, south of Ypres. Potentially the most significant military development of the year was the breakthrough by massed British tanks at Cambrai in November, but Haig by now did not have sufficient reserves to consolidate the gains made by the tanks, and the Germans recovered much of the land they had lost in a counter-attack ten days later.

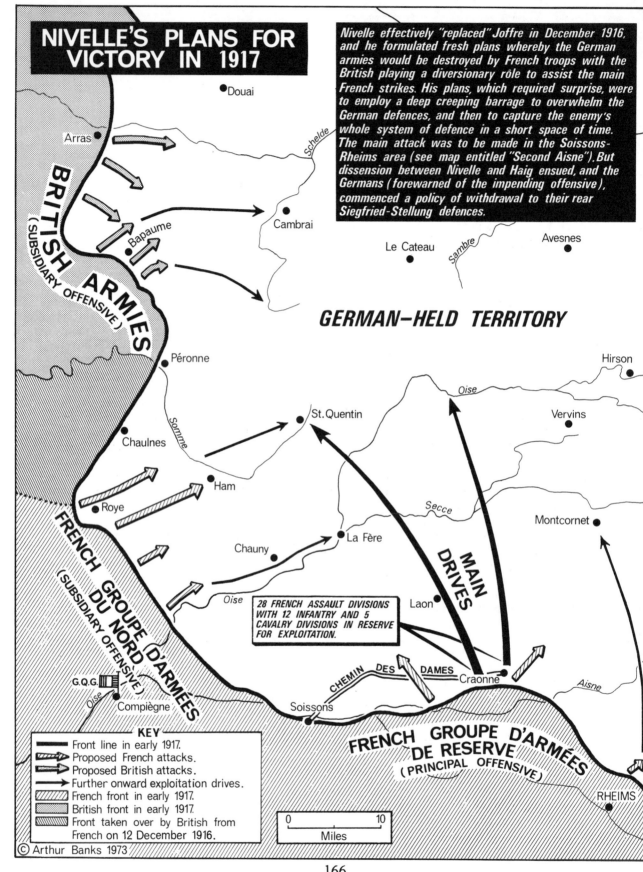

NIVELLE'S PLANS FOR VICTORY IN 1917

Nivelle effectively "replaced" Joffre in December 1916, and he formulated fresh plans whereby the German armies would be destroyed by French troops with the British playing a diversionary rôle to assist the main French strikes. His plans, which required surprise, were to employ a deep creeping barrage to overwhelm the German defences, and then to capture the enemy's whole system of defence in a short space of time. The main attack was to be made in the Soissons-Rheims area (see map entitled "Second Aisne"). But dissension between Nivelle and Haig ensued, and the Germans (forewarned of the impending offensive), commenced a policy of withdrawal to their rear Siegfried-Stellung defences.

Douai

Arras

BRITISH ARMIES (SUBSIDIARY OFFENSIVE)

Schelde

Bapaume

Cambrai

Le Cateau

Sambre

Avesnes

GERMAN—HELD TERRITORY

Péronne

Hirson

Oise

Vervins

St.Quentin

Somme

Chaulnes

Secce

Montcornet

Ham

Roye

FRENCH GROUPE DU NORD D'ARMÉES (SUBSIDIARY OFFENSIVE)

Chauny

La Fère

Oise

MAIN DRIVES

28 FRENCH ASSAULT DIVISIONS WITH 12 INFANTRY AND 5 CAVALRY DIVISIONS IN RESERVE FOR EXPLOITATION.

Laon

G.Q.G.

Oise

Compiègne

CHEMIN DES DAMES

Craonne

Aisne

Soissons

FRENCH GROUPE D'ARMÉES DE RESERVE (PRINCIPAL OFFENSIVE)

RHEIMS

KEY
— Front line in early 1917.
⇨ Proposed French attacks.
⇨ Proposed British attacks.
→ Further onward exploitation drives.
▨ French front in early 1917.
▨ British front in early 1917.
▨ Front taken over by British from French on 12 December 1916.

0   10
Miles

© Arthur Banks 1973

166

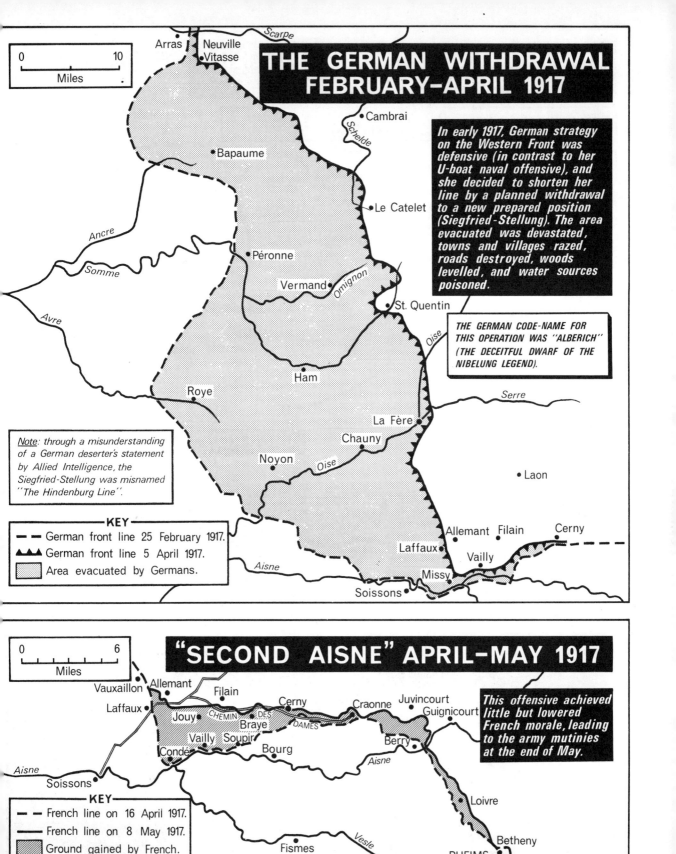

THE GERMAN WITHDRAWAL FEBRUARY–APRIL 1917

0 [scale] 10
Miles

In early 1917, German strategy on the Western Front was defensive (in contrast to her U-boat naval offensive), and she decided to shorten her line by a planned withdrawal to a new prepared position (Siegfried-Stellung). The area evacuated was devastated, towns and villages razed, roads destroyed, woods levelled, and water sources poisoned.

THE GERMAN CODE-NAME FOR THIS OPERATION WAS "ALBERICH" (THE DECEITFUL DWARF OF THE NIBELUNG LEGEND).

Note: through a misunderstanding of a German deserter's statement by Allied Intelligence, the Siegfried-Stellung was misnamed "The Hindenburg Line".

Arras
Neuville
Vitasse
Scarpe
Cambrai
Schelde
Bapaume
Le Catelet
Ancre
Somme
Péronne
Vermand
Omignon
St. Quentin
Avre
Oise
Ham
Roye
Serre
La Fère
Chauny
Noyon
Oise
Laon
Allemant Filain Cerny
Laffaux
Vailly
Aisne
Missy
Soissons

KEY
- - - German front line 25 February 1917.
▲▲▲ German front line 5 April 1917.
▒▒▒ Area evacuated by Germans.

"SECOND AISNE" APRIL–MAY 1917

0 [scale] 6
Miles

This offensive achieved little but lowered French morale, leading to the army mutinies at the end of May.

Vauxaillon Allemant
Filain
Laffaux
Cerny
Craonne Juvincourt
Guignicourt
Jouy CHEMIN DES
Braye
DAMES
Vailly Soupir
Condé
Bourg
Berry
Aisne
Aisne
Loivre
Fismes
Vesle
Betheny
RHEIMS
Soissons

KEY
- - - French line on 16 April 1917.
—— French line on 8 May 1917.
▨▨▨ Ground gained by French.

© Arthur Banks 1973

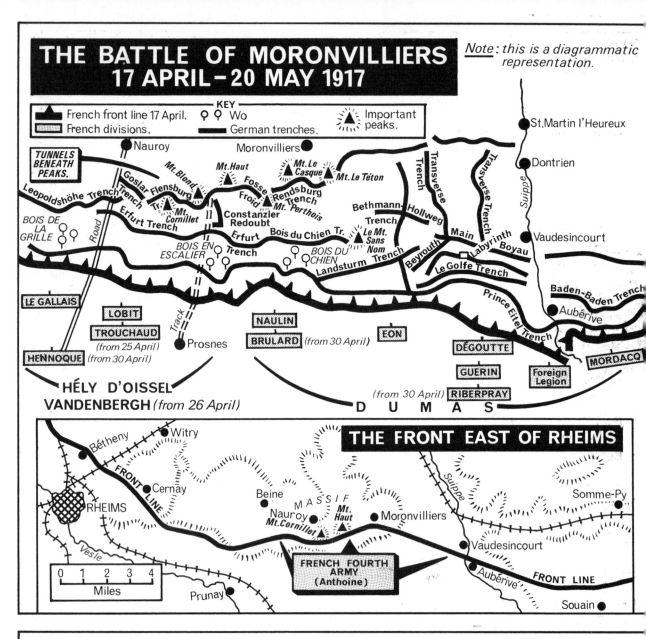

THE BATTLE OF MORONVILLIERS
17 APRIL – 20 MAY 1917

Note: this is a diagrammatic representation.

KEY
- French front line 17 April.
- French divisions.
- ♀ ♀ Wo
- German trenches.
- ▲ Important peaks.

TUNNELS BENEATH PEAKS.

Nauroy
Moronvilliers
St. Martin l'Heureux
Dontrien
Mt. Blond
Mt. Haut
Mt. Le Casque
Mt. Le Téton
Goslar Trench
Flensburg Tr.
Fosse
Rendsburg Trench
Transverse Trench
Transverse Trench
Leopoldshöhe Trench
Erfurt Trench
Mt. Cornillet
Froid
Mt. Perthois
Bethmann-Hollweg Trench
Vaudesincourt
Constanzler Redoubt
BOIS DE LA GRILLE
Road
Erfurt Trench
Bois du Chien Tr.
Le Mt. Sans Nom
Main
Labyrinth
Boyau
BOIS EN ESCALIER
BOIS DU CHIEN
Beyrouth
Le Golfe Trench
Landsturm Trench
Baden-Baden Trench
LE GALLAIS
LOBIT
TROUCHAUD *(from 25 April)*
NAULIN
EON
Prince Eitel Trench
Aubérive
HENNOQUE *(from 30 April)*
Track
Prosnes
BRULARD *(from 30 April)*
DÉGOUTTE
Foreign Legion
MORDACQ
HÉLY D'OISSEL
VANDENBERGH *(from 26 April)*
GUERIN
(from 30 April) RIBERPRAY
D U M A S

THE FRONT EAST OF RHEIMS

Béthény
Witry
FRONT LINE
Cernay
RHEIMS
Beine
MASSIF
Nauroy
Mt. Haut
Moronvilliers
Somme-Py
Mt. Cornillet
Suippe
Vesle
FRENCH FOURTH ARMY (Anthoine)
Vaudesincourt
Aubérive
FRONT LINE
Prunay
Souain

```
0  1  2  3  4
   Miles
```

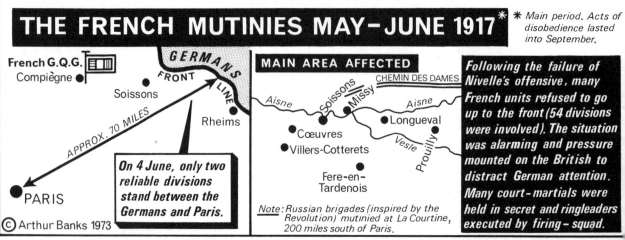

THE FRENCH MUTINIES MAY–JUNE 1917

✳ *Main period. Acts of disobedience lasted into September.*

French G.Q.G.
Compiègne
GERMANS FRONT LINE
Soissons
Rheims
APPROX. 70 MILES
PARIS

On 4 June, only two reliable divisions stand between the Germans and Paris.

© Arthur Banks 1973

MAIN AREA AFFECTED

CHEMIN DES DAMES
Aisne
Soissons
Missy
Aisne
Cœuvres
Longueval
Villers-Cotterets
Vesle
Prouilly
Fere-en-Tardenois

Note: Russian brigades (inspired by the Revolution) mutinied at La Courtine, 200 miles south of Paris.

Following the failure of Nivelle's offensive, many French units refused to go up to the front (54 divisions were involved). The situation was alarming and pressure mounted on the British to distract German attention. Many court-martials were held in secret and ringleaders executed by firing-squad.

168

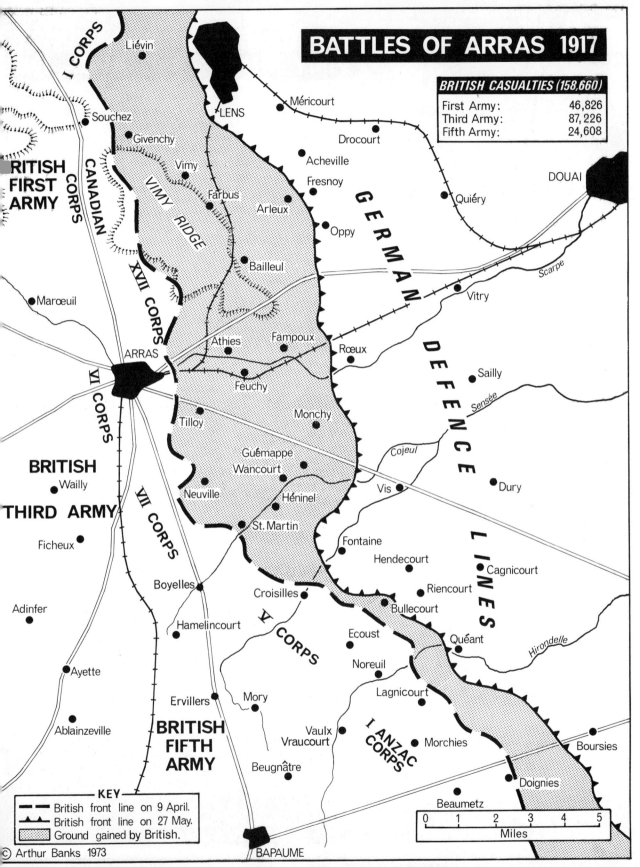

BATTLES OF ARRAS 1917

BRITISH CASUALTIES (158,660)

First Army:	46,826
Third Army:	87,226
Fifth Army:	24,608

I CORPS

Liévin

Souchez

BRITISH FIRST ARMY

CANADIAN CORPS

Givenchy

Vimy

VIMY RIDGE

Farbus

XVII CORPS

Maroeuil

ARRAS

VI CORPS

LENS

Méricourt

Drocourt

Acheville

Fresnoy

Arleux

Oppy

Bailleul

Athies

Fampoux

Rœux

Feuchy

Tilloy

Monchy

BRITISH

Wailly

THIRD ARMY

VII CORPS

Guémappe

Wancourt

Neuville

Héninel

Ficheux

St. Martin

Adinfer

Boyelles

Croisilles

Ayette

Hamelincourt

V CORPS

Ablainzeville

Ervillers

Mory

BRITISH FIFTH ARMY

Vaulx Vraucourt

Beugnâtre

GERMAN DEFENCE LINES

DOUAI

Quiéry

Vitry

Scarpe

Sailly

Sensée

Cojeul

Vis

Dury

Fontaine

Hendecourt

Cagnicourt

Riencourt

Bullecourt

Ecoust

Quéant

Hirondelle

Noreuil

Lagnicourt

I ANZAC CORPS

Morchies

Boursies

Doignies

Beaumetz

KEY

– – –	British front line on 9 April.
⌃⌃⌃	British front line on 27 May.
░░░	Ground gained by British.

© Arthur Banks 1973

0	1	2	3	4	5

Miles

BAPAUME

169

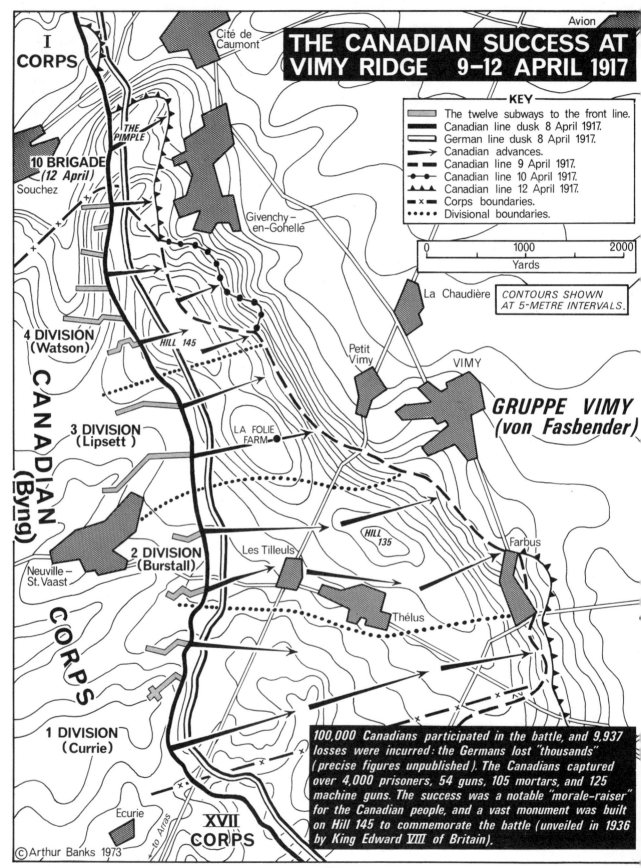

THE CANADIAN SUCCESS AT VIMY RIDGE 9–12 APRIL 1917

Avion

I CORPS

Cité de Caumont

KEY

▨	The twelve subways to the front line.
━━	Canadian line dusk 8 April 1917.
▭	German line dusk 8 April 1917.
→	Canadian advances.
▬ ▬	Canadian line 9 April 1917.
•—•—•	Canadian line 10 April 1917.
▲▲▲	Canadian line 12 April 1917.
—x—	Corps boundaries.
••••	Divisional boundaries.

THE PIMPLE

10 BRIGADE
(12 April)

Souchez

Givenchy–
en-Gohelle

0   1000   2000

Yards

La Chaudière

*CONTOURS SHOWN
AT 5-METRE INTERVALS.*

4 DIVISION
(Watson)

HILL 145

Petit
Vimy

VIMY

CANADIAN (Byng)

3 DIVISION
(Lipsett)

LA FOLIE
FARM

*GRUPPE VIMY
(von Fasbender)*

2 DIVISION
(Burstall)

Les Tilleuls

HILL
135

Farbus

Neuville –
St. Vaast

CORPS

Thélus

1 DIVISION
(Currie)

Ecurie

to Arras

XVII
CORPS

100,000 Canadians participated in the battle, and 9,937
losses were incurred: the Germans lost "thousands"
(precise figures unpublished). The Canadians captured
over 4,000 prisoners, 54 guns, 105 mortars, and 125
machine guns. The success was a notable "morale-raiser"
for the Canadian people, and a vast monument was built
on Hill 145 to commemorate the battle (unveiled in 1936
by King Edward VIII of Britain).

©Arthur Banks 1973

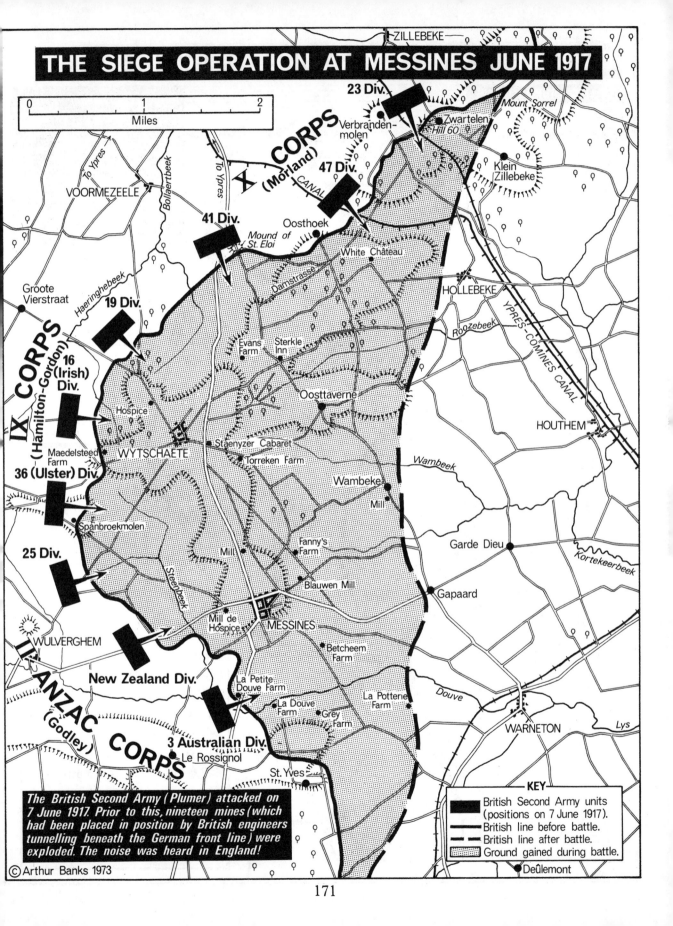

THE SIEGE OPERATION AT MESSINES JUNE 1917

0   1   2
Miles

ZILLEBEKE

23 Div.

Mount Sorrel

Verbranden-molen

Zwartelen

Hill 60

X CORPS (Morland)

CANAL

47 Div.

Klein Zillebeke

To Ypres

VOORMEZEELE

To Ypres

41 Div.

Oosthoek

Mound of St. Eloi

White Château

HOLLEBEKE

Damstrasse

Roozebeek

Groote Vierstraat

Bollaertbeek

Haeringhebeek

19 Div.

Evans Farm

Sterkle Inn

Oosttaverne

Wambeek

YPRES—COMINES CANAL

HOUTHEM

IX CORPS (Hamilton-Gordon)

16 (Irish) Div.

Hospice

WYTSCHAETE

Staenyzer Cabaret

Torreken Farm

Wambeke

Mill

Maedelsteed Farm

36 (Ulster) Div.

Garde Dieu

Kortekeerbeek

Spanbroekmolen

Mill

Fanny's Farm

25 Div.

Steenbeek

Blauwen Mill

Gapaard

Mill de Hospice

MESSINES

Betcheem Farm

WULVERGHEM

New Zealand Div.

La Petite Douve Farm

La Douve Farm

Grey Farm

La Potterie Farm

Douve

II ANZAC (Godley) CORPS

3 Australian Div.

Le Rossignol

WARNETON

Lys

St. Yves

KEY

◼ British Second Army units (positions on 7 June 1917).
— British line before battle.
– – – British line after battle.
▨ Ground gained during battle.

● Deûlemont

BRITISH PLANS FOR "WIPERS THREE" 1917

ALLIED DISPOSITIONS
- **N** Allied naval forces.
- **4** British Fourth Army.
- **B** Belgians.
- **F** French.
- **5** British Fifth Army.
- **2** British Second Army.

NORTH SEA

NOTE: IN FACT, THESE WERE SHORT-RANGE CRAFT.

U-BOATS

DUNES

ZEEBRUGGE

U-BOATS

U-BOATS OSTEND

U-BOATS

Haig (secretly under intense French pressure to distract German attention from their mutinous sectors) outlined these plans to a meeting of the Cabinet Committee on War Policy in London on 21 June. Jellicoe stressed the German U-boat threat: Haig stated that Bruges was his main objective.

GERMAN FLANDERS SUBMARINE BASE.

U-BOATS

DUNES
DUNES

Middelkerke

FEN COUNTRY

③ BRUGES

Nieuport

STRATEGIC

Yser (canalised)

Couckelaere

Aeltre

② Thourout Cortemarck

To Ghent (possible Fourth Objective).

Dixmude

RAILWAY

Thielt

Yser

Staden

ROULERS

LINE

Lys

Passchendaele

RIDGE

YPRES

① Gheluvelt

Hooge STIRLING CASTLE (chateau) Menin

COURTRAI

Known to British troops as "Wipers."

5

Wytschaete

Comines

Messines

Warneton

2

TOURCOING

Lys

ROUBAIX

Armentières

LILLE

| 0 | 5 | 10 |
Miles

© Arthur Banks 1973

KEY
- ━━━ Allied front line 21 June.
- ▨ Allied-held territory.
- ①➤ Opening assault.
- ▬ ▬ Haig's First Objective.
- ②➤ "Follow-up" assault.
- ▰▰▰ Haig's Second Objective.
- ➤ Main concentrated attack.
- ▨▨ Haig's Third (Main) Objective.
- ⇶ Flankguards along River Lys.
- ⟵ German U-boat routes to sea.
- ┴┴┴┴ Canals (note Bruges area).

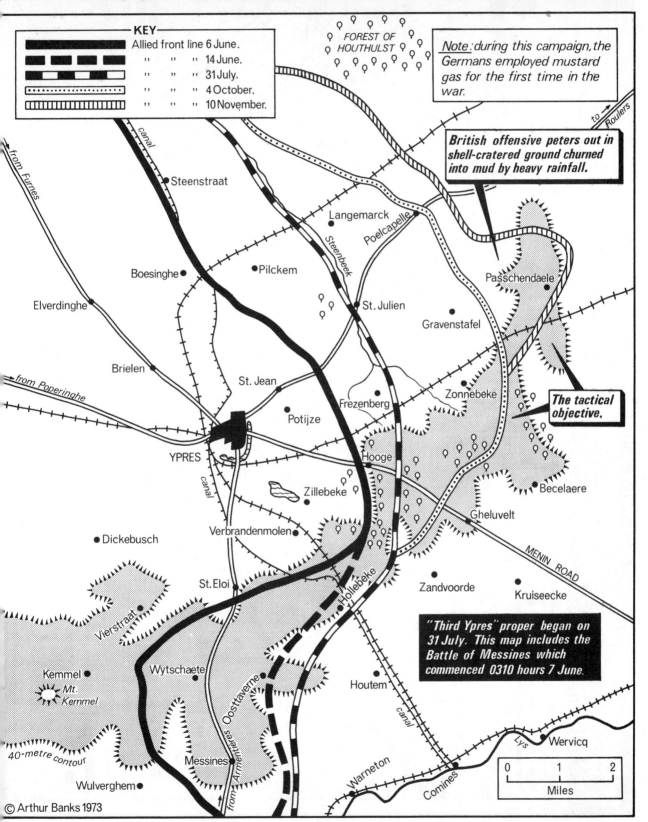

"THIRD YPRES"(PASSCHENDAELE): JULY – NOVEMBER 1917

KEY

Allied front line 6 June.
,, ,, ,, 14 June.
,, ,, ,, 31 July.
,, ,, ,, 4 October.
,, ,, ,, 10 November.

FOREST OF HOUTHULST

Note: during this campaign, the Germans employed mustard gas for the first time in the war.

to Roulers

British offensive peters out in shell-cratered ground churned into mud by heavy rainfall.

from Furnes

Steenstraat

Langemarck
Poelcapelle

Passchendaele

Boesinghe
Pilckem

Steenbeek

St. Julien

Gravenstafel

Elverdinghe

canal

The tactical objective.

Brielen

St. Jean

Frezenberg

Zonnebeke

from Poperinghe

Potijze

Becelaere

YPRES

canal

Hooge

Zillebeke

Gheluvelt

Verbrandenmolen

MENIN ROAD

Dickebusch

Zandvoorde

Kruiseecke

St. Eloi

Hollebeke

Oosttaverne

"Third Ypres" proper began on 31 July. This map includes the Battle of Messines which commenced 0310 hours 7 June.

Vierstraat

Wytschaete

Houtem

from Armentières

Kemmel
Mt. Kemmel

canal

Lys

Wervicq

40-metre contour

Messines

Warneton

0   1   2

Comines

Miles

Wulverghem

© Arthur Banks 1973

173

THE BRITISH TANK-SPEARHEADED OFFENSIVE AT CAMBRAI 1917

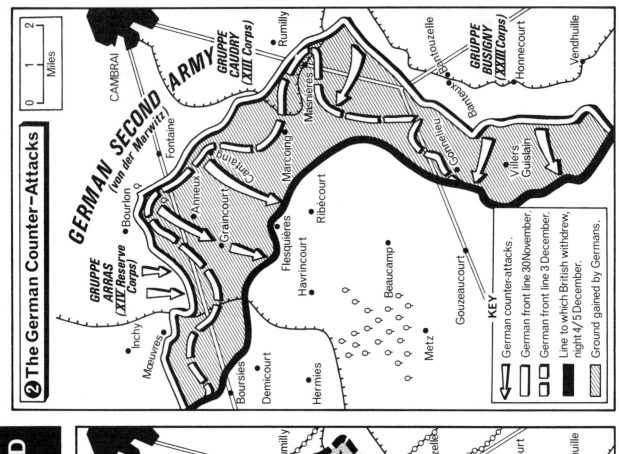

② The German Counter-Attacks

GERMAN SECOND ARMY (von der Marwitz)

GRUPPE CAUDRY (XIII Corps)

GRUPPE BUSIGNY (XXIII Corps)

GRUPPE ARRAS (XIV Reserve Corps)

CAMBRAI · Rumilly · Bantouzelle · Honnecourt · Vendhuille · Banteux · Masnières · Fontaine · Cantaing · Marcoing · Gonnelieu · Villers Guislain · Bourlon · Anneux · Graincourt · Ribécourt · Flesquières · Havrincourt · Beaucamp · Gouzeaucourt · Inchy · Mœuvres · Boursies · Demicourt · Hermies · Metz

KEY
- German counter-attacks.
- German front line 30 November.
- German front line 3 December.
- Line to which British withdrew, night 4/5 December.
- Ground gained by Germans.

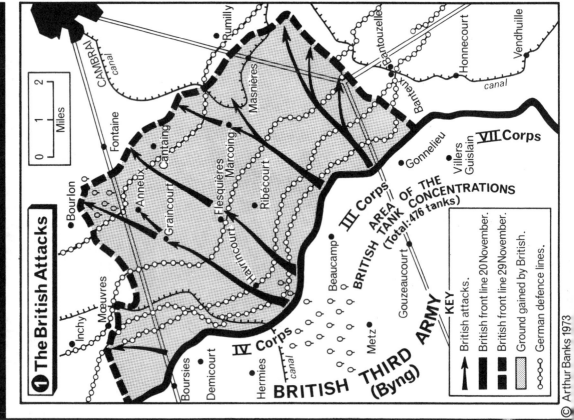

① The British Attacks

CAMBRAI · canal · Rumilly · Bantouzelle · Honnecourt · Vendhuille · Banteux · canal · Fontaine · Masnières · Cantaing · Marcoing · Ribécourt · Gonnelieu · Villers Guislain · **VII Corps** · Bourlon · Anneux · Graincourt · Flesquières · Havrincourt · **III Corps** · AREA OF THE BRITISH TANK CONCENTRATIONS (Total: 476 tanks) · Beaucamp · Gouzeaucourt · Mœuvres · Inchy · Boursies · Demicourt · **IV Corps** · Hermies · canal · Metz · **BRITISH THIRD ARMY (Byng)**

KEY
- British attacks.
- British front line 20 November.
- British front line 29 November.
- Ground gained by British.
- German defence lines.

174

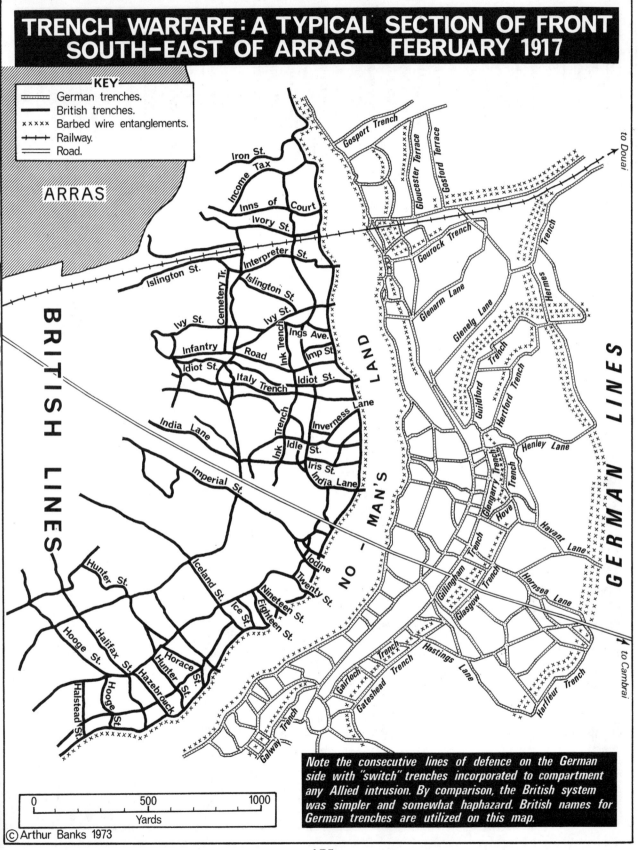

TRENCH WARFARE: A TYPICAL SECTION OF FRONT SOUTH-EAST OF ARRAS FEBRUARY 1917

KEY
- German trenches.
- British trenches.
- Barbed wire entanglements.
- Railway.
- Road.

ARRAS

BRITISH LINES

NO-MAN'S LAND

GERMAN LINES

to Douai

to Cambrai

Iron St.
Income Tax
Inns of Court
Ivory St.
Interpreter St.
Islington St.
Cemetery Tr.
Islington St.
Ivy St.
Ivy St.
Ink Trench
Ings Ave.
Infantry Road
Imp St.
Idiot St.
Italy Trench
Idiot St.
India Lane
Inverness Lane
Ink Trench
Idle St.
Iris St.
Imperial St.
India Lane
Iodine
Twenty St.
Iceland St.
Nineteen St.
Ice St.
Eighteen St.
Hunter St.
Halifax St.
Horace St.
Hooge St.
Hunter St.
Hazebrouck
Hooge St.
Halstead St.
Galway Trench
Gairloch Trench
Gateshead Trench
Hastings Lane
Harfleur Trench
Glasgow Trench
Gillingham Trench
Glengarry Trench
Hove
Havant Lane
Hornsea Lane
Henley Lane
Hertford Trench
Guildford Trench
Glenelg Lane
Glenarm Lane
Gourock Trench
Hermes Trench
Gosport Trench
Gloucester Terrace
Gosford Terrace

Note the consecutive lines of defence on the German side with "switch" trenches incorporated to compartment any Allied intrusion. By comparison, the British system was simpler and somewhat haphazard. British names for German trenches are utilized on this map.

0   500   1000
Yards

© Arthur Banks 1973

RUSSIA'S FINAL EFFORT IN 1917

② Central Powers' Backlash 19 July – 4 August

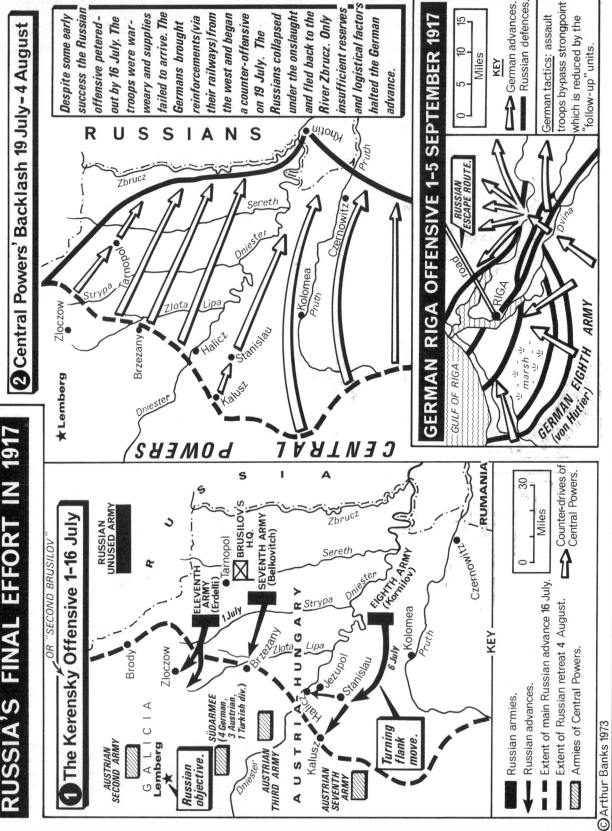

Despite some early success the Russian offensive petered-out by 16 July. The troops were war-weary and supplies failed to arrive. The Germans brought reinforcements (via their railways) from the west and began a counter-offensive on 19 July. The Russians collapsed under the onslaught and fled back to the River Zbrucz. Only insufficient reserves and logistical factors halted the German advance.

R U S S I A N S

Khotin

Zbrucz

Sereth

Dniester

Strypa

Tarnopol

Zloczow

Zlota Lipa

Brzezany

Halicz

Stanislau

Kalusz

Dniester

Czernowitz

Pruth

Kolomea

★ Lemberg

C E N T R A L   P O W E R S

GERMAN RIGA OFFENSIVE 1–5 SEPTEMBER 1917

KEY
Miles
0 5 10 15

⬆ German advances.
▮ Russian defences.

German tactics: assault troops by-pass strongpoint which is reduced by the "follow-up" units.

RUSSIAN ESCAPE ROUTE.

road

RIGA

Dvina

GULF OF RIGA

marsh

GERMAN EIGHTH ARMY (von Hutier)

① The Kerensky Offensive 1–16 July

OR "SECOND BRUSILOV"

RUSSIAN UNUSED ARMY

R U S S I A

Zbrucz

Sereth

Dniester

Tarnopol

BRUSILOV'S H.Q.

ELEVENTH ARMY (Erdelli)

1 July

SEVENTH ARMY (Belkovitch)

Strypa

EIGHTH ARMY (Kornilov)

Brody

Zloczow

Brzezany

Zlota Lipa

Jezupol

Halicz

Stanislau

6 July

Kolomea

Pruth

Czernowitz

RUMANIA

SÜDARMEE (4 German, 3 Austrian, 1 Turkish div.)

AUSTRIAN SECOND ARMY

G A L I C I A
★ Lemberg

Russian objective.

A U S T R I A - H U N G A R Y

AUSTRIAN THIRD ARMY

Dniester

Kalusz

Turning flank move.

AUSTRIAN SEVENTH ARMY

KEY
▮⬇ Russian armies.
⬇ Russian advances.
⌇⌇⌇ Extent of main Russian advance 16 July.
–– Extent of Russian retreat 4 August.
▨ Armies of Central Powers.
⬆ Counter-drives of Central Powers.

Miles
0 30

© Arthur Banks 1973

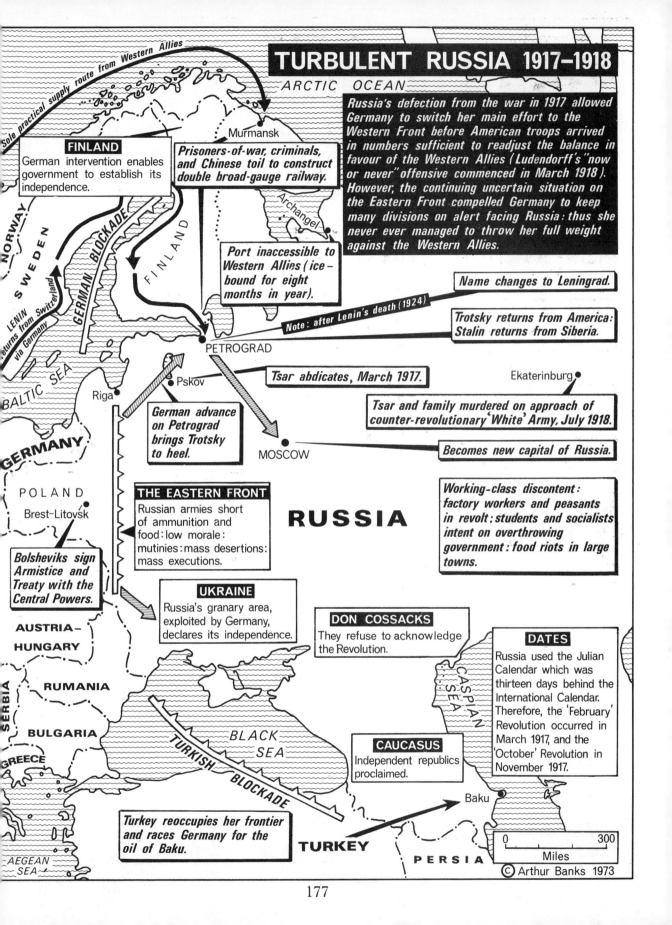

TURBULENT RUSSIA 1917-1918

ARCTIC OCEAN

Russia's defection from the war in 1917 allowed Germany to switch her main effort to the Western Front before American troops arrived in numbers sufficient to readjust the balance in favour of the Western Allies (Ludendorff's "now or never" offensive commenced in March 1918). However, the continuing uncertain situation on the Eastern Front compelled Germany to keep many divisions on alert facing Russia: thus she never ever managed to throw her full weight against the Western Allies.

Sole practical supply route from Western Allies

Murmansk

FINLAND
German intervention enables government to establish its independence.

Prisoners-of-war, criminals, and Chinese toil to construct double broad-gauge railway.

Archangel

NORWAY

SWEDEN

GERMAN BLOCKADE

FINLAND

LENIN returns from Switzerland via Germany

Port inaccessible to Western Allies (ice-bound for eight months in year).

Name changes to Leningrad.

Note: after Lenin's death (1924)

Trotsky returns from America: Stalin returns from Siberia.

PETROGRAD

BALTIC SEA

Pskov

Riga

Tsar abdicates, March 1917.

Ekaterinburg

German advance on Petrograd brings Trotsky to heel.

Tsar and family murdered on approach of counter-revolutionary 'White' Army, July 1918.

GERMANY

MOSCOW

Becomes new capital of Russia.

POLAND

Brest-Litovsk

THE EASTERN FRONT
Russian armies short of ammunition and food: low morale: mutinies: mass desertions: mass executions.

RUSSIA

Working-class discontent: factory workers and peasants in revolt: students and socialists intent on overthrowing government: food riots in large towns.

Bolsheviks sign Armistice and Treaty with the Central Powers.

UKRAINE
Russia's granary area, exploited by Germany, declares its independence.

AUSTRIA–HUNGARY

DON COSSACKS
They refuse to acknowledge the Revolution.

DATES
Russia used the Julian Calendar which was thirteen days behind the International Calendar. Therefore, the 'February' Revolution occurred in March 1917, and the 'October' Revolution in November 1917.

SERBIA

RUMANIA

CASPIAN SEA

BULGARIA

GREECE

TURKISH BLOCKADE

BLACK SEA

CAUCASUS
Independent republics proclaimed.

AEGEAN SEA

Baku

Turkey reoccupies her frontier and races Germany for the oil of Baku.

TURKEY

PERSIA

0 — 300
Miles

© Arthur Banks 1973

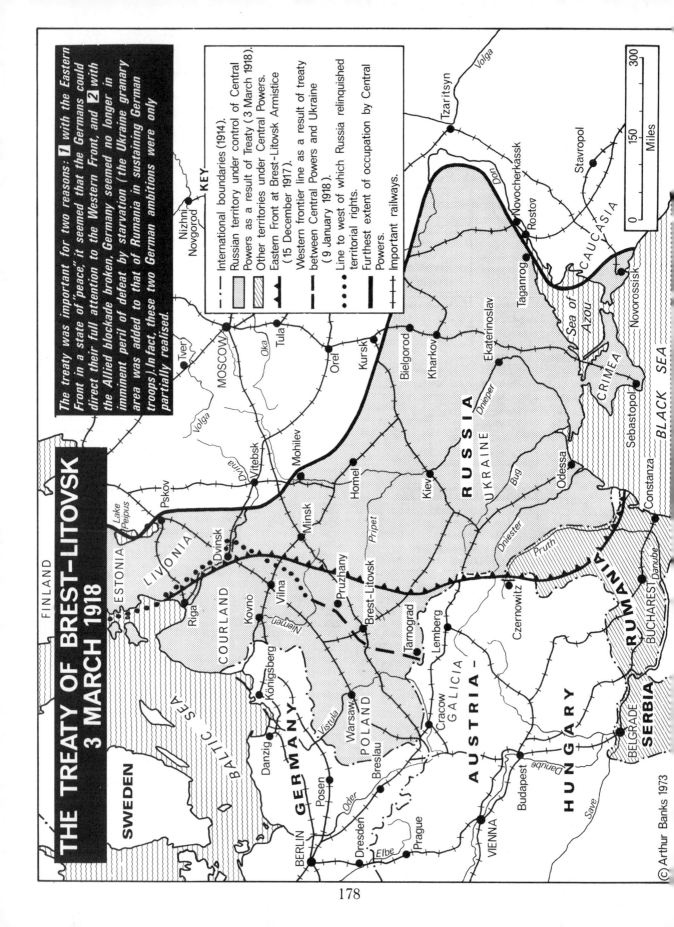

THE TREATY OF BREST-LITOVSK 3 MARCH 1918

The treaty was important for two reasons: **1** with the Eastern Front in a state of "peace" it seemed that the Germans could direct their full attention to the Western Front, and **2** with the Allied blockade broken, Germany seemed no longer in imminent peril of defeat by starvation (the Ukraine granary area was added to that of Rumania in sustaining German troops). In fact, these two German ambitions were only partially realised.

KEY

- _·_—_·_— International boundaries (1914).
- Russian territory under control of Central Powers as a result of Treaty (3 March 1918).
- Other territories under Central Powers.
- ⊢⊢⊢ Eastern Front at Brest-Litovsk Armistice (15 December 1917).
- ⊦ Western frontier line as a result of treaty between Central Powers and Ukraine (9 January 1918).
- • • • Line to west of which Russia relinquished territorial rights.
- ▬▬ Furthest extent of occupation by Central Powers.
- ⊢⊢⊢ Important railways.

© Arthur Banks 1973

178

THE WAR IN 1918

The war weariness which had assailed the Russian people at the start of winter in 1917–1918 threatened to spread to other countries which had been subjected to many years of heavy casualties and short rations. The German home front was hard-pressed by the British blockade while the British themselves had come close to disaster during the worst month of sinkings by U-boat, April 1917. There was widespread disaffection in Austria-Hungary, accentuated by conflicts between the nationalities within the Empire, and an extensive peace movement in Bulgaria, while desertions from the Turkish army in Palestine began to increase sharply. It was therefore essential for Hindenburg and Ludendorff to achieve a rapid military victory on the Western Front, using reinforcements from the East to defeat the British and French armies in the field before the Americans flooded in. In March 1917 there were three Allied soldiers to every two Germans in France and Belgium: a year later, the troop trains from Russia had changed the balance to four Germans to every three Allies.

The French and British prime ministers, Clemenceau and Lloyd George, anticipated a hard thrust by Germany; but no one believed it possible for Ludendorff to have achieved such concentration of firepower as the Germans mounted in March 1918. Within a week the Germans penetrated the Allied line to a depth of forty miles, although the Germans caused problems to themselves by outrunning their supplies. In April they struck farther north, penetrating a section of the Flanders Front held by inexperienced Portuguese troops; and in May Ludendorff succeeded in bringing the campaign back to the Marne and threatening Paris. His last great stroke, around Rheims on 15 July, was checked by astute defensive positioning on the part of Pétain. The German drive was brought to a standstill, with an exhausted army exposing the flanks of a series of salients to counter-attack.

The Allies had at last accepted the principle of unified command, entrusting Foch with the task of throwing back the Germans. American troops, disembarking in France at the rate of a quarter of a million each month, replenished the Allied armies. On 18 July tanks (as at Cambrai) provided the spearhead for Foch's counter-offensive although it was the German break in morale on 8 August which convinced Ludendorff Germany could not win the War. In September the Allied attacks seemed to lose impetus, but the British at last penetrated the Hindenburg Line on 29 September. At the same time news reached Supreme German Headquarters of collapse elsewhere: Bulgaria capitulated, after Franchet d'Espèrey's Salonika armies broke through on the Macedonian Front (page 204); Allenby and Lawrence's Arab Legion entered Damascus (3 October), and the Turks began to seek peace; at the end of October the Italians, with British and French support, launched a furious offensive on the Piave and induced Austria-Hungary to seek terms (page 203). Lloyd George, who had long believed in 'knocking away the props from under Germany', found his policy vindicated.

Hindenburg accepted the need for peace on 3 October, but he became more optimistic once he saw the Allies were themselves tiring. It was, in the end, bread riots, revolution and a mutiny of the fleet which convinced the German High Command the war was over. The tightening grip of the blockade prevented any hopes of further resistance, while a mass influenza epidemic lowered the morale of the civilian population. A German armistice delegation set out from Berlin on 6 November. The Armistice became effective five days later.

THE GERMAN OFFENSIVES 21 MARCH - 17 JULY 1918

German troop strengths in the west had increased by 30% between November 1917 and 21 March 1918, primarily due to transfer of troops from the east following the Treaty of Brest-Litovsk. British strengths had decreased by 25% since "Third Ypres" (Passchendaele) 1917 as they were content to wait upon the arrival of the fresh American troops.

KEY
GERMAN ARMIES

0 — 25 Miles

NORTH SEA

HOLLAND

Flushing

Zeebrugge

Ostend

Bruges

Ghent

ANTWERP

Nieuport

Thourout

④

Thielt

BRUSSELS

Furnes

Dixmude

Schelde

Dunkirk

Roulers

Hondschoote

Yser

Menin

Courtrai

Oudenarde

Calais

BELGIAN ARMY

Ypres

Tourcoing

⑥

Roubaix

Lys

BELGIUM

Boulogne

BRITISH SECOND ARMY

Cassel

St.Omer

Hazebrouck

Aire

Armentières

Georgette

LILLE

Tournai

RUPPRECHT A.G.H.Q. Charleroi

Béthune

La Bassée

St. Amand

Mons

Lens

Scarpe

G.H.Q. Montreuil

BRITISH FIRST ARMY

St.Pol

Douai

⑰

Valenciennes

Michael I

Maubeuge

Frévent

Arras

②

Sambre

Cambrai

Michael II

Doullens

Le Cateau

O.H.L. Avesnes

Abbeville

BRITISH THIRD ARMY

Bapaume

Albert

Somme

Péronne

Michael III

⑱

Hirson

Amiens

BRITISH FIFTH ARMY

Nesle

St.Quentin

Guise

Vervins

Aumale

Roye

Ham

Gneisenau

La Fère

Marle

⑦

FRANCE

Montdidier

Matz

Noyon

Barisis

Yorck

Laon

Blücher

Crâonne

①

Rethel

Beauvais

Compiègne

G.Q.G.

Aisne

CHEMIN DES DAMES

Aisne

Rheims

Clermont

Soissons

Vailly

Fismes

RHEIMS

Creil

Oise

Villers Cotterêts

Marne

FRENCH SIXTH ARMY

FRENCH SECOND ARMY

FRENCH FOURTH ARMY

Senlis

Chantilly

Meaux

Marne

Dormans

Épernay

Châlons -sur-Marne

Marne

PARIS

La Ferté

KEY

▨	'MICHAEL' 21 March - 5 April.
▦	'GEORGETTE' 9 - 11 April.
▥	'BLÜCHER-YORCK' 27 May.
▨	'GNEISENAU' 9 June.
▦	'MARNE-RHEIMS' 15 - 17 July.
·····	Army boundaries.
☐	Army General Headquarters.
☐	Army Headquarters.

© Arthur Banks 1973

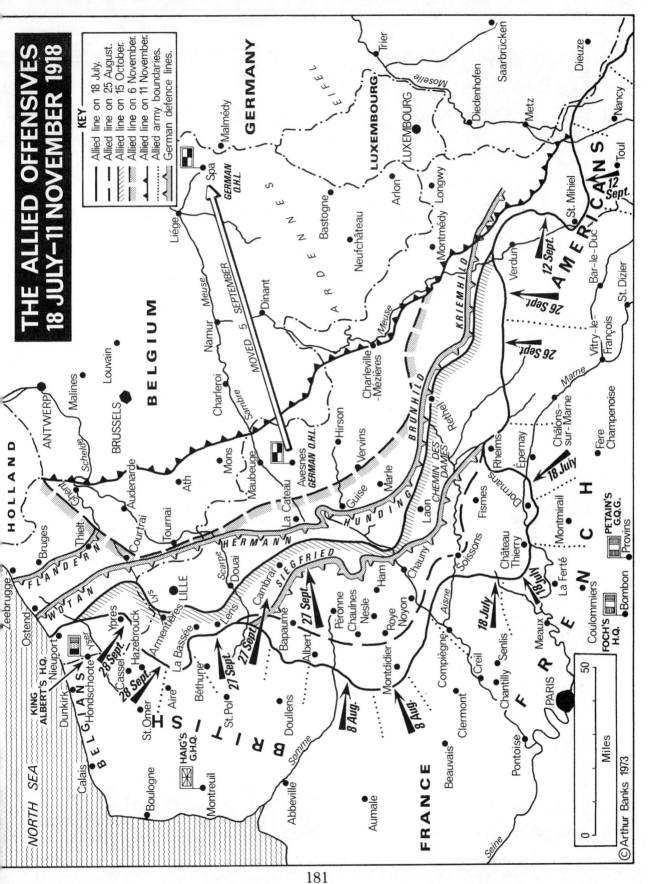

THE ALLIED OFFENSIVES
18 JULY–11 NOVEMBER 1918

KEY
Allied line on 18 July.
Allied line on 25 August.
Allied line on 15 October.
Allied line on 6 November.
Allied line on 11 November.
Allied army boundaries.
German defence lines.

NORTH SEA

HOLLAND

BELGIUM

GERMANY

LUXEMBOURG

FRANCE

GERMAN O.H.L. — Spa

MOVED 5 SEPTEMBER

GERMAN O.H.L. — Avesnes

Zeebrugge
Ostend
Bruges
Calais
Dunkirk
Boulogne
Nieuport
Ypres
Hazebrouck
Cassel
Hondschoote
St. Omer
Aire
Béthune
La Bassée
Armentières
LILLE
Lens
Courtrai
Thielt
Ghent
Audenarde
Tournai
Scarpe
Douai
Cambrai
Bapaume
Albert
Péronne
Chaulnes
Nesle
Roye
Noyon
Montdidier
Compiègne
Creil
Clermont
Beauvais
Montreuil
St. Pol
Doullens
Somme
Abbeville
Aumale
Pontoise
Chantilly
Senlis
PARIS
Meaux
Coulommiers
La Ferté
Château Thierry
Soissons
Chauny
Ham
Aisne
Laon
Fismes
Rheims
Épernay
Châlons-sur-Marne
Fère Champenoise
Montmirail
Provins
Dormans
Marne
Seine
Vitry-le-François
St. Dizier
Bar-le-Duc
Verdun
St. Mihiel
Toul
Nancy
Dieuze
Metz
Diedenhofen
Saarbrücken
Trier
Longwy
Montmédy
Arlon
Neufchâteau
Bastogne
Dinant
Namur
Charleroi
Charleville-Mézières
Rethel
Vervins
Marle
Guise
La Cateau
Maubeuge
Mons
Ath
Hirson
Sambre
Meuse
Meuse
Moselle
Liège
Malmédy
BRUSSELS
Louvain
Malines
ANTWERP
Schelde
Yser
Lys

BELGIANS
KING ALBERT'S H.Q.
HAIG'S G.H.Q.
BRITISH
FOCH'S H.Q. — Bombon
PETAIN'S G.Q.G. — Provins

AMERICANS
12 Sept.
26 Sept.
12 Sept.
26 Sept.

18 July
18 July
18 July
18 July

8 Aug.
8 Aug.

27 Sept.
27 Sept.
27 Sept.

28 Sept.
28 Sept.
28 Sept.

FLANDERN
WOTAN
HERMANN
SIEGFRIED
HUNDING
BRUNHILD
KRIEMHILD
CHEMIN DES DAMES

ARDENNES
EIFEL

© Arthur Banks 1973

0   Miles   50

181

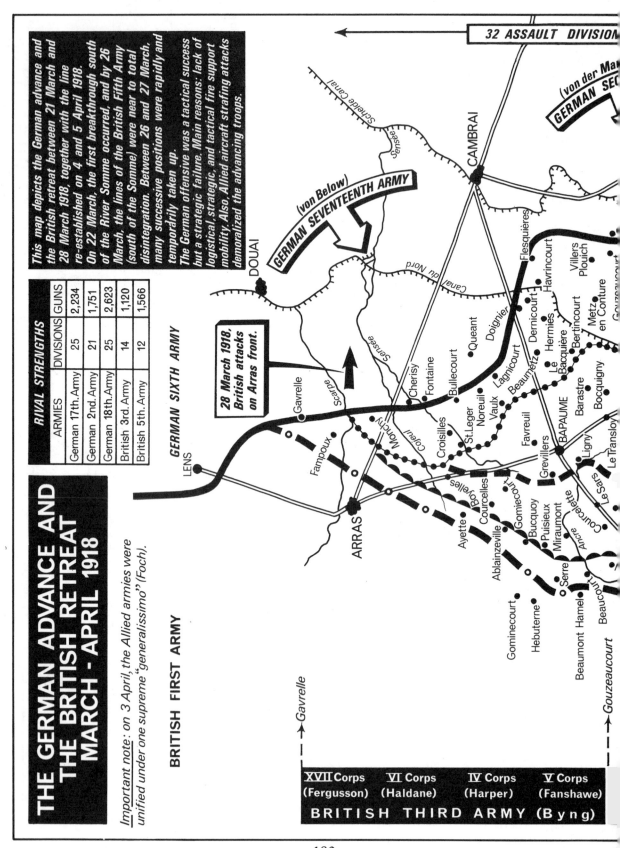

THE GERMAN ADVANCE AND THE BRITISH RETREAT MARCH - APRIL 1918

Important note: on 3 April, the Allied armies were unified under one supreme "generalissimo" (Foch).

This map depicts the German advance and the British retreat between 21 March and 28 March 1918, together with the line re-established on 4 and 5 April 1918. On 22 March, the first breakthrough south of the River Somme occurred, and by 26 March, the lines of the British Fifth Army (south of the Somme) were near to total disintegration. Between 26 and 27 March, many successive positions were rapidly and temporarily taken up.

The German offensive was a tactical success but a strategic failure. Main reasons: lack of logistical, strategic, and tactical fire support mobility. Also Allied aircraft strafing attacks demoralized the advancing troops.

RIVAL STRENGTHS

ARMIES	DIVISIONS	GUNS
German 17th. Army	25	2,234
German 2nd. Army	21	1,751
German 18th. Army	25	2,623
British 3rd. Army	14	1,120
British 5th. Army	12	1,566

GERMAN SIXTH ARMY

BRITISH FIRST ARMY

32 ASSAULT DIVISION

(von der Ma...) GERMAN SEC...

(von Below) GERMAN SEVENTEENTH ARMY

Schelde Canal

Sensée

CAMBRAI

DOUAI

Canal du Nord

Flesquières

Havrincourt

Villers Plouich

Queant

Doignier

Dernicourt

Le Hermies

Metz en Conture

Bertincourt

Bacquière

28 March 1918, British attacks on Arras front.

Gavrelle

Scarpe

Cherisy

Fontaine

Bullecourt

Lagnicourt

Beaumetz

Baraste

Bocquigny

LENS

Fampoux

Monchy

Copeul

St.Leger

Noreuil

Vaulx

Croisilles

Favreuil

Greviliers

BAPAUME

Ligny

LeTranslay

LeSars

Boyelles

Courcelles

Gomiecourt

Bucquoy

Puisieux

Miraumont

Ancre

Courcelette

ARRAS

Ayette

Ablainzeville

Serre

Beaucourt

Gomiecourt

Hebuterne

Beaumont Hamel

Beaucourt

Gouzeaucourt

→ Gavrelle

→ Gouzeaucourt

| XVII Corps (Fergusson) | VI Corps (Haldane) | IV Corps (Harper) | V Corps (Fanshawe) |

BRITISH THIRD ARMY (Byng)

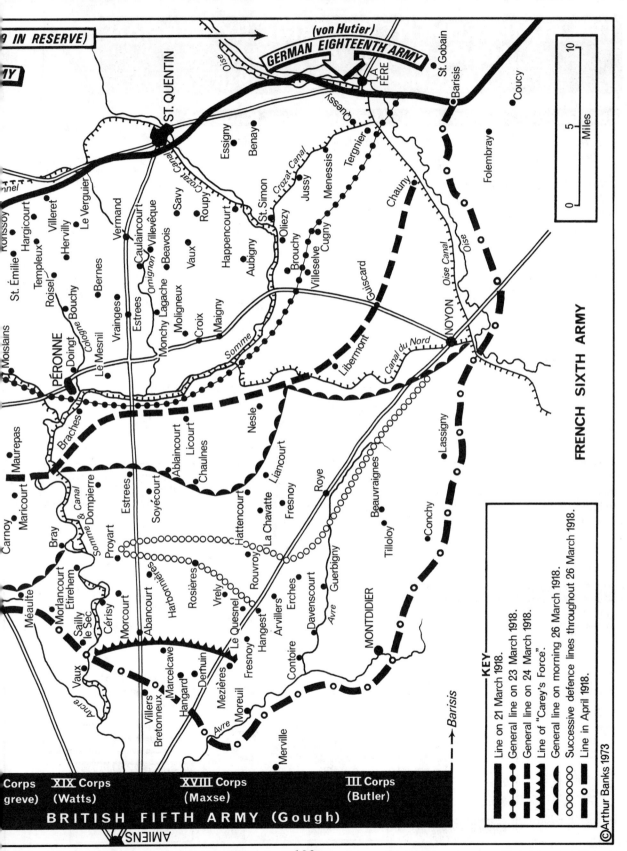

(9 IN RESERVE)

(von Hutier)

GERMAN EIGHTEENTH ARMY

Oise

St. Gobain

Coucy

Barisis

LA FÈRE

ST. QUENTIN

Folembray

Essigny

Benay

Crozat Canal

Ternier

Menessis

Jussy

Oise Canal

Oise

Villeret

Le Verguier

Hargicourt

Vermand

Caulaincourt

Villeveque

Savy

Roupy

Happencourt

St. Simon

Oliezy

Brouchy

Cugny

Chauny

Hervilly

Templeux

Bernes

Estrees

Beavois

Vaux

Aubigny

Villeselve

Guiscard

St. Émilie

Roisel

Bouchy

Vrainges

Monchy Lagache

Molineux

Maigny

NOYON

Moislains

Cologne

Le Mesnil

Croix

Somme

Libermont

Canal du Nord

FRENCH SIXTH ARMY

PÉRONNE

Doingt

Braches

Nesle

Maurepas

Licourt

Ablaincourt

Chaulnes

Liancourt

Roye

Lassigny

Carnoy

Maricourt

Bray

Somme & Canal

Dompierre

Estrees

Soyécourt

Hattencourt

La Chavatte

Fresnoy

Rouvroy

Beauvraignes

Conchy

Proyart

Rosières

Vrely

Guerbigny

Tilloloy

Morlancourt

Étirehem

Abancourt

Morcourt

Harbonnières

Le Quesnel

Arvillers

Erches

Davenscourt

Avre

MONTDIDIER

Méaulte

Sailly

le Sec

Cérisy

Hangest

Fresnoy

Contoire

Ancre

Vaux

Marcelcave

Hangard

Demuin

Mezières

Moreuil

Villers

Bretonneux

Avre

Merville

Barisis

Barisis

KEY

Line on 21 March 1918.

General line on 23 March 1918.

General line on 24 March 1918.

Line of "Carey's Force".

General line on morning 26 March 1918.

Successive defence lines throughout 26 March 1918.

Line in April 1918.

©Arthur Banks 1973

Corps   **XIX** Corps   **XVIII** Corps   **III** Corps
greve)   (Watts)   (Maxse)   (Butler)

BRITISH FIFTH ARMY (Gough)

AMIENS

Scale: 0 — 5 — 10 Miles

THE BOMBARDMENT OF PARIS BY GERMAN LONG-RANGE ARTILLERY 23 MARCH – 9 AUGUST 1918

The German "PARIS GUN" (Lange 21-cm. Kanone)

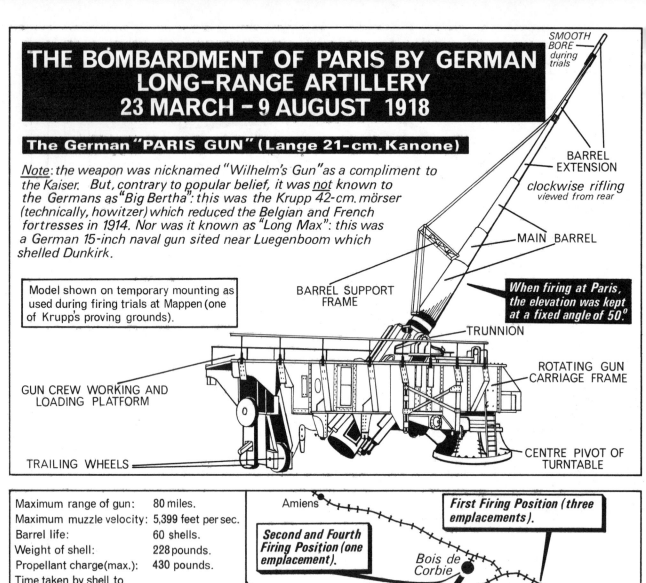

Note: the weapon was nicknamed "Wilhelm's Gun" as a compliment to the Kaiser. But, contrary to popular belief, it was _not_ known to the Germans as "Big Bertha": this was the Krupp 42-cm. mörser (technically, howitzer) which reduced the Belgian and French fortresses in 1914. Nor was it known as "Long Max": this was a German 15-inch naval gun sited near Luegenboom which shelled Dunkirk.

SMOOTH BORE _during trials_

BARREL EXTENSION

clockwise rifling _viewed from rear_

MAIN BARREL

Model shown on temporary mounting as used during firing trials at Mappen (one of Krupp's proving grounds).

BARREL SUPPORT FRAME

When firing at Paris, the elevation was kept at a fixed angle of 50.⁰

TRUNNION

ROTATING GUN CARRIAGE FRAME

GUN CREW WORKING AND LOADING PLATFORM

CENTRE PIVOT OF TURNTABLE

TRAILING WHEELS

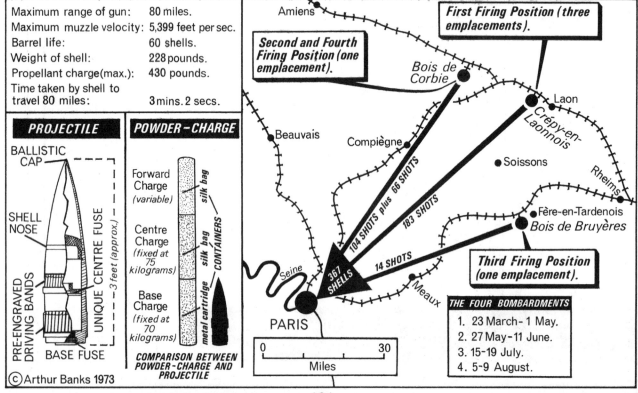

Maximum range of gun: 80 miles.
Maximum muzzle velocity: 5,399 feet per sec.
Barrel life: 60 shells.
Weight of shell: 228 pounds.
Propellant charge (max.): 430 pounds.
Time taken by shell to travel 80 miles: 3 mins. 2 secs.

PROJECTILE

BALLISTIC CAP

SHELL NOSE

UNIQUE CENTRE FUSE

—3 feet (approx.)

PRE-ENGRAVED DRIVING BANDS

BASE FUSE

POWDER–CHARGE

Forward Charge _(variable)_

Centre Charge _(fixed at 75 kilograms)_

Base Charge _(fixed at 70 kilograms)_

silk bag

silk bag

metal cartridge

CONTAINERS

COMPARISON BETWEEN POWDER-CHARGE AND PROJECTILE

Amiens

First Firing Position (three emplacements).

Second and Fourth Firing Position (one emplacement).

Bois de Corbie

Laon

Crépy-en-Laonnois

Beauvais

Compiègne

Soissons

Rheims

104 SHOTS plus 66 SHOTS

183 SHOTS

Fère-en-Tardenois
Bois de Bruyères

367 SHELLS

14 SHOTS

Seine

Third Firing Position (one emplacement).

Meaux

THE FOUR BOMBARDMENTS
1. 23 March – 1 May.
2. 27 May – 11 June.
3. 15-19 July.
4. 5-9 August.

PARIS

0   30
Miles

© Arthur Banks 1973

184

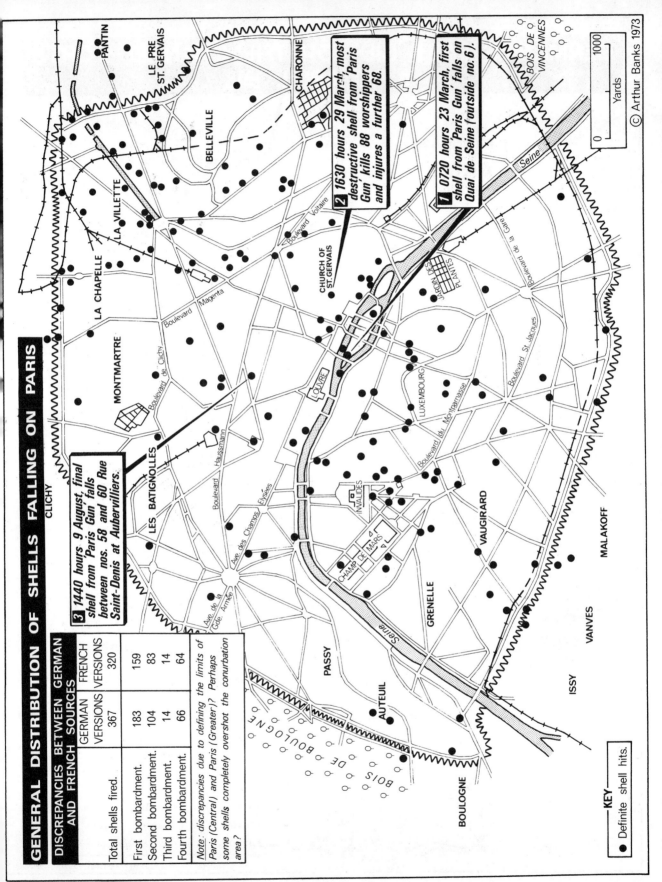

GENERAL DISTRIBUTION OF SHELLS FALLING ON PARIS

DISCREPANCIES BETWEEN GERMAN AND FRENCH SOURCES

	GERMAN VERSIONS	FRENCH VERSIONS
Total shells fired.	367	320
First bombardment.	183	159
Second bombardment.	104	83
Third bombardment.	14	14
Fourth bombardment.	66	64

Note: discrepancies due to defining the limits of Paris (Central) and Paris (Greater)? Perhaps some shells completely overshot the conurbation area?

3 1440 hours 9 August, final shell from Paris Gun' falls between nos. 58 and 60 Rue Saint-Denis at Aubervilliers.

2 1630 hours 29 March, most destructive shell from Paris Gun' kills 88 worshippers and injures a further 68.

1 0720 hours 23 March, first shell from Paris Gun' falls on Quai de Seine (outside no. 6).

© Arthur Banks 1973

1000
Yards
0

KEY

● Definite shell hits.

PANTIN
LE PRÉ ST. GERVAIS
BELLEVILLE
CHARONNE
BOIS DE VINCENNES
LA VILLETTE
LA CHAPELLE
MONTMARTRE
CLICHY
Boulevard de Clichy
Boulevard Magenta
Boulevard Voltaire
CHURCH OF ST. GERVAIS
Seine
JARDIN DES PLANTES
Boulevard de la Gare
LES BATIGNOLLES
Boulevard Haussmann
Ave. des Champs Élysées
LOUVRE
LUXEMBOURG
Boulevard du Montparnasse
Boulevard St. Jacques
Ave. de la Gde. Armée
INVALIDES
CHAMP DE MARS
GRENELLE
VAUGIRARD
MALAKOFF
PASSY
Seine
AUTEUIL
VANVES
ISSY
BOIS DE BOULOGNE
BOULOGNE

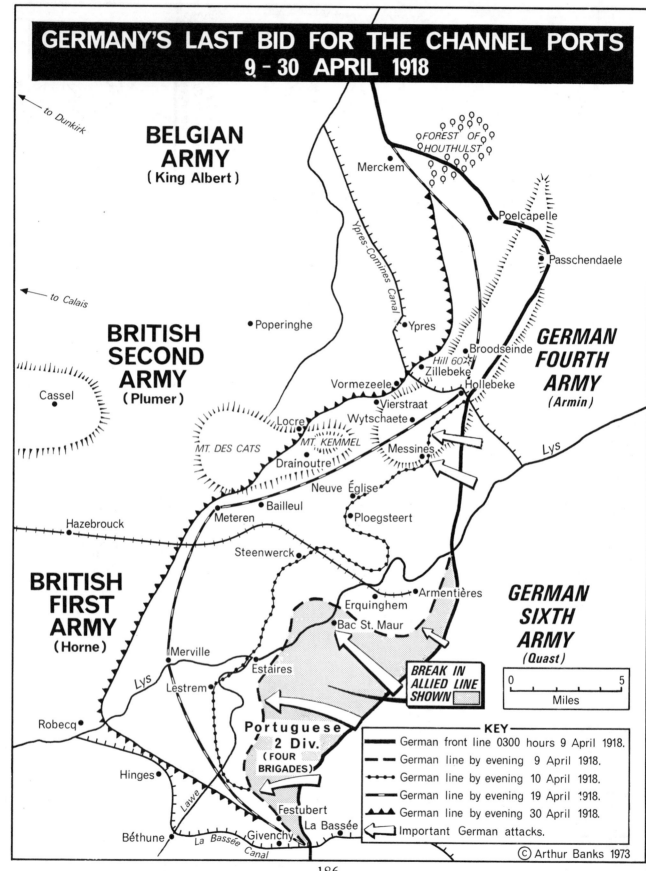

GERMANY'S LAST BID FOR THE CHANNEL PORTS
9 - 30 APRIL 1918

to Dunkirk

BELGIAN ARMY
(King Albert)

FOREST OF HOUTHULST

Merckem

Poelcapelle

Passchendaele

to Calais

BRITISH SECOND ARMY
(Plumer)

Poperinghe

Ypres-Comines Canal

Ypres

Broodseinde

Hill 60

GERMAN FOURTH ARMY
(Armin)

Cassel

Vormezeele

Zillebeke

Hollebeke

Vierstraat

Wytschaete

Locre

MT. DES CATS

MT. KEMMEL

Messines

Lys

Drainoutre

Neuve Église

Bailleul

Meteren

Ploegsteert

Hazebrouck

Steenwerck

Armentières

BRITISH FIRST ARMY
(Horne)

Erquinghem

Bac St. Maur

GERMAN SIXTH ARMY
(Quast)

Merville

Estaires

Lestrem

Lys

BREAK IN ALLIED LINE SHOWN

0   5
Miles

Robecq

Portuguese 2 Div.
(FOUR BRIGADES)

Hinges

Lawe

Festubert

La Bassée

Béthune

Givenchy

La Bassée Canal

KEY
▬▬▬	German front line 0300 hours 9 April 1918.
- - -	German line by evening 9 April 1918.
••••	German line by evening 10 April 1918.
▬○▬	German line by evening 19 April 1918.
▲▲▲	German line by evening 30 April 1918.
⟸	Important German attacks.

© Arthur Banks 1973

186

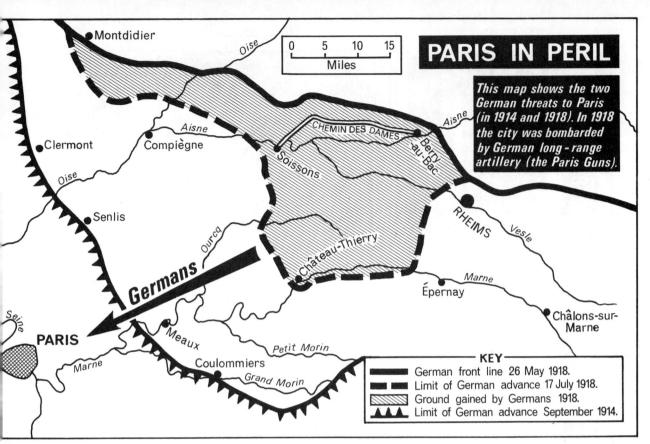

PARIS IN PERIL

This map shows the two German threats to Paris (in 1914 and 1918). In 1918 the city was bombarded by German long-range artillery (the Paris Guns).

Montdidier

Oise

0 5 10 15 Miles

Clermont

Aisne

CHEMIN DES DAMES

Compiègne

Soissons

Berry-au-Bac

Aisne

RHEIMS

Vesle

Oise

Senlis

Ourcq

Château-Thierry

Germans

Marne

Épernay

Châlons-sur-Marne

Seine

PARIS

Meaux

Marne

Petit Morin

Coulommiers

Grand Morin

KEY
— German front line 26 May 1918.
- - - Limit of German advance 17 July 1918.
▨ Ground gained by Germans 1918.
▲▲▲ Limit of German advance September 1914.

FOCH'S "COUNTERSTROKE"

This Allied attack was launched on 18 July 1918 with American and Moroccan divisions in the van supported by hundreds of small tanks. There was no artillery overture.

KEY
— German front line 18 July 1918.
- - - Allied line by 31 August 1918.
⊥ Allied divisions with names of army commanders.
* German 'Paris Gun' site 15–19 July 1918.

Aisne

Vailly

Aisne

Mangin FRENCH TENTH ARMY

18 JULY

SOISSONS

Vesle

Braine

Vierzy

Vesle

This road is first Allied objective (to cut off German supplies in the salient).

RHEIMS

Oulchy-le-Château

Ourcq

20 JULY

Berthelot FRENCH FIFTH ARMY

18 JULY

*
Bois de Bruyères

Belleau

Châtillon

Dégoutte FRENCH SIXTH ARMY

CHÂTEAU-THIERRY

20 JULY

Dormans

Marne

ÉPERNAY

Vesle

0 1 2 3 4 Miles

© Arthur Banks 1973

de Mitry **FRENCH NINTH ARMY**

187

THE AMERICAN EXPEDITIONARY FORCE IN EUROPE 1918

Note: the United States lost more soldiers from illness than it lost from all battles combined.

The United States declared war on Germany on 6 April 1917, and against Austria-Hungary on 7 December 1917. General John Joseph Pershing was appointed commander of the American Expeditionary Force to Europe, and a vast training and camp-building programme was commenced. By May 1918, there were over 500,000 U.S. troops in France, and by mid-July, over 1,000,000 men had arrived in Europe.

NUMBERS OF UNITED STATES TROOPS

EMBARKED FOR EUROPE AT:

New York	1,656,000 men
Newport News	288,000 men
Boston	46,000 men
Philadelphia	35,000 men
Portland	6,000 men
Baltimore	4,000 men

PLUS 45,000 TROOPS EMBARKED AT CANADIAN PORTS

Montreal	32,000 men
Quebec	11,000 men
Halifax	5,000 men
St. John's	1,000 men
	2,084,000 men

DISEMBARKED IN EUROPE AT:

Liverpool (including 4,000 at Manchester)	848,000 men
Brest	791,000 men
St. Nazaire	198,000 men
London	62,000 men
Southampton	57,000 men
Bassens (including Bordeaux)	50,000 men
Glasgow	45,000 men
Le Havre	13,000 men
Bristol	11,000 men
La Pallice (including La Rochelle)	4,000 men
Cherbourg	2,000 men
Marseilles	1,000 men
Plymouth	1,000 men
Falmouth	1,000 men
	2,08,000 men

Precise figs. 71 men were lost in Atlantic crossings.

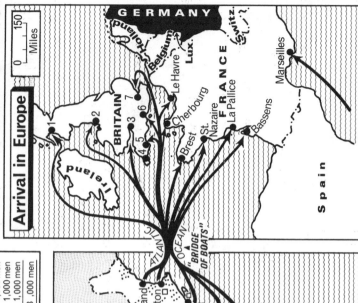

Arrival in Europe

0 — 150 Miles

KEY

Disembarkation ports shown ●

KEY TO BRITISH DISEMBARKATION PORTS

Mobilization

0 — 300

KEY

■ — National Guard camps.
□ — National Army camps.
∴ — Construction projects.

188

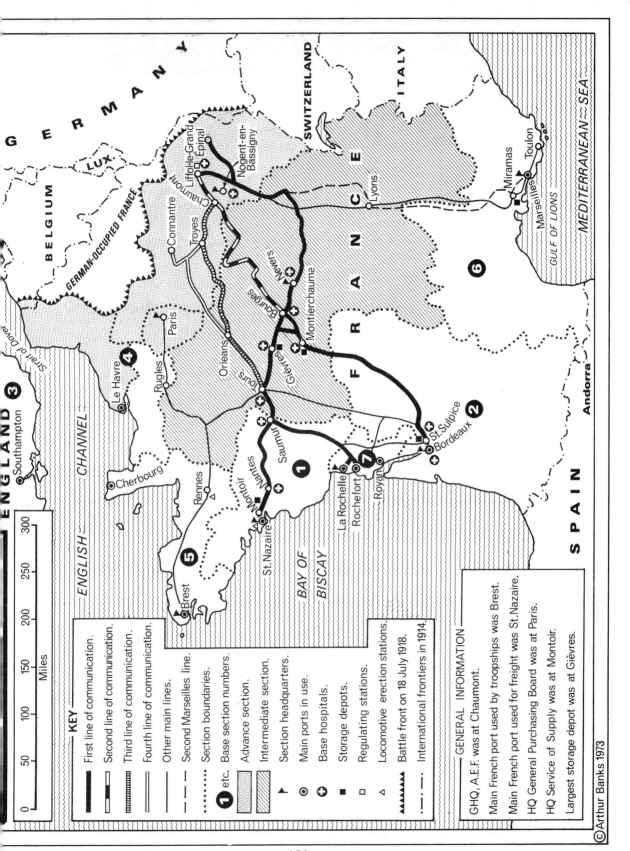

KEY

First line of communication.
Second line of communication.
Third line of communication.
Fourth line of communication.
Other main lines.
Second Marseilles line.
Section boundaries.
① etc. Base section numbers.
Advance section.
Intermediate section.
Section headquarters.
Main ports in use.
Base hospitals.
Storage depots.
Regulating stations.
Locomotive erection stations.
Battle front on 18 July 1918.
International frontiers in 1914.

GENERAL INFORMATION

GHQ, A.E.F. was at Chaumont.
Main French port used by troopships was Brest.
Main French port used for freight was St.Nazaire.
HQ General Purchasing Board was at Paris.
HQ Service of Supply was at Montoir.
Largest storage depot was at Gièvres.

© Arthur Banks 1973

Miles
0 50 100 150 200 250 300

189

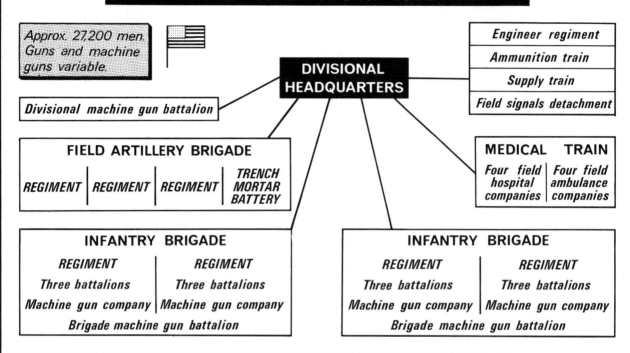

AMERICAN INFANTRY DIVISIONAL ORGANIZATION 1918

Approx. 27,200 men. Guns and machine guns variable

DIVISIONAL HEADQUARTERS

Divisional machine gun battalion

| Engineer regiment |
| Ammunition train |
| Supply train |
| Field signals detachment |

FIELD ARTILLERY BRIGADE

| REGIMENT | REGIMENT | REGIMENT | TRENCH MORTAR BATTERY |

MEDICAL TRAIN

| Four field hospital companies | Four field ambulance companies |

INFANTRY BRIGADE

REGIMENT	REGIMENT
Three battalions	Three battalions
Machine gun company	Machine gun company
Brigade machine gun battalion	

INFANTRY BRIGADE

REGIMENT	REGIMENT
Three battalions	Three battalions
Machine gun company	Machine gun company
Brigade machine gun battalion	

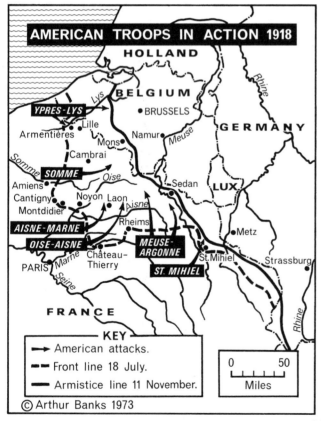

AMERICAN TROOPS IN ACTION 1918

HOLLAND
BELGIUM
GERMANY
BRUSSELS
Lille
Armentières
Mons
Namur
Cambrai
Meuse
Rhine
Lys
YPRES-LYS
Somme
SOMME
Oise
Amiens
Cantigny
Montdidier
Noyon
Laon
Aisne
Sedan
LUX.
Rheims
Metz
AISNE-MARNE
OISE-AISNE
Château-Thierry
MEUSE-ARGONNE
St.Mihiel
Strassburg
PARIS
Marne
Seine
ST. MIHIEL
Rhine
FRANCE

KEY
→ American attacks.
- - Front line 18 July.
— Armistice line 11 November.

0   50
Miles

© Arthur Banks 1973

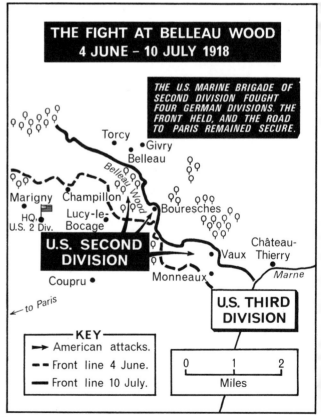

THE FIGHT AT BELLEAU WOOD
4 JUNE – 10 JULY 1918

THE U.S. MARINE BRIGADE OF SECOND DIVISION FOUGHT FOUR GERMAN DIVISIONS. THE FRONT HELD, AND THE ROAD TO PARIS REMAINED SECURE.

Torcy
Givry
Belleau
Belleau Wood
Marigny
Champillon
Bouresches
HQ. U.S. 2 Div.
Lucy-le-Bocage
U.S. SECOND DIVISION
Vaux
Château-Thierry
Coupru
Monneaux
Marne
to Paris
U.S. THIRD DIVISION

KEY
→ American attacks.
- - Front line 4 June.
— Front line 10 July.

0   1   2
Miles

"BLACK DAY OF THE GERMAN ARMY" 8 AUGUST 1918

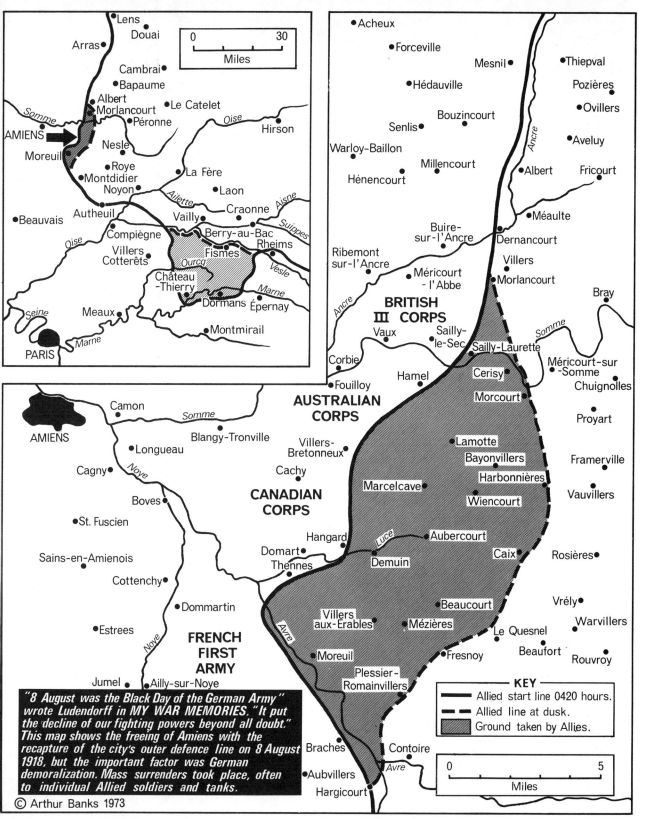

Lens
Douai
Arras
Cambrai
Bapaume
Albert
Morlancourt
Le Catelet
Péronne
Oise
Somme
Hirson
AMIENS
Nesle
Moreuil
Roye
La Fère
Montdidier
Noyon
Laon
Ailette
Aisne
Beauvais
Autheuil
Vailly
Craonne
Suippes
Oise
Compiègne
Berry-au-Bac
Rheims
Villers-
Cotterêts
Ourcq
Fismes
Vesle
Château-
Thierry
Marne
Dormans
Épernay
Seine
Meaux
Marne
Montmirail
PARIS

0   30   Miles

Acheux
Forceville
Mesnil
Thiepval
Hédauville
Pozières
Ovillers
Bouzincourt
Senlis
Aveluy
Warloy-Baillon
Millencourt
Albert
Fricourt
Hénencourt
Ancre
Méaulte
Buire-
sur-l'Ancre
Dernancourt
Villers
Morlancourt
Ribemont
sur-l'Ancre
Méricourt
- l'Abbe
Bray
BRITISH III CORPS
Vaux
Sailly-
le-Sec
Sailly-Laurette
Somme
Corbie
Méricourt-sur-
-Somme
Hamel
Chuignolles
Fouilloy
Cerisy
Proyart
AUSTRALIAN CORPS
Morcourt
Lamotte
Bayonvillers
Framerville
Villers-
Bretonneux
Harbonnières
Cachy
Marcelcave
Wiencourt
Vauvillers
CANADIAN CORPS
Hangard
Luce
Aubercourt
Domart
Caix
Rosières
Thennes
Demuin
Vrély
Beaucourt
Villers
aux-Erables
Mézières
Warvillers
Moreuil
Le Quesnel
Fresnoy
Beaufort
Rouvroy
FRENCH FIRST ARMY
Plessier-
Romainvillers
Braches
Contoire
Avre
Aubvillers
Hargicourt

Camon
Somme
Blangy-Tronville
AMIENS
Longueau
Noye
Cagny
Boves
St. Fuscien
Sains-en-Amienois
Cottenchy
Dommartin
Noye
Estrees
Jumel
Ailly-sur-Noye
Avre

KEY
— Allied start line 0420 hours.
--- Allied line at dusk.
▨ Ground taken by Allies.

0   5   Miles

*"8 August was the Black Day of the German Army"
wrote Ludendorff in MY WAR MEMORIES. "It put
the decline of our fighting powers beyond all doubt."
This map shows the freeing of Amiens with the
recapture of the city's outer defence line on 8 August
1918, but the important factor was German
demoralization. Mass surrenders took place, often
to individual Allied soldiers and tanks.*

© Arthur Banks 1973

191

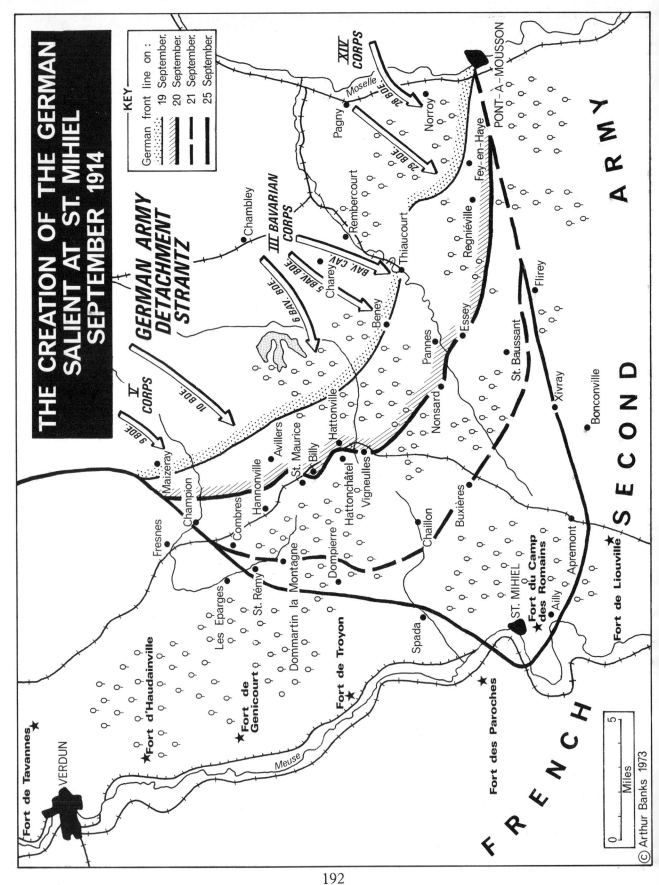

THE CREATION OF THE GERMAN SALIENT AT ST. MIHIEL SEPTEMBER 1914

KEY

German front line on :
.... 19 September.
///// 20 September.
– – – 21 September.
▬▬▬ 25 September.

GERMAN ARMY DETACHMENT STRANTZ

XII CORPS

III BAVARIAN CORPS

V CORPS

BAV. CAV.

28 BDE.
29 BDE.
5 BAV. BDE.
6 BAV. BDE.
9 BDE.
10 BDE.

PONT-À-MOUSSON

SECOND

FRENCH

ARMY

Moselle

Pagny
Norroy
Fey-en-Haye
Rembercourt
Thiaucourt
Regniéville
Chambley
Charey
Beney
Essey
Flirey
St. Baussant
Pannes
Xivray
Nonsard
Bonconville
Hattonville
Buxières
Avillers
St. Maurice
Billy
Hattonchâtel
Vigneulles
Hannonville
Maizeray
Champion
Combres
Chaillon
Apremont
Dompierre
ST. MIHIEL
Fort du Camp des Romains
Ailly
Fort de Liouville
Fresnes
St. Rémy
Dommartin la Montagne
Spada
Fort des Paroches
Les Eparges
Fort de Genicourt
Fort de Troyon
Fort d'Haudainville
Fort de Tavannes
VERDUN
Meuse

Miles
0   5

© Arthur Banks 1973

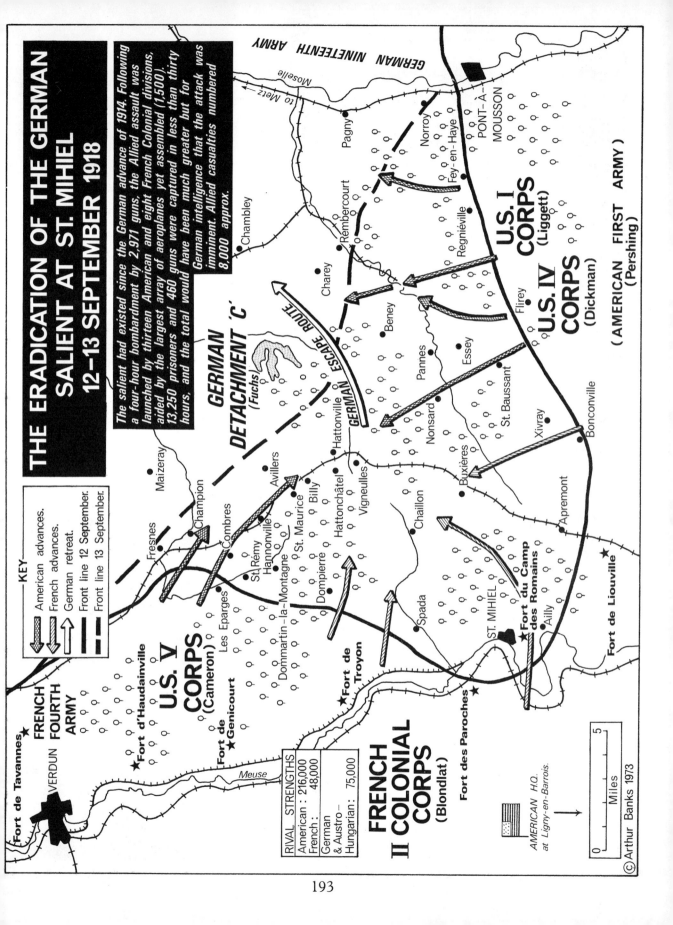

THE ERADICATION OF THE GERMAN SALIENT AT ST. MIHIEL 12–13 SEPTEMBER 1918

The salient had existed since the German advance of 1914. Following a four-hour bombardment by 2,971 guns, the Allied assault was launched by thirteen American and eight French Colonial divisions, aided by the largest array of aeroplanes yet assembled (1,500). 13,250 prisoners and 460 guns were captured in less than thirty hours, and the total would have been much greater but for German intelligence that the attack was imminent. Allied casualties numbered 8,000 approx.

GERMAN NINETEENTH ARMY

Moselle

to Metz

PONT-À-MOUSSON

Norroy

Fey-en-Haye

Pagny

Rembercourt

Regniéville

Chambley

U.S. I CORPS (Liggett)

U.S. IV CORPS (Dickman)

Charey

Flirey

Beney

(AMERICAN FIRST ARMY) (Pershing)

Pannes

Essey

GERMAN DETACHMENT 'C' (Fuchs)

ESCAPE ROUTE

Nonsard

St. Baussant

Hattonville

GERMAN

Bonconville

Maizeray

Avillers

Xivray

Buxières

Champion

Combres

Billy

St. Maurice

Hattonchâtel

Vigneulles

Apremont

Fresnes

St. Rémy

Hannonville

Chaillon

Dompierre

Les Eparges

Dommartin–la–Montagne

Fort de Troyon

Spada

ST. MIHIEL

Fort du Camp des Romains

Ailly

Fort de Liouville

FRENCH FOURTH ARMY

Fort d'Haudainville

U.S. V CORPS (Cameron)

Fort de Génicourt

FRENCH II COLONIAL CORPS (Blondlat)

Fort des Paroches

Fort de Tavannes

VERDUN

Meuse

KEY

- American advances.
- French advances.
- German retreat.
- Front line 12 September.
- Front line 13 September.

RIVAL STRENGTHS
American :	216,000
French :	48,000
German & Austro–Hungarian :	75,000

AMERICAN H.Q. at Ligny-en-Barrois.

Miles
0 5

© Arthur Banks 1973

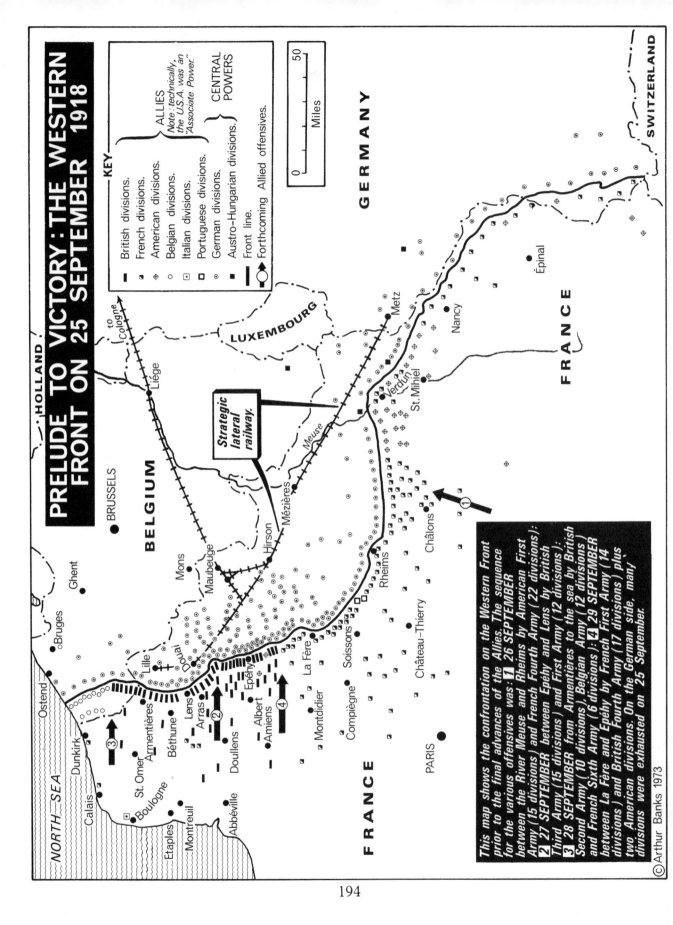

PRELUDE TO VICTORY: THE WESTERN FRONT ON 25 SEPTEMBER 1918

KEY

ALLIES
Note: technically, the U.S.A. was an "Associate Power."

▮	British divisions.
◪	French divisions.
⊕	American divisions.
○	Belgian divisions.
⊡	Italian divisions.
⊙	Portuguese divisions.
◻	German divisions.
⊙	Austro-Hungarian divisions.
▮	Front line.
⬤	Forthcoming Allied offensives.

CENTRAL POWERS

Miles
0   50

Strategic lateral railway.

to Cologne

HOLLAND
BELGIUM
LUXEMBOURG
GERMANY
SWITZERLAND
FRANCE

NORTH SEA

Ostend
Bruges
Ghent
BRUSSELS
Calais
Dunkirk
St. Omer
Boulogne
Montreuil
Étaples
Abbéville
Armentières
Béthune
Lille
Douai
Lens
Arras
Doullens
Albert
Amiens
Mons
Maubeuge
Hirson
Mézières
Liège
Métz
Verdun
St. Mihiel
Nancy
Épinal
Épehy
La Fère
Montdidier
Compiègne
Soissons
Rheims
Château-Thierry
Châlons
PARIS
Meuse

This map shows the confrontation on the Western Front prior to the final advances of the Allies. The sequence for the various offensives was: **1** *26 SEPTEMBER* between the River Meuse and Rheims by American First Army (15 divisions) and French Fourth Army (22 divisions); **2** *27 SEPTEMBER* between Epéhy and Lens by British Third Army (15 divisions) and First Army (12 divisions); **3** *28 SEPTEMBER* from Armentières to the sea by British Second Army (10 divisions), Belgian Army (12 divisions) and French Sixth Army (6 divisions); **4** *29 SEPTEMBER* between La Fère and Epéhy by French First Army (14 divisions) and British Fourth Army (17 divisions) plus two American divisions. On the German side, many divisions were exhausted on 25 September.

© Arthur Banks 1973

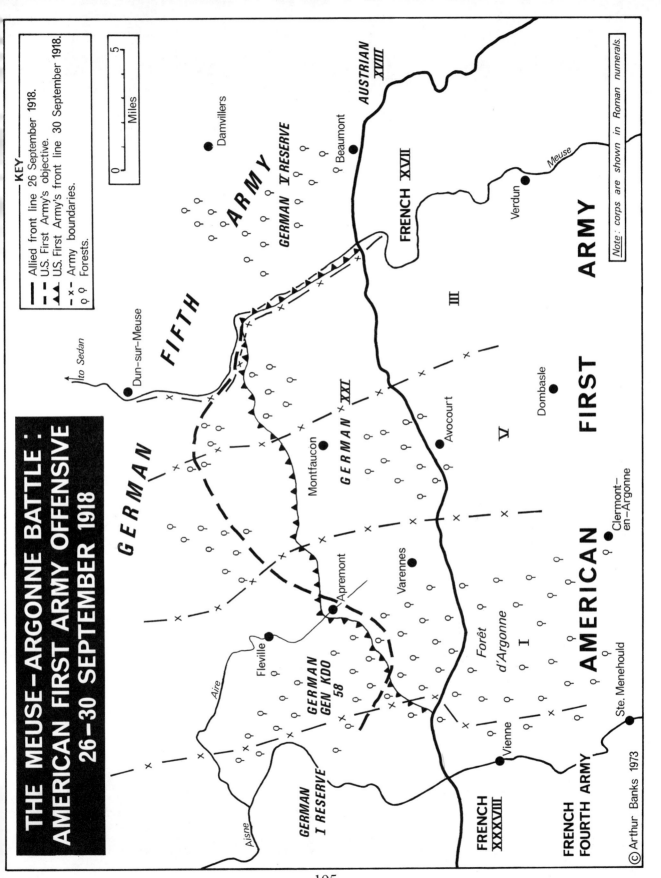

THE MEUSE-ARGONNE BATTLE : AMERICAN FIRST ARMY OFFENSIVE 26–30 SEPTEMBER 1918

KEY
- Allied front line 26 September 1918.
- U.S. First Army's objective.
- U.S. First Army's front line 30 September 1918.
- –×– Army boundaries.
- ⚲ ⚲ Forests.

Miles
0 ——— 5

Note: corps are shown in Roman numerals.

GERMAN FIFTH ARMY

GERMAN V RESERVE

AUSTRIAN XVIII

FRENCH XVII

GERMAN XXI

GERMAN GEN KDO 58

GERMAN I RESERVE

AMERICAN FIRST ARMY

FRENCH XXXVIII

FRENCH FOURTH ARMY

to Sedan

Dun-sur-Meuse

Damvillers

Beaumont

Meuse

Verdun

Montfaucon

Avocourt

Dombasle

III

V

Apremont

Varennes

Clermont–en–Argonne

Fleville

Forêt d'Argonne

I

Aire

Aisne

Vienne

Ste. Menehould

© Arthur Banks 1973

195

THE LIBERATION OF THE BELGIAN COAST
28 SEPTEMBER–25 OCTOBER 1918

HOLLAND

KEY

—— Allied front line morning 28 September 1918.
•••• Allied front line evening 28 September 1918.
– – Allied front line 29 September 1918.
—•— Allied front line 1 October 1918.
—▲— Allied front line 25 October 1918.
▒ Ground gained by Allies.
–×– Allied army boundaries.

0   5   10
Miles

Zeebrugge   Knocke
Blankenberghe   Westcapelle
Zuyenkerke
Middelburg
to Ostend
BRUGES
Jabbeke   Sysseele
Ghistelles
Lombartzyde   BELGIUM
Nieuport
Leke   Ferneghem
Pervyse   Ruddervoorde   Aeltre
Furnes   Thourout   Wynghene
Dixmude   Lichtervelde   BELGIANS
Zarren   Thielt
Woumen   Staden   Ardoye   FRENCH GROUP
Pierkenshoek   Roulers   to Ghent→
Iseghem   Ingelmunster   Lys
Poelcapelle
Boesinghe   Gravenstafel   BELGIANS
Becelaere   Harlebeke
Poperinghe   Ledeghem
Ypres   Hooge   COURTRAI
II
XIX   Wervicq   Menin
X   St. Genois
Kemmel Hill   Messines   BRITISH SECOND
XV   Comines   ARMY
Hill 63   Tourcoing
Bailleul   Quesnoy   Schelde
Nieppe   Roubaix
Armentières   to Tournai
Merville   Lys   FRANCE
Laventie   LILLE
XI   Haubourdin
Neuve Chapelle   BRITISH FIFTH
Fromelles   ARMY
Fournes   Faches
La Bassée

Yser
YSER-YPRES CANAL
BRUGES SHIP CANAL
GHENT CANAL

© Arthur Banks 1973

This map shows the Allied advance between
28 September and 25 October (when the King
and Queen of the Belgians made their state
entry into Bruges.) After 1 October the situation
became fluid, and the German retirement became
general until a line was reconstituted on 25 October.

196

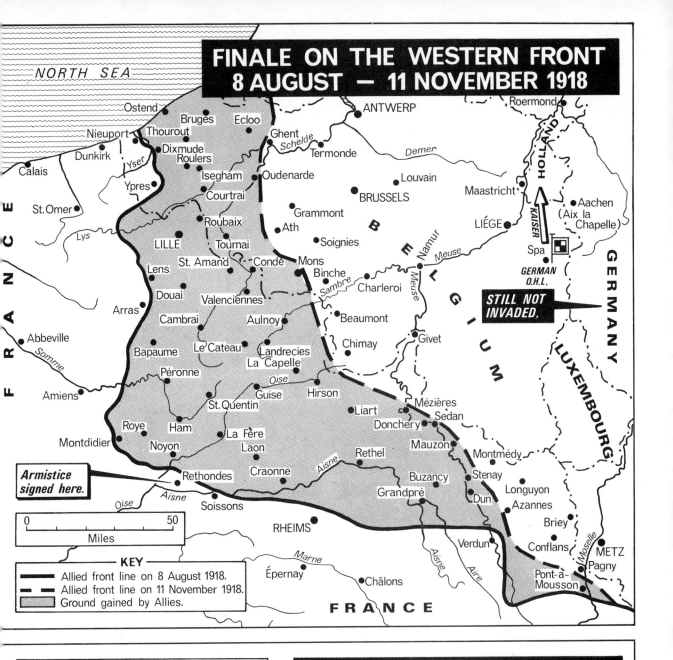

FINALE ON THE WESTERN FRONT
8 AUGUST — 11 NOVEMBER 1918

NORTH SEA

Roermond

Ostend

Bruges   Ecloo

Nieuport   Thourout   Ghent
           Dixmude   ANTWERP
Dunkirk   Roulers   Termonde   Demer
Calais   Yser   HOLLAND   Maastricht
St.Omer   Ypres   Isegham   Oudenarde   Louvain   Aachen
                    Courtrai   BRUSSELS   (Aix la
           Lys   Chapelle)
                 Roubaix   Grammont   LIÉGE
                          Ath   Namur
              LILLE   Tournai   Soignies   B   Spa
     Lens   St. Amand   Condé   Mons   E   GERMAN
Arras   Valenciennes   Binche   Sambre L   Meuse   O.H.L.   STILL NOT
     Douai   Charleroi   G   INVADED.
Abbeville   Cambrai   Aulnoy   Beaumont   I   Meuse   GERMANY
     Bapaume   Le Cateau   Chimay   U   Givet
Somme   Péronne   Landrecies   M   LUXEMBOURG
Amiens   La Capelle   Oise
                      Guise   Hirson   Mézières
           Roye   Ham   St.Quentin   Sedan
Montdidier   La Fère   Liart   Donchery
           Noyon   Laon   Mauzon   Montmédy
                               Rethel   Longuyon
**Armistice   Craonne   Buzancy   Stenay   Azannes
signed here.** Rethondes   Grandpré   Dun   Briey
        Oise Aisne   Conflans   METZ
              Soissons   Verdun   Pagny
0   50   RHEIMS   Aisne   Aire   Pont-à-
     Miles   Marne   Mousson
                   Épernay   Châlons
— KEY —
Allied front line on 8 August 1918.   F R A N C E
Allied front line on 11 November 1918.
Ground gained by Allies.

Since 18 July, when Foch sent Mangin
and Dégoutte to open the Allied attack,
the following prisoners had been taken:
188,000 (by the British), 140,000 (by the
French), 44,000, (by the Americans),
and 14,000 (by the Belgians). Plus some
7,000 guns captured. If German killed
and wounded are added, it is plain
that the German armies could not
continue to fight on effectively.

On 10 November, the Kaiser fled to Holland,
followed by the Crown Prince. The basic Armistice
terms signed at 1100 hours on 11 November were :
immediate cessation of hostilities : German evacuation
of invaded territory and of Alsace — Lorraine :
repatriation of Allied citizens and prisoners of war :
surrender of war materials and weapons : evacuation
of the Rhine's left bank and bridgeheads : surrender
of U-boats : internment of German surface warships :
a declaration that the Treaties of Bucharest and
Brest — Litovsk were null and void.

© Arthur Banks 1973

NOTE: MONS (FROM WHICH THE BRITISH RETREAT HAD BEGUN IN 1914) WAS RETAKEN BY THE
CANADIANS A FEW HOURS PRIOR TO THE ARMISTICE.

197

THE PERIPHERAL CAMPAIGNS

Throughout the War most military leaders in Britain and France were 'Westerners'; they believed the principal task of their armies was to defeat the enemy in the theatre of operations which the Germans had themselves selected for their main effort. All other campaigns were dangerous 'sideshows', eating up men and munitions; and it was not until the final months of the war that a resolute effort was made to gain victories against Germany's allies in northern Italy, the Balkans, and the Middle East.

In practice these peripheral campaigns fall strategically into three categories. Some were intended, at least originally, as offensive thrusts against the central bloc from new points of the compass: the Italian and Macedonian Fronts, for example. Others were forced on the allies by Turkey's adhesion to the Germano-Austrian side: the need to defend the Suez lifeline by a campaign in Palestine, and to secure Anglo-Persian oil supplies by an offensive up the Shatt-el-Arab. Finally there was the fighting in Africa, and notably in German East Africa, where General von Lettow-Vorbeck waged colonial warfare throughout the four years of the European conflict, eventually surrendering a fortnight after the Armistice in France.

The character of several of these campaigns changed as the war dragged on: thus operations to safeguard oil refineries and counter intrigues in the Middle East developed into a lengthy campaign in Mesopotamia, with the possibility of a strike against the interior of Turkey. Conversely, the Italian Front, where it was hoped in 1915 that Austria-Hungary would drain away her last resources, became a burden for Italy's allies, although the Italian troops fought at first with fiercely whipped-up patriotic courage. They suffered from inadequate supplies of munitions and artillery, from poor training, and from the assumption that frontal assaults were the sole method of achieving victory. The Italians sustained 600,000 casualties in eleven offensives along the river Isonzo from mid-June 1915 to mid-September 1917; and after all this terrible fighting, they succeeded in advancing the front line only seven miles. The twelfth Isonzo battle, the combined German and Austrian offensive at Caporetto in October 1917, pushed the Italians back fifty miles to the river Piave. Eventually, on the first anniversary of Caporetto, the Italians launched an attack on the Austrian positions which cost them 25,000 casualties in sixty hours of grim combat, before the Austrians lost their headquarters at Vittorio Veneto and sued for peace.

The Salonika Front, originating with the Austro-German-Bulgarian offensive against Serbia (page 160) was for long quiescent, although joint operations by Serbs, Italians, Russians and French liberated Serbian Monastir in November 1916 and the British were heavily engaged with the Bulgarians around Lake Doiran and the River Struma in the spring of 1917. Disease, especially malaria, caused the heaviest casualties in Macedonia. The final offensive of 1918 involved an initial assault by the French and the Serbs on a formless ridge known as the Dobropolje, more than 7,000 feet above sea-level. Subsequently Franchet d'Espèrey's army made the swiftest long advance of the war, sweeping up to the Danube and the plains of Hungary, and preparing to march on Berlin by way of Budapest and Dresden.

In Palestine General Allenby, with elaborate deception and imaginative use of cavalry pushed the Turks (and the German 'Asia Corps') rapidly northwards into the Lebanon and Syria in the autumn of 1918. His advanced cavalry reached Aleppo before Turkish delegates concluded an armistice at Mudros on 30 October, with the commander-in-chief of the British Mediterranean Fleet. Both Allenby in Palestine and Franchet d'Espèrey in Salonika had shown the need for unconventional commanders filled with offensive spirit in the fringe theatres of war. So, indeed, did Lettow-Vorbeck in East Africa.

THE ITALIAN FRONT 1915-1918

① The Battleground

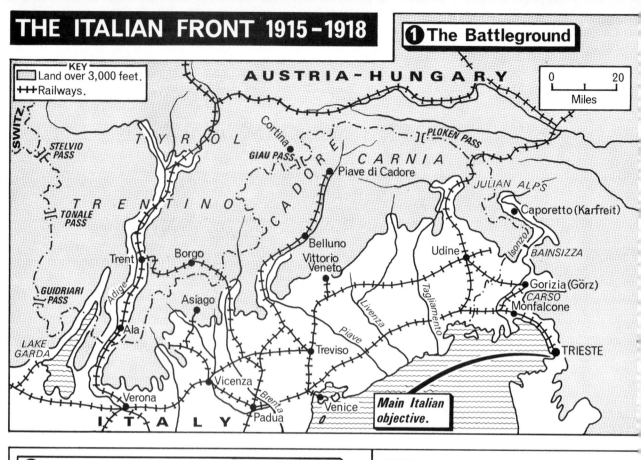

KEY
- ☐ Land over 3,000 feet.
- +++ Railways.

AUSTRIA-HUNGARY

SWITZ.

STELVIO PASS

TYROL

Cortina

GIAU PASS

CADORE

CARNIA

PLOKEN PASS

Piave di Cadore

JULIAN ALPS

Caporetto (Karfreit)

TONALE PASS

TRENTINO

Belluno

BAINSIZZA

Isonzo

Trent · Borgo

Vittorio Veneto

Udine

Gorizia (Görz)

GUIDRIARI PASS

Asiago

Livenza

Tagliamento

CARSO

Monfalcone

Ala

Piave

LAKE GARDA

Treviso

TRIESTE

Vicenza

Brenta

Verona

Venice

Main Italian objective.

Padua

ITALY

0 ——— 20 Miles

② The Opposing Forces (Land and Air)

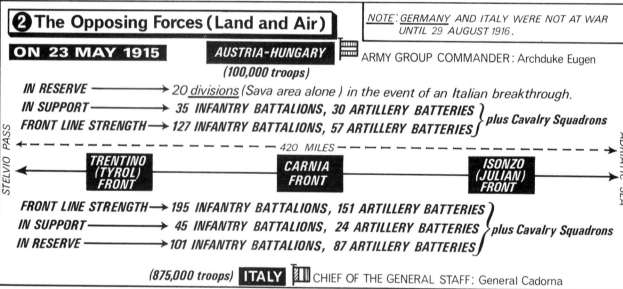

NOTE: GERMANY AND ITALY WERE NOT AT WAR UNTIL 29 AUGUST 1916.

ON 23 MAY 1915   AUSTRIA-HUNGARY (100,000 troops)   ARMY GROUP COMMANDER: Archduke Eugen

IN RESERVE → 20 divisions (Sava area alone) in the event of an Italian breakthrough.

IN SUPPORT → 35 INFANTRY BATTALIONS, 30 ARTILLERY BATTERIES ⎞
FRONT LINE STRENGTH → 127 INFANTRY BATTALIONS, 57 ARTILLERY BATTERIES ⎠ plus Cavalry Squadrons

STELVIO PASS ←——————— 420 MILES ———————→ ADRIATIC SEA

TRENTINO (TYROL) FRONT   CARNIA FRONT   ISONZO (JULIAN) FRONT

FRONT LINE STRENGTH → 195 INFANTRY BATTALIONS, 151 ARTILLERY BATTERIES ⎞
IN SUPPORT → 45 INFANTRY BATTALIONS, 24 ARTILLERY BATTERIES ⎬ plus Cavalry Squadrons
IN RESERVE → 101 INFANTRY BATTALIONS, 87 ARTILLERY BATTERIES ⎠

(875,000 troops) **ITALY**   CHIEF OF THE GENERAL STAFF: General Cadorna

BY 15 JUNE 1915

	ITALY	AUSTRIA-HUNGARY
INFANTRY BATTALIONS	415	234
ARTILLERY BATTERIES	326	155
CAVALRY SQUADRONS	116	21

Note: figures are deceptive.

Austria was stronger in heavy artillery and machine guns and many of her troops were already battle-experienced.

IN THE AIR

ITALY
77 Aircraft
including seaplanes
7 Airships

AUSTRIA-HUNGARY
136 Aircraft
including seaplanes
1 Airship

© Arthur Banks 1973

200

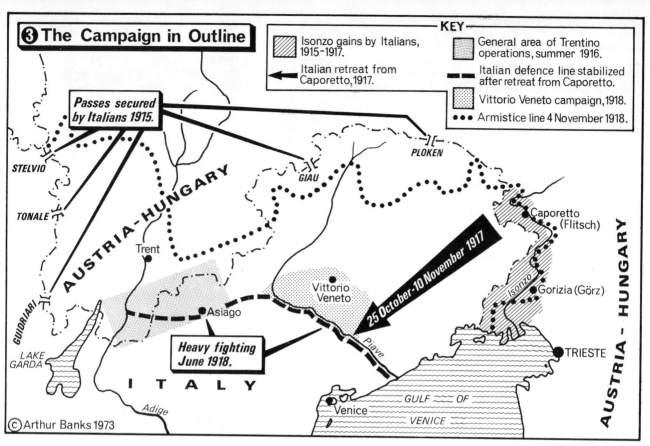

❸ The Campaign in Outline

KEY

- Isonzo gains by Italians, 1915-1917.
- Italian retreat from Caporetto, 1917.
- General area of Trentino operations, summer 1916.
- Italian defence line stabilized after retreat from Caporetto.
- Vittorio Veneto campaign, 1918.
- Armistice line 4 November 1918.

Passes secured by Italians 1915.

STELVIO

TONALE

GUIDRIARI

AUSTRIA-HUNGARY

Trent

GIAU

PLOKEN

Caporetto (Flitsch)

Isonzo

Gorizia (Görz)

25 October-10 November 1917

Vittorio Veneto

Asiago

Heavy fighting June 1918.

Piave

LAKE GARDA

ITALY

TRIESTE

AUSTRIA - HUNGARY

Adige

Venice

GULF — OF — VENICE

© Arthur Banks 1973

---

❹ The Eleven Isonzo Battles 1915-1917 *

* The Twelfth is generally known as **CAPORETTO**

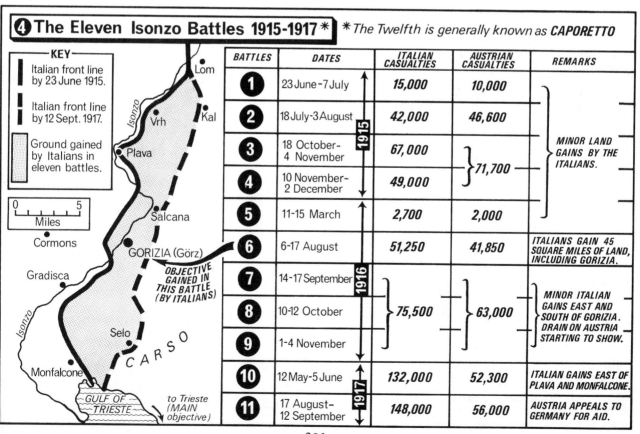

KEY

- Italian front line by 23 June 1915.
- Italian front line by 12 Sept. 1917.
- Ground gained by Italians in eleven battles.

0 — 5 Miles

Lom

Isonzo

Vrh

Kal

Plava

Salcana

Cormons

GORIZIA (Görz)

OBJECTIVE GAINED IN THIS BATTLE (BY ITALIANS)

Gradisca

Isonzo

Selo

CARSO

Monfalcone

GULF OF TRIESTE

to Trieste (MAIN objective)

BATTLES	DATES	ITALIAN CASUALTIES	AUSTRIAN CASUALTIES	REMARKS
❶	23 June-7 July	15,000	10,000	MINOR LAND GAINS BY THE ITALIANS.
❷	18 July-3 August	42,000	46,600	
❸	18 October-4 November	67,000	} 71,700	
❹	10 November-2 December	49,000		
❺	11-15 March	2,700	2,000	
❻	6-17 August	51,250	41,850	ITALIANS GAIN 45 SQUARE MILES OF LAND, INCLUDING GORIZIA.
❼	14-17 September	} 75,500	} 63,000	MINOR ITALIAN GAINS EAST AND SOUTH OF GORIZIA. DRAIN ON AUSTRIA STARTING TO SHOW.
❽	10-12 October			
❾	1-4 November			
❿	12 May-5 June	132,000	52,300	ITALIAN GAINS EAST OF PLAVA AND MONFALCONE.
⓫	17 August-12 September	148,000	56,000	AUSTRIA APPEALS TO GERMANY FOR AID.

(1915 / 1916 / 1917 marked along the date column)

THE ITALIAN FRONT – continued

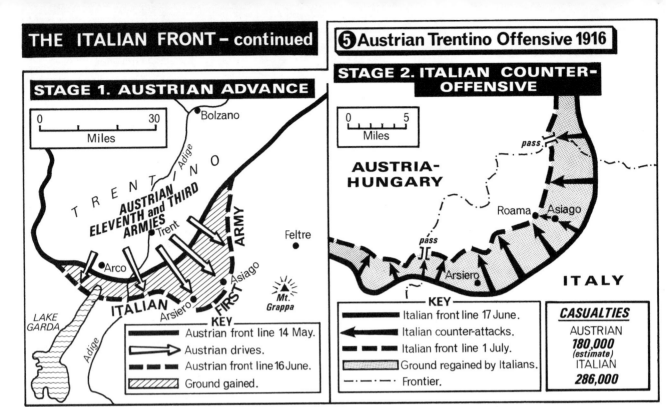

STAGE 1. AUSTRIAN ADVANCE

Bolzano

0 — 30 Miles

T R E N T I N O

Adige

AUSTRIAN ELEVENTH and THIRD ARMIES

Trent

Arco

FIRST ARMY

Feltre

Asiago

Arsiero

ITALIAN

Mt. Grappa

LAKE GARDA

Adige

KEY
— Austrian front line 14 May.
⇨ Austrian drives.
╾╾ Austrian front line 16 June.
▨ Ground gained.

⑤ Austrian Trentino Offensive 1916

STAGE 2. ITALIAN COUNTER-OFFENSIVE

0 — 5 Miles

AUSTRIA-HUNGARY

pass

Roama   Asiago

pass

Arsiero

ITALY

KEY
— Italian front line 17 June.
← Italian counter-attacks.
╾╾ Italian front line 1 July.
▨ Ground regained by Italians.
–·–· Frontier.

CASUALTIES
AUSTRIAN
180,000
(estimate)
ITALIAN
286,000

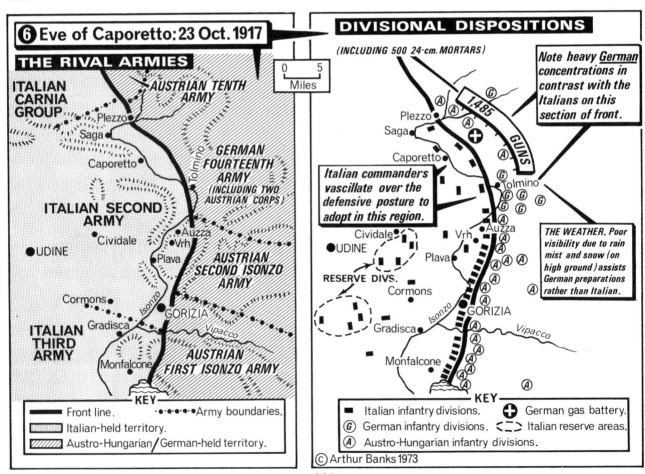

⑥ Eve of Caporetto: 23 Oct. 1917

THE RIVAL ARMIES

0 — 5 Miles

ITALIAN CARNIA GROUP

AUSTRIAN TENTH ARMY

Plezzo

Saga

Caporetto

GERMAN FOURTEENTH ARMY (INCLUDING TWO AUSTRIAN CORPS)

Tolmino

ITALIAN SECOND ARMY

Cividale

Auzza

Vrh

UDINE

Plava

AUSTRIAN SECOND ISONZO ARMY

Cormons

Isonzo

GORIZIA

Gradisca

Vipacco

ITALIAN THIRD ARMY

Monfalcone

AUSTRIAN FIRST ISONZO ARMY

KEY
— Front line.   ····· Army boundaries.
▨ Italian-held territory.
▧ Austro-Hungarian/German-held territory.

DIVISIONAL DISPOSITIONS

(INCLUDING 500 24-cm. MORTARS)

Note heavy German concentrations in contrast with the Italians on this section of front.

Plezzo

Saga

1485 GUNS

Caporetto

Tolmino

Italian commanders vascillate over the defensive posture to adopt in this region.

Cividale

UDINE

RESERVE DIVS.

Vrh

Auzza

Plava

Cormons

Gradisca

GORIZIA

Vipacco

THE WEATHER. Poor visibility due to rain mist and snow (on high ground) assists German preparations rather than Italian.

Monfalcone

KEY
■ Italian infantry divisions.   ✛ German gas battery.
Ⓖ German infantry divisions.   ⊂⊃ Italian reserve areas.
Ⓐ Austro-Hungarian infantry divisions.

© Arthur Banks 1973

❼ The Italian Retreat from Caporetto to the River Piave Position 1917

KEY

- ⬅️ Main German-led 'punch' attack 24 October 1917.
- ⬅️ Other attacks by Central Powers October 1917.
- ⬅️ Abortive attempt to intercept Italians.
- ••• Italian front line 23 October 1917.
- ⬅️ Italian retreat to the Piave 24 Oct.-10 Nov.1917.
- – – – Line where Italians attempted to stand.
- ▬▬ Final Italian defence line 10 November 1917.

The Germans and Austrians attacked on 24 October. A huge bombardment (including gas shells) preceded the infantry. The demoralized Italians fell back, tried to halt at the River Tagliamento, but were eventually pushed back to the Piave.

• Belluno

AUSTRIANS

31 Oct

November

12 Nov.

Caporetto

Isonzo

Italian G.H.Q.

🔲 • Cividale

• Udine 28 Oct.

9 *November, General Diaz replaces General Cadorna as Italian Chief of the General Staff. He implements the latter's defensive plans.*

31 Oct.

Piave

10 Nov.

5 Nov.

Livenza

7 Nov.

5 Nov.

31 Oct.

Tagliamento

• Gorizia

31 Oct.

FRENCH & BRITISH TROOPS ARRIVING TO AID ITALIANS.

7 Nov.

5 Nov.

7 Nov.

These Italians retreating to avoid being trapped.

0 — 15
Miles

---

❽ 1918 : Vittorio Veneto: The Armistice

0 ————— 50
Miles

KEY

- – – – Allied line 24 October 1918.
- ▒▒▒ Ground gained by Allies in late October.
- ▬▬ Armistice line 4 November 1918.
- –·–·– Frontier.

MAIN EVENTS

1 15-16 June, Battle of Asiago.

2 15-24 June, Battle of the Piave.

3 30 June, American infantry arrive in Italy.

4 24 October, Battle of Vittorio Veneto opens. British take Papadopoli.

5 27 October, Austria asks Italy for armistice.

6 2 November, Hungarians ordered to disarm.

7 3 November, armistice signed near Padua: takes effect 1500 hours 4 Nov.

SWITZ.

AUSTRIA - HUNGARY

• Glurns

• Bolzano

• Piave di Cadore

Piave

• Tolmezzo

• Caporetto

I T A L Y

• Trent

• Belluno

• Udine

• Vittorio Veneto

• Gorizia

• Asiago

Papadopoli Island

Piave

Heavy fighting in June 1918.

• Treviso

TRIESTE

LAKE GARDA

• Vicenza

• Verona

• Padua

• VENICE

3 November 1918, Italian landing party is received by the Yugoslav National Council which has taken over the port.

ⓒ Arthur Banks 1973

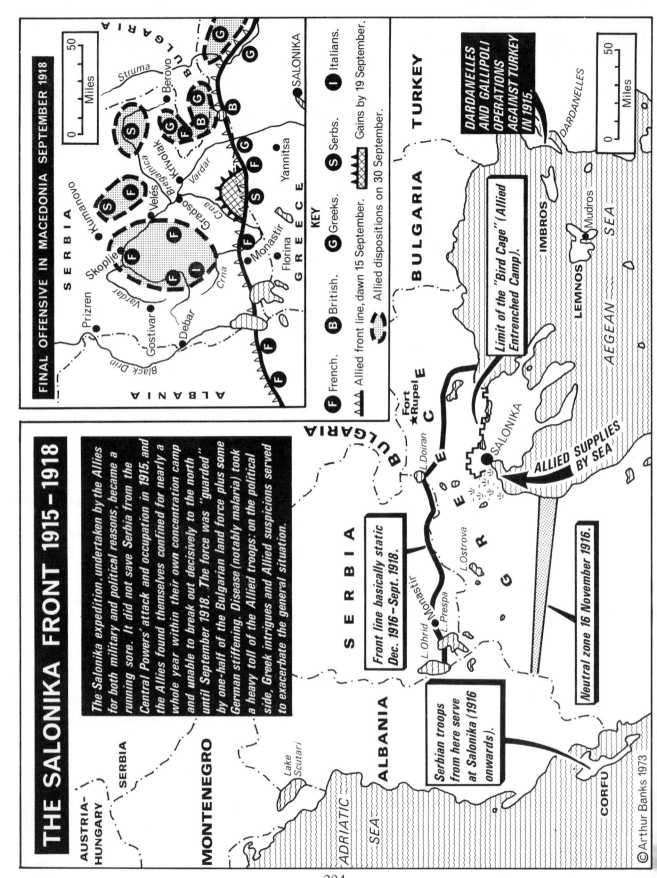

THE SALONIKA FRONT 1915–1918

The Salonika expedition, undertaken by the Allies for both military and political reasons, became a running sore. It did not save Serbia from the Central Powers' attack and occupation in 1915, and the Allies found themselves confined for nearly a whole year within their own concentration camp and unable to break out decisively to the north until September 1918. The force was "guarded" by one-half of the Bulgarian land force plus some German stiffening. Disease (notably malaria) took a heavy toll of the Allied troops: on the political side, Greek intrigues and Allied suspicions served to exacerbate the general situation.

AUSTRIA-HUNGARY

SERBIA

MONTENEGRO

Lake Scutari

ALBANIA

ADRIATIC SEA

CORFU

© Arthur Banks 1973

Serbian troops from here serve at Salonika (1916 onwards).

Front line basically static Dec. 1916 – Sept. 1918.

L. Ohrid
L. Prespa
Monastir
L. Ostrova
L. Doiran

SERBIA

GREECE

Neutral zone 16 November 1916.

Fort Rupel ★
E C E
E
R
G
E
θ

BULGARIA

Limit of the "Bird Cage" (Allied Entrenched Camp).

SALONIKA

ALLIED SUPPLIES BY SEA

DARDANELLES AND GALLIPOLI OPERATIONS AGAINST TURKEY IN 1915.

TURKEY

BULGARIA

IMBROS

LEMNOS

Mudros

DARDANELLES

AEGEAN SEA

FINAL OFFENSIVE IN MACEDONIA SEPTEMBER 1918

50 Miles
0

BULGARIA

Struma
Berovo
Krivolek
Bregalnica
Vardar
Vardar
Crna
Crna

SERBIA

Prizren
Gostivar
Debar
Black Drin
Skopje
Velés
Gradsko
Kumanovo

ALBANIA

GREECE

Monastir
Florina
Yannitsa
SALONIKA

KEY

F French.	**B** British.	**G** Greeks.	**S** Serbs.
	I Italians.		

△△△ Allied front line, dawn 15 September.

⟲ Gains by 19 September.

▨ Allied dispositions on 30 September.

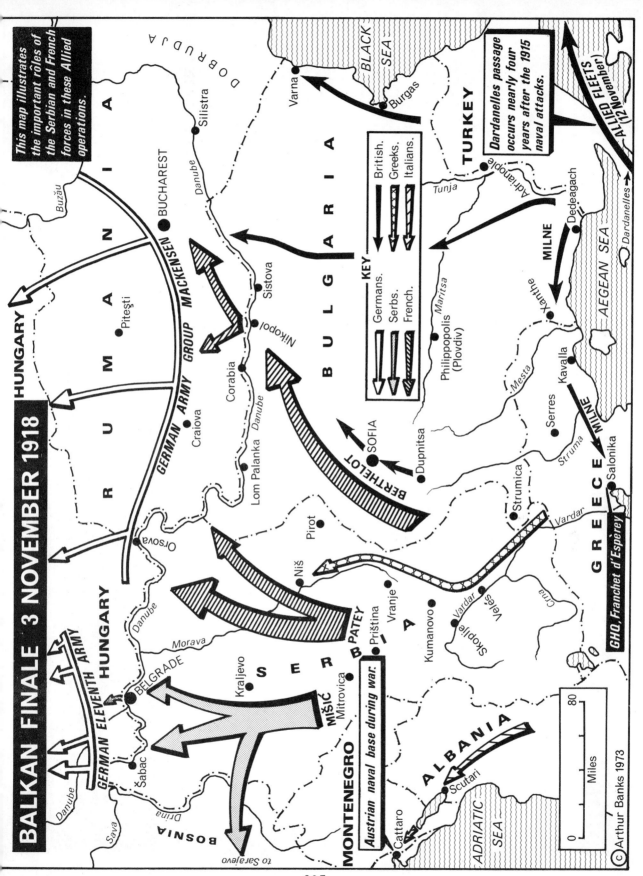

BALKAN FINALE 3 NOVEMBER 1918

This map illustrates the important rôles of the Serbian and French forces in these Allied operations.

Dardanelles passage occurs nearly four years after the 1915 naval attacks.

KEY

Germans.	Serbs.	French.
British.	Greeks.	Italians.

Austrian naval base during war.

GHQ, Franchet d'Espèrey

0 — 80 Miles

© Arthur Banks 1973

BLACK SEA
Varna
Burgas
DOBRUDJA
Silistra
BUCHAREST
Buzău
Piteşti
Craiova
Corabia
Nikopol
Sistova
Lom Palanka
Danube
RUMANIA
Orsova
HUNGARY
GERMAN ARMY GROUP MACKENSEN
BULGARIA
SOFIA
Dupnitsa
Pirot
Niš
Vranje
Kumanovo
Priština
Mitrovica
Kraljevo
BELGRADE
SERBIA
Morava
Danube
Šabac
Drina
Sava
BOSNIA
to Sarajevo
MONTENEGRO
Cattaro
ALBANIA
Scutari
ADRIATIC SEA
GERMAN ELEVENTH ARMY
MIŠIĆ
PATEY
BERTHELOT
Vardar
Veles
Skoplje
Crna
Strumica
Struma
Serres
Kavalla
Mesta
Philippopolis (Plovdiv)
Maritsa
Xanthe
Dedeagach
Adrianople
Tunja
TURKEY
MILNE
AEGEAN SEA
Dardanelles
GREECE
Salonika
ALLIED FLEETS (12 November)

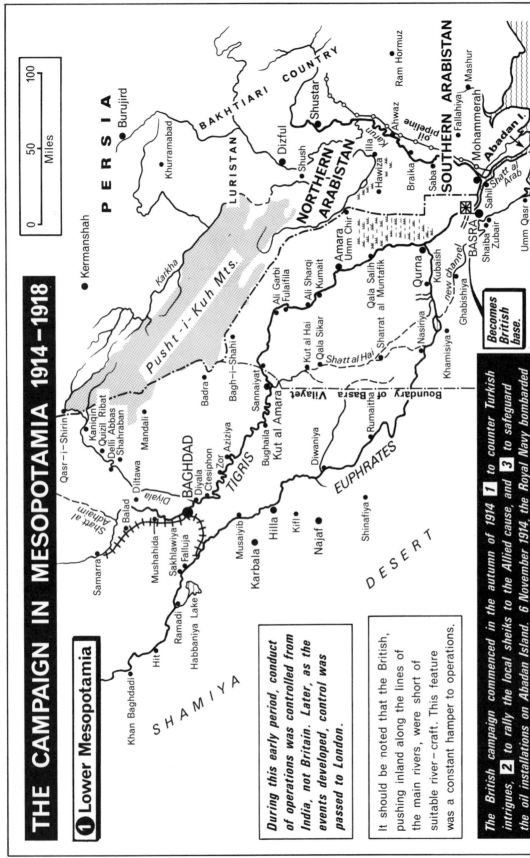

THE CAMPAIGN IN MESOPOTAMIA 1914–1918

① Lower Mesopotamia

During this early period, conduct of operations was controlled from India, not Britain. Later, as the events developed, control was passed to London.

It should be noted that the British, pushing inland along the lines of the main rivers, were short of suitable river-craft. This feature was a constant hamper to operations.

The British campaign commenced in the autumn of 1914 ① to counter Turkish intrigues, ② to rally the local sheiks to the Allied cause, and ③ to safeguard the oil installations on Abadan Island. 6 November 1914, the Royal Navy bombarded Fao and landed a small force. Despite some Turkish resistance, reinforcements (6th Indian Division) soon arrived and the Turks fell back (17 November). Pushing in-land, the Allies took Basra (22 November) and Qurna (9 December). In April 1915, Ahwaz was occupied to check any Turkish advance from the north-east (the oil pipeline was defended by local khans). Note: on map, "Shatt" means "river bank".

Becomes British base.

Boundary of Basra Vilayet

BRITISH ATTACK

© Arthur Banks 1973

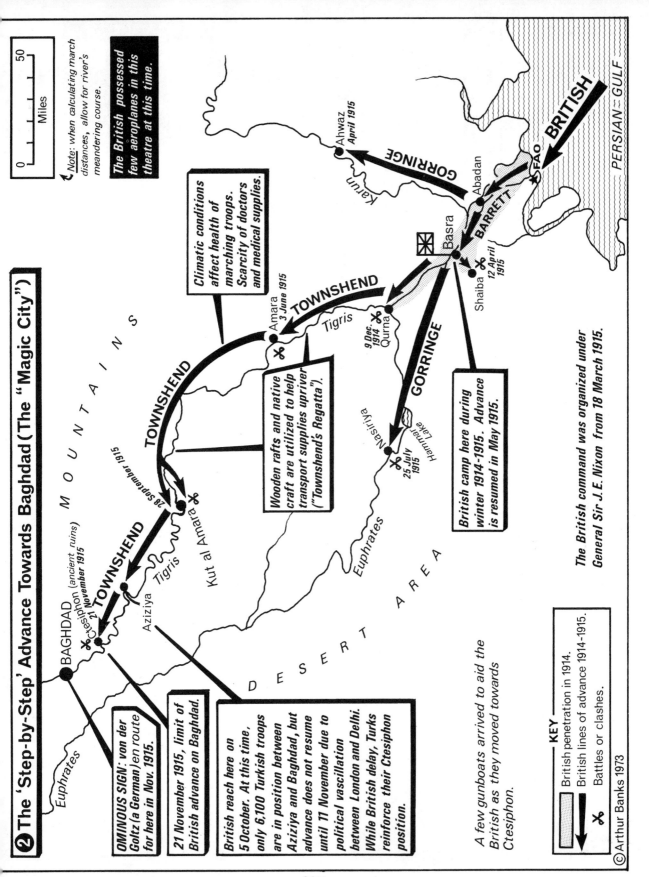

② The 'Step-by-Step' Advance Towards Baghdad (The "Magic City")

Note: when calculating march distances, allow for river's meandering course.

The British possessed few aeroplanes in this theatre at this time.

0 50 Miles

PERSIAN ~ GULF

BRITISH

GORRINGE

Ahwaz April 1915

Karun

Abadan

FAO

BARRETT

Basra

Shaiba 12 April 1915

Climatic conditions affect health of marching troops. Scarcity of doctors and medical supplies.

Amara 3 June 1915

TOWNSHEND

Tigris

9 Dec. 1914 Qurna

GORRINGE

TOWNSHEND

Wooden rafts and native craft are utilized to help transport supplies upriver ("Townshend's Regatta").

MOUNTAINS

Nasiriya

Hammar Lake

25 July 1915

British camp here during winter 1914-1915. Advance is resumed in May 1915.

28 September 1915

Kut al Amara

Tigris

Aziziya

Euphrates

DESERT AREA

BAGHDAD (ancient ruins)

Ctesiphon

21 November 1915

TOWNSHEND

OMINOUS SIGN: von der Goltz (a German) en route for here in Nov. 1915.

21 November 1915, limit of British advance on Baghdad.

British reach here on 5 October. At this time, only 6,100 Turkish troops are in position between Aziziya and Baghdad, but advance does not resume until 11 November due to political vascillation between London and Delhi. While British delay, Turks reinforce their Ctesiphon position.

Euphrates

A few gunboats arrived to aid the British as they moved towards Ctesiphon.

The British command was organized under General Sir J.E. Nixon from 18 March 1915.

KEY
British penetration in 1914.
British lines of advance 1914-1915.
Battles or clashes.

© Arthur Banks 1973

207

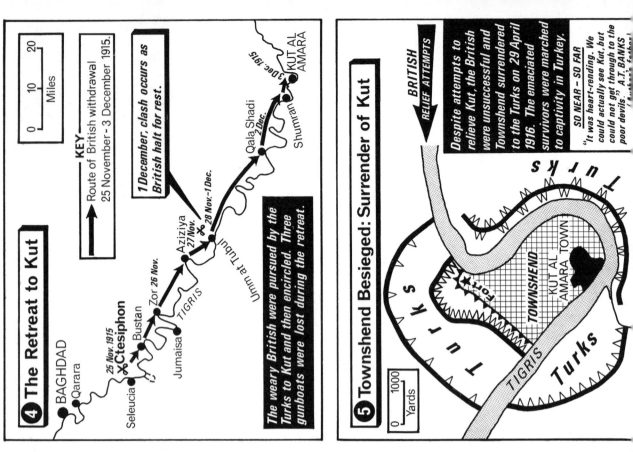

4 The Retreat to Kut

KEY

↑ Route of British withdrawal
25 November – 3 December 1915.

Miles 0 10 20

BAGHDAD
Qarara

25 Nov. 1915
✗Ctesiphon
Seleucia
Bustan
Jumaisa
Zor 26 Nov.
TIGRIS
Aziziya 27 Nov.
Umm at Tubul
28 Nov.–1 Dec.
Qala Shadi 2 Dec.
Shumran
3 Dec. 1915
KUT AL AMARA

1 December, clash occurs as British halt for rest.

The weary British were pursued by the Turks to Kut and then encircled. Three gunboats were lost during the retreat.

5 Townshend Besieged: Surrender of Kut

Turks
Turks
FORT
TOWNSHEND
KUT AL AMARA TOWN
TIGRIS

Yards 0 1000

BRITISH RELIEF ATTEMPTS

Despite attempts to relieve Kut, the British were unsuccessful and Townshend surrendered to the Turks on 29 April 1916. The emaciated survivors were marched to captivity in Turkey.

SO NEAR – SO FAR
"It was heart-rending. We could not see Kut, but could not get through to the poor devils." A.T. BANKS

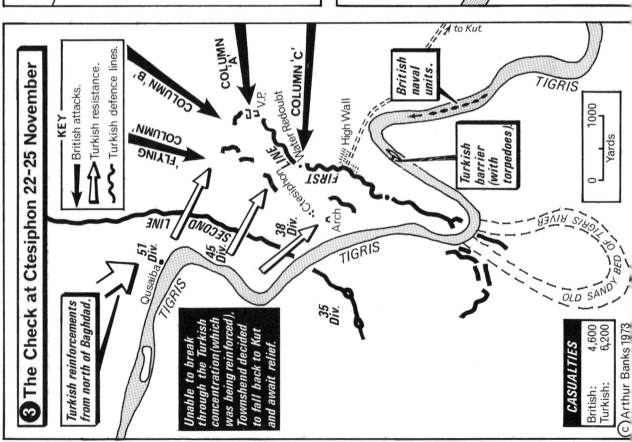

3 The Check at Ctesiphon 22–25 November

KEY

⬇ British attacks.
⬆ Turkish resistance.
〜 Turkish defence lines.

Turkish reinforcements from north of Baghdad.

COLUMN 'A'
COLUMN 'B'
COLUMN 'C'
'FLYING' COLUMN
V.P.
Water Redoubt
High Wall
Arch
FIRST Ctesiphon LINE
SECOND LINE
51 Div.
45 Div.
38 Div.
35 Div.
Qusaiba
TIGRIS
TIGRIS
OLD SANDY BED OF TIGRIS RIVER

British naval units.
TIGRIS

Turkish barrier (with torpedoes).

Yards 0 1000

to Kut

Unable to break through the Turkish concentration (which was being reinforced), Townshend decided to fall back to Kut and await relief.

CASUALTIES
British: 4,600
Turkish: 6,200

© Arthur Banks 1973

208

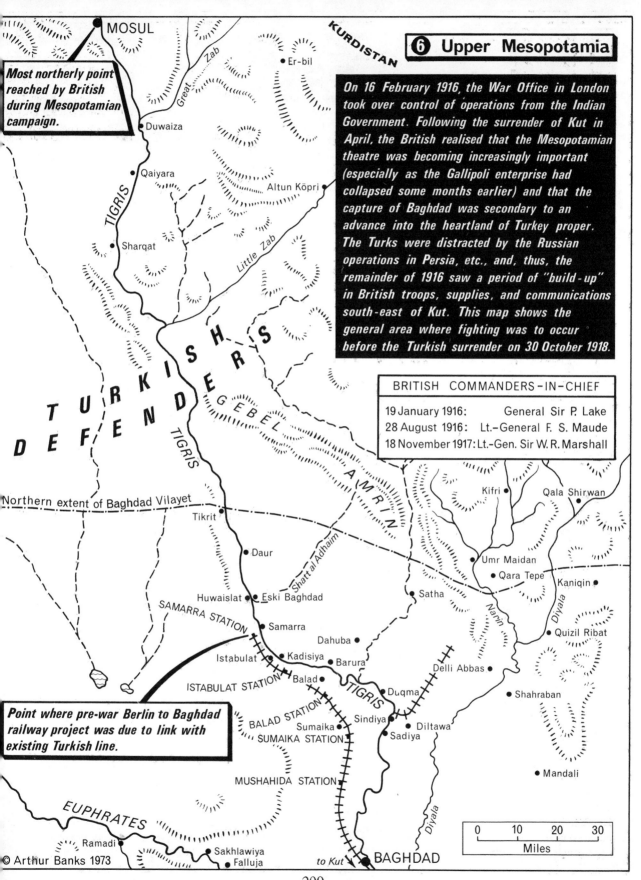

MOSUL

KURDISTAN

⑥ Upper Mesopotamia

Most northerly point reached by British during Mesopotamian campaign.

• Er-bil

Great Zab

• Duwaiza

• Qaiyara

Altun Köpri •

TIGRIS

• Sharqat

Little Zab

On 16 February 1916, the War Office in London took over control of operations from the Indian Government. Following the surrender of Kut in April, the British realised that the Mesopotamian theatre was becoming increasingly important (especially as the Gallipoli enterprise had collapsed some months earlier) and that the capture of Baghdad was secondary to an advance into the heartland of Turkey proper. The Turks were distracted by the Russian operations in Persia, etc., and, thus, the remainder of 1916 saw a period of "build-up" in British troops, supplies, and communications south-east of Kut. This map shows the general area where fighting was to occur before the Turkish surrender on 30 October 1918.

BRITISH COMMANDERS–IN–CHIEF

19 January 1916:   General Sir P. Lake
28 August 1916:   Lt.–General F. S. Maude
18 November 1917: Lt.–Gen. Sir W. R. Marshall

T U R K I S H

D E F E N D E R S

GEBEL

Kifri •

Qala Shirwan

AMRIN

TIGRIS

Northern extent of Baghdad Vilayet

• Tikrit

Umr Maidan •

• Qara Tepe

Kaniqin •

• Daur

Diyala

Shatt al Adhaim

• Satha

Huwaislat • Eski Baghdad

• Quizil Ribat

SAMARRA STATION

• Samarra

Dahuba •

Delli Abbas •

Istabulat

• Kadisiya

• Barura

• Shahraban

ISTABULAT STATION

Balad •

TIGRIS

• Duqma

Point where pre-war Berlin to Baghdad railway project was due to link with existing Turkish line.

BALAD STATION

Sumaika

Sindiya •

• Diltawa

SUMAIKA STATION

Sadiya

• Mandali

MUSHAHIDA STATION

EUPHRATES

Diyala

| 0 | 10 | 20 | 30 |

Miles

© Arthur Banks 1973

• Ramadi

• Sakhlawiya
• Falluja

to Kut

BAGHDAD

209

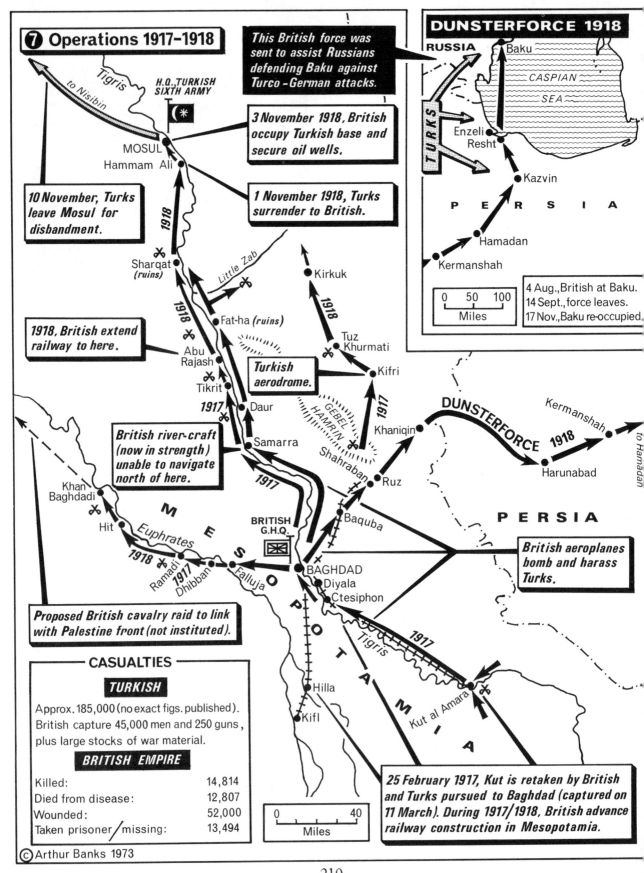

⑦ Operations 1917-1918

This British force was sent to assist Russians defending Baku against Turco-German attacks.

DUNSTERFORCE 1918

RUSSIA

CASPIAN SEA

TURKS

Baku

Enzeli
Resht

Kazvin

PERSIA

Hamadan

Kermanshah

| 0 | 50 | 100 |
Miles

4 Aug., British at Baku.
14 Sept., force leaves.
17 Nov., Baku re-occupied.

Tigris
to Nisibin

H.Q. TURKISH SIXTH ARMY

3 November 1918, British occupy Turkish base and secure oil wells.

MOSUL
Hammam Ali

10 November, Turks leave Mosul for disbandment.

1918

1 November 1918, Turks surrender to British.

Sharqat (ruins)

Little Zab

Kirkuk

1918

1918, British extend railway to here.

Fat-ha (ruins)

Tuz Khurmati

Abu Rajash

Turkish aerodrome.

Kifri

Tikrit

Daur

1917

1917

Samarra

Khaniqin

GEBEL HAMRIN

DUNSTERFORCE

Kermanshah

British river-craft (now in strength) unable to navigate north of here.

1917

Shahraban

Ruz

1918

Harunabad

to Hamadan

Khan Baghdadi

Hit

MESOPOTAMIA

Baquba

PERSIA

Euphrates

BRITISH G.H.Q.

British aeroplanes bomb and harass Turks.

1918

Ramadi
Dhibban

1917

Falluja

BAGHDAD
Diyala
Ctesiphon

Proposed British cavalry raid to link with Palestine front (not instituted).

Tigris

1917

Hilla

Kifl

Kut al Amara

CASUALTIES

TURKISH

Approx. 185,000 (no exact figs. published).
British capture 45,000 men and 250 guns, plus large stocks of war material.

BRITISH EMPIRE

Killed:	14,814
Died from disease:	12,807
Wounded:	52,000
Taken prisoner/missing:	13,494

© Arthur Banks 1973

| 0 | 40 |
Miles

25 February 1917, Kut is retaken by British and Turks pursued to Baghdad (captured on 11 March). During 1917/1918, British advance railway construction in Mesopotamia.

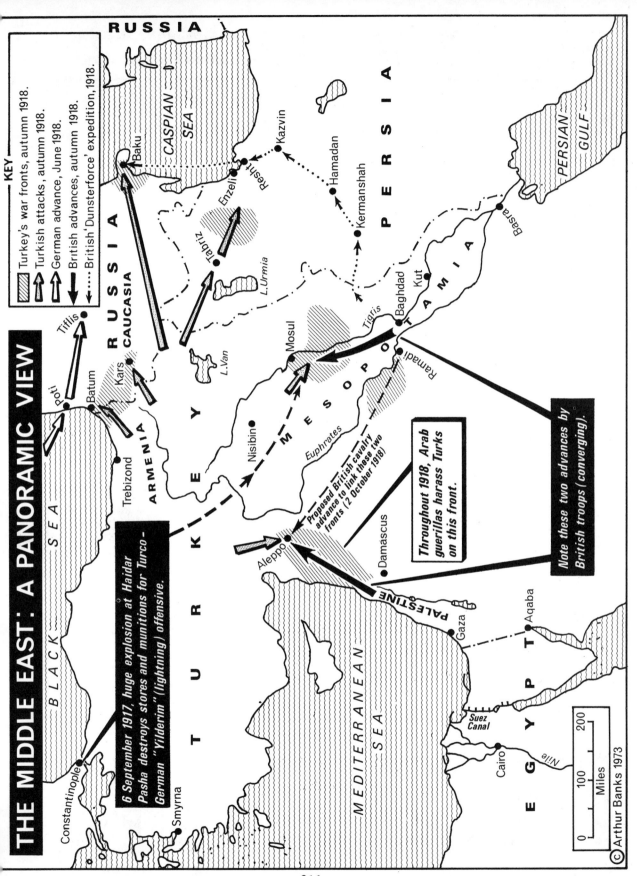

THE MIDDLE EAST: A PANORAMIC VIEW

KEY
- Turkey's war fronts, autumn 1918.
- Turkish attacks, autumn 1918.
- German advance, June 1918.
- British advances, autumn 1918.
- British 'Dunsterforce' expedition, 1918.

RUSSIA

CASPIAN SEA

PERSIA

PERSIAN GULF

Baku

Kazvin

Resht

Enzeli

Hamadan

Kermanshah

Tabriz

L. Urmia

Basra

RUSSIA

CAUCASIA

Tiflis

Mosul

Baghdad

Kut

Ramadi

Tigris

MESOPOTAMIA

Poti

Batum

Kars

ARMENIA

TURKEY

L. Van

Nisibin

Euphrates

Trebizond

Damascus

Proposed British cavalry advance to link these two fronts (2 October 1918)

Throughout 1918, Arab guerillas harass Turks on this front.

Note these two advances by British troops (converging).

Aleppo

PALESTINE

Gaza

Aqaba

EGYPT

6 September 1917, huge explosion at Haidar Pasha destroys stores and munitions for Turco–German "Yilderim" (lightning) offensive.

BLACK SEA

Constantinople

Smyrna

MEDITERRANEAN SEA

Suez Canal

Cairo

Nile

0   100   200
Miles

© Arthur Banks 1973

211

EGYPT, PALESTINE, AND THE ARAB REVOLT

The canal was opened in 1869.

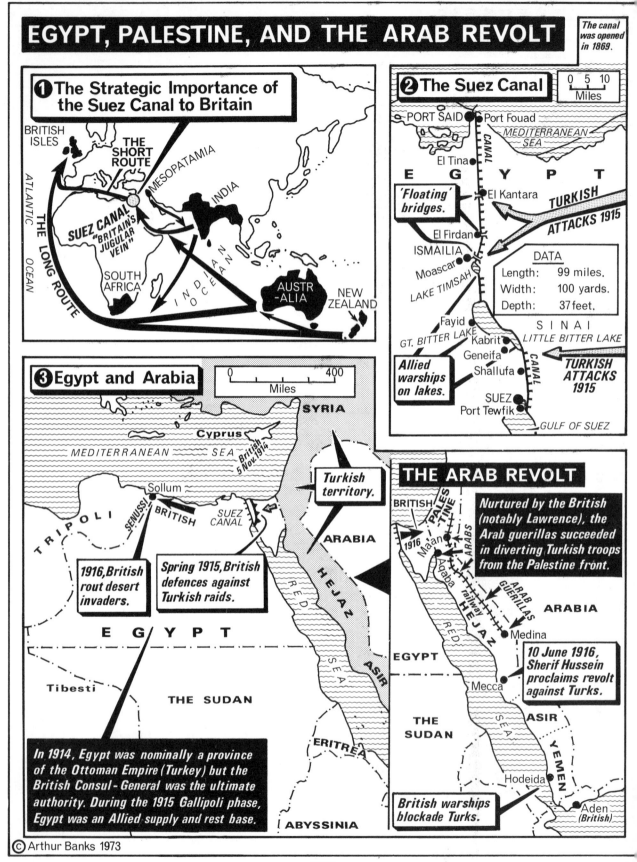

❶ The Strategic Importance of the Suez Canal to Britain

BRITISH ISLES
THE SHORT ROUTE
THE LONG ROUTE
ATLANTIC OCEAN
MESOPATAMIA
INDIA
SUEZ CANAL "BRITAIN'S JUGULAR VEIN"
SOUTH AFRICA
INDIAN OCEAN
AUSTR-ALIA
NEW ZEALAND

❷ The Suez Canal

0 5 10 Miles

PORT SAID — Port Fouad
MEDITERRANEAN SEA
El Tina
EGYPT
El Kantara
'Floating' bridges.
TURKISH ATTACKS 1915
El Firdan
ISMAILIA
Moascar
LAKE TIMSAH

DATA
Length: 99 miles.
Width: 100 yards.
Depth: 37 feet.

Fayid
GT. BITTER LAKE
Kabrit
Geneifa
Shallufa
Allied warships on lakes.
SINAI
LITTLE BITTER LAKE
CANAL
TURKISH ATTACKS 1915
SUEZ
Port Tewfik
GULF OF SUEZ

❸ Egypt and Arabia

0 400 Miles

SYRIA
Cyprus
MEDITERRANEAN SEA
British 5 Nov. 1914
Sollum
SENUSSI
BRITISH
SUEZ CANAL
Turkish territory.
ARABIA
TRIPOLI

1916, British rout desert invaders.

Spring 1915, British defences against Turkish raids.

EGYPT
RED SEA
HEJAZ
ASIR
Tibesti
THE SUDAN
ERITREA
ABYSSINIA

In 1914, Egypt was nominally a province of the Ottoman Empire (Turkey) but the British Consul-General was the ultimate authority. During the 1915 Gallipoli phase, Egypt was an Allied supply and rest base.

THE ARAB REVOLT

Nurtured by the British (notably Lawrence), the Arab guerillas succeeded in diverting Turkish troops from the Palestine front.

BRITISH
PALESTINE
1916
Ma'an
ARABS
Aqaba
ARAB GUERILLAS
railway
HEJAZ
ARABIA
Medina

10 June 1916, Sherif Hussein proclaims revolt against Turks.

EGYPT
Mecca
RED SEA
ASIR
THE SUDAN
YEMEN
Hodeida
Aden (British)

British warships blockade Turks.

© Arthur Banks 1973

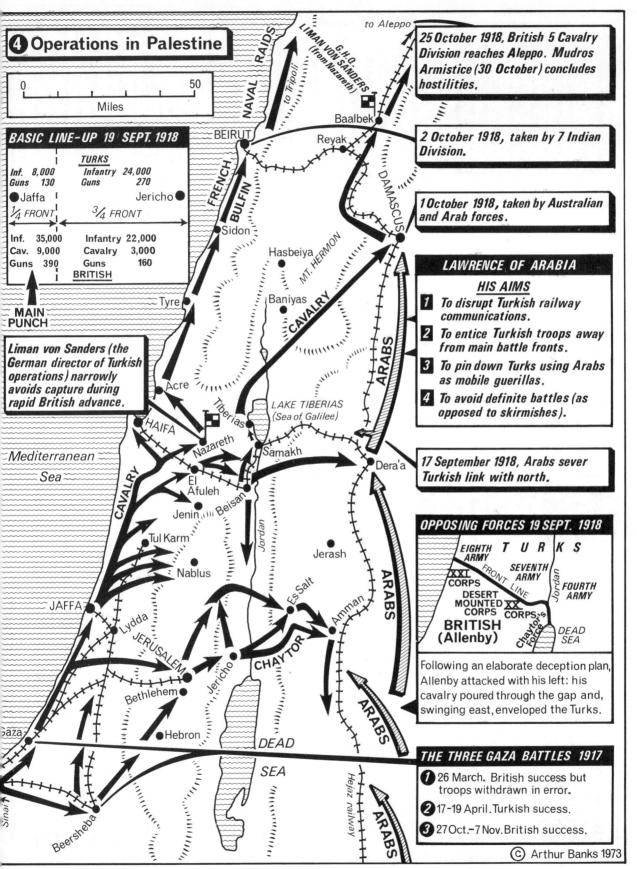

④ Operations in Palestine

Miles 0 — 50

BASIC LINE-UP 19 SEPT. 1918

TURKS
Inf. 8,000	Infantry 24,000
Guns 130	Guns 270
● Jaffa	Jericho ●

¼ FRONT | ¾ FRONT

Inf. 35,000	Infantry 22,000
Cav. 9,000	Cavalry 3,000
Guns 390	Guns 160

BRITISH

MAIN PUNCH

Liman von Sanders (the German director of Turkish operations) narrowly avoids capture during rapid British advance.

25 October 1918, British 5 Cavalry Division reaches Aleppo. Mudros Armistice (30 October) concludes hostilities.

2 October 1918, taken by 7 Indian Division.

1 October 1918, taken by Australian and Arab forces.

LAWRENCE OF ARABIA

HIS AIMS

1 To disrupt Turkish railway communications.

2 To entice Turkish troops away from main battle fronts.

3 To pin down Turks using Arabs as mobile guerillas.

4 To avoid definite battles (as opposed to skirmishes).

17 September 1918, Arabs sever Turkish link with north.

OPPOSING FORCES 19 SEPT. 1918

T U R K S

EIGHTH ARMY

SEVENTH ARMY

FOURTH ARMY

XXI CORPS

DESERT MOUNTED CORPS

XX CORPS

FRONT LINE

Chaytor's Force

DEAD SEA

BRITISH (Allenby)

Following an elaborate deception plan, Allenby attacked with his left: his cavalry poured through the gap and, swinging east, enveloped the Turks.

THE THREE GAZA BATTLES 1917

❶ 26 March. British success but troops withdrawn in error.

❷ 17-19 April. Turkish sucess.

❸ 27 Oct.-7 Nov. British success.

© Arthur Banks 1973

Map labels: to Aleppo, NAVAL RAIDS, to Tripoli, G.H.Q. LIMAN VON SANDERS (from Nazareth), Baalbek, Reyak, BEIRUT, DAMASCUS, FRENCH, BULFIN, Sidon, Hasbeiya, MT. HERMON, Baniyas, CAVALRY, ARABS, Tyre, Acre, Tiberias, LAKE TIBERIAS (Sea of Galilee), HAIFA, Nazareth, Samakh, Dera'a, Mediterranean Sea, CAVALRY, El Afuleh, Jenin, Beisan, Jordan, Jerash, Tul Karm, Nablus, ARABS, JAFFA, Es Salt, Amman, Lydda, JERUSALEM, CHAYTOR, ARABS, Bethlehem, Jericho, Hebron, DEAD SEA, Hejaz railway, Gaza, Sinai, Beersheba, ARABS

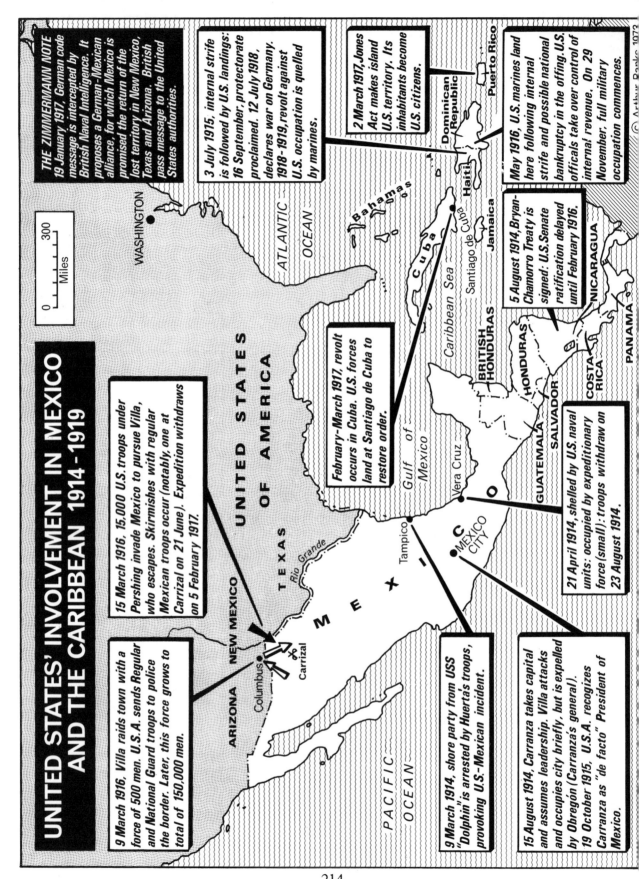

UNITED STATES' INVOLVEMENT IN MEXICO AND THE CARIBBEAN 1914-1919

THE ZIMMERMANN NOTE 19 January, 1917, German code message is intercepted by British Naval Intelligence. It proposes a German-Mexican alliance, for which Mexico is promised the return of the lost territory in New Mexico, Texas and Arizona. British pass message to the United States authorities.

9 March 1916, Villa raids town with a force of 500 men. U.S.A. sends Regular and National Guard troops to police the border. Later, this force grows to total of 150,000 men.

15 March 1916, 15,000 U.S. troops under Pershing invade Mexico to pursue Villa, who escapes. Skirmishes with regular Mexican troops occur (notably one at Carrizal on 21 June). Expedition withdraws on 5 February 1917.

9 March 1914, shore party from USS "Dolphin" is arrested by Huerta's troops, provoking U.S.-Mexican incident.

15 August 1914, Carranza takes capital and assumes leadership. Villa attacks and occupies city briefly, but is expelled by Obregón (Carranza's general). 19 October 1915, U.S.A. recognizes Carranza as "de facto" President of Mexico.

21 April 1914, shelled by U.S. naval units: occupied by expeditionary force (small): troops withdraw on 23 August 1914.

February–March 1917, revolt occurs in Cuba. U.S. forces land at Santiago de Cuba to restore order.

3 July 1915, internal strife is followed by U.S. landings: 16 September, protectorate proclaimed. 12 July 1918, declares war on Germany. 1918-1919, revolt against U.S. occupation is quelled by marines.

2 March 1917, Jones Act makes island U.S. territory. Its inhabitants become U.S. citizens.

May 1916, U.S. marines land here following internal strife and possible national bankruptcy in the offing. U.S. officials take over control of internal revenue. On 29 November, full military occupation commences.

5 August 1914, Bryan-Chamorro Treaty is signed: U.S. Senate ratification delayed until February 1916.

WASHINGTON

ATLANTIC OCEAN

PACIFIC OCEAN

UNITED STATES OF AMERICA

ARIZONA   NEW MEXICO   TEXAS

Rio Grande

Columbus   Carrizal

MEXICO

MEXICO CITY

Tampico

Vera Cruz

Gulf of Mexico

Bahamas

Cuba

Santiago de Cuba   Haiti

Jamaica

Caribbean Sea

Dominican Republic

Puerto Rico

BRITISH HONDURAS

GUATEMALA

HONDURAS

SALVADOR

NICARAGUA

COSTA RICA

PANAMA

0   300
Miles

© Arthur Banks 1973

SOUTH AMERICA 1914-1918

KEY

- ■ At war against the Central Powers 1917-1918.
- □ Neutral states.
- ▨ British territory.
- ▧ French territory.
- ⇨ Track of SMS 'Dresden' from 8 December 1914 to 14 March 1915.

0 — 500 Miles

Panama Canal

VENEZUELA

DUTCH GUIANA

BRITISH GUIANA

FRENCH GUIANA

COLOMBIA

ECUADOR

PERU

B R A Z I L

April 1917, the 'Paraná' is sunk by a German submarine.
11 April 1917, Brazil severs her relations with Germany and on 1 June 1917, revokes neutrality in favour of the Allies.
26 October 1917, Brazil declares war upon the Central Powers.

1914, revolt led by Benavides ends in the overthrow of President Billinghurst. Pardo is president from 1914 to 1919; breaks off diplomatic relations with Germany in 1917.

BOLIVIA

PACIFIC OCEAN

ATLANTIC OCEAN

PARAGUAY

14 March 1915, SMS 'Dresden' is destroyed following action with HMS 'Glasgow' and 'Kent'.

Juan Fernandez Islands

Coronel

URUGUAY

Buenos Aires

1917, three Argentinian ships are sunk by German submarines. After secret diplomatic exchanges, the German minister is withdrawn from Buenos Aires.

1 November 1914, naval battle.

C H I L E

A R G E N T I N A

HUNTED BY BRITISH WARSHIPS

German cruiser SMS 'Dresden' is the sole survivor from the Falkland Islands naval battle.

'Dresden' hides in this area from 11 December 1914 to 8 February 1915.

Falkland Islands

8 December 1914, naval battle.

Brazil was the sole Latin American state at war with the Central Powers. In 1918, a Brazilian squadron served for nine months with the Allies off the African coast, and on 10 November 1918, Brazilian warships entered the Mediterranean Sea for further duty with the Allies.

© Arthur Banks 1973

215

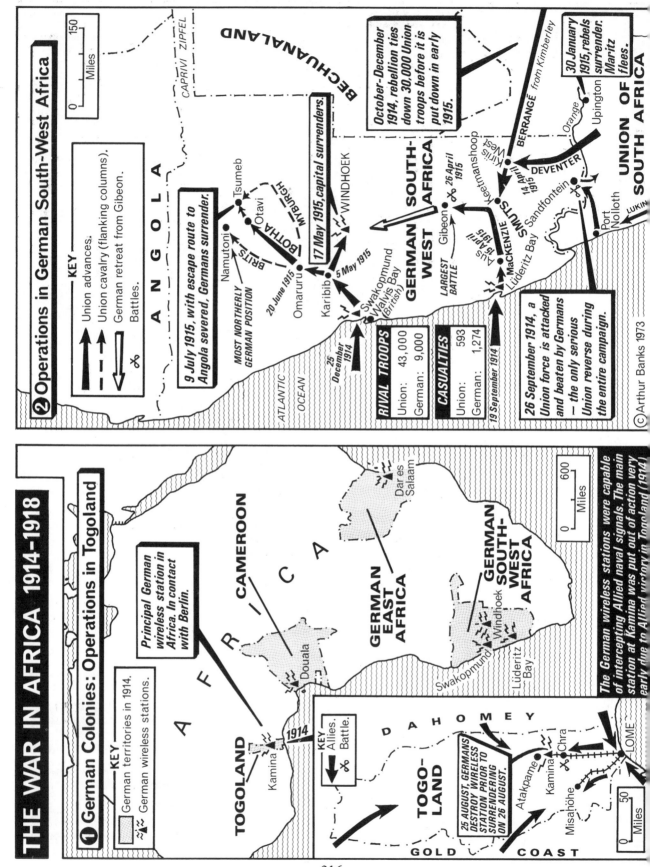

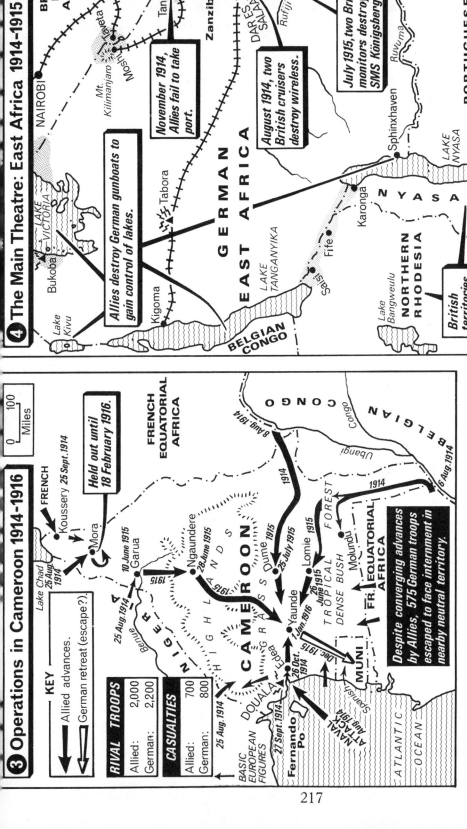

④ Operations in Cameroon 1914–1916

KEY
→ Allied advances.
⇨ German retreat (escape?).

RIVAL TROOPS
Allied: 2,000
German: 2,200

CASUALTIES
Allied: 700
German: 800

BASIC EUROPEAN FIGURES

FRENCH Koussery 25 Sept. 1914

Held out until 18 February 1916.

FRENCH EQUATORIAL AFRICA

Lake Chad
Mora
Garua 10 June 1915
25 Aug. 1914
Benue 1915
Ngaundere 28 June 1915
N I G E R I A
G R A S S L A N D S
Dume 25 July 1915
H I G H L A N D S
Lomie 1915
Yaunde 26 June 1915
C A M E R O O N
Edea 1 Jan. 1916
DOUALA 26 Oct. 1914 Dec. 1915
Molundu
TROPICAL DENSE BUSH
EQUATORIAL FOREST
FR. EQUATORIAL AFRICA
MUNI
Fernando Po
NAVAL ATTACK Aug. 1914
27 Sept. 1914
Spanish
25 Aug. 1914
ATLANTIC OCEAN

8 Aug. 1914
6 Aug. 1914
Ubangi
Congo
B E L G I A N   C O N G O

Despite converging advances by Allies, 575 German troops escaped to face internment in nearby neutral territory.

0 ———— 100 Miles

---

④ The Main Theatre: East Africa 1914–1915

ALLIED NAVAL BLOCKADE

BRITISH EAST AFRICA
Mombasa
Gazi
Tanga
Taveta
Moshi
Mt. Kilimanjaro
NAIROBI

November 1914, Allies fail to take port.

Zanzibar
DAR ES SALAAM
Rufiji

August 1914, two British cruisers destroy wireless.

July 1915, two British monitors destroy SMS Königsberg.

Ruvuma
INDIAN OCEAN
MOZAMBIQUE
PORTUGUESE EAST AFRICA

G E R M A N   E A S T   A F R I C A

Tabora
LAKE VICTORIA
Bukoba
Lake Kivu
Kigoma
LAKE TANGANYIKA
BELGIAN CONGO

Allies destroy German gunboats to gain control of lakes.

Saisi
Fife
Karonga
LAKE NYASA
Sphinxhaven
N Y A S A L A N D
ZOMBA
Lake Chilwa
Blantyre
Lake Bangweulu
NORTHERN RHODESIA

British territories.

KEY
▨ Areas where fighting occurred.
⚡ Wireless stations.

0 ——— 150 Miles

© Arthur Banks 1973

SMS 'KÖNIGSBERG'

The German light cruiser 'Königsberg' sank HMS 'Pegasus' in Zanzibar harbour in September 1914 but later was blockaded in the Rufiji river. She was destroyed on 11 July 1915 after an action with British monitors and two aircraft, but her guns were salvaged and used by the Germans in east Africa.

217

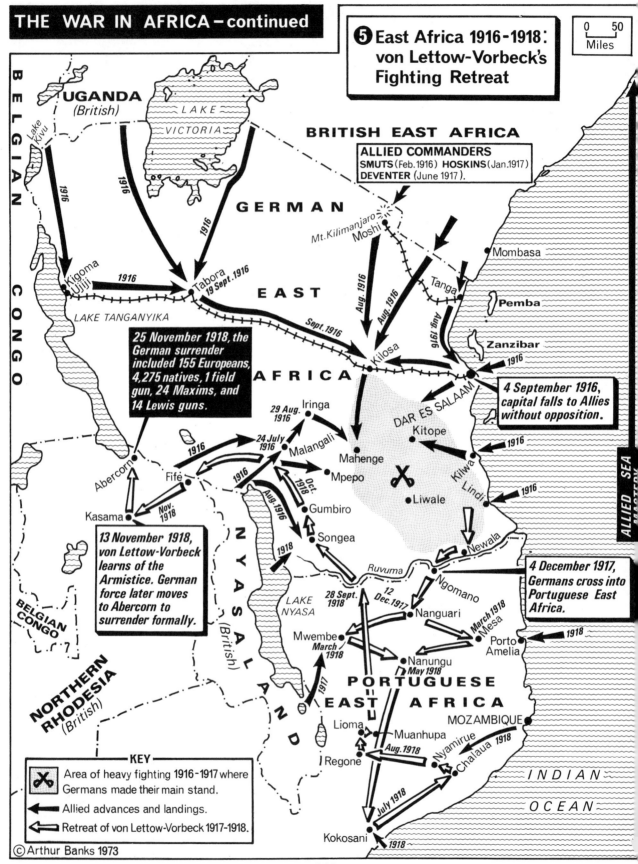

THE WAR IN AFRICA – continued

⑤ East Africa 1916-1918: von Lettow-Vorbeck's Fighting Retreat

0   50
Miles

UGANDA
(British)

LAKE VICTORIA

BRITISH EAST AFRICA

ALLIED COMMANDERS
SMUTS (Feb.1916) HOSKINS (Jan.1917)
DEVENTER (June 1917).

GERMAN

Mt.Kilimanjaro Moshi

Mombasa

B E L G I A N   C O N G O

Lake Kivu

1916

1916

1916

Kigoma Ujiji

1916

Tabora
19 Sept. 1916

E A S T

Aug.1916

Aug.1916

Aug.1916

Tanga

Pemba

LAKE TANGANYIKA

Sept. 1916

Zanzibar

1916

25 November 1918, the German surrender included 155 Europeans, 4,275 natives, 1 field gun, 24 Maxims, and 14 Lewis guns.

A F R I C A

Kilosa

DAR ES SALAAM

4 September 1916, capital falls to Allies without opposition.

Kitope

29 Aug. 1916   Iringa

1916

24 July 1916   Malangali

Mahenge

Mpepo

Oct. 1918

1916

Abercorn

Fife

1916

Aug. 1916

Gumbiro

Songea

Liwale

Kilwa

Lindi

1916

1916

Kasama

Nov. 1918

13 November 1918, von Lettow-Vorbeck learns of the Armistice. German force later moves to Abercorn to surrender formally.

1918

N Y A S A L A N D
(British)

LAKE NYASA

28 Sept. 1918

12 Dec. 1917

Ruvuma

Ngomano

Newala

4 December 1917, Germans cross into Portuguese East Africa.

Nanguari

March 1918   Mesa

Porto Amelia

1918

BELGIAN CONGO

NORTHERN RHODESIA
(British)

1917

Mwembe
March 1918

Nanungu
May 1918

P O R T U G U E S E   E A S T   A F R I C A

MOZAMBIQUE

Lioma   Muanhupa

Regone

Aug. 1918

Nyamirue   Chalaua   1918

I N D I A N

O C E A N

─── **KEY** ───

✂ Area of heavy fighting 1916-1917 where Germans made their main stand.

◀ Allied advances and landings.

◁ Retreat of von Lettow-Vorbeck 1917-1918.

July 1918

Kokosani   1918

© Arthur Banks 1973

ALLIED SEA BLOCKADE

WEAPONS

During the half century preceding the First World War military science had taken note of technological developments but had not appreciated the extent to which they revolutionised traditional concepts of warfare. French infantrymen armed with the *chassepot* breech-loading rifle had wrought havoc with the German attackers in 1870 and convinced military authorities that rifles would henceforth strengthen the defensive position of troops, especially if they were also supported by artillery. But because the original French machine guns —the *mitrailleuses*—of 1870 had proved ineffectual, the potentialities of this weapon were ignored. The trench fighting of the Russo-Japanese War (1905–1905) should have awakened an interest in the machine gun, for Maxim's water-cooled weapon of 1884, firing 2,000 rounds in three minutes, was very different from the prototypes of the Franco-Prussian campaign; and it was eventually the German Maxim which proved so terribly effective on the first day of the Somme (compare pages 152–153 and page 224). Without well-sited machine guns and barbed-wire entanglements, there would have been no war of stalemate on the Western Front.

At first it was assumed that mobility could be restored to warfare by artillery power. This, at least, had been a lesson of the Russo-Japanese War, and in the ten years before Sarajevo much attention was given to the development of howitzers, the heaviest models being used to reduce the Belgian fortifications in 1914 (pages 33 and 62). The most effective field gun was the French 75-mm (page 33), with a buffer recoil system which allowed a fire rate of 20/30 rounds a minute. By contrast, the British 18-pounder had a rate of fire of only 8 rounds a minute, and this was faster than the best German and Austrian guns. During the First World War three-quarters of the wounds caused by guns came from shells, high explosive or shrapnel, rather from bullets.

The experience of the long barrages used as preparation for offensives in 1915 showed that artillery was a less decisive weapon in the field than the experts had anticipated. Concrete pill-boxes stood up against most normal field artillery, while the barrages ruled out all element of surprise and made soft ground impassable to heavily encumbered infantry. It was partly to overcome these problems that petrol driven armoured vehicles with caterpillar tracks were introduced, first as 'tanks' in the British army and then into the armies of other countries. No commander, however, felt sufficiently confident to develop the tank as a revolutionary weapon in its own right. On the Somme in 1916 tanks suffered as much as infantry from shell craters, and at Cambrai in 1917 (page 174) no attempt was made to follow penetration by exploitation with vehicles mounted on caterpillar tracks. Moreover, although use was made of armoured cars, lorries (notably at Verdun), and the famous Paris taxis (page 55), the value of the internal combustion engine was only slowly perceived.

This hardly is surprising: military minds did not rapidly assimilate the changed patterns of daily life. Thus, although the transport of armies by rail from one war zone to another dates from 1862–1863 (both Confederate and Union forces in the American Civil War), it was not until the outbreak of the First World War that the smooth running of a railway transport system was recognised as an essential prerequisite for offensive operations. General Groener, who succeeded Ludendorff as virtual field commander in the last days of the War, was the first military leader to have 'graduated' as a railway specialist.

By contrast, trench warfare brought new forms of old weapons: clubs, knives, canisters of burning oil, pistols and revolvers. The greatest innovations of all, however, were in the skies and under the waves.

British 4·5-inch howitzer

Length of gun (overall):	13 feet, 6 inches.
Weight of gun in action:	3,004 pounds.
Range:	7,000 yards.
Elevation:	–5 to +45 degs.
Barrel length:	13·33 calibres.
Weight of shell:	35 pounds.
Muzzle velocity:	1,010 ft./sec.
Rate of fire:	4 rds. per min.

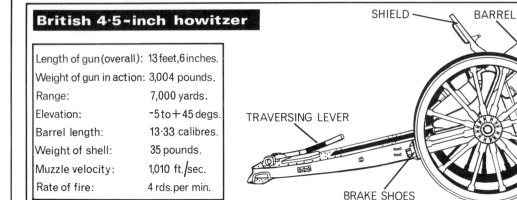

SHIELD BARREL

RECOIL MECHANISM

TRAVERSING LEVER

BRAKE SHOES

British 60-pounder field gun

Length of gun (overall):	21 feet, 7 inches.
Weight of gun in action:	11,705 pounds.
Range:	10,300 yards.
Elevation:	21°30′.
Barrel length:	33·61 calibres.
Weight of shell:	60 pounds.
Muzzle velocity:	2,149 ft./sec.
Rate of fire:	2 rds. per min.
Traverse:	4° left/4° right.
Calibre:	5 inches.

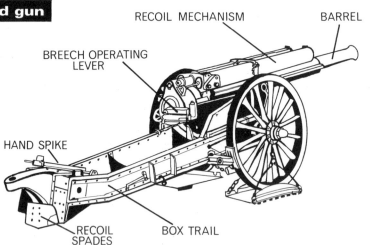

RECOIL MECHANISM BARREL

BREECH OPERATING LEVER

HAND SPIKE

RECOIL SPADES BOX TRAIL

British 9·2-inch (Mark I) howitzer

Length of gun (overall):	11 feet, 15 inches.
Weight of gun in action:	25,906 pounds.
Range:	10,000 yards.
Elevation:	55°.
Barrel length:	14·5 calibres.
Weight of shell:	290 pounds.
Muzzle velocity:	1,187 ft./sec.
Rate of fire:	2 rds. per min.
Traverse:	30° left/30° right.
Height:	8 feet, 6 inches.

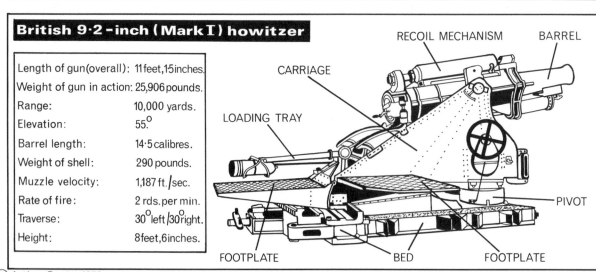

RECOIL MECHANISM BARREL

CARRIAGE

LOADING TRAY

PIVOT

FOOTPLATE BED FOOTPLATE

German 10·5-cm. howitzer 1916

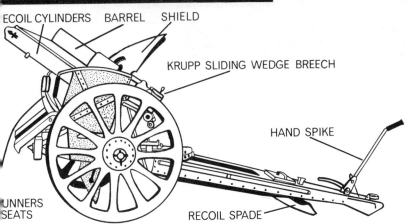

RECOIL CYLINDERS   BARREL   SHIELD

KRUPP SLIDING WEDGE BREECH

HAND SPIKE

GUNNERS SEATS

RECOIL SPADE

Length of gun (overall):	12 feet.
Weight of gun in action:	3,036 pounds.
Range:	6,250 yards.
Elevation:	$40°$
Barrel length:	22 calibres.
Weight of shell:	34·5 pounds.
Muzzle velocity:	1,400 ft./sec.
Rate of fire:	4 rds. per min.
Traverse:	$4°$ left/$4°$ right.

(note: unusual nine increment cartridge).

German 13-cm. (Model 1913) field gun

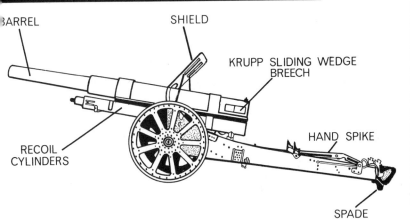

BARREL   SHIELD

KRUPP SLIDING WEDGE BREECH

HAND SPIKE

RECOIL CYLINDERS

SPADE

Length of gun (overall):	22 feet.
Weight of gun in action:	12,768 pounds.
Range:	15,750 yards.
Elevation:	$26°$
Barrel length:	35 calibres.
Weight of shell:	89 pounds.
Muzzle velocity:	2,280 ft./sec.
Rate of fire:	2 rds. per min.
Traverse:	$2°$ left/$2°$ right.

(note: shrapnel shell contains 1,170 lead bullets).

German 21-cm. "mörser"

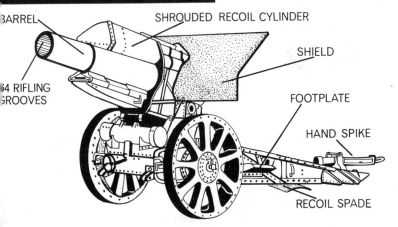

BARREL   SHROUDED RECOIL CYLINDER

SHIELD

64 RIFLING GROOVES

FOOTPLATE

HAND SPIKE

RECOIL SPADE

Length of gun (overall):	20 feet.
Weight of gun in action:	9,828 pounds.
Range:	10,280 yards.
Elevation:	$70°$
Barrel length:	12 calibres.
Weight of shell:	184 pounds.
Muzzle velocity:	1,203 ft./sec.
Rate of fire:	2 rds. per min.
Traverse:	$2°$ left/$2°$ right.

(note: H.E. shell contains 17 pounds of amatol).

TWELVE IMPORTANT ARTILLERY WEAPONS–continued

French 155-mm. Grande Puissance Filloux gun

Length of gun (overall):	29 feet, 7 inches.
Weight of gun in action:	24,640 pounds.
Range:	19,650 yards.
Elevation:	35°.
Barrel length:	38·2 calibres.
Weight of shell:	97 pounds.
Muzzle velocity:	2,339 ft./sec.
Rate of fire:	2 rds. per min.

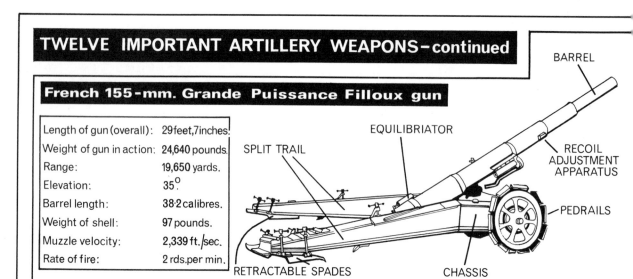

BARREL

EQUILIBRIATOR

SPLIT TRAIL

RECOIL ADJUSTMENT APPARATUS

PEDRAILS

RETRACTABLE SPADES

CHASSIS

British 18-pounder (Mark I) field gun

Length of gun (overall):	13 feet, 8 inches.
Weight of gun in action:	2,904 pounds.
Range:	7,000 yards.
Calibre:	3·3 inches.
Elevation:	−5 to +6 degs.
Barrel length:	28 calibres.
Weight of shell:	18 pounds.
Muzzle velocity:	1,614 ft./sec.
Rate of fire:	8 rds. per min.

(note: developed from the lessons of the Boer War).

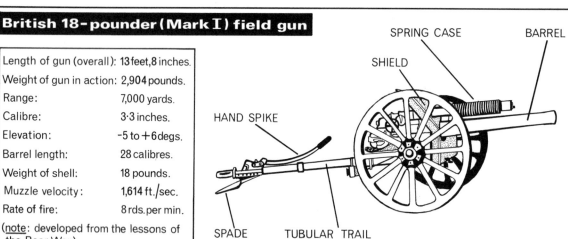

SPRING CASE

BARREL

SHIELD

HAND SPIKE

SPADE

TUBULAR TRAIL

British 12-inch (Mark III) railway howitzer

Length of mounting:	41 feet, 3 inches.
Weight of gun in action:	76 tons.
Range:	14,300 yards.
Elevation:	40°.
Barrel length:	17·3 calibres.
Weight of shell:	750 pounds.
Muzzle velocity:	1,474 ft./sec.
Rate of fire:	1 rd. per min.
Traverse:	5° left/5° right.

(note: most used British railway howitzer).

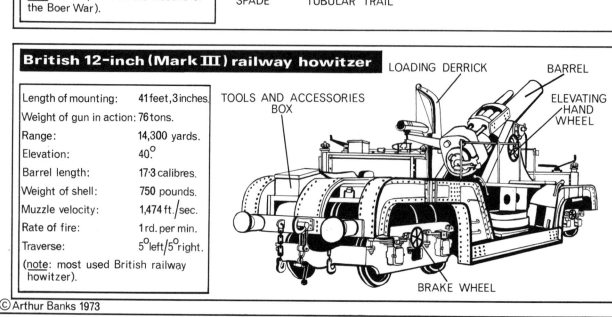

LOADING DERRICK

BARREL

ELEVATING HAND WHEEL

TOOLS AND ACCESSORIES BOX

BRAKE WHEEL

German 10-cm. (Model 1917) field gun

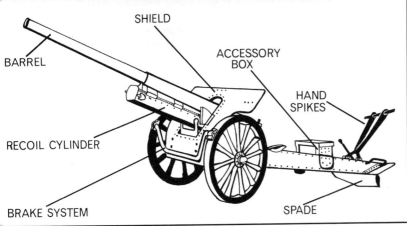

BARREL

SHIELD

ACCESSORY BOX

HAND SPIKES

RECOIL CYLINDER

BRAKE SYSTEM

SPADE

Length of gun(overall):	20 feet.
Weight of gun in action:	6,104 pounds.
Range:	12,085 yards.
Elevation:	-5 to +30 degs.
Barrel length:	35 calibres.
Weight of shell:	39·5 pounds.
Muzzle velocity:	1,923 ft./sec.
Rate of fire:	2 rds. per min.
Traverse:	2°left/2°right.

(note: smallest high-velocity gun in field use during 1914-1918 war).

Austrian 10·4-cm. field gun M.14

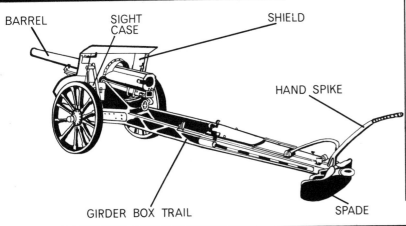

BARREL

SIGHT CASE

SHIELD

HAND SPIKE

GIRDER BOX TRAIL

SPADE

Length of gun(overall):	14 feet.
Weight of gun in action:	5,040 pounds.
Range:	13,670 yards.
Elevation:	-10 to +30 degs.
Barrel length:	35 calibres.
Weight of shell:	38·5 pounds.
Muzzle velocity:	2,230 ft./sec.
Rate of fire:	4 rds. per min.
Traverse:	3°left/3°right.

(note: first Austrian steel field gun: previous guns were bronze).

French 370-mm. mortar

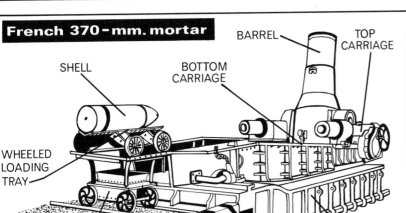

BARREL

TOP CARRIAGE

SHELL

BOTTOM CARRIAGE

WHEELED LOADING TRAY

AMMUNITION TRUCK

BED

Length of gun:	13 feet.
Weight of gun in action:	30 tons.
Range:	8,820 yards.
Elevation:	60°.
Barrel length:	8 calibres.
Weight of shell:	1,076 pounds.
Muzzle velocity:	1,230 ft./sec.
Rate of fire:	1 rd. per 2 mins.
Traverse:	Nil.

(note: shell contains 262 pounds of high explosive).

SIX IMPORTANT MACHINE GUNS 1914–1918

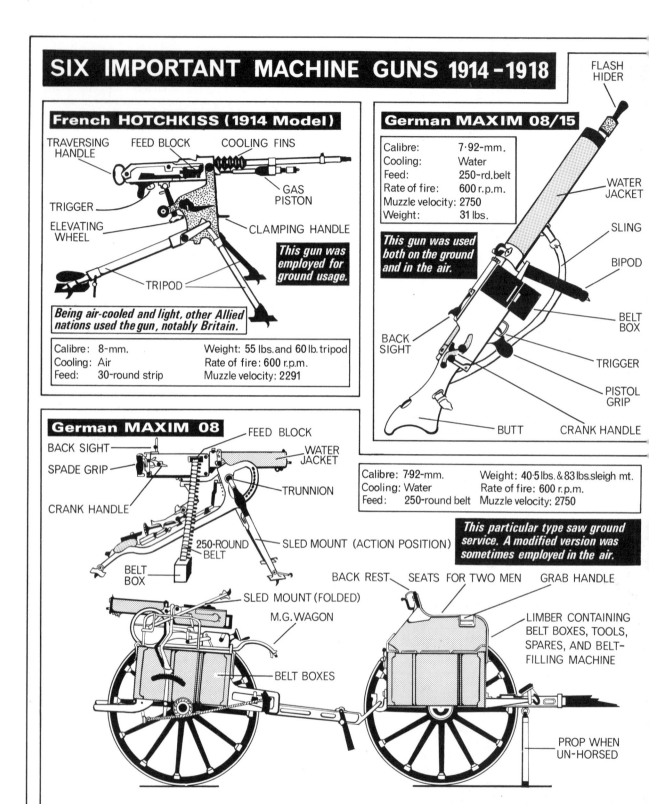

French HOTCHKISS (1914 Model)

TRAVERSING HANDLE
FEED BLOCK
COOLING FINS
GAS PISTON
TRIGGER
ELEVATING WHEEL
CLAMPING HANDLE
TRIPOD

This gun was employed for ground usage.

Being air-cooled and light, other Allied nations used the gun, notably Britain.

Calibre: 8-mm.	Weight: 55 lbs. and 60 lb. tripod
Cooling: Air	Rate of fire: 600 r.p.m.
Feed: 30-round strip	Muzzle velocity: 2291

German MAXIM 08/15

Calibre:	7·92-mm.
Cooling:	Water
Feed:	250-rd.belt
Rate of fire:	600 r.p.m.
Muzzle velocity:	2750
Weight:	31 lbs.

This gun was used both on the ground and in the air.

FLASH HIDER
WATER JACKET
SLING
BIPOD
BELT BOX
TRIGGER
PISTOL GRIP
CRANK HANDLE
BUTT
BACK SIGHT

German MAXIM 08

BACK SIGHT
SPADE GRIP
CRANK HANDLE
FEED BLOCK
WATER JACKET
TRUNNION
250-ROUND BELT
SLED MOUNT (ACTION POSITION)
BELT BOX

Calibre: 7·92-mm.	Weight: 40·5 lbs. & 83 lbs.sleigh mt.
Cooling: Water	Rate of fire: 600 r.p.m.
Feed: 250-round belt	Muzzle velocity: 2750

This particular type saw ground service. A modified version was sometimes employed in the air.

SLED MOUNT (FOLDED)
M.G. WAGON
BELT BOXES
BACK REST
SEATS FOR TWO MEN
GRAB HANDLE
LIMBER CONTAINING BELT BOXES, TOOLS, SPARES, AND BELT-FILLING MACHINE
PROP WHEN UN-HORSED

This gun was the "slayer" of 1 July 1916, the opening day of the Allied infantry offensive at the Battle of the Somme. Its devastating fire-power accounted for 90% of the 60,000 Allied casualties (mainly British) incurred on that one day.

© Arthur Banks 1973

224

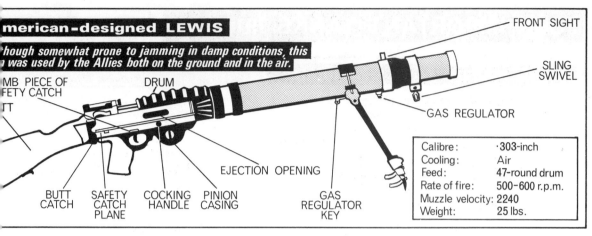

merican-designed LEWIS

*hough somewhat prone to jamming in damp conditions, this
 was used by the Allies both on the ground and in the air.*

FRONT SIGHT

SLING SWIVEL

MB PIECE OF
FETY CATCH

TT

DRUM

GAS REGULATOR

BUTT CATCH

SAFETY CATCH PLANE

COCKING HANDLE

PINION CASING

EJECTION OPENING

GAS REGULATOR KEY

Calibre:	·303-inch
Cooling:	Air
Feed:	47-round drum
Rate of fire:	500-600 r.p.m.
Muzzle velocity:	2240
Weight:	25 lbs.

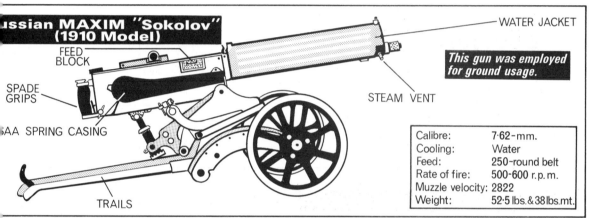

ussian MAXIM "Sokolov" (1910 Model)

WATER JACKET

FEED BLOCK

SPADE GRIPS

AA SPRING CASING

STEAM VENT

TRAILS

**This gun was employed
for ground usage.**

Calibre:	7·62-mm.
Cooling:	Water
Feed:	250-round belt
Rate of fire:	500-600 r.p.m.
Muzzle velocity:	2822
Weight:	52·5 lbs. & 38 lbs.mt.

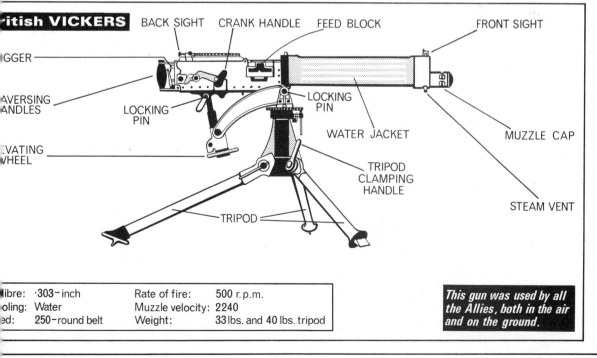

ritish VICKERS

BACK SIGHT

CRANK HANDLE

FEED BLOCK

FRONT SIGHT

IGGER

AVERSING ANDLES

LOCKING PIN

LOCKING PIN

WATER JACKET

MUZZLE CAP

VATING WHEEL

TRIPOD CLAMPING HANDLE

TRIPOD

STEAM VENT

libre:	·303-inch	Rate of fire:	500 r.p.m.	
oling:	Water	Muzzle velocity:	2240	
ed:	250-round belt	Weight:	33 lbs. and 40 lbs. tripod	

**This gun was used by all
the Allies, both in the air
and on the ground.**

FOUR IMPORTANT TANKS 1916-1918

Weight:	14 tons.
Speed:	8·3 m.p.h.
Range:	80 miles.
Crew:	3.
Engines:	2 Tylor (total: 90 h.p

British Medium Mark A "Whippet"

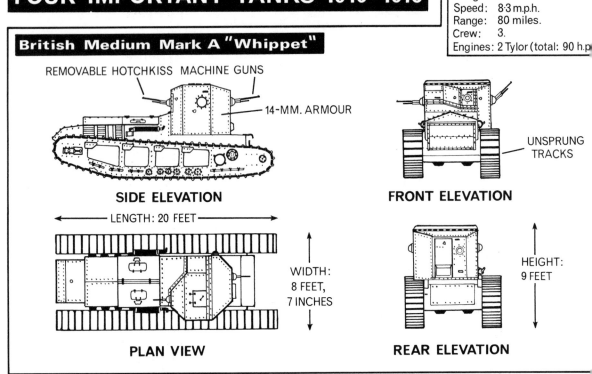

REMOVABLE HOTCHKISS MACHINE GUNS

14-MM. ARMOUR

SIDE ELEVATION

UNSPRUNG TRACKS

FRONT ELEVATION

← LENGTH: 20 FEET →

WIDTH: 8 FEET, 7 INCHES

HEIGHT: 9 FEET

PLAN VIEW

REAR ELEVATION

German A7V Sturmpanzerwagen

Weight: 30 tons.   Speed: 8 m.p.h.   Crew:
Engines: 2 Daimler four-cylinder (total: 200 h.p.).

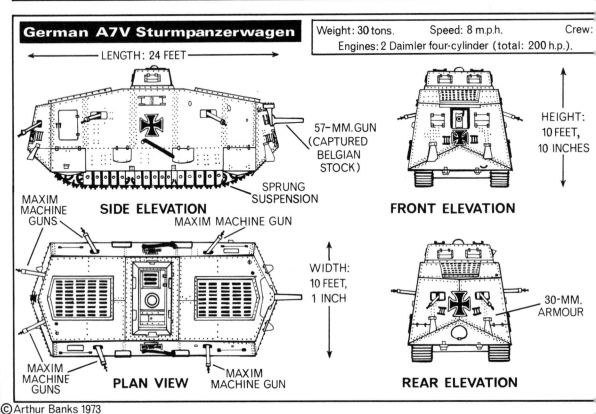

← LENGTH: 24 FEET →

57-MM. GUN (CAPTURED BELGIAN STOCK)

SPRUNG SUSPENSION

MAXIM MACHINE GUNS

SIDE ELEVATION

MAXIM MACHINE GUN

HEIGHT: 10 FEET, 10 INCHES

FRONT ELEVATION

WIDTH: 10 FEET, 1 INCH

30-MM. ARMOUR

MAXIM MACHINE GUNS

PLAN VIEW

MAXIM MACHINE GUN

REAR ELEVATION

French Schneider M.16 CA1

Weight:	13·5 tons.
Speed:	4·5 m.p.h.
Range:	25 miles.
Crew:	6/7.
Engine:	Schneider, four-cylinder, watercooled, 55 h.p.

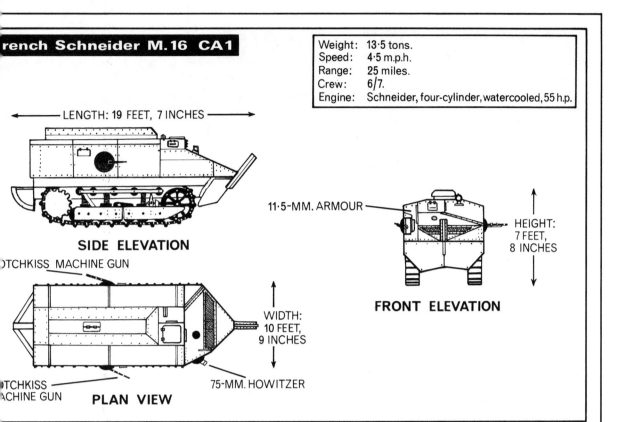

← LENGTH: 19 FEET, 7 INCHES →

SIDE ELEVATION

11·5-MM. ARMOUR

HEIGHT: 7 FEET, 8 INCHES

FRONT ELEVATION

HOTCHKISS MACHINE GUN

WIDTH: 10 FEET, 9 INCHES

HOTCHKISS MACHINE GUN

75-MM. HOWITZER

PLAN VIEW

French Light Renault FT 17

Weight: 6·4 tons	Speed: 4·8 m.p.h.	Crew: 2.
	Engine: Renault, four-cylinder, 35 h.p.	

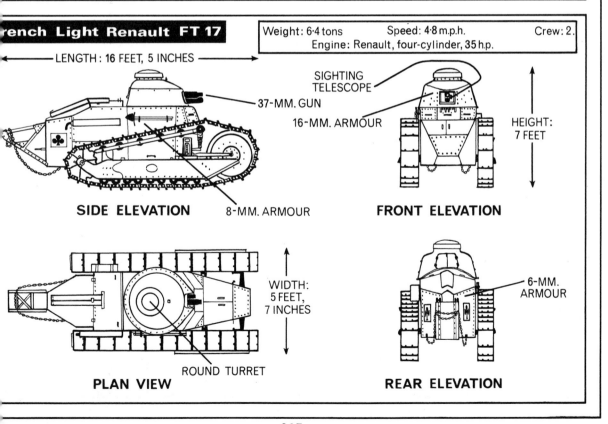

← LENGTH: 16 FEET, 5 INCHES →

SIGHTING TELESCOPE

37-MM. GUN

16-MM. ARMOUR

HEIGHT: 7 FEET

SIDE ELEVATION

8-MM. ARMOUR

FRONT ELEVATION

WIDTH: 5 FEET, 7 INCHES

6-MM. ARMOUR

ROUND TURRET

PLAN VIEW

REAR ELEVATION

227

NINE IMPORTANT RIFLES 1914-1918

The rifles of the 1914–1918 war were basically similar in performance. All incorporated hand-operated bolt actions, some straight pull, others turn-bolt. Reliability varied somewhat, but no single rifle had any outstanding advantage over the others. In 1918, efforts were made to produce rifles of a self-loading nature, but only one type saw some limited service. The vast majority of rifles used were of the basic types shown on these pages.

THE BRITISH REGULAR ARM

Prior to the war, the British Regular Army paid particular attention to training its infantry in marksmanship and "rapid fire" techniques and by outbreak in August 1914, regiment contained riflemen with ability to fire at rates of 15-20 rounds per minute with great accuracy.

German "MAUSER" (Model 1898)

BACK SIGHT
EXPOSED BARREL
UNPROTECTED FRONT SIGHT
MAGAZINE (totally enclosed)
STACKING FITTING

Calibre:	7·92-mm.
Length overall:	49·25 inche
Barrel length:	29·15 inche
Magazine (full):	5 rounds
Weight:	9·5 lbs.
Muzzle velocity:	2,500 ft./se

French "LEBEL" (Model 1916)

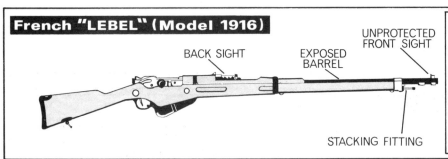

BACK SIGHT
EXPOSED BARREL
UNPROTECTED FRONT SIGHT
STACKING FITTING

Calibre:	8-mm.
Length overall:	51·3 inches
Barrel length:	31·4 inches
Magazine (full):	8 rounds
Weight:	9·35 lbs.
Muzzle velocity:	2,380 ft./se

United States "SPRINGFIELD" (Model 1903)

TURNED-DOWN BOLT HANDLE
(important in rapid fire)
BACK SIGHT
UNPROTECTED FRONT SIGHT

Calibre:	30.06
Length overall:	43·25 inche
Barrel length:	24 inches
Magazine (full):	5 rounds
Weight:	8·69 lbs.
Muzzle velocity:	2,500 ft./se

United States (Model 1917)

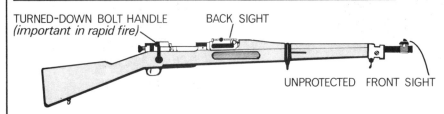

BACK SIGHT (within protective ears)
FRONT SIGHT (within protective ears)
TURNED-DOWN BOLT HANDLE
(important in rapid fire)

Experimental British rifle produced in U.S.A. for the British Empire to alleviate S.M.L.E. shortage. Later made to take American cartridge to relieve U.S.A. shortage.

Calibre:	30.06
Length overall:	46·25 inche
Barrel length:	26 inches
Magazine (full):	5 rounds
Weight:	9·62 lbs.
Muzzle velocity:	2,600 ft./se

British SHORT MAGAZINE "LEE-ENFIELD" Mark III

TURNED-DOWN BOLT HANDLE
(important in
rapid fire)

BACK SIGHT

FRONT SIGHT
(within protective
ears)

DETACHABLE BOX

Introduced in 1907

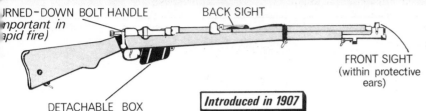

Calibre:	·303-inch
Length overall:	44·5 inches
Barrel length:	25·19 inches
Magazine (full):	10 rounds
Weight:	8·12 lbs.
Muzzle velocity:	2,060 ft./sec.

Canadian "ROSS" Mark III B

BACK SIGHT

UNPROTECTED FRONT SIGHT

UNPROTECTED BARREL

Produced in 1916

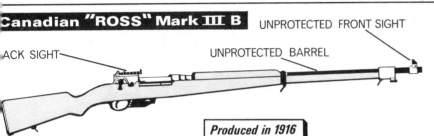

Calibre:	·303-inch
Length overall:	50·5 inches
Barrel length:	30·5 inches
Magazine (full):	5 rounds
Weight:	9·75 lbs.
Muzzle velocity:	2,060 ft./sec.

Russian "MOISIN—NAGANT" (Model 1891)

BACK SIGHT

UNPROTECTED FRONT SIGHT

STACKING FITTING

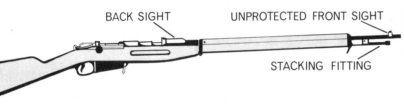

Calibre:	7·62–mm.
Length overall:	51·37 inches
Barrel length:	31·6 inches
Magazine (full):	5 rounds
Weight:	9·62 lbs.
Muzzle velocity:	2,660 ft./sec.

Austrian "MÄNNLICHER" (Model 1895)

*Diagram and main details refer
to the long version.*

BACK SIGHT

UNPROTECTED
FRONT SIGHT

SHORT VERSION (variations)
Length overall: 40 inches
Barrel length: 19 inches
Weight: 7·8 lbs.

Calibre:	8–mm.
Length overall:	50 inches
Barrel length:	30 inches
Magazine (full):	5 rounds
Weight:	8·4 lbs
Muzzle velocity:	2,030 ft./sec.

Italian "MÄNNLICHER—CARCANO" (Model 1891)

BACK SIGHT

EXPOSED BARREL

UNPROTECTED
FRONT SIGHT

STACKING FITTING

Calibre:	6·5–mm.
Length overall:	50·75 inches
Barrel length:	30·7 inches
Magazine (full):	6 rounds
Weight:	9 lbs.
Muzzle velocity:	2,200 ft./sec.

TWENTY TRENCH WEAPONS AND MUNITIONS

German 240-mm. old style Minenwerfer "Iko"
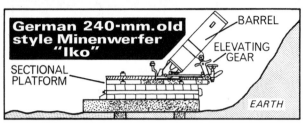
BARREL
ELEVATING GEAR
SECTIONAL PLATFORM
EARTH

British "Jam Tin" Bomb
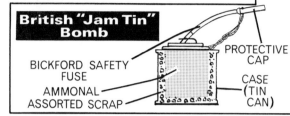
BICKFORD SAFETY FUSE
AMMONAL
ASSORTED SCRAP
PROTECTIVE CAP
CASE (TIN CAN)

German 75-mm. new style Minenwerfer

RECOIL CYLINDER
REAR SIGHT
ELEVATING LEVER
TRAVERSING LEVER
BARREL
RECOIL SPADE
EARTH

British Newton Pippin Rifle Grenade (Mark I)
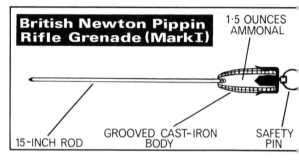
1·5 OUNCES AMMONAL
15-INCH ROD
GROOVED CAST-IRON BODY
SAFETY PIN

British 2-inch Trench Mortar "Toffee Apple"
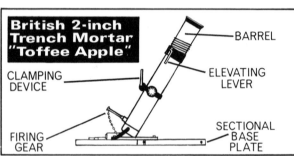
BARREL
ELEVATING LEVER
CLAMPING DEVICE
FIRING GEAR
SECTIONAL BASE PLATE

British Mills Hand Grenade (1915)
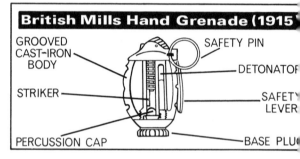
GROOVED CAST-IRON BODY
SAFETY PIN
DETONATOR
STRIKER
SAFETY LEVER
PERCUSSION CAP
BASE PLUG

British 3-inch Stokes Mortar
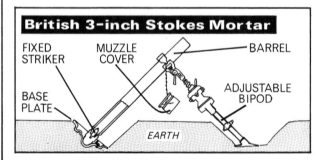
FIXED STRIKER
MUZZLE COVER
BARREL
BASE PLATE
ADJUSTABLE BIPOD
EARTH

German Stick Grenade
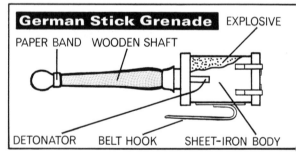
EXPLOSIVE
PAPER BAND
WOODEN SHAFT
DETONATOR
BELT HOOK
SHEET-IRON BODY

French 2.58 Trench Mortar (Mark II)
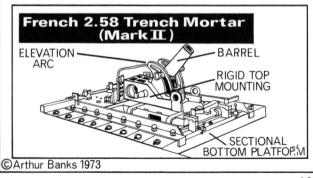
ELEVATION ARC
BARREL
RIGID TOP MOUNTING
SECTIONAL BOTTOM PLATFORM

French V. B. Launcher & Grenade
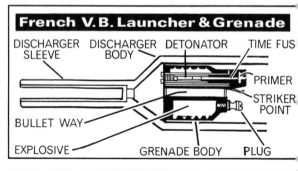
DISCHARGER SLEEVE
DISCHARGER BODY
DETONATOR
TIME FUSE
PRIMER
STRIKER POINT
BULLET WAY
EXPLOSIVE
GRENADE BODY
PLUG

Typical High Explosive Shell

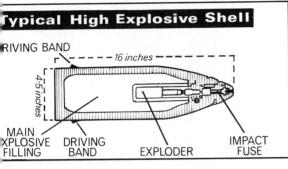

DRIVING BAND
16 inches
4·5 inches
MAIN EXPLOSIVE FILLING
DRIVING BAND
EXPLODER
IMPACT FUSE

German 76-mm. Minenwerfer Message Shell

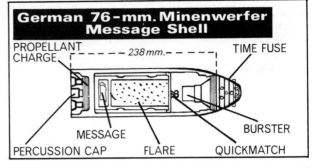

PROPELLANT CHARGE
238 mm.
TIME FUSE
MESSAGE
BURSTER
PERCUSSION CAP
FLARE
QUICKMATCH

Typical Shrapnel Shell

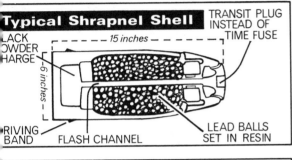

BLACK POWDER CHARGE
15 inches
TRANSIT PLUG INSTEAD OF TIME FUSE
6 inches
DRIVING BAND
FLASH CHANNEL
LEAD BALLS SET IN RESIN

Trench Club

IMPROVISED IN THE TRENCHES

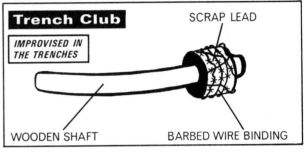

SCRAP LEAD
WOODEN SHAFT
BARBED WIRE BINDING

Typical Gas Shell

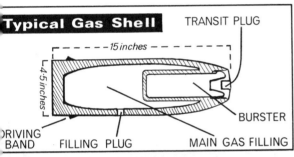

TRANSIT PLUG
15 inches
4·5 inches
BURSTER
DRIVING BAND
FILLING PLUG
MAIN GAS FILLING

Old Welsh Knife

TRADITIONAL FROM DAYS OF THE LONGBOW

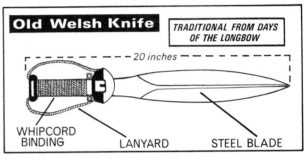

20 inches
WHIPCORD BINDING
LANYARD
STEEL BLADE

Typical Semi Armour–Piercing Shell

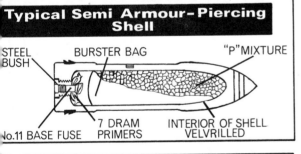

STEEL BUSH
BURSTER BAG
"P" MIXTURE
No.11 BASE FUSE
7 DRAM PRIMERS
INTERIOR OF SHELL VELVRILLED

Knuckleduster Knife

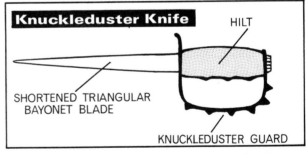

HILT
SHORTENED TRIANGULAR BAYONET BLADE
KNUCKLEDUSTER GUARD

Typical Incendiary (Thermite) Shell

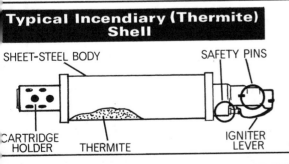

SHEET-STEEL BODY
SAFETY PINS
CARTRIDGE HOLDER
THERMITE
IGNITER LEVER

British Webley (Mark VI) Stock & Bayonet

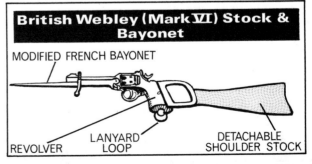

MODIFIED FRENCH BAYONET
REVOLVER
LANYARD LOOP
DETACHABLE SHOULDER STOCK

EIGHT IMPORTANT PISTOLS AND REVOLVERS 1914 – 1918

United States COLT M1917

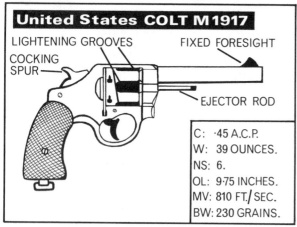

LIGHTENING GROOVES
FIXED FORESIGHT
COCKING SPUR
EJECTOR ROD

C: ·45 A.C.P.
W: 39 OUNCES.
NS: 6.
OL: 9·75 INCHES.
MV: 810 FT./SEC.
BW: 230 GRAINS.

British WEBLEY Mark VI

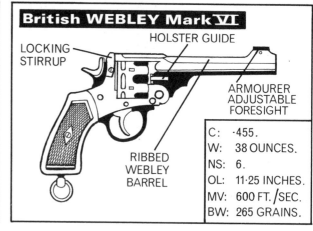

HOLSTER GUIDE
LOCKING STIRRUP
ARMOURER ADJUSTABLE FORESIGHT
RIBBED WEBLEY BARREL

C: ·455.
W: 38 OUNCES.
NS: 6.
OL: 11·25 INCHES.
MV: 600 FT./SEC.
BW: 265 GRAINS.

British COLT

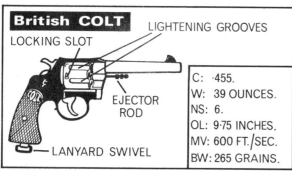

LIGHTENING GROOVES
LOCKING SLOT
EJECTOR ROD
LANYARD SWIVEL

C: ·455.
W: 39 OUNCES.
NS: 6.
OL: 9·75 INCHES.
MV: 600 FT./SEC.
BW: 265 GRAINS.

British WEBLEY-FOSBERY

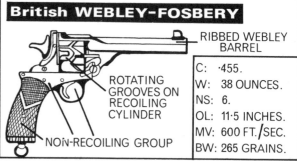

RIBBED WEBLEY BARREL
ROTATING GROOVES ON RECOILING CYLINDER
NON-RECOILING GROUP

C: ·455.
W: 38 OUNCES.
NS: 6.
OL: 11·5 INCHES.
MV: 600 FT./SEC.
BW: 265 GRAINS.

German MAUSER

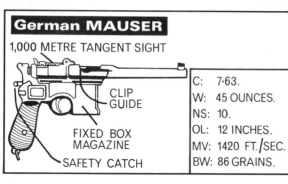

1,000 METRE TANGENT SIGHT
CLIP GUIDE
FIXED BOX MAGAZINE
SAFETY CATCH

C: 7·63.
W: 45 OUNCES.
NS: 10.
OL: 12 INCHES.
MV: 1420 FT./SEC.
BW: 86 GRAINS.

German LUGER (Parabellum)

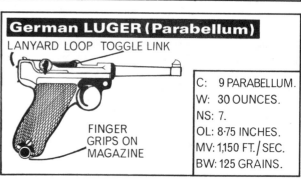

LANYARD LOOP   TOGGLE LINK
FINGER GRIPS ON MAGAZINE

C: 9 PARABELLUM.
W: 30 OUNCES.
NS: 7.
OL: 8·75 INCHES.
MV: 1,150 FT./SEC.
BW: 125 GRAINS.

Italian GLISENTI

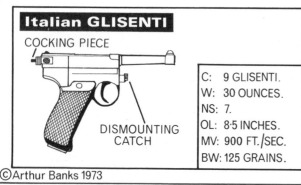

COCKING PIECE
DISMOUNTING CATCH

C: 9 GLISENTI.
W: 30 OUNCES.
NS: 7.
OL: 8·5 INCHES.
MV: 900 FT./SEC.
BW: 125 GRAINS.

Japanese NAMBU

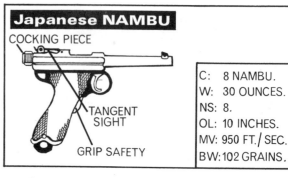

COCKING PIECE
TANGENT SIGHT
GRIP SAFETY

C: 8 NAMBU.
W: 30 OUNCES.
NS: 8.
OL: 10 INCHES.
MV: 950 FT./SEC.
BW: 102 GRAINS.

FIVE IMPORTANT ANTI-AIRCRAFT GUNS 1914-1918

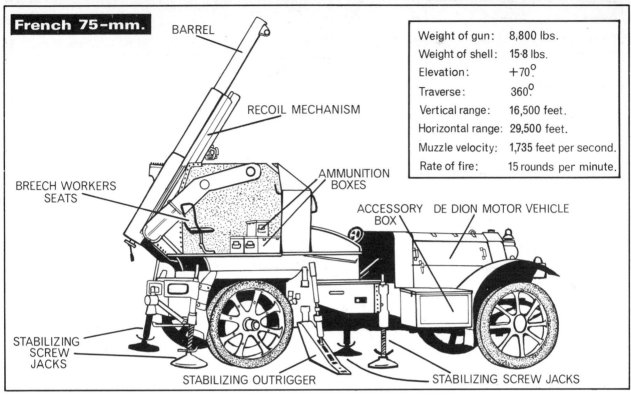

French 75-mm.

BARREL

RECOIL MECHANISM

Weight of gun:	8,800 lbs.
Weight of shell:	15·8 lbs.
Elevation:	+70°.
Traverse:	360°.
Vertical range:	16,500 feet.
Horizontal range:	29,500 feet.
Muzzle velocity:	1,735 feet per second.
Rate of fire:	15 rounds per minute.

AMMUNITION BOXES

BREECH WORKERS SEATS

ACCESSORY BOX   DE DION MOTOR VEHICLE

STABILIZING SCREW JACKS

STABILIZING OUTRIGGER

STABILIZING SCREW JACKS

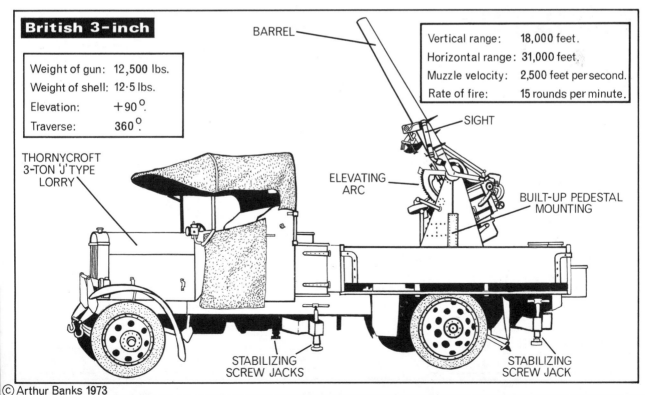

British 3-inch

BARREL

Vertical range:	18,000 feet.
Horizontal range:	31,000 feet.
Muzzle velocity:	2,500 feet per second.
Rate of fire:	15 rounds per minute.

Weight of gun:	12,500 lbs.
Weight of shell:	12·5 lbs.
Elevation:	+90°.
Traverse:	360°.

SIGHT

THORNYCROFT 3-TON 'J' TYPE LORRY

ELEVATING ARC

BUILT-UP PEDESTAL MOUNTING

STABILIZING SCREW JACKS

STABILIZING SCREW JACK

© Arthur Banks 1973

233

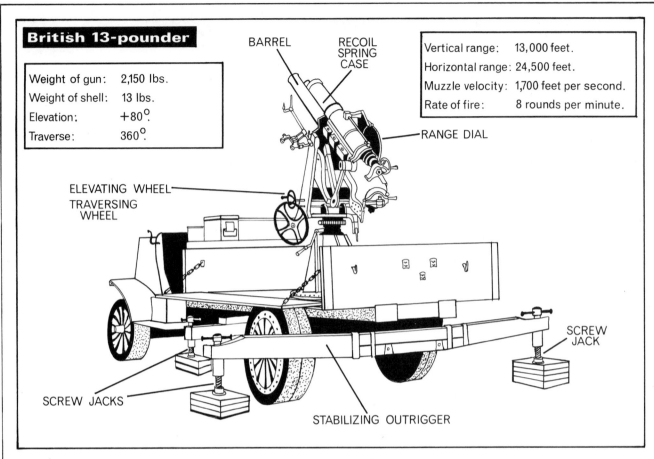

British 13-pounder

Weight of gun:	2,150 lbs.
Weight of shell:	13 lbs.
Elevation:	$+80°$
Traverse:	$360°$

BARREL

RECOIL SPRING CASE

Vertical range:	13,000 feet.
Horizontal range:	24,500 feet.
Muzzle velocity:	1,700 feet per second.
Rate of fire:	8 rounds per minute.

RANGE DIAL

ELEVATING WHEEL

TRAVERSING WHEEL

SCREW JACK

SCREW JACKS

STABILIZING OUTRIGGER

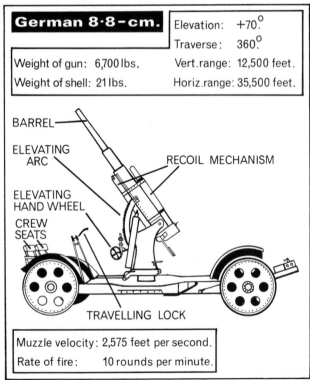

German 8·8-cm.

Elevation:	$+70°$
Traverse:	$360°$

Weight of gun:	6,700 lbs.
Weight of shell:	21 lbs.
Vert. range:	12,500 feet.
Horiz. range:	35,500 feet.

BARREL

ELEVATING ARC

RECOIL MECHANISM

ELEVATING HAND WHEEL

CREW SEATS

TRAVELLING LOCK

Muzzle velocity: 2,575 feet per second.
Rate of fire: 10 rounds per minute.

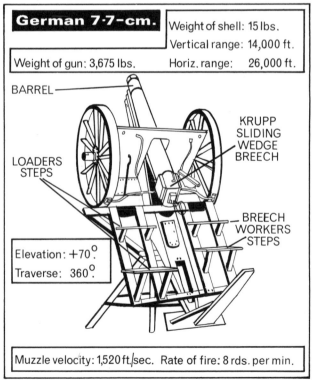

German 7·7-cm.

Weight of shell:	15 lbs.
Vertical range:	14,000 ft.
Weight of gun: 3,675 lbs.	Horiz. range: 26,000 ft.

BARREL

KRUPP SLIDING WEDGE BREECH

LOADERS STEPS

BREECH WORKERS STEPS

Elevation:	$+70°$
Traverse:	$360°$

Muzzle velocity: 1,520 ft./sec. Rate of fire: 8 rds. per min.

234

THE WAR AT SEA

During the first decade of the century a radical change in warship construction led to the development of 'all big gun' battleships. The first British vessel of this type was H.M.S. *Dreadnought* (ten 12-inch guns and a speed of 21 knots), laid down in October 1905, launched February 1906, at sea by October 1906. The Dreadnoughts could outrange and outpace all previous battleships, which were soon made obsolete. Other countries followed Britain's lead: a German dreadnought, the *Nassau*, was launched in 1907. The Royal Navy in 1914 had twenty dreadnoughts or 'super-dreadnoughts' based in home waters: Germany, the second largest naval power in Europe, had fifteen. Everyone awaited a dreadnought Trafalgar. A difference in concepts of naval strategy postponed the clash. The Germans hoped to offset their numerical inferiority by splitting the British Grand Fleet by a feint, enabling their battle squadrons to fall on the enemy a portion at a time; the British, on the other hand, were content to use dreadnoughts as a distant deterrent, exercising naval supremacy in home waters from Scapa Flow, in the Orkneys. The prospect of a great naval battle receded.

Meanwhile, the British, French, Russian and Japanese navies were confronted with the problem of German cruisers in distant seas. The battle-cruiser *Goeben* and the cruiser *Breslau* succeeded in evading pursuit in the Mediterranean and took refuge at Constantinople, where their transference to the Turkish fleet played a considerable part in inducing the Turks to enter the war. The German Pacific Squadron (Spee) inflicted, off Coronel, the first defeat sustained by the Royal Navy since the 1812 War with America, sinking an outdated armoured cruiser and a light cruiser. Coronel was avenged at the Falkland Islands five weeks later, while the lone raider *Emden* was tracked down by the Australian cruiser *Sydney* in the Indian Ocean. The chivalrous seamanship of the commanders of the German surface vessels won high regard; but the development by the Germans of submarine warfare, and especially the increasing number of underwater attacks on merchantmen and passenger liners, aroused anger and resentment in Britain and the

United States. On the other hand, the Americans also resented the British imposition of a naval blockade on Germany and her allies. British submarine activity was especially effective in the Sea of Marmara, off Constantinople, and in the Baltic.

In January 1915 the battle-cruisers of the Grand Fleet, under Beatty, intercepted Admiral Hipper's 'scouting group' off the Dogger Bank and pursued the Germans but lost contact after Beatty's flagship was immobilised. The German armoured cruiser *Blücher* was sunk, and the Germans concentrated for the remainder of the year on U-boat activity. In February 1916 Admiral Scheer took command of the High Seas Fleet at Wilhelmshaven, and planned to tempt Beatty into another battle-cruiser engagement, with a pack of U-boats waiting to intercept the dreadnoughts of the Grand Fleet (Jellicoe) as they moved south. Surface, submarine and Zeppelin activity was, however, not as co-ordinated as Scheer wished. The British were remarkably well-informed of German movements (by wireless interception), and were prepared for a major battle in May 1916.

Jutland, the largest naval action in world history, was essentially a battle of feints and manoeuvres. It involved 151 British warships and 99 German vessels although the dreadnoughts themselves (28 British, 16 German) were in action against each other for only twenty minutes during the evening of 31 May. Beatty, realising the German cruisers were seeking to draw his squadron towards the heavy guns of the High Seas Fleet, himself tried to lure the Germans towards Jellicoe's squadron. The British battle-cruisers suffered heavily from accurate German fire, but tactically trapped Scheer into allowing the Grand Fleet to get between his vessels and his home port. Jellicoe hoped to bring Scheer to battle next morning, but the Germans evaded him at night, partly through sheer speed and partly through better training for a running battle by night. British casualties and losses were far higher than those of the Germans at Jutland; but it was harder for the Germans to fill the gaps in their fleet. Strategically Jutland was a British victory, for it reinforced the Kaiser's inclination to preserve his navy intact, rather than risk another encounter with the Grand Fleet.

After Jutland there was little surface conflict between rival warships. The Austro-Hungarian fleet made a number of sorties on the barrage which the Allies sought to establish across the Strait of Otranto, so as to seal off the Adriatic from the Mediterranean; and there were occasional alarms in the Black Sea, where the Russian and Turkish fleets had already clashed briefly off the southern tip of the Crimea in November 1914. It is often said that the German High Seas Fleet remained inactive off Heligoland and Kiel for the remainder of the War until a break in morale led to mutiny in 1918. Yet, though the Kaiser was opposed to offensive action, Scheer took the Fleet to sea again in the third week of August 1916 and, for the last time, in April 1918. These sweeps seem, however, to have been intended as diversions rather than as preliminaries to another battle, and no contact was made with British surface vessels. It should, of course, be noted (page 276) that the rival fleets were increasingly hemmed in by minefields.

Both the British and German Admiralties had anticipated that attempts would be made in any war to strangle the economy of a country, and cut off its food supply, by means of a blockade. The British system (for which a separate Government department, the Ministry of Blockade, was eventually established early in 1916) was basically an extension of the controversial rights exercised during the Napoleonic Wars: an Order in Council of March 1915 authorising the seizure by British warships of goods destined for Germany by way of a neutral port provoked similar hostility to the notorious Orders in Council of 1807, although German submarine ruthlessness assuaged the wrath of some neutral countries. Neither the British nor the Germans had worked out the implications of using the submarine as a destroyer of commerce; but by the spring of 1916 the U-boat was recognised in Berlin as the most effective of all naval weapons. Attempts were made later that summer to counter the U-boat menace with new minefields, increased defensive nets and disguised 'mystery ships' (Q-ships). Yet the tonnage of merchant shipping sunk by U-boat averaged 300,000 a month in the last quarter of 1916 and rose dramatically in February when the Germans began unrestricted submarine warfare. Over half a million tons of British merchant shipping was lost in April 1917, one in four vessels leaving British ports never returning there again. Corn supplies in England were down to six weeks.

The U-boat menace was mastered by a return to the eighteenth century concept of convoys, imposed on a reluctant Admiralty by the Prime Minister Lloyd George, in May 1917 (see page 266). The addition of American naval strength to Atlantic patrols helped ensure the effectiveness of convoying. At the same time, new anti-submarine techniques were perfected, notably the depth-charge. The Admiralty remained concerned over the use which the Germans made of the Belgian ports as U-boat bases. In April 1918 a raid was made on Zeebrugge—the prototype of amphibious commando raids in the Second World War—which sought to block the canal to Bruges, where there were docking facilities for destroyers and as many as 30 U-boats. An attempt was also made on the Bruges–Ostend Canal. The Zeebrugge Raid (for which eight Victoria Crosses were awarded) was only partially successful and the accompanying raid on Ostend (which won another three Victoria Crosses) was so disappointing that a second assault had to be made a fortnight later. It, too, proved largely abortive. But the Zeebrugge-Ostend operations sealed off the U-boats and destroyers at Bruges, even if the shallow-draught boats were soon able to move again out to sea. The chief effect of the raids was as a fillip to lagging morale in Britain.

A final plan to challenge the Grand Fleet in the hopes of securing better Armistice terms in 1918 came to nothing when the German naval ratings mutinied, first at the fleet anchorage off Wilhelmshaven on 29 October and later at Kiel. It was the beginning of the revolution which, within a fortnight, turned Germany from an autocracy to a republic.

THE PURSUIT AND ESCAPE OF SMS 'GOEBEN' AND 'BRESLAU', AUGUST 1914

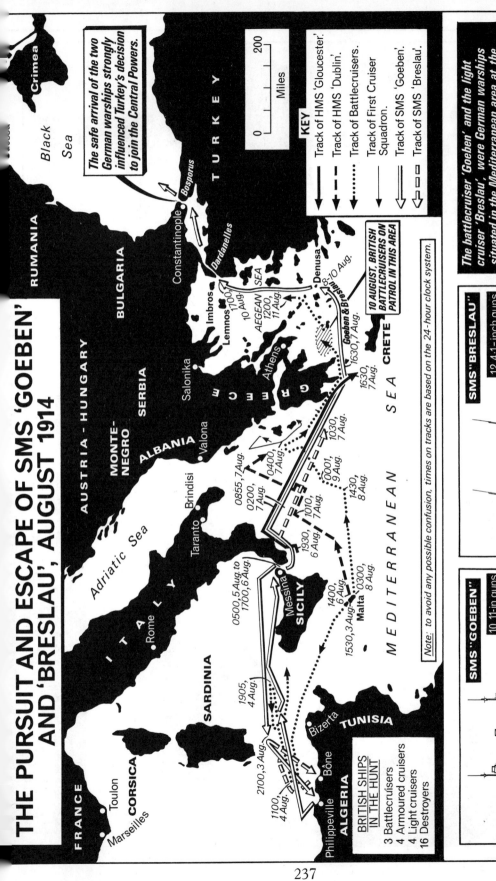

The safe arrival of the two German warships strongly influenced Turkey's decision to join the Central Powers.

KEY

→	Track of HMS 'Gloucester.'
- →	Track of HMS 'Dublin.'
⋯→	Track of Battlecruisers.
→	Track of First Cruiser Squadron.
⇨	Track of SMS 'Goeben'.
⇠⇠	Track of SMS 'Breslau'.

10 AUGUST, BRITISH BATTLECRUISERS ON PATROL IN THIS AREA

Goeben & Breslau, 1630, 7 Aug.

1700, 10 Aug.

1200, 11 Aug.

8-10 Aug.

1630, 7 Aug.

1030, 7 Aug.

0400, 7 Aug.

0001, 9 Aug.

1430, 8 Aug.

0300, 8 Aug.

0855, 7 Aug.

0200, 7 Aug.

1010, 7 Aug.

1930, 6 Aug. to 7 Aug.

1400, 6 Aug.

Malta 0300, 8 Aug.

0500, 5 Aug. to 1700, 6 Aug.

1905, 4 Aug.

2100, 3 Aug.

1530, 3 Aug.

1100, 4 Aug.

Note: to avoid any possible confusion, times on tracks are based on the 24-hour clock system.

BRITISH SHIPS IN THE HUNT
3 Battlecruisers
4 Armoured cruisers
4 Light cruisers
16 Destroyers

Black Sea

Crimea

RUMANIA

TURKEY

BULGARIA

Bosporus

Constantinople

Dardanelles

AEGEAN SEA

Imbros

Lemnos

Denusa

SERBIA

MONTE-NEGRO

ALBANIA

Valona

Salonika

Athens

G R E E C E

CRETE

M E D I T E R R A N E A N   S E A

AUSTRIA – HUNGARY

Brindisi

Taranto

Adriatic Sea

I T A L Y

Rome

SARDINIA

CORSICA

FRANCE

Toulon

Marseilles

Messina

SICILY

Bizerta

Bône

Philippeville

ALGERIA

TUNISIA

0   200
Miles

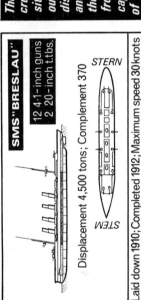

The battlecruiser 'Goeben' and the light cruiser 'Breslau', were German warships situated in the Mediterranean area at the outbreak of the war. After attempting to disrupt French troop convoys between Africa and France by bombarding Algerian ports, they were hunted by British naval units from Messina to the Dardanelles. To escape capture, they were sold to Turkey for a sum of £3,800,000, and then used against Russia.

SMS "BRESLAU"
12 4.1-inch guns
2 20-inch t.tbs.

STERN
STEM

Displacement 4,500 tons; Complement 370
Laid down 1910; Completed 1912; Maximum speed 30knots

SMS "GOEBEN"
10 11-in.guns
12 6-in.guns
12 24-pdrs.
4 20-in.t.t.s.

STERN
STEM

Displacement 23,000tons; Complement 1,107
Laid down 1909; Completed 1912; Maximum speed 28knots

© Arthur Banks 1973

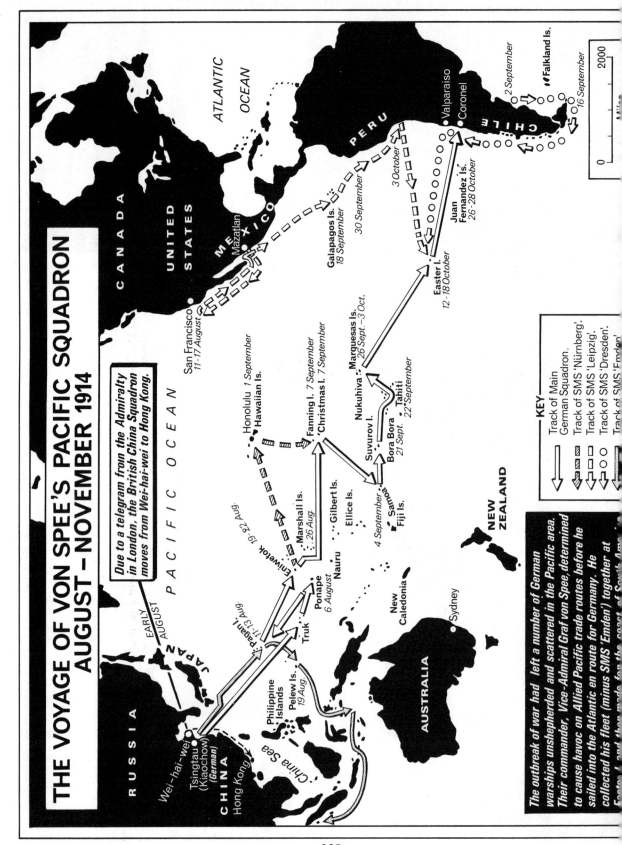

THE VOYAGE OF VON SPEE'S PACIFIC SQUADRON
AUGUST–NOVEMBER 1914

Due to a telegram from the Admiralty in London, the British China Squadron moves from Wei-hai-wei to Hong Kong.

ATLANTIC OCEAN

PACIFIC OCEAN

CANADA

UNITED STATES

MEXICO

San Francisco
11–17 August

Mazatlan

PERU

CHILE

Valparaiso
Coronel

2 September

Falkland Is.

16 September

Juan Fernandez Is.
26–28 October

3 October

30 September

Galapagos Is.
18 September

Easter I.
12–18 October

Marquesas Is.
26 Sept.–3 Oct.

Nukuhiva

Tahiti
22 September

Bora Bora
21 Sept.

Suvurov I.

4 September

Samoa
Fiji Is.

Honolulu *1 September*
Hawaiian Is.

Fanning I. *7 September*
'Christmas I. 7 September'

Marshall Is.
26 Aug.

Gilbert Is.

Ellice Is.

Eniwetok
19–22 Aug.

Nauru

Ponape
6 August

Truk

Pagan I.
11–13 Aug.

Pelew Is.
19 Aug.

Philippine Islands

China Sea

Hong Kong

CHINA

Wei-hai-wei

Tsingtau (Kiaochow)
(German)

JAPAN

RUSSIA

EARLY AUGUST

NEW ZEALAND

NEW Caledonia

Sydney

AUSTRALIA

2000

0

Miles

KEY
- ⇨ Track of Main German Squadron.
- ⇨ Track of SMS 'Nürnberg'.
- ▨ Track of SMS 'Leipzig'.
- ⬜ Track of SMS 'Dresden'.
- ○ Track of SMS 'Emden'

The outbreak of war had left a number of German warships unshepherded and scattered in the Pacific area. Their commander, Vice-Admiral Graf von Spee, determined to cause havoc on Allied Pacific trade routes before he sailed into the Atlantic en route for Germany. He collected his fleet (minus SMS 'Emden') together at

238

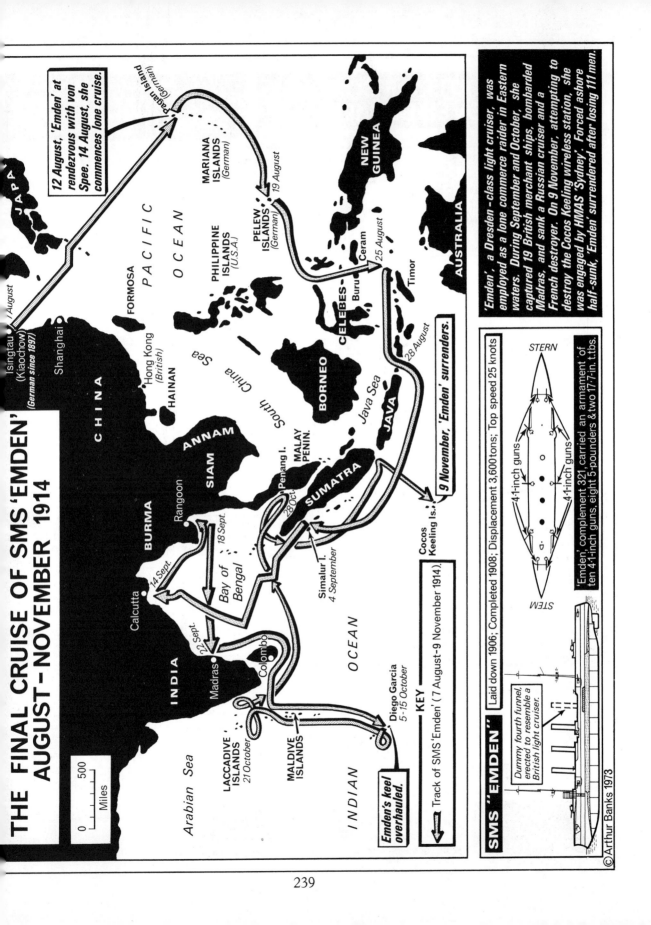

THE FINAL CRUISE OF SMS 'EMDEN' AUGUST–NOVEMBER 1914

12 August, 'Emden' at rendezvous with von Spee. 14 August, she commences lone cruise.

JAPAN

Isingtau (Kiaochow) (German since 1897)

7 August

Pagan Island (German)

Shanghai

CHINA

FORMOSA

Hong Kong (British)

HAINAN

PACIFIC

OCEAN

MARIANA ISLANDS (German)

PHILIPPINE ISLANDS (U.S.A.)

PELEW ISLANDS (German)

19 August

NEW GUINEA

South China Sea

BORNEO

CELEBES

Buru

Ceram

25 August

Timor

AUSTRALIA

Java Sea

JAVA

28 August

9 November, 'Emden' surrenders.

ANNAM

SIAM

Rangoon

BURMA

MALAY PENIN.

Penang I.

SUMATRA

28 Oct.

14 Sept.

18 Sept.

Bay of Bengal

Simalur I. 4 September

Cocos Keeling Is.

Calcutta

22 Sept.

INDIA

Madras

Colombo

INDIAN

OCEAN

Diego Garcia 5–15 October

LACCADIVE ISLANDS 21 October

MALDIVE ISLANDS

Arabian Sea

Emden's keel overhauled.

KEY

➡ Track of SMS 'Emden' (7 August–9 November 1914).

0   500
Miles

'Emden', a Dresden-class light cruiser, was employed as a lone commerce raider in Eastern waters. During September and October, she captured 19 British merchant ships, bombarded Madras, and sank a Russian cruiser and a French destroyer. On 9 November, attempting to destroy the Cocos Keeling wireless station, she was engaged by HMAS 'Sydney'. Forced ashore half-sunk, 'Emden' surrendered after losing 111 men.

SMS "EMDEN"   Laid down 1906; Completed 1908; Displacement 3,600 tons; Top speed 25 knots

STERN

4·1-inch guns

4·1-inch guns

STEM

'Emden', complement 321, carried an armament of ten 4·1-inch guns, eight 5-pounders & two 17·7-in. t.tbs.

Dummy fourth funnel, erected to resemble a British light cruiser.

© Arthur Banks 1973

239

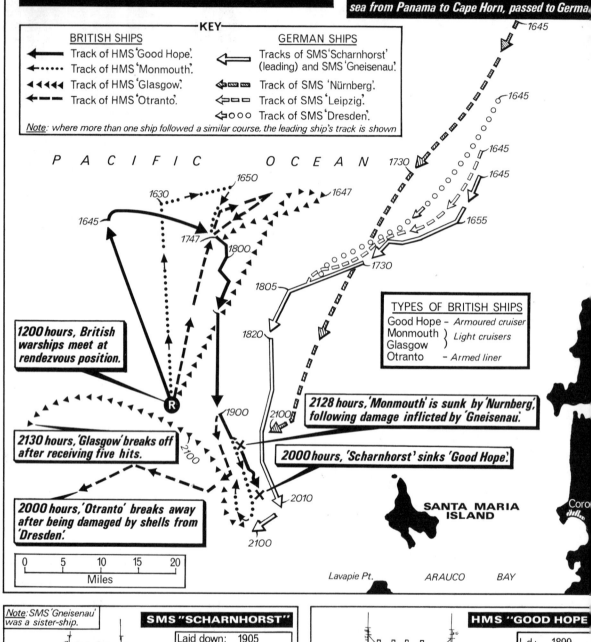

THE BATTLE OF CORONEL 1 NOVEMBER 1914

The Battle of Coronel resulted in a German victory. It was the first major British naval reverse for over a century, and command of th[e] sea from Panama to Cape Horn, passed to Germa[ny.]

──KEY──

BRITISH SHIPS
- Track of HMS 'Good Hope'.
- Track of HMS 'Monmouth'.
- Track of HMS 'Glasgow'.
- Track of HMS 'Otranto'.

GERMAN SHIPS
- Tracks of SMS 'Scharnhorst' (leading) and SMS 'Gneisenau'.
- Track of SMS 'Nürnberg'.
- Track of SMS 'Leipzig'.
- Track of SMS 'Dresden'.

Note: where more than one ship followed a similar course, the leading ship's track is shown

PACIFIC OCEAN

1200 hours, British warships meet at rendezvous position.

2128 hours, 'Monmouth' is sunk by 'Nurnberg', following damage inflicted by 'Gneisenau'.

2130 hours, 'Glasgow' breaks off after receiving five hits.

2000 hours, 'Scharnhorst' sinks 'Good Hope'.

2000 hours, 'Otranto' breaks away after being damaged by shells from 'Dresden'.

TYPES OF BRITISH SHIPS
- Good Hope – Armoured cruiser
- Monmouth ⎫
- Glasgow ⎬ Light cruisers
- Otranto – Armed liner

SANTA MARIA ISLAND

Cor[o...]

0 5 10 15 20
Miles

Lavapie Pt.   ARAUCO   BAY

Note: SMS 'Gneisenau' was a sister-ship.

SMS "SCHARNHORST"

Laid down:	1905
Completed:	1907
Max speed:	21 knots
Displacem't:	11,600 tons
Complement:	765

Eight 8·2-inch guns
Six 6-inch guns
Twenty 24-pdr. guns
Four 18-inch torp.tubes
Flagship of Vice-Admiral von Spee

HMS "GOOD HOPE"

L.d.:	1899
Cd.:	1902
M.s.:	24 knots
Dis.:	14,100 ton[s]
Ct.:	900

Two 9·2-in.guns
Sixteen 6-in.guns
Twelve 12-pdrs.
Three 3-pdrs.
Two 18-in.t.tubes
Flagship of Rear-Admiral Sir C.Cradock

STEM   STERN

© Arthur Banks 1973

240

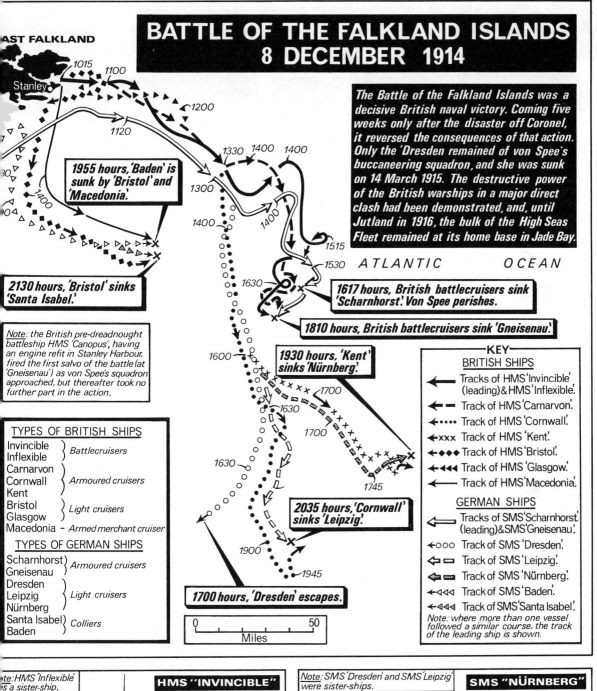

BATTLE OF THE FALKLAND ISLANDS
8 DECEMBER 1914

AST FALKLAND

Stanley

1015
1100
1120
1200
1330
1400
1400
1300
1400
1400
1515
1530
1630
1515

The Battle of the Falkland Islands was a decisive British naval victory. Coming five weeks only after the disaster off Coronel, it reversed the consequences of that action. Only the 'Dresden' remained of von Spee's buccaneering squadron, and she was sunk on 14 March 1915. The destructive power of the British warships in a major direct clash had been demonstrated, and, until Jutland in 1916, the bulk of the High Seas Fleet remained at its home base in Jade Bay.

ATLANTIC OCEAN

1955 hours, 'Baden' is sunk by 'Bristol' and 'Macedonia'.

2130 hours, 'Bristol' sinks 'Santa Isabel'.

Note: the British pre-dreadnought battleship HMS 'Canopus', having an engine refit in Stanley Harbour, fired the first salvo of the battle (at 'Gneisenau') as von Spee's squadron approached, but thereafter took no further part in the action.

1617 hours, British battlecruisers sink 'Scharnhorst'. Von Spee perishes.

1810 hours, British battlecruisers sink 'Gneisenau'.

1930 hours, 'Kent' sinks 'Nürnberg'.

1600
1630
1700
1700
1630
1630
1745

2035 hours, 'Cornwall' sinks 'Leipzig'.

1900
1945

1700 hours, 'Dresden' escapes.

TYPES OF BRITISH SHIPS

Invincible Inflexible	} Battlecruisers
Carnarvon Cornwall Kent	} Armoured cruisers
Bristol Glasgow	} Light cruisers
Macedonia	- Armed merchant cruiser

TYPES OF GERMAN SHIPS

Scharnhorst Gneisenau	} Armoured cruisers
Dresden Leipzig Nürnberg	} Light cruisers
Santa Isabel Baden	} Colliers

0 _____ 50
Miles

─KEY─
BRITISH SHIPS

←	Tracks of HMS 'Invincible' (leading) & HMS 'Inflexible'.
←---	Track of HMS 'Carnarvon'.
←••••	Track of HMS 'Cornwall'.
←xxx	Track of HMS 'Kent'.
←♦♦♦	Track of HMS 'Bristol'.
←◄◄◄	Track of HMS 'Glasgow'.
←	Track of HMS 'Macedonia'.

GERMAN SHIPS

⇐	Tracks of SMS 'Scharnhorst' (leading) & SMS 'Gneisenau'.
←ooo	Track of SMS 'Dresden'.
⇐▭	Track of SMS 'Leipzig'.
⇐▬	Track of SMS 'Nürnberg'.
←◄◄◄	Track of SMS 'Baden'.
←◄◄◄	Track of SMS 'Santa Isabel'.

Note: where more than one vessel followed a similar course, the track of the leading ship is shown.

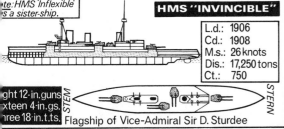

Note: HMS 'Inflexible' was a sister-ship.

HMS "INVINCIBLE"

L.d.:	1906
Cd.:	1908
M.s.:	26 knots
Dis.:	17,250 tons
Ct.:	750

ght 12-in.guns
xteen 4-in.gs.
ree 18-in.t.ts. Flagship of Vice-Admiral Sir D. Sturdee

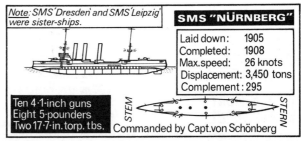

Note: SMS 'Dresden' and SMS 'Leipzig' were sister-ships.

SMS "NÜRNBERG"

Laid down:	1905
Completed:	1908
Max.speed:	26 knots
Displacement:	3,450 tons
Complement:	295

Ten 4·1-inch guns
Eight 5-pounders
Two 17·7-in. torp. tbs. Commanded by Capt. von Schönberg

241

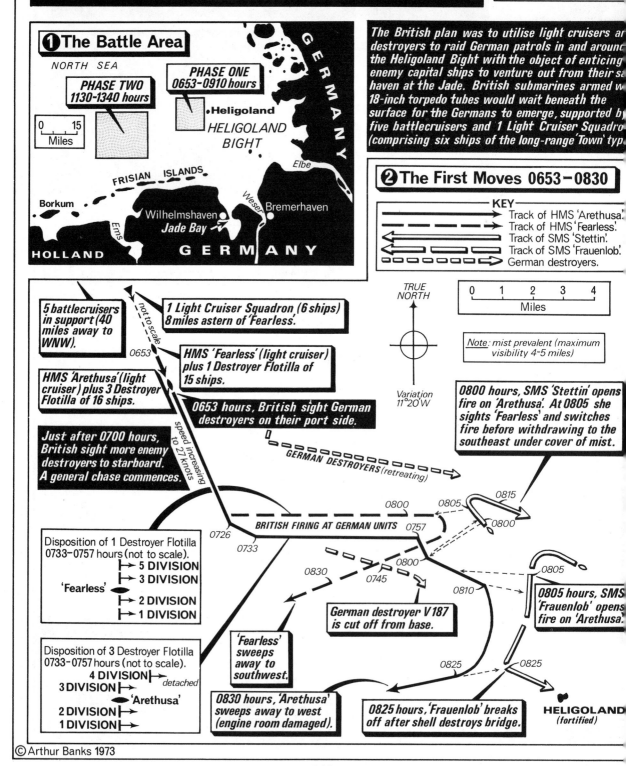

THE BATTLE OF HELIGOLAND BIGHT 28 AUGUST 1914

NOTE: GREENWICH MEAN TIME HAS BEEN ADOPTED FOR TRACK CALCULATION

❶ The Battle Area

NORTH SEA

GERMANY

PHASE TWO 1130-1340 hours

PHASE ONE 0653-0910 hours

Heligoland

HELIGOLAND BIGHT

0   15
Miles

Elbe

FRISIAN ISLANDS

Weser

Borkum

Ems

Bremerhaven

Wilhelmshaven
Jade Bay

HOLLAND   GERMANY

The British plan was to utilise light cruisers and destroyers to raid German patrols in and around the Heligoland Bight with the object of enticing enemy capital ships to venture out from their safe haven at the Jade. British submarines armed with 18-inch torpedo tubes would wait beneath the surface for the Germans to emerge, supported by five battlecruisers and 1 Light Cruiser Squadron (comprising six ships of the long-range 'Town' type).

❷ The First Moves 0653–0830

━━━━━━━ KEY ━━━━━━━
Track of HMS 'Arethusa'.
Track of HMS 'Fearless'.
Track of SMS 'Stettin'.
Track of SMS 'Frauenlob'.
German destroyers.

TRUE NORTH

0   1   2   3   4
Miles

Variation 11°20'W

Note: mist prevalent (maximum visibility 4-5 miles)

5 battlecruisers in support (40 miles away to WNW).

not to scale

0653

1 Light Cruiser Squadron (6 ships) 8 miles astern of 'Fearless'.

HMS 'Fearless' (light cruiser) plus 1 Destroyer Flotilla of 15 ships.

HMS 'Arethusa' (light cruiser) plus 3 Destroyer Flotilla of 16 ships.

0653 hours, British sight German destroyers on their port side.

0800 hours, SMS 'Stettin' opens fire on 'Arethusa'. At 0805 she sights 'Fearless' and switches fire before withdrawing to the southeast under cover of mist.

Just after 0700 hours, British sight more enemy destroyers to starboard. A general chase commences.

speed increasing to 27 knots

GERMAN DESTROYERS (retreating)

0815

0800   0805

0726   BRITISH FIRING AT GERMAN UNITS   0757   0800

0733

Disposition of 1 Destroyer Flotilla 0733-0757 hours (not to scale).
├─ 5 DIVISION
├─ 3 DIVISION
'Fearless'
├─ 2 DIVISION
├─ 1 DIVISION

0830   0745   0810   0805

German destroyer V 187 is cut off from base.

0805 hours, SMS 'Frauenlob' opens fire on 'Arethusa'.

Disposition of 3 Destroyer Flotilla 0733-0757 hours (not to scale).
4 DIVISION ├─ detached
3 DIVISION ├─
'Arethusa'
2 DIVISION ├─
1 DIVISION ├─

'Fearless' sweeps away to southwest.

0825   0825

0830 hours, 'Arethusa' sweeps away to west (engine room damaged).

0825 hours, 'Frauenlob' breaks off after shell destroys bridge.

HELIGOLAND (fortified)

© Arthur Banks 1973

The Sinking of German Destroyer V 187

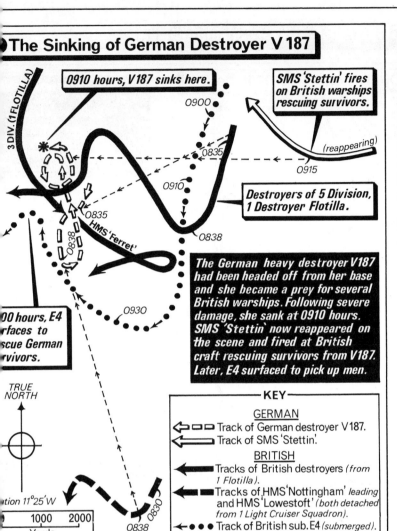

0910 hours, V 187 sinks here.

0900

SMS 'Stettin' fires on British warships rescuing survivors.

3 DIV (1 FLOTILLA)

0835

(reappearing)

0915

0910

Destroyers of 5 Division, 1 Destroyer Flotilla.

0835

HMS 'Ferret'

0838

0838

0910

The German heavy destroyer V 187 had been headed off from her base and she became a prey for several British warships. Following severe damage, she sank at 0910 hours. SMS 'Stettin' now reappeared on the scene and fired at British craft rescuing survivors from V 187. Later, E4 surfaced to pick up men.

0930

00 hours, E4 rfaces to scue German rvivors.

TRUE NORTH

tion 11°25'W

1000   2000
Yards

0830

0838

KEY

GERMAN
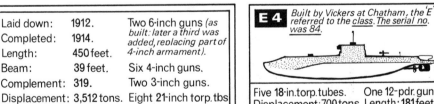 Track of German destroyer V 187.
Track of SMS 'Stettin'.

BRITISH
Tracks of British destroyers (from 1 Flotilla).
Tracks of HMS 'Nottingham' leading and HMS 'Lowestoft' (both detached from 1 Light Cruiser Squadron).
Track of British sub. E4 (submerged).

SMS 'STETTIN'

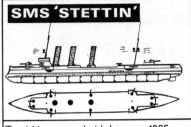

Ten 4·1-in. guns.	Laid down:	1905.
Eight 5-pdrs.	Completed:	1908.
Length: 360 feet.	Complement: 320.	
Beam: 44 feet.	Displacement: 3,450 tons.	

SMS 'FRAUENLOB'

Ten 4·1-in guns.	Laid down:	1900.
Ten 1-pdrs.	Completed:	1903.
Length: 330 feet.	Complement: 265.	
Beam: 40 feet.	Displacement: 2,715 tons.	

V 187

Note: the letter 'V' referred to the Vulkan construction yard at Stettin.

Two 24-pdr. guns. Complement: 84.
Three 18-in. torp. tbs. Max. speed: 35 knots.

E4

Built by Vickers at Chatham, the 'E' referred to the class. The serial no. was 84.

Five 18-in. torp. tubes.   One 12-pdr. gun.
Displacement: 700 tons. Length: 181 feet.
Complement: 30.   Beam: 22·5 feet.

MS 'ARETHUSA'

Light cruiser of 'Arethusa' class.

Laid down:	1912.	Two 6-inch guns (as built: later a third was added, replacing part of 4-inch armament).
Completed:	1914.	
Length:	450 feet.	
Beam:	39 feet.	Six 4-inch guns.
Complement:	319.	Two 3-inch guns.
Displacement:	3,512 tons.	Eight 21-inch torp. tbs
Max. speed:	29 knots.	(four above water).

MS 'FEARLESS'

Scout light cruiser of 'Active' class.

Laid down:	1911.	Ten 4-inch guns.
Completed:	1913.	Four 3-pounder guns.
Length:	385 feet.	Two 21-inch torp. tbs.
Beam:	41·5 feet.	Armour: nil.
Complement:	320.	(double skin amidships).
Displacement:	3,440 tons.	Mean draught: 14 feet.
Max. speed:	26 knots.	H.P. 18,000.

The German battlecruisers were "trapped" behind the sand bar at the Jade and could not move out until high tide. Meanwhile, several cruisers were despatched at full speed to engage the enemy (unaware of the British battlecruisers being near at hand). SMS 'Strassburg' and SMS 'Mainz' were the first arrivals.

0   10,00
Yards

❹ Start of Phase Two: Operations 1130–1200 hours

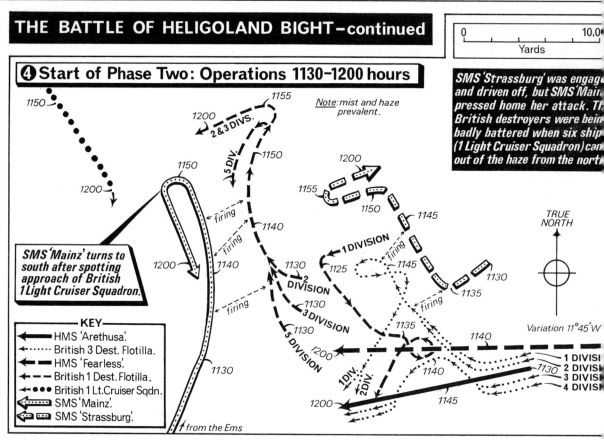

Note: mist and haze prevalent.

SMS 'Strassburg' was engage and driven off, but SMS 'Main. pressed home her attack. Th British destroyers were bein badly battered when six ship (1 Light Cruiser Squadron) can out of the haze from the nort

SMS 'Mainz' turns to south after spotting approach of British 1 Light Cruiser Squadron.

TRUE NORTH

Variation 11°45'W

KEY
- ← HMS 'Arethusa'.
- ←···· British 3 Dest. Flotilla.
- ←-- HMS 'Fearless'.
- ←--- British 1 Dest. Flotilla.
- ←••• British 1 Lt. Cruiser Sqdn.
- ⇐▭▭ SMS 'Mainz'.
- ⇐▭▭ SMS 'Strassburg'.

❺ Operations 1205–1230 hours

0   6,000
Yards

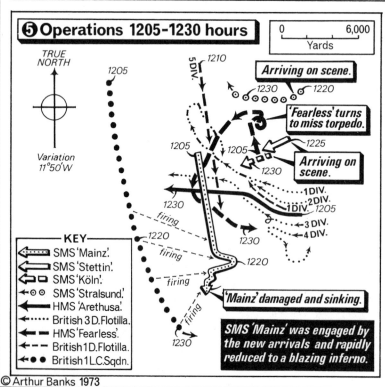

TRUE NORTH

Variation 11°50'W

Arriving on scene.

'Fearless' turns to miss torpedo.

Arriving on scene.

'Mainz' damaged and sinking.

SMS 'Mainz' was engaged by the new arrivals and rapidly reduced to a blazing inferno.

KEY
- ⇐▭▭ SMS 'Mainz'.
- ⇐ SMS 'Stettin'.
- ⇐▭ SMS 'Köln'.
- ←⊙⊙ SMS 'Stralsund'.
- ← HMS 'Arethusa'.
- ←···· British 3 D. Flotilla.
- ←-- HMS 'Fearless'.
- ←--- British 1 D. Flotilla.
- ←••• British 1 L.C. Sqdn.

HMS 'SOUTHAMPTON'

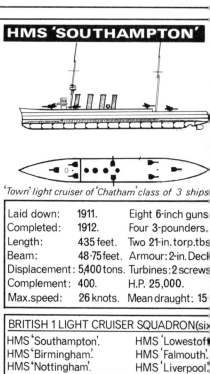

'Town' light cruiser of 'Chatham' class of 3 ships

Laid down:	1911.	Eight 6-inch guns
Completed:	1912.	Four 3-pounders,
Length:	435 feet.	Two 21-in. torp. tbs
Beam:	48.75 feet.	Armour: 2-in. Deck
Displacement:	5,400 tons.	Turbines: 2 screws
Complement:	400.	H.P. 25,000.
Max. speed:	26 knots.	Mean draught: 15

BRITISH 1 LIGHT CRUISER SQUADRON (six
- HMS 'Southampton'.   HMS 'Lowestof
- HMS 'Birmingham'.   HMS 'Falmouth'.
- HMS 'Nottingham'.   HMS 'Liverpool'.

© Arthur Banks 1973

The Final Moves: 1230-1340 hours

ealizing that sizable German reinforcements were arriving on
e scene, the British battlecruisers were called into action.
eir fire-power proved decisive: SMS 'Köln' was sunk and SMS
riadne' severely damaged (sinking later). Only the mist shroud
evented the remaining German ships from suffering like fates.

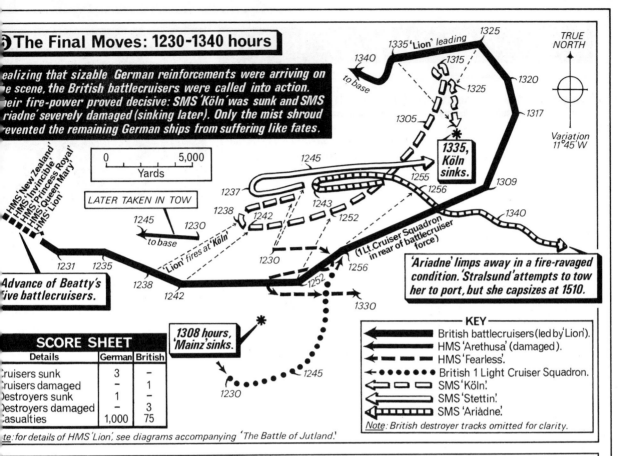

1325
1335 'Lion' leading
1340
1315
1325
1320
1317
to base
1305
1335, Köln sinks.

TRUE NORTH

Variation 11°45'W

0 — 5,000
Yards

1245
1255
1256
1309
1340

LATER TAKEN IN TOW
1245
1230
to base
1237
1238
1242
1243
1252

HMS 'New Zealand'
HMS 'Invincible'
HMS 'Princess Royal'
HMS 'Queen Mary'
HMS 'Lion'

Lion fires at 'Köln'
1230

(1 Lt. Cruiser Squadron in rear of battlecruiser force)

'Ariadne' limps away in a fire-ravaged condition. 'Stralsund' attempts to tow her to port, but she capsizes at 1510.

1231 1235
1238
1242
1230
1252
1256
1330

Advance of Beatty's five battlecruisers.

1308 hours, 'Mainz' sinks.

1245
1230

KEY
➤	British battlecruisers (led by 'Lion').
←	HMS 'Arethusa' (damaged).
⇠	HMS 'Fearless'.
••••	British 1 Light Cruiser Squadron.
⟸	SMS 'Köln'.
⟸	SMS 'Stettin'.
⟸	SMS 'Ariàdne'.

Note: British destroyer tracks omitted for clarity.

SCORE SHEET

Details	German	British
Cruisers sunk	3	–
Cruisers damaged	–	1
Destroyers sunk	1	–
Destroyers damaged	–	3
Casualties	1,000	75

Note: for details of HMS 'Lion', see diagrams accompanying 'The Battle of Jutland.'

SMS 'MAINZ' & SMS 'KÖLN'

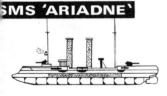

Note: both ships were light cruisers of the 'Kolberg' class.

Laid down: 1907	} 'Mainz'	Twelve 4·1-inch guns.	
Completed: 1909		Four 5-pounder guns.	
Laid down: 1908	} 'Köln'	Four machine guns.	
Completed: 1910		Two 18-inch torpedo tubes.	
Length:	428 feet.	Complement:	375.
Beam:	46 feet.	Max. speed:	27 knots.
Displacement:	4,350 tons.	Max. draught:	18 feet.

SMS 'ARIADNE'

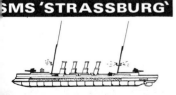

Protected cruiser of 'Nymphe' class.

Laid down:	1899.	Ten 4·1-inch guns.
Completed:	1901.	Fourteen 1-pounder guns.
Length:	328 feet.	Four machine guns.
Beam:	40 feet.	Two 17·7-inch torp. tubes.
Complement:	265.	Max. draught: 17·25 feet.
Displacement:	2,670 tons.	Armour: 2-in. Deck (amid.).
Max. speed:	21 knots.	" 1-in. Deck (ends).

SMS 'STRASSBURG'

Note: SMS 'Stralsund' was a sister-ship. (Similar details, including later armament alterations).

Light cruiser of 'Breslau' class.

Laid down:	1910.	Twelve 4·1-inch guns.
Completed:	1912.	*(Note: later altered to seven 5·9-inch and two 3·4-inch A.A. guns).*
Length:	445 feet.	
Beam:	43 feet.	
Complement:	370.	Two 20-inch torp. tubes.
Displacement:	4,550 tons.	Mean draught: 16·5 feet.
Max. speed:	28 knots.	Armour: 2-in. Deck (amid.).

245

SUBMARINE WARFARE IN 1914

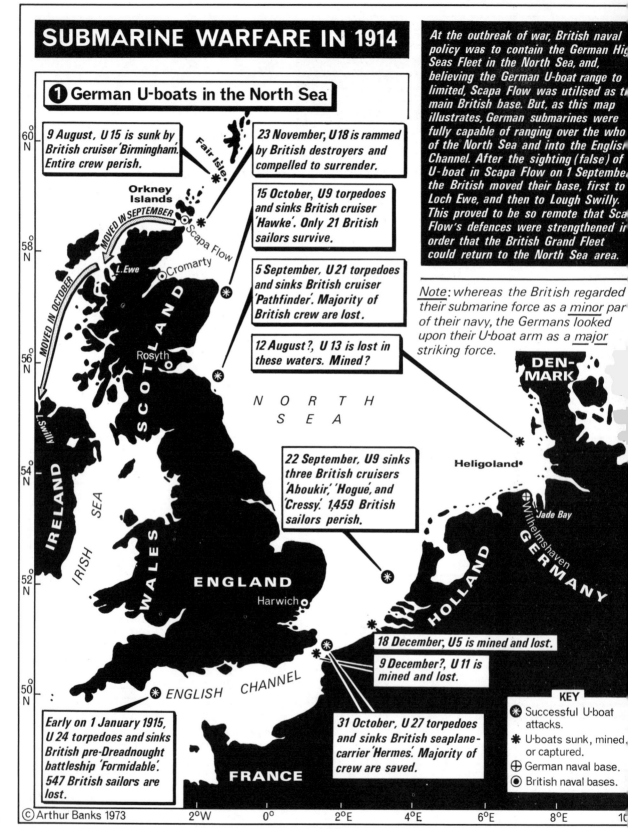

① German U-boats in the North Sea

9 August, U 15 is sunk by British cruiser 'Birmingham'. Entire crew perish.

23 November, U 18 is rammed by British destroyers and compelled to surrender.

15 October, U 9 torpedoes and sinks British cruiser 'Hawke'. Only 21 British sailors survive.

5 September, U 21 torpedoes and sinks British cruiser 'Pathfinder'. Majority of British crew are lost.

12 August?, U 13 is lost in these waters. Mined?

22 September, U 9 sinks three British cruisers 'Aboukir', 'Hogué', and 'Cressy'. 1,459 British sailors perish.

18 December, U 5 is mined and lost.

9 December?, U 11 is mined and lost.

31 October, U 27 torpedoes and sinks British seaplane-carrier 'Hermes'. Majority of crew are saved.

Early on 1 January 1915, U 24 torpedoes and sinks British pre-Dreadnought battleship 'Formidable'. 547 British sailors are lost.

At the outbreak of war, British naval policy was to contain the German High Seas Fleet in the North Sea, and, believing the German U-boat range to limited, Scapa Flow was utilised as the main British base. But, as this map illustrates, German submarines were fully capable of ranging over the whole of the North Sea and into the English Channel. After the sighting (false) of U-boat in Scapa Flow on 1 September the British moved their base, first to Loch Ewe, and then to Lough Swilly. This proved to be so remote that Scapa Flow's defences were strengthened in order that the British Grand Fleet could return to the North Sea area.

<u>Note</u>: whereas the British regarded their submarine force as a <u>minor</u> part of their navy, the Germans looked upon their U-boat arm as a <u>major</u> striking force.

MOVED IN SEPTEMBER

MOVED IN OCTOBER

Fair Isle

Orkney Islands

Scapa Flow

L. Ewe

Cromarty

SCOTLAND

Rosyth

L. Swilly

IRELAND

IRISH SEA

WALES

ENGLAND

Harwich

ENGLISH CHANNEL

FRANCE

NORTH SEA

DEN-MARK

Heligoland

Wilhelmshaven

Jade Bay

GERMANY

HOLLAND

KEY
- ✱ Successful U-boat attacks.
- ✻ U-boats sunk, mined, or captured.
- ⊕ German naval base.
- ◉ British naval bases.

© Arthur Banks 1973

2°W 0° 2°E 4°E 6°E 8°E 10

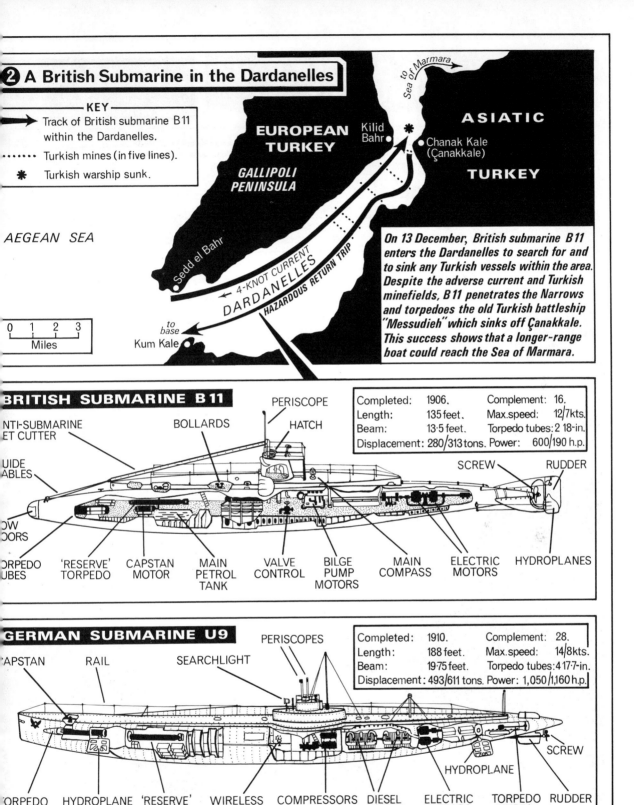

❷ A British Submarine in the Dardanelles

KEY

→ Track of British submarine B 11 within the Dardanelles.

⋯⋯ Turkish mines (in five lines).

✳ Turkish warship sunk.

to Sea of Marmara

ASIATIC

EUROPEAN TURKEY Kilid Bahr ✳ • Chanak Kale (Çanakkale)

GALLIPOLI PENINSULA **TURKEY**

AEGEAN SEA

Sedd el Bahr

4-KNOT CURRENT DARDANELLES HAZARDOUS RETURN TRIP

0 1 2 3
Miles

to base
Kum Kale

On 13 December, British submarine B 11 enters the Dardanelles to search for and to sink any Turkish vessels within the area. Despite the adverse current and Turkish minefields, B 11 penetrates the Narrows and torpedoes the old Turkish battleship "Messudieh" which sinks off Çanakkale. This success shows that a longer-range boat could reach the Sea of Marmara.

BRITISH SUBMARINE B 11

PERISCOPE

BOLLARDS   HATCH

ANTI-SUBMARINE
NET CUTTER

GUIDE
CABLES

BOW
DOORS

Completed:	1906.	Complement:	16.
Length:	135 feet.	Max. speed:	12/7 kts.
Beam:	13·5 feet.	Torpedo tubes:	2 18-in.
Displacement: 280/313 tons.		Power:	600/190 h.p.

SCREW   RUDDER

TORPEDO
TUBES   'RESERVE' TORPEDO   CAPSTAN MOTOR   MAIN PETROL TANK   VALVE CONTROL   BILGE PUMP MOTORS   MAIN COMPASS   ELECTRIC MOTORS   HYDROPLANES

GERMAN SUBMARINE U9

PERISCOPES

CAPSTAN   RAIL   SEARCHLIGHT

Completed:	1910.	Complement:	28.
Length:	188 feet.	Max. speed:	14/8 kts.
Beam:	19·75 feet.	Torpedo tubes:	4 17·7-in.
Displacement: 493/611 tons.		Power:	1,050/1,160 h.p.

SCREW

HYDROPLANE

TORPEDO
TUBES   HYDROPLANE   'RESERVE' TORPEDO   WIRELESS CABIN   COMPRESSORS   DIESEL ENGINES   ELECTRIC MOTORS   TORPEDO TUBES   RUDDER

247

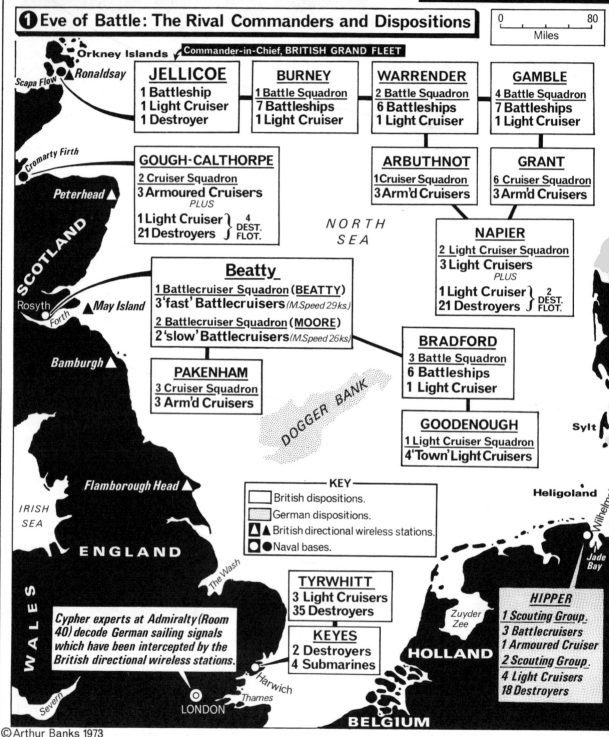

BATTLE OF THE DOGGER BANK 24 JANUARY 1915

Note: in August 1914, SMS 'Magdeburg'(a German light cruiser of the 'Breslau' class) was lost in the Baltic. The Russians recovered its signal code book and passed them to the Admiralty in London. British cypher experts utilised these for decoding purposes.

❶ Eve of Battle: The Rival Commanders and Dispositions

0 ___ 80
Miles

Orkney Islands
▲Ronaldsay
Scapa Flow
Cromarty Firth
Peterhead ▲
SCOTLAND
Rosyth
May Island ▲
Forth
Bamburgh ▲
Flamborough Head ▲
IRISH SEA
ENGLAND
WALES
Severn
The Wash
Thames
Harwich
LONDON
BELGIUM
NORTH SEA
DOGGER BANK
Heligoland
Wilhelmshaven
Jade Bay
Sylt
Zuyder Zee
HOLLAND

Commander-in-Chief, BRITISH GRAND FLEET

JELLICOE
1 Battleship
1 Light Cruiser
1 Destroyer

BURNEY
1 Battle Squadron
7 Battleships
1 Light Cruiser

WARRENDER
2 Battle Squadron
6 Battleships
1 Light Cruiser

GAMBLE
4 Battle Squadron
7 Battleships
1 Light Cruiser

GOUGH-CALTHORPE
2 Cruiser Squadron
3 Armoured Cruisers
PLUS
1 Light Cruiser } 4 DEST. FLOT.
21 Destroyers }

ARBUTHNOT
1 Cruiser Squadron
3 Arm'd Cruisers

GRANT
6 Cruiser Squadron
3 Arm'd Cruisers

NAPIER
2 Light Cruiser Squadron
3 Light Cruisers
PLUS
1 Light Cruiser } 2 DEST. FLOT.
21 Destroyers }

Beatty
1 Battlecruiser Squadron (**BEATTY**)
3 'fast' Battlecruisers *(M.Speed 29 ks.)*
2 Battlecruiser Squadron (**MOORE**)
2 'slow' Battlecruisers *(M.Speed 26 ks.)*

PAKENHAM
3 Cruiser Squadron
3 Arm'd Cruisers

BRADFORD
3 Battle Squadron
6 Battleships
1 Light Cruiser

GOODENOUGH
1 Light Cruiser Squadron
4 'Town' Light Cruisers

KEY
□ British dispositions.
▨ German dispositions.
△▲ British directional wireless stations.
○● Naval bases.

Cypher experts at Admiralty (Room 40) decode German sailing signals which have been intercepted by the British directional wireless stations.

TYRWHITT
3 Light Cruisers
35 Destroyers

KEYES
2 Destroyers
4 Submarines

HIPPER
1 Scouting Group.
3 Battlecruisers
1 Armoured Cruiser
2 Scouting Group.
4 Light Cruisers
18 Destroyers

© Arthur Banks 1973

248

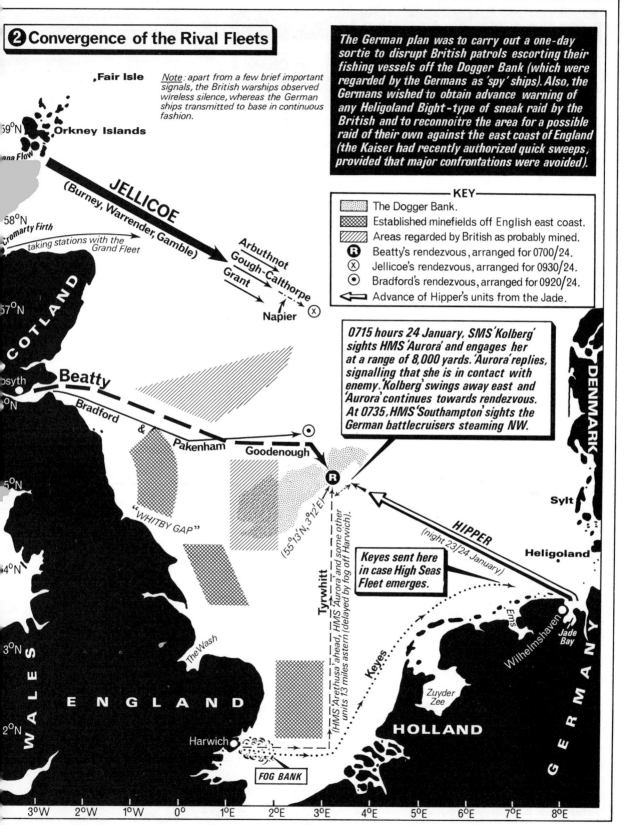

❷ Convergence of the Rival Fleets

Fair Isle

Note: apart from a few brief important signals, the British warships observed wireless silence, whereas the German ships transmitted to base in continuous fashion.

Orkney Islands

59°N

Scapa Flow

58°N

Cromarty Firth

57°N

JELLICOE
(Burney, Warrender, Gamble)

taking stations with the Grand Fleet

Arbuthnot
Gough-Calthorpe
Grant

Napier

Ⓧ

The German plan was to carry out a one-day sortie to disrupt British patrols escorting their fishing vessels off the Dogger Bank (which were regarded by the Germans as 'spy' ships). Also, the Germans wished to obtain advance warning of any Heligoland Bight-type of sneak raid by the British and to reconnoitre the area for a possible raid of their own against the east coast of England (the Kaiser had recently authorized quick sweeps, provided that major confrontations were avoided).

— KEY —

- The Dogger Bank.
- Established minefields off English east coast.
- Areas regarded by British as probably mined.
- Ⓡ Beatty's rendezvous, arranged for 0700/24.
- Ⓧ Jellicoe's rendezvous, arranged for 0930/24.
- ⊙ Bradford's rendezvous, arranged for 0920/24.
- ⇐ Advance of Hipper's units from the Jade.

0715 hours 24 January, SMS 'Kolberg' sights HMS 'Aurora' and engages her at a range of 8,000 yards. 'Aurora' replies, signalling that she is in contact with enemy. 'Kolberg' swings away east and 'Aurora' continues towards rendezvous. At 0735, HMS 'Southampton' sights the German battlecruisers steaming NW.

SCOTLAND

Rosyth

56°N

Beatty

Bradford

&

Pakenham

Goodenough

⊙

Ⓡ

(55°13'N, 3°12'E)

55°N

"WHITBY GAP"

54°N

DENMARK

Sylt

HIPPER
(night 23/24 January)

Heligoland

Keyes sent here in case High Seas Fleet emerges.

Tyrwhitt

(HMS 'Arethusa' ahead, HMS 'Aurora' and some other units 13 miles astern (delayed by fog off Harwich).

Keyes

Ems

Wilhelmshaven

Jade Bay

The Wash

3°N

Zuyder Zee

2°N

WALES

ENGLAND

Harwich

FOG BANK

HOLLAND

GERMANY

| 3°W | 2°W | 1°W | 0° | 1°E | 2°E | 3°E | 4°E | 5°E | 6°E | 7°E | 8°E |

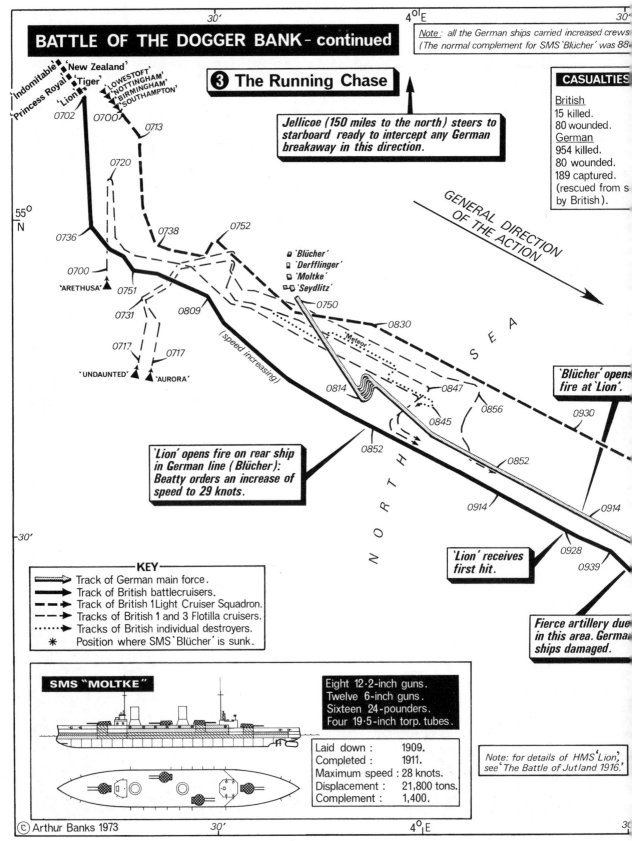

BATTLE OF THE DOGGER BANK - continued

Note: all the German ships carried increased crews (The normal complement for SMS 'Blücher' was 88...

❸ The Running Chase

Jellicoe (150 miles to the north) steers to starboard ready to intercept any German breakaway in this direction.

CASUALTIES

British
15 killed.
80 wounded.
German
954 killed.
80 wounded.
189 captured.
(rescued from s...
by British).

GENERAL DIRECTION OF THE ACTION

'Indomitable' 'New Zealand'
'Princess Royal' 'Tiger'
'Lion'
0702
0700
0713

LOWESTOFT
'NOTTINGHAM'
'BIRMINGHAM'
'SOUTHAMPTON'

0720

55° N

0736

0738

0752

🅑 'Blücher'
🅑 'Derfflinger'
🅑 'Moltke'
🅑🅑 'Seydlitz'

0700

'ARETHUSA' 0751

0731 0809

0750

0830

'Meteor'

0717 0717

'UNDAUNTED' 'AURORA'

(speed increasing)

0814

0847

0856

0930

0845

0852

'Blücher' opens fire at 'Lion'.

N O R T H   S E A

'Lion' opens fire on rear ship in German line (Blücher): Beatty orders an increase of speed to 29 knots.

0852

0914

0914

'Lion' receives first hit.

0928

0939

KEY

- ⇒ Track of German main force.
- ➤ Track of British battlecruisers.
- - - ➤ Track of British 1 Light Cruiser Squadron.
- – – ➤ Tracks of British 1 and 3 Flotilla cruisers.
- ······➤ Tracks of British individual destroyers.
- ✱ Position where SMS 'Blücher' is sunk.

Fierce artillery due... in this area. Germa... ships damaged.

SMS "MOLTKE"

Eight 12·2-inch guns.
Twelve 6-inch guns.
Sixteen 24-pounders.
Four 19·5-inch torp. tubes.

Laid down :	1909.
Completed :	1911.
Maximum speed :	28 knots.
Displacement :	21,800 tons.
Complement :	1,400.

Note: for details of HMS 'Lion', see 'The Battle of Jutland 1916.'

Ⓒ Arthur Banks 1973

30'

4° E

250

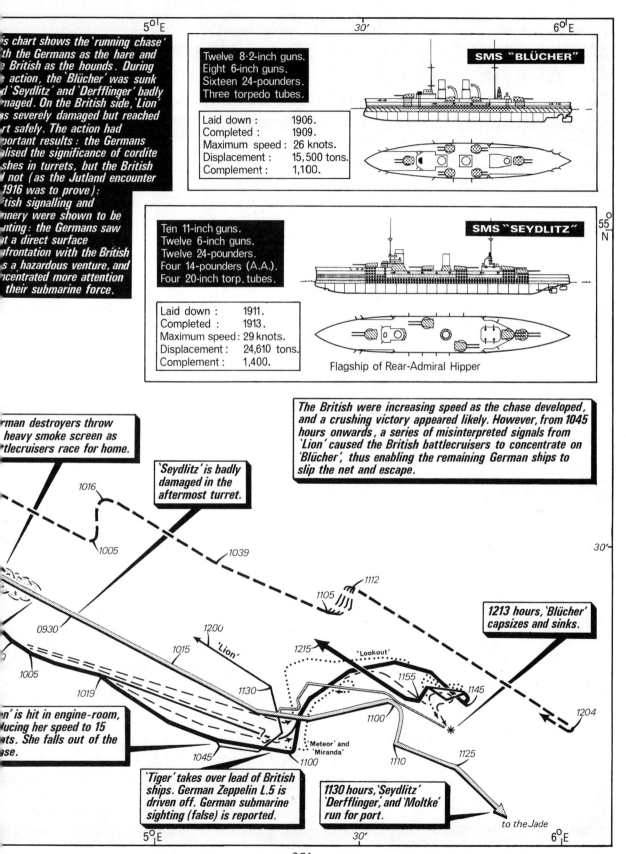

is chart shows the 'running chase' th the Germans as the hare and e British as the hounds. During action, the 'Blücher' was sunk d 'Seydlitz' and 'Derfflinger' badly maged. On the British side, 'Lion' s severely damaged but reached rt safely. The action had portant results: the Germans alised the significance of cordite shes in turrets, but the British not (as the Jutland encounter 1916 was to prove): tish signalling and nnery were shown to be nting: the Germans saw a direct surface frontation with the British s a hazardous venture, and ncentrated more attention their submarine force.

Twelve 8·2-inch guns.
Eight 6-inch guns.
Sixteen 24-pounders.
Three torpedo tubes.

SMS "BLÜCHER"

Laid down:	1906.
Completed:	1909.
Maximum speed:	26 knots.
Displacement:	15,500 tons.
Complement:	1,100.

Ten 11-inch guns.
Twelve 6-inch guns.
Twelve 24-pounders.
Four 14-pounders (A.A.).
Four 20-inch torp. tubes.

SMS "SEYDLITZ"

Laid down:	1911.
Completed:	1913.
Maximum speed:	29 knots.
Displacement:	24,610 tons.
Complement:	1,400.

Flagship of Rear-Admiral Hipper

The British were increasing speed as the chase developed, and a crushing victory appeared likely. However, from 1045 hours onwards, a series of misinterpreted signals from 'Lion' caused the British battlecruisers to concentrate on 'Blücher', thus enabling the remaining German ships to slip the net and escape.

rman destroyers throw heavy smoke screen as tlecruisers race for home.

'Seydlitz' is badly damaged in the aftermost turret.

1213 hours, 'Blücher' capsizes and sinks.

n' is hit in engine-room, ucing her speed to 15 ts. She falls out of the se.

'Tiger' takes over lead of British ships. German Zeppelin L.5 is driven off. German submarine sighting (false) is reported.

1130 hours, 'Seydlitz' 'Derfflinger', and 'Moltke' run for port.

to the Jade

'Lion'
'Lookout'
'Meteor' and 'Miranda'

1016
1005
1039
1112
1105
0930
1200
1215
1155
1145
1015
1130
1100
1204
1005
1019
1045
1100
1110
1125

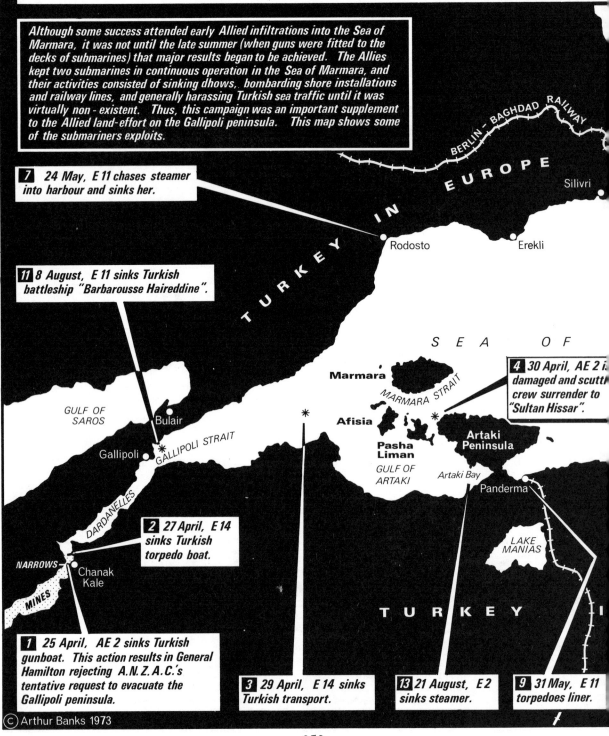

THE SUCCESSFUL ALLIED SUBMARINE CAMPAIGN AT THE TIME OF THE GALLIPOLI EXPEDITION MAY - DECEMBER 1915

Although some success attended early Allied infiltrations into the Sea of Marmara, it was not until the late summer (when guns were fitted to the decks of submarines) that major results began to be achieved. The Allies kept two submarines in continuous operation in the Sea of Marmara, and their activities consisted of sinking dhows, bombarding shore installations and railway lines, and generally harassing Turkish sea traffic until it was virtually non - existent. Thus, this campaign was an important supplement to the Allied land-effort on the Gallipoli peninsula. This map shows some of the submariners exploits.

7 24 May, E 11 chases steamer into harbour and sinks her.

11 8 August, E 11 sinks Turkish battleship "Barbarousse Haireddine".

4 30 April, AE 2 i... damaged and scutt... crew surrender to "Sultan Hissar".

2 27 April, E 14 sinks Turkish torpedo boat.

1 25 April, AE 2 sinks Turkish gunboat. This action results in General Hamilton rejecting A.N.Z.A.C.'s tentative request to evacuate the Gallipoli peninsula.

3 29 April, E 14 sinks Turkish transport.

13 21 August, E 2 sinks steamer.

9 31 May, E 11 torpedoes liner.

TURKEY IN EUROPE

BERLIN - BAGHDAD RAILWAY

Silivri

Rodosto

Erekli

SEA OF

Marmara

MARMARA STRAIT

Afisia

Pasha Liman

Artaki Peninsula

GULF OF ARTAKI

Artaki Bay

Panderma

LAKE MANIAS

GULF OF SAROS

Bulair

Gallipoli

GALLIPOLI STRAIT

DARDANELLES

NARROWS

Chanak Kale

MINES

TURKEY

© Arthur Banks 1973

252

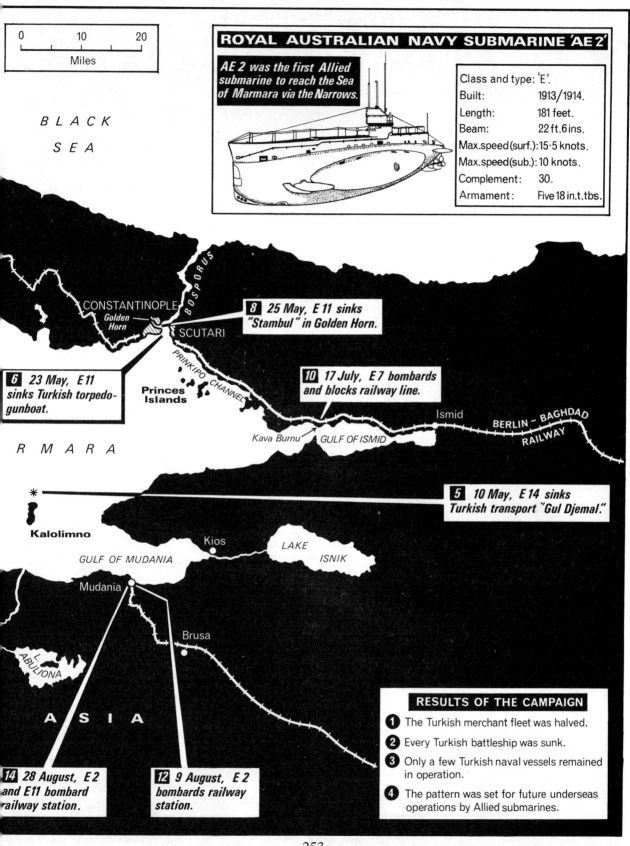

BLACK SEA

ROYAL AUSTRALIAN NAVY SUBMARINE 'AE 2'

AE 2 was the first Allied submarine to reach the Sea of Marmara via the Narrows.

Class and type: 'E'.
Built: 1913/1914.
Length: 181 feet.
Beam: 22 ft. 6 ins.
Max. speed (surf.): 15·5 knots.
Max. speed (sub.): 10 knots.
Complement: 30.
Armament: Five 18 in. t. tbs.

0   10   20
Miles

BOSPORUS

CONSTANTINOPLE
Golden Horn
SCUTARI

8 25 May, E 11 sinks "Stambul" in Golden Horn.

6 23 May, E 11 sinks Turkish torpedo-gunboat.

PRINKIPO CHANNEL

Princes Islands

10 17 July, E 7 bombards and blocks railway line.

Ismid

BERLIN – BAGHDAD RAILWAY

Kava Burnu GULF OF ISMID

R M A R A

5 10 May, E 14 sinks Turkish transport "Gul Djemal."

Kalolimno

Kios   LAKE ISNIK

GULF OF MUDANIA

Mudania

L. ABULIONA

Brusa

A S I A

RESULTS OF THE CAMPAIGN

1 The Turkish merchant fleet was halved.

2 Every Turkish battleship was sunk.

3 Only a few Turkish naval vessels remained in operation.

4 The pattern was set for future undersea operations by Allied submarines.

14 28 August, E 2 and E11 bombard railway station.

12 9 August, E 2 bombards railway station.

BRITISH BATTLESHIP LOSSES DURING THE GALLIPOLI CAMPAIGN MAY 1915

On 12 May, HMS "Queen Elizabeth" was ordered home from the Aegean area to strengthen the British Grand Fleet. On 13 May, the British battleship HMS "Goliath" was sunk by a Turkish destroyer, and later in the month the U21 sank two more British battleships. The Allied heavy warships were withdrawn from the Gallipoli operations leaving the land troops with no large naval guns to support them until the new monitors arrived in August.

KEY

✳ Positions of the three British battleships when sunk during May.

★ Main forts.

Boghali

Gaba Tepe

2 1225 hours 25 May, U21 torpedoes HMS "Triumph" in full view of A.N.Z.A.C. troops. 3 British officers and 70 men are lost. De Robeck promptly recalls all large warships to Mudros: this causes a demoralizing effect upon the Allied troops on land. HMS "Majestic" is ordered to 'W' Beach on 26 May.

Maidos

GALLIPOLI PENINSULA

DARDANELLES

Kilid Bahr

Chanak Kale

AEGEAN SEA

Krithia

0 1 2 3
Miles

'W' Beach

Cape Helles

Morto Bay

Eski Hissarlik Pt.

ROUTE OF U21 TO THE AEGEAN

U21 DEPARTS 25 APRIL.

U21 ARRIVES HERE ON 13 MAY. CREW RESTS FOR ONE WEEK WHILE SUBMARINE IS REFUELLED AND STORES REPLENISHED.

Wilhelmshaven

Cattaro

Cape Helles

1 0116 hours 13 May, HMS "Goliath" is sunk by Turkish destroyer "Muavenet-i-Miliet." Operating under cover of a thick mist, the destroyer fires three torpedoes. 570 British officers and men are lost. This is the largest single disaster suffered by the Royal Navy throughout the entire Dardanelles and Gallipoli campaign.

3 0645 hours 27 May, U21 fires two torpedoes at HMS "Majestic". The "fish" penetrate the protecting torpedo-nets and British battleship sinks with the loss of 40 men.

0 600
Miles

25 MAY, U21 ARRIVES OFF CAPE HELLES.

© Arthur Banks 1973

NORTH SEA RIVAL STRATEGIES

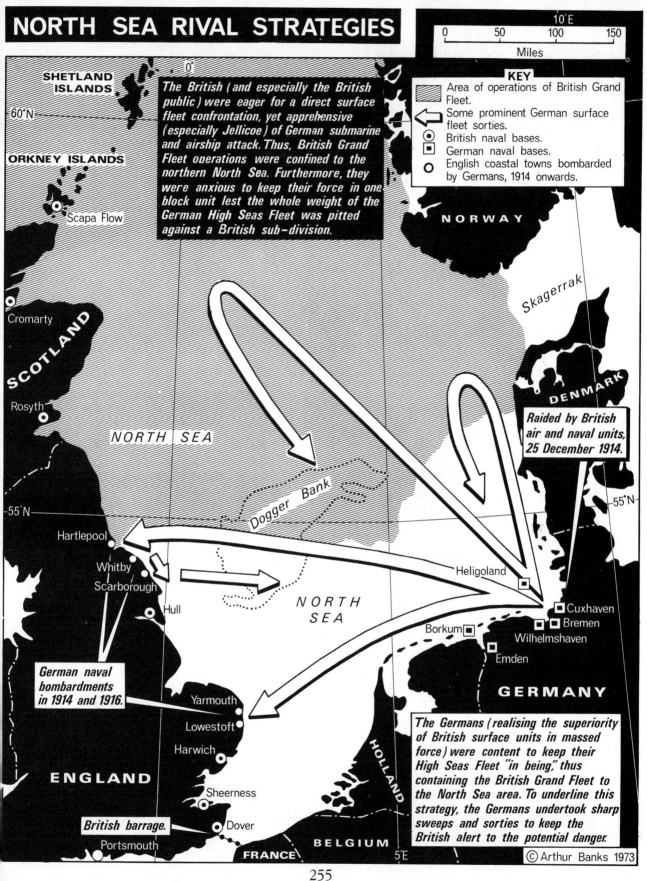

KEY

Area of operations of British Grand Fleet.

Some prominent German surface fleet sorties.

⊙ British naval bases.

▣ German naval bases.

○ English coastal towns bombarded by Germans, 1914 onwards.

10°E

| 0 | 50 | 100 | 150 |

Miles

SHETLAND ISLANDS

60°N

ORKNEY ISLANDS

Scapa Flow

The British (and especially the British public) were eager for a direct surface fleet confrontation, yet apprehensive (especially Jellicoe) of German submarine and airship attack. Thus, British Grand Fleet operations were confined to the northern North Sea. Furthermore, they were anxious to keep their force in one block unit lest the whole weight of the German High Seas Fleet was pitted against a British sub-division.

NORWAY

Cromarty

SCOTLAND

Rosyth

NORTH SEA

Skagerrak

DENMARK

Raided by British air and naval units, 25 December 1914.

55°N

Dogger Bank

55°N

Hartlepool

Whitby

Scarborough

Hull

NORTH SEA

Heligoland

Borkum

□ Cuxhaven
□ Bremen
Wilhelmshaven
Emden

German naval bombardments in 1914 and 1916.

Yarmouth

Lowestoft

Harwich

GERMANY

ENGLAND

Sheerness

HOLLAND

British barrage.

Dover

Portsmouth

FRANCE

BELGIUM

5°E

The Germans (realising the superiority of British surface units in massed force) were content to keep their High Seas Fleet "in being," thus containing the British Grand Fleet to the North Sea area. To underline this strategy, the Germans undertook sharp sweeps and sorties to keep the British alert to the potential danger.

© Arthur Banks 1973

255

THE BATTLE OF JUTLAND 31 MAY 1916

Note; to avoid any possi confusion, times are bas on the 24-hour clock syst

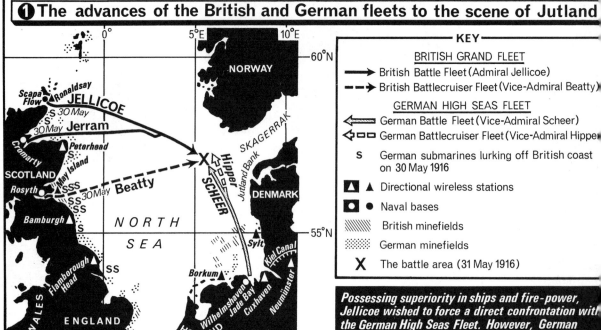

① The advances of the British and German fleets to the scene of Jutland

KEY

BRITISH GRAND FLEET
→ British Battle Fleet (Admiral Jellicoe)
⇢ British Battlecruiser Fleet (Vice-Admiral Beatty)

GERMAN HIGH SEAS FLEET
⬅ German Battle Fleet (Vice-Admiral Scheer)
⬅□ German Battlecruiser Fleet (Vice-Admiral Hipper)

S German submarines lurking off British coast on 30 May 1916
▲ Directional wireless stations
● Naval bases
British minefields
German minefields
X The battle area (31 May 1916)

Possessing superiority in ships and fire-power, Jellicoe wished to force a direct confrontation with the German High Seas Fleet. However, German naval strategy was designed to avoid a head-on clash, but to contain the British Grand Fleet in the North Sea area by the very presence of their large fleet which might venture out of port at any time.

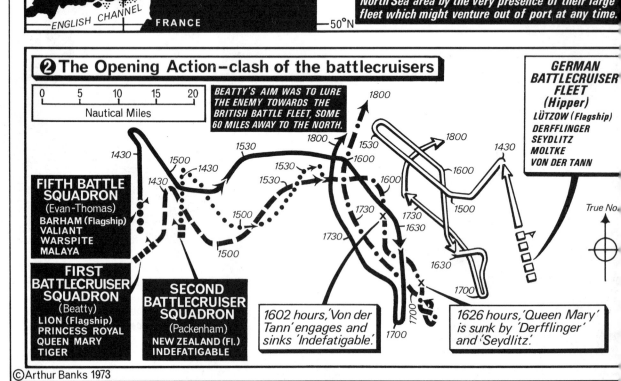

② The Opening Action—clash of the battlecruisers

GERMAN BATTLECRUISER FLEET (Hipper)
LÜTZOW (Flagship)
DERFFLINGER
SEYDLITZ
MOLTKE
VON DER TANN

0 5 10 15 20 Nautical Miles

BEATTY'S AIM WAS TO LURE THE ENEMY TOWARDS THE BRITISH BATTLE FLEET, SOME 60 MILES AWAY TO THE NORTH.

FIFTH BATTLE SQUADRON (Evan-Thomas)
BARHAM (Flagship)
VALIANT
WARSPITE
MALAYA

FIRST BATTLECRUISER SQUADRON (Beatty)
LION (Flagship)
PRINCESS ROYAL
QUEEN MARY
TIGER

SECOND BATTLECRUISER SQUADRON (Packenham)
NEW ZEALAND (Fl.)
INDEFATIGABLE

1602 hours, 'Von der Tann' engages and sinks 'Indefatigable'.

1626 hours, 'Queen Mary' is sunk by 'Derfflinger' and 'Seydlitz'.

© Arthur Banks 1973

256

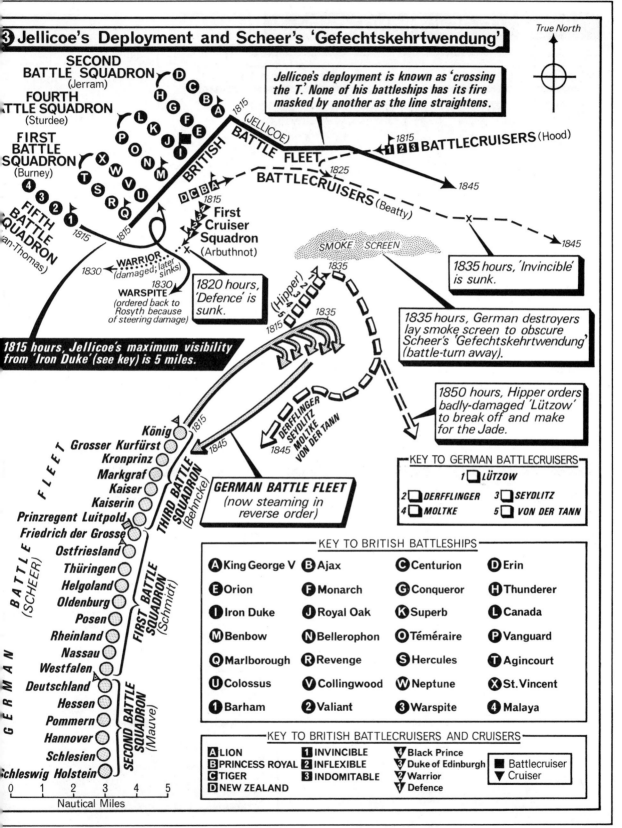

3 Jellicoe's Deployment and Scheer's 'Gefechtskehrtwendung'

True North

SECOND BATTLE SQUADRON (Jerram)

FOURTH BATTLE SQUADRON (Sturdee)

FIRST BATTLE SQUADRON (Burney)

FIFTH BATTLE SQUADRON (an-Thomas)

Jellicoe's deployment is known as 'crossing the T.' None of his battleships has its fire masked by another as the line straightens.

(JELLICOE)

BRITISH BATTLE FLEET

1815 BATTLECRUISERS (Hood)

BATTLECRUISERS (Beatty)

First Cruiser Squadron (Arbuthnot)

1835 hours, 'Invincible' is sunk.

SMOKE SCREEN

WARRIOR (damaged; later sinks)

WARSPITE (ordered back to Rosyth because of steering damage)

1820 hours, 'Defence' is sunk.

(Hipper)

1835 hours, German destroyers lay smoke screen to obscure Scheer's 'Gefechtskehrtwendung' (battle-turn away).

1850 hours, Hipper orders badly-damaged 'Lützow' to break off and make for the Jade.

1815 hours, Jellicoe's maximum visibility from 'Iron Duke' (see key) is 5 miles.

DERFFLINGER
SEYDLITZ
MOLTKE
VON DER TANN

König
Grosser Kurfürst
Kronprinz
Markgraf
Kaiser
Kaiserin
Prinzregent Luitpold
Friedrich der Grosse
Ostfriesland
Thüringen
Helgoland
Oldenburg
Posen
Rheinland
Nassau
Westfalen
Deutschland
Hessen
Pommern
Hannover
Schlesien
Schleswig Holstein

FLEET

THIRD BATTLE SQUADRON (Behncke)

FIRST BATTLE SQUADRON (Schmidt)

SECOND BATTLE SQUADRON (Mauve)

GERMAN BATTLE FLEET (now steaming in reverse order)

BATTLE (SCHEER)

GERMAN

KEY TO GERMAN BATTLECRUISERS
1 LÜTZOW
2 DERFFLINGER
3 SEYDLITZ
4 MOLTKE
5 VON DER TANN

KEY TO BRITISH BATTLESHIPS
A King George V	**B** Ajax	**C** Centurion	**D** Erin
E Orion	**F** Monarch	**G** Conqueror	**H** Thunderer
I Iron Duke	**J** Royal Oak	**K** Superb	**L** Canada
M Benbow	**N** Bellerophon	**O** Téméraire	**P** Vanguard
Q Marlborough	**R** Revenge	**S** Hercules	**T** Agincourt
U Colossus	**V** Collingwood	**W** Neptune	**X** St. Vincent
1 Barham	**2** Valiant	**3** Warspite	**4** Malaya

KEY TO BRITISH BATTLECRUISERS AND CRUISERS
A LION	**1** INVINCIBLE	**4** Black Prince	■ Battlecruiser
B PRINCESS ROYAL	**2** INFLEXIBLE	**3** Duke of Edinburgh	▼ Cruiser
C TIGER	**3** INDOMITABLE	**2** Warrior	
D NEW ZEALAND		**V** Defence	

0 1 2 3 4 5
Nautical Miles

THE BATTLE OF JUTLAND - continued

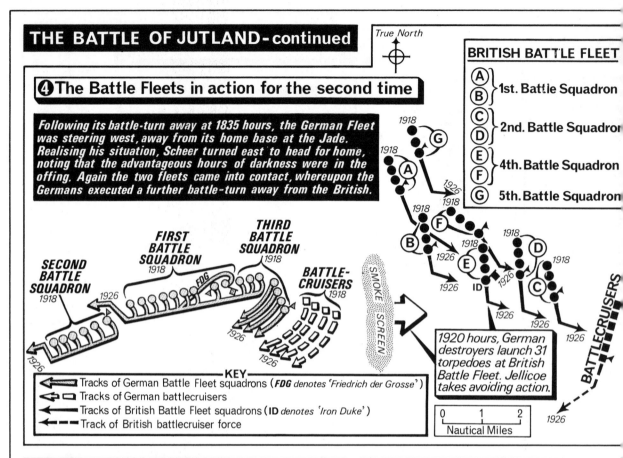

❹ The Battle Fleets in action for the second time

Following its battle-turn away at 1835 hours, the German Fleet was steering west, away from its home base at the Jade. Realising his situation, Scheer turned east to head for home, noting that the advantageous hours of darkness were in the offing. Again the two fleets came into contact, whereupon the Germans executed a further battle-turn away from the British.

BRITISH BATTLE FLEET

(A) (B) — 1st. Battle Squadron
(C) (D) — 2nd. Battle Squadron
(E) (F) — 4th. Battle Squadron
(G) — 5th. Battle Squadron

SECOND BATTLE SQUADRON 1918
FIRST BATTLE SQUADRON 1918
THIRD BATTLE SQUADRON 1918
BATTLE-CRUISERS 1918

SMOKE SCREEN

1920 hours, German destroyers launch 31 torpedoes at British Battle Fleet. Jellicoe takes avoiding action.

BATTLECRUISERS

KEY
Tracks of German Battle Fleet squadrons (**FDG** denotes 'Friedrich der Grosse')
Tracks of German battlecruisers
Tracks of British Battle Fleet squadrons (**ID** denotes 'Iron Duke')
Track of British battlecruiser force

0   1   2
Nautical Miles

A BRITISH BATTLECRUISER GUN TURRET

The loss of three British battlecruisers at Jutland was attributed to lack of adequate anti-flash screening between magazine and handling-room.

GUN HOUSE
GUN
RAMMER
MOUNTING
WORKING CHAMBER
RAMMERS
MAIN TRUNK
HANDLING ROOM
HANDLING ROOM
CORDITE CHARGES
MAGAZINE
CAGE
SHELL ROOM
SHELL ROOM

A shell exploding in the gun house of a turret could ignite a chain of charges down to the magazine section.

BRITISH AND GERMAN LOSSES AT JUTLAND

DETAILS	BRITISH	GERMAN
Total of ships engaged	151	99
Total of men employed	60,000	36,000
Battleships sunk	0	1
Battlecruisers sunk	3	1
Armoured cruisers sunk	3	0
Light cruisers sunk	0	4
Destroyers sunk	8	5
Casualties	6,097	2,551

The Battle of Jutland (known to the Germans as the 'Skagerrak') was a German success in terms of ships sunk and men lost, and contributed to Russia's exit from the war. Allied supplies to the hard-pressed Russian armies could not be guaranteed, as the Baltic approaches remained in possession of the High Seas Fleet. A controversy commenced in Britain to apportion the blame for the result, and a Jellicoe versus Beatty campaign ensued. Nevertheless, the German Fleet had been badly mauled, and U-boat warfare against British commerce was a consequence.

❺ The escape of the German Fleet–the night chase

0 — 50 Miles

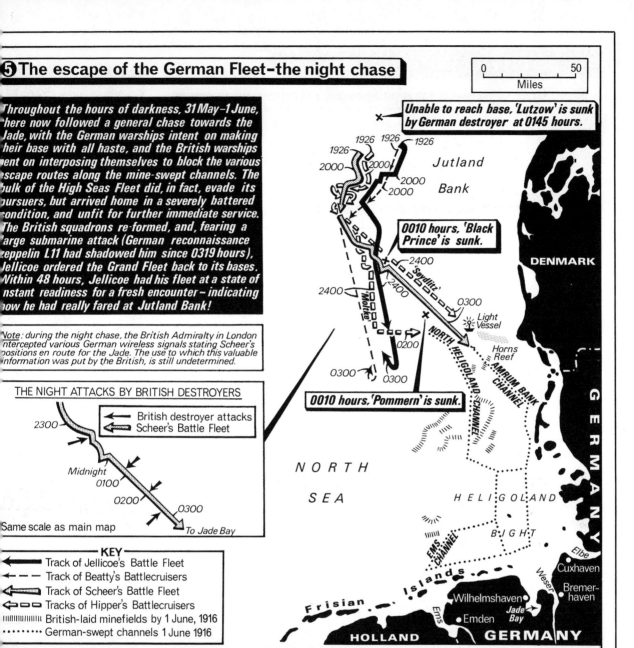

Throughout the hours of darkness, 31 May–1 June, there now followed a general chase towards the Jade, with the German warships intent on making their base with all haste, and the British warships bent on interposing themselves to block the various escape routes along the mine-swept channels. The bulk of the High Seas Fleet did, in fact, evade its pursuers, but arrived home in a severely battered condition, and unfit for further immediate service. The British squadrons re-formed, and, fearing a large submarine attack (German reconnaissance zeppelin L11 had shadowed him since 0319 hours), Jellicoe ordered the Grand Fleet back to its bases. Within 48 hours, Jellicoe had his fleet at a state of instant readiness for a fresh encounter – indicating how he had really fared at Jutland Bank!

Note: during the night chase, the British Admiralty in London intercepted various German wireless signals stating Scheer's positions en route for the Jade. The use to which this valuable information was put by the British, is still undetermined.

THE NIGHT ATTACKS BY BRITISH DESTROYERS

2300
Midnight
0100
0200
0300
To Jade Bay

← British destroyer attacks
⬅ Scheer's Battle Fleet

Same scale as main map

Unable to reach base, 'Lutzow' is sunk by German destroyer at 0145 hours.

1926 1926 1926
2000 2000
2000
2000

Jutland Bank

0010 hours, 'Black Prince' is sunk.

2400
'Seydlitz'
2400
2400
'Moltke'
0300
0200
Light Vessel
Horns Reef
0300
0300
0010 hours, 'Pommern' is sunk.

DENMARK

NORTH, HELIGOLAND, CHANNEL

AMRUM BANK CHANNEL

NORTH SEA

HELIGOLAND

BIGHT

EMS CHANNEL

GERMANY

Frisian Islands

Elbe
Cuxhaven
Bremer-haven
Weser
Wilhelmshaven
Emden
Jade Bay
Ems

HOLLAND   GERMANY

KEY
← Track of Jellicoe's Battle Fleet
←- - Track of Beatty's Battlecruisers
⬅ Track of Scheer's Battle Fleet
⬅□□ Tracks of Hipper's Battlecruisers
▥▥▥ British-laid minefields by 1 June, 1916
⋯⋯⋯ German-swept channels 1 June 1916

Smaller units were operating with the British and German Battle and Battlecruiser Fleets — these are listed below
Abbreviations:– S = Squadron, F = Flotilla, AC = Armoured Cruiser, LC = Light Cruiser, D = Destroyer, SG = Scouting Group

BRITISH BATTLE FLEET		BRITISH BATTLECRUISER FLEET		GERMAN BATTLE FLEET		GERMAN BATTLECRUISER FLEET	
1st. ACS	4 ships	1st. LCS	4 ships	4th. SG (LC)	5 ships	2nd. SG (LC)	4 ships
2nd. ACS	4 ships	2nd. LCS	4 ships	LC	1 ship	LC	1 ship
4th. LCS	5 ships	3rd. LCS	4 ships	1st. DF (half)	4 ships	2nd. DF	10 ships
5th. LCS (attached)	6 ships	1st. DF	10 ships	3rd. DF	7 ships	6th. DF	9 ships
4th. DF	19 ships	9th. & 10th. DF (comb.)	8 ships	5th. DF	11 ships	9th. DF	11 ships
11th. DF	16 ships	13th. DF	11 ships	7th. DF	9 ships		
12th. DF	16 ships						
plus		plus					
Minelayers	1 ship	Seaplane Carriers	1 ship				
Tenders	1 ship						

259

THE BATTLE OF JUTLAND – continued

HMS "IRON DUKE" (Flagship of Admiral Jellicoe)

The 'Iron Duke' was a Dreadnought battleship, and the class was named after her. Sister-ships were 'Benbow', 'Emperor of India', and 'Marlborough'.

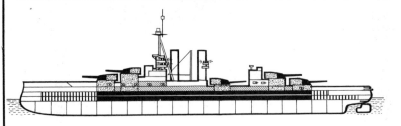

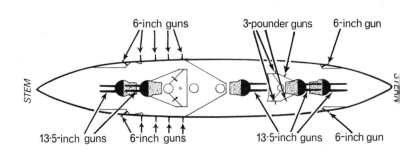

6-inch guns   3-pounder guns   6-inch gun

STEM

STERN

13·5-inch guns   6-inch guns   13·5-inch guns   6-inch gun

Laid down:	1912
Completed:	1914
Displacement:	25,000 tons
Waterline length:	620 feet
Maximum speed:	23 knots
Complement:	900

HMS "LION" (Flagship of Vice-Admiral Beatty)

The 'Lion' was a battle-cruiser, and the class was named after her. There was one sister-ship, 'Princess Royal'.

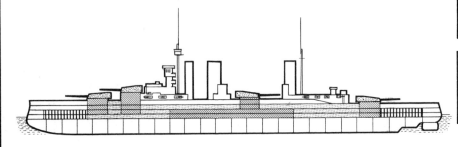

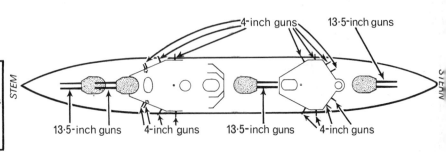

4-inch guns   13·5-inch guns

STEM

STERN

13·5-inch guns   4-inch guns   13·5-inch guns   4-inch guns

Laid down:	1909
Completed:	1912
Displacement:	26,350 tons
Waterline length:	675 feet
Maximum speed:	29 knots
Complement:	1,000

260

SMS "FRIEDRICH DER GROSSE"(Flagship of Vice-Admiral Scheer)

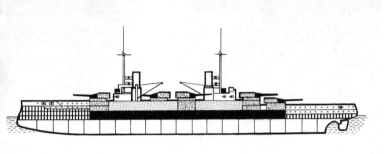

ARMAMENT

Ten 12-inch guns

Fourteen 6-inch guns

Twelve 24-pounder guns

Four 14-pounder anti-aerial guns

Five 20-inch torpedo tubes

The 'Friedrich der Grosse' was a Dreadnought battleship of the 'Kaiser' class. Sister-ships were 'Kaiser', 'Kaiserin', 'Prinzregent Luitpold', and 'König Albert'.

Laid down:	1909
Completed:	1912
Displacement:	24,700 tons
Waterline length:	564 feet
Maximum speed:	23 knots
Complement:	1,088

12-inch guns   6-inch guns   24-pounder guns

STEM   STERN

24-pounder guns   6-inch guns   12-inch guns   6-inch guns   12-inch guns

---

SMS "LÜTZOW"(Flagship of Vice-Admiral Hipper)

ARMAMENT

Eight 12-inch guns

Twelve 6-inch guns

Twelve 24-pounder guns

Five 22-inch torpedo tubes

Note: during the battle, Hipper transferred his flag from the badly-damaged 'Lützow' to the 'Moltke'.

The 'Lützow' was a battle-cruiser, and sister-ships were 'Derfflinger' and 'Ersatz Hertha'.

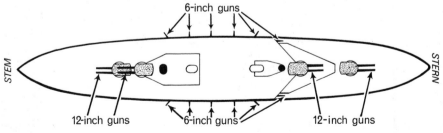

Laid down:	1912
Completed:	1915
Displacement:	28,000 tons
Waterline length:	590 feet
Maximum speed:	29 knots
Complement:	1,100

6-inch guns

STEM   STERN

12-inch guns   6-inch guns   12-inch guns

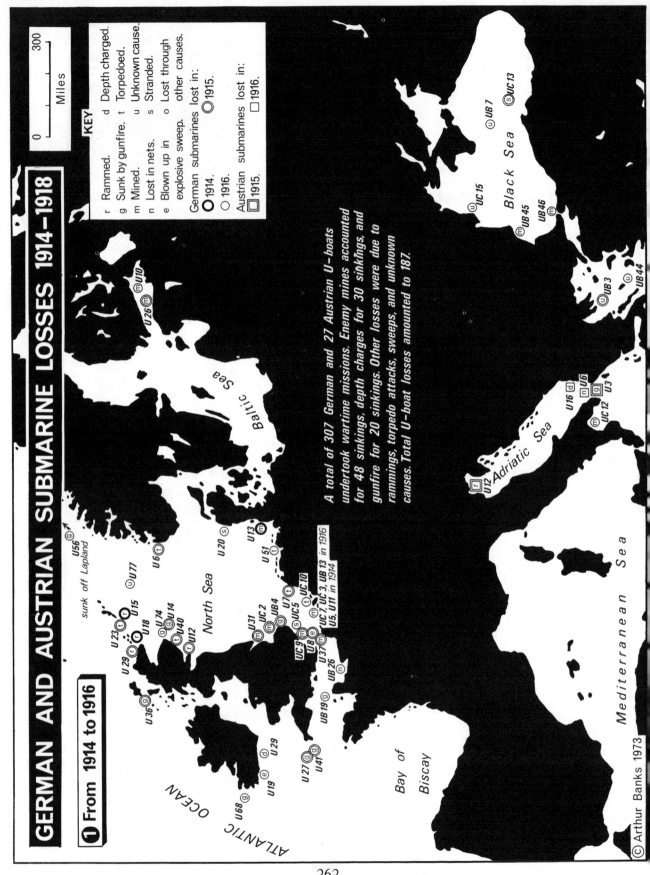

GERMAN AND AUSTRIAN SUBMARINE LOSSES 1914–1918

1 From 1914 to 1916

KEY

r Rammed.
g Sunk by gunfire.
m Mined.
n Lost in nets.
e Blown up in explosive sweep.

d Depth charged.
t Torpedoed.
u Unknown cause.
s Stranded.
o Lost through other causes.

German submarines lost in:
◯ 1914. ◯ 1915.
◯ 1916.

Austrian submarines lost in:
▢ 1915. ▢ 1916.

A total of 307 German and 27 Austrian U-boats undertook wartime missions. Enemy mines accounted for 48 sinkings, depth charges for 30 sinkings, and gunfire for 20 sinkings. Other losses were due to rammings, torpedo attacks, sweeps, and unknown causes. Total U-boat losses amounted to 187.

© Arthur Banks 1973

262

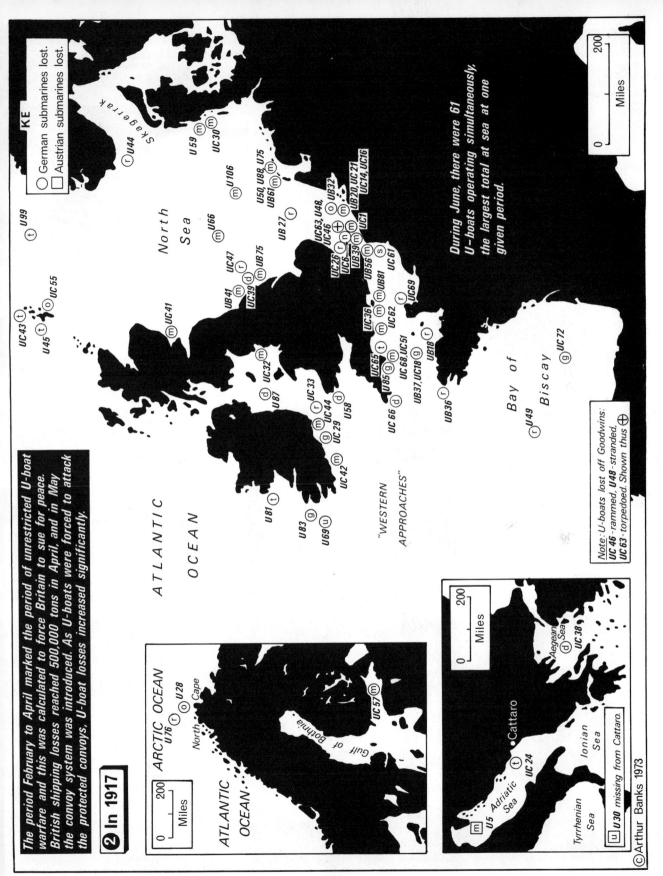

KE
○ German submarines lost.
□ Austrian submarines lost.

The period February to April marked the period of unrestricted U-boat warfare and this was calculated to force Britain to sue for peace. British shipping losses reached 500,000 tons in April, and in May the convoy system was introduced. As U-boats were forced to attack the protected convoys, U-boat losses increased significantly.

② In 1917

North Sea

Skagerrak

ⓣ U99

U44 ⓣ

ⓜ U59   U30 ⓜ

U106 ⓜ

U50, U88, U75
UB61 ⓜ

U66 ⓜ

UB32

UB27 ⓡ

UC63, U48,
UC46 ⓡ   ⊕

UC14, UC16
UB20, UC21
UC1

UC26 ⓡ   UC39 ⓜ   UC61 ⓢ
UC6 ⓝ   UB56 ⓜ

UC47 ⓡ   UB75 ⓜ

UB41   UC39 ⓓ

UC41 ⓜ

UC55 ◎
U45 ⓣ   u99
UC43 ⓣ

UC32 ⓜ

U87 ⓓ
UC33 ⓡ
UC44 ⓜ
UC29 ⓖ   U58 ⓓ

U42 ⓜ

U81 ⓣ

U83 ⓖ
U69 ⓤ

ATLANTIC
OCEAN

UB81 ⓝ

UC36 ⓜ   UC62 ⓜ
UC65 ⓣ   UC68, UC51 ⓖ
U85 ⓖ   UB37, UC18 ⓓ
UC66 ⓓ

UB18 ⓡ

UB36 ⓡ

U69 ⓡ

"WESTERN
APPROACHES"

Bay of
Biscay

UC72 ⓖ

During June, there were 61 U-boats operating simultaneously, the largest total at sea at one given period.

Note: U-boats lost off Goodwins:
UC 46 - rammed, **U48** - stranded.
UC 63 - torpedoed. Shown thus ⊕

ARCTIC OCEAN

U76 ⓡ   U28 ◎

North Cape

ATLANTIC
OCEAN

Gulf of Bothnia

UC 57 ⓜ

200
Miles

Aegean
Sea   UC 38 ⓓ

Cattaro

Ionian
Sea

Adriatic
Sea   UC 24 ⓣ

Tyrrhenian
Sea   U5 ⓜ

ⓤ **U30** missing from Cattaro.

©Arthur Banks 1973

263

GERMAN AND AUSTRIAN SUBMARINE LOSSES~continued

3 In 1918

0 ___ 150
Miles

ATLANTIC OCEAN

North Sea

Skagerrak

UB116 (m)
UB83 (d)
U156, UB123 (m)
U92, UB104, UB127, U102 (m)
U90 (t)

UB124 (d)
U110 (d)
(r) U89
UB82 (d)
UB115 (d)
U78 (t)
UB22 (m)

UB85 (g)

UB63 (d)
UB119 (u)
UB110, UB107, UB30, UC70 (d)
UC75 (r)

UB17 (u)

UB16 (t)
U104 (d)
U61 (d) (r) U84
UB65 (○)
UB12 (u)
UC11, UB31, UB55 UB109
UB35 (m) (d)
UB57
UC79, UC78 (m)
UB103, UC64, UB33, U95, UB58, UB38, U109

UC49 (d)
UB74 (d)
UC77
UC50
U93 (r)
(r) U103
UB72 (t)
UB54 (u)
UB78 (r)
UB113, UB108 (u)

The great weakness of the U-boat lay in its dependency on heavy batteries for undersea work. Prolonged tracking by enemy surface ships could eventually exhaust the U-boat's batteries, forcing it to surface.

KEY
○ German submarines lost.
□ Austrian submarines lost.

0 ___ 200
Miles

U10 (m)
U20 (t)
UB70 (u)
Adriatic Sea

UB52 (t)
(e) U23
UB53 (m)

UC35 (g)
Tyrrhenian Sea
U64 (g)
Ionian Sea

Mediterranean Sea

U154 (t)
U34 (d)
(d) UB71
UB69 (e)

U32 (d)
UB66 (d)
(g) UB68

© Arthur Banks 1973

264

A SPECIALLY-CONSTRUCTED BRITISH 'Q'-SHIP : HMS "HYDERABAD"

Built by John I. Thorneycroft & Co. Ltd., in four months during 1917.

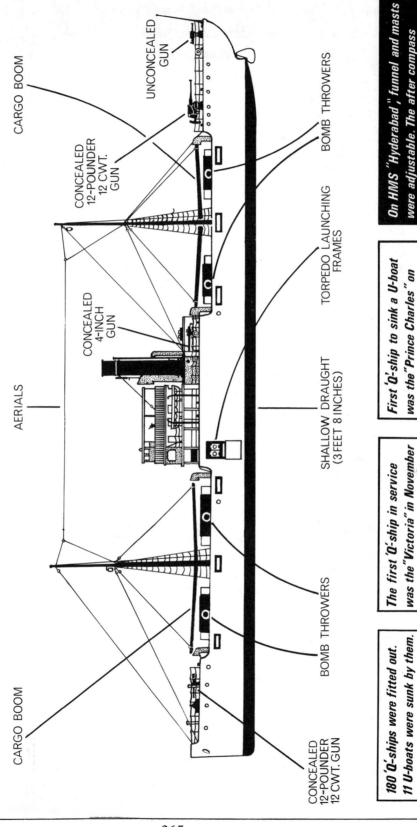

CARGO BOOM

UNCONCEALED GUN

CONCEALED 12-POUNDER 12 CWT. GUN

CONCEALED 4-INCH GUN

AERIALS

BOMB THROWERS

TORPEDO LAUNCHING FRAMES

SHALLOW DRAUGHT (3 FEET 8 INCHES)

BOMB THROWERS

CARGO BOOM

CARGO BOOM

CONCEALED 12-POUNDER 12 CWT. GUN

On HMS "Hyderabad", funnel and masts were adjustable. The after compass pedestal and wheel collapsed to improve field of fire.

First 'Q'-ship to sink a U-boat was the "Prince Charles" on 24 July 1915.

The first 'Q'-ship in service was the "Victoria" in November 1914.

180 'Q'-ships were fitted out. 11 U-boats were sunk by them.

© Arthur Banks 1973

THE U-BOAT WAR AGAINST ALLIED MERCHANT SHIPPING IN 1917

April to July was the most worrying period for Britain. In April alone, 373 Allied ships were sunk (highest monthly loss total of the war).

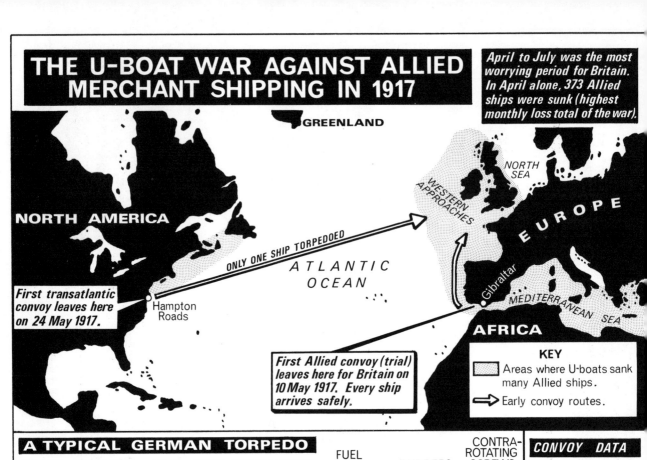

GREENLAND

NORTH AMERICA

NORTH SEA

WESTERN APPROACHES

EUROPE

ATLANTIC OCEAN

ONLY ONE SHIP TORPEDOED

Gibraltar

MEDITERRANEAN SEA

AFRICA

First transatlantic convoy leaves here on 24 May 1917.

Hampton Roads

First Allied convoy (trial) leaves here for Britain on 10 May 1917. Every ship arrives safely.

KEY
- Areas where U-boats sank many Allied ships.
- ⇨ Early convoy routes.

A TYPICAL GERMAN TORPEDO

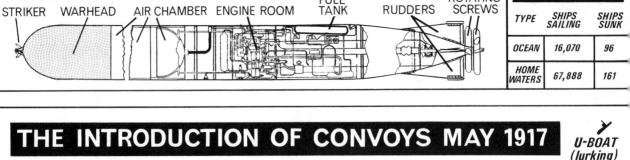

STRIKER WARHEAD AIR CHAMBER ENGINE ROOM FUEL TANK RUDDERS CONTRA-ROTATING SCREWS

CONVOY DATA

TYPE	SHIPS SAILING	SHIPS SUNK
OCEAN	16,070	96
HOME WATERS	67,888	161

THE INTRODUCTION OF CONVOYS MAY 1917

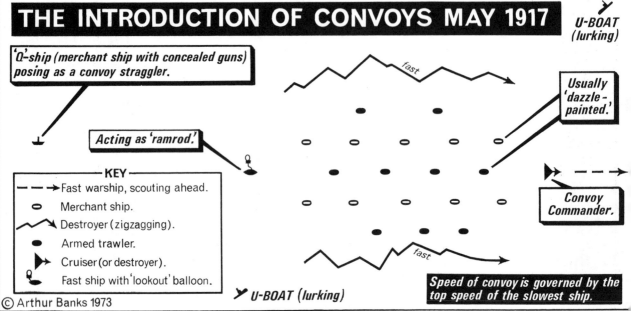

U-BOAT (lurking)

'Q'-ship (merchant ship with concealed guns) posing as a convoy straggler.

Acting as 'ramrod.'

fast

Usually 'dazzle-painted.'

Convoy Commander.

KEY
- – – → Fast warship, scouting ahead.
- ⊖ Merchant ship.
- ⋏⋎ Destroyer (zigzagging).
- ● Armed trawler.
- ▶ Cruiser (or destroyer).
- ♀ Fast ship with 'lookout' balloon.

fast

Speed of convoy is governed by the top speed of the slowest ship.

U-BOAT (lurking)

© Arthur Banks 1973

266

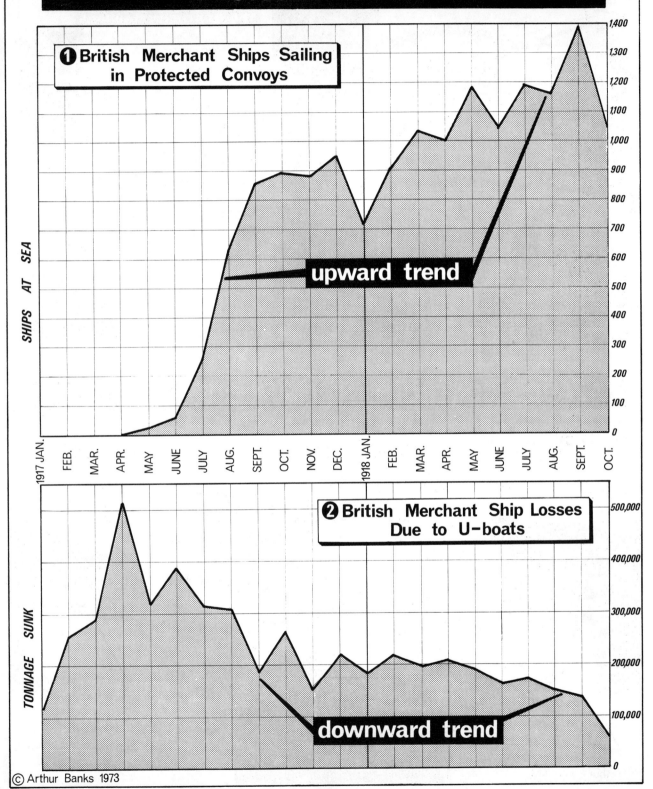

THE EFFECTIVENESS OF THE BRITISH CONVOY SYSTEM 1917–1918

1 British Merchant Ships Sailing in Protected Convoys

SHIPS AT SEA

upward trend

2 British Merchant Ship Losses Due to U-boats

TONNAGE SUNK

downward trend

© Arthur Banks 1973

267

HAZARDS CONFRONTING GERMAN-BASED U-BOATS

DIAGRAMMATIC

NORTHERN BARRAGE

NORWAY

Scapa Flow

BRITISH ARMED TRAWLERS (with hydrophones)

MINES

Cromarty

Rosyth

NORTH SEA

Skagerrak

BRITAIN

MINEFIELDS

BRITISH NAVAL PATROLS

DOGGER BANK

DEN-MARK

BRITISH SUBMARINES

MINES

HELIGOLAND

Kiel Canal

CUXHAVEN

WILHELMSHAVEN

EMDEN

MINES

MINES

HOLLAND

Harwich

MINES

0 — 100 Miles

SEALING THE NORTH SEA

THE NORTHERN BARRAGE

American-laid mines: 56,000
British-laid mines: 13,000

ATLANTIC OCEAN

NORWAY

SCOTLAND

AREA 'B'

AREA 'A'

AREA 'C'

NORTH SEA

Skagerrak

THE DOVER BARRAGE

ENGLAND

Dover

Folke-stone

Mines laid: 9,000

SHORE-OPERATED MINES

THE VARNE

DEEP AND SURFACE MINES

STRAIT OF DOVER

SEARCHLIGHTS

LE COLBART (The Ridge)

AT NIGHT

Calais

FRANCE

SHORE-OPERATED MINES

HAZARDS CONFRONTING FLANDERS-BASED U-BOATS

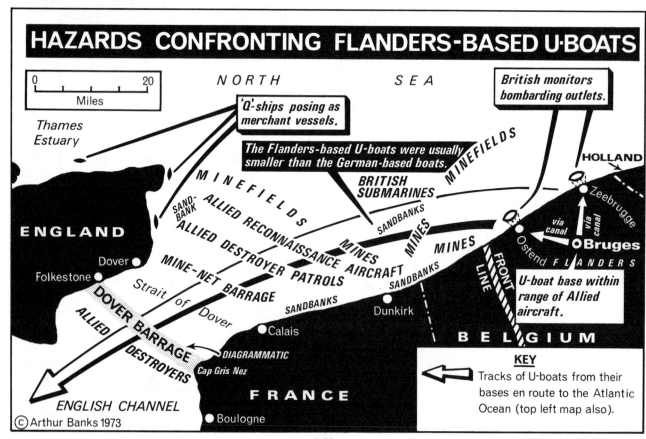

0 — 20 Miles

NORTH SEA

'Q'-ships posing as merchant vessels.

British monitors bombarding outlets.

Thames Estuary

MINEFIELDS

The Flanders-based U-boats were usually smaller than the German-based boats.

BRITISH SUBMARINES

MINEFIELDS

HOLLAND

Zeebrugge

ENGLAND

SAND-BANK

ALLIED RECONNAISSANCE AIRCRAFT

ALLIED DESTROYER PATROLS

MINEFIELDS

SANDBANKS

MINES

MINES

MINES

via canal

via canal

Ostend

Bruges

FLANDERS

Dover

Folkestone

MINE-NET BARRAGE

Strait of Dover

SANDBANKS

Dunkirk

SANDBANKS

FRONT LINE

U-boat base within range of Allied aircraft.

DOVER BARRAGE

ALLIED DESTROYERS

DIAGRAMMATIC

Cap Gris Nez

Calais

BELGIUM

ENGLISH CHANNEL

© Arthur Banks 1973

FRANCE

Boulogne

KEY

Tracks of U-boats from their bases en route to the Atlantic Ocean (top left map also).

BRITISH SUBMARINES IN THE BALTIC

© Arthur Banks 1973

0   100
Miles

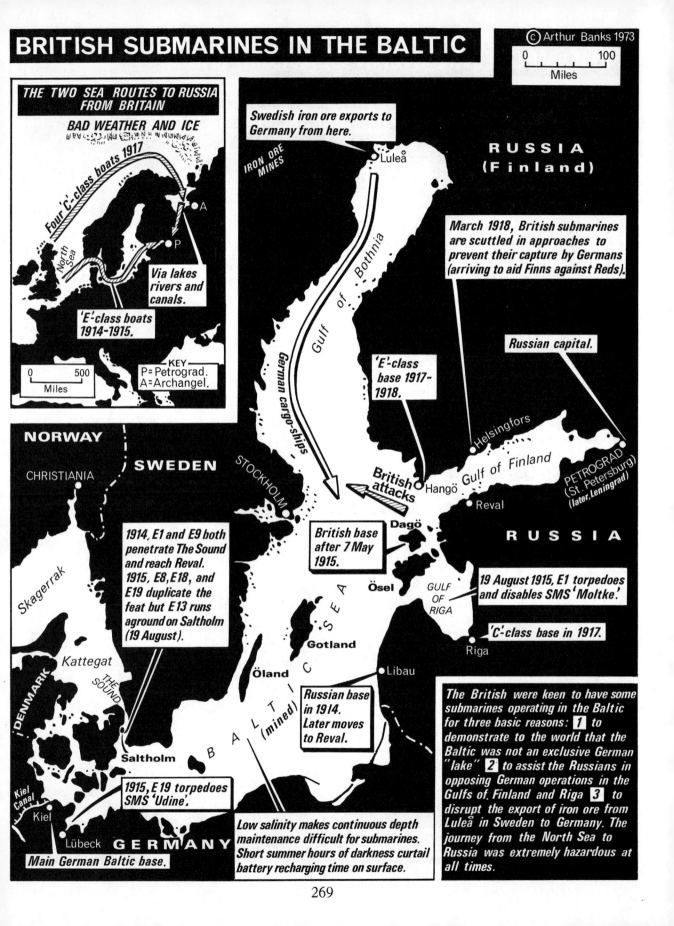

THE TWO SEA ROUTES TO RUSSIA FROM BRITAIN

BAD WEATHER AND ICE

Four 'C'-class boats 1917

A

P

North Sea

Via lakes rivers and canals.

'E'-class boats 1914-1915.

0   500
Miles

KEY
P= Petrograd.
A= Archangel.

Swedish iron ore exports to Germany from here.

IRON ORE MINES

Luleå

RUSSIA (Finland)

March 1918, British submarines are scuttled in approaches to prevent their capture by Germans (arriving to aid Finns against Reds).

Gulf of Bothnia

German cargo-ships

'E'-class base 1917-1918.

Russian capital.

Helsingfors

Gulf of Finland

PETROGRAD (St. Petersburg) (later, Leningrad)

British attacks

Hangö

Reval

NORWAY

SWEDEN

CHRISTIANIA

STOCKHOLM

1914, E1 and E9 both penetrate The Sound and reach Reval. 1915, E8, E18, and E19 duplicate the feat but E13 runs aground on Saltholm (19 August).

British base after 7 May 1915.

Dagö

RUSSIA

Ösel

GULF OF RIGA

19 August 1915, E1 torpedoes and disables SMS 'Moltke.'

Skagerrak

Kattegat

Gotland

'C'-class base in 1917.

THE SOUND

Öland

B A L T I C   S E A

Libau

Riga

DENMARK

Saltholm

Russian base in 1914. Later moves to Reval.

(mined)

Kiel Canal

Kiel

1915, E 19 torpedoes SMS 'Udine'.

Lübeck

GERMANY

Main German Baltic base.

Low salinity makes continuous depth maintenance difficult for submarines. Short summer hours of darkness curtail battery recharging time on surface.

The British were keen to have some submarines operating in the Baltic for three basic reasons: **1** to demonstrate to the world that the Baltic was not an exclusive German "lake" **2** to assist the Russians in opposing German operations in the Gulfs of Finland and Riga **3** to disrupt the export of iron ore from Luleå in Sweden to Germany. The journey from the North Sea to Russia was extremely hazardous at all times.

THE MEDITERRANEAN SEA 1914–1918

During 1917 alone, nearly 900 Allied merchant ships were sunk.

❶ The U-boat Offensive Against Allied Merchant Shipping

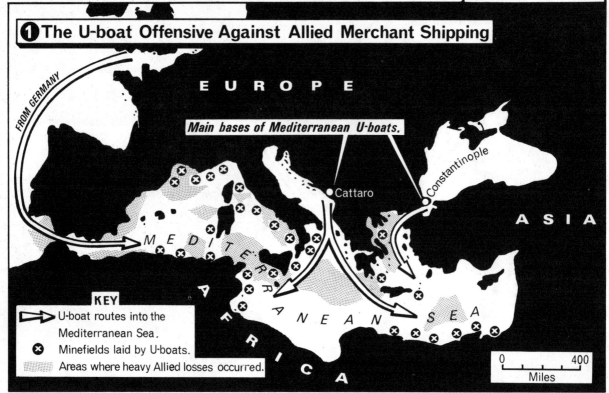

EUROPE

FROM GERMANY

Main bases of Mediterranean U-boats.

Constantinople

Cattaro

ASIA

MEDITERRANEAN SEA

AFRICA

KEY

⇨ U-boat routes into the Mediterranean Sea.

⊗ Minefields laid by U-boats.

Areas where heavy Allied losses occurred.

0   400
Miles

❷ Allied Anti-U-boat Naval Patrol Zones

These zones were in use from early 1916 onwards.

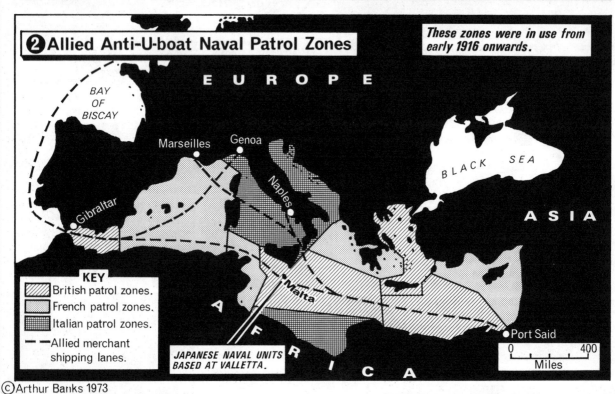

EUROPE

BAY OF BISCAY

Marseilles   Genoa

Naples

BLACK SEA

Gibraltar

ASIA

Malta

AFRICA

Port Said

KEY

▨ British patrol zones.

▢ French patrol zones.

▦ Italian patrol zones.

– – – Allied merchant shipping lanes.

JAPANESE NAVAL UNITS BASED AT VALLETTA.

0   400
Miles

© Arthur Banks 1973

THE ADRIATIC SEA 1914-1918

0 — 50 Miles

Battle squadron, torpedo craft, etc.

Railway used to transport U-boats in sections from Germany to Pola.

Night 31 October 1918, an Italian miniature torpedo-style craft sinks Austrian battleship 'Viribus Unitis' in harbour.

Main Austrian surface fleet base.

ITALY

Trieste

Venice

● Fiume

Pola

ADRIATIC

AUSTRIA – HUNGARY

KEY

Allied Otranto Barrage.

⊕ Italian naval base.

Ⓢ Italian seaplane base.

▨ Austro-Hungarian naval base.

✗ Naval action.

✳ Capital ship sunk.

⇨ U-boat routes from Adriatic to Mediterranean Sea.

Ancona ●

S E A

Night 9 December 1917, Italian motor boat torpedoes and sinks Austrian battleship 'Wien'.

10 June 1918, Italian motor boat torpedoes Austrian battleship 'Szent Istvan'. 89 Austrian sailors are lost in sinking ship.

Main Austrian U-boat base and advance surface fleet anchorage.

≋ Cattaro

Night 11 December 1916, Italian battleship 'Regina Margherita' hits mine and sinks.

Night 14/15 May 1917, Austrian cruisers raid Barrage and sink 14 Allied drifters.

I T A L Y

ALBANIA

● Durazzo

In use by British, French, and Italian ships.

Valona

Barrage is never 100% effective in containing U-boats in Adriatic Sea.

THE ALLIED ANTI–U-BOAT OTRANTO BARRAGE

1 Early 1915, British fishing vessels employed with 30-feet deep wire drift nets: Allied destroyers "on call": U-boats able to dive beneath nets.

2 Barrage weakened by drifters being transferred to assist in Salonika operations and Serbian evacuation to Corfu: remaining ships to port at night to avoid surface attacks.

3 Fixed net barrage commenced in April 1918: completed in September. Nets 150 feet deep, submerged 30 feet below surface, secured to moored buoys, mines attached. The whole complex patrolled by drifters with hydrophones, destroyers, sea-planes (from Otranto), American "sub-chasers" (based on Corfu).

⊕ Brindisi

Taranto ⊕

Otranto Ⓢ

Main Italian naval base.

Corfu

21 December 1914, French battleship 'Jean Bart' is sunk by U-boat.

French naval base in the area.

GREECE

The Austro-Hungarian surface fleet, locked in the Adriatic "lake" by Allied control of the Strait of Otranto, was restricted to hit-and-run sorties, whereas the U-boats were able to penetrate into the Mediterranean on numerous occasions to sink Allied shipping

© Arthur Banks 1973

S I C I L Y

271

THE BLACK SEA 1914-1917

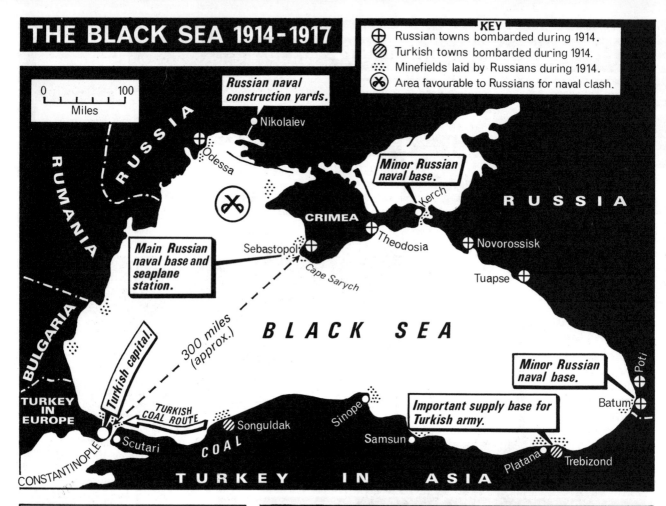

Russian naval construction yards.

Nikolaiev

RUSSIA

RUMANIA

Odessa

Minor Russian naval base.

CRIMEA

Kerch

RUSSIA

Main Russian naval base and seaplane station.

Sebastopol

Theodosia

Novorossisk

Cape Sarych

Tuapse

BULGARIA

Turkish capital.

300 miles (approx.)

BLACK SEA

Minor Russian naval base.

Poti

TURKEY IN EUROPE

TURKISH COAL ROUTE

COAL

Songuldak

Sinope

Important supply base for Turkish army.

Batum

Scutari

Samsun

Platana

Trebizond

CONSTANTINOPLE

TURKEY   IN   ASIA

RIVAL NAVAL STRENGTHS IN 1914

RUSSIAN FLEET

5 Pre-Dreadnought Battleships.
2 Cruisers.
4 Destroyers.
4 Submarines.

(3 Dreadnought Battleships and 2 Cruisers under construction)

TURKISH/GERMAN FLEET

1 Battlecruiser (SMS 'Goeben').
3 Pre-Dreadnought Battleships.
3 Cruisers (including SMS 'Breslau').
2 Destroyers.

The importance of the German warships must be stressed. SMS 'Goeben' was the most powerful warship in the area in 1914.

In 1914, the Black Sea naval scene was basically as follows : the Turkish/German fleet was intent on sorties from Constantinople to bombard Russian ports (spearheaded by SMS 'Goeben', the most powerful warship in the area). The Russians, eager to disrupt Turkish coal supplies by sea from Songuldak to Constantinople (there was no land railway link), yearned for a supply base on the Bulgarian coastline to shorten the distance between Sebastopol and Constantinople. They laid minefields off Turkish ports to impede enemy sorties, and entertained hopes that if a major naval confrontation occurred, it would take place between Odessa and Sebastopol, within range of Russian seaplanes.

THE NAVAL CLASH OFF CAPE SARYCH 18 NOVEMBER 1914

MIST

CLEAR WEATHER

SMS 'Breslau'
SMS 'GOEBEN'

firing

1221 hours
Russian cruisers
RUSSIAN BATTLE FLEET

This 14-minute action marked the first encounter between 'Goeben' and Russian capital ships. The old pre-dreadnoughts equalled the 'Goeben's' hit-rate of 10% from salvoes fired before the Germans broke off. There were 14 hits on 'Goeben' causing casualties of 115 killed and 59 wounded.

During 1915, two new dreadnoughts came into service with the Russian Black Sea fleet. These battleships, "Imperatritsa Maria" and "Ekaterina II," altered the naval balance of power, although the former was sunk at Sebastopol in the following year (27 October 1916). SMS "Goeben" made her final Black Sea sortie on 8 January 1916. In September 1915, U-boats appeared in the Black Sea, and in that year Bulgaria joined the Central Powers. Rumania became involved in 1916. There was no all-out naval clash, but several fights took place, sometimes involving Russian seaplanes. Russian troops were transported across the sea to fight on the Turkish shore. Trebizond was captured in April 1916 and used as a military port.

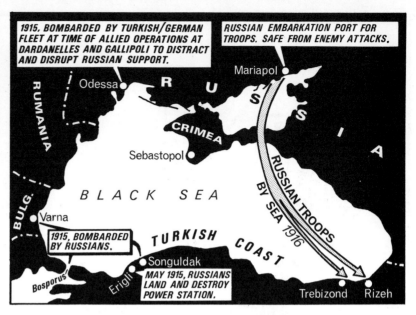

1915, BOMBARDED BY TURKISH/GERMAN FLEET AT TIME OF ALLIED OPERATIONS AT DARDANELLES AND GALLIPOLI TO DISTRACT AND DISRUPT RUSSIAN SUPPORT.

RUSSIAN EMBARKATION PORT FOR TROOPS. SAFE FROM ENEMY ATTACKS.

1915, BOMBARDED BY RUSSIANS.

MAY 1915, RUSSIANS LAND AND DESTROY POWER STATION.

RUSSIAN TROOPS BY SEA 1916

BLACK SEA

TURKISH COAST

RUMANIA • Odessa • Mariapol • Sebastopol • Varna • BULG. • Bosporus • Eregli • Songuldak • Trebizond • Rizeh

CRIMEA

R U S S I A

THE UNSUCCESSFUL BRITISH AERIAL BID TO SINK SMS "GOEBEN" MAY–JULY 1916

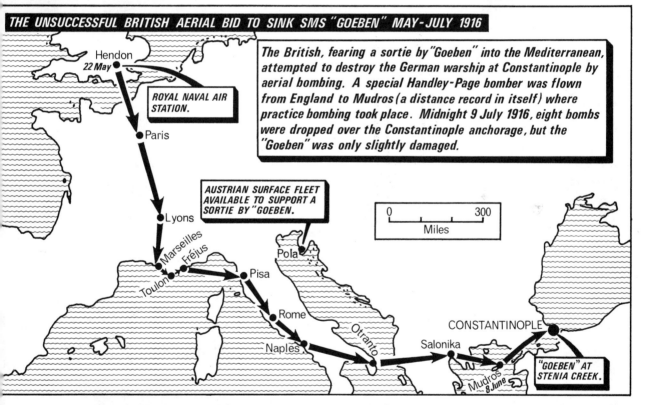

The British, fearing a sortie by "Goeben" into the Mediterranean, attempted to destroy the German warship at Constantinople by aerial bombing. A special Handley-Page bomber was flown from England to Mudros (a distance record in itself) where practice bombing took place. Midnight 9 July 1916, eight bombs were dropped over the Constantinople anchorage, but the "Goeben" was only slightly damaged.

ROYAL NAVAL AIR STATION.

AUSTRIAN SURFACE FLEET AVAILABLE TO SUPPORT A SORTIE BY "GOEBEN.

"GOEBEN" AT STENIA CREEK.

Hendon 22 May • Paris • Lyons • Marseilles • Fréjus • Toulon • Pisa • Rome • Naples • Pola • Otranto • Salonika • Mudros 8 June • CONSTANTINOPLE

0 — 300 Miles

"GOEBEN" AND "BRESLAU" IN THE AEGEAN 20 JANUARY 1918

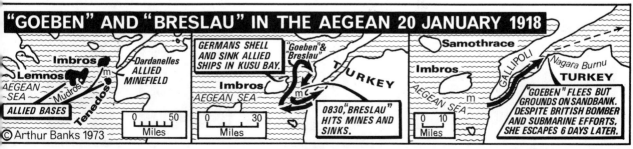

Imbros • Lemnos • Mudros • Tenedos • Dardanelles ALLIED MINEFIELD
AEGEAN SEA
ALLIED BASES
0 — 50 Miles

GERMANS SHELL AND SINK ALLIED SHIPS IN KUSU BAY.
"Goeben" & "Breslau"
TURKEY
Imbros
AEGEAN SEA
0830, "BRESLAU" HITS MINES AND SINKS.
0 — 30 Miles

Samothrace
Imbros
AEGEAN SEA
GALLIPOLI • Nagara Burnu • TURKEY
"GOEBEN" FLEES BUT GROUNDS ON SANDBANK. DESPITE BRITISH BOMBER AND SUBMARINE EFFORTS, SHE ESCAPES 6 DAYS LATER.
0 — 10 Miles

© Arthur Banks 1973

273

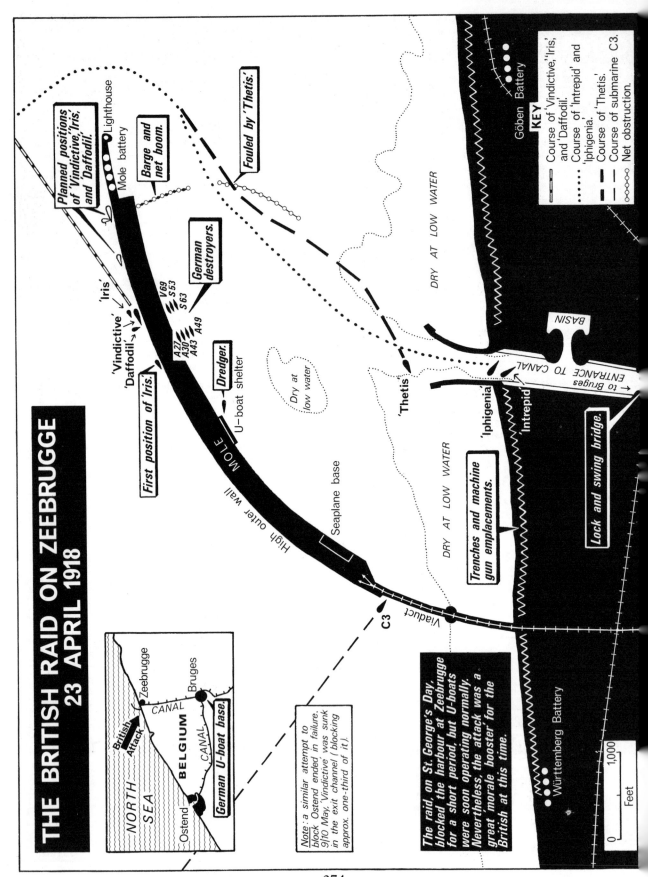

THE BRITISH RAID ON ZEEBRUGGE 23 APRIL 1918

Planned positions of 'Vindictive,'Iris,' and 'Daffodil.'

Lighthouse

Mole battery

Barge and net boom.

Fouled by 'Thetis.'

'Iris'

'Vindictive'

'Daffodil'

First position of 'Iris.'

German destroyers.

V 69
S 53
S 63
A 49
A 27
A 30
A 43

Dredger.

U–boat shelter

High outer wall

MOLE

Dry at low water

Seaplane base

'Thetis'

DRY AT LOW WATER

DRY AT LOW WATER

Trenches and machine gun emplacements.

'Iphigenia'

'Intrepid'

← to Bruges ENTRANCE TO CANAL

BASIN

Lock and swing bridge.

Göben Battery

KEY

▭ Course of 'Vindictive,'Iris,' and 'Daffodil.'

⋯ Course of 'Intrepid' and 'Iphigenia.'

▬ ▬ Course of 'Thetis.'

— — Course of submarine C3.

ooooo Net obstruction.

C3

Viaduct

Würtemberg Battery

NORTH SEA

Zeebrugge

Bruges

British Attack

CANAL

BELGIUM

CANAL

Ostend

German U-boat base.

<u>Note</u>: a similar attempt to block Ostend ended in failure. 9/10 May, Vindictive was sunk in the exit channel (blocking approx. one-third of it).

The raid, on St. George's Day, blocked the harbour at Zeebrugge for a short period, but U-boats were soon operating normally. Nevertheless, the attack was a great morale booster for the British at this time.

0

1,000

Feet

274

GERMAN PLANS FOR A FINAL NAVAL CONFRONTATION OCTOBER 1918

0 — 100
Miles

Night 28 October, UB116 is destroyed by electrically-detonated loop-style minefield in Hoxa Sound.

Note: the Germans appeared to consider Scapa Flow as the main British naval base. In fact, this had been moved to Rosyth in April 1918.

Shetland Islands

Fair Isle

ATLANTIC OCEAN

Orkney Islands

UB116 ○ *Scapa Flow*

NORWAY

seven Zeppelins to be sent to report Grand Fleet's movements

assumed British line of approach

U-boats to patrol this area.

SCOTLAND

28 October, U78 is torpedoed and sunk by the British sub. G2.

Skagerrak

British naval base.

Rosyth

N O R T H   S E A

DENMARK

IRELAND

IRISH SEA

German light cruisers to lay mines in British path.

○ U78

Germans hope to bring about the action in this area (favourable for them).

Jade Bay

Frisian Islands

Wilhelmshaven

WALES

ENGLAND

Harwich

HOLLAND

German naval base.

GERMANY

Light cruiser sorties to entice the British south from Scapa.

BELGIUM

English Channel

In an attempt to influence the Armistice negotiations,* the German naval authorities formulated plans to bring about the long-awaited clash between the German and British battle fleets. It came to naught due to mutinies and demoralization among the German crews. However, twenty-five U-boats actually set sail on 25 October, and two were destroyed by the British.

Historical note: In June 1667, de Ruyter's Dutch raid on the Medway influenced the peace negotiations for the Treaty of Breda in July 1667.

FRANCE

© Arthur Banks 1973

275

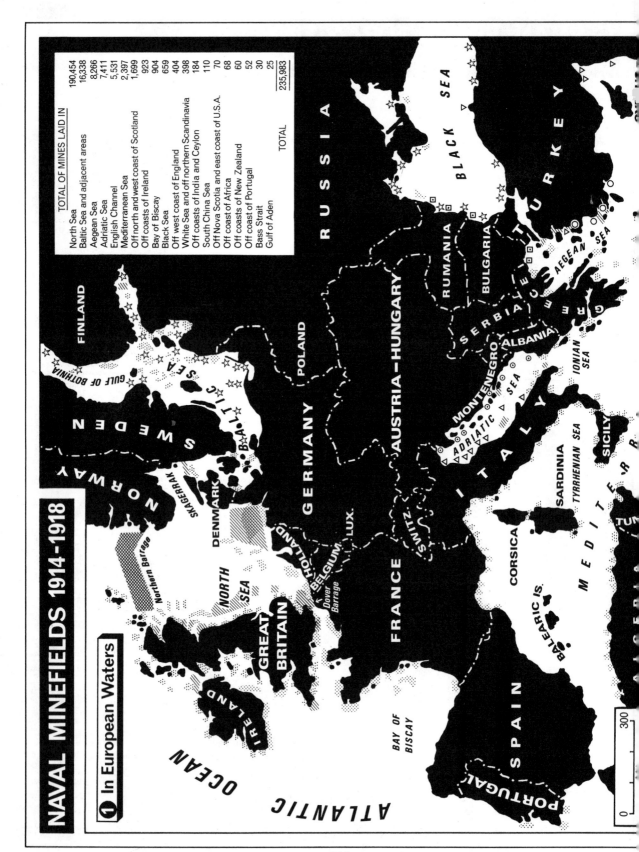

NAVAL MINEFIELDS 1914–1918

① In European Waters

TOTAL OF MINES LAID IN	
North Sea	190,454
Baltic Sea and adjacent areas	16,338
Aegean Sea	8,266
Adriatic Sea	7,411
English Channel	5,531
Mediterranean Sea	2,397
Off north and west coast of Scotland	1,699
Off coasts of Ireland	923
Bay of Biscay	904
Black Sea	659
Off west coast of England	404
White Sea and off northern Scandinavia	398
Off coasts of India and Ceylon	184
South China Sea	110
Off Nova Scotia and east coast of U.S.A.	70
Off coasts of Africa	68
Off coasts of New Zealand	60
Off coast of Portugal	52
Bass Strait	30
Gulf of Aden	25
TOTAL	235,983

RUSSIA

FINLAND

GULF OF BOTHNIA

BALTIC SEA

SWEDEN

NORWAY

Northern Barrage

SKAGERRAK

DENMARK

NORTH SEA

GREAT BRITAIN

IRELAND

ATLANTIC OCEAN

HOLLAND

BELGIUM LUX.

Dover Barrage

GERMANY

POLAND

AUSTRIA–HUNGARY

SWITZ.

FRANCE

BAY OF BISCAY

SPAIN

PORTUGAL

BALEARIC IS.

CORSICA

SARDINIA

MEDITER

ALGERIA

TUN

RUMANIA

SERBIA

BULGARIA

MONTENEGRO

ALBANIA

ADRIATIC SEA

ITALY

TYRRHENIAN SEA

SICILY

IONIAN SEA

GREECE

AEGEAN SEA

TURKEY

BLACK SEA

0   300

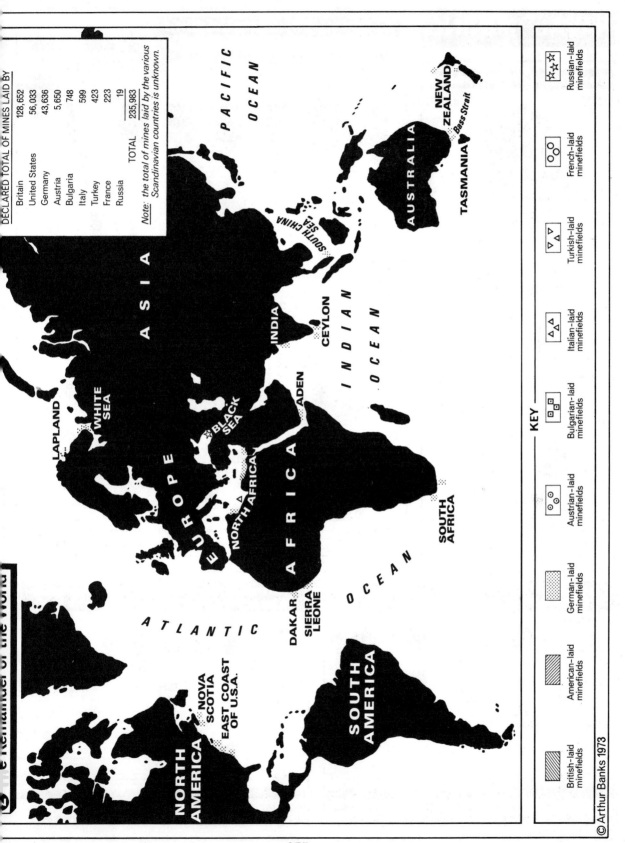

The Remainder of the World

DECLARED TOTAL OF MINES LAID BY

Britain	128,652
United States	56,033
Germany	43,636
Austria	5,650
Bulgaria	748
Italy	599
Turkey	423
France	223
Russia	19
TOTAL	235,983

Note: the total of mines laid by the various Scandinavian countries is unknown.

PACIFIC OCEAN

ASIA

NEW ZEALAND

AUSTRALIA

TASMANIA   Bass Strait

SOUTH CHINA SEA

INDIA

CEYLON

INDIAN OCEAN

LAPLAND

WHITE SEA

BLACK SEA

EUROPE

NORTH AFRICA

ADEN

AFRICA

SOUTH AFRICA

DAKAR

SIERRA LEONE

ATLANTIC OCEAN

NORTH AMERICA

NOVA SCOTIA

EAST COAST OF U.S.A.

SOUTH AMERICA

KEY

British-laid minefields	American-laid minefields	German-laid minefields	Austrian-laid minefields	Bulgarian-laid minefields	Italian-laid minefields	Turkish-laid minefields	French-laid minefields	Russian-laid minefields

NAVAL MINING

German contact mine

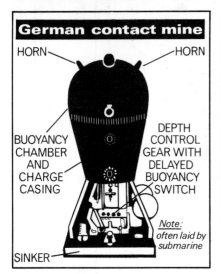

HORN — HORN

BUOYANCY CHAMBER AND CHARGE CASING

DEPTH CONTROL GEAR WITH DELAYED BUOYANCY SWITCH

SINKER

Note: often laid by submarine

An Observation Minefield

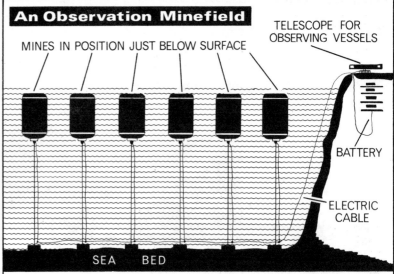

MINES IN POSITION JUST BELOW SURFACE

TELESCOPE FOR OBSERVING VESSELS

BATTERY

ELECTRIC CABLE

SEA BED

This system was employed at harbour entrances. Shore observers fired the mines by electrical methods at the moment when a hostile ship passed over the line.

The Antenna Mine

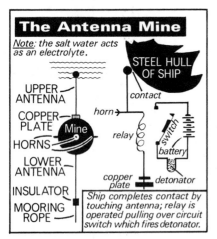

Note: the salt water acts as an electrolyte.

STEEL HULL OF SHIP

contact

UPPER ANTENNA

COPPER PLATE

HORNS

LOWER ANTENNA

INSULATOR

MOORING ROPE

Mine

horn

relay

switch

battery

copper plate

detonator

Ship completes contact by touching antenna; relay is operated pulling over circuit switch which fires detonator.

Hydrostatic depth-taking

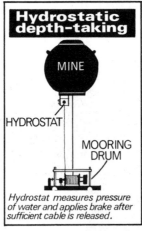

MINE

HYDROSTAT

MOORING DRUM

Hydrostat measures pressure of water and applies brake after sufficient cable is released.

The "HERZ" Horn

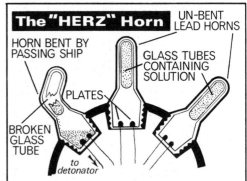

HORN BENT BY PASSING SHIP

UN-BENT LEAD HORNS

GLASS TUBES CONTAINING SOLUTION

PLATES

BROKEN GLASS TUBE

to detonator

The inside of the horn is similar to an electrical battery. A bichromate solution comes in contact with zinc and carbon plates, thus making voltage.

Plummet system of automatic depth-taking (non-buoyant unit)

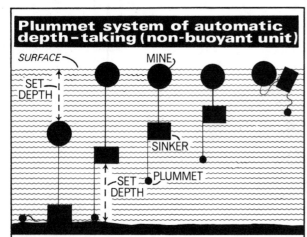

SURFACE

MINE

SET DEPTH

SINKER

PLUMMET

SET DEPTH

Mine parts from sinker upon laying; thus, an unknown length of wire spins out before unit settles, making laying haphazard.

Plummet system of automatic depth-taking (buoyant unit)

SET DEPTH

SURFACE

MINE

SINKER

PLUMMET

SET DEPTH

Mine stays with sinker until equilibrium is established. Thus, depth-taking with this system is more accurate and precise.

© Arthur Banks 1973

SEVEN IMPORTANT NAVAL MINES 1914–1918

TYPES OF MINE

CONTROLLED MINES (employed defensively, e.g. placed at harbour entrances). Fired from shore via electric wire.

INDEPENDENT MINES (employed both offensively and defensively in open sea, off coasts, etc. Types included moored, sea-bed, drifting, creeping, and oscillating.

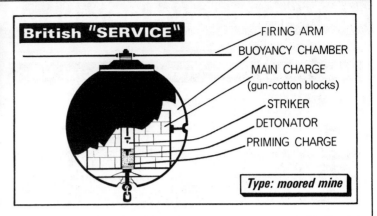

British "SERVICE"

- FIRING ARM
- BUOYANCY CHAMBER
- MAIN CHARGE (gun-cotton blocks)
- STRIKER
- DETONATOR
- PRIMING CHARGE

Type: moored mine

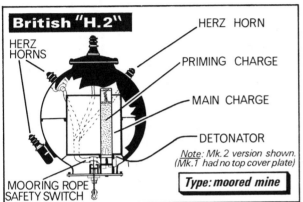

British "H.2"

- HERZ HORN
- HERZ HORNS
- PRIMING CHARGE
- MAIN CHARGE
- DETONATOR
- MOORING ROPE SAFETY SWITCH

Note: Mk.2 version shown. (Mk.1 had no top cover plate)

Type: moored mine

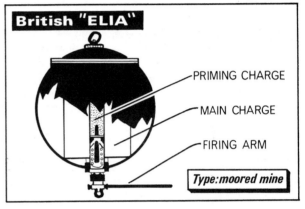

British "ELIA"

- PRIMING CHARGE
- MAIN CHARGE
- FIRING ARM

Type: moored mine

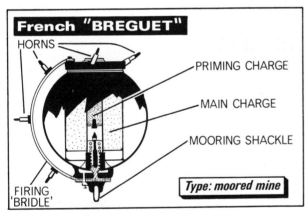

French "BREGUET"

- HORNS
- PRIMING CHARGE
- MAIN CHARGE
- MOORING SHACKLE
- FIRING 'BRIDLE'

Type: moored mine

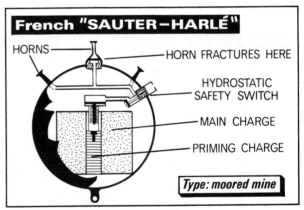

French "SAUTER-HARLÉ"

- HORNS
- HORN FRACTURES HERE
- HYDROSTATIC SAFETY SWITCH
- MAIN CHARGE
- PRIMING CHARGE

Type: moored mine

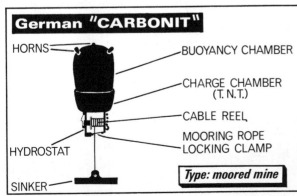

German "CARBONIT"

- HORNS
- BUOYANCY CHAMBER
- CHARGE CHAMBER (T.N.T.)
- CABLE REEL
- MOORING ROPE LOCKING CLAMP
- HYDROSTAT
- SINKER

Type: moored mine

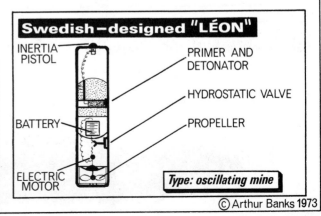

Swedish-designed "LÉON"

- INERTIA PISTOL
- PRIMER AND DETONATOR
- HYDROSTATIC VALVE
- BATTERY
- PROPELLER
- ELECTRIC MOTOR

Type: oscillating mine

SUBMARINE DEVELOPMENT DURING THE WAR

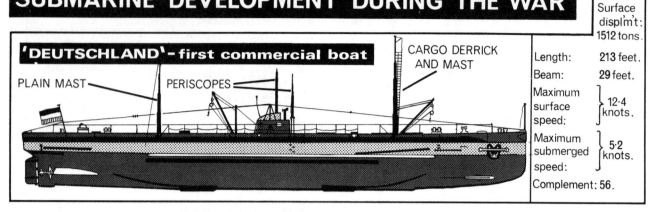

'DEUTSCHLAND' - first commercial boat

PLAIN MAST

PERISCOPES

CARGO DERRICK AND MAST

Surface displm't: 1512 tons.

Length: 213 feet.

Beam: 29 feet.

Maximum surface speed: } 12·4 knots.

Maximum submerged speed: } 5·2 knots.

Complement: 56.

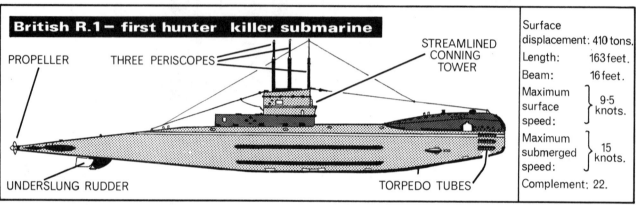

British R.1 – first hunter killer submarine

PROPELLER

THREE PERISCOPES

STREAMLINED CONNING TOWER

UNDERSLUNG RUDDER

TORPEDO TUBES

Surface displacement: 410 tons.

Length: 163 feet.

Beam: 16 feet.

Maximum surface speed: } 9·5 knots.

Maximum submerged speed: } 15 knots.

Complement: 22.

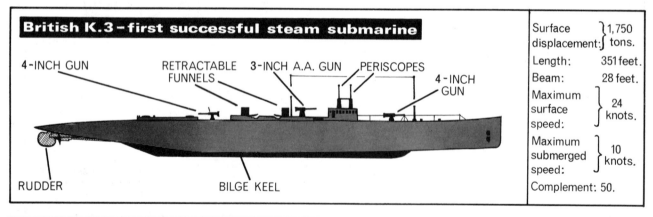

British K.3 - first successful steam submarine

4-INCH GUN

RETRACTABLE FUNNELS

3-INCH A.A. GUN

PERISCOPES

4-INCH GUN

RUDDER

BILGE KEEL

Surface displacement: } 1,750 tons.

Length: 351 feet.

Beam: 28 feet.

Maximum surface speed: } 24 knots.

Maximum submerged speed: } 10 knots.

Complement: 50.

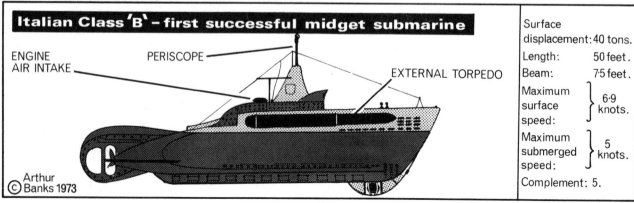

Italian Class 'B' – first successful midget submarine

ENGINE AIR INTAKE

PERISCOPE

EXTERNAL TORPEDO

Arthur © Banks 1973

Surface displacement: 40 tons.

Length: 50 feet.

Beam: 7·5 feet.

Maximum surface speed: } 6·9 knots.

Maximum submerged speed: } 5 knots.

Complement: 5.

THE WAR IN THE AIR

On 1 November 1911 a primitive Italian aeroplane, supporting military operations in Libya, dropped four specially modified grenades on Turkish troops near Zuwarah. The pilot of the aircraft, Lieutenant Cavotti, was thus inaugurating a new and terrible phase of warfare, less than eight years since the first heavier-than-air machine had lifted off the ground. The French, German and American armies were already, in 1911, experimenting with aircraft, though they were uncertain how to use them. The British War Secretary, Haldane, took the lead in establishing a Royal Flying Corps in 1912, while at the Admiralty Churchill warmly supported the aeronautical enterprises (and himself took flying lessons). But by 1914 military and naval leaders, if not actively hostile to 'an air arm', saw in planes and airships little more than reconnaissance machines and gunnery spotters.

The only combatant possessing an aerial fleet of any significance was Germany, with eleven rigid airships, all except one manufactured by Count Zeppelin. During the early months of the war these craft bombed Liége, Antwerp and Warsaw. They proved, however, vulnerable to gunfire when used in close support of the army, and, at the beginning of 1915, it was decided that they would be most effective against targets in England, bringing 'terror to the people of London'. Navigational difficulties saved London from raids on several occasions (and similarly ruled out projected attacks on Petrograd), but the British capital was attacked by Zeppelins twelve times between May 1915 and October 1917. There were forty other raids on Britain, with bombs dropped in the Midlands, Liverpool, Newcastle and Hull as well as East Anglia and the Home Counties. Night bombing by Zeppelins interfered with efficiency in vital factories. Subsequently this role was assumed by aircraft, and the ten night raids of September–October 1917 (see page 296) had a particularly bad effect on civilian morale.

The Zeppelins which raided England in August 1915 were faster and bigger than the craft of a year earlier: they carried twice the weight of bombs. Without these technological improvements, it would have been impossible to mount what was, in effect, a strategic air offensive against civilian and military targets. But improvements to airships were equalled by developments in aeroplane construction. The most revolutionary of these was Anthony Fokker's invention of an interrupter, a cam which could stop a machine gun firing when the propeller blade swept across the muzzle. This device made the fighter aircraft a weapon in itself. German Fokkers were able to check the mounting pressure by the French bombing planes, an arm in which Joffre himself had long been interested. The British developed DH 4s and DH 9s as light bombers to attack front line troops, and depended on the manoeuvrable Sopwith Camel and S.E. 5a as the principal fighters. The Royal Naval Air Service used seaplane carriers during the Dardanelles Operations and experimented with dropping torpedoes from aircraft, a technique which could be perfected only with more powerful engines, giving a greater impetus.

The 'dog fight', a new form of combat creating its own tactics, gave the opportunity for individualists to make themselves reputations as 'aces'. Yet by the spring of 1917 the most famous of these German aces, Richthofen, was himself perfecting a 'circus', a squadron which was standardising at a rate technical level the accumulated skills of air fighting. Nor were these developments limited to the German side.

By the last winter in the war the British Government had so far accepted the significance of air power that on 1 April 1918, it created a third military service, a Royal Air Force with an 'Air Staff', totally independent of army and navy. The light bombers of the R.A.F. played a prominent part in the final defeat of the Bulgarians in the Balkan mountains and of the Turks in the coastal plain of Palestine; but the authorities were more interested in the effects of strategic bombing on Germany's factories.

GERMAN AIRSHIPS

GERMAN AIRSHIP RAIDS ON BRITAIN 1915-1918

YEAR	NUMBER OF RAIDS	BOMBS DROPPED (All types)	CIVILIANS KILLED	CIVILIANS INJURED
1915	20	1,525	207	533
1916	22	3,458	293	691
1917	7	580	40	75
1918	4	188	16	59
TOTALS	53*	5,751	556	1,358

*Note: London was attacked on twelve occasions

NORTH-WEST GERMAN AIRSHIP BASES

NORTH SEA

BALTIC SEA

Tondern

Kiel

Nordholz

Fuhlsbüttel

Hage

Wittmundhaven

Alhorn   Wildeshausen

HOLLAND

GERMANY

HQ Naval Airship Division
14 Oct. 1914 - 25 July 1917
10 Jan. 1918 - 9 Nov. 1918

HQ Naval Airship Division
25 July 1917 - 10 Jan. 1918

L.3 – First Zeppelin to raid Britain

Complement: 16 men ← GAS CELLS → Maximum speed: 48 m.p.h.

1 2 3 4 5 6 7 8 9 10 11 12 13 14 15 16 17 18

PROPELLER   OPEN GONDOLAS   PROPELLER

Completed: 11 May 1914	Gas volume: 794,500 cubic ft.
Commissioned: 23 May 1914	Height: 60 ft. 3 ins.
Length: 518 ft. 2 ins.	Diameter: 48 ft. 6 ins.

Zeppelin "P" Type

Length: 536 ft. 5 ins.   Maximum speed: 59 m.p.h.   Gas volume: 1,126,400 cubic ft.
Diameter: 61 ft. 4 ins.   Complement: 16 men   Height: 79 ft. 4 ins.

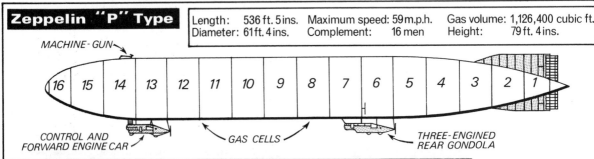

MACHINE-GUN

16 15 14 13 12 11 10 9 8 7 6 5 4 3 2 1

CONTROL AND FORWARD ENGINE CAR   GAS CELLS   THREE-ENGINED REAR GONDOLA

NAVAL NUMBER	COMMISSIONED	ACTUAL RAIDS	TOTAL FLIGHTS	TERMINATION OF SERVICE
L.10	17 May 1915	5	28	3 September 1915: destroyed off Neuwerk I.
L.11	8 June 1915	18	118	24 November 1917: dismantled at Hage.
L.12	22 June 1915	1	14	10 August 1915: burned at Ostend.
L.13	25 July 1915	17	159	11 December 1917: dismantled at Hage.
L.14	10 August 1915	17	127	23 June 1919: wrecked at Nordholz.
L.15	12 September 1915	3	36	1 April 1916: sank in sea at Knock Deep.
L.16	24 September 1915	16	132	19 October 1917: wrecked at Nordholz.
L.17	22 October 1915	11	73	28 December 1916: burned at Tondern.
L.18	6 November 1915	0	4	17 November 1915: burned at Tondern.
L.19	22 November 1915	1	14	2 February 1916: sank in North Sea.

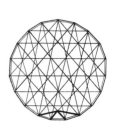

MAIN RING BRACING

THE THREE BASIC TYPES OF AIRSHIP

1 Non-rigid
A balloon, the shape of which was held by internal pressure.

2 Semi-rigid
A shaped balloon with a rigid girder to which the main weights were slung.

3 Rigid
A group of balloons inside a rigid frame with, usually, a fabric cover.

During the war, the Germans manufactured two main types of rigid airships, the Schütte-Lanz and the Zeppelin. The early S.L.'s were wooden-framed, and the Zeppelins metal-framed (the metal used was duralumin). Hydrogen was the gas employed, and Germany paid particular attention to purity to avoid explosions.

© Arthur Banks 1973

282

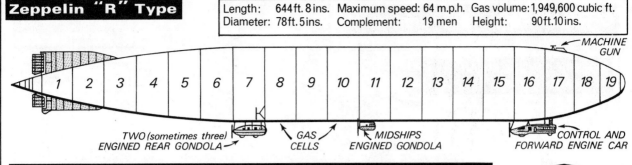

Zeppelin "R" Type

Length: 644 ft. 8 ins.　Maximum speed: 64 m.p.h.　Gas volume: 1,949,600 cubic ft.
Diameter: 78 ft. 5 ins.　Complement: 19 men　Height: 90 ft. 10 ins.

MACHINE GUN

TWO (sometimes three) ENGINED REAR GONDOLA

GAS CELLS

MIDSHIPS ENGINED GONDOLA

CONTROL AND FORWARD ENGINE CAR

NAVAL NUMBER	COMMISSIONED	ACTUAL RAIDS	TOTAL FLIGHTS	TERMINATION OF SERVICE
L.30	30 May 1916	9	115	Broken up in 1920: parts to Belgium.
L.31	14 July 1916	8	19	2 October 1916: destroyed at Potters Bar.
L.32	7 August 1916	3	13	24 September 1916: destroyed at Gt. Burstead.
L.33	2 September 1916	1	10	24 Sept. 1916: captured at Little Wigborough.
L.34	22 September 1916	2	11	27 November 1916: destroyed off Hartlepool.
L.35	12 October 1916	5	54	September 1918: broken up at Jüterbog.
L.36	7 November 1916	1	20	7 February 1917: crashed on frozen River Aller.
L.37	27 November 1916	4	50?	Broken up in 1920: parts to Japan.
L.38	26 November 1916	1	10	29 December 1916: captured at Seemuppen.
L.39	18 December 1916	1	24	17 March 1917: destroyed at Compiègne.
L.40	7 January 1917	2	30	17 June 1917: dismantled at Nevenwald.
L.41	30 January 1917	4	36	23 June 1919: destroyed at Nordholz.
L.45	7 April 1917	3	27	20 October 1917: captured at Sisteron.
L.47	3 May 1917	4	44	5 January 1918: destroyed at Alhorn.
L.50	12 June 1917	2	19	20 October 1917: lost in Mediterranean.

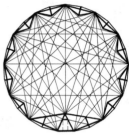

MAIN RING BRACING

Note: there were minor design variations in certain of the 'R'-type airships. Gondolas were altered here and there to improve the performance of engines and propellers.

GERMAN AIRSHIP BASES IN THE EASTERN BALTIC

On 26 January 1915, the German Naval Airship Division lost its first airship of the war when the Parseval PL.19 set out from the Army shed near Königsberg to raid the Russian naval base at Libau. It crashed in the Baltic seven miles from the coast after severe icing which jammed a propellor and fractured an engine. Finally, the envelope buckled due to loss of pressure.

Wainoden (from 1916)

Libau

RUSSIA

Baltic Sea

Telshi

Memel

Tilsit

GULF OF DANZIG

Königsberg

Seerappen

Seddin

EAST PRUSSIA

Danzig

Elbing

0　　50
Miles

GERMANY　Bases shown thus ⊙

During the night of 21-22 March 1915, three German army airships attempted to raid Paris. The ZX and the LZ.35 dropped seven high explosive and 45 incendiaries on Paris and its suburbs, killing one civilian and injuring a further eight. Hit by ground fire, the ZX was destroyed at St. Quentin on the return trip. Damaged by gunfire, the third airship (Schütte-Lanz SL.2) never reached the French capital, but distributed her bombs over Compiègne.

During the war, both the naval and the army airship services made unsuccessful attempts to raid the Russian capital of St. Petersburg (Petrograd). Distance alone prevented success during the early period, but the main problem throughout was bad weather. Ice and snow fouled engines and propellors, congealed oil, and made airships top-heavy and unstable.

Airships worked as scouts with the German navy and were present at a number of sea battles, such as Jutland and Dogger Bank. However, they were never used in conjunction with the U-boat offensive in the Atlantic.

GERMAN AIRSHIPS – continued

AIRSHIP CONSTRUCTION PLANTS AND INLAND BASES

BALTIC SEA

NORTH SEA

HOLLAND

G E R M A N Y

RUSSIA

POLAND

BELGIUM

LUX.

FRANCE

main Zeppelin plant

SWITZ.

AUSTRIA-HUNGARY

RUMANIA

SERBIA

BULGARIA

KEY
⑦ The 'Central Powers'.

Scale: 0 – 100 – 200 Miles

ARMY BASES
① Evere
② Berchem Ste. Agathe
③ Gontrode
④ Düsseldorf
⑤ Hanover
⑥ Schneidemühl
⑦ Kovno

NAVY BASES
Ⓐ Namur
Ⓑ Düren
Ⓒ Jüterbog
Ⓓ Johannisthal
Ⓔ Leipzig
Ⓕ Dresden
Ⓖ Jamboli

CONSTRUCTION PLANTS
❶ Friedrichshafen
❷ Löwenthal
❸ Potsdam
❹ Zeesen
❺ Tegel
❻ Staaken
❼ Bitterfeld
❽ Leipzig
❾ Mannheim

On 5 January 1918, five German airships were destroyed in a sudden and still-unexplained fire at Alhorn. Zeppelins L.46, L.47, L.51, and L.58, plus the Schütte-Lanz SL.20, were involved and the German Naval Airship Division lost 10 men dead, 30 seriously injured, and 104 slightly injured. A further 4 civilian technicians were killed. The most widely held theory is that the blaze originated in the rear gondola of L.51 through the use of petroleum as a cleaning agent by civilian workmen. The German airship service never properly recovered from this disaster.

Airship SCHÜTTE-LANZ
Designed by Professor Schütte and Dr. Lanz. Built in October 1912.

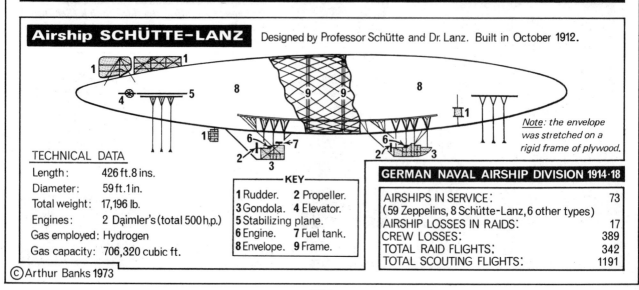

Note: the envelope was stretched on a rigid frame of plywood.

TECHNICAL DATA
Length:	426 ft. 8 ins.
Diameter:	59 ft. 1 in.
Total weight:	17,196 lb.
Engines:	2 Daimler's (total 500 h.p.)
Gas employed:	Hydrogen
Gas capacity:	706,320 cubic ft.

KEY
1 Rudder.   2 Propeller.
3 Gondola.   4 Elevator.
5 Stabilizing plane.
6 Engine.   7 Fuel tank.
8 Envelope. 9 Frame.

GERMAN NAVAL AIRSHIP DIVISION 1914-18
AIRSHIPS IN SERVICE:	73
(59 Zeppelins, 8 Schütte-Lanz, 6 other types)	
AIRSHIP LOSSES IN RAIDS:	17
CREW LOSSES:	389
TOTAL RAID FLIGHTS:	342
TOTAL SCOUTING FLIGHTS:	1191

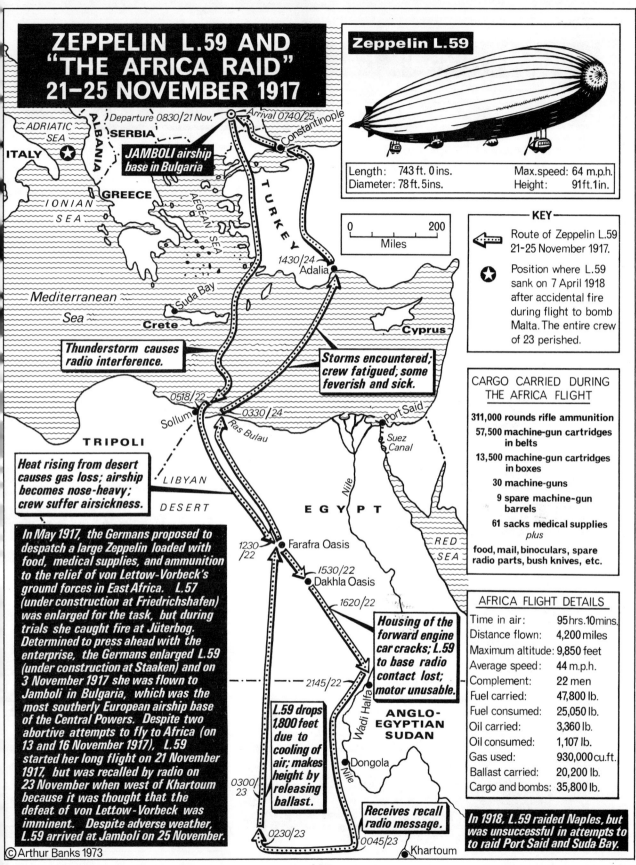

ZEPPELIN L.59 AND "THE AFRICA RAID" 21–25 NOVEMBER 1917

Zeppelin L.59

| Length: | 743 ft. 0 ins. | Max. speed: | 64 m.p.h. |
| Diameter: | 78 ft. 5 ins. | Height: | 91 ft. 1 in. |

Departure 0830/21 Nov.

Arrival 0740/25

Constantinople

JAMBOLI airship base in Bulgaria

ADRIATIC SEA

SERBIA

ALBANIA

ITALY

GREECE

IONIAN SEA

AEGEAN SEA

TURKEY

0 — 200 Miles

KEY

⬅ Route of Zeppelin L.59 21–25 November 1917.

★ Position where L.59 sank on 7 April 1918 after accidental fire during flight to bomb Malta. The entire crew of 23 perished.

1430/24

Adalia

Suda Bay

Mediterranean Sea

Crete

Cyprus

Thunderstorm causes radio interference.

Storms encountered; crew fatigued; some feverish and sick.

0518/22

Sollum

0330/24

Ras Bulau

Port Said

Suez Canal

TRIPOLI

Heat rising from desert causes gas loss; airship becomes nose-heavy; crew suffer airsickness.

LIBYAN DESERT

E G Y P T

Nile

CARGO CARRIED DURING THE AFRICA FLIGHT

311,000 rounds rifle ammunition

57,500 machine-gun cartridges in belts

13,500 machine-gun cartridges in boxes

30 machine-guns

9 spare machine-gun barrels

61 sacks medical supplies

plus

food, mail, binoculars, spare radio parts, bush knives, etc.

1230/22

Farafra Oasis

RED SEA

In May 1917, the Germans proposed to despatch a large Zeppelin loaded with food, medical supplies, and ammunition to the relief of von Lettow-Vorbeck's ground forces in East Africa. L.57 (under construction at Friedrichshafen) was enlarged for the task, but during trials she caught fire at Jüterbog. Determined to press ahead with the enterprise, the Germans enlarged L.59 (under construction at Staaken) and on 3 November 1917 she was flown to Jamboli in Bulgaria, which was the most southerly European airship base of the Central Powers. Despite two abortive attempts to fly to Africa (on 13 and 16 November 1917), L.59 started her long flight on 21 November 1917, but was recalled by radio on 23 November when west of Khartoum because it was thought that the defeat of von Lettow-Vorbeck was imminent. Despite adverse weather, L.59 arrived at Jamboli on 25 November.

1530/22

Dakhla Oasis

1620/22

Housing of the forward engine car cracks; L.59 to base radio contact lost; motor unusable.

AFRICA FLIGHT DETAILS

Time in air:	95 hrs. 10 mins.
Distance flown:	4,200 miles
Maximum altitude:	9,850 feet
Average speed:	44 m.p.h.
Complement:	22 men
Fuel carried:	47,800 lb.
Fuel consumed:	25,050 lb.
Oil carried:	3,360 lb.
Oil consumed:	1,107 lb.
Gas used:	930,000 cu. ft.
Ballast carried:	20,200 lb.
Cargo and bombs:	35,800 lb.

2145/22

L.59 drops 1,800 feet due to cooling of air; makes height by releasing ballast.

ANGLO-EGYPTIAN SUDAN

Wadi Halfa

Dongola

Nile

0300/23

Receives recall radio message.

0230/23

0045/23

Khartoum

In 1918, L.59 raided Naples, but was unsuccessful in attempts to raid Port Said and Suda Bay.

© Arthur Banks 1973

285

GERMAN AIRSHIP RAIDS ON BRITAIN 1915–1918

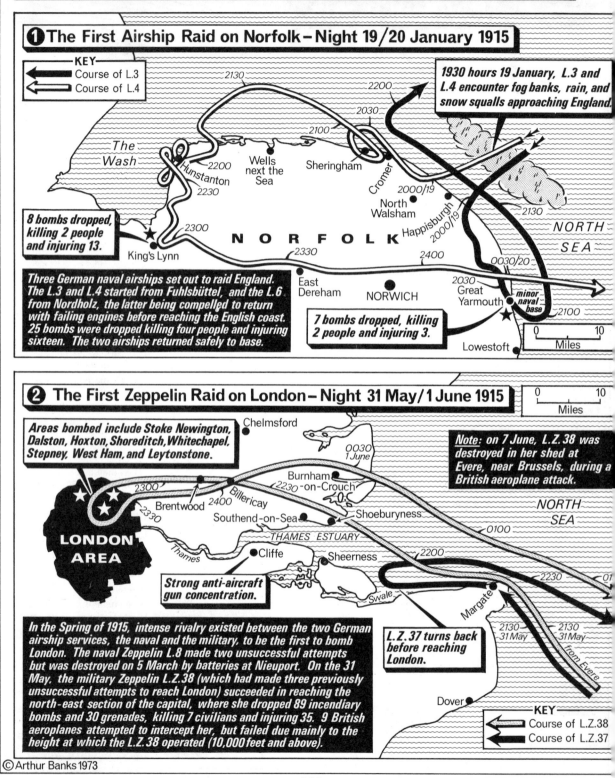

❶ The First Airship Raid on Norfolk – Night 19/20 January 1915

KEY
Course of L.3
Course of L.4

1930 hours 19 January, L.3 and L.4 encounter fog banks, rain, and snow squalls approaching England.

The Wash

Hunstanton 2200 2230
2100
2130
Wells next the Sea
Sheringham
Cromer
2030
2200
2000/19
North Walsham
Happisburgh 2000/19
2130

NORTH SEA

2300
King's Lynn
N O R F O L K
2330
East Dereham
NORWICH
2400
Great Yarmouth
0030/20
minor naval base
2030
2100

8 bombs dropped, killing 2 people and injuring 13.

7 bombs dropped, killing 2 people and injuring 3.

Lowestoft

0   10
Miles

Three German naval airships set out to raid England. The L.3 and L.4 started from Fuhlsbüttel, and the L.6 from Nordholz, the latter being compelled to return with failing engines before reaching the English coast. 25 bombs were dropped killing four people and injuring sixteen. The two airships returned safely to base.

❷ The First Zeppelin Raid on London – Night 31 May/1 June 1915

0   10
Miles

Areas bombed include Stoke Newington, Dalston, Hoxton, Shoreditch, Whitechapel, Stepney, West Ham, and Leytonstone.

Chelmsford
0030 1 June
Burnham-on-Crouch 2230
2300
2400 Billericay
Brentwood
2330
Southend-on-Sea
Shoeburyness

Note: on 7 June, L.Z.38 was destroyed in her shed at Evere, near Brussels, during a British aeroplane attack.

NORTH SEA

LONDON AREA
Thames
Cliffe
THAMES ESTUARY
Sheerness
2200
Swale
0100
2230
01

Strong anti-aircraft gun concentration.

Margate
2130 31 May
2130 31 May
from Evere

Dover

L.Z.37 turns back before reaching London.

In the Spring of 1915, intense rivalry existed between the two German airship services, the naval and the military, to be the first to bomb London. The naval Zeppelin L.8 made two unsuccessful attempts but was destroyed on 5 March by batteries at Nieuport. On the 31 May, the military Zeppelin L.Z.38 (which had made three previously unsuccessful attempts to reach London) succeeded in reaching the north-east section of the capital, where she dropped 89 incendiary bombs and 30 grenades, killing 7 civilians and injuring 35. 9 British aeroplanes attempted to intercept her, but failed due mainly to the height at which the L.Z.38 operated (10,000 feet and above).

KEY
Course of L.Z.38
Course of L.Z.37

© Arthur Banks 1973

286

❸ Early Tyneside Raids-April/June 1915

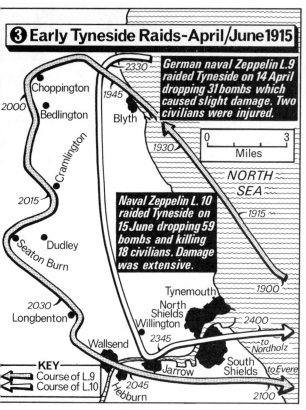

German naval Zeppelin L.9 raided Tyneside on 14 April dropping 31 bombs which caused slight damage. Two civilians were injured.

2330
2000 Choppington
1945
Bedlington
Blyth
Cramlington
1930
2015
NORTH SEA
1915
Seaton Burn
Dudley
1900
Longbenton
2030
Tynemouth
North Shields
Willington
2345
2400
Wallsend
to Nordholz
Jarrow
to Evere
South Shields
2045
Hebburn
2100

Naval Zeppelin L.10 raided Tyneside on 15 June dropping 59 bombs and killing 18 civilians. Damage was extensive.

0 Miles 3

KEY
⬅ Course of L.9
⬅ Course of L.10

❹ First Humber Raid- 6/7 June 1915

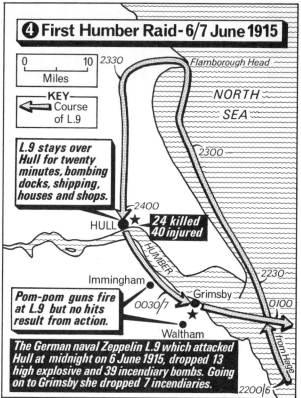

0 Miles 10
2330
Flamborough Head
NORTH SEA
2300

KEY
⬅ Course of L.9

L.9 stays over Hull for twenty minutes, bombing docks, shipping, houses and shops.

2400
HULL ★
24 killed 40 injured

Immingham
0030/7
Grimsby
HUMBER
2230
0100

Pom-pom guns fire at L.9 but no hits result from action.

Waltham
from Hage
2200/6

The German naval Zeppelin L.9 which attacked Hull at midnight on 6 June 1915, dropped 13 high explosive and 39 incendiary bombs. Going on to Grimsby she dropped 7 incendiaries.

❺ The First Sizable Raid on the Midlands–Night 31 January/1 February 1916

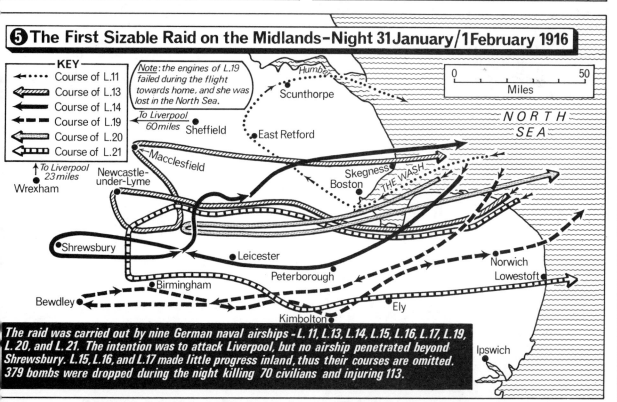

KEY
⬅⋯ Course of L.11
⬅ Course of L.13
⬅ Course of L.14
⬅- - Course of L.19
⬅ Course of L.20
⬅ Course of L.21

To Liverpool 23 miles
Wrexham

Note: the engines of L.19 failed during the flight towards home, and she was lost in the North Sea.

To Liverpool 60 miles
Sheffield

Humber
Scunthorpe
East Retford

NORTH SEA

0 Miles 50

Macclesfield
Newcastle-under-Lyme
Skegness
Boston
THE WASH

Shrewsbury
Leicester
Peterborough
Norwich
Lowestoft

Bewdley
Birmingham
Kimbolton
Ely
Ipswich

The raid was carried out by nine German naval airships - L.11, L.13, L.14, L.15, L.16, L.17, L.19, L.20, and L.21. The intention was to attack Liverpool, but no airship penetrated beyond Shrewsbury. L.15, L.16, and L.17 made little progress inland, thus their courses are omitted. 379 bombs were dropped during the night killing 70 civilians and injuring 113.

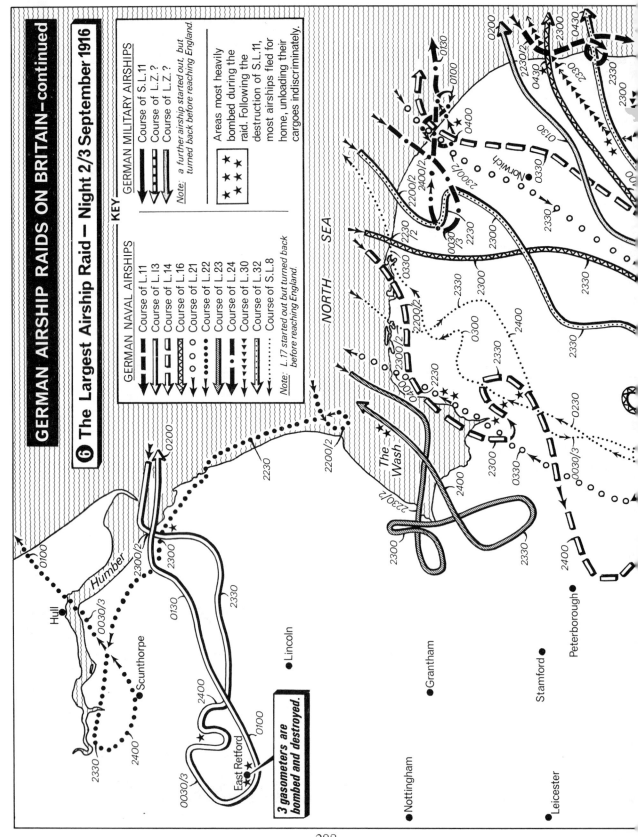

GERMAN AIRSHIP RAIDS ON BRITAIN—continued

❻ The Largest Airship Raid – Night 2/3 September 1916

KEY

GERMAN MILITARY AIRSHIPS

- Course of S.L.11
- Course of L.Z.?
- Course of L.Z.?

Note: a further airship started out, but turned back before reaching England.

Areas most heavily bombed during the raid. Following the destruction of S.L.11, most airships fled for home, unloading their cargoes indiscriminately.

GERMAN NAVAL AIRSHIPS

- Course of L.11
- Course of L.13
- Course of L.14
- Course of L.16
- Course of L.21
- Course of L.22
- Course of L.23
- Course of L.24
- Course of L.30
- Course of L.32
- Course of S.L.8

Note: L.17 started out but turned back before reaching England.

NORTH SEA

Norwich

The Wash

Humber

Hull

Scunthorpe

Lincoln

3 gasometers are bombed and destroyed.

East Retford

Nottingham

Grantham

Leicester

Stamford

Peterborough

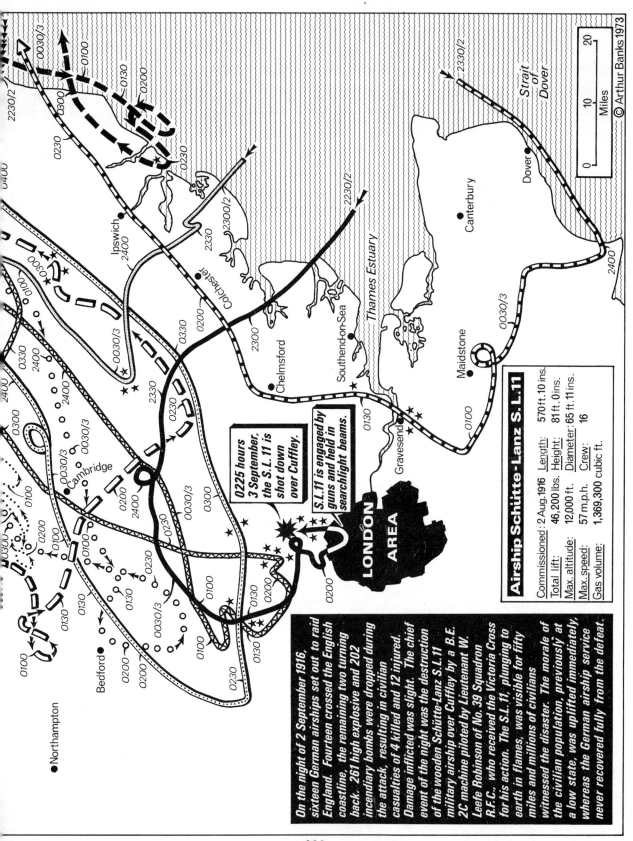

Airship Schütte-Lanz S.L.11

Commissioned: 2 Aug. 1916	Length:	570 ft. 10 ins.
Total lift: 46,200 lbs.	Height:	81 ft. 0 ins.
Max. altitude: 12,000 ft.	Diameter:	65 ft. 11 ins.
Max. speed: 57 m.p.h.	Crew:	16
Gas volume: 1,369,300 cubic ft.		

0225 hours 3 September, the S.L.11 is shot down over Cuffley.

S.L.11 is engaged by guns and held in searchlight beams.

On the night of 2 September 1916, sixteen German airships set out to raid England. Fourteen crossed the English coastline, the remaining two turning back. 261 high explosive and 202 incendiary bombs were dropped during the attack, resulting in civilian casualties of 4 killed and 12 injured. Damage inflicted was slight. The chief event of the night was the destruction of the wooden Schütte-Lanz S.L.11 military airship over Cuffley by a B.E. 2C machine piloted by Lieutenant W. Leefe Robinson of No. 39 Squadron R.F.C., who received the Victoria Cross for his action. The S.L.11, plunging to earth in flames, was visible for fifty miles and millions of civilians witnessed the disaster. The morale of the civilian population, previously at a low state, was uplifted immediately, whereas the German airship service never recovered fully from the defeat.

LONDON AREA

Thames Estuary

Strait of Dover

© Arthur Banks 1973

Miles

Northampton
Bedford
Cambridge
Ipswich
Colchester
Chelmsford
Southend-on-Sea
Gravesend
Maidstone
Canterbury
Dover

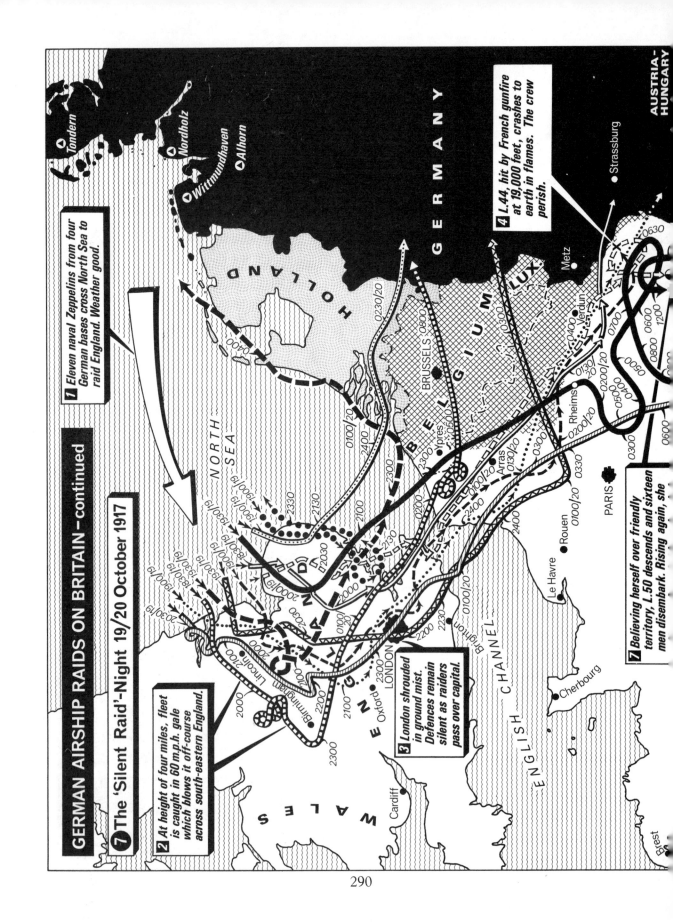

GERMAN AIRSHIP RAIDS ON BRITAIN—continued

7 The 'Silent Raid'–Night 19/20 October 1917

1 Eleven naval Zeppelins from four German bases cross North Sea to raid England. Weather good.

2 At height of four miles, fleet is caught in 60 m.p.h. gale which blows it off-course across south-eastern England.

3 London shrouded in ground mist. Defences remain silent as raiders pass over capital.

4 L.44, hit by French gunfire at 19,000 feet, crashes to earth in flames. The crew perish.

7 Believing herself over friendly territory, L.50 descends and sixteen men disembark. Rising again, she

Map labels:

Tondern
Nordholz
Wittmundhaven
Alhorn

HOLLAND

GERMANY

AUSTRIA-HUNGARY

Strassburg

Metz

BRUSSELS

BELGIUM

LUX.

Ypres
Arras
Rheims
Verdun

PARIS

Le Havre
Rouen
Cherbourg

NORTH SEA

ENGLAND

Lincoln
Birmingham
Oxford
LONDON
Brighton

WALES

Cardiff

ENGLISH CHANNEL

Brest

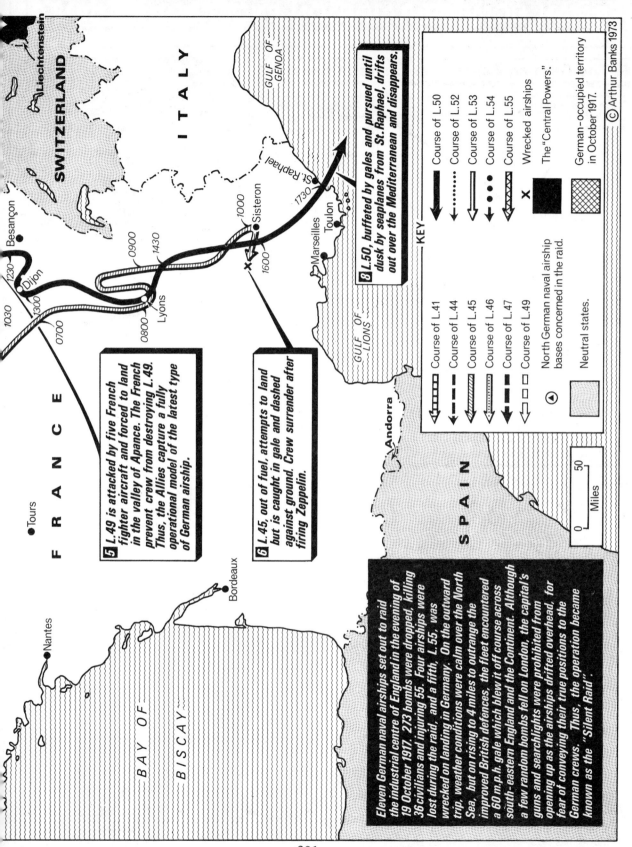

SWITZERLAND

Liechtenstein

ITALY

GULF OF GENOA

St. Raphael

1730

8 L.50, buffeted by gales and pursued until dusk by seaplanes from St. Raphael, drifts out over the Mediterranean and disappears.

Besançon

Dijon

1030

1230

1300

0700

0800

Lyons

0900

1430

1000

Sisteron

1600

X

Marseilles

Toulon

GULF OF LIONS

KEY

Course of L.50
Course of L.52
Course of L.53
Course of L.54
Course of L.55

Course of L.41
Course of L.44
Course of L.45
Course of L.46
Course of L.47
Course of L.49

X   Wrecked airships

The "Central Powers".

German-occupied territory in October 1917.

© Arthur Banks 1973

North German naval airship bases concerned in the raid.

Neutral states.

FRANCE

Tours

5 L.49 is attacked by five French fighter aircraft and forced to land in the valley of Apance. The French prevent crew from destroying L.49. Thus, the Allies capture a fully operational model of the latest type of German airship.

6 L.45, out of fuel, attempts to land but is caught in gale and dashed against ground. Crew surrender after firing Zeppelin.

Bordeaux

Nantes

BAY OF

BISCAY

Andorra

SPAIN

0   50
Miles

Eleven German naval airships set out to raid the industrial centre of England in the evening of 19 October 1917. 273 bombs were dropped, killing 36 civilians and injuring 55. Four airships were lost during the raid, and a fifth, L.55, was wrecked on landing in Germany. On the outward trip, weather conditions were calm over the North Sea, but on rising to 4 miles to outrange the improved British defences, the fleet encountered a 60 m.p.h. gale which blew it off course across south-eastern England and the Continent. Although a few random bombs fell on London, the capital's guns and searchlights were prohibited from opening up as the airships drifted overhead, for fear of conveying their true positions to the German crews. Thus, the operation became known as the "Silent Raid".

GERMAN BOMBER RAIDS ON ENGLAND 1917-1918

① The German Bases near Ghent in Belgium

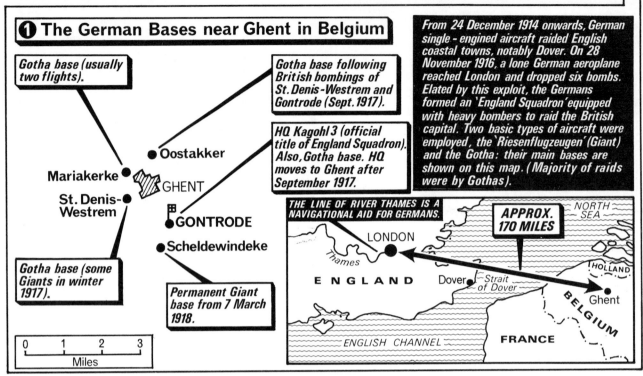

Gotha base (usually two flights).

Gotha base following British bombings of St. Denis-Westrem and Gontrode (Sept. 1917).

HQ Kagohl 3 (official title of England Squadron). Also, Gotha base. HQ moves to Ghent after September 1917.

Gotha base (some Giants in winter 1917).

Permanent Giant base from 7 March 1918.

● Oostakker

Mariakerke

St. Denis-Westrem

GHENT

GONTRODE

● Scheldewindeke

From 24 December 1914 onwards, German single-engined aircraft raided English coastal towns, notably Dover. On 28 November 1916, a lone German aeroplane reached London and dropped six bombs. Elated by this exploit, the Germans formed an 'England Squadron' equipped with heavy bombers to raid the British capital. Two basic types of aircraft were employed, the 'Riesenflugzeugen' (Giant) and the Gotha: their main bases are shown on this map. (Majority of raids were by Gothas).

THE LINE OF RIVER THAMES IS A NAVIGATIONAL AID FOR GERMANS.

APPROX. 170 MILES

NORTH SEA

LONDON

Thames

ENGLAND

Dover — Strait of Dover

HOLLAND

BELGIUM

Ghent

ENGLISH CHANNEL

FRANCE

0 1 2 3
Miles

② The Main Target: LONDON

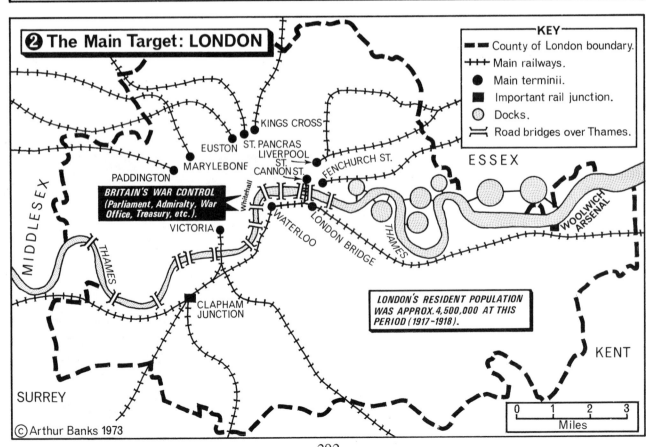

KEY
- ▬ ▬ County of London boundary.
- ┼┼┼ Main railways.
- ● Main terminii.
- ■ Important rail junction.
- ◉ Docks.
- ⌗ Road bridges over Thames.

KINGS CROSS

EUSTON
ST. PANCRAS
LIVERPOOL ST.
FENCHURCH ST.
MARYLEBONE
CANNON ST.
PADDINGTON

ESSEX

BRITAIN'S WAR CONTROL (Parliament, Admiralty, War Office, Treasury, etc.).

Whitehall

WATERLOO

LONDON BRIDGE

Thames

WOOLWICH ARSENAL

VICTORIA

MIDDLESEX

THAMES

CLAPHAM JUNCTION

LONDON'S RESIDENT POPULATION WAS APPROX. 4,500,000 AT THIS PERIOD (1917-1918).

KENT

SURREY

© Arthur Banks 1973

0 1 2 3
Miles

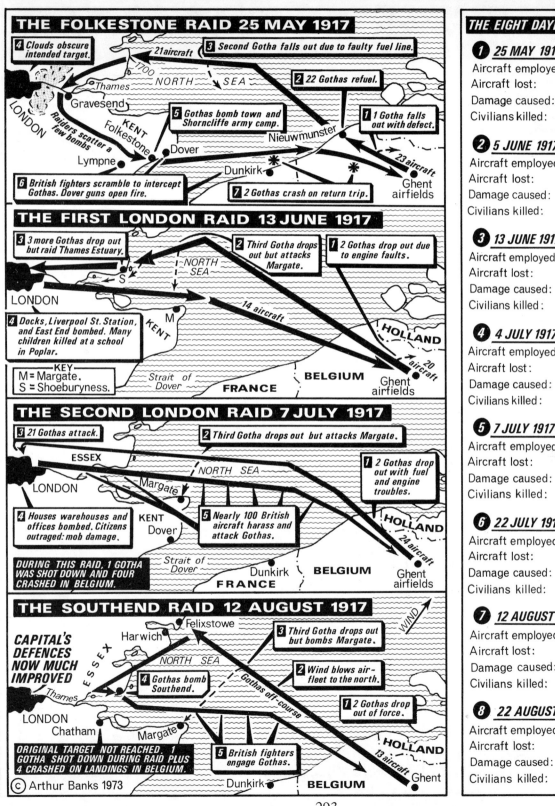

Employing Gotha bombers, the Germans made eight mass-attacks in daylight against England in 1917. 165 aircraft flights were involved and nearly 73,000 lbs. of bombs were dropped, killing or injuring 1,364 English civilians. Seventeen Gothas were destroyed during the period 25 May – 22 August 1917. Four of the attacks are shown below.

THE FOLKESTONE RAID 25 MAY 1917

4 Clouds obscure intended target.

3 Second Gotha falls out due to faulty fuel line.

21 aircraft

1700

NORTH SEA

Thames

Gravesend

2 22 Gothas refuel.

5 Gothas bomb town and Shorncliffe army camp.

1 1 Gotha falls out with defect.

LONDON

Raiders scatter a few bombs

KENT

Folkestone

Dover

Nieuwmunster

23 aircraft

Lympne

Dunkirk

Ghent airfields

6 British fighters scramble to intercept Gothas. Dover guns open fire.

7 2 Gothas crash on return trip.

THE FIRST LONDON RAID 13 JUNE 1917

3 3 more Gothas drop out but raid Thames Estuary.

2 Third Gotha drops out but attacks Margate.

1 2 Gothas drop out due to engine faults.

NORTH SEA

S

LONDON

14 aircraft

HOLLAND

4 Docks, Liverpool St. Station, and East End bombed. Many children killed at a school in Poplar.

KENT

M

20 aircraft

BELGIUM

KEY
M = Margate.
S = Shoeburyness.

Strait of Dover

FRANCE

Ghent airfields

THE SECOND LONDON RAID 7 JULY 1917

3 21 Gothas attack.

2 Third Gotha drops out but attacks Margate.

ESSEX

1 2 Gothas drop out with fuel and engine troubles.

NORTH SEA

LONDON

Margate

4 Houses warehouses and offices bombed. Citizens outraged: mob damage.

KENT

Dover

5 Nearly 100 British aircraft harass and attack Gothas.

HOLLAND

24 aircraft

DURING THIS RAID, 1 GOTHA WAS SHOT DOWN AND FOUR CRASHED IN BELGIUM.

Strait of Dover

Dunkirk

BELGIUM

FRANCE

Ghent airfields

THE SOUTHEND RAID 12 AUGUST 1917

CAPITAL'S DEFENCES NOW MUCH IMPROVED

Felixstowe

Harwich

3 Third Gotha drops out but bombs Margate.

WIND

ESSEX

NORTH SEA

Gothas off-course

2 Wind blows air-fleet to the north.

4 Gothas bomb Southend.

Thames

1 2 Gothas drop out of force.

LONDON

Chatham

Margate

HOLLAND

13 aircraft

ORIGINAL TARGET NOT REACHED. 1 GOTHA SHOT DOWN DURING RAID PLUS 4 CRASHED ON LANDINGS IN BELGIUM.

5 British fighters engage Gothas.

Dunkirk

BELGIUM

Ghent

© Arthur Banks 1973

THE EIGHT DAYLIGHT RAIDS

1 **25 MAY 1917**
Aircraft employed: 23.
Aircraft lost: 2.
Damage caused: £19,500.
Civilians killed: 95.

2 **5 JUNE 1917**
Aircraft employed: 22.
Aircraft lost: 1.
Damage caused: £5,000.
Civilians killed: 13.

3 **13 JUNE 1917**
Aircraft employed: 20.
Aircraft lost: Nil.
Damage caused: £129,500.
Civilians killed: 162.

4 **4 JULY 1917**
Aircraft employed: 25.
Aircraft lost: Nil.
Damage caused: £2,100.
Civilians killed: 17.

5 **7 JULY 1917**
Aircraft employed: 24.
Aircraft lost: 5.
Damage caused: £205,500.
Civilians killed: 57.

6 **22 JULY 1917**
Aircraft employed: 23.
Aircraft lost: 1.
Damage caused: £2,800.
Civilians killed: 13.

7 **12 AUGUST 1917**
Aircraft employed: 13.
Aircraft lost: 5.
Damage caused: £9,600.
Civilians killed: 32.

8 **22 AUGUST 1917**
Aircraft employed: 15.
Aircraft lost: 3.
Damage caused: £17,200.
Civilians killed: 12.

Because of the increasing efficiency of Britain's defences, the Germans switched from daylight to darkness for their attacks. 19 raids were carried out between 3 September 1917 and 20 May 1918 and often several towns were bombed during a single raid. At one period, 300,000 Londoners sought refuge at Underground stations.

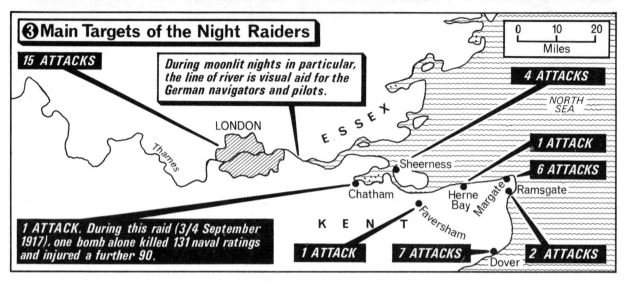

❸ Main Targets of the Night Raiders

15 ATTACKS

During moonlit nights in particular, the line of river is visual aid for the German navigators and pilots.

4 ATTACKS

NORTH SEA

ESSEX

LONDON

Thames

1 ATTACK

6 ATTACKS

Sheerness

Chatham

Herne Bay

Margate

Ramsgate

1 ATTACK. During this raid (3/4 September 1917), one bomb alone killed 131 naval ratings and injured a further 90.

KENT

Faversham

1 ATTACK

7 ATTACKS

Dover

2 ATTACKS

0 10 20
Miles

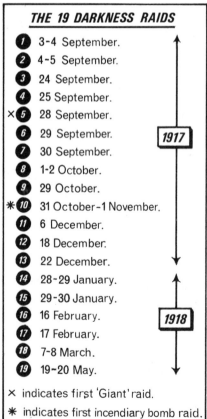

THE 19 DARKNESS RAIDS

1. 3-4 September.
2. 4-5 September.
3. 24 September.
4. 25 September.
× 5. 28 September.
6. 29 September.
7. 30 September.
8. 1-2 October.
9. 29 October.
* 10. 31 October-1 November.
11. 6 December.
12. 18 December.
13. 22 December.
14. 28-29 January.
15. 29-30 January.
16. 16 February.
17. 17 February.
18. 7-8 March.
19. 19-20 May.

1917

1918

× indicates first 'Giant' raid.

* indicates first incendiary bomb raid.

THE GERMAN 'ELEKTRON' BOMB (AUGUST 1918)

Weighing approx. one kilogram, this incendiary device ignited upon contact. Constructed of magnesium, its main feature was that when sprayed with water, the existing fire became even fiercer. The Germans planned to drop large numbers on London (and Paris), but the Allied offensives in the autumn of 1918 frustrated this idea.

GERMAN BOMBER LOSSES

43 Gothas (from 383 flights) } ALL ATTACKS, { shot down, crashed,
2 Giants (from 30 flights) } NIGHT AND DAY { missing, etc.

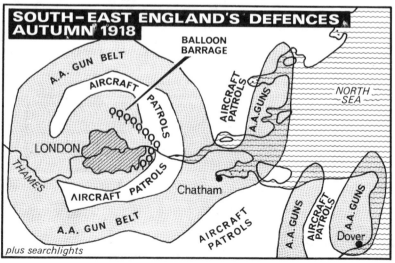

SOUTH-EAST ENGLAND'S DEFENCES, AUTUMN 1918

BALLOON BARRAGE

A.A. GUN BELT

AIRCRAFT PATROLS

NORTH SEA

AIRCRAFT PATROLS

A.A. GUNS

LONDON

THAMES

AIRCRAFT PATROLS

Chatham

A.A. GUN BELT

AIRCRAFT PATROLS

A.A. GUNS

AIRCRAFT PATROLS

A.A. GUNS

Dover

plus searchlights

GERMAN Zeppelin-Staaken R.VI (Giant) Bomber

One R.VI, the R.39, delivered the greatest bomb-load of any single aeroplane during the war (26,000 kilograms in 20 raids). It dropped the only 3 1,000 kg. bombs to fall on Britain.

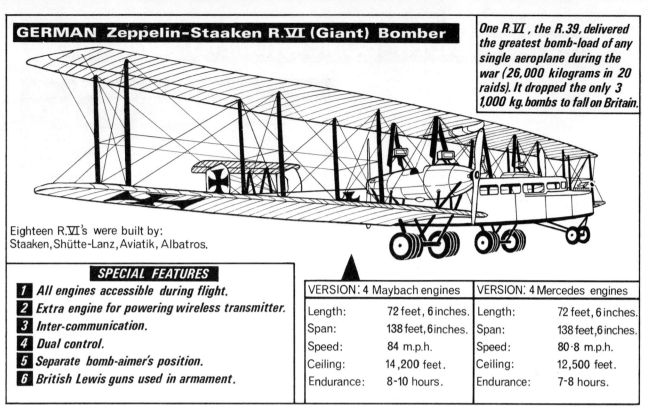

Eighteen R.VI's were built by: Staaken, Shütte-Lanz, Aviatik, Albatros.

SPECIAL FEATURES

1 All engines accessible during flight.
2 Extra engine for powering wireless transmitter.
3 Inter-communication.
4 Dual control.
5 Separate bomb-aimer's position.
6 British Lewis guns used in armament.

VERSION: 4 Maybach engines		VERSION: 4 Mercedes engines	
Length:	72 feet, 6 inches.	Length:	72 feet, 6 inches.
Span:	138 feet, 6 inches.	Span:	138 feet, 6 inches.
Speed:	84 m.p.h.	Speed:	80·8 m.p.h.
Ceiling:	14,200 feet.	Ceiling:	12,500 feet.
Endurance:	8-10 hours.	Endurance:	7-8 hours.

④ British Fighter Airfields: Autumn 1918

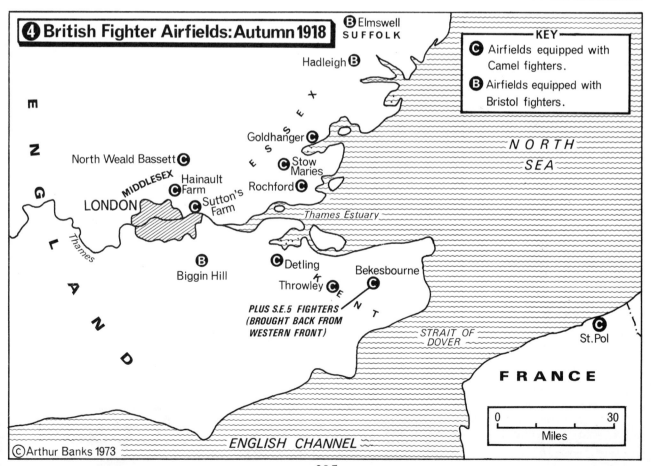

KEY

C Airfields equipped with Camel fighters.

B Airfields equipped with Bristol fighters.

© Arthur Banks 1973

295

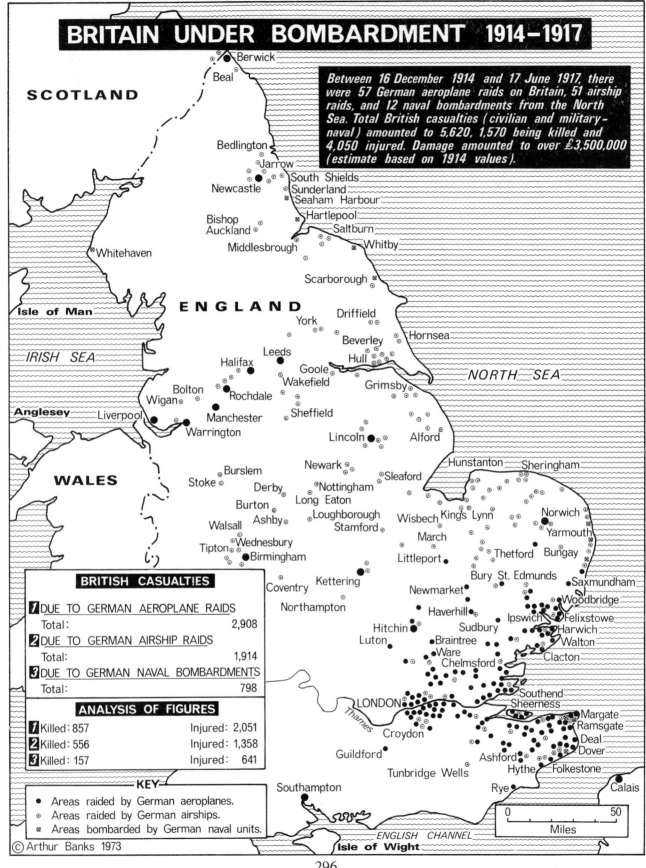

BRITAIN UNDER BOMBARDMENT 1914–1917

SCOTLAND

Between 16 December 1914 and 17 June 1917, there were 57 German aeroplane raids on Britain, 51 airship raids, and 12 naval bombardments from the North Sea. Total British casualties (civilian and military-naval) amounted to 5,620, 1,570 being killed and 4,050 injured. Damage amounted to over £3,500,000 (estimate based on 1914 values).

ENGLAND

WALES

IRISH SEA

Isle of Man

Anglesey

NORTH SEA

Berwick
Beal
Bedlington
Jarrow
Newcastle
South Shields
Sunderland
Seaham Harbour
Bishop Auckland
Hartlepool
Saltburn
Middlesbrough
Whitby
Scarborough
Driffield
York
Beverley
Hornsea
Leeds
Hull
Halifax
Goole
Wakefield
Grimsby
Bolton
Rochdale
Wigan
Sheffield
Liverpool
Manchester
Warrington
Lincoln
Alford
Whitehaven
Newark
Hunstanton
Sheringham
Burslem
Sleaford
Stoke
Derby
Nottingham
Norwich
Long Eaton
Burton
Ashby
Loughborough
Wisbech
King's Lynn
Yarmouth
Walsall
Stamford
March
Thetford
Bungay
Tipton
Wednesbury
Littleport
Birmingham
Bury St. Edmunds
Saxmundham
Coventry
Kettering
Newmarket
Woodbridge
Northampton
Haverhill
Ipswich
Felixstowe
Hitchin
Sudbury
Harwich
Luton
Braintree
Walton
Ware
Clacton
Chelmsford
LONDON
Southend
Sheerness
Croydon
Margate
Ramsgate
Guildford
Deal
Ashford
Dover
Tunbridge Wells
Hythe
Folkestone
Southampton
Rye
Calais
Thames
Isle of Wight
ENGLISH CHANNEL

BRITISH CASUALTIES

1 DUE TO GERMAN AEROPLANE RAIDS		
Total:		2,908
2 DUE TO GERMAN AIRSHIP RAIDS		
Total:		1,914
3 DUE TO GERMAN NAVAL BOMBARDMENTS		
Total:		798

ANALYSIS OF FIGURES

1 Killed: 857		Injured: 2,051
2 Killed: 556		Injured: 1,358
3 Killed: 157		Injured: 641

KEY
- ● Areas raided by German aeroplanes.
- ⊙ Areas raided by German airships.
- ⊠ Areas bombarded by German naval units.

0 ———— 50
Miles

© Arthur Banks 1973

296

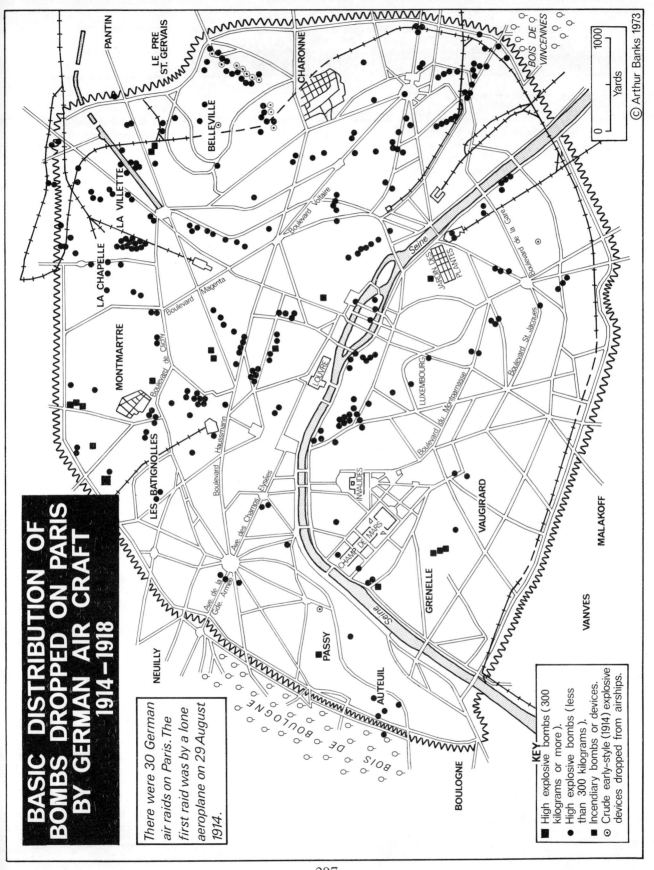

BASIC DISTRIBUTION OF BOMBS DROPPED ON PARIS BY GERMAN AIR CRAFT 1914–1918

There were 30 German air raids on Paris. The first raid was by a lone aeroplane on 29 August 1914.

KEY
■ High explosive bombs (300 kilograms or more).
● High explosive bombs (less than 300 kilograms).
■ Incendiary bombs or devices.
⊙ Crude early-style (1914) explosive devices dropped from airships.

© Arthur Banks 1973

0 — 1000 Yards

297

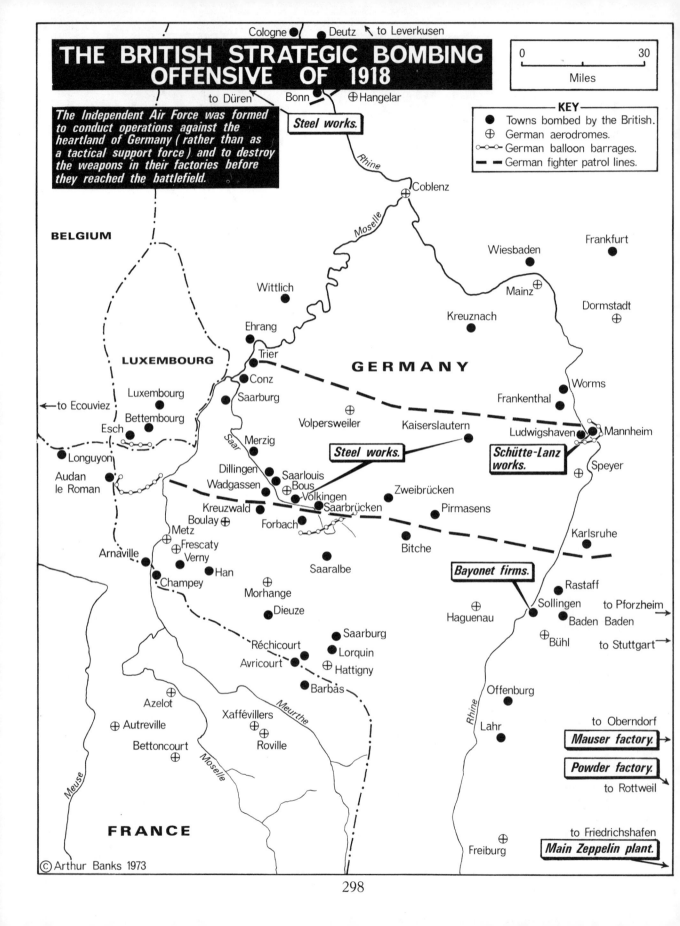

THE BRITISH STRATEGIC BOMBING OFFENSIVE OF 1918

The Independent Air Force was formed to conduct operations against the heartland of Germany (rather than as a tactical support force) and to destroy the weapons in their factories before they reached the battlefield.

0   30
Miles

KEY
● Towns bombed by the British.
⊕ German aerodromes.
○—○—○ German balloon barrages.
– – – German fighter patrol lines.

Cologne ● ● Deutz ↖ to Leverkusen

to Düren → Bonn ⊕ Hangelar

Steel works.

BELGIUM

Rhine

Coblenz ⊕

Moselle

Frankfurt

Wiesbaden

Wittlich

Mainz ⊕   Dormstadt

Ehrang

GERMANY

Trier   Kreuznach

Conz

LUXEMBOURG   Saarburg   Worms

Luxembourg   Frankenthal

Bettembourg   Volpersweiler ⊕   Kaiserslautern ●   Ludwigshaven ● ● Mannheim

to Ecouviez →   Esch   Merzig   **Steel works.**   **Schütte-Lanz works.**   Speyer ⊕

Longuyon ●   Dillingen   Zweibrücken   ⊕

Audan le Roman   Wadgassen   Saarlouis   Bous ⊕   Pirmasens

Kreuzwald   Völkingen   Saarbrücken   Karlsruhe

Boulay ⊕   Forbach   Bitche   Rastaff

Metz   ⊕Frescaty   Saaralbe   **Bayonet firms.**   Sollingen   Baden Baden

Arnaville   Verny   Han   Morhange ⊕   Haguenau ⊕   Bühl ⊕   to Pforzheim →

Champey   Dieuze   to Stuttgart →

Saarburg ●

Réchicourt   Lorquin   Offenburg   to Oberndorf

Azelot ⊕   Avricourt   Hattigny ⊕   Lahr   **Mauser factory.**

Autreville ⊕   Xaffévillers   Barbas ●   Rhine   **Powder factory.**

Bettoncourt ⊕   Roville ⊕   Meurthe   to Rottweil

FRANCE   Meuse   Moselle   Freiburg ⊕   to Friedrichshafen   **Main Zeppelin plant.**

© Arthur Banks 1973

298

DEVELOPMENTS IN AERIAL SURVEYING 1914-1918

❶ Balloon Photography

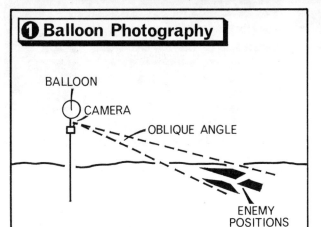

From the cartographic viewpoint, this method was unsatisfactory due to distortion of scale. What was required was overhead 'plan view' photography.

❷ Overhead Photography

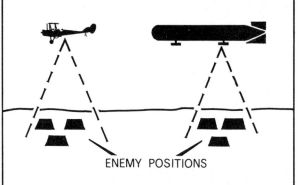

By utilising aeroplanes and airships, overhead views could be obtained. Battle maps improved both in scale accuracy and in detail shown.

❸ The Mosaic Map

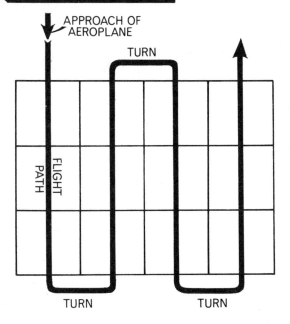

To cover large areas, photographs were butt-jointed together to form one vast panoramic spread.

❹ The Overlap Refinement

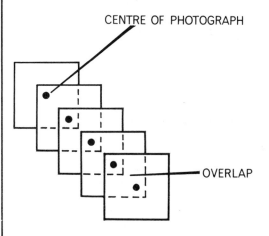

The mosaic map left much to be desired as only the centres of photographs were true to scale, and these varied individually. By regulating camera shutters at fixed intervals while aircraft maintained a consistent height, resulting prints could be overlapped to register uniformly.

THE FIGHTER 'ACES'

Note: main decorations only shown.

THE INTERNATIONAL TOP TEN SCORERS

POSITION	NAME	COUNTRY	'KILLS'
1	RICHTHOFEN	GERMANY	80
2	FONCK	FRANCE	75 ?
3	MANNOCK	BRITAIN	73 ?
4	BISHOP	CANADA	72
5	UDET	GERMANY	62
6	COLLISHAW	CANADA	60
7	McCUDDEN	BRITAIN	57
8	BEAUCHAMP-PROCTOR	SOUTH AFRICA	54
8	MacLAREN	CANADA	54
8	GUYNEMER	FRANCE	54

GERMAN TOP SCORERS

1	Rittmeister Manfred von Richthofen	80 kills
2	Oberleutnant Ernst Udet	62 kills
3	Oberleutnant Erich Loewenhardt	53 kills
4	Leutnant Werner Voss	48 kills
5	Hauptmann Rudolph Berthold	44 kills
6	Leutnant Paul Bäumer	43 kills

All six aces won Pour le Mérite (in Germany an 'ace' implied 10 or more victories).

FRENCH TOP SCORERS

1	Capitaine Rene Paul Fonck, L d'H, C de G with 28 Palms, MC, CK	75 kills
2	Capitaine Georges M.L.J. Guynemer, L d'H, MM, C de G (26 Palms)	54 kills
3	Lieutenant Charles E J M Nungesser, L d'H, MM, C de G	45 kills
4	Capitaine Georges Felix Madon, L d'H, MM, C de G	41 kills
5	Lieutenant Maurice Bayau, L d'H, MM, C de G	35 kills
6	Lieutenant Michel Coifford, L d'H, MM, C de G	34 kills

BRITISH EMPIRE TOP SCORERS

1	Major Edward Mannock, VC, DSO and 2 bars, MC and bar	73 kills
2	Lt. Colonel William A. Bishop, VC, DSO and bar, MC, DFC, L d H	72 kills
3	Lt. Colonel Raymond Collishaw, DSO and bar, DSC, DFC, C de G	60 kills
4	Major James T.B. McCudden, VC, DSO and bar, MC and bar, MM	57 kills
5	Captain Anthony W. Beauchamp-Proctor, VC, DSO, MC and bar	54 kills
6	Major Donald R. MacLaren, DSO, MC and bar, DFC, L d'H, C de G	54 kills

RUSSIAN TOP SCORERS

1	Staff Captain Alexander A. Kazakov, (13 Russian), DSO, MC, DFC	17 kills
2	Captain d'Argueeff (Argeyev ?), Order of St. George	15 kills
3	Lt. Commander Alexander Prokofieff de Seversky, (all high Russian)	13 kills

THE RED BARON

Manfred von Richthofen was the highest scoring German fighter pilot 'ace' of the 1914-1918 war. He was credited with 80 enemy aircraft destroyed, and although the majority of these were reconnaissance machines, this total made him the top individual scorer of any country involved in the war.

He began flying as an active fighter pilot in March 1916, and was associated with the red Fokker triplane, the machine gun of which was synchronised to fire through the propeller.

He formed the group of squadrons known by the British as Richthofen's "circus", and was awarded the Pour le Mérite (the Blue Max) in February 1917. He was finally shot down on 21 April 1918, and was buried by the British with full military honours at Bertangles in France.

After the war he was reburied with much pomp and ceremony in Berlin.

AUSTRO-HUNGARIAN TOP SCORER

Hauptmann Godwin Brumowski	40 kills

BELGIAN TOP SCORER

Second Lieutenant Willy Coppens de Houthulst, DSO	37 kills

ITALIAN TOP SCORER

Maggiore Francesco Baracca	34 kills

UNITED STATES' TOP SCORER

Captain Edward V. Rickenbacker, CMH	26 kills

DECORATIONS: abbreviations employed here

VC = Victoria Cross.
MC = Military Cross.
DSO = Distinguished Service Order.
MM = Military Medal.
DSC = Distinguished Service Cross.
L d'H = Légion d'Honneur.
DFC = Distinguished Flying Cross.
C de G = Croix de Guerre.
CK = Cross of Karageorgevitch.
CMH = Congressional Medal of Honor.

EUROPEAN RANKINGS: Approx. equivalents

note: army ranks

Rittmeister = Cavalry captain.
Hauptmann = Captain.
Oberleutnant = Lieutenant.
Leutnant = Second Lieutenant.
Maggiore = Major.
Capitaine = Captain.

© Arthur Banks 1973

300

THE LOOP

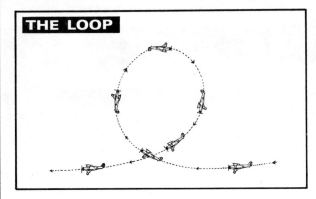

HALF ROLL ON TOP OF LOOP

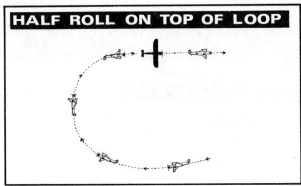

SLOW ROLL

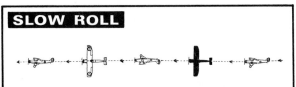

THE TOP SCORER : AN ANALYSIS

MANFRED VON RICHTHOFEN : THE RED BARON

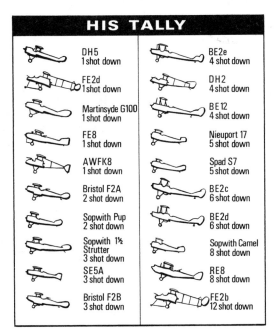

HIS TALLY		
DH5 — 1 shot down	BE2e — 4 shot down	
FE2d — 1 shot down	DH2 — 4 shot down	
Martinsyde G100 — 1 shot down	BE12 — 4 shot down	
FE8 — 1 shot down	Nieuport 17 — 5 shot down	
AWFK8 — 1 shot down	Spad S7 — 5 shot down	
Bristol F2A — 2 shot down	BE2c — 6 shot down	
Sopwith Pup — 2 shot down	BE2d — 6 shot down	
Sopwith 1½ Strutter — 3 shot down	Sopwith Camel — 8 shot down	
SE5A — 3 shot down	RE8 — 8 shot down	
Bristol F2B — 3 shot down	FE2b — 12 shot down	

SOME OTHER FAMOUS 'ACES'	KILLS
AUSTRALIAN Captain Robert A. Little, DSO and bar, DSC, C de G	47
BRITISH Captain Albert Ball, VC, DSO and 2 bars, MC	44
GERMAN Hauptmann Oswald Boelcke, Pour le Mérite	40
GERMAN Oberleutnant Max Immelmann, Pour le Mérite	15

ATTACK FROM ASTERN ➊

FIXED MACHINE GUN FIRING FORWARD.

LINE OF ATTACK

HEIGHT ADVANTAGE (CLEAR VIEW).

This position was advantageous to the rear aircraft when the front machine carried only one occupant.

ATTACK FROM ASTERN ➋

OWN FUSELAGE IMPEDES REAR MACHINE GUNNER'S LINE OF FIRE.

LINE OF ATTACK

This position was advantageous to the rear aircraft when the front machine carried two occupants.

THE DECEPTIVE SIDE TURN

PLAN VIEW

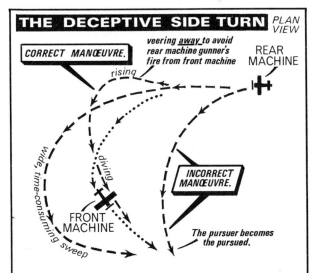

CORRECT MANŒUVRE.

veering *away* to avoid rear machine gunner's fire from front machine

REAR MACHINE

rising

wide, time-consuming sweep

diving

FRONT MACHINE

INCORRECT MANŒUVRE.

The pursuer becomes the pursued.

This diagram illustrates problems confronting a pilot when his quarry turned or banked to escape attack.

TWELVE IMPORTANT AIRCRAFT 1914-1918

BRITISH B.E. 2C

FRONT ELEVATION

SIDE ELEVATION

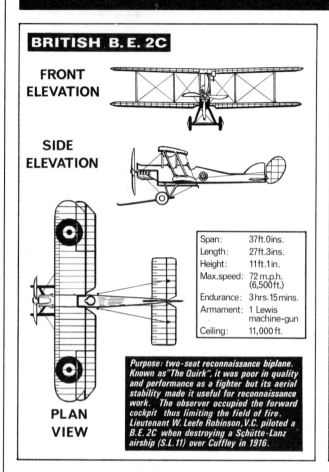

PLAN VIEW

Span:	37ft.0ins.
Length:	27ft.3ins.
Height:	11ft.1in.
Max.speed:	72 m.p.h. (6,500 ft.)
Endurance:	3 hrs.15 mins.
Armament:	1 Lewis machine-gun
Ceiling:	11,000 ft.

Purpose: two-seat reconnaissance biplane. Known as "The Quirk", it was poor in quality and performance as a fighter but its aerial stability made it useful for reconnaissance work. The observer occupied the forward cockpit thus limiting the field of fire. Lieutenant W. Leefe Robinson, V.C. piloted a B.E. 2C when destroying a Schütte-Lanz airship (S.L.11) over Cuffley in 1916.

FRENCH Nieuport 17 C.1

FRONT ELEVATION

SIDE ELEVATION

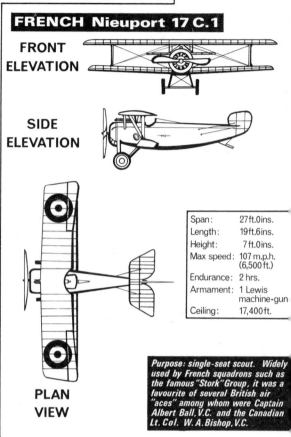

PLAN VIEW

Span:	27ft.0ins.
Length:	19ft.6ins.
Height:	7ft.0ins.
Max speed:	107 m.p.h. (6,500 ft.)
Endurance:	2 hrs.
Armament:	1 Lewis machine-gun
Ceiling:	17,400 ft.

Purpose: single-seat scout. Widely used by French squadrons such as the famous "Stork" Group, it was a favourite of several British air "aces" among whom were Captain Albert Ball, V.C. and the Canadian Lt. Col. W. A. Bishop, V.C.

GERMAN Albatros D-1

SIDE ELEVATION

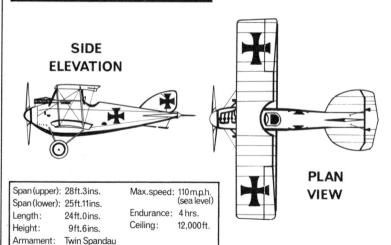

PLAN VIEW

FRONT ELEVATION

Span (upper):	28ft.3ins.	Max.speed: 110 m.p.h. (sea level)
Span (lower):	25ft.11ins.	Endurance: 4 hrs.
Length:	24ft.0ins.	Ceiling: 12,000ft.
Height:	9ft.6ins.	
Armament:	Twin Spandau machine-guns	

Purpose: single-seat scout. First deliveries to squadrons commenced on 3 September 1916, and the famous German "ace" Oswald Boelcke shot down eleven Allied aircraft within a short period of 16 days. It was supreme during the winter of 1916-1917 and its twin synchronised guns feature became incorporated into the design of all subsequent German and Allied fighters.

BRITISH Bristol F.2B

SIDE ELEVATION

FRONT ELEVATION

PLAN VIEW

Span:	39ft.4ins.	Armament:	1 Vickers machine-gun for the pilot
Length:	26ft.2ins.		
Height:	10ft.1in.		1 or 2 Lewis guns for the observer
Max.speed:	125 m.p.h. (sea level)		
Endurance:	3 hrs.		Racks for light bombs
Ceiling:	20,000 ft.		

Purpose: two-seat fighter/reconnaissance aircraft. Possibly the finest all-round fighter of the Allies in the war, it was extremely manœuvrable and carried the advantage of a "sting in the tail". Known as the "Brisfit" or "Biff", it was a favourite of British "ace" Captain McKeever who won most of his thirty victories with this type.

FRENCH Spad S-7 C.1

SIDE ELEVATION

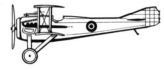

FRONT ELEVATION

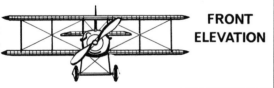

PLAN VIEW

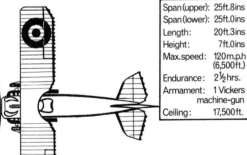

Span (upper):	25ft.8ins
Span (lower):	25ft.0ins
Length:	20ft.3ins
Height:	7ft.0ins
Max.speed:	120m.p.h (6,500ft.)
Endurance:	2½ hrs.
Armament:	1 Vickers machine-gun
Ceiling:	17,500ft.

Purpose: single-seat scout. First flown in July 1916, over 5,000 Spad S-7's were built in France, and 400 in England. The famous French "Stork" Group, of which the "ace" Georges Guynemer was a member, flew this type.

GERMAN Fokker Dr-1 Triplane

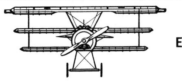

FRONT ELEVATION

SIDE ELEVATION

Span (upper):	23ft.7ins.
Span (centre):	20ft.6ins.
Span (lower):	18ft.9ins.
Length:	19ft.0ins.
Height:	9ft.0ins.
Max.speed:	122m.p.h. at 8,000ft.
Endurance:	2hrs.30mins.
Armament:	Twin Spandau machine-guns
Ceiling:	20,000ft.

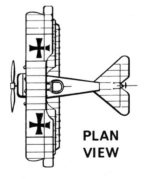

PLAN VIEW

Purpose: single-seat scout. First employed in August 1917, it was a favourite of German "aces" such as Manfred von Richthofen and Werner Voss and was the supreme German "dogfighter" of the war.

TWELVE IMPORTANT AIRCRAFT-continued

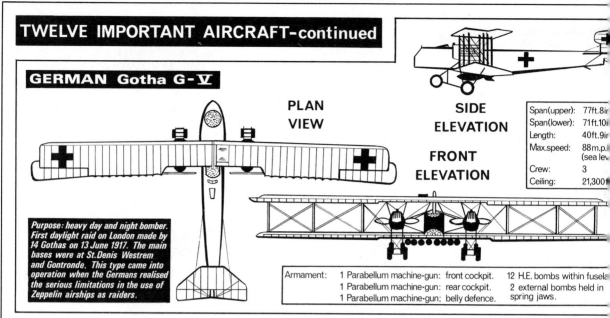

GERMAN Gotha G-V

PLAN VIEW

SIDE ELEVATION

FRONT ELEVATION

Span(upper):	77ft.8in
Span(lower):	71ft.10in
Length:	40ft.9in
Max.speed:	88m.p.h (sea lev
Crew:	3
Ceiling:	21,300ft

Purpose: heavy day and night bomber. First daylight raid on London made by 14 Gothas on 13 June 1917. The main bases were at St.Denis Westrem and Gontronde. This type came into operation when the Germans realised the serious limitations in the use of Zeppelin airships as raiders.

Armament:	1 Parabellum machine-gun: front cockpit.	12 H.E. bombs within fusela
	1 Parabellum machine-gun: rear cockpit.	2 external bombs held in
	1 Parabellum machine-gun: belly defence.	spring jaws.

BRITISH Sopwith F.1 "Camel"

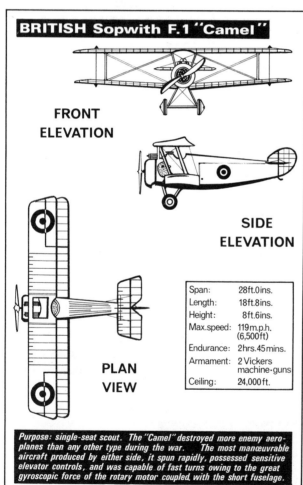

FRONT ELEVATION

SIDE ELEVATION

PLAN VIEW

Span:	28ft.0ins.
Length:	18ft.8ins.
Height:	8ft.6ins.
Max.speed:	119m.p.h. (6,500ft)
Endurance:	2hrs.45mins.
Armament:	2 Vickers machine-guns
Ceiling:	24,000ft.

Purpose: single-seat scout. The "Camel" destroyed more enemy aeroplanes than any other type during the war. The most manœuvrable aircraft produced by either side, it spun rapidly, possessed sensitive elevator controls, and was capable of fast turns owing to the great gyroscopic force of the rotary motor coupled with the short fuselage.

BRITISH S.E.5a

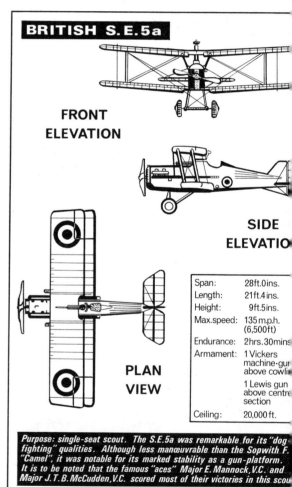

FRONT ELEVATION

SIDE ELEVATIO

PLAN VIEW

Span:	28ft.0ins.
Length:	21ft.4ins.
Height:	9ft.5ins.
Max.speed:	135m.p.h. (6,500ft)
Endurance:	2hrs.30mins
Armament:	1 Vickers machine-gun above cowli
	1 Lewis gun above centre section
Ceiling:	20,000ft.

Purpose: single-seat scout. The S.E.5a was remarkable for its "dog-fighting" qualities. Although less manœuvrable than the Sopwith F. "Camel", it was notable for its marked stability as a gun-platform. It is to be noted that the famous "aces" Major E. Mannock,V.C. and Major J.T.B.McCudden,V.C. scored most of their victories in this scou

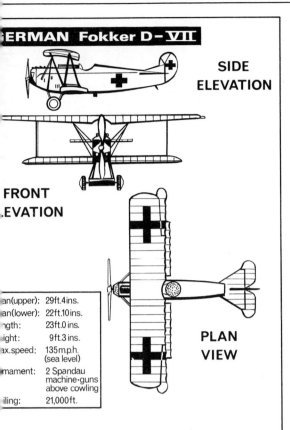

GERMAN Fokker D–VII

SIDE ELEVATION

FRONT ELEVATION

PLAN VIEW

Span(upper): 29ft.4ins.
Span(lower): 22ft.10ins.
Length: 23ft.0 ins.
Height: 9ft.3 ins.
Max.speed: 135m.p.h. (sea level)
Armament: 2 Spandau machine-guns above cowling
Ceiling: 21,000ft.

Purpose: single-seat scout. Possibly the finest of all German fighters produced during the 1914-1918 war, it was credited with 565 victims in August 1918 alone. Hermann Goering (also of 1939-1945 war fame) flew this type. By the autumn of 1918 every German scout squadron on the Western Front was equipped with this aircraft.

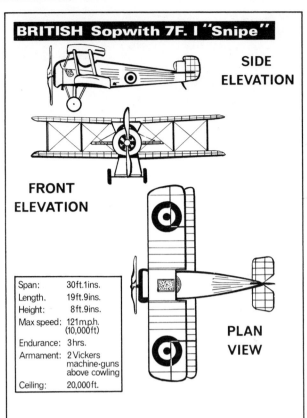

BRITISH Sopwith 7F. I "Snipe"

SIDE ELEVATION

FRONT ELEVATION

PLAN VIEW

Span: 30ft.1ins.
Length: 19ft.9ins.
Height: 8ft.9ins.
Max speed: 121m.p.h. (10,000ft)
Endurance: 3hrs.
Armament: 2 Vickers machine-guns above cowling
Ceiling: 20,000ft.

Purpose: single-seat scout. Although operational during only the final three months of the war, it showed itself to be a first-class fighter. Among those who piloted this type was the famous Canadian "ace" Major W.G.Barker, V.C. In all 264 "Snipes" were built, 97 being used on the Western Front. The plan was to fully replace the "Camel" with this newest scout, but the Armistice closed its brief military career.

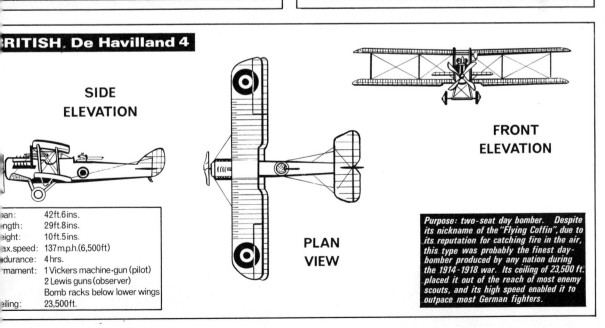

BRITISH, De Havilland 4

SIDE ELEVATION

PLAN VIEW

FRONT ELEVATION

Span: 42ft.6ins.
Length: 29ft.8ins.
Height: 10ft.5ins.
Max.speed: 137m.p.h.(6,500ft)
Endurance: 4hrs.
Armament: 1 Vickers machine-gun (pilot)
2 Lewis guns (observer)
Bomb racks below lower wings
Ceiling: 23,500ft.

Purpose: two-seat day bomber. Despite its nickname of the "Flying Coffin", due to its reputation for catching fire in the air, this type was probably the finest day-bomber produced by any nation during the 1914-1918 war. Its ceiling of 23,500 ft. placed it out of the reach of most enemy scouts, and its high speed enabled it to outpace most German fighters.

General Index*

* Prepared by Mrs Brenda Hall, Society of Indexers.

Capinghem, 75, 76–7
Caporetto (Karfreit), 200, 203
Caporetto, battle of, 165, 199, 201, 202–3
'Carbonit' mines, 279
Carden, Vice-Admiral, 110–11, 115
Carency, 144
Carey's force, 182–3
Caribbean, United States' involvement in, 214
Carlowitz, General, 67, 139
Carnia, 200
Carnoy, 182–3
Carpathian Mountains, 85–6; see also Galicia
Carranza, President, 214
Carrizal, 214
Carso, 200
Cartography, military, contribution of aerial surveying to, 299
Cassel, 38–9
Casualties
among airship crews, 284, 285, 290–1; among submarine crews, 246; at battle of Masurian Lakes, 85–6; at battle of the Somme, 152–3, 219, 224; at battle of Verdun, 147, 148–9; at Jutland, 235–6, 258; at Loos, 147; at St Mihiel Salient, 193; at Tannenberg, 96–7; at Vimy, 170; at 2 Ypres, 141, 143; caused by artillery fire, 219; civilian, in air raids, 282, 283, 286–7, 288–9, 290–1, 293, 294, 296; during Brusilov offensive, 161; during war of movement, trench war, compared, 13–15; in Artois offensives, 144; in battle of Dogger Bank, 250–1; in battle of Neuve Chapelle, 131, 136–7; in battles of Arras, 169; in bombardment of Paris, 185; in campaigns in Africa, 216, 217; in campaigns in Caucasus, 163; in Gallipoli, 109, 120, 121, 122, 128–9, 254; in Macedonia, caused by malaria, 199; in Mesopotamia, 208, 210; in naval action off Cape Sarych, 273; in naval actions in Dardanelles, 113, 115, 116–17; in Serbian campaign, 99; in ships sunk by U-boats, 246; in S.M.S. Emden, 239; on Italian front, 199, 201, 202
Caterpillar Wood, 152–3, 154–5
Catholic Serbs, minority group in Hungary, 5
Cattaro, U-boat base at, 205, 254, 270, 271
Caucasus
aid (Dunsterforce) for Russian defence of Baku, 210, 211; campaigns in, 163, 211; creation of independent republics, 177; Grand Duke Nicholas transferred

to, 147; Russian supply routes to, 273; Turkish ambitions in, 108, 109, 110–11
Caudry, 50
Caulaincourt, 182–3
Cavalry
British reliance on, in 1914, 4; British use of, in Palestine, 199; contestants' strength, in Palestine, 213; contestants' strength on Italian front, 200; in divisional organization, 34–5, 36–7; Russian, Austro-Hungarian deployment of, distinguished, 100
Cavan, F. R., Earl of, 80–2, 83
Cavotti, Lieutenant, first bombs dropped by, 281
Central Powers
alignment in 1914, 1, 2, 3, 11, 106–7; dispositions in 1914, 194; military appraisal, 4; response to Kerensky offensive, 176; see also Triple alliance and under individual nations
Cerisy, 182–3, 191
Cernay, 168
Cerny, 167
Chaillon, 192, 193
Chalaua, Portuguese East Africa, 218
Châlons-sur-Marne, 16, 23, 48–9, 58, 134, 180
Chamlik, 110–11
Champagne, 131, 144
Champion, 192, 193
Champneuville, 148–50
Champney, bombing of, 298
Chanak Kale, Dardanelles, 110–11, 119
Channel Ports,
and the race to the sea, 1914, 13–15, 59, 65, 66; German last bid for, 1918, 186
Chapelle-lez-Herlaimont, 43
Charleroi, 17, 23, 33, 38–9, 43, 48–9
Charleville-Mézières, 181
Charny, 148–50
Chasseur Cyclist Groups, French, 36
Chatalja Armistice, 1912, 8, 9
Chatalja, battle of, 1912, 8
Château Farm, Ypres, 138
Château-Salins, 30–1
Château-Thierry, 16, 17, 48–9, 54–7, 58, 181, 187, 191
Chatham, air raids on, 293, 294
'Chatham' class of light cruisers, 244
Chatillon, 187
Chaulnes, 181, 182–3
Chaumes, 47
Chaumont, 189
Chauny, 27, 167, 181, 182–3
Chelmsford, air raid on, 296
Chemenlik Fort, Dardanelles, 110–11, 116–17
Chemin des Dames, 17, 166, 167

Cherbourg, U.S. troops passing through, 188–9
Chimay, 38–9, 43, 48–9
China, British, German colonies in, 238, 239
Chivres, 59
Chlorine gas see Gas warfare
Chocolate Hill, Gallipoli, 123, 124–5
Choisy, 58–9
Chomak Dere, Gallipoli, 110–11
Chomak Tenkir Dere, Gallipoli, 110–11
Chra, Togoland, 216
Chunuk Bair, Gallipoli, 110–11, 123
Churchill, Winston
pioneer of military, naval aircraft, 281; strategy in Dardanelles, 109; visit to Antwerp, 1914, 13–15
Ciney, 38–9
Cividale, 202, 203
Civilians
casualties among, through bombing raids, 282, 283, 286–7, 288–9, 290–1, 293, 294, 296; effect of raids on morale of, 281, 288–9
Clacton, air raids on, 296
Claer, General, 76–7
Claye Souilly, 56, 57
Clemenceau, Georges, 179
Clermont, 16, 187
Cléry-sur-Somme, 152–3, 156
Cliffe, anti-aircraft defences at, 286
Climate, problems in Mesopotamia, 207
Clubs, trench, 219, 231
Coblenz
fortifications, 26, 36; German air base at, 298
Coeuvres, 57, 168
Coifford, Lieutenant Michael, 300
Collier ships, 241
Colmar, 31
Cologne
bombing of, 298; fortifications, 26, 30
Colonialism, conflicting interests in, 1
Colt revolvers, pistols, 232
Columbus, Arizona, Mexican raid on, 214
Combles, 152–3, 156, 158, 182–3
Combres, 192, 193
Comines, 75, 196
Commercy, 16
Communications
problems following German advance, 1914, 48–9; Russian weakness in, 4; see also Wireless
Compiègne, 16, 17, 23, 48–9, 134, 168, 180, 187
Conchy, 182–3
Concrete pill-boxes, effectiveness against artillery fire, 219
Condé, 46, 47, 48–9, 167, 197

Ghistelles, 196
'Giant' bombers, German, 292, 294
Giau Pass, 200, 201
Gibeon, 216
Gièvres, U.S. storage depot, 189
Ginchy, 152–3, 154–5, 156, 158
Givenchy, 17, 169
Givet (Fort de Charlemont), 16, 26, 38–9, 52
Glasgow, U.S. troops disembarkation point, 188
Glisenti pistols, Italian, 232
Gneisenau, German offensive, 1918, 180
Godley, General, 171
Goering, Hermann, 30?
Gold Coast, advance on Togoland from, 216
Golden Horn, submarine attack on 'Stambul' in, 252–3
Goldhanger, Essex, airfield at, 295
Goltz, General von der, 94, 95, 96–7, 207
Gomiecourt, 182–3
Gonnelieu, 174
Gontrode, air base at, 284, 292
Goodenough, Rear-Admiral W. E., 248–51
Goole, air raid on, 296
Gorizia (Görz), 200, 201, 202–3
Gorlice, 131, 135
Gorringe, Lieutenant-General, 207
Goslar Trench, Moronvilliers, 168
Gotha G-V aircraft, German, 292, 293, 294, 304
Gough, General Sir H., 145, 182–3
Gough-Calthorpe, Rear-Admiral, 248–51
Gourko, General Basil, 88–9
Gouzeaucourt, 182–3
Grabez, Trifko, 10
Gradisca, 202
Graincourt, 174
Grand Morin, River, 16, 17, 52, 54–7
Grande Puissance Filloux gun, French, 222
Grant, Captain H. W., 248–51
Graudenz, 18, 87
Gravelines, 66
Gravenstafel, 138–41, 143, 173, 196
Gravenstafel Ridge, Ypres, 138
Great Bitter Lake, defence of, 212
Great Yarmouth, air raid on, 286, 296
Greece
    involvement in, repercussions of Balkan Wars, 8, 9; Salonika front, 199, 204; union with Crete, 7
Greek army, 204, 205
Green cross gas see Gas warfare
Grenades, 230
Grevillers, 182–3
Grimsby, air raid on, 287, 296
Grodno, 18, 135

Groener, General, 219
Guémappe, 169
Guépratte, Vice-Admiral, 116–17
Guerbigny, 182–3
Guérin, General, 168
Guidriari Pass, 200, 201
Guildford, air raid on, 296
Guillemont, 152–3, 154–5, 156, 158
Guiscard, 182–3
Guise, 16, 23, 47, 48–9, 51, 180, 181, 197
Gulf of Aden, minefields, 276–7
Gulf of Saros, strategic significance, 119
Gully Beach, Gallipoli, 121
Gumbinnen, action at, 1914, 85–6, 88–9
Gumbiro, German East Africa, 218
Gun turrets, structural defects in British battlecruisers, 250–1, 258
Gunboats
    British, in flotilla bombarding coast in battle of the Yser, 68; use on Tigris, 207, 208; *German* destruction on African lakes, 217
Gunfire, submarines sunk by, 262–4
Guns see Artillery *and under individual weapons, types of weapon*
Gusyatin, 161
Guynemer, Capitaine Georges, 300, 303
Guyot de Salins, General, 159

Hadleigh, fighter airfield at, 295
Hage, airship base, 282
Haguenau, air base, 298
Haidar Pasha, explosion at, 211
Haifa, 213
Haig, Field Marshal Sir Douglas, 46, 131, 137, 147, 166, 172
Hainault, 60
Hainault Farm, fighter airfield, 295
Haiti
    declaration of war on Germany, 214; United States' involvement in, 214
Haldane, General J. A. L., 182–3
Haldane, Lord, 281
Halicz, 176
Halifax, Nova Scotia, U.S. embarkation port, 188
Halifax, Yorks, air raid on, 296
Halluin, 75
Ham, 47, 166, 167, 180, 181, 197
Ham-sur-Sambre, 43
Hamadan, 210, 211
Hamidieh, Dardanelles, 110–11
Hamidieh II, Gallipoli, 110–11
Hamilton, General, 120, 252–3
Hamilton, Lieutenant-General Gordon, 171
Hamman Ali, 210
Hampshire Farm, Ypres, 138
Han, bombing of, 298

Hand grenades, British, 230
Handley-Page bombers, 273
Hangard, 182–3
Hangelar, air base, 298
Hangest, 182–3
Hankey, Lord, 109
Hannonville, 192, 193
Hanover, airship base, 284
Happencourt, 182–3
Harbonnières, 182–3, 191
Harbour entrances, mining of, 178, 179
Hardaumont Battery, Verdun, 148–9
Hardecourt au Bois, 152–3, 156, 158
Hargicourt, 182–3
Harlebeke, 196
Harper, Lieutenant-General, 182–3
Hartlepool, bombardment of, 255, 296
Harunabad, 210
Harwich
    air raid on, 296; naval base at, 246, 255
Hasselt, 30
Hastière, 38–9
Hattencourt, 182–3
Hattigny, air base at, 298
Hattonchâtel, 192, 193
Hattonville, 192, 193
Haubourdin, 196
Haucourt, 50, 148–50
Haumont, 148–50
Hauptmann, rank of, British equivalents, 300
Hausen, 30, 38–9, 48–9, 51, 54
Hauslar, Gallipoli, 110–11
Haussner, Konrad, 33
Haverhill, air raid on, 296
Havrincourt, 174, 182–3
Hayes-Sadler, Rear-Admiral A., 116–17
Hebburn, Tyneside, air raid on, 287
Hebron, 213
Heeringen, 30–1, 45
Heinrichsdorf, 92–3
Hejaz, 212
Hejaz Railway, 213
Heligoland, naval base at, 255
Heligoland Bight, battle of, 108, 242–3
Helles
    Allied bombardment of, 112–14; contestants' trench lines, 123, 126–7; defences, 110–11, 112–14; evacuation, 129
Hellimer, 44
Hem, 152–3, 156, 158
Hendon, Royal Naval Air Station, 273
Héninel, 169
Hennoque, 168
Herbecourt, 156, 158
Herenthage Wood, Ypres, 80
Hermann defence line, 181

317

'Jack Johnsons', 59
Jade Bay, naval harbour, 241, 242
Jaffa, 213
Jäger battalions, in divisional organization, 36
'Jam tin' bombs, British, 230
Jamboli, airship base, 284, 285
Janina, 8
Japanese armed forces
capture of German Pacific colonies, 108; pistols used by, 232; units based at Malta, 270
Jarrow, air raid on, 287, 296
Jassy, 162
Javary see Armed Forces Index, British Navy, H.M.S. Humber
Jedwabno, 90, 96–7
Jerram, Vice-Admiral Sir Martyn, 257–9
Jellicoe, Earl, 172, 235, 248–51, 255, 256–9, 260
Jenin, 213
Jenlain, 46, 47
Jericho, 213
Jerusalem, 118, 165, 213
Jezupol, 176
Jilinsky, General, 95
Joffre, Field-Marshal J. J. C.
appointment as C. in C. French army, 31; interest in potential of bombing aircraft, 281; replacement as C. in C., 159, 165, 166; request for Belgian sorties from Antwerp, 60; strategic concepts, 13–15, 25, 53, 131, 134, 144, 147; supremacy in French army, 147
Joffre's Wall, 133
Johannisthal, airship base, 284
Jones Act, 1917, 214
Joppé, General, 142
Josef Ferdinand, Archduke, 101, 161
Jouy, 167
Juan Fernandez Islands, sinking of S.M.S. Dresden off, 215
Julian Alps, 200
Julian Calendar, use in Russia, 177
Julian front, 200; see also Isonzo River, region
Jussy, 182–3
Jüterbog, airship base, 284, 285
Jutland, battle of, 147, 250–1, 283
Juvigny, 58

'Kaiser' class of battleships, 26!
Kaiserlautem, bombing of, 298
Kaledin, General, 161
Kalusz, 176
Kamenets-Poddski, 161
Kamina, Togoland, 216
Karakilise, 163
Karantina, Dardanelles, 110–11
Karfreit see Caporetto
Karibib, South West Africa, 216
Karlsruhe, bombing of, 298

Kars, Caucasia, 211
Kasama, Northern Rhodesia, 218
Kazakov, Staff Captain Alexander A., 300
Kazvin, 210, 211
Keetmanshoop, South West Africa, 216
Kemmel, 64–5, 75, 78–82
Kephez, Dardanelles, 110–11, 115, 116–17
Kerch, Russian naval base, 272
Kerensky offensive, 165, 176
Kereves Dere, Gallipoli, 110–11
Kermansha, 210, 211
Kettering, air raid on, 296
Keyem, 67, 68, 70–1
Keyes, Vice-Admiral Sir Roger, 116–17, 248–51
Khan Baghdadi, 210
Khaniqin, 210
Khotin, 176
Kiaochow, 108
Kiel
airship base, 282; naval base, 269; naval mutiny at, 236
Kiel Canal, 5, 21
Kifri, 210
Kigoma, German East Africa, 218
Kilid Bahr, Gallipoli, 110–11, 116–17, 119
Kilosa, German East Africa, 218
Kilwa, German East Africa, 218
Kimbolton, airship flight over, 287
Kimpolung, 161
King's Lynn, air raid on, 286, 296
Kiretch Tepe, Gallipoli, 119
Kirk Kilisse, battle of, 1912, 8
Kirkuk, 210
Kirlis West, South West Africa, 216
Kitchener, Lord, 13–15, 109, 147
'Kitchener's Divisions', 152–3
Kitchener's Wood, Ypres, 138, 140
Kitope, German East Africa, 218
Kleist, General, 67
Kluck, General Alexander von, 13–15, 23, 30, 38–9, 48–9, 51, 53, 56
Klyuchev, General, 92–3, 96–7
Knives, used in trench warfare, 219, 231
Knocke, 196
Knuckleduster knives, 231
Koja Chemen Tepe, Gallipoli, 110–11
Koja Dere, Dardanelles, 110–11
Kokosani, Portuguese East Africa, 218
'Kolberg' class of light cruisers, 245
Kolomea, 161, 176
Komoron, 18
Kondratovich, General, 94, 96–7
Königsberg
airship base near, 283; fortified town, 18, 87; Russian push towards, 24, 85–6, 87, 90

Koprukoy, 163
Kornilov, General, 176
Kortekeer, 72–82
Kortewilde, 78–82
Koussery, Cameroon, 217
Kövess, General, 100, 160
Kovno,
airship base, 284; battle for, 1915, 135; fortified town, 18; Russian surrender of, at Brest-Litovsk, 178
Kragujevac, 99, 160
Kreuznach, bombing of, 298
Kreuzwald, bombing of, 298
Kriemhild defence line 1918, 181
Krithia, 119, 122
Kruiseecke, 75, 78–82
Krupp artillery see Howitzers Mortars
Kum Burnu, Gallipoli, 110–11
Kum Kale, Dardanelles, 109, 110–11, 112–14, 115, 119, 122
Kumanovo, battle of, 1912, 8
Kummer, General, 100
Kut, 165
Kut al Amara, 206–8, 210–11
Kuty, 161

La Bassée, 17, 64–5, 72–4, 181, 196
La Boiselle, 152–3, 154–5, 156, 158
La Boutillerie, 76–7
La Capelle, 197
La Chavatte, 182–3
La Courtine, 168
La Fère, 16, 17, 22, 23, 26, 27, 48–9, 52, 166, 167, 180, 197
La Ferté Gaucher, 54–5
La Ferté Milon, 54–6
La Ferté-sous-Jouarre, 47, 54–7
La Folie Farm, Vimy Ridge, 170
La Pallice, U.S. troops passing through, 188–9
'La Revanche' see Alsace-Lorraine
La Rochelle, U.S. troops passing through, 188–9
La Targette, 144
Ladins, minority group in Austria-Hungary, 5
Laffaux, 167
Laffert, General, 76–7
Lagache, 182–3
Lagny, 47, 48–9
Lagricourt, 182–3
Lahore, troops from, on Western Front, 13–15; see also Armed Forces Index, British Commonwealth Forces
Lahr, bombing of, 298
Lake, General Sir P., 209
Lake Donau, 199
Lake Nysau, destruction of German gunboats on, 217
Lake Tanganyika, destruction of German gunboats on, 217

321

Namur—*contd.*
following defeat at, 60; fortifications, 16, 26, 28; relation to static Western Front lines, 17, 134; siege of, 23, 39, 42, 48–9, 51, 115
Namutoni, South West Africa, 216
Nancy, 16, 17, 30–1, 53, 134
Nanguari, Portuguese East Africa, 218
Nanichevanski, General Khan, 88–9
Nanteuil, 47, 48–9, 55–7
Nanungu, Portuguese East Africa, 218
Napier, Rear-Admiral T. D. W., 248–51
Naples, Zeppelin raid on, 285
Narrows *see* Dardanelles, Sea of Marmara
Nasiriya, 207
Naulin, General, 168
Nauroy, 168
Naval blockades, techniques, strategies, 108, 147, 177, 179, 212, 235–6
Naval guns
German ('Long Max'), shelling of Dunkirk by, 184; German long-range shelling of Verdun, 150; Hotchkiss Automatic, on British Monitors, 69; inaccuracy in trench warfare, 122; Maxims, on 'London' Class of battleships, 69; use of British 6-pounder on early tanks, 157; types used in bombardments in Dardanelles, 112, 115; 38-cm. long-range, German, 150; 4-inch, 112; 4.7-inch, 69; 6-inch, 69, 112, 115; 6.4-inch, 112; 12-inch, 69, 112; 15-inch, 115; 3-pounder, 69, 115; 12-pounder, 69, 115
Naval supremacy *see* Sea power
Nazareth, 213
Neidenburg, 90–3, 94, 96–7
Néry, 47, 48–9
Nesle, 48–9, 180, 181, 182–3
Nets, submarine losses in, 262–4
Neu-Breisach, 26, 31, 45
Neuenburg, 26
Neufchâteau, 16, 26
Neuve Chapelle, 17, 74, 76–7, 134
Neuve Chapelle, battle of, 131, 136–7
Neuve Église, 75, 186
Neuville, 169
Neuville-St.-Vaast, 144
Neuville Vitasse, 167
New York, U.S. embarkation port, 188
New Zealand, coastal minefields, 276–7
New Zealand armed forces
capture of German colonies in Pacific, 108; in battle of Messines, 165; in Gallipoli campaign, 109; *see also* Anzac forces
Newala, German East Africa, 218

Newark, air raid on, 296
Newcastle on Tyne, air raids on, 281, 287, 296
Newcastle under Lyme, air raid on, 287
Newmarket, air raid on, 296
Newport News, U.S. troops embarkation point, 188
Newton Pippin rifle grenades, British, 230
Ngaundere, Cameroon, 217
Ngomano, Portuguese East Africa, 218
Nibrunesi Beach, Gallipoli, 123
Nibrunesi Point, Gallipoli, 119
Nicaragua, Bryan-Chamorro Treaty with, 214
Nicholas, Grand Duke, 85–6, 147
Nicholas II, Tsar, 147, 177
Nieppe, 75, 76–7
Nieumunster, air base, 293
Nieuport
battle for, 66, 68, 69; inundation of, 13–15, 70–1, 83; relation to static Western Front lines, 17
Nieuport 17 C.1 French aircraft, 302
Nigeria, Allied advance into Cameroon from, 217
Nikolaiev, naval construction yards at, 272
Nivelle, Robert Georges, 159, 165, 166
Nivelles, 16
Nixon, General Sir J. E., 207
Nonsard, 192, 193
Noord Vaart Siphon, 71
Nordenburg, 87, 88–9
Nordholz, airship base, 282, 286, 290–1
Noreuil, 182–3
Norfolk
air raids on, 286, 296; naval bombardment on coast of, 296
Norroy, 192, 193
North Africa *see* Africa, North
North Sea
contestants' naval strategies in, 235–6, 255, 256, 275; Franco-British agreement on naval supremacy in, 2, 3; German access to, 5, 21; minefields, 236, 246, 249, 256, 259, 268, 276; U-boats in, in 1914, 246; *see also* Sea, War at, Submarine warfare, *and individual battles*
North Weald Bassett, fighter airfield, 295
Northampton, air raid on, 296
Northern Rhodesia, advance on German East Africa from, 218
Norwich, air raids on, 287, 296
Nottingham, air raid on, 296
Novo-Georgievsk, 18, 91, 100, 135

Noyon, 16, 17, 47, 48–9, 58–9, 134, 167, 180, 181, 182–3, 197
Nungesser, Lieutenant Charles E. J. M., 300
Nun's Copse, Ypres, 80
Nurlu, 182–3
Nyamirue, Portuguese East Africa, 218
Nyasaland, advance into German, Portuguese East Africa from, 218
'Nymphe' class of protected cruisers, 245

Oberleutnant, rank of, equivalents, 300
Oblong Farm, Ypres, 138
Obrégon, Alvaro, 214
Observation balloons, 152–3
Odessa, bombardment of, 272, 273
Offenburg, bombing of, 298
Oil
contestants' strategies for securing of supplies, 177, 199, 206, 210; use of burning, in trench warfare, 219
Oise River, region, 16, 17, 52, 53, 190
Oisy, 47
Old Contemptibles, 13–15
Oliezy, 182–3
Olleris, General, 81–2
Omaruru, South West Africa, 216
Omecourt, 158
Oostakker, air base, 292
Oostaverne, 173
Oostniewkerke, 75
Oranovski, General, 88–9
Orkanie, Dardanelles, 110–11, 112–14, 119
Ornes, 148–50
Ortelsburg, 90–1, 95–7
Oscillating mines, 279
Ossowiec, 87
Ostend
Allied bombardment of, 68; battles for, 181, 197; British attempt to block harbour, 236, 274; minefield laid outside, 68; relation to Western Front lines, 17; strategic importance, 66, 68, 172; submarine base at, 268
Osterode, 96–7
Ostrolenka, 87, 90, 91
Otranto, 236, 271
Ottoman Empire *see* Turkey
Ouchy, Treaty of, 7
Oudenarde, 197
Ouderdom, 141
Ourcq, River, 16, 54–7
Ourthe, River, 16, 52
Ovillers la Boisselle, 154–5, 156, 158

Pacific Ocean, area
German squadron in, 108, 238; loss of German colonies in, 108

Quebec, U.S. embarkation point, 188
Quedecourt, 156, 152–3, 158
Quesnoy, 196
Quessy, 182–3
Quick-firers, Turkish use of, in Dardanelles, 110–11, 112
'Quirk, The', 302
Qurna, 206, 207

Race to the Sea, 1914, 13–15, 17, 59, 64–5
Radinghem, 75, 76–7
Radom, 103
Railways
Arab severance of Hejaz, 213; Belgian cyclists' sortie to destroy, 60; Berlin–Baghdad, 5, 18, 209, 252–3; different gauges of German, Russian, 18; German control of, to Middle East, 131; importance in German strategy, 4, 13–15, 18, 21, 24, 103, 134, 152–3, 158; network on Western Front, 16; on Italian Front, 200; Russian attempt to construct broad gauge, 177; Russian capture of strategic, 1916, 161; significance for efficient military operations, 118, 134, 176, 194, 213, 219; use to transport U-boats overland, 271
Ramadi, 210, 211
Ramming, submarines lost by, 262–4
Ramsgate, air raid on, 294, 296
Rancourt, 152–3, 156, 158, 182–3
Rankings, European equivalents, 300
Rastaff, bombing of, 298
Rastenburg, 90
Rathen, General, 139
Rattevalle, 67
Rava Russka, 102
Rawlinson, General Sir H. S., 67, 145
Réchicourt, 298
Reconnaissance, aerial, 22, 53, 59, 139, 299, 302–5
Red Baron see Richthofen
Red Sea, British blockade of, 212
Regiments, in divisional organization, 34–7, 190
Regina Trench, Somme, 152–3
Regniéville, 192, 193
Regone, Portuguese East Africa, 218
Rembercourt, 192
Renault FT i7 Tanks, 227
Rendsburg Trench, Moronvilliers, 168
Rennenkampf, General, 87, 88–9, 90, 92, 95, 97, 98
Resht, 210, 211
Retal, 47
Rethel, 16, 22, 48–9, 180, 181, 197
Rethondes, Armistice signed at, 197
Reumont, 50

Reutel, 78–9
Reval, Russian naval base, 269
Revolvers, used by contestants, 219, 232
Rheims
battles in region of, 1914, 1918, 23, 48–9, 52, 57, 58–9, 179, 180; bombardment of, 59; fortifications, 16, 26, 27; Nivelle's proposed offensive at, 166; relation to Western Front lines, 17, 134, 168
Rhine, River, evacuation of left bank, a term of Armistice, 197
Rhodes, seizure by Italy, 7
Ribécourt, 58, 174
Ribemont, 27
Riberpray, General, 168
Richthofen, General, 105
Richthofen, Manfred von, 281, 300, 301, 303
Rickenbacker, Captain Edward V., 300
Riesenburg, 90, 91
Riesenflugzeugen ('Giant') bombers, German, 292, 294
Rifle grenades, British, 230
Rifles
British rapid-fire techniques, 80, 228; British reliance on, in 1914, 4; experimental self-loading, 228; types used by contestants, 219, 228–9
Riga
German offensive towards, 1917, 269; naval base, 269; surrender by Russia at Brest-Litovsk, 178
Rittmeiser, rank of, British equivalents, 300
Rivers, systems on Western Front, 16, 17; see also individual rivers
Rizeh, 273
Roads, destruction by retreating Germans, 167
Roama, 202
Robeck, Rear Admiral de, 115–17, 254
Robertson, Sir William, 147
Robinson, Lieutenant W. Leefe, 288–9, 302
Rochdale, air raid on, 296
Rochford, fighter airfield, 295
Rocroi, 48–9
Rodosto, 252–3
Roisel, 182–3
Ronaldsay, wireless station, 248
Ronarc'h, Rear Admiral, 66
Ronssoy, 182–3
Rosières, 182–3
'Ross' Mark III rifles, Canadian, 229
Rosyth, naval base at, 246, 255, 275
Rother Thurm Pass, 162
Roubaix, 196, 197
Roucy, 59
Rouen, 17

Rouges Bancs, 76–7
Roulers, 64–5, 75, 196–7
Roupy, 182–3
Rouvroy, 182–3
Roville, air base at, 298
Roye, 48–9, 166, 167, 180, 181, 182–3, 197
Rozoy, 47, 48–9
Ruddervoorde, 196
Rudolf, Crown Prince, 10
Rue du Bois, 76–7
Ruffey, General, 30–1, 44
Rufiji River, destruction of S.M.S. Königsberg in, 217
Rumania
Allied advance through, 1918, 205; defeat, 147; entry into war, 147; German dependence on grain from, 178; German success in, 1916, 162; physical, regional geography, 18; policies during Balkan Wars, 8, 9
Rumanians
minority group in Austria-Hungary, 5; percentage in Austro-Hungarian army, 102
Rumili Medjidieh, Gallipoli, 110–11
Rupprecht of Bavaria, Crown Prince, 30–1, 44, 75–7, 78–82, 144, 180
Russia
alliances, 1, 2, 3; barren terrain policies, 90; declarations of war, 11; desire for Allied second front in Dardanelles, 110–11; difficulties of supply routes to, 109, 177, 269; effect of separate peace with, on troop ratios on Western Front, 179; effect on morale of casualties, 161; gauge of railways, 18, 177; isolation following withdrawal from Gallipoli, 109; military appraisal, 4; mobilization speed, 20, 22; naval strategy in Black Sea, 272–3; physical, regional geography, 18; policies in Balkans, 1908–13, 7; reasons for going to war, 2; support for Slavs in Austria-Hungary, 5; terms of Treaty of Brest Litovsk, 178; war plans in 1914, 24; war weariness, disaffection in, 1, 2, 161, 165, 168, 177, 179; see also Eastern front, Russian armed forces, Russian Revolution
Russian armed forces
Army assumption of command by Tsar, 147; brigades serving in France, mutiny amongst, 168; British aid for defence of Baku, 210, 211; campaigns in Caucasia, 163; casualties suffered by, 96–7, 131, 135, 161; dispositions during Rumanian campaign, 162; dis-

329

Warnelle Ravine, 50
Warneton, 38–9, 75, 78–82
Warrington, air raid on, 296
Warsaw
    battles for, 85–6, 135; bombing of, 281; fortifications, 18, 100; Russian surrender of, at Brest Litovsk, 178
Warships, internment of German, a term of Armistice, 194; *see also individual types of ship and under* Armed Forces Index
Waterloo, 38–9
Waterlot Farm, Somme, 154–5
Watson, General, 170
Watts, Lieutenant-General, 182–3
Weather, significance at Caporetto, 202
Webley Mark VI pistols, 232
Webley-Fosbery pistols, 232
Wednesbury, air raid on, 296
Wei-hai-wei, removal of British China Squadron from, **238**
Welch Farm, Ypres, 138
Welsh knives, 231
Wervicq, 75, 196
West Ham, air raid on, 286
Westcapelle, 196
Westende, bombardment during battle of the Yser, 68
Western Front
    Allied offensives, 1918, 181, 194; Allied strategic concepts, 1916, 147; basic stages of war, 17; disposition of contestants at beginning of trench war, 83; disposition of contestants in September 1918, 194; effect of arrival of American troops, 177; effects of Bolshevik propaganda, 165; effect on, of Russian withdrawal from war, 177, 178; fortifications, 1914, 16, 26–9; French offensives in Artois, Champagne, 144; German divisions transferred to East from, 13–15, 47–8, 96–7, 103, 177; German initiatives, 1916, 147; German offensives, 1918, 179, 182–3; limits of German advance, 1914, 17; line at Armistice, 17; numbers, disposition of contestants' troops, 1914, 13–15, 30–1; physical characteristics, 16; stabilized lines of trench warfare, 106–7, 108, 133, 134, 166, 168; *see also individual battles*
Westhoek, 78–82, 138–41, 143
Westroosebeke, 75
Wez Macquart, 75, 76–7

Whippet tanks, British, 226
Whitby, naval bombardment of, 255, 296
White Château Farm, Ypres, 138
White Sea, minefields, 276
Whitechapel, air aid on, 286
Whitehaven, naval bombardment of, 296
Wieltje, 78–82, 138–43
Wiencourt, 191
Wierzbolovo, 87
Wiesbaden, bombing of, 298
Wigan, air raid on, 296
Wildeshausen, airship base, 282
Wilhelm II, Kaiser, 2, 5, 7, 13–15, 21, 30, 108, 147, 197
Wilhelm, Imperial Crown Prince of Germany, 30–1
'Wilhelm's Gun' (Lange 21-cm. Kanone), 184, 185, 187
Wilhelmshaven, naval base at, 236, 246, 255
Windhoek, German South West Africa, 216
Wipers *see* Ypres
Wireless
    British interception of German naval signals, 235, 248, 259; contestants' use of, during battle of Dogger Bank, 235, 249; effectiveness of German, on Eastern Front, 90, 91; German stations in Africa, 216, 217–18; interception of Russian open signals, 85–6, 90, 91, 102, 103, 104; use by Zeppelin L 59 on African mission, 285
Wireless detachments, in divisional organization, 34, 36
Wisbech, air raid on, 296
Witry, 168
Wittlich, bombing of, 298
Wittmundhaven, airship base, 282, 290–1
Wonder Work, Somme, 152–3
Woodbridge, air raid on, 296
Worms, bombing of, 298
Wotan defence line, 1918, 181
Woumen, 196
Woyrsch, General, 32
Wulverghem, 75
Württemberg, Grand Duke of, 30, 78–82
Wynghene, 196
Wytschaete, 64–5, 75, 78–81, 171, 173, 186

Xaffevillers, air base at, 298
Xivray, 192, 193

Yanov, 90, 96–7
Yarmouth, naval bombardment of, 255
Yaunde, Cameroon, 217
Yepanchin, General, 88–9
Yidiz, Gallipoli, 110–11
Yorck, German offensive, 1918, 180
York, air raid on, 296
Young Bosnia, secret society, 10
Young Turk revolt, 7
Ypres
    battles round, 1914, 13–15, 64–5, 72–82; creation, line of salient, 83; final penetration of German positions, 13–15, 196; involvement of American troops near, 190; names given to farms round, 138; relation to Western Front lines, 17, 133, 134; second battle of, 1915, 13–15, 138–43; strategic, psychological significance, 13–15; third battle of, *see* Passchendaele; use of gas in German offensive, 1915, 131; villages round, 138; war graves at, 13–15; *see also* Yser, battle of
Ypres Ridge, 138
Yser, battle of, 13–15, 64–5, 67–71

Zanvoorde, 75, 78–82
Zanzibar harbour, sinking of H.M.S. Pegasus in, 217
Zarren, 196
Zbrucz, River, 176
Zeebrugge
    liberation, 196; raid on, 236, 274; relation to Western Front lines, 17; submarine base at, 268
Zeesen, airship construction plant, 284
Zeppelin airships
    bombing of Britain, 131, 281, 286–96; losses, 282, 283, 284, 286, 287, 288–9, 290–1; types, construction, performance, 281, 282–3, 284, 285; *see also* Airships *and* Armed Forces Index
Zeppelin-Staaken R VI (Giant) Bomber, 295
Zillebeke, 78–82, 173, 186
Zillebeke Ridge, Ypres, 138
Zimmerman Note, 165, 214
Zollern Redoubt, 152–3
Zollern Trench, 152–3
Zonnebeke, 75, 78–82, 138–43, 173
Zonnebeke Ridge, Ypres, 138
Zouave Regiments, 13–15
Zuyenkerke, 196
Zweibrücken, bombing of, 298

Armed Forces Index *

* Prepared by Mrs Brenda Hall, Society of Indexers.

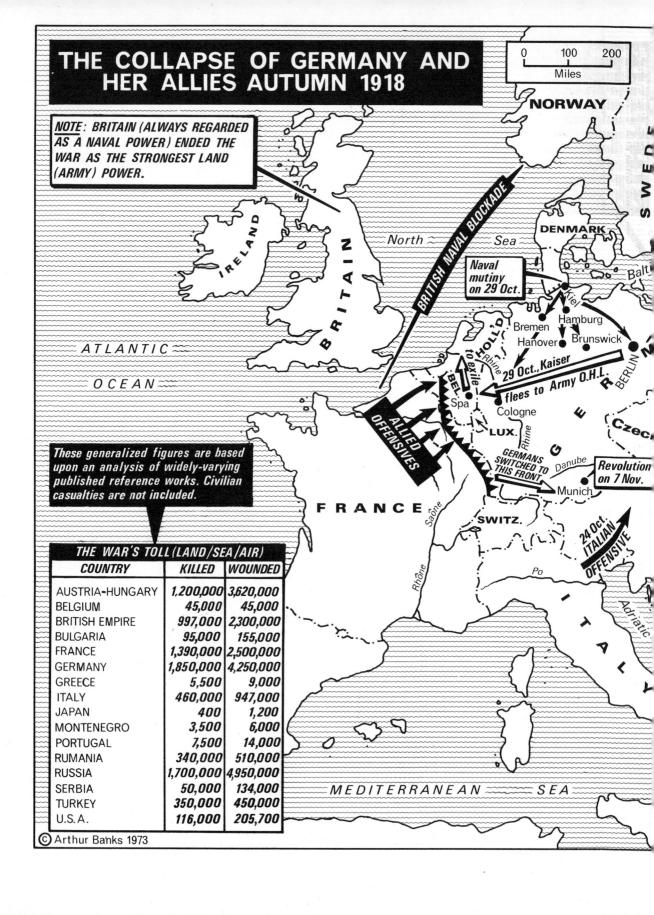

THE COLLAPSE OF GERMANY AND HER ALLIES AUTUMN 1918

NOTE: BRITAIN (ALWAYS REGARDED AS A NAVAL POWER) ENDED THE WAR AS THE STRONGEST LAND (ARMY) POWER.

BRITISH NAVAL BLOCKADE

Naval mutiny on 29 Oct.

ALLIED OFFENSIVES

29 Oct., Kaiser flees to Army O.H.L.

to exile

GERMANS SWITCHED TO THIS FRONT

Revolution on 7 Nov.

24 Oct. ITALIAN OFFENSIVE

These generalized figures are based upon an analysis of widely-varying published reference works. Civilian casualties are not included.

THE WAR'S TOLL (LAND/SEA/AIR)		
COUNTRY	KILLED	WOUNDED
AUSTRIA-HUNGARY	1,200,000	3,620,000
BELGIUM	45,000	45,000
BRITISH EMPIRE	997,000	2,300,000
BULGARIA	95,000	155,000
FRANCE	1,390,000	2,500,000
GERMANY	1,850,000	4,250,000
GREECE	5,500	9,000
ITALY	460,000	947,000
JAPAN	400	1,200
MONTENEGRO	3,500	6,000
PORTUGAL	7,500	14,000
RUMANIA	340,000	510,000
RUSSIA	1,700,000	4,950,000
SERBIA	50,000	134,000
TURKEY	350,000	450,000
U.S.A.	116,000	205,700